W9-BJG-161

DESKTOP PUBLISHING
by DESIGN

▲▲▲▲▲▲▲▲▲▲▲▲▲▲▲▲▲▲▲▲▲

Praise for Aldus® PageMaker® edition

▶ ▶ ▶ ▶ ▶

"Best How-To Book of 1989."— *Computer Press Association*

"A treasure trove of useful, detailed examples and tips designed to help readers create desktop-published documents that get attention. It's an enjoyable introduction to a field where taste and judgement are just as important as technical expertise; a practical, hands-on workbook with plenty of useful examples; and an excellent reference work for anyone who is designing and creating documents with PageMaker. I loved it!"— Richard Landry, Editor-in-Chief, *PC World*

"This thorough, well-crafted work offers something for every PageMaker user— a manual for all seasons."— *Aldus Magazine*

"If you're still looking for an overall introductory text in desktop publishing, this may well be the best yet…. Microsoft Press simply doesn't seem to do anything but top-notch books. This is one more in a long string of high-quality texts that simply can't fail to satisfy…. A splendid book."— *Computing Now*

"The Strunk and White of desktop publishing…. A brilliantly thought-out and classically executed work…. For anyone already experimenting with desktop publishing, or contemplating doing so, it belongs in the most frequently used section of your library."—*Woodstock Times*

"Real-life examples are liberally captioned with appropriate insights…all presented in a cogent and fluid style."—*The Page*

"An excellent resource for electronic visual communicators."
—*Step by Step Electronic Design*

DESKTOP PUBLISHING
by DESIGN

Blueprints for Page Layout
Using
Aldus® PageMaker®
on IBM® and
Apple® Macintosh®
Computers.
Includes
Hands-On Projects.

Ronnie Shushan
and
Don Wright

PUBLISHED BY
Microsoft Press
A Division of Microsoft Corporation
One Microsoft Way
Redmond, Washington 98052-6399

Library of Congress Cataloging-in-Publication Data
Shushan, Ronnie.
   Desktop publishing by design: Aldus Pagemaker edition / Ronnie
  Shushan, Don Wright. -- 2nd ed.
     p. cm.
  Includes bibliographical references and index.
  ISBN 1-55615-364-3
    1. Desktop publishing--Computer programs.   2. PageMaker (Computer
program)   I. Wright, Don   II. Title.
Z286.D47S59   1991
686.2'2544536--dc20   91-10065
                                                CIP

Printed and bound in the United States of America.

1 2 3 4 5 6 7 8 9 MLML 6 5 4 3 2 1

Distributed to the book trade in Canada by Macmillan of Canada,
a division of Canada Publishing Corporation.

Distributed to the book trade outside the United States and Canada by Penguin Books Ltd.

Penguin Books Ltd., Harmondsworth, Middlesex, England
Penguin Books Australia Ltd., Ringwood, Victoria, Australia
Penguin Books N.Z. Ltd., 182-190 Wairau Road, Auckland 10, New Zealand

British Cataloging-in-Publication Data available.

Acquisitions Editor: Dean Holmes
Project Editor: Mary Ann Jones
Manuscript Editor: Alice Copp Smith
Technical Editor: Rebecca Pepper

To all the pioneers

scientists and artists
engineers and designers
programmers and publishers

who have shown the way

►►► CONTENTS ◄◄◄

Preface to the Second Edition

In revising the original PageMaker edition of *Desktop Publishing by Design*, we found that the sections addressing graphic design needed very little revision at all, and the PageMaker tutorials required almost a complete rewrite. The moral, which isn't very surprising, is that the principles of good design are timeless, while technology is in a constant state of change.

To be sure, trends plays an important role in our media-saturated culture. But even the most undisciplined of today's graphic styles are based on a traditional repertoire of visual principles. In the first two sections of the book, we look at how those principles are applied to business publications in today's desktop-publishing environment.

The hands-on projects, which make up the second half of the book, have been completely revised for PageMaker 4. Six of the nine projects are new to this edition. And of the three that are carried over from the first edition, two have been rewritten to take advantage of the increased capabilities of the software.

As in the first edition, we would like to acknowledge the contribution of the many designers who took the time to send us their work and talk about their experience with this marriage of art and technology. One of the rewards of working in this field is the generosity of other enthusiasts who willingly share their knowledge and experience.

Thanks, also, to our friends and colleagues at Microsoft Press for making the first edition successful enough to warrant a second; to the technical support staff at Aldus, whose help was invaluable to us as authors and as typical users; to Bob Schaffel at Sprintout, for seeing us through the uncertainties of Linotronic output; and to Megan Denver, for always coming through.

Ronnie Shushan
Don Wright

INTRODUCTION

This book is about two dramatically different and wonderfully complementary tools of communication: graphic design and electronic page assembly. The first is a tradition as old as recorded history, the second a technology unimaginable to most of us even seven years ago. In addition to changing the way we produce documents and publications of every kind, the combination of these tools is introducing more people than ever before to the art and technology of publishing.

Technology has always had an impact on visual communication, which is essentially what graphic design is. At every stage of the evolution of the communication arts—from prehistoric cave paintings to Gutenberg's movable type to today's computerized typesetting and imaging systems—technology has increased the potential for communication with audiences that are both broader and more specialized than before.

The computer is by all odds the most extraordinary of the technological clothing ever devised by man, since it is an extension of our central nervous system. Beside it the wheel is a mere hula-hoop.
—Marshall McLuhan

In the past, especially in the last half century or so during which graphic design as a commercial art has flourished, people entered the field through formal training in art schools and apprenticeships with experienced designers. The almost overnight proliferation of desktop-publishing technology has attracted and, through management expectations, forced many people with no training in the visual arts to take responsibility for a wide range of printed material. Increased access to publishing tools has motivated many businesses to produce in-house publications that were previously done, in whole or in part, by outside contractors. At the same time, the promise and the inevitable hype surrounding desktop publishing has raised expectations about internal and external communications of all kinds.

While expanding the number of people involved in printed communication, desktop typesetting and electronic page assembly are also dramatically changing the day-to-day operations of an increasing number of publishers, design studios, corporate art departments, and independent freelancers. Writers and editors who cannot draw a straight line find themselves assembling pages in electronic templates. Designers used to specifying type on manuscripts are setting and manipulating it themselves. Production managers used to trafficking hard copy from one department to another are wrestling with the management of electronic files. And pasteup artists with T-squares and ruling pens are, quite simply, an endangered species.

Although they approach desktop publishing from different perspectives, people within both the business community and the publishing industry share a need for two different kinds of training. This book focuses on that need. It is not a general overview of desktop publishing. It assumes that you already appreciate the potential benefits the technology offers: the ability to integrate text and graphics electronically, to see and alter on-screen what the printed page will look like, and to print that page on a variety of different printers, depending upon the quality you require. The book does not try to convince you of the ways in which desktop publishing can save you time or money, enhance the creative process, or give you more control over the pages you produce. It assumes you're already convinced. Instead, it reviews the fundamental elements of graphic design for the many people without any training or experience in the visual arts who are suddenly responsible for producing—or who want to learn to produce—business publications. And it provides hands-on tutorials for using Aldus PageMaker, the most popular electronic page layout program for both Macintosh and IBM-compatible computers.

There are very few rules in graphic design. A relatively subjective craft, it requires the designer to make one judgment after another based on such intangible criteria as "look" and "feel." Even if you have no inkling of the formal traditions and techniques taught in design schools, you have some personal experience with the elements designers work with—words, lines, colors, pictures.

On the other hand, there are hundreds and hundreds of rules for using Aldus PageMaker. Even with its user-friendly mouse, pull-down menus, and familiar drawing-board metaphor, PageMaker is not—for most people—a program you just jump into and start producing pages with. It requires learning which commands to use and how to respond to dialog boxes and how the same commands in difference sequences produce different results. Sometimes the program appears to have a mind of its own. It can display your headline in one style when you know you specified another. It can refuse to place your graphic. It can appear to eat your text. It can tell you there's a bad hole record index detected by the line walker. (A bad what?)

One important quality common to designing printed pages and assembling them in PageMaker is that both tasks become intuitive as you gain experience. The variety of typefaces that intimidates a novice designer, for example, becomes a rich resource once you gain a feeling for the often subtle distinctions between them. The apparent mysteries of layout grids become time-saving production tools when you understand the simple principles that govern their use. Similarly, the endless rules that slow down the PageMaker rookie provide control and flexibility to the experienced user.

There are many techniques that can be applied in the search for visual solutions. Here are some of the most often used and easily identified:

Contrast	Harmony
Instability	Balance
Asymmetry	Symmetry
Irregularity	Regularity
Complexity	Simplicity
Fragmentation	Unity
Intricacy	Economy
Exaggeration	Understatement
Spontaneity	Predictability
Activeness	Stasis
Boldness	Subtlety
Accent	Neutrality
Transparency	Opacity
Variation	Consistency
Distortion	Accuracy
Depth	Flatness
Juxtaposition	Singularity
Randomness	Sequentiality
Sharpness	Diffusion
Episodicity	Repetition

—Donis A. Dondis,
A Primer of Visual Literacy

Think of buying a computer as like buying a car. A car just moves your body; your computer, though, is the chariot of your mind, carrying it through the whole universe. How much is your mind worth to you?
—Ted Nelson,
Computer Lib

In a sense, this book tries to simulate experience both in graphic design and in using PageMaker. Section 1, "The Elements of Design," is a sort of primer of visual literacy as it relates to the printed page. It provides a working vocabulary of graphic design in the context of desktop technology.

Section 2, "A PageMaker Portfolio" (and the chapter on Creating a Grid in Section 1) show sample pages from more than a hundred documents along with notes about design elements such as grid structure, type treatment, and use of art. Although these documents can't replace personal experience, they can provide the novice designer with a sense of the many different solutions to common design problems, and they can help you develop an eye for effective combinations. All of the publications were created using PageMaker (along with other applications for word processing and graphics), so these samples also illustrate both simple and complex applications of this program.

The third section, "Hands-On Projects," provides actual experience. Here you'll find nine different tutorials, each with step-by-step instructions for creating a particular publication. The purpose is to help you learn and become more confident with PageMaker's tools and techniques by applying them to actual documents. PageMaker operates almost identically on the Macintosh and on IBM-compatibles, so you can do the projects on either type of computer. (Keystroke combinations are given for both types.)

The book was conceived to be used as a resource, rather than to be read from start to finish. If you want to start right in working with Page-Maker, begin in Section 3. If you want to review publications of a particular kind, flip through Section 2. And if you want some grounding in design basics, start with Section 1. Even within each section, the chapters are organized so that you can begin at whatever point suits your needs and experience. If you stumble across an unfamiliar term, refer to the glossary at the back of the book.

Visual communication of any kind, whether persuasive or informative, from billboards to birth announcements, should be seen as the embodiment of form and function: the integration of the beautiful and the useful.
—Paul Rand,
Thoughts on Design

Throughout this book, we emphasize that the computer is only a tool. Good design is not one of its default settings. PageMaker can enable you to draw a straight line, but it can't tell you how heavy to make it or where to put it on the page. It places text in perfectly aligned columns, but it doesn't tell you how wide the columns should be or how much white space is needed to make the page appealing to read. It offers hundreds of typefaces but requires your visual judgment to select and size the one that's right for your publication.

PageMaker is a wonderful, powerful tool, getting better and more sophisticated every day. But it is only an extension of your creativity. We hope this book will help you gain some of the skill, experience, and visual discrimination needed to use it well.

THE ELEMENTS OF DESIGN

CHAPTER 1

EFFECTIVE COMMUNICATION IN AN INFORMATION ENVIRONMENT

Past	Present	Future
Data	Information	Knowledge
Control	Access	Exploration
Calculation	Presentation	Communication

—*Stuart Greene,*
Apple viewpoints

The electronic age has given us an almost magical ability to store, retrieve, and analyze data. Whether you're making travel plans, checking the status of an insurance policy, or changing an assumption in a five-year plan, the computer can provide almost instantaneous answers to questions that only a decade ago might have remained unanswered for a day, a week, or even a month.

But the electronic age has not given us a paperless office. In fact, in a single year computers are said to churn out some 1200 pages of print for every man, woman, and child in the United States. Although they help us manage individual pieces of data, computers have increased our information overload.

In the midst of this overload, desktop publishing reaffirms the fundamental power of print. Print is tangible; it has a life of its own. You can read it when you want, at your own pace, and keep it for future reference. And now, with desktop publishing, the newest darling of the electronic age, you can produce more pages faster and cheaper than ever before.

But can you produce effective pages?

In the information environment, competition for the ever-shrinking attention span is fierce. We are saturated both as senders (too much to say, too little space) and as receivers (too much to read, too little time). The result is often information that is confusing, that you can't find when you need it, or that simply sits unread in a rotating stack of other communications that failed to deliver their messages. The cumulative result is an enormous amount of wasted effort. The hidden costs, whether in sales or productivity or corporate image, are difficult to calculate.

The elements that make up a successful document—careful writing, thoughtful organization, effective design—grow out of an understanding of your message, your audience, and your resources. The publication checklist below can help guide you toward that understanding. The questions it raises force you to think through a great many variables and even some unpleasant realities. Some of the answers may raise more questions. The purpose of the checklist is to help you define your communication problem so that you can use graphic design as a way of solving it. We'll briefly consider each item on the checklist after a look at a few diverse examples of effective communication.

An erroneous conception of the graphic designer's function is to imagine that in order to produce a "good layout" all he need do is make a pleasing arrangement of miscellaneous elements. What is implied is that this may be accomplished simply by pushing these elements around until something happens. At best, this procedure involves the time-consuming uncertainties of trial and error, and at worst, an indifference to plan, order, or discipline.
—Paul Rand
Thoughts on Design

PUBLICATION CHECKLIST

- What is the purpose of your publication?

- Why is it needed?

- Who is the intended audience?

- What kind of information will your publication include?

- What kind of image do you want to project?

- Does the publication need to fit into a larger program or conform to a corporate style?

- What is the overall format?

- What kinds of art and photography—and how much—will be needed?

- What are the printing specifications?

- What will you use for camera-ready pages?

- How will the publication be reproduced?

- How will it be distributed?

- When is it needed?

- What is the budget?

The dramatically different documents reproduced on this and the following two pages illustrate the rich range of visual form that effective communication can take. Each of the four samples successfully solves a very different design problem, and their contrasting styles say a great deal about the different purpose and audience of each message.

A poster is one of the simplest and most direct forms of communication. It delivers a message that is as brief as it is bold. Although many posters rely heavily on graphics, this one is a reminder of the power of words.

The street language is well suited to the young audience; the rhythm of the words is in their own vernacular.

The typography follows the cadence of the words, so that the visual rhythm literally echoes the verbal message. Reverse type on a red background supports the jazzy rhythm and the serious message.

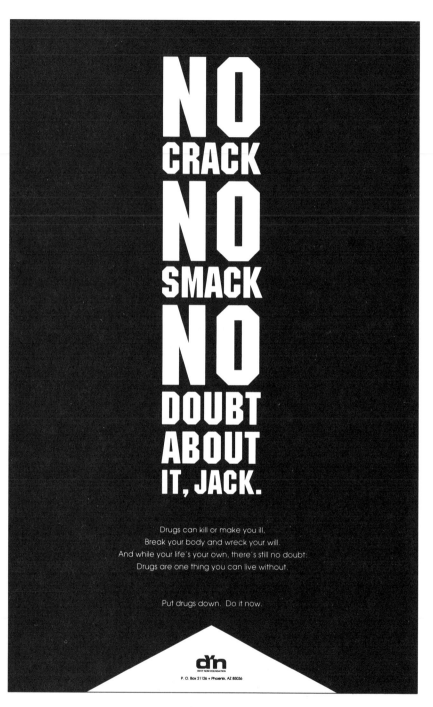

Design: Jim Parker (Phoenix, AZ)
Poster produced by the Do It Now Foundation.
Trim size: 12 by 19

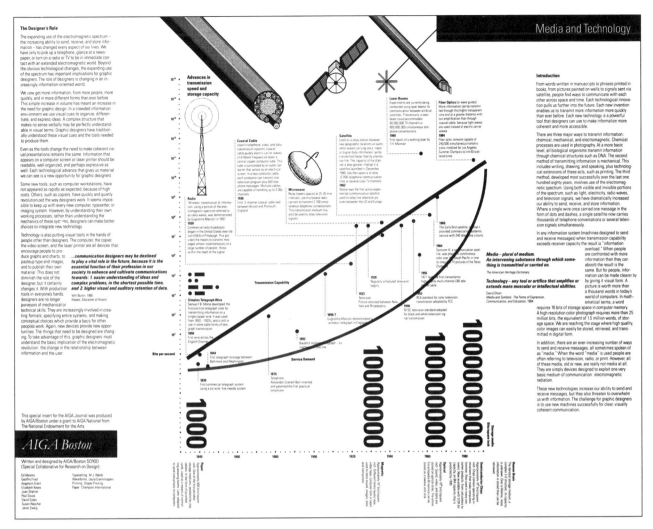

The carefully organized collection of information above is at the opposite end of the communications spectrum from the poster. The subject is media and technology; the audience is sophisticated (the document was designed as an insert for a graphic arts journal) and so is the delivery of information.

The chart encapsulates advances in transmission speed and storage capacity of media in the context of a time line. In addition to providing a great deal of information in a very small space, it cuts through the stereotypical image of charts as bland and linear.

Quotations inset between the running text and the chart provide a point of easy access in this complex page as well as another layer of historical context:

…communication designers may be destined to play a vital role in the future, because it is the essential function of their profession in our society to enhance and cultivate communications towards: 1. easier understanding of ideas and complex problems, in the shortest possible time, and 2. higher visual and auditory retention of data.
—Will Burtin, 1965

Design: Paul Souza, Ed Abrams, and Susan Wascher (Boston, MA)

Insert for the American Institute of Graphic Arts journal produced by AIGA/ Boston.

Trim size: 22 by 17

The conceptual illustration on the cover of this quarterly publication brings to bear the personal and subjective vision of the artist. It invites the reader to participate and engages the imagination.

The single-word title is very focused. It succinctly states the subject but leaves you curious as to how it will be addressed.

The overall image of the cover combines a feeling of accomplishment and success with the need for innovation and a sense of work yet to be done. Each element, as well as the whole, echoes the nature of leadership itself.

The dramatic photo composition on the cover of this PBS-series program guide has an emotional content that touches the reader in a way that straight typography cannot. The juxtaposition of a mushroom cloud against the outstretched hands of Gorbachev and Reagan evokes the terror and hope, the despair and optimism of our time. The photos also suggest the mix of historical and contemporary components in the series.

The title over the photos suggests that the series will be comprehensive. The wording is restrained and sets a tone that encourages the viewer to suspend moral judgments temporarily .

Design: Alison Kennedy (Boston, MA)

Program guide produced by WGBH and Central Independent Television.
Trim size: 8-1/2 by 11

Design: Weisz Yang Dunkelberger Inc. (Westport, CT)

Periodical published by Lefkoe & Associates, a management consulting and training organization.
Trim size: 9 by 12

What is the purpose of your publication?

Desktop publishing can be used to produce documents as diverse as calling cards and novels. This book is concerned primarily with business documents, which usually fall into several categories. Identifying the category to which your document belongs (it may be more than one) can help you develop the right approach for the purpose.

Information technology was supposed to let us taper off paper.... From 1959 to 1986 America's consumption of writing and printing paper increased from 6.83 million to 21.99 million tons, or 320 percent, while the real [GNP] rose 280 percent.

—Edward Tenner, Harvard Magazine, cited in The Computer Desk Reference & Appointment Calendar 1989

Documents that persuade
Advertisements
Invitations
Fund raisers
Posters
Press releases
Promotional flyers
Prospectuses
Sales brochures

Documents that identify
Business cards
Certificates
Labels
Stationery

Documents that inform
Brochures
Bulletins
Curriculum listings
Fact sheets
Marketing plans
Product lists
Programs
Rate cards
Specification sheets

Periodicals that inform
Magazines
Newsletters
Newspapers
Reports

Documents that elicit response
Applications
Order forms
Surveys

Documents that provide reference
Calendars
Directories
Lists
Parts lists
Schedules
Timetables

Documents that give how-to information
Curriculum guides
Instruction manuals
Training guides

Why is your publication needed?

One of the most important questions to ask yourself is why the reader needs or wants the information in your document. If you can zero in on that need, you can use it in your headlines and art to get the reader's attention. Keeping the reader's needs in mind also helps focus your writing.

Desktop publishers get carried away with their tools. They...spend more time on the aesthetics of a document than the content of it.
—Boeing's DTP product manager, in an article in MacWEEK

In many cases the reader is at best indifferent and at worst resistant to the information you want to convey. If you acknowledge that indifference, you can try to devise some way of overcoming it. In the face of audience resistance, you might want to put extra effort and money into the cover. Or consider printing a strong opening sentence or two in large type on the cover to lure readers in. Puzzles, quizzes, and other involvement techniques can sometimes draw readers to a subject they might otherwise ignore. A headline that poses a bold question is a simpler version of this same approach and can work if your audience is likely to want to know the answer. (Readers can often be hooked by a question even if it's one they think they can answer.) Humor, where appropriate, can also cajole the audience into reading on. The technique depends on the publication, the audience, and the budget. But do try something. If you ignore audience indifference when you write and design a document, you can guarantee that it won't be read.

Who is your audience?

Unless you write like Stephen King or address a subject as important to your reader as his or her bank balance, you can't assume that your intended reader will actually read your document. You may have a target audience or even a captive audience, but you don't have a reader until you've involved that person through words or pictures or an overall impression. Identifying your audience helps you choose the techniques that engage readers. Are they colleagues? Customers? Potential investors? Clients? What style is appropriate? How much do they know about your subject? How much time are they likely to spend with your publication? What other information do they have on the subject? Is this their only source?

The business of reaching the audience is no different than before.
—Ben Bagdikian,
in a New York Times *interview about desktop publishing*

Think in terms of interaction rather than one-way communication. It doesn't hurt to think of yourself as an entertainer or a sales person anticipating your audience's reaction. Consider readers' responses so that you can adjust your approach.

As you develop your publication, put yourself in the readers' position:

- How quickly can they pick out the highlights? Most readers scan. They want a sense of what you have to say before they make a commitment to read on. They want the highlights before the details.

- Can they find the items that are relevant to their particular concerns? Many publications have a mix of information, with different subjects, themes, or types of material. In a company newsletter, for example, one employee may be interested in educational assistance while another is concerned with after-hours security. Understanding your readers' special interests helps you organize the material.

- How quickly can they read the text? Remember the problem of information overload. Your text should be clear and lean. Less is more in print.

- Can your readers understand the information? Have you assumed knowledge they don't have?

Instruction manuals and reference books require careful organization and graphic devices that help the reader to find what he or she needs. One study of computer documentation revealed that of all the questions phoned in to the technical support staff, 80 percent were covered in the manual; the users either couldn't find the answers quickly enough or didn't understand them.

What kind of information will be included?

Different kinds of publications have different elements. A brochure for a professional conference may require a program, a workshop schedule, brief biographies of the speakers, and a map. An advertisement may consist entirely of slogans, tag lines, and little pieces of information such as prices or an address. A press release needs the name of a person to contact for more information. A technical manual needs a glossary. Review the different kinds of information—text and visual—early on so that you'll have space for all the pieces and avoid oversights.

An awareness of the elements needed in your document also affects your format and pacing. For a newsletter with several short articles and small photographs, you might choose a four-column format, whereas a newsletter with one major article and a number of short, newsy items might work best in two unequal columns. You can't possibly make an intelligent decision about format until you have a fix on the kinds of information you'll be formatting.

What kind of image do you want to project?

Everything about a publication, from the style of the prose to the quality of the paper it's printed on, contributes to the image it conveys about the sender. And the single most important guideline in fashioning that image is appropriateness. The elements you select and the way you assemble and reproduce them become a matter not so much of good or bad design as of design that is appropriate for your purpose and audience. Even the crammed-full, poorly printed advertisements for discount department stores cannot be dismissed as "bad" design when put to the tests of appropriate and effective communication.

The layout of the circus under canvas is more like the plan of the Acropolis than anything else; it is a beautiful organic arrangement established by the boss canvas man and the lot boss.... The concept of "appropriateness," this "how-it-should-be-ness," has equal value in the circus, in the making of a work of art, and in science.

—Charles Eames

If you are promoting a financial service, you want prose that is well informed and authoritative and design and printing that is prosperous without being indulgent. A company that has had a bad year, on the other hand, wants to appear careful and restrained without creating concern about quality. And you want an entrepreneurial business plan to appear energetic, bold, and thorough all at the same time.

A travel brochure for a Caribbean cruise might use color photos to suggest escape, adventure, and celebration, and an ad for a new restaurant in the theater or art district might use words and decorative motifs to project a similar experience close to home.

As you consider the elements and design of your publication, write down a list of impressions you want to make. Formal. Informal. Friendly. Playful. Elegant. Stylish. Trendy. Classic. Adventurous. Conservative. Scholarly. Provocative. Diverse. Spirited. Generous. Concerned. How do you want your audience to perceive you?

Must your publication fit into a program or conform to a corporate style?

For a new program that requires continuity—say a series of health seminars, each with a promotional mailing before the event, a seminar program distributed at the event, and a follow-up questionnaire after the event—you'll want to develop a design that establishes an identity for the series and that can be followed for each event.

The issue of corporate identity has emerged as some companies have discovered that desktop publishing encourages more creativity than their image can handle. The logo begins appearing in different sizes and positions on the page. Documents from one department have a streamlined, stylized look, whereas documents from another use Victorian clip art. The corporate response is to establish formats and design standards so that different kinds of documents—order forms, product sheets, newsletters, reports, and so on—all have a consistent look. You may feel that having to adhere to these standards puts a damper on your style, but in fact it will probably free you to concentrate on the clarity and effectiveness of the elements within the established format.

What is the overall format?

Format includes everything from the organization of material to the page size to the underlying structure, or grid, of your layout. You rarely start a publication with an idea of what the format should be; rather, the format evolves out of the material and often changes as your understanding of the publication changes.

In developing your format, consider first the common elements in the publication. How many levels of headlines will you need? How will you separate items that appear on the same page?

Readers want what is important to be clearly laid out; they will not read anything that is troublesome to read.
—Jan Tschichold,
writing in 1935, cited in
Thirty Centuries of Graphic Design

Look at the formats of other publications, keep a file of what you like, and adapt those techniques to fit your needs. Professional designers do this all the time. Don't limit your file to the kinds of publications you will produce. You may never create an accordion-fold brochure, but some aspect of the format may help you solve a problem in your own publication.

Keep in mind that readers scan printed matter, and consider techniques to facilitate this:

- A strong visual framework will separate one item from another and indicate relative importance.

- Several short stories are almost always more accessible and inviting than one long one.

- Use sidebars or boxed copy to break the text into accessible chunks.

- Every headline and caption is a hook, a potential entry point for busy readers.

- Pay attention to the pacing: Balance text with visuals and offset "quick reads" with more demanding material.

- Use graphic devices to move the reader's eye from one place on the page to another, especially to key points or to little bits of information that you think are particularly interesting.

- Keep in mind also that many readers scan from back to front; can you get their attention in the middle of a story?

For magazines, newsletters, and other periodicals, develop your format with great care so that you can maintain a consistent style from one issue to the next. What departments and features will be included in every issue? Where will they appear?

What kinds of art or photography will be included?

You can produce professional, attractive documents without any art, but pictures unquestionably draw readers in more easily than words, and illustrations can greatly enhance your message. Art and photography can illustrate the text, provide additional information, create a mood, provoke questions in the reader's mind, and set the overall tone of a publication. Charts and graphs can squeeze a lot of facts into a small amount of space and be visually interesting at the same time. Even abstract geometric shapes can intrigue and invite and add movement to the page. Graphic devices such as borders, boxes, and tinted areas, along with icons such as arrows, bullets, and ballot boxes, all help create a strong sense of organization and move the reader from one part of the page to another. Consider these devices as ways to break up the text and make your pages more interesting, more accessible, and more informative. Keep in mind that you don't necessarily need a lot of art; often one or two strong images are more effective than half a dozen mediocre ones.

We learn language by applying words to visual experiences, and we create visual images to illustrate verbal ideas. This interaction of word and image is the background for contemporary communication.
—Allen Hurlburt,
The Design Concept

You will need to consider the amount and type of art to be used early on, because it will affect your format and will also generate loose odds and ends of text. Will you have captions? Numbers to identify figures? Sources for charts? Where will the art credits appear?

The art will affect the schedule, too. Will you have the printer make conventional halftones from black-and-white photos? Or will you scan the photos to place as digital halftones in the PageMaker file? Or will you have a service bureau do the scans? Each method requires a slightly different schedule. Color art requires similar considerations. Conventional color separations can take anywhere from three days to two weeks, depending on your relationship with the printer and the extent of the color corrections you require.

What are the printing specifications?

Specifications—including page size, number of pages, type of binding, paper stock, quantity to be printed, and use of color, if any—are inextricably related to the overall format. Changing one often affects the other. Review your options early on with any outside vendors you plan to use (commercial printers, color separators, full-service copy centers); your specifications must be consistent with their capabilities and requirements.

If you've come to desktop publishing without any experience in working with printed materials, you'll encounter a new set of jargon as you move into printing and binding. It's just trade talk, and you'll pick it up in time. If your printer can print in four- and eight-page signatures as well as in sixteens, that might affect the number of pages you produce. If you can get a good price on an odd-size paper that works for your needs, you might want to adjust your page size. The binding you select may affect your page margins. See the Resources section in the back of this book for production guides that will help you understand the fundamentals of commercial printing.

What will you use for camera-ready pages?

For many documents, the 300-dots-per-inch output from a laser printer is sufficient for camera-ready pages. For others, you may want the higher resolution provided by an imagesetter such as the Linotronic. Again, your decision here will affect your schedule and your budget.

When you plan to use Linotronic output, be sure to run test pages of your format early on. Rules, shades, and type weight are lighter at higher resolutions, and you may want to adjust your specs when you see the early tests. You'll want to work with the service center that will provide your Linotronic output just as you do with your printer. Find out what kind of compatibility the service center requires in order to print your files—what versions of programs they use, which fonts they have, what backup you must provide, whether they use screen fonts for boldface and italic styles or require that you apply these from the Type style menu. Knowledgeable personnel at good service centers are a valuable resource and can help you troubleshoot problems early on.

How will your document be reproduced?

For any but those jobs you consider routine, talk with the printer as early in the planning as possible.... Describe your needs and ask whether your piece can be printed practically. Consider suggestions about alternate papers, design changes, and other ideas about how to save time and money.... [But] remember that they want your business. By suggesting changes which take advantage of particular presses or papers, a printer may be shaping your job to fit that shop. Keep in mind that you are getting consultation and may not be ready to write specifications.

—Mark Beach,
Getting It Printed

As is the case with many aspects of publishing, the new technology has expanded the ways in which documents are reproduced. Will you use the office photocopy machine? A full-service copy center? A quick printer with offset presses and binderies? Or a commercial printer for higher-quality reproduction? Your printing needs will be determined by the number of copies, the quality desired, and your budget.

If you will be using commercial printers on a regular basis and you are new to publishing, try to develop a working relationship with local printers and learn more about that end of the business. Printing is a fine art but an inconsistent one; even highly experienced professionals fear the nasty surprises that can happen on press. Poor communication between publisher and printer can result in poor quality. Let your printer know what you expect. If you're not satisfied with the quality, follow up after you receive printed copies to find out what the problem was. Often the printer will blame it on the paper (which is rarely as good as you'd like it to be) or on the size of the run (it is difficult to maintain certain standards in large press runs, but the printer is supposed to have quality-control mechanisms to catch problems as they come up), or on some other plausible factors. But sometimes the problem could have been avoided. Perhaps your photograph was cut off because you didn't leave enough space between your art and the trim; next time you'll know to determine the tolerance and adjust your margins accordingly. By asking, you'll let the printer know you care about quality, and you may learn something.

How will it be distributed?

Whether your document is distributed through interoffice mail, given away in stores, or sent through the mail or some other delivery service, you want the purpose to be easily discernible. What is the reader's first impression? Is a person as likely to see the back cover first as the front? If the publication is folded, will the pacing of the words and images keep the recipients moving through the folds? If a flyer is to be tacked on a bulletin board, can the headline be read from a distance?

If your document will be mailed, it must conform to postal regulations for the appropriate mailing class. This may affect the size, the way the publication is folded, the placement of the mailing label, and the amount of space for the address if the publication is a self-mailer.

An early understanding of the restrictions and requirements of your distribution method can save you time and money and can affect certain decisions about your format as well.

When is it needed?

Regardless of your experience and that of your staff, expect productivity to drop in the beginning, as everyone learns the new system.... It will probably take at least three production cycles before you can get all the kinks out.... Many organizations continue to use traditional production methods in parallel with their new desktop systems, phasing in the new methods gradually. This means you won't see your cost savings right away, but you're not putting all your eggs in one new and untested basket.
—Janet Millenson, writing in Publish! *magazine*

Schedules are a blessing and a curse. On the one hand there is the feeling that there's not enough time to do the job the way you'd like, but on the other hand everyone knows that any project will expand to fill the time available. Scheduling is especially sensitive when you are working with new technology. Desktop publishing is supposed to shave days off a project that would have taken a week, and weeks off one that would have taken a month. That can happen, but not the first week you have your system. You need time to learn, time to find out what you can and can't do with your particular configuration.

Most schedules are determined backwards, starting with when you want the document in your reader's hands. You then figure in the time required for distribution, printing, and other outside services, and finally you determine not how long you *need* to create the publication, but how long you *have*.

Schedules are a reality factor. The tighter the schedule, the simpler your format should be.

What is the budget?

Money is also a reality factor. It so affects everything about a publication that it's often the first consideration. We've put it last on the checklist, not out of disregard for its importance, but out of a belief that first you should think about what you want to do, and then you should look at what you can do. It's the nature of dreams to make us reach, and even when we can't grab hold of what we want, dreams often produce good ideas that can be scaled down to fit a budget. Take your budget and your schedule seriously, but don't let them be ever-present blinders.

CHAPTER 2

THE PRINCIPLES OF TYPOGRAPHY

Typographic arrangement should achieve for the reader what voice tone conveys to the listener.
—*El Lissitzky*

The ability to set type, to modify it on-screen, to compose it in pages, and then print the result in camera-ready form is the foundation of desktop publishing. Suddenly, the fundamental building block of graphic design is in the hands of anyone with a few thousand dollars. What are we to make of this access to such a rich tradition, one developed over 500 years of practice?

The answer, of course, varies widely. Typography at its most basic is simply the selection and arrangement of typefaces, sizes, and spacing on the printed page. But faced with the raw material for a page that isn't printed, how do you style the elements so that the page is inviting and easy to read, so that the eye can distinguish the relative importance of items and pick out the ones of interest, so that the overall appearance is both varied and unified?

In addition to the utilitarian functions implied in those questions, typography also gives a page a certain personality (formal or informal, modern or classic, ornate or sturdy) and an overall feeling (dense or open, light or dramatic). How do you choose from among the many typefaces available to project the desired image and to give your publication a distinctive and recognizable personality?

As much as in any other area of graphic design, the answers come largely from experience. Some of that experience we all have as readers. A great deal more can be gained by looking carefully at how type is styled in the whole range of printed materials. And finally, the computer makes it possible to discover the nuances of type through hands-on experimentation.

Computers have given us an invaluable control over typography, but they have also made possible a counterproductive versatility. In desktop publishing we have so many typefaces available and so many special effects, we can change so readily from one size and style to another, that undisciplined typography can as easily fragment the message as help hold it together. Use the control to experiment, to find the right face and size and spacing for your purpose, but don't use the versatility to pack your pages with a half dozen or more styles that confuse more than they communicate.

The power to control typography from the desktop is all the more miraculous when you review the history of typesetting and see the

72 dots per inch (screen image)

300 dpi

1270 dpi

2540 dpi

There is a story, no doubt apocryphal, that a fifteenth-century scribe, upon examining one of Gutenberg's press sheets, exclaimed, "It's nice, but it's not calligraphy."

progression from a craftsman's handling of each individual letter to a computer operator's ability to send electrical impulses around the world. In the fifteenth century, Johann Gutenberg liberated the printed word from the painstaking craft of handscripting with what now seems the almost equally painstaking craft of individually setting each metal character. With the introduction of linotype machines in the 1880s, keyboard operators could type in the text and the machine would cast an entire line in a single slug of hot metal. Phototypesetting eliminated the actual type altogether and produced text by projecting the images of characters on light-sensitive film or paper. Today's computer-driven laser printers have turned letters into patterns of dots and computer owners and operators into typographers.

This most recent "democratization" of typography has created something of a holy war between the traditionalists and the new breed of desktop publishers. The traditionalists—designers of typefaces and graphic designers who have worked with commercial type throughout their careers—lament the distortion of letterforms in standard faces, the uneven spacing between letters and words, and the lower resolution in the type created on desktop systems. The desktop publishers see savings in time and money and, in some documents, a quality that is far superior to the previous typewritten and mimeographed forms.

The real miracle, which it is the nature of holy wars to overlook, is choice. The laser printer resolution of 300 dots per inch (dpi) is perfectly adequate as well as cost effective for many newsletters, reports, bulletins, price sheets, and a great many other documents. The higher resolution of a Linotronic 100 or 300 (1270 and 2540 dots per inch, respectively) is appropriate for many brochures, books, catalogs, technical manuals, magazines, and annual reports; in these situations the desktop computer serves as the front end for commercial typesetting and still gives the user greater control and considerable savings of time and money over traditional typesetting. High-quality, commercial typesetting is still available for advertising agencies, design studios, and publishers of fine books and magazines whose products require, and can afford, the cleanest, sharpest, most beautifully proportioned type. It's a matter of choosing the quality of type appropriate for your needs and budget, and then using that type as well as you possibly can.

This chapter is about the many ways of using type. The main purpose is not to put forth rules you must remember but to suggest ways of looking at type on the printed page. As Sumner Stone, the director of typography at Adobe Systems, said in a *Publish!* magazine roundtable discussion on typography, "It's like learning how to appreciate different flavors of wine." Drink up.

A VISUAL GLOSSARY OF TYPOGRAPHY

The terminology used to describe type and its appearance on the printed page is a colorful and useful jargon. As with any specialized language, it enables people to communicate unambiguously, so that the instruction "align baseline of flush right caption with bottom of art" means the same thing to everyone involved in a job. But the language of typography also describes the subtlety and diversity among letterforms. This glossary is intended to display some of that richness in the process of setting forth basic definitions.

TYPEFACE

The name of a typeface refers to an entire family of letters of a particular design. (Historically, face referred to the surface of the metal type piece that received the ink and came into contact with the printing surface.) The faces shown on this spread are resident on most Post-Script printers. Hundreds of faces are available for desktop production today; by the end of 1990, the number will be in the thousands.

Avant Garde

ABCDEFGHIJKLMNOPQRSTUVWXYZ
abcdefghijklmnopqrstuvwxyz
1234567890!$,""?
ABCDEFGHIJKLMNOPQRSTUVWXYZ
abcdefghijklmnopqrstuvwxyz
1234567890!$,""?

Bookman

ABCDEFGHIJKLMNOPQRSTUVWXYZ
abcdefghijklmnopqrstuvwxyz
1234567890!$,""?
ABCDEFGHIJKLMNOPQRSTUVWXYZ
abcdefghijklmnopqrstuvwxyz
1234567890!$,""?

Courier

ABCDEFGHIJKLMNOPQRSTUVWXYZ
abcdefghijklmnopqrstuvwxyz
1234567890!$,""?
ABCDEFGHIJKLMNOPQRSTUVWXYZ
abcdefghijklmnopqrstuvwxyz
1234567890!$,""?

Helvetica

ABCDEFGHIJKLMNOPQRSTUVWXYZ
abcdefghijklmnopqrstuvwxyz
1234567890!$,""?
ABCDEFGHIJKLMNOPQRSTUVWXYZ
abcdefghijklmnopqrstuvwxyz
1234567890!$,""?

New Century
Schoolbook

ABCDEFGHIJKLMNOPQRSTUVWXYZ
abcdefghijklmnopqrstuvwxyz
1234567890!$,""?
ABCDEFGHIJKLMNOPQRSTUVWXYZ
abcdefghijklmnopqrstuvwxyz
1234567890!$,""?

Palatino

ABCDEFGHIJKLMNOPQRSTUVWXYZ
abcdefghijklmnopqrstuvwxyz
1234567890!$,""?
ABCDEFGHIJKLMNOPQRSTUVWXYZ
abcdefghijklmnopqrstuvwxyz
1234567890!$,""?

Times Roman

ABCDEFGHIJKLMNOPQRSTUVWXYZ
abcdefghijklmnopqrstuvwxyz
1234567890!$,""?
ABCDEFGHIJKLMNOPQRSTUVWXYZ
abcdefghijklmnopqrstuvwxyz
1234567890!$,""?

Zapf Chancery

ABCDEFGHIJKLMNOPQRSTUVWXYZ
abcdefghijklmnopqrstuvwxyz
1234567890!$,""?

ABCDEFGHIJKLMNOPQRSTUVWXYZ
abcdefghijklmnopqrstuvwxyz
1234567890!$,""?

For all of the variety found across thousands of typefaces, most of them can be grouped into three basic styles—serif, sans serif, and script. The samples shown on these two pages suggest the variation available in each style. These samples (and the ones throughout this chapter) are PostScript fonts from Adobe Systems.

Some legibility studies have found that serif typefaces are easier to read, the theory being that the serifs help move the eye from one letter to the next without the letters blurring together. On the other hand, sans serif typefaces are generally thought to be easier to read at very large and especially at very small sizes. It's difficult to make any hard-and-fast rules because legibility is affected not only by typeface but also by size, length of line, amount of leading, amount of white space on the page, and even by the quality of the paper.

SANS SERIF

Sans serif typefaces do not have finishing strokes at the end of the letterforms. The name comes from the French *sans*, meaning "without." Sans serif faces are also referred to as Gothic.

Helvetica   Futura   Univers

Avant Garde   Franklin Gothic

Eurostile   News Gothic   Optima

SCRIPT

Script faces simulate handwriting, with one letter connected to another visually if not physically.

Freestyle Script   *Zapf Chancery*

SERIF

Serifs are lines or curves projecting from the end of a letterform. Typefaces with these additional strokes are called serif faces. They are also referred to as Roman faces because the serifs derived from the marks made chiseling letters into Roman monuments. (Note that when describing serif faces, the word Roman is capitalized; when describing vertical letters as distinguished from italic ones, roman is lowercase.)

Palatino   Times Roman   Garamond

New Century Schoolbook   Caslon

Bookman   Century Old Style

Goudy Old Style   Glypha

Bodoni   American Typewriter

Trump Mediæval   Galliard

Lubalin Graph   New Baskerville

SIZE

Type is measured by its vertical height, in points. (There are 12 points to a pica and about 6 picas to an inch.) But if you use a pica ruler to measure from the highest ascender to the lowest descender in any font, the result will be less than the size you've specified. That's because, despite all the revolutions in typesetting technology, type size still allows for the shoulder above and below the letter in a piece of metal type.

Height Height Height Height Height Height Height Height

6 pt 8 pt 10 pt 12 pt 14 point 18 point 36 point 72 point

WEIGHT

Weight refers to the density of letters, to the lightness or heaviness of the strokes. It is described as a continuum: light, regular, book, demi, bold, heavy, black, extra bold. Not all typefaces are available for all weights, and the continuum varies in some faces.

HELVETICA LIGHT HELVETICA REGULAR
HELVETICA BOLD HELVETICA BLACK

WIDTH

The horizontal measure of letters is described as condensed, normal, or expanded. Resident typefaces such as Times Roman and Helvetica are generally normal. You can condense and expand type in PageMaker using the Set Width option on the Type menu. Be careful, though, of extreme settings that distort the letterforms. If you want to use a condensed typeface for large amounts of body text, choose one that's available as a downloadable font rather than using the Set Width option.

CONDENSED NORMAL EXPANDED

SLANT

Slant is the angle of a type character, either vertical or inclined. Vertical type is called roman (in PageMaker it is called Normal, and in some word-processing programs, Plain). Inclined type is called italic or oblique.

roman & *italic*

STYLE

In PageMaker, style refers to options such as bold, italic, and underline that you can choose as part of your type specifications. All the styles shown below are available in the Macintosh version of PageMaker; the outline and shadow styles are not available in the Windows version.

STYLE **STYLE** *STYLE* STYLE

STYLE STYLE STYLE STYLE

FAMILY

All of the variations of a single typeface—the different weights, widths, slants, and styles—constitute a type family. Some families have more styles than others, providing for considerable type contrast within a document without the need to change typefaces. In addition to the Helvetica styles shown below, the family includes Compressed, Thin, Ultra Light, and Heavy variations. Some other families with many variations are Bodoni, Futura, Univers, and Stone.

Helvetica
Helvetica Italic
Helvetica Bold
Helvetica Bold Italic
Helvetica Condensed Light
Helvetica Condensed Light Oblique
Helvetica Condensed
Helvetica Condensed Oblique
Helvetica Condensed Bold
Helvetica Condensed Bold Oblique
Helvetica Condensed Black
Helvetica Condensed Black Oblique
Helvetica Light
Helvetica Light Oblique
Helvetica Black
Helvetica Black Oblique

ANATOMY

In designing, measuring, and identifying type, a precise vocabulary is essential. Here are the basics:

LEADING

The vertical space between lines of type is called leading (pronounced "led•ing"). It is measured in points and is expressed as the sum of the type size and the space between two lines. For example, 10-point type with 2 points between the lines is described as 10-point type on 12-point leading. It is written 10/12 and spoken "10 on 12." The term was originally used to describe the narrow metal strips inserted between lines of hand-set type.

Type with a generous amount of space between lines is said to have open leading; type with relatively little space between lines is said to be set tight. Type without any space between lines (such as the 10/10 and the 30/30 samples below) is said to be set solid. Leading that is less than the point size, as in the 30/26 sample, is called negative, or minus, leading; it is used primarily for large type sizes set in all caps.

10/10 Times Roman

These three type samples are all set in 10-point Times Roman. The first is set solid (10/10), the second is set tight (10/11), and the third (10/12) is set with PageMaker's automatic leading (120% of the point size).

10/11 Times Roman

These three type samples are all set in 10-point Times Roman. The first is set solid (10/10), the second is set tight (10/11), and the third (10/12) is set with PageMaker's automatic leading (120% of the point size).

10/12 Times Roman

These three type samples are all set in 10-point Times Roman. The first is set solid (10/10), the second is set tight (10/11), and the third (10/12) is set with PageMaker's automatic leading (120% of the point size).

30/26 Helvetica Condensed Black

THIS DISPLAY TYPE IS SET MINUS

30/30 Helvetica Condensed Black

THIS DISPLAY TYPE IS SET SOLID

30/34 Helvetica Condensed Black

THIS DISPLAY TYPE IS SET OPEN

LINE LENGTH

The length of a line of type is called the measure and is traditionally specified in picas. Fractions of picas are expressed as points (there are 12 points to a pica), not as decimals. So a column that is 10 and one-quarter picas wide is 10 picas 3 points, or 10p3.

Generally, the longer the line length the larger the type should be.

This is set to a 12p measure and can be easily read with a relatively small type size. This sample is 9/11.

This is set to a 20p measure and needs a larger type size for ease of reading. This sample is 10/12.

This is set to a 37p6 measure and needs a larger type size to be easily read. This measure is too wide for most running text and is best used for subheads, blurbs, and other short display type. This sample is set 13/15.

ALIGNMENT

Alignment refers to the shape of the type block relative to the margins. PageMaker offers five settings: flush left, centered, flush right, justified, and force justified. Body text is generally set flush left or justified, but justified type requires more attention to the spacing between letters and words, as you can see from the examples below.

Flush left

The lines of text are even on the left edge (flush with the left margin) and uneven, or ragged, on the right. Flush left is the recommended alignment for body text in desktop publishing. It is easy to read and allows even word spacing.

Centered

Each line is centered;
thus, both left and right margins
are ragged.
Centered text is often used
for headlines and
other display type,
as well as for formal invitations
and announcements.

Flush right

The lines of text are even on the right and uneven on the left. This alignment is sometimes used for captions, display type, and advertising copy but is not recommended for body text. We are used to reading from left to right; if the left edge of the text is not well defined, the eye falters, and the text is more difficult to read.

Justified

The type is flush, or even, on both the right and the left margins. Because the normal space between letters and words is altered in order to justify text, justification sometimes results in uneven spacing, with "rivers" of white space running through the type. The narrower the measure, the more uneven the spacing is likely to be, as you can see by comparing these side-by-side examples.

Justified

The type is flush, or even, on both the right and the left margins. Because the normal space between letters and words is altered in order to justify text, justification sometimes results in uneven spacing, with "rivers" of white space running through the type. The narrower the measure, the more uneven the spacing is likely to be, as you can see by comparing these side-by-side examples.

Rag left and rag right

A less common setting is rag left and rag right.
This is sometimes used for display type.
It gives the page a poetic feeling without being formal.
This setting cannot be achieved automatically:
You must specify the indent for each individual line.

RULES

Rules are also typographic elements and are measured in points. Use PageMaker's Line command (on the Element menu) to specify the style and weight of rules. You can import rules with additional weights and styles from drawing programs.

TYPE SPECIMEN SHEETS

Designers have traditionally relied on specimen sheets to select and specify type in their publications. "Spec" sheets, as they are known, simply display typefaces in various sizes, weights, and styles so that you can judge the appropriateness of a particular face for the publication you're about to design, as well as the readability, color, and overall look of frequently used sizes. Spec sheets are also useful when you want to identify a typeface that you see and like in another publication.

Commercial typesetters generally supply spec sheets to their customers as a sort of catalog of what is available. You can also buy books of spec sheets, and some are now available specifically for desktop publishing. (See the Resources section in the back of this book.)

Type is the first impression you have of what you're about to read. Each typeface, like a human face, has a subtle character all its own. Depending on which face you choose, the same word can have many different shades of meaning. And since you must have type in order to have words, why not make sure those words are presented in the most elegant, or the most powerful, or the softest way possible.
—Roger Black
from an interview in Font & Function

You can also make your own spec sheets for the typefaces available on your own system or network. The little time it takes will repay you generously every time you need to design a publication. In addition to providing you with a useful resource, making spec sheets is a good way to begin learning the nuances of type.

The page at right shows one format for a spec sheet. Depending upon the kind of publication work you do, you may want to vary the components, with more or less display type, more or less running text, more or fewer small-size settings for captions, data, and so on. You may also want more variation in line length than our sample shows. Expand it to two pages, include character counts for various settings—in short, do whatever will be most useful to you. Once you have a format worked out and have set up one complete spec sheet as an electronic page, you can simply open a copy of that page for each typeface in your system, change the typeface, and then type over the identifying names for the new typeface. By using the same words and style for each sheet, you'll get a true comparison between the faces that are available to you.

In the sample, we've kerned the name of the typeface at the very top of the page, adding space between letters where needed so that none of the letters butt. You want to be able to see the shape of each letter when you use the spec sheets as an identification aid.

GARAMOND

Garamond Light
Garamond Light Italic
Garamond Bold
Garamond Bold Italic

ABCDEFGHIJKLMNOPQRSTUVWXYZ
abcdefghijklmnopqrstuvwxyz
1234567890!@#$%^&*( )+[ ] , ; " " ?

WALDEN BY HENRY DAVID THOREAU   12/14
WALDEN BY HENRY DAVID THOREAU

WALDEN BY HENRY DAVID THOREAU   caps/sm caps
WALDEN BY HENRY DAVID THOREAU

Walden by Henry David Thoreau
Walden by Henry David Thoreau

14/16

When I wrote the following pages, I lived alone, in the woods, a mile from any neighbor, in a house which I had built myself, on the shore of Walden Pond.

9/11

I lived alone, in the woods, a mile from any neighbor, in a house which I had built myself, on the shore of Walden

I lived alone, in the woods, a mile from any neighbor, in a house which I had built myself, on the shore of

11/13

When I wrote
the following pages,
or rather
the bulk of them,
I lived alone, in the woods,
a mile from any neighbor,
on the shore of Walden Pond.

36

Aa Ee Gg Tt Ww
1234567890 $? ' '

9/11

When I wrote the following pages, or rather the bulk of them, I lived alone, in the woods, a mile from any neighbor, in a house which I had built myself, on the shore of Walden Pond, in Concord, Massachusetts, and earned my living by the labor of my hands only. I lived there two years and two months. At present I am a sojourner in civilized life again.

I should not obtrude my affairs so much on the notice of my readers if very

W 72

When I wrote the following pages, or rather the bulk of them, I lived alone, in the woods, a mile from any neighbor, in a house which I had built myself, on the shore of Walden Pond, in Concord, Massachusetts, and earned my living by the labor of my hands only. I lived there two years and two months. At present I am a sojourner in civilized life again.

I should not obtrude my affairs so much on the notice of my readers if

10/12

11/13

When I wrote the following pages, or rather the bulk of them, I lived alone, in the woods, a mile from any neighbor, in a house which I had built myself, on the shore of Walden Pond, in Concord, Massachusetts, and earned my living by the labor of my hands only. I lived there two years and two months. At present I am a sojourner in civilized life again.

I should not obtrude my affairs so much on the notice of my

12/14

When I wrote the following pages, or rather the bulk of them, I lived alone, in the woods, a mile from any neighbor, in a house which I had built myself, on the shore of Walden Pond, in Concord, Massachusetts, and earned my living by the labor of my hands only. I lived there two years and two months. At present I am a sojourner in civilized life again.

I should not obtrude my affairs so much on the notice of

Using key letters to identify type

When using spec sheets to identify type from other publications, look for key letters that tend to be distinctive, including the T, g, and M shown here (all 60 point). Numbers and question marks are also good indicators. You quickly learn to look for the shape of the serif (straight, triangular, rounded, or square), whether the bowls of the Ps and Rs and the tails of the g's are open or closed, the contrast between thick and thin parts of the letter, and so on.

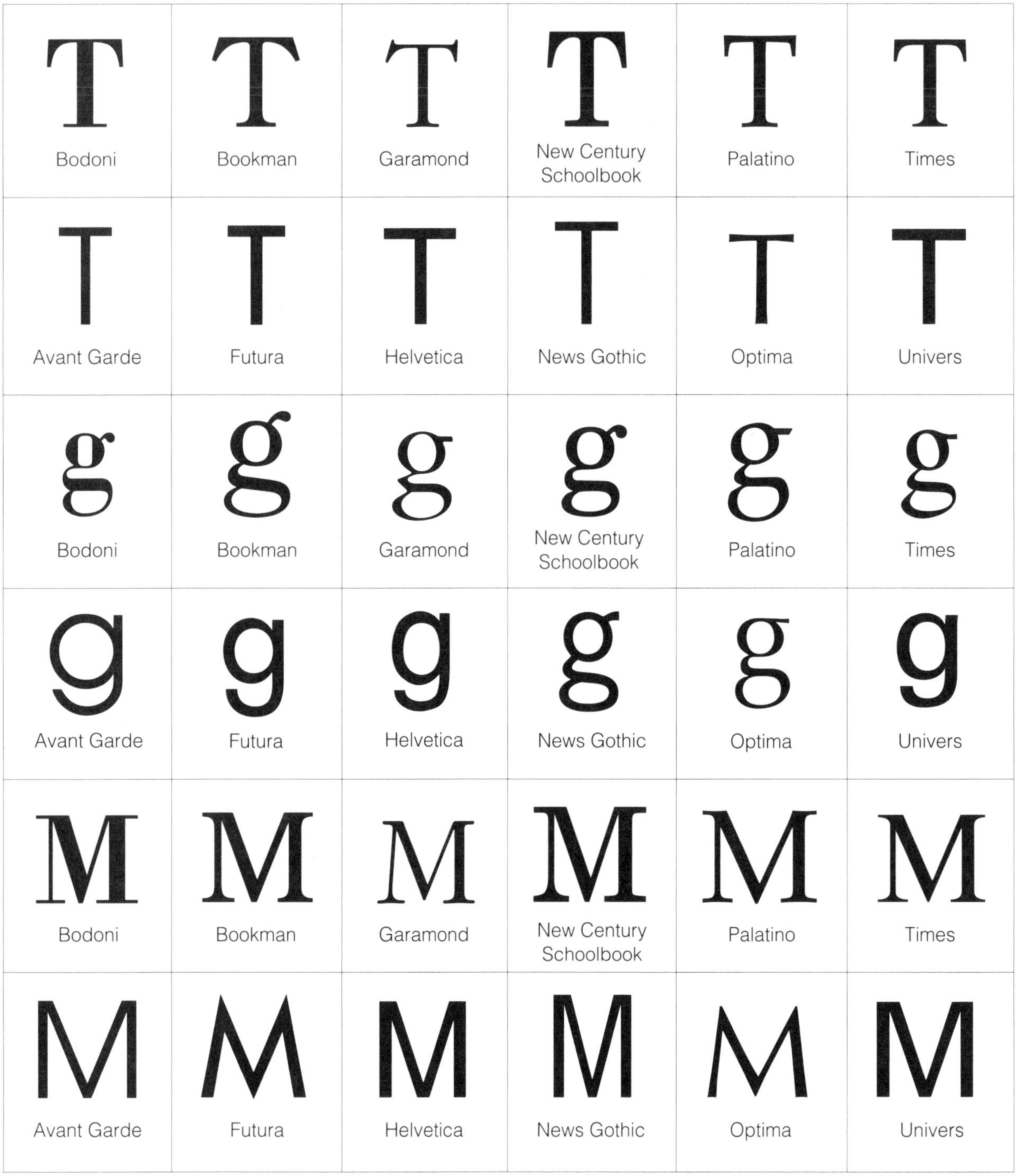

T	T	T	T	T	T
Bodoni	Bookman	Garamond	New Century Schoolbook	Palatino	Times

T	T	T	T	T	T
Avant Garde	Futura	Helvetica	News Gothic	Optima	Univers

g	g	g	g	g	g
Bodoni	Bookman	Garamond	New Century Schoolbook	Palatino	Times

g	g	g	g	g	g
Avant Garde	Futura	Helvetica	News Gothic	Optima	Univers

M	M	M	M	M	M
Bodoni	Bookman	Garamond	New Century Schoolbook	Palatino	Times

M	M	M	M	M	M
Avant Garde	Futura	Helvetica	News Gothic	Optima	Univers

The color of type

The addition of a second color (or several colors) can enhance the typographic design of a publication in many ways. But even when printed in black and white, type has a color on the printed page. Color in this sense means the overall tone, or texture, of the type; the lightness or darkness, which varies from one typeface and style to another; and also the evenness of the type as determined by the spacing. Spec sheets provide valuable guides to the color of different typefaces, which, as you can see in the samples below, vary considerably.

A large rose-tree stood near the entrance of the garden: the roses growing on it were white, but there were three gardeners at it, busily painting them red. Alice thought this a very curious thing, and she went nearer to watch....
—Futura Light

A large rose-tree stood near the entrance of the garden: the roses growing on it were white, but there were three gardeners at it, busily painting them red. Alice thought this a very curious thing, and she went nearer to...
—Goudy Old Style

A large rose-tree stood near the entrance of the garden: the roses growing on it were white, but there were three gardeners at it, busily painting them red. Alice thought this a very curious thing, and she went nearer to...
—Optima

A large rose-tree stood near the entrance of the garden: the roses growing on it were white, but there were three gardeners at it, busily painting them red. Alice thought this a very curious thing, and she went nearer...
—Palatino

A large rose-tree stood near the entrance of the garden: the roses growing on it were white, but there were three gardeners at it, busily painting them red. Alice thought this a very curious thing, and she went nearer to...
—Garamond

A large rose-tree stood near the entrance of the garden: the roses growing on it were white, but there were three gardeners at it, busily painting them red. Alice thought this a very curious thing...
—Avant Garde

A large rose-tree stood near the entrance of the garden: the roses growing on it were white, but there were three gardeners at it, busily painting them red. Alice thought this a very curious thing...
—Univers

A large rose-tree stood near the entrance of the garden: the roses growing on it were white, but there were three gardeners at it, busily painting them red. Alice thought this a very curious thing, and she went nearer...
—Franklin Gothic Demi

A large rose-tree stood near the entrance of the garden: the roses growing on it were white, but there were three gardeners at it, busily painting them red. Alice thought this a very curious thing, and she went nearer...
—Helvetica

A large rose-tree stood near the entrance of the garden: the roses growing on it were white, but there were three gardeners at it, busily painting them red. Alice thought this a very curious thing, and she went nearer to watch....
—New Baskerville Bold

A large rose-tree stood near the entrance of the garden: the roses growing on it were white, but there were three gardeners at it, busily painting them red. Alice thought this a very curious thing...
—Souvenir Demi

A large rose-tree stood near the entrance of the garden: the roses growing on it were white, but there were three gardeners at it, busily painting them red. Alice thought this a very curious thing...
—Bookman Demi

A large rose-tree stood near the entrance of the garden: the roses growing on it were white, but there were three gardeners at it, busily painting them red. Alice thought this a very curious thing, and she went nearer to watch....
—Glypha

A large rose-tree stood near the entrance of the garden: the roses growing on it were white, but there were three gardeners at it, busily painting them red. Alice thought this a very curious thing, and she went nearer to watch....
—Century Old Style Bold

A large rose-tree stood near the entrance of the garden: the roses growing on it were white, but there were three gardeners at it, busily painting them red. Alice thought this a very curious thing and she went ...
—Am. Typewriter Bold

A large rose-tree stood near the entrance of the garden: the roses growing on it were white, but there were three gardeners at it, busily painting them red. Alice thought this a very curious...
—Futura Extra Bold

The many personalities of type

Every typeface has its own personality, a look that makes it more or less suited for a particular type of publication. Confident, elegant, casual, bold, novel, romantic, friendly, stylish, nostalgic, classic, delicate, modern, crisp...the possibilities are endless. You have only to know the feeling you want, select an appropriate face, and then test it for legibility and effectiveness within your overall design.

The faces shown on these pages merely suggest the range available to today's desktop publisher. Having to choose from the many faces available can be intimidating to new designers. Begin by using a few faces and learning them well: how to achieve contrast through different styles and spacing within those families, which letter pairs require kerning, which counters fill in at small sizes, and so on.

Take note of typefaces you like in other publications and identify them using a type book. Then gradually add new faces to your system, learning their unique subtleties as you did the few faces that you started with. As one designer cautioned in the same *Publish* roundtable on typography quoted earlier in this chapter, "There are only two kinds of typefaces: those you know how to use and those you don't."

GEOMETRY AND PRECISION
WHEN YOU WANT THE CUTTING EDGE

USE AVANT GARDE. IT'S MODERN WITHOUT BEING FORMAL AND GIVES A PAGE A VERY CRISP LOOK. IT SETS BEST IN ALL CAPS AND BENEFITS FROM KERNING SO THAT THE LETTERS SNUGGLE UP TIGHT AGAINST ONE ANOTHER.

A REPORT THAT SUGGESTS
The Writer Has Big Shoulders

would work well in Bookman. It's a sturdy, highly legible typeface, used in many newspapers and often described as a workhorse because it's so versatile. In both its light and bold faces, it has relatively little contrast between the thick and thin strokes.

WHEN YOU WANT TO KNOW THE SCORE

MACHINE IS THERE TO DELIVER IT IN A VERY BOLD WAY. IT IS A FACE WITH NO CURVES, ONLY ANGLES, AND IT SETS VERY CONDENSED. IT SHOULD BE USED FOR SHORT DISPLAY COPY ONLY AND NO SMALLER THAN 18 POINT (WHICH IS WHY THIS 9-POINT DESCRIPTION IS SET IN HELVETICA LIGHT RATHER THAN IN MACHINE). FOR BEST VISUAL RESULTS, MACHINE SHOULD BE KERNED. IN THE SAMPLE ABOVE, WE'VE KERNED TO TIGHTEN UP BOTH THE LETTER AND THE WORD SPACE.

This message demands your immediate attention...

so it is set in American Typewriter, which has the immediacy of a standard typewriter face but is more sophisticated. Type sets more economically, with more words per line, in this face than in true typewriter faces such as Courier.

If the plan is to
GET ON THE FAST TRACK

try Lubalin Graph Demi. It's actually a serif version of Avant Garde with a square, Egyptian-style serif that is both modern and utilitarian. (Both Lubalin Graph Demi and Avant Garde were created by renowned designer Herb Lubalin.)

LIGHT AS THE ESSENCE OF SUNSHINE
AND BOLD AS A MOONLESS NIGHT

is the broad personality of Futura. It's a classic typeface: Born of the machine age in the twenties, it continues to be a designer favorite. Its versatility ranges from advertising to editorial, from fashion to technology. It comes in a wide selection of weights and widths. An all-time favorite combination is Futura Light and Extra Bold, shown above. This text is Futura Light Condensed.

If the need is to be
DRAMATIC AND SOPHISTICATED
AT THE SAME TIME

then look no further than the Bodoni family. It is very urban, with a touch of the theatrical. This is especially true with Bodoni Poster, used above. This text is in Bodoni Bold.

THE ANNUAL MESSAGE FROM
THE EXECUTIVE OFFICES

might well be set in Garamond. It's an extremely graceful, refined, and legible face that suggests the confidence that comes from success. The italic face is highly legible (many italic faces are not), as you can see from these few lines set in Garamond Light Italic.

The efficiency of type

The number of characters per line varies from one typeface to another, even when the same size type is specified. A typeface that has a relatively high character count per line is said to set efficiently (or tightly or economically), and is likely to look smaller than a less efficient typeface set in the same size.

Traditional type charts (and some books on typography) provide tables for determining the character count of each typeface in various sizes and line lengths. These may not translate with 100 percent accuracy to your desktop system because there are subtle differences in the same typeface from one manufacturer to another. Still, they can be helpful for determining the relative efficiency of different faces, as well as the approximate character count for your type specifications.

The words in these twelve blocks of text are exactly the same, and each text block is set 10/12. But the length varies from 10 to 15 lines because some typefaces set more economically than others, with more characters per line. Note also that the type in the shortest text block does not look the smallest. A condensed typeface with a large x-height sets tighter than a noncondensed face but still looks larger.

—Times Roman

The words in these twelve blocks of text are exactly the same, and each text block is set 10/12. But the length varies from 10 to 15 lines because some typefaces set more economically than others, with more characters per line. Note also that the type in the shortest text block does not look the smallest. A condensed typeface with a large x-height sets tighter than a noncondensed face but still looks larger.

—Garamond

The words in these twelve blocks of text are exactly the same, and each text block is set 10/12. But the length varies from 10 to 15 lines because some typefaces set more economically than others, with more characters per line. Note also that the type in the shortest text block does not look the smallest. A condensed typeface with a large x-height sets tighter than a noncondensed face but still looks larger.

—New Baskerville

The words in these twelve blocks of text are exactly the same, and each text block is set 10/12. But the length varies from 10 to 15 lines because some typefaces set more economically than others, with more characters per line. Note also that the type in the shortest text block does not look the smallest. A condensed typeface with a large x-height sets tighter than a noncondensed face but still looks larger.

—Helvetica Condensed Light

The words in these twelve blocks of text are exactly the same, and each text block is set 10/12. But the length varies from 10 to 15 lines because some typefaces set more economically than others, with more characters per line. Note also that the type in the shortest text block does not look the smallest. A condensed typeface with a large x-height sets tighter than a noncondensed face but still looks larger.

—Futura

The words in these twelve blocks of text are exactly the same, and each text block is set 10/12. But the length varies from 10 to 15 lines because some typefaces set more economically than others, with more characters per line. Note also that the type in the shortest text block does not look the smallest. A condensed typeface with a large x-height sets tighter than a noncondensed face but still looks larger.

—News Gothic

The samples on these two pages show the relative efficiency of a number of popular faces, with the serif faces across the top and the sans serif faces across the bottom. (All are from Adobe Systems.) In general, the more efficient faces have a smaller x-height; in addition to getting more characters per line, these faces require less lead because there is more built-in white space between the lines. Note the relatively small visual size and open lines of the New Baskerville setting, for example, compared to the larger, visually tighter look of Bookman or Avant Garde.

When efficiency is extremely important, consider using a condensed face with a large x-height. Note that the Helvetica Condensed Light sample looks larger than some of the others even though it sets the most economically.

The words in these twelve blocks of text are exactly the same, and each text block is set 10/12. But the length varies from 10 to 15 lines because some typefaces set more economically than others, with more characters per line. Note also that the type in the shortest text block does not look the smallest. A condensed typeface with a large x-height sets tighter than a noncondensed face but still looks larger.

—Palatino

The words in these twelve blocks of text are exactly the same, and each text block is set 10/12. But the length varies from 10 to 15 lines because some typefaces set more economically than others, with more characters per line. Note also that the type in the shortest text block does not look the smallest. A condensed typeface with a large x-height sets tighter than a noncondensed face but still looks larger.

—New Century Schoolbook

The words in these twelve blocks of text are exactly the same, and each text block is set 10/12. But the length varies from 10 to 15 lines because some typefaces set more economically than others, with more characters per line. Note also that the type in the shortest text block does not look the smallest. A condensed typeface with a large x-height sets tighter than a noncondensed face but still looks larger.

—Bookman

The words in these twelve blocks of text are exactly the same, and each text block is set 10/12. But the length varies from 10 to 15 lines because some typefaces set more economically than others, with more characters per line. Note also that the type in the shortest text block does not look the smallest. A condensed typeface with a large x-height sets tighter than a noncondensed face but still looks larger.

—Helvetica

The words in these twelve blocks of text are exactly the same, and each text block is set 10/12. But the length varies from 10 to 15 lines because some typefaces set more economically than others, with more characters per line. Note also that the type in the shortest text block does not look the smallest. A condensed typeface with a large x-height sets tighter than a noncondensed face but still looks larger.

—Univers

The words in these twelve blocks of text are exactly the same, and each text block is set 10/12. But the length varies from 10 to 15 lines because some typefaces set more economically than others, with more characters per line. Note also that the type in the shortest text block does not look the smallest. A condensed typeface with a large x-height sets tighter than a noncondensed face but still looks larger.

—Avant Garde

STYLING TYPE IN PAGEMAKER

MAC TIPS

Keyboard shortcuts for formatting text can save you time when you are testing different specifications. Here are some of the most useful:

Bold	Command-Shift-B
Italic	Command-Shift-I
Plain text	Com-Shift-Spbar
Outline	Command-Shift-D
Shadow	Command-Shift-W
All caps	Command-Shift-K
Small caps	Command-Shift-H
Subscript	Command-Shift- -
Superscript	Command-Shift-+
Align left	Command-Shift-L
Align right	Command-Shift-R
Justify	Command-Shift-J
Center	Command-Shift-C
Force justify	Command-Shift-F
1 point larger	Option-Com-Shift->
1 point smaller	Option-Com-Shift-<
1 graphic size larger*	Command-Shift->
1 graphic size smaller*	Command-Shift-<

PC TIPS

Keyboard shortcuts for formatting text can save you time when you are testing different specifications. Here are some of the most useful:

Normal text	Ctrl-Shift-Sp or F5
Bold	Ctrl-Shift-B or F6
Italic	Ctrl-Shift-I or F7
Reverse	Ctrl-Shift-V or F9
All caps	Ctrl-Shift-K
Small caps	Ctrl-Shift-H
Subscript	Ctrl-\ (backslash)
Superscript	Ctrl-Shift-\
Align left	Ctrl-Shift-L
Align right	Ctrl-Shift-R
Justify	Ctrl-Shift-J
Center	Ctrl-Shift-C
Force justify	Ctrl-Shift-F
1 point larger	Ctrl-Sh-> or F4
1 point smaller	Ctrl-Sh-< or F3
1 graphic size larger*	Ctrl->
1 graphic size smaller*	Ctrl-<

* These "sizes" refer to the point sizes listed in the Size submenu.

It is very difficult to give general rules for specifying type. The variables are so numerous—the size of the page, the type of reading material, how the text is broken up, the resolution of the output, the quality of the printing, and on and on and on.

Although type design involves a multitude of subtle judgments, there are two ways to develop your skills in this area. The first is to examine printed material and note what, to your eye, does and doesn't work. Does the type get your attention? Is it easy to read? Does it help move your eye from one part of the page to another? Does it clarify the relationship between different items? Do special typographic effects further or hinder the communication? The more closely you look at type in other publications, the better you'll be able to evaluate your own type design.

The second way to learn about type is to experiment. Desktop publishing facilitates experimentation to an unprecedented degree, which alone is likely to speed the learning curve of anyone coming into the field of graphic design today. Even a seasoned designer may try several settings before getting just the right relationship of display to body text, the desired contrast between captions or sidebars and the main story, and the balance of size, leading, and column width for the amount of text on a page. With commercial typesetting, both the cost and the turnaround time limit the ability to test different possibilities; when you work on the desktop, the time is your own (a mixed blessing, to be sure), and the cost of laser printouts is a few cents each.

Take advantage of this ability to experiment once you're comfortable with the mechanics of changing and controlling type in PageMaker. In fact, "playing" with type styles is a good way to explore the mechanics of the program and the nuances of type design at the same time. To experiment with different type settings in the early stages of a project, use text in whatever stage it exists or create a text file of dummy type. You might want to create a *lorem ipsum* file, which looks like Latin but really isn't. (You'll see it in many of the sample documents we created for this book.) Some designers prefer using *lorem ipsum* to real text in the early stages because it encourages people to focus on the format and design rather than on reading the copy. If you have PageMaker 3.0, keep the *lorem ipsum* file that was included with the program. It's been replaced in PageMaker 4.0 by a file called Copy Fit. The Copy Fit file is useful for estimating copy length (see Project 2), but because it consists entirely of five-letter words, it gives the type a homogeneous appearance that makes it worthless for evaluating type specs.

When you begin to develop the format for a project, try several settings of two or three different typefaces. The ability to specify both type and leading in increments of 0.1 point gives you tremendous flexibility. Vary the margins and the space between columns. Stretch the windowshade

TIP

In addition to the options available through the Paragraph and Tabs commands, you can insert typographic spaces as needed. They are all nonbreaking spaces, so called because PageMaker will not break a line on either side of them. An em space is the width of the point size; an en is half that, and a thin space is half an en. So in 12-point type, an em is 12 points, an en is 6 points, and a thin space is 3 points. A fixed space is the width of a word space for the specified font; it is inserted between two words when you don't want to see a line break between them, such as the name of your company or the numeral following the word "Chapter."

Space	Macintosh	PC
em	Command-Shift-M	Ctrl-Shift-M
en	Command-Shift-N	Ctrl-Shift-N
thin	Command-Shift-T	Ctrl-Shift-T
fixed	Option-Spacebar	Ctrl-Sp

handles horizontally to see different line lengths. Try different headline treatments in relation to the body text—different sizes and styles, with different amounts of space between the headline and the text.

Learn early on to use the Paragraph Specifications dialog box to specify paragraph indents and space between paragraphs or between different text elements, such as headlines and body text. For many new users, the familiar typewriter functions of the Spacebar and the carriage return seem easier, but it is virtually impossible to maintain consistency using them, or to remember, when you compare different samples, how much space you inserted. (When several people work on the same job, Spacebar and carriage-return spacing can really wreak havoc.)

A lot of people have trouble setting tabs properly, but if you need tabs, you won't get them right until you learn to use the Indents/Tabs dialog box. (It's called Indents/Tabs because you can also set left, first, and right indents in this dialog box.) Don't even be tempted to use the Spacebar to set tabs; it simply won't work. (See Projects 5, 6, and 7 for hands-on practice with tabs.)

Learn to define and use a style sheet. It will save you more time than any other feature of the program. It will also help you maintain consistency throughout the publication and enable you to make global changes that would be a real headache to do manually. A style is simply the name you give to a collection of type attributes—typeface, size, leading, alignment, indents, and so on. You can apply all those attributes to a paragraph just by selecting the paragraph and clicking on the name of the style. It's much faster than going through two or three different dialog boxes to specify each attribute individually, and much easier than trying to remember the attributes for the chart headline on page 3 when you need to specify those same attributes for the chart headline on page 12. (See Project 4 for working with style sheets.)

MEASURING TYPE

As mentioned previously, type is measured vertically, in points, and line lengths are measured in picas. If you haven't worked with points and picas before, you will soon appreciate the small unit of measure this system provides:

12 points = 1 pica
6 picas = 1 inch

To measure type in printed samples, you will need a type gauge, a special ruler with several slots running for most of its length and various sizes (usually ranging from 5 or 6 to 15 points) marked along the sides of different slots. You

can buy a type gauge in any art supply store; they're very inexpensive. (The most common one is called a Haberule.)

When using a traditional type gauge, keep in mind that the conversion from picas to inches is slightly different from that used on the computer: 6 picas (72 points) is 0.996 inches on a traditional type ruler; the conversion has been rounded off in most desktop-publishing systems, where the 72-dots-per-inch resolution of many monitors converts so easily to 72 points to the inch.

TYPOGRAPHIC REFINEMENTS

Even the simplest publication is likely to have some element of type that doesn't look quite right using the default setting: the line breaks in a headline, the shape of the right margin in flush left text, the two-word line that ends a paragraph at the top of a column. Part of what distinguishes professional from amateur typography is the fine-tuning of these details. This section addresses some of the problem areas, so you'll know what to look for, but the actual solutions tend to be unique to each design. For a close look at the visual and mechanical process of solving typographic problems in real documents, see the projects in Section 3.

Pay attention to headlines

Headlines almost always require some typographic refinement. It's not simply that their size and styling make them such a dominant element on the page but also that larger type sets differently than body text. In general, headlines and other display type hold together better and look crisper if they are set tight. Of course many designs use open spacing for a desired effect, but the *problem* to look for is headlines that are unintentionally too loose.

In general, large type sizes require proportionally less leading than body text. PageMaker's automatic leading of 120% adds 2 points to 10- or 11-point reading text but more than 7 points of lead in a 36-point headline. Headlines, especially when set in all caps, usually look better set solid or with minus leading so that the lines hold together as a unit.

Large type sizes also generally require tighter word spacing and letterspacing. To achieve this, you can use the Tracking options, the Spacing command, or manual kerning.

The tracking option on the Type menu provides six preset levels for increasing and decreasing word spacing and letterspacing uniformly

No Track (default setting)	Endless Typographic Details
Very Loose	Endless Typographic Details
Loose	Endless Typographic Details
Normal	Endless Typographic Details
Tight	Endless Typographic Details
Very Tight	Endless Typographic Details
Tight Track with 1/100 of an em space added across the entire text block	Endless Typographic Details

To tighten space
1/100th of em: Op-Del (or Bksp)
1/25th of em: Com-Del (or Bksp)

To open up space
1/100th of em: Op-Shift-Del (or Bksp)
1/25th of em: Com-Shift-Del (or Bksp)

To remove kerning
Select the characters and press Command-Option-K.

To kern over a range of text
Select the text and press the appropriate key combination.

To tighten space
1/100th of em: Ctrl-Shift-Minus
1/25th of em: Ctrl-Bksp or Ctrl-Minus (on the numeric keypad)

To open up space
1/100th of em: Ctrl-Shift-Plus
1/25th of em: Ctrl-Shift-Bksp or Ctrl-Plus (on the num keypad)

To remove kerning
Select the characters and press Ctrl-Sh-0 (zero on numeric keypad).

To kern over a range of text
Select the text and press the appropriate key combination.

across a range of selected text. The amount of adjustment increases with the size of the type. PageMaker includes built-in tracking values for the 35 standard laser printer fonts, but for most other fonts it uses default settings that may require further refinements. Manual kerning and values that you specify in the Spacing dialog box (both of which will be explained shortly) are added on top of the track setting. You can also customize values for downloadable fonts using a third-party program such as PM Tracker from Edco Systems.

Kerning is the process of adjusting the space between individual letters for better overall balance. The shape of some letter pairs, such as Wo, Ya, and Tu, makes the space between the letters seem too big. The shape of other letters, such as Mi and Il, makes the letters seem too close together. Mechanically, it is very easy to adjust the space in PageMaker using the keyboard combinations in the tips at left. But how much space to add or delete is a subjective visual judgment.

When you kern, the goal is to achieve an overall balance of spacing across the entire headline. One approach is to imagine pouring sand between the letters and then to add or delete space so that there would be a nearly equal volume of sand between each pair. Another approach is to visually isolate three letters to see if the space on both sides of the center one is equal; you can quickly "scan" an entire headline this way.

In the examples below, the top two headlines are set 30/30, the bottom two 30/20. The headlines with the tighter leading hold together much better as a unit and are easier to read. The top two samples have not been kerned. Note that the unkerned Times Roman setting (top left) is better balanced than the unkerned Helvetica Condensed setting to its right; in general, serif typefaces are more forgiving of spacing imbalances because the serifs form a visual connection between the letters.

PAY ATTENTION TO HEADLINES

PAY ATTENTION TO HEADLINES

Letterspacing and leading are too open

Good letterspacing and leading

PAY ATTENTION TO HEADLINES

PAY ATTENTION TO HEADLINES

Spacing

Sometimes you'll want to alter the word spacing and letterspacing built into a typeface. Before considering some examples, you might want to bring up PageMaker's Spacing dialog box, which is accessed through the Paragraph command on the Type menu. Note that for both Word and Letter Space, there are Minimum, Desired, and Maximum settings. In flush left text, PageMaker can generally break lines without deviating from the specs for Desired spacing. But in justified text, if a line can't be composed within the Desired spacing, PageMaker will try to adhere to the range specified for Maximum and Minimum spacing.

Some designers prefer body text set a little tight, and even in flush left text they will adjust the Desired Word Space to 80% or 90% and the Desired Letter Space to anywhere from -2% to -8%. The setting varies depending on the typeface and the kind of reading material.

Open spacing is often used in display type. For example, the running heads in this book have the Desired Letter Space adjusted to 100% (the default is 0), doubling the space between letters. When you alter the Desired Letter Space, the word spacing is adjusted proportionally (the result of the adjustment to the character preceding the word space and to the width of the Spacebar character itself).

For justified text, you'll need to experiment with different settings over a wide range of text to determine the optimal spacing. The example below is based on only a single paragraph, but it will give you an idea of how different values can affect the setting, and how you rarely solve all the spacing problems without some manual fine-tuning. The order of the values for each setting follows the order in the Spacing dialog box: Minimum, Desired, and then Maximum. For the range kerning used in the third sample, we selected the text in line 7, which was too tight, and pressed Option-Shift-Delete (on a Mac) to add 1/100th of an em to the letterspacing in that line. This forced the word "of" to the next line, but left lines 7 and 8 with excessively open word spacing. We selected both lines, and pressed Option-Shift-Delete three times. This opened the letterspace (and in doing so removed some of the excess word space), making the overall color of the type more even. If you plan to use justified type, be prepared to spend time making these sorts of adjustments.

TIP

To find out where PageMaker has set lines tighter or looser than you've specified in the Spacing dialog box, turn on the Loose/Tight Lines option in the Preferences dialog box. PageMaker will highlight those lines in your screen display. You can then manually adjust those lines, either by kerning a range of selected text (as in the third example below), by adjusting the hyphenation parameters, or by editing the text. If a lot of lines are highlighted, you probably need to change the design in some way—a wider column or a different type size, for example.

TIP

Spacing is a paragraph-level attribute, so you can specify Spacing parameters as part of a Style definition. You can make small adjustments to individual paragraphs for copyfitting purposes, but check your printouts carefully to be sure the variation from one paragraph to another is acceptable.

Default Spacing Word Space: 50/100/200 Letter Space: -5/0/25	Custom Spacing Word Space: 50/85/150 Letter Space: -8/-3/15	Custom Spacing as at left + Range Kerning in lines 7 and 8
The ability to set type, to modify it on-screen, to com- pose it in pages, and then print the result in camera- ready form is the foundation of desktop publishing. Sud- denly, the fundamental building block of graphic de- sign is in the hands of anyone with a few thousand dollars.	The ability to set type, to mod- ify it on-screen, to compose it in pages, and then print the result in camera-ready form is the foundation of desktop publishing. Suddenly, the fundamental building block of graphic design is in the hands of anyone with a few thousand dollars.	The ability to set type, to mod- ify it on-screen, to compose it in pages, and then print the result in camera-ready form is the foundation of desktop publishing. Suddenly, the fundamental building block of graphic design is in the hands of anyone with a few thousand dollars.

Hyphenation

TIP

To add a manual hyphen: Set an insertion point in the text and then press Command-hyphen on a Mac, Ctrl-hyphen on a PC. These are called discretionary hyphens because PageMaker inserts them only if the word breaks at the end of a line; if editing alters the line breaks, you won't end up with a hyphen in the middle of a line.

To delete an undesirable hyphen: Insert a discretionary hyphen immediately preceding the first character of the word, thus forcing the word to the next line. (Or edit the text to change the line break.) Use this technique when PageMaker hyphenates a proper noun, or when a tight line of justified text ends in a hyphen.

To enter a nonbreaking hyphen: Press Command-Option-hyphen on a Mac, Ctrl-Shift-hyphen on a PC (and ^~ in dialog boxes). Use this when you don't want a line break in the middle of a hyphenated compound word.

Hyphenation is an area of trade-offs. A line break in the middle of a word slows down reading. But disallowing hyphenation can be distracting, too: In justified text, it adds to uneven word spacing and letterspacing; in flush left text, it can create line lengths that are so uneven as to look odd. Use the Hyphenation command (on the Type menu) to control this aspect of your typography. Like Spacing, hyphenation is a paragraph-level command and can be incorporated into the definition of a style.

Hyphenation off: Generally you should not have hyphens in headlines and other display copy, in captions set to a narrow measure, and in center-aligned type.

Manual hyphenation: PageMaker allows only discretionary hyphens that you insert manually. See the Tip at left.

Dictionary hyphenation: PageMaker allows word breaks according to its own hyphenation dictionaries (which you can edit).

Algorithm hyphenation: PageMaker allows word breaks according to certain rules of logic, which may not coincide with traditional hyphenation rules.

Limit Consecutive Hyphens: To avoid having two consecutive lines hyphenated, type *1* in the box. To avoid having more than two consecutive lines hyphenated, type *2* in the text box. Try to avoid stacking more than two hyphens in a row if you possibly can (even though PageMaker's default is No Limit).

Hyphenation Zone: This determines how close to the end of a line PageMaker can insert a hyphen. In justified text and in narrow columns, specify 1 or 2 picas. This allows hyphens close to the end of the line, resulting in a softer rag in flush left text and in more even spacing in justified text. But it also allows more hyphens after only two letters of a word. In wider columns, a harder rag (hyphenation zone of 3 or 4 picas) with less hyphenation often looks better.

Regardless of your hyphenation settings, for professional-looking typography you should review your pages and make some manual corrections, for both typographical and grammatical reasons. Occasionally, you'll need to edit the text in order to avoid a bad line break.

Very hard rag (Hyphenation: Off)	Hard rag (Hyphenation Zone: 3)	Soft rag (Hyphenation Zone: 1)
The great error in Rip's composition was an insuperable aversion to all kinds of profitable labour. It could not be from the want of assiduity or perseverance; for he would sit on a wet rock, with a rod as long and heavy as a Tartar's lance, and fish all day without a murmur, even though he should not be encouraged by a single nibble.	The great error in Rip's composition was an insuperable aversion to all kinds of profitable labour. It could not be from the want of assiduity or perseverance; for he would sit on a wet rock, with a rod as long and heavy as a Tartar's lance, and fish all day without a murmur, even though he should not be encouraged by a single nibble.	The great error in Rip's composition was an insuperable aversion to all kinds of profitable labour. It could not be from the want of assiduity or perseverance; for he would sit on a wet rock, with a rod as long and heavy as a Tartar's lance, and fish all day without a murmur, even though he should not be encouraged by a single nibble.

Understanding proportional leading

Some of PageMaker's typographic controls—such as paragraph rules and the position of subscripts and superscripts—are specified relative to the baseline of the text. In order to use these features, you have to know where that baseline is. PageMaker's default uses proportional leading, with two-thirds of the leading above the baseline and one-third below it. So in the example below, which is set 20/24, the leading is calculated with 16 points above the baseline and 8 points below it.

This type has proportional leading

24 points lead

24 points lead

16 points above baseline

8 points below baseline

A few words about emphasis

When used for emphasis, some type styles have the opposite result of what is intended. **Boldface, for example,** is generally the most effective way to make type stand out. But some typefaces, such as the Palatino used here, don't have much contrast between the bold and regular faces. And as with anything else, too much can be counterproductive. Too much boldface, for example, makes the page look uneven and dark. In addition, when used in small sizes, boldface type can fill in the open space in letters such as o, e, and b; this is of particular concern when you use a 300 dots-per-inch printer for final output, and in poor-quality printing in general.

Italic type may be the most misused of all forms of emphasis because it is actually softer, not bolder, than roman text. The calligraphic nature of italic text also makes it relatively difficult to read. Used for captions,

A HANDFUL OF TYPOGRAPHIC CONVENTIONS

• **Space between sentences** It's difficult to get used to this if you've spent years pressing a typewriter space bar twice between sentences, but typesetting requires only one space after periods, question marks, exclamation points, and colons.

• **Dash** Type Option-Shift-hyphen (Alt-0151 on a PC with a PostScript printer) to get a long dash—also called an em dash—rather than typing two hyphens as you do on a typewriter.

For an en dash, used to indicate continuing or inclusive numbers as in 1988–91, type Option-hyphen (Ctrl-= on a PC).

• **Quotation Marks and Apostrophe** Type Option-[to open a quote and Option-Shift-[to close a quote. (On a PC, type Ctrl-Shift-[to open quotes and Ctrl-Shift-] to close them.) This gives you true "typeset" quotation marks designed for the font you are using instead of straight, "typewriter-style" marks. When you place text in PageMaker from a word-processing program, you can get typeset-style quotation marks automatically by selecting the Convert Quotes option in the Place dialog box, but you will need to use the keyboard sequence for quotation marks that you type in PageMaker.

For single quote marks, the keyboard sequences are Option-] to open the quote and Option-Shift-] to close the quote. (On a PC, type Ctrl-[to open single quotes and Ctrl-] to close them.)

For an apostrophe, use the Option-Shift-] sequence (Ctrl-] on a PC).

quotes, display type, marginalia, leadins, and other short items, *italic type can provide a subtle contrast to the main text, but it does not provide emphasis.* As with boldface, some typefaces have more contrast than others between their italic and roman styles; the Palatino used here is one of them.

ALL CAPS should be avoided for sustained reading. Words set in upper- and lowercase have distinctive and recognizable shapes. WORDS SET IN ALL CAPS LOOK LIKE RECTANGLES OF DIFFERENT LENGTHS AND ARE MORE DIFFICULT TO READ, ESPECIALLY IN RUNNING TEXT, WHERE THERE ISN'T MUCH WHITE SPACE. It's fine to use all caps sparingly to get attention in headlines. But don't overdo it.

Underlining is a holdover from typewriters, where it is one of the few means of emphasis available. It can still be useful in electronic publishing, especially in the presentation of data. But PageMaker's underline style is heavy and sets too close to the body text in many typefaces. If you want to use underlining, draw a hairline rule with the perpendicular line tool. Remember, though, that if you edit the text, you'll have to move the underline manually. And when you use underlining for labels (as we've done for samples in this chapter), use a placeholder to maintain a uniform distance between the baseline of the text and the underline.

> In this type sample, we used the Underline style on Page-Maker's Type menu.
>
> In this type sample, we used a hairline-weight rule to achieve an underline style.

Widows and orphans

Desktop publishing has spawned more definitions of widows and orphans than we can count. To take advantage of PageMaker's controls, define them as follows: A widow is the first 1, 2, or 3 lines of a paragraph at the end of a column; an orphan is the last 1, 2, or 3 lines of a paragraph at the top of a column. If you specify 2 lines in the Widow Control option (in the Paragraph Specs dialog box), PageMaker will not allow the first one or two lines of a paragraph to fall at the bottom of a column but rather will force them to the top of the next column. Similarly, if you specify 3 lines in the Orphan Control option, PageMaker will not allow the last 3 lines of a paragraph to fall at the top of a column but rather will push a fourth line forward to keep them company, as it were.

In publications with continuous running text—a long report, for example, or a two-column journal without much illustrative material—these controls can help you produce better-looking pages more efficiently. But in highly formatted publications, with art and display type, editing around the problem may be a better solution than the uneven column breaks created by automatically forcing lines forward and backward. It depends on how loose or tight your format is.

In traditional publishing, we always defined a widow as a single word or two that forms the last line of a paragraph. PageMaker has no option for controlling these kinds of lines; you'll have to look for them yourself.

What's the big deal? However you define them, widows and orphans can have one of two unfortunate effects. They can be eyesores (a single word line at the top of a column looks awful). And they can interrupt the reader's flow (a single line of a new paragraph at the bottom of a column does this, especially if the reader must turn the page to continue).

SPECIAL CHARACTERS & SYMBOLS

Both the Macintosh and the PC have extended character sets that enable you to incorporate special symbols—copyright and register marks, pound and yen signs, accents used in foreign languages, and so on—into your documents.

On the Macintosh, you can review the special characters by selecting the Key Caps desk accessory from the Apple menu. This displays the Key Caps window, which displays a typewriter keyboard. When this window is active, the usual PageMaker menu bar is replaced by the Key Caps menu bar. Point to the Key Caps menu, hold down the mouse button, and scroll to select the typeface you want. The keyboard in the Key Caps window will correspond to that typeface. With the Key Caps window still visible, press Option and Option-Shift to see the extended characters available for each key in the selected typeface. To insert a special character in your document, close the Key Caps window, set an insertion point with the text tool, check that the correct typeface is selected, and then type the appropriate key combinations.

In PC PageMaker, the situation is more complex because it is less uniform: Different printer fonts have different extended character sets, and there is no on-screen equivalent to the sort of directory provided by the Macintosh Key Caps accessory. Appendix C of the PC Page-Maker *Reference Manual* lists the ANSI character set used in Windows. It's possible, though, that what you see on the screen will not match what is printed. In that situation, you'll need to keep a list of the characters, the keyboard commands, and the screen characters displayed for each.

Here are a few often-used characters. (A blank means that a special font is required for that character.) PC users note: All numbers in Alt key combinations must be entered on the numeric keypad. Typing Alt + 0 + the subsequent three-digit number instructs PageMaker to remap the standard ASCII code to the ANSI code used in Windows.

> **TIP**
>
> Although some fonts come with built-in fraction characters, most do not. When you need proper fractions (such as ½ or ²¹/₃₂) you must format each character individually.
> - Specify the **numerator** as a superscript (using the Case option in the Type Specs dialog box).
> - Type the **slash** as a fraction bar character (Option-Shift-1 on a Mac, Alt-0164 in the Symbol font on a PC).
> - Specify the **denominator** as a subscript (again using the Case option).
>
> Then select all three characters, bring up the Type Specs dialog box, press the Options button, and customize the superscript and subscript values. The values used in the fractions in this tip, which work well for many typefaces in body text size, were:
> - Super/subscript size: 60%
> - Superscript positon: 30%
> - Subscript position: 0%
>
> You may need to kern around the slash for some numbers.

Char	Macintosh	PC
®	Option-r	Ctrl-Shift-R
©	Option-g	Ctrl-Shift-C
™	Option-2	
£	Option-3	Alt-0163
¢	Option-4	Alt-0162
¥	Option-y	Alt-0165
§	Option-6	Ctrl-Shift-M
¶	Option-7	Ctrl-Shift-7
•	Option-8	Ctrl-Shift-8
∞	Option-5	
÷	Option-/	
√	Option-v	

Char	Macintosh	PC
´	Option-e then type letter	*Accents not separated from letters; see the PageMaker Reference Manual for list.*
¨	Option-u then type letter	
^	Option-i then type letter	
~	Option-n then type letter	
ç	Option-c	Alt-0231
Ç	Option-Shift-C	Alt-0199
¿	Option-Shift-/	Alt-0191
¡	Option-1	Alt-0161

ZAPF DINGBATS

The Zapf Dingbats typeface provides useful typographic embellishments. It is resident on many PostScript printers and available as a downloadable font from Adobe. The characters are shown below with the key combinations used to produce them. (The Shift and Option keys are abbreviated as "Sh" and "Op," respectively.) PC users: For characters in columns 4, 5, and 6, you must hold down the Alt key and use the numeric keypad to type 0 and the three numbers listed.

Ch	Mac/PC	Ch	Mac/PC
	Sh-1		Sh-C
	Sh-'		Sh-D
	Sh-3		Sh-E
	Sh-4		Sh-F
	Sh-5		Sh-G
	Sh-7		Sh-H
	'		Sh-I
	Sh-9		Sh-J
	Sh-0		Sh-K
	Sh-8		Sh-L
	Sh-=		Sh-M
	,		Sh-N
	-		Sh-O
	.		Sh-P
	/		Sh-Q
	0		Sh-R
	1		Sh-S
	2		Sh-T
	3		Sh-U
	4		Sh-V
	5		Sh-W
	6		Sh-X
	7		Sh-Y
	8		Sh-Z
	9		[
	Sh-;		\
	;		]
	Sh- ,		Sh-6
	=		Sh- -
	Sh-.		`
	Sh-/		a
	Sh-2		b
	Sh-A		c
	Sh-B		d

Ch	Mac/PC	Ch	Mac	PC	Ch	Mac	PC	Ch	Mac	PC
	e		Sh-Op-8	161		Sh-Op-/	192		Sh-Op-6	223
	f		Op-4	162		Op-1	193		Sh-Op-7	224
	g		Op-3	163		Op-l	194		Sh-Op-9	225
	h		Op-6	164		Op-v	195		Sh-Op-0	226
	i		Op-8	165		Op-f	196		Sh-Op-W	227
	j		Op-7	166		Op-x	197		Sh-Op-E	228
	k		Op-s	167		Op-j	198		Sh-Op-R	229
	l		Op-r	168		Op-\	199		Sh-Op-T	230
	m		Op-g	169		Sh-Op-\	200		Sh-Op-Y	231
	n		Op-2	170		Op-;	201		Sh-Op-U	232
	o		Op-e	171		Op-spbar	202		Sh-Op-I	233
	p		Op-u	172		(PC only)	203		Sh-Op-S	234
	q		Op-=	173		(PC only)	204		Sh-Op-D	235
	r		Sh-Op-'	174		(PC only)	205		Sh-Op-F	236
	s		Sh-Op-O	175		Sh-Op-Q	206		Sh-Op-G	237
	t		Op-5	176		Op-q	207		Sh-Op-H	238
	u		Sh-Op-=	177		Op- -	208		Sh-Op-J	239
	v		Op-,	178		Sh-Op- -	209		Sh-Op-L	241
	w		Op-.	179		Op-[	210		Sh-Op-;	242
	x		Op-y	180		Sh-Op-[	211		Sh-Op-Z	243
	y		Op-m	181		Op-]	212		Sh-Op-X	244
	z		Op-d	182		Sh-Op-]	213		Sh-Op-B	245
	Sh-[		Op-w	183		Op-/	214		Sh-Op-N	246
	Sh-\		Sh-Op-P	184		Sh-Op-V	215		Sh-Op-M	247
	Sh-]		Op-p	185		(PC only)	216		Sh-Op-,	248
	Op-n (Mac) / Alt-0-126 (PC)		Op-b	186		Sh-Op-`	217		Sh-Op-.	249
			Op-9	187		Sh-Op-1	218		Op-H	250
			Op-0	188		Sh-Op-2	219		Op-K	251
			Op-z	189		Sh-Op-3	220		(PC only)	252
			Op-'	190		Sh-Op-4	221		(PC only)	253
			Op-o	191		Sh-Op-5	222		(PC only)	254

CHAPTER 3

CREATING A GRID: THE UNDERLYING STRUCTURE OF PAGE COMPOSITION

A major virtue of the grid system is the discipline it imposes on the untrained designer. As a teacher of publication design, I have found that it is only when the student divides and analyzes the space he is working with that he is able to achieve a cohesive design solution.
—Allen Hurlburt, The Grid

There is nothing mysterious about a grid. It is simply an underlying structure that defines where to put things on the page. A letter typed on an old manual typewriter uses a grid; so does a handwritten list on a sheet of paper in which you note the names of items on the left and the costs on the right. Although grids used in publication design can be considerably more complex than that, they can also be that simple.

The grid itself is a series of nonprinting vertical and horizontal lines that divide the page. This technique has been the dominant approach to publication design for at least twenty years, primarily because it provides such an effective way of organizing the page and speeds up layout time considerably. A well-constructed grid can make a lot of decisions for you—where to place the headlines, text, and art and how to handle the many details that inevitably turn up. A grid gives a publication a planned, cohesive look and helps ensure consistency from one page to the next. It also sets visual ground rules that everyone involved in a publication can follow.

The grid system is perfectly matched to designing on computers, where the basic unit is a square pixel. It works on the same principle as modular furniture, storage units, and old-fashioned wooden building blocks. In fact, constructing and using a grid has the same tactile tidiness and infinite variety as playing with blocks.

Of course, not all graphic designers use the grid system in their work. Some use other formal techniques, such as perspective, and some use a more intuitive, more purely aesthetic approach to page design. In general, however, designers find it far easier to introduce diversity and visual interest to a formal grid than to impose order and balance on a free-form approach.

This chapter looks at the grids found in a wide variety of publications, some of them real, some of them hypothetical documents created for this book. (The real publications carry a credit identifying the designer and the purpose of the document; the hypothetical publications, which generally use a Latin *lorem ipsum* file for running text, do not carry that credit.) The chapter begins with simple one-column grids and proceeds to increasingly complex formats. By following the progression from simple to complex, you should get a good feel for how grids work and how to use them in your publications.

Because grids provide the underlying structure of the page, we've used them as a sort of lens for looking at the other elements of page composition—typography and art. Type size and leading are inextricably related to column width, as are the size and position of graphic elements. So although the organizing principle of this chapter is grids, you will also find information about styling type and working with art. Terms that may be unfamiliar to some readers, whether having to do with graphic design or electronic page assembly, are defined in the glossary.

Throughout the chapter there are blueprints for grids that you can adapt for your own needs. Each blueprint is based on one of the hypothetical documents; your own documents may have different elements. If you use a different typeface, it might look better a little smaller or a little larger than the one in the document on which the blueprint was based. If your headline is longer than the one in the sample, you might need to adjust the space between the head and the text. The blueprints are only guidelines; as you change one element, be sure to reevaluate the others to see if additional changes are needed.

Before moving on to the structure of the page, we'll look at the shape of the page and the elements that are often found on it.

THE ANATOMY OF A PAGE

Designing and assembling pages, whether by hand or on a computer, is more than a mechanical or electronic task. It's a way of looking at a page as having a certain size, shape, and proportion.

Look through the printed material around you and you'll see that most of the pages are 8.5 by 11 inches, the same size as the letters we read and the memos we send. It's the most efficient cut of paper, it stacks up in newsstand racks with other printed material, and it fits nicely in files. But it's the vertical, or portrait shape—more than the size—that feels so familiar.

Although the page itself is usually vertical, in multipage documents the reader sees two facing pages as a horizontal unit with the slight interruption of the gutter down the center. Take advantage of this wider, more expansive unit as you organize your material and design the actual pages. And think of consecutive pages as part of a three-dimensional whole that exists in time as the reader turns the pages.

In addition to its shape, the printed page has a vocabulary that enables editors, designers, layout artists, and printers to communicate unambiguously about a job. Turn the page for a visual glossary of terms you're likely to encounter in this book and elsewhere.

THE ANATOMY OF A PRINTED PAGE

Byline The author's name, which may appear after the headline or at the end of an article.

Overline (also called a kicker or eyebrow) A brief tag over the headline that categorizes the story.

Headline The title of an article.

Deck (also called a tag line) A line that gives more information about the story.

Stick-up cap An enlarged initial letter extending above the body text.

Bleed art A photo, drawing, or tint that runs off the edge of the page.

Picture window A rectangle that indicates the position and size of art to be stripped into the page.

Caption The text describing a photograph or illustration.

Body text The main text, also called running text.

Folio The page number.

Running foot A line across the bottom of the page that helps orient the reader within a document. Here it contains the folio and date.

Verso Left-hand page (literally, the reverse, with the right-hand page considered the front).

THE COMPANY BULLETIN

Cover story

The Headline Goes Here

Optional secondary lines follow the headline to guide the reader into the story.

by John Hamilton

Lorem ipsum dolor sit amet, consectetuer adipiscing elit, sed diam nonummy nibh euismod tincidunt ut laoreet dolore magna aliquam erat volutpat. Ut wisi enim ad minim veniam, quis nostrud exerci tation ullamcorper suscipit lobortis nisl ut aliquip ex ea commodo consequat.

Duis autem vel eum iriure dolor in hendrerit in vulputate velit esse molestie consequat, vel illum dolore eu feugiat nulla facilisis at vero eros et accumsan et iusto odio dignissim qui blandit praesent luptatum zzril delenit augue duis dolore te feugait nulla facilisi. Lorem ipsum dolor sit amet, consectetuer adipiscing elit, sed diam nonummy nibh euismod tincidunt ut laoreet dolore magna aliquam erat volutpat.

Ut wisi enim ad minim veniam, quis nostrud exerci tation ullamcorper suscipit lobortis nisl ut aliquip ex ea commodo consequat. Duis autem vel eum iriure dolor in hendrerit in vulputate velit esse molestie consequat, vel illum dolore eu feugiat nulla facilisis at vero eros et accumsan et iusto odio dignissim qui blandit praesent luptatum zzril delenit augue duis dolore te feugait nulla facilisi.

Nam liber tempor cum soluta nobis eleifend option congue nihil imperdiet doming id quod mazim placerat facer possim assum. Lorem ipsum dolor sit amet, consectetuer adipiscing elit, sed diam nonummy nibh euismod tincidunt ut laoreet dolore magna aliquam erat volutpat. Ut wisi enim ad minim veniam, quis nostrud exerci tation ullamcorper suscipit lobortis nisl ut aliquip ex ea commodo consequat. Duis autem vel eum iriure dolor in hendrerit in vulputate velit esse molestie conse-

quat, vel illum dolore eu feugiat nulla facilisis at vero eros et accumsan et iusto odio dignissim qui blandit praesent luptatum zzril delenit augue duis dolore te feugait nulla facilisi. Lorem ipsum dolor sit amet, consectetuer adipiscing elit, sed diam nonummy nibh euismod

Duis autem vel eum iriure

Ttincidunt ut laoreet dolore magna aliquam erat volutpat.Ut wisi enim ad minim veniam, quis nostrud exerci tation ullamcorper suscipit lobortis nisl ut aliquip ex ea commodo consequat. Duis autem vel eum iriure dolor in hendrerit in vulputate velit esse molestie consequat, vel illum dolore eu feugiat nulla facilisis at.

Vero eros et accumsan et iusto odio dignissim qui blandit praesent luptatum zzril delenit augue duis dolore te feugait nulla facilisi. Lorem ipsum dolor sit amet, consectetuer adipiscing elit, sed diam nonummy nibh euismod tincidunt ut laoreet dolore magna aliquam erat volutpat. Ut wisi enim ad minim veniam, quis nostrud exerci tation ullamcorper suscipit lobortis nisl ut aliquip ex ea commodo consequat. Duis autem vel eum iriure dolor in hendrerit in vulputate velit esse molestie consequat, vel illum dolore eu feugiat nulla facilisis at vero eros et accumsan et iusto odio dignissim qui blandit prae-

The caption helps entice the reader into the text of your story and also provides information about the art and photography.

Alley The space between columns.

Wraparound text Copy that wraps around a graphic.

Subhead A phrase that identifies a subtopic.

Inside margin The space between the binding edge of the page and the text.

Sidebar A smaller story inside a larger one, boxed with its own headline to set it apart from the main text. (It can be positioned anywhere on the page.)

Breakout (also called a pull quote or blurb) A sentence or passage excerpted from the body copy and set in large type.

Top margin The distance from the top trim to the top of the text area. Running heads and feet and folios are often positioned in the top or bottom margin.

THE COMPANY BULLETIN

This display type is another technique to grab the reader's attention and pull him or her into the article.

Running head A line of text across the top of the page that helps orient the reader within a document. It might include the document's title, author, chapter, subject of current page, or page number.

Callout A label that identifies part of an illustration.

Sidebar heading is centered over the text in the sidebar

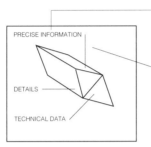

PRECISE INFORMATION

DETAILS

TECHNICAL DATA

Leader A rule that moves the eye from a callout to the part of the illustration it describes.

S equat, vel illum dolore eu feugiat nulla facilisis at vero eros et accumsan et iusto odio dignissim qui blandit praesent luptatum zzril delenit augue duis dolore te feugait nulla facilisi.

Lorem ipsum dolor sit amet, consectetuer adipiscing elit, sed diam nonummy nibh euismod tincidunt ut laoreet dolore magna aliquam erat volutpat. Ut wisi enim ad minim veniam, quis nostrud exerci tation ullamcorper suscipit lobortis nisl ut aliquip ex ea commodo consequat.

Duis autem vel eum iriure dolor in hendrerit in vulputate velit esse molestie consequat, vel illum dolore eu feugiat nulla facilisis at vero eros et accumsan et iusto odio dignissim qui blandit praesent luptatum zzril delenit augue duis dolore te feugait nulla facilisi. Lorem ipsum dolor sit amet, consectetuer adipiscing elit, sed diam.

Nonummy nibh euismod tincidunt ut laoreet dolore magna aliquam erat volutpat. Ut wisi enim ad minim veniam, quis nostrud exerci tation ullamcorper suscipit lobortis nisl ut aliquip ex ea commodo consequat.

The caption helps entice the reader into the text of your story and provides additional information about the art and photography.

❖ ❖ ❖

sent luptatum zzril delenit augue duis dolore te feugait nul ummy nibh euismod tincidunt ut laoreet dol magna aliquam erat volutpat.

Ut wisi enim ad minim veniam, quis nostrud exerci tation ullamcorper suscipit lobortis nisl ut aliquip ex ea commodo consequat. Duis autem vel eum iriure dolor in hendrerit in vulputate velit esse molestie consequat, vel illum dolore eu feugiat nulla facilisis at vero eros et accumsan et iusto odio dignissim qui blandit praesent luptatum zzril delenit augue dolore te feugait nulla facilisi. Lorem ipsum dolor sit amet, consectetuer adipiscing elit, sed diam nonummy nibh euismod tincidunt ut laoreet dolore magna aliquam erat volutpat. Ut wisi enim ad minim veniam, quis nostrud exerci tation ullamcorper suscipit lobortis nisl ut aliquip ex ea

Continued on page 11

JANUARY 1989 9

Dingbat A decorative or symbolic device used to separate items on the page or denote items in a list.

Outside margin The space between the outside trim and the text.

Continued line (also called jumpline) A line of text indicating the page on which an article continues. Its counterpart on the continuation page is a carryover line identifying the story that is being continued.

Bottom margin The space between the bottom trim and the baseline of the last line of text.

Drop cap An enlarged initial letter that drops below the first line of body text.

Screen (also called tone) A tint, either a percentage of black or a second color, behind text or art.

Printing rule A rule that traps a screen or surrounds a text block or a piece of art.

Page trim The edge of the page. In commercial printing, the size of the page after it is cut during the binding process.

Gutter The space between two facing pages.

Recto Right-hand page.

ONE-COLUMN GRIDS

The fewer the columns, the easier a grid is to work with. A simple one-column format requires relatively little planning and allows you to place text quickly. When done well, this format has an unstudied, straightforward look in which the hand of the designer is relatively invisible. That lack of "fuss" suggests a serious purpose that is appropriate for business plans, reports, proposals, press releases, announcements, simple manuals, and various forms of internal communications. Even when you use a two-column grid for these types of documents, consider a one-column format for the opening page to create the feeling of a foreword. When you mix grids in this way, be sure to maintain consistent margins throughout.

The generous margins and leading and the frequent subheads make this page very open for a one-column format. The text is 10/16 Helvetica with an 8-pica left margin and a 7-pica right margin.

The sans serif Helvetica face used here has a straightforward look that is well suited to factual or practical information. By comparsion, the serif type in the sample on the facing page suggests a narrative, essay-like writing style.

The 6-point rules at the top and bottom give the page structure. Note that with an anchor such as this you can vary the depth of the text from one page to the next and still maintain continuity of page format.

The justified text balances the overall openness, creating a strong right margin that completes the definition of the image area. The page would not hold together nearly as well with ragged right text.

Charts and diagrams (not shown) run as half or full pages centered left to right.

Design: Wadlin & Erber (New Paltz, NY)

Page from a manual that addresses the subject of radon occurrence in homes for an audience of building inspectors, architects, and contractors.
Trim size: 8-1/2 by 11

REDUCING INDOOR RADON

UNIT I

RADON OCCURRENCE AND HEALTH EFFECTS

Introduction

Radon is a colorless, odorless, and tasteless gas produced by the normal decay of uranium and radium. It is a naturally occuring radioactive gas produced in most soil or rock which surrounds houses. As a result, all houses will have some radon. It is an inert gas, which means it tends to be chemically inactive. Since radon is not chemically bound or attached to other materials, it can move easily through all gas permeable materials.

Radioactive Decay

Radioactive decay is the disintegration of the nucleus of atoms in a radioactive element by spontaneous emission of charged particles, often accompanied by photon (gamma) emission. As these charged particles are released, new elements are formed. The radioactive decay chain for radon begins with **uranium** producing **radium**, which in turn produces **radon**. Each of these elements has a different "half-life" (the time required for half of the atoms of a radioactive element to decay). The "half-life" is important because its length determines the time available for decay products to be dispersed into the environment.

Types of Radiation

The three types of radiation are gamma, beta, and alpha.

Gamma radiation is photon "parcels of energy" which operate at much higher energy levels than visible light. These rays are relatively high in penetrating power. They can travel much more deeply into objects than alpha or beta particles, and can pass through the body.

Beta radiation involves an energized particle emitted from the nucleus of a radioactive atom. It has a negative charge, and has a mass equal to one electron. Beta particles have medium penetrating power, and can penetrate up to about 0.5 centimeter of surface tissue, or about a millimeter of lead.

1

The simpler grids are generally "quiet." They don't allow for as much variety in art and headline treatment as the multicolumn formats, but with the typefaces, rules, and other simple graphic devices available in desktop publishing these pages can be effective and smart-looking.

Keep in mind that longer lines are more difficult to read than shorter ones because the eye has to travel farther from the end of one line to the beginning of the next. One-column pages risk becoming dense, dull, and uninviting. To compensate for this, use generous margins and space between lines and a relatively large typeface (10 to 13 points). Space between paragraphs also helps keep the page open.

The Past, Present and Future of Lotteries

People prefer to play on-line games

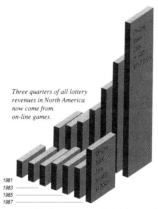

Three quarters of all lottery revenues in North America now come from on-line games.

1981
1983
1985
1987

Lottery sales are booming. In North America, the combined annual revenues from state-run lotteries have risen from approximately $3 billion in 1980 to over $15.7 billion in 1987.

Approximately 75 percent of the total revenues generated by North American lotteries is now derived from on-line games. The attraction of the on-line games lies in the daily drawing of the Numbers game and the frequent, multimillion-dollar jackpots of the Lotto games. These huge and enticing Lotto jackpots are the result of the top-prize pot "rolling over." The pot rolls over when all the numbers drawn were not picked by any player, and the unclaimed money rolls back into the pot for the next drawing. Rollovers cause wagering on the game to soar which, in turn, pushes the jackpot even higher until, finally, one or more lucky players win by matching the numbers drawn and the prize money is paid.

Outside of North America, those lottery jurisdictions that have added on-line technology to their operations have experienced great increases in revenues. For example, GTECH provided the first lottery-specific on-line system in Asia for Singapore Pools, Singapore's government-owned lottery company. The accompanying chart demonstrates the impact in sales gained by Singapore Pools after the GTECH network began operation.

In May 1986, Singapore Pools added on-line games. By the end of the year its sales had climbed 1600%, to average $8 million Singapore per week.

$8 million

on-line operations begin

months

5

The continuous running text in this sample requires a different treatment than the broken blocks of copy on the facing page. The inset art shortens the line length and makes the page more readable than it would be if the text were solid.

The margins are 6 picas top and bottom and 7 picas left and right.

The text is 12/16 Times Roman with a ragged right margin.

The headline treatment borrows editorial and typographic techniques used in magazines, with the contrasting style and size unified by the flush right alignment. The relationship of the two sizes is very nice here: The headline is 24-point Times Roman, and the tag line is 18-point Times Roman italic.

The chart, graph, and angled type were created in Adobe Illustrator. The ability to create dramatic, three-dimensional art for charts and graphs without having to be a technical illustrator is a great asset of desktop technology.

Design: Tom Ahern (Providence, RI)

Page from a capabilities brochure for GTECH, which provides on-line games for lottery networks.
Trim size: 8-1/2 by 11

Wide-margin one-column

A one-column grid with a wide margin is perhaps the most useful of all the designs in this book for internal reports, press releases, proposals, prospectuses, and other documents that have unadorned running text and need to be read fast. You may be tempted, with desktop publishing, to take something you used to distribute as a typewritten page and turn it into a multicolumn format, simply because you can. The danger is that you'll devote time to layout that would be better spent on content. As the hypothetical documents on the next three pages show, this simple one-column format can be smart, authoritative, and well planned. And though the line length is long, the white space provided by the wide margin gives the eye room to rest and makes the copy more inviting to read.

This format is especially well suited for single-sided documents that are either stapled or intended for three-ring binders. Use the left side of the page for the wide margin so that the space will look planned. (If you use the right side, it may look as though you ran out of copy and couldn't fill the page.) Although none are shown in these pages, headlines and subheads could extend into the margin for visual interest. So could short quotes, diagrams, and even small photos. When you want to make extensive use of the margin in this way, consider the "one + one-column" format discussed later in this section.

Extremely open leading facilitates quick scanning of a press release (on facing page), which usually commands less than a minute of the reader's time. The body text here is 11/20 Times Roman. With this much leading you probably would not want space between paragraphs; so you need an indent that is markedly wider than the space between lines. The indent in the sample shown is 3 picas for all paragraphs except the first.

The first paragraph is not indented. With flush left text, you rarely need to indent the opening paragraph or any paragraph that immediately follows a headline or a subhead. An indent would create an unnecessary visual gap at a place where the start of a new paragraph is obvious to the reader. To achieve this in running text where your paragraph indent is specified, for example, as 1 pica, you will need to select the opening paragraph and change its first line indent to 0.

The logo treatment can vary. The symbol could be flush with the left edge of the 6-point rule; a company name or logo could run across the top of the page, replacing the symbol and release line shown. (See the following page for an example.)

The headline should be short and straightforward. This is not the place to be clever.

The names of contacts for more information are positioned on a grid of two equal columns within the single-column format. The type is 9/12 Helvetica for contrast with the body text. If there is only one contact to list, position it in the right column of the two-column grid and move the "for immediate release" line to the left so that it is aligned left with the contact name.

The blueprint for this page appears on the following spread.

XYZ Corporation Announces New Plant Opening

For more information contact:

High Profile Publicity
Ann Millard
5432 Schoolhouse Road
Santa Monica, CA 92131
213-555-4664

XYZ Corporation
Marilyn Ferguson
1104 Beltway Drive
Los Angeles, CA 92111
213-555-3030

SANTA MONICA, CA. APRIL 10, 1989—Lorem ipsum dolor sit amet, consectetuer adipiscing elit, sed diam   nonummy nibh euismod tincidunt ut laoreet dolore magna aliquam erat volutpat. Ut wisi enim ad minim veniam, quis nostrud exerci tation ullamcorper suscipit lobortis nisl ut aliquip ex ea commodo consequat. Duis autem vel eum iriure dolor in hendrerit in vulputate velit esse molestie consequat, vel illum dolore eu feugiat nulla facilisis at vero eros et accumsan et iusto odio dignissim qui blandit praesent luptatum zzril delenit augue duis dolore te feugait nulla facilisi. Lorem ipsum dolor sit amet, consectetuer adipiscing elit, sed diam nonummy nibh euismod tincidunt ut laoreet dolore magna aliquam erat volutpat. Ut wisi enim ad minim veniam, quis nostrud exerci tation ullamcorper suscipit lobortis nisl ut aliquip ex ea commodo consequat.

Duis autem vel eum iriure dolor in hendrerit in vulputate velit esse molestie consequat, vel illum dolore eu feugiat nulla facilisis at vero eros et accumsan et iusto odio dignissim qui blandit praesent luptatum zzril delenit augue duis dolore te feugait nulla facilisi. Nam liber tempor cum soluta nobis eleifend option congue nihil imperdiet doming id quod mazim placerat facer possim assum. Lorem ipsum dolor sit amet, consectetuer adipiscing elit, sed diam nonummy nibh euismod tincidunt ut laoreet dolore magna aliquam erat volutpat. Ut wisi enim ad minim veniam, quis nostrud exerci tation ullamcorper suscipit lobortis nisl ut aliquip ex ea commodo consequat. Duis autem vel eum iriure dolor in hendrerit in vulputate velit esse molestie consequat, vel illum

The basic grid for the documents on this page is the same as the one used for the press release. Tighter leading here (11/15 Times Roman) is balanced with a full line space (15 points) between paragraphs.

The business plan above has 6 picas between the left trim and the rule. The text block is 12 picas from the top trim.

Boldface subheads are the same size as the body text. Omitting paragraph space after the subheads visually connects each subhead to its respective text block.

The company name is 14-point Times Roman bold italic.

The caption is inset in the box around the art (a style commonly found in reports and business plans) and set in 10/12 Times Roman italic.

In the proposal at right, the art is the full column width with the caption (10/13 Times Roman italic) in the margin. Note the alignment of the date, folio, rules at the top and bottom of the page, and left margin of the caption. This alignment is important: It creates an implied border that gives structure to the page.

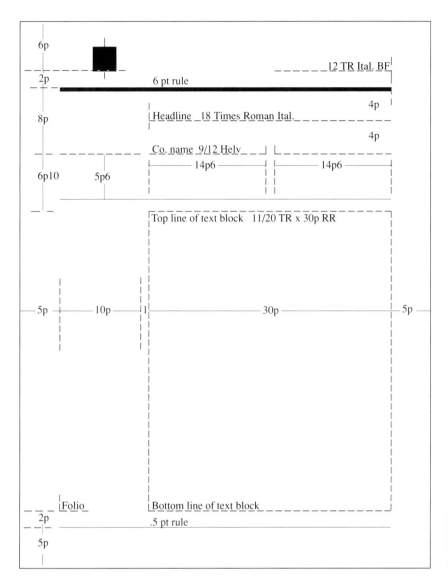

6p

12 TR Ital. BF

2p 6 pt rule

4p

8p Headline 18 Times Roman Ital.

4p

Co. name 9/12 Helv

6p10 5p6 14p6 14p6

Top line of text block 11/20 TR x 30p RR

5p 10p 30p 5p

Folio Bottom line of text block

2p .5 pt rule

5p

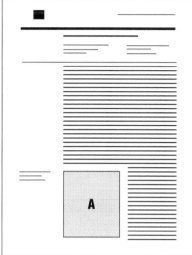

A

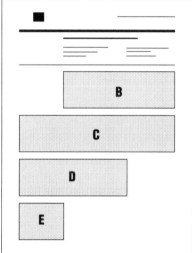

B

C

D

E

This blueprint shows the grid and type specifications for the press release on the preceding spread. The documents on the facing page use the same grid (except as noted in the annotations) but, for the most part, different type sizes.

A mixed grid structure is useful even in this simple format. Divide the text column into two equal units with a 1-pica space between. This creates two additional grid lines for placing small text and sizing art.

Blueprint measurements throughout the book are given in picas unless otherwise noted. The notation "x 30p" describes the measure, or length, of a text line. "RR" denotes a ragged right margin.

Guidelines for placing art on this grid

- Size all art to one of the following widths:
  A: 14p6—half the width of the text column with 1p between the art and the wraparound text
  B: 30 picas—the full width of the text column
  C: 41 picas—from the left edge of the 6-point rule to the right margin
  D: 25 picas—from the left edge of the 6-point rule to a point 1 pica short of the midpoint of the text column
  E: 10 picas—in the wide margin (if you have small mug shots)

- Avoid placing half-column art in the text column. Small charts and illustrations should be boxed with a 0.5- or 1-point rule to the sizes suggested.

- Placement is best at the bottom of the page, as shown in the examples at left. The top of the page is acceptable; the middle is not.

- For art that extends the full width of the column, the space between the text and the art should be equal to or greater than the leading.

- Place captions in the margin or inset them in a box around the art, as shown. Captions generally should be set one size smaller than the body text with tighter leading. Italic or a contrasting typeface is often used.

Attention to graphic detail makes the designer's hand more apparent in these documents than in the ones on the preceding pages. Both use a strong organization identity for external communication.

The large vertical headline fills the wide margin and establishes a distinctive style for a series of information sheets. Vertical type should always read upward unless the words themselves suggest downward motion.

The underlined headlines and bullets (which are gray) add variety to the simple page design.

Bulleted paragraphs with hanging indents are very effective when a message can be broken down into small chunks of information. The text immediately following the bullet should align exactly with subsequent lines.

The typeface is Palatino throughout.

IMAGESET :
First in Digital Graphic Design and
Desktop Publishing

Services

GRAPHIC DESIGN SERVICES

▪ ImageSet provides professional graphic design services for creating state-of-the-art computer graphics and page layouts for a variety of businesses, firms, and publications.

▪ Brochures, newsletters, magazine covers, advertisements, menus, logos, annual reports, and corporate identity programs can be designed from start to finish by our graphic design department. If there is a special design problem, ImageSet will find a solution.

▪ ImageSet offers electronic design templates that can be purchased and modified for a client's use. Design templates are preformatted designs that can be quickly adapted to just about any publication task (newsletters, flyers, price lists, etc.).

▪ ImageSet offers graphic design consultation for companies and individuals using desktop publishing technology. ImageSet can provide graphic design consultancy to assist the client in designing templates for newsletters, brochures, logos, or even help develop a coherent corporate identity program which can be utilized for all the client's desktop publishing applications.

▪ Should the need arise, ImageSet offers individual and group instruction on computer graphics and page layout programs.

DESKTOP PUBLISHING SERVICES

▪ ImageSet offers an output service of high resolution print for individuals and organizations whose publishing tasks demand higher quality typeset than laser printer (300 dpi) resolution. To implement this service, ImageSet utilizes a Mergenthaler Linotype L100 commercial laser phototypesetting device.

*Design:
Mark Beale,
ImageSet Design
(Portland, OR)*

*One of a series of information sheets in the promotional literature for ImageSet Associates.
Size: 8-1/2 by 11*

A distinctive logo gives this simple page a unique personality. The descriptive line explains the otherwise cryptic name.

The black and gray border echoes the logo style and gives structure to what could have been an overly loose composition. Borders provide a very simple and effective way to add graphic interest to a page. To create a gray border in PageMaker, create a rectangle with a Paper fill inside a rectangle with a gray fill. You cannot define the line and the fill of a single rectangle as two different colors (gray and white, in this case).

Initial caps add variety to the text and help draw the reader into the page. Like the bullets in the sample above, the initial caps facilitate the "quick scan" nature of information presented in short paragraphs.

The typeface, Galliard throughout, has a calligraphic feeling that is more friendly than formal.

Stick Your Neck Out

*Thanks for re-enlisting
in the Giraffe Campaign*

To show you how much we appreciate that, we've enclosed our official H.W.C.S.F.F.* telling the world that your membership in the Giraffe Project is in good standing and that you're entitled to all the rights and privileges thereof.

You'll also find an updated membership card, an *Instant Giraffe Citation* and a new campaign button — we're assuming that you, like so many other members, have been hit up for your old button by a friend or one of your kids.

People's faces do light up when they see Giraffe stuff — instead of letting them take yours, you can use the enclosed order form to get them their own buttons, mugs, shirts — and memberships. And don't forget to order more *Instant Giraffe Citations* yourself. Members who are using these report maximum satisfaction in being able to cite a Giraffe on-the-spot for meritorious action.

There will be exciting New Ideas and new "giraffenalia" in your upcoming year's worth of *Giraffe Gazettes*. We think you'll be surprised and delighted.

Keep scouting for new Giraffes and reporting your sightings to Giraffe Headquarters. We couldn't do the job without you.

And thanks again for your renewed vote of confidence in Giraffeness.

* Handsome Wall Certificate Suitable For Framing

*Design:
Scot Louis Gaznier
(Langley, WA)*

*Page acknowledging membership in the Giraffe Project, an organization that encourages people to "stick their neck out for the common good."
Size: 8-1/2 by 11*

Centering text inside a border creates a more formal image. The style of the border subtly changes the look of a page; experiment with the borders in PageMaker and clip art files to find a style appropriate for your needs.

The justified text and centered headline add to the formality. Positioning the border slightly off center keeps the design from being quite so rigid.

On subsequent pages the border would be repeated and the position of the first line of text would remain constant, leaving the space occupied by the headline open.

The 33-pica line length is the widest of the one-column formats shown in this section. The density of the running text (11/15 New Century Schoolbook) is maximum for a readable page, and you should avoid paragraphs longer than the last one shown here (11 lines).

The inset text helps relieve the density of the long text lines. Use this device on as many pages as possible in a document with this wide a column.

This blueprint defines the guidelines for the proposal above.

Charts, graphs, financials, and other art should be centered horizontally within the text block, inset at least 2 picas from the left and right margins. Graphics of various sizes can be accommodated, as shown in the schematics at far right. If you have data or art on several consecutive pages, placing them in the same vertical position on the page suggests care and planning. (It also takes a little more time.)

Southside Coolant Incorporated

**A Proposal for Temperature Control
in the Mesa School District**

Lorem ipsum dolor sit amet, consectetuer adipiscing elit, sed diam nonummy nibh euismod tincidunt ut laoreet dolore magna aliquam erat volutpat. Ut wisi enim ad minim veniam, quis nostrud exerci tation ullamcorper suscipit lobortis nisl ut aliquip ex ea commodo consequat. Duis autem vel eum iriure dolor in hendrerit in vulputate velit esse molestie consequat, vel illum dolore eu feugiat nulla facilisis at vero eros et accumsan et iusto odio dignissim qui blandit

Praesent luptatum zzril delenit augue duis dolore te feugait nulla facilisi. Lorem ipsum dolor sit amet, consectetuer adipiscing elit, Sed diam nonummy nibh euismod tincidunt ut laoreet dolore magna aliquam erat volutpat. Ut wisi enim ad minim veniam, quis nostrud exerci tation ullamcorper suscipit lobortis nisl ut aliquip ex ea commodo consequat. Duis autem vel eum iriure dolor in hendrerit in vulputate velit esse molestie consequat, vel illum dolore eu feugiat nulla facilisis at vero eros et accumsan et iusto odio dignissim qui blandit praesent luptatum zzril delenit augue duis dolore te feugait

Nulla facilisi. Nam liber tempor cum soluta nobis eleifend option congue nihil imperdiet doming id quod mazim placerat facer possim assum. Lorem ipsum dolor sit amet, consectetuer adipiscing elit, sed diam nonummy nibh euismod tincidunt ut laoreet dolore magnaAliquam erat volutpat. Ut wisi enim ad minim veniam, quis nostrud exerci tation ullamcorper suscipit lobortis nisl ut aliquip ex ea commodo consequat. Duis autem vel eum iriure dolor in hendrerit in vulputate velit esse molestie

Consequat, vel illum dolore eu feugiat nulla facilisis at vero eros et accumsan et iusto odio dignissim qui blandit praesent luptatum zzril delenit augue duis dolore te feugait. Lorem ipsum dolor sit amet, consectetuer adipiscing elit, sed diam nonummy nibh euismod tincidunt ut laoreet dolore magna aliquam erat volutpat.Ut wisi enim ad minim veniam, quis nostrud exerci tation ullamcorper suscipit lobortis nisl ut aliquip ex ea Commodo consequat. Duis autem vel eum iriure Dolor in hendrerit in vulputate velit esse molestie consequat, vel illum dolore eu feugiat nulla facilisis at vero eros et accumsan et iusto odio dignissim qui blandit praesent luptatum zzril delenit augue duis dolore te feugait nulla facilisi. Lorem ipsum dolor sit amet, consectetuer adipiscing elit, sed diam nonummy nibh euismod tincidunt ut laoreet dolore magna aliquam erat

3

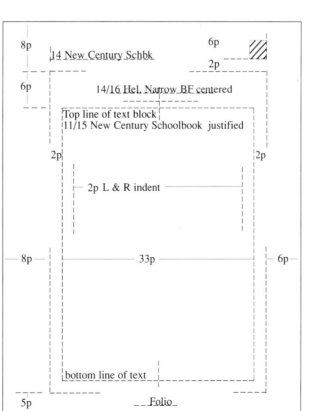

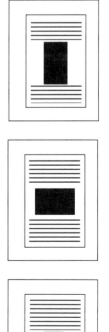

One-column grid with display heads

Many complex reports and proposals contain straight running text separated by subheads that recur throughout the document. The wide, one-column measure is ideal for the running text, and when the subheads are set fairly large and given plenty of white space and structural rules, the effect is well organized and easy to scan.

The highly structured report shown below contains a single topic on each page, with two recurring subheads placed in the same position on every page. You can adapt this format for a less structured document, placing the topic headline anywhere on the page with running text continuing from one page to the next as needed.

Bulleted text is used here to summarize the contents of each page. This technique works particularly well in long documents: The reader can make a horizontal pass through the pages for the highlights and then drop vertically into the running text for details. The ballot boxes are 11-point Zapf Dingbats.

The rules and generous white space (3 to 4 picas above each 0.5-point rule) provide a strong horizontal grid that facilitates scanning.

Art can be centered in the text column or inset on one side with the text wrapped around it, as shown in the schematics below.

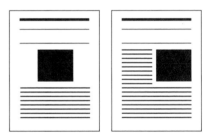

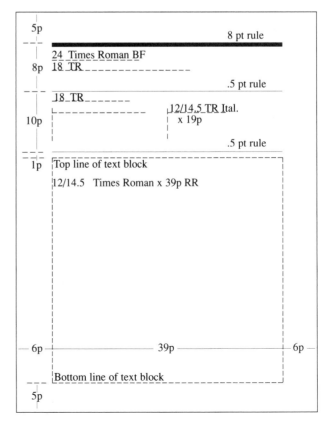

One + one-column grid

The combination of one narrow and one wide column might be considered either a one- or a two-column grid. The narrow column isn't a true text column, but it is wide enough to use for different kinds of text, graphics, and display type without crowding.

Whether you set up this format as one or two columns on the screen may well depend on the length of the document: In a long document with a great deal of running text, setting up as one column enables you to "autoflow" the text; in a short document, setting up as two columns eliminates the need to "drag place" the text in the narrow column.

Whatever you call it and however you set it up, keep this format in mind. It's extremely useful for a wide variety of reports, newsletters, bulletins, and data sheets.

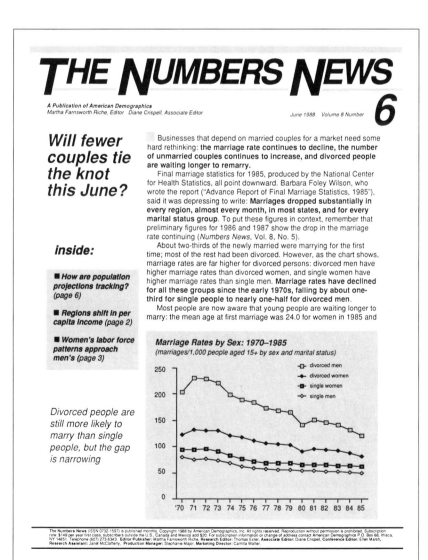

This newsletter uses the narrow column on the cover for headlines, contents listings, and story highlights. On inside pages the use is even more versatile, accommodating charts, graphs, news items, product notes, and conference listings.

The narrow column is 11p6, the wide column is 29 picas, and the space in between is 1 pica. The inside margins are 4p6, wide enough to accommodate the holes for a three-ring binder.

The tinted boxes run the full column measure without rules. Once you adopt this style, you should maintain it throughout. Text inside the boxes is indented 1 pica at both the left and right margins.

The logo uses the currently popular technique of enlarging the initial caps in an all cap name. Here the caps drop below the other letters, and tie in with the large issue number, a good device for quick reference and continuity.

The 2-point rules at the bottom of the page enclose publishing and masthead information. This type can be as small as 5 or 6 points.

Design: Carol Terrizzi (Ithaca, NY)

The Numbers News is published monthly by American Demographics. Trim size: 8-1/2 by 11

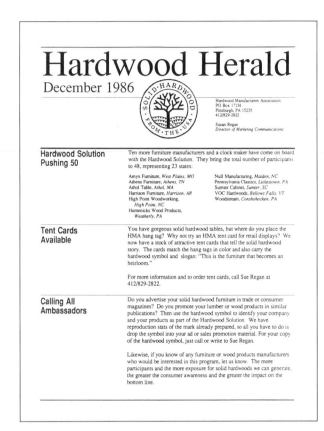

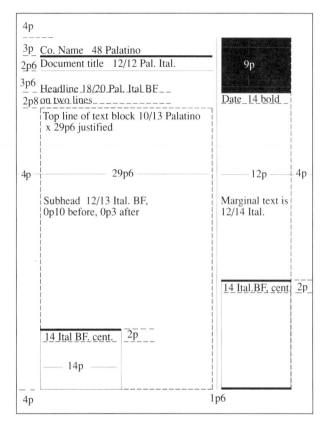

A deep space at the top of the page for the company identification, a narrow column for headlines and overhanging rules, and a wide column for body text create a very simple, effective format.

The text column is divided into two equal columns for listings. The address above the text area follows this grid.

The main headline and the running text are Times Roman; the headlines in the narrow column are Helvetica Narrow. Although Helvetica Narrow is considered a resident font in many laser printers, it is not a true PostScript font; the printer scales it from Helvetica. If you send a file to a service bureau for high-resolution output, you must tell them if you've used Helvetica Narrow so they can load the scaling information into their printer.

The text column is 29 picas. The outside margins are 3 picas, and the top and bottom margins are 4 picas.

This blueprint matches the monthly report on the facing page. You can adapt the grid for either of the other publications shown in this section by reversing the narrow and wide columns and adjusting the margins.

The text is Palatino throughout.

The bold rules are 4 point; the lighter ones are 0.5 point.

The sales highlights box in the lower left has a 1-pica standoff for the text wraparound. The type in the sample is 12/14, with 1p3 left and right indents. The tab is set at 7p.

The type in the contents box is 10/11.5 italic with 1p3 left and right indents, a leadered tab at 9 picas, and 6 points after each listing.

The screens in both of the boxes are 10%.

The maple leaf logo was created from clip art (DrawArt from Desktop Graphics) in MacDraw.

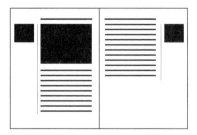

You can use four art sizes, as shown above. Another approach is to hang the art from a horizon line, as in the second schematic.

Design: Agnew Moyer Smith (Pittsburgh, PA)

The Hardwood Herald *is published by the Hardwood Manufacturers Association. Trim size: 8-1/2 by 11*

University Press

The Monthly Report on Sales, Promotion, and Product Development

Political History and Economics Titles Continue to Boost Overseas Sales

March 1990

Lorem ipsum dolor sit amet, consectetuer adipiscing elit, sed diam nonummy nibh euismod tincidunt ut laoreet dolore magna aliquam erat volutpat. Ut wisi enim ad minim veniam, quis nostrud exerci tation ullamcorper suscipit lobortis nisl ut aliquip ex ea commodo consequat. Duis autem vel eum iriure dolor in hendrerit in vulputate velit esse molestie consequat, vel illum dolore eu feugiat nulla facilisis at vero eros et accumsan et iusto odio dignissim qui blandit.

Praesent luptatum zzril delenit augue duis dolore te feugait nulla facilisi. Lorem ipsum dolor sit amet, consectetuer adipiscing elit, sed diam nonummy nibh euismod tincidunt ut laoreet dolore magna aliquam erat volutpat. Ut wisi enim ad minim veniam, quis nostrud exerci tation ullamcorper suscipit lobortis nisl ut aliquip ex ea commodo consequat.

Duis autem vel eum iriure dolor in hendrerit in vulputate velit esse molestie consequat, vel illum dolore eu feugiat nulla facilisis at vero eros et accumsan et iusto odio dignissim qui blandit praesent luptatum zzril delenit augue duis dolore te feugait nulla facilisi. Nam liber tempor cum soluta nobis eleifend option congue nihil imperdiet doming id quod mazim placerat facer possim assum. Lorem ipsum dolor sit amet, consectetuer adipiscing elit, sed diam nonummy nibh euismod tincidunt ut laoreet dolore magna aliquam erat volutpat.

London office to open this summer

Ut wisi enim ad minim veniam, quis nostrud exerci tation ullamcorper suscipit lobortis nisl ut aliquip ex ea commodo consequat. Duis autem vel eum iriure dolor in hendrerit in vulputate velit esse molestie consequat, vel illum dolore eu feugiat nulla facilisis at vero eros et accumsan et iusto odio dignissim qui blandit praesent luptatum zzril delenit augue duis dolore te feugait nulla facilisi. Lorem ipsum dolor sit amet, consectetuer adipiscing elit, sed diam nonummy nibh euismod tincidunt ut laoreet dolore magna aliquam erat volutpat.

Ut wisi enim ad minim veniam, quis nostrud exerci tation ullamcorper suscipit lobortis nisl ut aliquip ex ea commodo consequat. Duis autem vel eum iriure dolor in hendrerit in vulputate velit esse molestie consequat, vel illum dolore eu feugiat nulla facilisis at vero eros et accumsan et iusto odio dignissim qui blandit praesent luptatum zzril delenit augue duis dolore te feugait nulla facilisi. Lorem ipsum lobortis nisl ut aliquip ex ea commodo consequat. Duis autem vel eum iriure dolor elit, sed diam nonummy nibh euismod tincidunt ut laoreet dolore magna aliquam erat volutpat. Ut wisi enim ad minim veniam, quis nostrud exerci tation ullamcorper suscipit lobortis nisl ut aliquip ex ea commodo consequat.

Duis autem vel eum iriure dolor in hendrerit in vulputate velit esse molestie consequat, vel illum dolore eu feugiat nulla facilisis at vero eros et accumsan et

University Press authors Jonathan Pritchard and Michelle Colibier are honored by the United States Library of Congress; see page 6.

Overseas Sales

FY 85	16, 365
FY 86	25,347
FY 87	36,897
FY 88	47,356
FY 89	59,000

TWO-COLUMN GRIDS

Two-column grids have a more designed and polished look than the one-column formats, yet they don't require a great deal of planning and can be assembled fairly quickly in PageMaker. They're useful for a wide variety of publications, including newsletters, brochures, annual reports, bulletins, menus, fact sheets, and catalog listings. When done well, they can range from honest simplicity to punchy straightforwardness. When done poorly, they can be boring or heavy-handed.

With two equal columns, the line length in an 8.5- by 11-inch page is usually between 16 and 21 picas, depending on the margins and the space between the columns. The type can drop down to 10/12 and still be quite readable. These factors make this format very economical in that you can fit quite a lot of text on a page. The greatest danger of the

Each editorial topic is contained on a single page, giving this brief annual report a simple, consistent, accessible style. The text does not have to fill out to the bottom margin. When your message can be broken down into one and two page units, this is a very effective format that is quite simple to produce.

The narrow margins (3 picas on the outside and bottom, 5 picas on the inside) work here because of the undersized page, the simple design, the open leading, and the white space at the top of the page. You wouldn't want margins any narrower than this, and without the compensating factors just mentioned wider margins would be essential.

The inset photos with wraparound text keep the running text from being too symmetrical. The depth of the photos varies according to the picture and the amount of text on the page. Photos can also run the full column width or extend halfway into the second column.

The body text is 10/14 Times Roman with 36-point initial caps. The headlines are 22 point.

PATIENT SERVICES

A kidney patient faces hardships that most healthy people never encounter. The Kidney Foundation of Maryland attempts to help these patients by providing an extensive array of patient programs and services.

The second annual Kids Having Fun Camp for pediatric renal patients was held during the weekend of August 23 at the pastoral YMCA Camp Letts in Edgewater, Maryland. This year's camp attracted 13 young renal patients from a three-state area. Smiles were abundant as the youngsters enjoyed a carefree weekend away from the all-too-familiar medical environment. Exciting activities such as horseback riding and boating, as well as the more traditional sports of tennis, softball and volleyball, thrilled the campers and volunteers alike. The camp also provided a respite from the constant demands imposed by kidney disease on the patients' parents.

December is an unlikely time to have a picnic. The Kidney Foundation, however, chose to beat summer's heat and hold a "Picnic in December" for its annual patient party for the second consecutive year. The University of Maryland Medical School Teaching Facility was the site for the party attended by special guests Mr. and Mrs. Santa, who presented gifts donated by Santa Claus Anonymous, to over 40 children. Volunteers from Maryland Casualty Company portrayed the visitors from the North Pole, as well as a snowman and other storybook characters. The Boys Latin Magicians' Guild provided entertainment that delighted the entire audience.

The Patient Emergency Assistance Program provided one-time grants to kidney patients in need of financial help. Patients were awarded nearly $2,000 in emergency grants.

The Medication Discount Program allowed dialysis, transplant, and chronic kidney disease patients to purchase medication at the lowest possible cost. Patients were registered for the program by their physicians. Under this program, all prescription drugs related to the patient's kidney condition can be purchased at wholesale price through the Kidney Foundation, which pays the pharmacist's fees and handling costs.

Transplant and dialysis patients also received free medical identification jewelry. This jewelry alerts medical personnel to the patient's kidney condition and is especially valuable in emergency situations.

Young kidney patients from Maryland and Washington, D.C. had an opportunity to show off their creativity in the Foundation's "Gift of Life" poster contest, held on November 15 at the Top of the World Trade Center in Baltimore. The youngsters' artwork was displayed and judged by such celebrities as Ken Matz of WMAR-TV and Bob MacAvan of the Baltimore Blast. Eight-year-old Mario Velez, of Baltimore, won third prize in his category and was awarded a trip for his entire family to the Six Flags Power Plant in Baltimore. First prize winners in each category advanced to the National "Gift of Life" poster contest in Washington, D.C.

PUBLIC EDUCATION

Kidney disease is an intricate and complex subject. One of the Kidney Foundation's primary responsibilities is to educate the public about kidney disease and the benefits of organ donation.

Over 78,000 Americans die each year of kidney disease. Many of these patients die because a suitable organ donor cannot be found. As a result, the Kidney Foundation has expanded its efforts to promote voluntary organ donation through its "Give the Gift of Life" campaign.

In December and January the Maryland affiliate participated in a nationwide campaign based on the theme, "Sign an organ donor card....It's one New Year's resolution that's easy to keep." The Foundation distributed public service announcements to the major Baltimore TV stations and to radio stations across the state. Public service ads and fact sheets were also provided to area newspapers.

Public information efforts were intensified during Organ Donation Awareness Week in April. NKF-Maryland held an organ donor sign-in at Johns Hopkins Hospital, and area radio stations gave frequent air play to public service announcements about organ donation. Although April marked the height of the organ donor campaign, "Gift of Life" materials were used extensively by the media throughout the year.

Health fairs provided an excellent opportunity for Foundation representatives to personally

speak with the public about kidney disease and organ donation. During the year Kidney Foundation staff and volunteers were on hand at many health fairs throughout the area. The KF newsletter, refreshed with a new format, continued to inform thousands of readers with interesting information about kidney disease issues and the many activities of the Foundation. Educational brochures, on topics ranging from "Transplantation" to "Nutritional Considerations for the Patient on Dialysis," were available to the public free of charge.

The KF Membership Drive held in the spring featured an effective plea for funds by WMAR-TV anchorman Ken Matz and infant kidney patient Jason Ogle. The drive culminated in May, with a three-night phone-a-thon from the offices of the Baltimore Gas and Electric Company. Friends of the Foundation generously responded to the drive, contributing a total of nearly $10,000 to the fight against kidney disease.

Since organ donation is a key step in solving the problem of kidney disease, the Foundation strongly supported the efforts of Delegate Paula Hollinger to pass a state law requiring the "routine inquiry" issue. The law now states that parents of a deceased minor must be approached by a hospital medical staff member concerning post-mortem organ donation.

Design: Carl A. Schuetz, Foxglove Communications (Baltimore, MD)

Pages from the annual report of the National Kidney Foundation of Maryland.
Trim size: 7-1/2 by 10

two-column grid, however, is that you will try to fit in too much text and create pages that are dense and difficult to read. When in doubt, add an extra pica to the margins rather than to the text block.

With two columns you have more options in both the size and placement of headlines. You need to be careful, however, of the position of the heads—they shouldn't be too close to the top or the bottom of a column. (The very top of a column is, of course, okay). Also, take care that headlines in adjoining columns do not align with one another.

The off-center page created by a wide outer margin adds variety and sophistication to a two-column grid. This format is especially well suited to house organs.

A tight grid structure and well-defined image area is established by the extension of visual elements into the side and top margins and by the strong graphic treatment of the folios at the bottom of the page.

The graphic style of the breakout, folios, and logo and the contemporary headline treatment with bracket-style rules give the format a personal signature, as well as a consistency of visual style from one page to the next. The overall feeling is restrained without being bland.

Photos can be sized as shown here or, in the case of mug shots, used in half-column width with wrap-around text filling out the other half column. The rules around the photos crisp up the otherwise soft edges.

The text is Palatino throughout.

Design: Michael Waitsman, Synthesis Concepts (Chicago, IL)

The Wildman Herald *is the national newsletter of Wildman, Harrold, Allen & Dixon, a law firm.*
Trim size: 8-1/2 by 11

Judge Turner and his wife Kay (right) enjoy themselves at the Federal Bar Association reception following the swearing-in ceremony.

In 1967 Turner hired on with the firm of Canada, Russell & Turner (Memphis predecessor of Wildman, Harrold), where his father Cooper Turner had helped establish a thriving practice. He became a partner in 1974, the year of his father's death.

In 20 years of private practice with the firm, Turner earned a reputation as one of the Mid South area's top civil litigators. Working in state and federal courts throughout the region, he ran the gamut — commercial and corporate cases, products liability, banking, insurance defense, you name it. His most recent success was the recovery of a summary judgment in favor of Richards Medical Company, requiring that

The ABA declared him "well qualified," a rating not often given, and the nomination sailed through the Judiciary Committee and the full Senate.

Richards' parent company turn over $13 million in pension plan assets to Richards. (The parent has appealed.)
Over the years Turner has also found time for various civic endeavors. He worked in the successful campaigns of Rep. Don Sundquist, a Memphis-area congressman, and he has filled numerous offices and

committee positions with the local bar, which he now serves as president.
With this kind of background, Turner was as ready as one can be for the intricate and sometimes intrusive process of becoming a federal judge. "There was a form for Department of Justice, a form for the FBI, a form for the ABA, a form for the Federal Bar Association..." the nominee recounted with a weary sigh. Scores of friends and family members were interviewed by men in dark suits. Detailed financial disclosure forms had to be completed.
After being put through the washer and dryer, though, he emerged clean — and more. The ABA declared him "well qualified," a rating not often given, and once the Senate finally got past the logjam over the Battle of Bork, the Turner nomination sailed through the Judiciary Committee and the full Senate.
A few days before his swearing in, Turner, along with another large gathering of the legal profession, attended the funeral of Judge Marion Boyd. The father of Memphis partner Boots Boyd, Judge Boyd was the first man to occupy the seat which Judge Turner now occupies. He was known for his honesty, fairness, timeliness, and strictness in sentencing. As the eulogist reviewed Judge Boyd's long career of public service, Turner felt a special kinship with his early predecessor. "I would like to be seen after a number of years as being completely honest, with a good temperament, polite and courteous, as one who knows his law and does his work and comes up with fair results. If I can do all of that I will be a great judge."
Because of his caseload, with 370 civil cases and an unknown number of criminal cases awaiting him when he first arrived, it is difficult to see how Judge Turner will find time for his hobbies, which include tennis, bird hunting, and gardening. But he vows to make time for his family, who have been his biggest boosters throughout the long nominating process: wife Kay Farese Turner, herself a practicing attorney, and five children, Park (18), Alexandra (14), Oliver (13), Christian (12), and Whitney (9).
Looking back on his private practice, Turner noted that leaving the firm was not easy. "I have practiced law with most of the lawyers here longer than I have been with anyone else in my life, and I've liked it. I've liked the firm, and I respect the integrity of the lawyers here. I hope I'll be lucky enough to enjoy my job as judge as much as I have enjoyed practicing law."
Janet Wilson has something special to remember, too. "Can you believe it?" she marvelled. "I put the President on hold!"

THE WILDMAN HERALD

March 1988

Firm Promotes Valuable European Contacts
by Robert Keel

In November, 1987, Tom Smith of the New York office and Bob Keel of the Toronto office visited Rome and London. The visit to Rome was arranged by Keel to introduce Smith to clients of the Toronto office. Moreover, Keel Cottrelle maintains an office in Rome in association with Avvocato Francesco Ruggieri and Avvocato Giovanni Iasilli. The trip therefore, presented an opportunity to introduce this affiliated office to a member of the national management committee. Indeed, Bob and Tom were delighted to discover that there are now two affiliated offices in Italy because Avv. Ruggieri now maintains an office in Milan. Avv. Ruggieri made it clear that both the Rome and Milan offices are available to anyone in the firm, either for business or merely to drop in to get acquainted. The Rome office is in the center of the city at 95 Via Barberini, which is just around the corner from the American Embassy.

While they were in Italy, Keel and Smith devoted a considerable amount of time to client business. Among other things, Bob introduced Tom to a number of multi-national corporate clients. As you might expect, the trip was not all work. The hospitality extended to them by clients and by Avv. Ruggieri and Avv. Iasilli was delightful and occupied a considerable amount of otherwise billable hours. Moreover, Tom's wife Terry, who also made the trip, convinced Tom to take a side trip to Venice.
After Rome, Tom, Terry and Bob flew on to London. This time, it was Smith's turn to show Keel around. Tom visited his business acquaintances at Shell International. Bob and Tom also visited an acquaintance at Hambros Bank. They spent some time with representatives of Network Security Management Limited, which is based in London. Keel managed to squeeze in visits with a number of business acquaintances who are now doing business in London.
With our expanding practice and our shrinking world, our European contacts will assume increasing importance. We should all be aware of the global networks that are in place.

Left to right:
Bob Keel,
Giovanni Iasilli,
Tom Smith, and
Francesco Ruggieri.

Four wide-margin, two-column designs

Wide margins are the foundation for an open, two-column format that is very appealing and highly readable. All four documents in this section were designed using the grid in the blueprint on the following spread, but the kind of information, the intended audience, and the styles of the publications differ considerably.

The most varied and dynamic of the four designs (facing page) divides the vertical grid into horizontal story areas. This modular format requires more time and planning to execute than the others; you may have to adjust the depth of the text blocks several times to balance all the elements on the page.

The overall busyness of the design elements is appropriate here because it evokes the adventure of travel. You can create a more conservative look with this horizontal format by using a simpler nameplate and more uniform art styles. The format works for all-text documents, too, though to very different effect.

The nameplate at the top of the page uses the multiple headline style commonly found in newsstand magazines. Note the bold contents list and also the "Summer Specials" stamp, which is similar to the diagonal banner on many magazine covers. Deft handling of typography is critical in composing so many elements with varying emphases into a unified, readable whole.

The pictures use the grid effectively precisely because they break out of it. The mountains seem more expansive because they exceed the margins; the balloon seems to float off the page. The range of art styles, from realistic to schematic, adds to the feeling of adventure that a travel bulletin wants to project. The pictures are all from clip art files. (The stamp and mountains are from WetPaint; the compass and balloon are from The Mac Art Dept.; the plane is from Artware; and the ship is from Images with Impact.)

The type used throughout is Futura. The combination of Futura Light, Extra Bold, and Oblique in the headlines creates a colorful contrast without introducing another typeface. The unity of a single type family balances the complex nameplate treatment and the different styles of art.

Type specifications
Nameplate overline: 16-point Futura
  Light
Going: 96-point Light
Places: 36-point Futura Extra Bold
  Oblique
Contents: 14/14 Extra Bold
Lead story headline: 28/29 Light
Second story head: 18/18 Extra Bold
Body text: 10/12.5 Light

SUMMER SPECIALS

GOING PLACES

RIVERBOAT RACES

GRAND TETONS

GREAT BARRIER REEF

AROUND THE WORLD IN SO MANY WAYS

Lorem ipsum dolor sit amet, consectetuer adipiscing elit, sed diam nonummy nibh euismod tincidunt ut laoreet dolore magna aliquam erat volutpat. Ut wisi enim ad minim veniam, quis nostrud exerci tation ullamcorper suscipit lobortis nisl ut aliquip ex ea commodo Consequat. Duis

PLUS THE MANY ADVENTURES THAT AWAIT YOU CLOSE TO HOME

Autem vel velit esse molestie Consequat, vel illum dolore eu feugiat nulla facilisis at vero eros et accumsan et iusto odio dignissim qui blandit praesent luptatum zzril delenit augue duis dolore te feugait nulla facilisi. Lorem ipsum dolor sit amet, consectetuer adipiscing elit, sed diam nonummy nibh euismod tincidunt ut laoreet dolore magna aliquam erat volutpat. Ut wisi enim ad minim veniam, quis nostrud exerci tation ullamcorper suscipit lobortis nisl ut aliquip ex ea commodo consequat.

Duis autem vel eum iriure dolor in hendrerit in vulputate velit esse molestie consequat, vel illum dolore eu feugiat nulla facilisis at vero eros et accumsan et iusto odio dignissim qui blandit

praesent luptatum zzril delenit augue duis dolore te feugait nulla facilisi. Nam liber tempor cum soluta nobis eleifend option congue nihil imperdiet doming id quod mazim placerat facer pos assum.

Lorem ipsum dolor sit amet, consectetuer adipiscing elsed diam nonummy nibh euismod tincidunt ut laoreet magna aliquam erat volutpat. Ut wisi enim ad minveniam, quis nostrud exerci tation ullamcorper suscipit lobortis nisl ut aliquip ex ea commodo

The Symonton Foundation

What We've Accomplished

Lorem ipsum dolor sit amet, consectetuer adipiscing elit, sed diam nonummy nibh euismod tincidunt ut laoreet dolore magna aliquam erat volutpat. Ut wisi enim ad minim veniam, quis nostrud exerci tation ullamcorper suscipit lobortis nisl ut aliquip ex ea commodo consequa te feugait nulla facilisi t.

The Centerville Nursing Home
Duis autem vel eum iriure dolor in hendrerit in vulputate velit esse molestie consequat, vel illum dolore eu feugiat nulla facilisis at vero eros et accumsan et iusto odio dignissim qui blandit praesent luptatum zzril delenit augue duis dolore te feugait nulla facilisi. Lorem ipsum dolor sit amet, consectetuer adipiscing elit, sed diam nonummy nibh euismod tin-

cidunt ut laoreet dolore magna aliquam erat volutpat. Ut wisi enim ad minim veniam, quis nostrud exerci tation ullamcorper suscipit lobortis nisl ut aliquip ex ea commodo consequat te feugait nulla

Duis autem vel eum iriure dolor in hendrerit in vulputate velit esse molestie consequat, vel illum dolore eu feugiat nulla facilisis at vero eros et accumsan et iusto odio dignissim qui blandit praesent luptatum zzril delenit augue duis dolore te feugait nulla facilisi. Nam liber tempor cum soluta nobis eleifend option congue nihil imperdiet doming id quod mazim placerat facer possim assum.

Job Training Program for Disadvantaged Youth
Lorem ipsum dolor sit amet, consectetuer adipiscing elit, sed diam nonummy nibh euismod tincidunt ut laoreet dolore magna aliquam erat volutpat. Ut wisi enim ad minim veniam, quis nostrud exerci tation ullamcorper suscipit lobortis nisl ut aliquip ex ea commodo consequat. Duis autem vel eum iriure dolor in hendrerit in vulputate velit esse molestie consequat, vel illum dolore eu feugiat nulla facilisis at vero eros et accumsan et iusto odio dignissim qui blandit praesent luptatum zzril delenit augue duis dolore te feugait nulla facilisi. Lorem ipsum dolor sit amet, consectetuer adipiscing elit, sed diam nonummy nibh euismod tincidunt ut laoreealiquam erat volut

The Symonton Foundation

What We Need to Do

Ut wisi enim ad minim veniam, quis nostrud exerci tation ullamcorper suscipit lobortis nisl ut aliquip ex ea commodo consequat. Duis autem vel eum iriure dolor in hendrerit in vulputate velit esse molestie consequat, vel illum dolore eu feugiat nulla facilisis at vero eros et accumsan et iusto odio dignissim qui blandit praesent luptatum zzril delenit augue duis dolore te feugait nulla facilisi.

Capital Fund
Lorem ipsum dolor sit amet, consectetuer adipiscing elit, sed diam nonummy nibh euismod tincidunt ut laoreet dolore magna aliquam erat volutpat. Ut wisi enim ad minim veniam, quis nostrud exerci tation ullamcorper suscipit lobortis nisl ut aliquip ex ea commodo consequat. Duis autem vel eum iriure dolor in hendrerit in vulputate velit esse molestie con-sequat, vel illum dolore eu feugiat nulla facilisis at vero eros et accumsan et iusto odio dignis-sim qui blandit praesent luptatum zzril delenit augue duis dolore te feugait nulla facilisi.

Lorem ipsum dolor sit amet, consectetuer adipiscing elit, sed diam nonummy nibh euismod tincidunt ut laorealiquam eratorem Lorem ipsum dolor sit amet, consectetuer adipiscing elit, sed diam nonummy nibh euismod tincidunt ut laoreet dolore magna.

ipsum dolor sit amet, consectetuer adipiscing elit, sed diam nonummy nibh euismod tin-cidunt ut laoreet dolore magna erat volutpat. Ut wisi enim ad minim veniam, quis nostrud exerci tation ullamcorper suscipit lobortis nisl ut aliquip ex ea commodo conse-quat. Duis autem vel eum iriure dolor in hendrerit in vulputate velit esse molestie consequat, vel illum dolore eu feugiat nulla volutpat orem ipsum dolor sit amet, con-sectetuer adipiscing elit, sed diam nonummy nibh euismod tincidunt ut laoreet dolore magna aliquam erat volutpat. Ut wisi enim ad minim veniam, quis nostrud exerci tation ullamcorper suscipit lobortis nisl ut aliquip ex ea commodo consequat. Duis autem vel eum iriure dolor in hendrerit in vulputate velit esse molestie consequat, vel illum dolore eu feugiat

Staff Expansion
Ut wisi enim ad minim veniam, quis nostrud exerci tation ullamcorper suscipit lobortis nisl ut aliquip ex ea commodo consequat. Duis autem vel eum iriure dolor in hendrerit in vulputate velit esse molestie consequat, vel illum dolore eu feugiat nulla facilisis at vero eros et accumsan et iusto odio dignissim qui blandit praesent luptatum zzril delenit augue duis dolore te feugait nulla facilisi. Lorem ipsum dolor sit amet, consectetuer adipiscing elit, sed diam nonummy nibh euismod tin

duis dolore te feugait nulla facilisi. Nam liber tempor cum soluta nobis eleifend option congue nihil imperdiet doming id quod mazim placerat facer possim assum.
Lorem ipsum dolor sit amet, consectetuer adipiscing elit, sed diam nonummy nibh euismod tincidunt ut laoreet dolore magna aliquam erat volutpatillum.

This document shares the dignified simplicity found in the annual report reproduced at the beginning of the two-column grid section. It is designed to accommodate a subject head over a 0.5-point rule at the top of each page. If you omit that head, leave the rule in place.

The text seems to hang from the rule under the main headline. This strong structure provides consistency from page to page regardless of the column depth. The variable column depth gives you flexibility and speed when you assemble the pages on screen.

The banner, the main headline, and the rule below that headline extend 3 picas past the left text margin shown in the blueprint on the facing page. The banner is 2 picas deep with 14-point Garamond Bold type.

The main headlines are 30-point Bodoni Bold.

The body text is 10/13 Helvetica Light. The subheads are 10/12 Helvetica Black under 0.5-point rules.

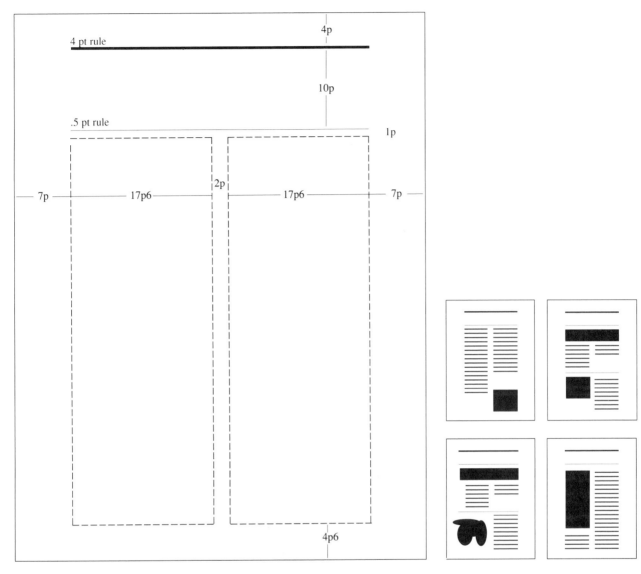

The blueprint above shows the basic grid for the four documents on the previous three and following two pages.

The column width (17p6) is excellent for easy reading.

The generous margins require a generous space between the columns.

The grid is centered on the page. If you shift the grid to one side for an off-center page, the wider margin can be used for annotations, notes, small pieces of art, and other marginalia.

A variation with a more structured nameplate and headline treatment is shown on the next spread.

Art can be placed on the grid as shown in the schematics or as shown in the sample pages.

1989 PROGRAM OF EVENTS

SCHOOL OF PHYSICAL SCIENCES

SOUTHEAST STATE UNIVERSITY
70TH SCIENTIFIC FORUM

MONDAY, MAY 8, 1989   FULTON AUDITORIUM

MORNING PROGRAM

7:45   Registration
> Hendrerit in vulputate velit esse molestie consequat, vel illum dolore eu feugiat.

7:45   Continental Breakfast
> Nonummy nibh euismod tincidunt ut laoreet dolore magna aliquam erat volutpat. Ut wisi enim ad minim.

9:00   Introduction
> Veniam, quis nostrud exerci tation ullamcorper suscipit lobortis nisl ut aliquip ex ea commodo consequat. Duis autem vel eum iriure dolor in.

10:00   Break
> Hendrerit in vulputate velit esse molestie consequat, vel illum dolore eu feugiat nulla facilisis at vero eros et accumsan et iusto odio dignissim qui.

10:30   Opening Address
> Blandit praesent luptatum zzril delenit augue duis dolore te feugait nulla facilisi. Lorem ipsum dolor sit amet, consectetuer adipiscing elit, sed diam.

12:00   Open House and Lunch
> Nonummy nibh euismod tincidunt ut laoreet dolore magna aliquam erat volutpat. Ut wisi enim ad minim.

AFTERNOON PROGRAM

2:00   Overview of Seminars
> Veniam, quis nostrud exerci tation ullamcorper suscipit lobortis nisl ut aliquip ex ea commodo consequat.

3:00   Faculty Roundtable
> Duis autem vel eum iriure dolor in hendrerit in vulputate velit esse molestie consequat, vel illum dolore eu feugiat nulla facilisis at vero eros et accumsan et iusto odio dignissim qui blandit praesent luptatum zzril delenit augue duis dolore te feugait nulla facilisi. Nam liber tempor cum soluta.

4:00   The Year in Review
> Option congue nihil imperdiet doming id quod mazim placerat facer possim assum. Lorem ipsum dolor sit amet.,

4:30   Agenda for the Nineties
> Consectetuer adipiscing elit, sed diam nonummy nibh euismod tincidunt ut laoreet dolore magna aliquam erat volutpat. Ut wisi enim ad minim veniam, quis nostrud exerci tation.

5:00   Discussion Period
> UlLamcorper suscipit lobortis nisl ut aliquip ex ea commodo consequat. Duis autem vel eum iriure dolor in hendrerit in vulputate velit esse.

EVENING PROGRAM

6:30   School of Chemistry Buffet
> Consequat, vel illum dolore eu feugiat nulla facilisis at vero eros et.

8:00   Class Reunion
> Et iusto odio dignissim qui blandit praesent luptatum zzril delenit augue duis dolore te feugait nulla facilisi. Lorem ipsum dolor sit amet, con.

Programs with many items briefly described, like the one shown here, work very well in this two-column format. The column measure is wide enough to contain the agenda listings on single lines, but short enough so that the indented descriptions run over, creating visual separation between the headings.

A classic, traditional feeling appropriate for an academic program is created by the centered text in the open space at the top of the page and by the use of Garamond, a very refined and graceful typeface.

Nameplate type
1989 Program: 18-point Garamond
Top rule: 4 point
School of…: 12 point
Southeast State…: 18/21
Date and place: 10 point
Bottom rule: 0.5 point

The three subheads (Morning Program, etc.) are 10-point Garamond small caps. The double rules below them are from PageMaker's Lines menu. The hand-placed rules under the agenda listings are 0.5 point, to match the weight of the double rules. You should maintain consistency in line weight throughout a page. The typeface underscore would be too heavy here.

The boldface time for each part of the program adds a different color to the type, which keeps the page from being too monotonous.

The program listings are 10/12 Garamond. The event after the time is tabbed to 3 picas from the left margin; the descriptive copy is set with a 3-pica left indent so that it is flush with the tabbed text.

The space between listings in the sample is specified as 1 pica paragraph space before each event heading and 4 points after it.

A newsletter style is adapted here for a sales department's monthly bulletin. The rules, bold heads with tag lines, and initial caps dress up and give a newsy image to what could be a pedestrian report.

The highly structured name-plate shows another way of using the open space at the top of the grid. (See the blueprint detail below right for specifications.)

The strong headline treatment requires white space around the various elements and makes separation of headlines in adjoining columns essential.

The initial caps are 60-point Helvetica Condensed Black. Often found in the editorial pages of magazines to highlight points of entry on a page, initial caps are generally underused in business publications. They are especially effective in complex pages such as this sample.

The wide, 3-pica paragraph indent is proportional to the initial cap. Be aware that very narrow letters (such as I) and very wide letters (M and W) will not conform to this proportion. The price of a truly professional document is editing to avoid these letters. Really.

The body text is 10/12 Bookman.

The illustration was created with PageMaker's drawing tools. The box around it uses a 2-point rule and a 10% shade. The headline is 10-point Helvetica Black Oblique, and the descriptive lines are 9/9 Helvetica Light with Helvetica Black numbers. The caption is 10/12 Bookman italic, centered.

The centered folio (10-point Helvetica Light) and the flush right continued line (9-point Helvetica Light Oblique) are aligned at their baselines 2 picas below the bottom margin.

THE GREAT OUTDOORS STORE

Month in Review

July 1989

BRISK START FOR CAMPING AND BACKPACKING EQUIPMENT

Fewer travelers abroad spurs sales in do it yourself activities.

Lorem ipsum dolor sit amet, consectetuer adipiscing elit, sed diam nonummy nibh euismod tincidunt ut laoreet dolore magna aliquam erat volutpat. Ut wisi enim ad minim veniam, quis nostrud exerci tation ullamcorper suscipit lobortis nisl ut aliquip ex ea commodo consequat. Duis autem vel eum iriure dolor in hendrerit in vulputate velit esse molestie consequat, vel illum dolore eu feugiat nulla facilisis at vero eros et accumsan et iusto odio dignissim qui blandit praesent luptatum zzril delenit augue duis dolore te feugait nulla facilisi.

Lorem ipsum dolor sit amet, consectetuer adipiscing elit, sed diam nonummy nibh euismod tincidunt ut laoreet dolore magna aliquam erat volutpat. Ut wisi enim ad minim veniam, quis nostrud exerci tation ullamcorper suscipit lobortis nisl ut aliquip ex ea commodo consequat. Duis autem vel eum iriure dolor in hendrerit in vulputate velit esse molestie consequat, vel illum dolore eu feugiat nulla facilisis at vero eros et accumsan et iusto odio dignissim qui blandit praesent luptatum zzril delenit augue duis dolore te feugait nulla facilisi. Nam liber tempor cum soluta nobis eleifend option congue nihil imperdiet doming id quod mazim placerat facer possim assum.

Lorem ipsum dolor sit amet, consectetuer adipiscing elit, sed diam nonummy nibh euismod tincidunt ut laoreet dolore magna aliquam erat volutpat. Utwisi enim ad minim veniam, quis nostrud wisi enim ad minim veniam, quis nostrud exerci tation ex ea commodo

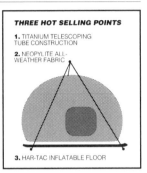

THREE HOT SELLING POINTS

1. TITANIUM TELESCOPING TUBE CONSTRUCTION

2. NEOPYLITE ALL-WEATHER FABRIC

3. HAR-TAC INFLATABLE FLOOR

The newly introduced two-person model X-2000-2 tent

WEATHERMAN PREDICTS ANOTHER HOT SUMMER. EXPECT BOOST IN WATER SPORTS GEAR

Jump in on the action in the new colorful inflatable water toys.

Nconsequat. Duis autem vel eum iriure dolor in hendrerit in vulputate velit esse molestie consequat, vel illum dolore eu feugiat nulla facilisis at vero eros et accumsan et iusto odio dignissim qui blandit praesent luptatum zzril delenit augue duis dolore te feugait nulla facilisi.

Lorem ipsum dolor sit amet, consectetuer adipiscing elit, sed diam nonummy nibh euismod tincidunt ut laoreet dolore magna aliquam erat volut. Lorem ipsum dolor sit amet, consectetuer adipiscing elit, sed diam nonummy nibh euismod tincidunt ut laoreet dolore magna

1

Continued on page 3

---

	4 pt rule	4p
Co. name 24 pt Machine	.5 pt rule	2p6
Pub. Name 48 pt Bookman Ital.		5p6
Date 12 pt Bookman		2p
	1p	
Head 14/13 Helv. Cond. Black	4 pt rule	
	2p3	
Tag line 11/13 Helv. L. Oblique		
	1p	2 pt rule
Top line of body text		

12p

3p

5p3

Wide-measure two-column grids

When you need to put a lot of running text or data on a page but still want a fairly simple format, consider a two-column grid with narrow margins and wide columns. You can see from the documents in this section—a newsletter, a catalog, an instruction sheet, and a journal—how adaptable this grid is to many different kinds of publications. Each of the examples uses this format in a completely different way and creates a very different image through typography and art.

A self-contained cover story emphasizes the importance of the topic, in this case a substantial contribution to a small boarding school.

The sidebar inset in the two-column grid is used here to quote the donor. The box is 14 picas wide with a 12p6 column measure. The use of a second color, blue, for the italic type draws the reader's attention to this statement.

Blue is also used in the banner, with reverse type, and for the display text.

The typeface on the cover is Galliard throughout.

A bolder, busier style for an inside story is created by the large headline, the recurrent subheads, and the bold rule around the photo. The banner, headline, and subheads print in blue.

The column width—22 picas—is the absolute maximum for running text on an 8.5- by 11-inch page. With a rule down the center of the page, you don't have to align the text in adjoining columns.

Other pages of the newsletter use a three-column grid, maintaining the banner, page frame, and rules

between columns for continuity. Mixing grids within a publication in this way accommodates a mix of short and long stories and different-size pictures and gives the publication a varied texture.

The body text is Galliard. The headlines are Helvetica Black Oblique.

Design: Scot Louis Gaznier (Langley, WA)

Pages from The Solebury School newsletter. Trim size: 8-1/2 by 11

The Newsletter

EDITOR: *Daniel Lusk* • ASSOCIATE EDITOR: *Jean Shaw Gaznier '53* • DESIGN: *Scot Louis Gaznier*

SPRING 1988

Pledge to Build New Dorm Spurs Board to Consider Long-Range Capital Campaign

A RECENT PLEDGE of $250,000 for capital construction by Carol Chianese VanDuyne '52 has provided the impetus for the trustees of Solebury School to look into the feasibility of launching a full-scale campaign.

A feasibility study to explore options and create plans for faculty and student housing is going forward at this time, according to Bruce Bergquist, HEAD OF SCHOOL.

The study, authorized by the BOARD OF TRUSTEES at its January meeting, will consider three options with respect to improvement of present boys' living quarters: to renovate the existing facility, to rebuild the present dormitory, or to construct a new building in a different location on campus.

Bruce said that the Planning Committee has met frequently since the Board meeting, has selected an architect to act as consultant for the study, and is currently exploring options for location of a new building. It also is reviewing the feasibility of a new wing for the current dorm, which he said seems at this point a less likely option for providing the housing needed to meet both immediate and long-range goals for the school.

The Board also authorized preparation of a more formal long-range plan by administration and Board leadership. A written document is being created to clarify and project long-range goals for future development of the school — in essence to update and focus a long-range plan completed in 1985 by an ad hoc committee of students, faculty, administration and Board members.

When completed, the current study will provide schematics of a proposed new building, lay out a timetable for construction, and project costs.

Bruce anticipates completion of the study by April 15, in time for the Board to decide in May which of the options under consideration to include in a case statement

"I have made this decision because I believe in Solebury's future, and I feel fortunate and proud to be able to help the school reach its goals in such a substantial way. I also want this pledge to be used as an incentive for others to reach as deeply as they can into their own pockets and help. My two years at Solebury gave me more of a total education than any schools before or after that time. I want to make certain that students just like me continue to be able to have the Solebury experience. I am just as certain that all of you reading this have much to thank Solebury for. It helped us create our future as adults, and now it is time for us to repay that debt and help Solebury's future."

being prepared by Bruce and Board CHAIRMAN Bill Berkeley. The latter statement will present the case for a capital campaign for the school.

Balanced Budget

While the tenor of the Board's open session in January was cautious, dominated by realistic assessment and close examination, there was an obvious undercurrent of excitement. For the first time in a decade a Board faced the prospect of a balanced budget — a budget that not only projected realistic income figures and expenditures that do not exceed them; it also projected nominal salary increases and substantial reduction of indebtedness.

Members acknowledged a need to improve on the current rate of annual giving, citing a general caution on the part of donors that reflects current economic trends in the country. The Board targeted annual giving donations in the $5,000 – $10,000 range as critical to the continuing, improved health of the school.

Given a balanced budget for the coming fiscal year, and given long-range goals, the Board is considering major steps involving possible construction of new facilities in order to accommodate the proposed growth of the student body.

With Carol VanDuyne's pledge of $250,000 already a beginning for a capital campaign, the question now before the Board is whether the time is right for proceeding with a major fund drive that will accomodate the growth of the student body, enhance the quality of life for faculty, and in the process affect the growth of curriculum and programs and focus more clearly the character of the school.

The present challenge, said Bruce, "is to clarify our priorities and to act on them. We have come a long way, and we know what we want. Now we have some even harder decisions to make."

CLEVE: SOMETHING EXTRA

CLEVE IS ONE of those talented part-time people there have been so many of in our little history. We tend to take them, once they are here, for granted. And, when they are specialists like Cleve Christie, we may not even know their names, much less meet them.

Cleve is easy to talk about because the numbers we can use are beautiful: 18 and 2, 22 and 1. Those are the season records, wins and losses of his Solebury boys varsity basketball team for the past two seasons.

Yet, while those are pretty numbers, they are far from being the whole story of Cleve's impact on his players or even on our school; they aren't even the interesting part.

Coaching our team is only one of the things Cleve does, and one might hurry to say that, while it may appear to be the shiny part, it is not a separate thing from the other parts of his life.

ROMEO AND JULIET'S

Dignified, tough, and generally soft-spoken, Cleve works for the Trenton Housing Authority and manages a number of public housing projects. That's a very important part of his life. He has always made things happen.

He grew up in Trenton in a neighborhood that used to be known as *Dogpatch*. He lived with his grandmother on Southard Street, not far from where he took me for lunch — a cafe called Romeo and Juliet's. Cleve says the place was smaller when he was a kid and used to shovel snow for the people who owned it.

He recalls that he and his friends had one of the first basketball courts in the area. When a couple of houses were moved out of the neighborhood, they asked the township for some dirt to cover the bricks and refuse that were left behind. The Ewing Township trucks brought dirt and dumped it in huge piles and went away. Cleve was organized the kids, got the lemonade, and together they spread out that dirt to make a court.

"When the township people saw our initiative," he recalls, "they came and put up baskets. Putting in time on the court kept me out of trouble."

LOFTY GOALS

Like many young kids, his idols were the basketball super stars of the day — Elgin Baylor, Jerry West, Bob Koosy — immortals of the game. "You set lofty goals, and if you

get halfway there, you're a lot farther than you might have been."

In high school, Cleve "lettered" in basketball and soccer, and continued to play basketball during the 4½ years he was in the Air Force, stationed in Istanbul, Turkey. Twice he made the service all-star team. He returned then to Trenton, married, but left again to go back to school. He attended High Point College and graduated from Ashmore Business College in Thomasville, North Carolina.

Coaching grew quite naturally, he says, out of playing (he still plays in a couple of 30-and-older type leagues, "to get rid of hostilities," and to be with friends) and out of concern for kids.

Since 1970 he has coached in the Unlimited League, a part of the Trenton summer basketball program. His Merryman team has won the championship three times.

Besides coaching from 1984–1986 in the Pro-Am League in Camden — a development league for young professionals sponsored by the National Basketball Association (NBA) — Cleve coached for five years (1981–1986) in the Police Athletic League (PAL) for girls 12 years and under.

Cleve now directs the Summer Program. He says it "helps a lot of guys to get into college." NBA fans will recognize the names of John Battle of the Atlanta Hawks and Roy Hinson of the Philadelphia '76ers, both of whom are graduates of his summer program.

ROLE MODELS

Cleve is very conscious that he is a role model for kids and young people. "In the inner city, the only role models are the guys dealing drugs with their pockets bulging with money. I know it was tough when I came up — but not tough compared to now. I stay involved and give them some time; I have their ear."

For a time he was the director of an after-school pro

The two-column grid is used in this book catalog to create an extremely open, well-organized, easily referenced format.

The long line length (maximum measure is 20p6) minimizes runover lines, so it's easy to pick out the title, author, and other details in each listing.

The small type size (8/11 Friz Quadrata) helps contain the lines, but the leading and white space are designed so that readability isn't compromised. This typeface has a good contrast of boldface to light-face that makes the book titles stand out. The use of boldface, roman, italics, and all caps is handled care-fully to delineate clearly what could have been a hodgepodge of details.

The hard left edge created by the type and the hairline rules contrasts with the openness of the very uneven right margin. Open at the top and the bottom, the page has a strong sense of verticality, which is emphasized by the weight of the category heads.

The headline type is Aachen Bold. The weight of the headlines is emphasized by the bold rules below. Note that in a two-line head the length of the bold rule is determined by the short second line; the hairline rule above the bold rule extends to the maximum measure.

The faceted sphere, with its mathematical precision and crystal-line structure, is appropriate for the scientific line of books being sold. The art was created in Pro3D, using one of the generic solids available in that program, and imported into PageMaker as a PICT file. Because PICT-file tones print differently on LaserWriters and Linotronics (the final output was from an L300), the Pro3D art was kept a little lighter and lower in contrast on-screen than was desired in the printed piece.

Design: John Odam (San Diego, CA)

Catalog from Academic Press, Harcourt Brace Jovanovich, Publishers.

Trim size: 24-3/4 by 11 inches, folded twice

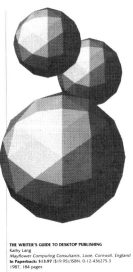

PHYSICAL SCIENCES

THE REWIRING OF AMERICA
The Fiber Optics Revolution
C. David Chaffee
Atlantic Information Services, Inc., Washington, D.C.
1987, 256 pages. **$17.47** ($24.95)
ISBN: 0-12-166360-4

THE FOUNDATIONS OF MAGNETIC RECORDING
John C. Mallinson
Center for Magnetic Recording Research, University of California, San Diego
1987, 175 pages. **$20.97** ($29.95)
ISBN: 0-12-466625-6

ELECTRONS IN SOLIDS
An Introductory Survey
Second Edition
Richard H. Bube
Stanford University, California
1988, 328 pages. **$27.65** ($39.50)
ISBN: 0-12-138552-3

ENCYCLOPEDIA OF PHYSICAL SCIENCE AND TECHNOLOGY
edited by
Robert A. Meyers
TRW Electronics and Defense Sector, Redondo Beach, California
1987, 15-volume set. **$1750.00** ($2500.00)

HANDBOOK OF DIGITAL SIGNAL PROCESSING
ENGINEERING APPLICATIONS
edited by
Douglas F. Elliott
Rockwell International Corporation, Anaheim, California
1987, 999 pages. **$94.50** ($135.00)
ISBN: 0-12-237075-9

ISOTOPE CHRONOSTRATIGRAPHY
Theory and Methods
Douglas F. Williams and Ian Lerche
University of South Carolina, Columbia
W.E. Full
Wichita State University, Kansas
May 1988, 333 pages. **$34.97** ($49.95, tentative)
ISBN: 0-12-754560-3

HISTORICAL SEISMOGRAMS AND EARTHQUAKES
OF THE WORLD
edited by
W.H.K. Lee
U.S. Geological Survey, Menlo Park, California
H. Meyers
National Oceanic and Atmospheric Administration Boulder, Colorado
K. Shimazaki
University of Tokyo, Japan
1988, 528 pages. **$31.50** ($45.00)
ISBN: 0-12-440870-2

COMPUTER SCIENCE

PROLOG FOR PROGRAMMERS
Feliks Kluzniak and Stanislaw Szpakowicz
Warsaw University, Poland
With a contribution by Janusz S. Bien
Paperback Reprint: $17.47 ($24.95)/ISBN: 0-12-416521-4
1987, 320 pages
Casebound: $47.25 ($67.50)/ISBN: 0-12-416520-6
1985, 400 pages

INTRODUCTION TO COMMON LISP
Taiichi Yuasa and Masami Hagiya
Kyoto University, Japan
translated by
Richard Weyhrauch and Yasuko Kitajima
1987, 293 pages. **$20.97** ($29.95)
ISBN: 0-12-774860-1

U.S. and Canadian Customers
CALL TOLL FREE
1-800-321-5068
During normal working hours, weekdays only.
In Missouri, Alaska, or Hawaii
call 1-314-528-8110.
*For detailed sales and discount information
call our National Sales Desk
at 1-619-699-6345*

THE WRITER'S GUIDE TO DESKTOP PUBLISHING
Kathy Lang
Mayflower Computing Consultants, Looe, Cornwall, England
In Paperback: $13.97 ($19.95)/ISBN: 0-12-436275-3
1987, 184 pages

COLOR AND THE COMPUTER
edited by
H. John Durrett
Interactive Systems Laboratories, San Marcos, Texas
1987, 299 pages. **$41.30** ($59.00)
ISBN: 0-12-225210-1

PARALLEL COMPUTER VISION
edited by
Leonard Uhr
University of Wisconsin-Madison
1987, 320 pages. **$20.97** ($29.95)
ISBN: 0-12-706958-5

MATHEMATICS AND ECONOMICS

MATHEMATICS FOR DYNAMIC MODELING
Edward Beltrami
State University of New York at Stony Brook
1987, 277 pages. **$19.25** ($27.50)
ISBN: 0-12-085555-0

RANDOM SIGNAL ANALYSIS IN ENGINEERING SYSTEMS
John J. Komo
Clemson University, South Carolina
1987, 302 pages. **$27.97** ($39.95)
ISBN: 0-12-418660-2

ALGEBRAIC D-MODULES
A. Borel et al.
Princeton University, New Jersey
Volume 2 in the PERSPECTIVES IN MATHEMATICS Series
1987, 355 pages. **$23.10** ($33.00)
ISBN: 0-12-117740-8

THE BOOK OF SQUARES
Leonardo Pisano
(Fibonacci)
An annotated translation into Modern English by
L.E. Sigler
Bucknell University, Lewisburg, Pennsylvania
1987, 124 pages. **$13.97** ($19.95)
ISBN: 0-12-643130-2

INDUSTRIAL POLICY OF JAPAN
edited by
Ryutaro Komiya and Masahiro Okuno
University of Tokyo, Bunkyo-ku, Japan
Kotaro Suzumura
Hitotsubashi University, Kunitachi, Tokyo, Japan
Kazuo Sato
Rutgers University, Newark, New Jersey
March 1988, 590 pages. **$34.97** ($49.95, tentative)
ISBN: 0-12-418650-5

MACROECONOMIC THEORY
Second Edition
Thomas J. Sargent
University of Minnesota and Federal Reserve Bank, Minneapolis and Hoover Institution Stanford University, California
1987, 528 pages. **$31.15** ($44.50)
ISBN: 0-12-619751-2

AN INTRODUCTORY THEORY OF SECURITY MARKETS
J.D. Duffie
Stanford University, California
April 1988, 350 pages. **$27.65** ($39.50, tentative)
ISBN: 0-12-223345-X

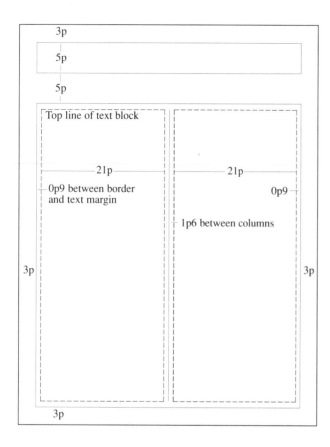

3p

5p

5p

Top line of text block

21p   21p

0p9 between border
and text margin   0p9

1p6 between columns

3p   3p

3p

This blueprint was used for both documents on these two pages.

Equal margins on all four sides work best in this format. If you vary from that, do it decisively, as in a deep top margin, rather than subtly.

The depth of the panel at the top of the page and the space between the panel and the text block can vary depending on the elements to be included.

Art is best sized to the width of a single column. Small diagrams can be accommodated as shown in the instruction sheet at right. Art can also be inset in the text, like the quote in the page below.

The illustrations in the instruction sheet were scanned with a Datacopy 730 and traced in Aldus FreeHand for the purpose of position only. Using a scanner in this way provides an opportunity to test sizes in the layout and to eliminate elements of the art that are unnecessary. The printer strips in the halftones to match the size and position in the layout.

Type specs for instruction sheet
Company name: 18-point Bookman with
     20-point caps
Headline: 16/15 Helvetica Black
Subheads: 12-point Helvetica Black
Text: 10/10 Helvetica Light with 6 points
     between paragraphs, Helvetica Black
     numbers, and a 1p4 hanging indent
Numbers in diagrams: 18-point Helvetica
     Black

 The Journal of Contemporary Mythology

WINTER 1990

IN SEARCH OF
THE MODERN MYTH

By Raymond Chavoustier

orem ipsum dolor sit amet, consectetuer adipiscing elit, sed diam nonummy nibh euismod tincidunt ut laoreet dolore magna aliquam erat volutpat. Ut wisi enim ad minim veniam, quis nostrud exerci tation ullamcorper suscipit lobortis nisl ut aliquip ex ea commodo consequat hendrerit in velit esse molestie.

Duis autem vel eum iriure dolor in hendrerit in vulputate velit esse molestie consequat, vel illum dolore eu feugiat nulla facilisis at vero eros et accumsan et iusto odio dignissim qui blandit praesent luptatum zzril delenit augue duis dolore te feugait nulla facilisi. Lorem ipsum dolor sit amet, consectetuer adipiscing elit, sed diam nonummy nibh euismod tincidunt ut laoreet dolore magna aliquam erat volutpat. Ut wisi enim ad minim veniam, quis nostrud exerci tation ullamcorper suscipit lobortis nisl ut aliquip ex ea commodo consequat. Duis autem vel eum iriure dolor in hendrerit in vulputate velit esse molestie consequat, vel illum dolore eu feugiat nulla facilisis at vero eros et accumsan et iusto odio dignissim qui blandit praesent luptatum zzril delenit augue duis dolore te feugait nulla facilisi. Nam liber tempor cum soluta nobis eleifend option.Ut enim ad minim veniam, quis nostrud exerci

Congue nihil imperdiet doming id quod mazim placerat facer possim assum. Lorem ipsum dolor sit amet, consectetuer adipiscing elit, sed diam nonummy nibh euismod tincidunt ut laoreet dolore magna aliquam erat volutpat. Ut wisi enim ad minim veniam, quis nostrud exerci tation ullamcorper suscipit lobortis nisl ut aliquip ex ea commodo consequat.

Duis autem vel eum iriure dolor in hendrerit in vulputate velit esse molestie consequat, vel illum dolore eu feugiat nulla facilisis at vero eros et accumsan et iusto odio dignissim qui blandit praesent luptatum zzril delenit augue duis dolore te feugait nulla facilisi.

gue duis dolore te feugait nulla facilisi. Lorem ipsum dolor sit amet, consectetuer adipiscing elit, sed diam nonummy nibh euismod tincidunt ut laoreet dolore magna aliquam erat qui blandit praesent luptatumvolutpatquis augue duis dolore tenostrud exerci.

Ut wisi enim ad minim veniam, quis nostrud exerci tation ullamcorper suscipit lobortis nisl ut aliquip ex ea commodo consequat. Duis autem vel eum iriure dolor in hendrerit in vulputate velit esse molestie consequat, vel illum dolore eu feugiat nulla facilisis at vero eros et accumsan et iusto odio dignissim qui blandit praesent luptatum zzril delenit augue duis dolore te feugait nulla facilisihendrerit in vulputate velit esse molestie.

Lorem ipsum dolor sit amet, consectetuer adipiscing elit, sed diam nonummy nibh euismod tincidunt ut laoreet dolore magna aliquam erat volutpat. Ut wisi enim ad minim veniam, quis nostrud exerci tation ullamcorper suscipit lobortis nisl ut aliquip ex ea commodo consequat. Duis autem vel eum iriure dolor in hendrerit in vulputate velit esse molestie consequat, vel illum dolore eu feugiat nulla facilisis at vero eros et accumsan et iusto odio dignissim qui blandit praesent luptatum zzril delenit augue duis dolore te feugait nulla facilisi.Lorem ipsum dolor sit amet, consectetuer adipiscing elit, sed diam nonummy nibh euismod tincidunt ut laoreet dolore magna aliquam erat volutpat. Ut wisi enim ad minim veniam, quis nostrud exerci tation ullamcorper suscipit lobortis nisl ut aliquip ex ea commodo consequat. Duis autem vel eum iriure dolor in hendrerit in vulputate velit esse molestie consequat.

Vel illum dolore eu feugiat nulla facilisis at vero eros et accumsan et iusto odio dignissim qui blandit praesent luptatum zzril delenit augue duis dolore te feugait nulla facilisi. Lorem ipsum dolor sit amet, consectetuer adipiscing elit, sed diam nonummy nibh euismod tincidunt ut

> We have not even to risk
> the adventure alone,
> for the heroes of all time have
> gone before us.
> The labyrinth is thoroughly
> known. We have only to follow
> the thread
> of the hero path,
> ... and where we had thought
> to be alone,
> we will be with all the world.
> —Joseph Campbell

23

The journal page at left is obviously designed for an audience predisposed to sustained reading.

The white box for the inset quote is the same width as the text columns. The 12-point rule anchors the quote so that it doesn't float in empty space. The type is 16/18 Helvetica Condensed Bold, centered, and contrasts with the classic feeling of the rest of the page.

The running text is Palatino. The initial cap is 96-point Zapf Chancery followed by a 5p6 indent.

The border decoration is clip art from DeskTop Art Borders & Mortises (Dynamic Graphics).

AUTOMATIC ICE MAKER INSTALLATION KIT
FOR TWO-DOOR SIDE-BY-SIDE REFRIGERATOR

IMPORTANT

The refrigerator must be level to ensure proper operation of the ice maker. See your owner's manual.

TOOLS YOU WILL NEED

Phillips head screwdriver
Drill with 1/4" bit
Adjustable open-end wrench
Needlenose pliers

PARTS LIST

1. Harness and fill-tube grommet.

2. Water supply unit with hose nut, rubber washer, water valve, and compression nuts.

3. Rectangular clip (4) for end assembly unit and split grommet (2).

4. Screws and nuts (See screw identification chart on page 3).

5. Fill spout.

6. Plastic fill tube for ice maker harness.

STEPS IN THIS PROCEDURE

Ut wisi enim ad minim veniam, quis nostrud exerci tation ullamcorper suscipit lobortis nisl ut aliquip ex ea commodo consequat. Duis autem vel eum iriure dolor in hendrerit in vulputate velit esse molestie consequat, vel illum dolore eu feugiat nulla facilisis

1. At vero eros et accumsan et iusto odio dignissim qui blandit praesent luptatum zzril delenit augue duis dolore te feugait

2. Nulla facilisihendrerit in vulputate velit esse molestie . Lorem ipsum dolor sit amet, consectetuer adipiscing elit, sed diam nonummy nibh euismod tincidunt ut laoreet dolore magna aliquam erat volutpat.

3. Ut wisi enim ad minim veniam, quis nostrud exerci tation ullamcorper suscipit lobortis nisl ut aliquip ex ea commodo consequat.

4. Duis autem vel eum iriure dolor in hendrerit in vulputate velit esse molestie consequat, vel illum dolore eu feugiat nulla facilisis at vero eros et accumsan et iusto odio dignissim qui blandit praesent luptatum zzril delenit augue

5. Duis dolore te feugait nulla facilisi.Lorem ipsum dolor sit amet, consectetuer adipiscing elit, sed diam nonummy nibh euismod tincidunt ut laoreet dolore magna

2

Duis autem vel eum iriure dolor in hendrerit

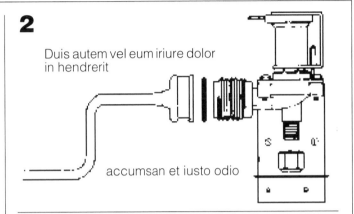

accumsan et iusto odio

3

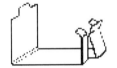

Ut wisi enim ad minim veniam, quis exerci tation

4

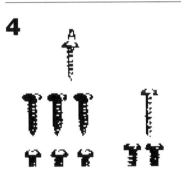

accumsan et iusto odio

5

Duis autem vel eum iriure dolor in hendrerit

1

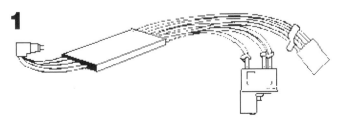

Ut wisi enim ad minim veniam, quis exerci tation

6

Nulla facilisihendrerit in vulpu

THREE-COLUMN GRIDS

The three-column grid is the most common format in publishing, widely used in magazines, newspapers, newsletters, catalogs, and annual reports. It is popular because it is so flexible, allowing you to place headlines, art, boxed copy, and other elements across any one, two, or even all three columns. This enables you to break the material into small chunks or modules, using various graphic devices to indicate the relative importance of items and relationships between them.

In the short line length, usually 12 to 14 picas, type sets efficiently in relatively small sizes (9- or 10-point type is frequently used for running

This informal, three-column format shows the value of simplicity. With the controls available in desktop publishing, these pages are probably easier to produce than a single-column typewritten document. A stapled, four-page statement of purpose, this was created when the organization first converted to desktop publishing. Three years later, they print the same information in an 11-by-17, three-color folder with computer-drawn art.

The horizontal rules provide a consistent structure that is balanced by open, ragged right type. The two-column heads, the angled, bit-mapped initial caps, and the playful art keep the three-column grid from feeling rigid and also suggest the personality of a foundation trying to reach young people.

The headline type is Bookman (with open spacing in the foundation's name). The running text is Avant Garde, a sans serif face with a large x-height. When generously leaded, as it is here, it is distinctive and inviting.

Lists of names work very well in the three-column format.

Design: Jim Parker (Phoenix, AZ)

Pages from a statement of purpose by the Do It Now Foundation.
Trim size: 8-1/2 by 11

text) that is still easy for readers to scan. The three-column grid also accommodates small pictures and large ones equally well, so that a really terrific photo can be given adequate space while a not-very-good mug shot can be kept appropriately sized to the width of a single column. This range enables you to use contrast in sizing art as a design element.

So why doesn't everyone use a three-column grid? One of the disadvantages of the format is that so many people do, and it can be difficult to devise a style that distinguishes your publication from all the others.

Page frames and column rules create a classic, three-column newsletter format. A second color, used for banners, breakouts, art, and sidebar tints, adds to the appeal.

Note the many devices used to vary the page composition: inset art, two-column tables and breakouts, sidebars that run the full page width in a two-column format rather than a three-column one. Note

also how the horizontal rules turn into the page on one or both sides of the center column; often, the facing page runs the horizontal rule across all three columns for contrast.

The shatter outline of the art (below left) contrasts sharply with the page structure. In general, irregularly shaped art helps keep a tight grid from being too rigid.

The reverse type in the banners is Avant Garde with open letter spacing, which greatly improves the legibility of reverse type. The breakout is Avant Garde italic, the headlines are Helvetica, and the running text is Times Roman.

Design: Jim Parker (Phoenix, AZ)

Pages from Newservice, *published by the Do It Now Foundation.*
Trim size: 8-1/2 by 11

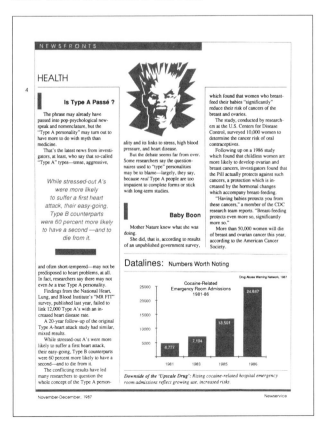

Modular verticals

The easiest way to lay out a three-column page is to run the text continuously in vertical columns. And one of the easiest ways to keep those verticals from being dull is through the use of tones. Whether shades of gray or a second color, tones can be used to separate, isolate, emphasize, or unify. Three different treatments are shown on these two pages.

The tones used in headline banners both unify and separate different elements on the page. The headline banners in this newsletter are 8-point rules (which print 60% black) on top of 20% black boxes, which vary in depth according the length of the headline. The two-line heads are centered in 3p9-deep boxes, the one-line heads in 3p-deep boxes. You can leave a master banner for each headline size on the pasteboard of your document, and then make copies of them as needed.

The caption also prints in a 20% box. A three-line caption fits in the same 3p9 box as a two-line head.

The clip art is from the Metro ImageBase NewsletterMaker.

Nashville, the type used for the publication name, is from Agfa Compugraphic, a phototypesetter that is releasing its library to the desktop market. When Nashville is set tightly, its slab-serif style works well, and the word "NewsBeat" has been kerned to bring out that characteristic. The date, set in 9-point Futura, is set with 200% letter space for additional contrast with the type above.

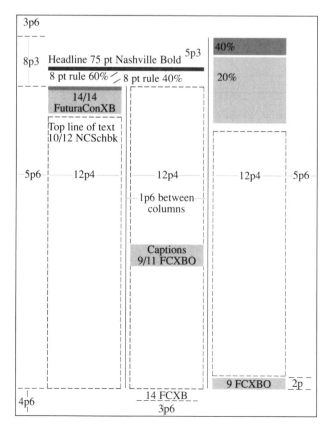

Art, headlines, and color tints are placed loosely in the grid to create a collage-like feeling in the first sample. The effect is casual and gives an inviting sense of the unexpected, which is relatively rare in three-column newsletters.

Color is a strong element in this design. The tone unifying the two related stories under a single headline is orange; it drops out to create a white border around the photos, which print over a blue tint. The two-column headline, initial caps, 8-point rules, and exclamation point also print in orange. The logo prints orange and blue.

The distinctive logo collages small sans serif type, boxed and angled, over the larger Roman-style title. An effective way to integrate the company and newsletter names, this device is relatively easy to execute if you have a good eye for proportioning type.

The Times Roman running text is set in relatively narrow columns surrounded by generous white space. For contrast, the display type is set in a bold Helvetica.

In the bottom sample, the tone is used behind secondary material—the issue highlights on the cover and sidebars on inside pages—rather than behind features.

The structured rules, justified text, and even column bottoms represent a completely different approach to page design than the previous sample. Each sets a style appropriate for its audience.

Design (top): Tom Ahern (Providence, RI)

Dateline *is published quarterly by GTECH Lottery.*
Size: 8-1/2 by 11

Design (bottom): Kimberly Mancebo, Robert Bryant Associates (Campbell, CA)

TeleVisual Market Strategies *is published by Telecommunications Productivity Center.*
Size: 8-1/2 by 11

Introducing the horizontal

A true grid has a precise horizontal structure that is generally determined by the type specifications of the dominant text face, so that a given number of lines will fit in each grid unit. The construction of the grid must also take into account the space between grid units. For example, if your type is 10/12, each grid unit and the space beween two units will be in multiples of 12 points, or 1 pica. If your type is 11/13, then the grid units will be in multiples of 13 points, obviously a less convenient measurement to work with.

Visual elements are sized to fit different combinations of these units, allowing for varied sizes and shapes which, because of their relationship to the underlying structure, are in proportion to one another and to the page as a whole. In some ways, the truly modular grid simplifies layout more than the mostly vertical structures apparent in many of the samples reproduced in this book. But an orthodox grid is also more difficult to construct. If you find the mathematically determined horizontal structure confusing or inhibiting, then adopt a more informal approach to placing the elements vertically on the page. If, on the other hand, you are drawn to the possibilities inherent in the technique introduced on these and the following two pages, you'll find a number of useful books listed in the resource section.

If you want to study an expertly used horizontal grid, see the Pitney Bowes publication toward the beginning of the Brochure section in Chapter 5.

The sample on the facing page is built on an 18-unit grid, with 3 vertical divisions and 6 horizontal ones. This schematic shows the placement of the sample's visual elements on the grid. You can see how the structure facilitates decision making by suggesting both size and placement; note also how the design overrides the grid when needed. Turn the page for additional diagrams, grid specifications, and another, very different design based on the same grid.

Type Specifications
Overline: 10/12 Avant Garde reverse, centered, +200% letterspace
Publication name: 48-point Avant Garde, –20% letterspace
Story heads: 24/24 Bodoni Bold Italic
Body text: 10/12 Bodoni
Captions: 11/12 Bodoni Bold Italic

The clip art is from Metro ImageBase NewsletterMaker. The trumpet image was created by silhouetting, in DeskPaint, one of a trio that were all the same size; that silhouette was placed in PageMaker, copied, and resized to produce the trio you see here. The other images were used as is, except for the party scene in which we moved a balloon or two and some confetti (again in DeskPaint) to fit the image area. This sort of manipulation is typical of how clip art is adapted to suit specific layouts.

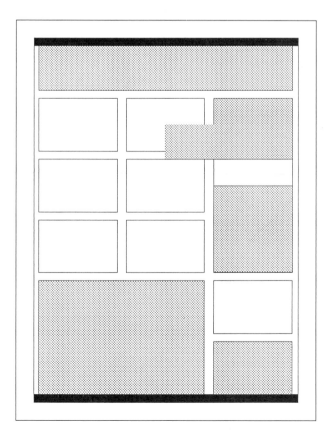

Triangle Hotel Trumpet

EAT, DRINK AND BE MERRY

Lorem ipsum dolor sit amet, consectetuer adipiscing elit, sed diam nonummy nibh euismod tincidunt ut laoreet dolore magna aliquam erat volutpat. Ut wisi enim ad minim veniam, quis nostrud exerci tation ullamcorper suscipit lobortis nisl ut aliquip ex ea commodo consequat.

Duis autem vel eum iriure dolor in hendrerit in vulputate velit esse molestie consequat, vel illum dolore eu feugiat nulla facilisis at vero eros et accumsan et iusto odio dignissim qui blandit praesent luptatum zzril delenit augue duis dolore te feugait nulla facilisi. Lorem ipsum dolor sit amet, consectetuer adipiscing elit, sed diam nonummy nibh euismod tincidunt ut laoreet dolore magna aliquam erat volutpat. Ut wisi enim ad minim veniam, quis nostrud exerci tation ullamcorper suscipit lobortis nisl ut aliquip ex ea commodo consequat.

Duis autem vel eum iriure dolor in hendrerit in vulputate velit esse molestie consequat, vel illum dolore eu feugiat nulla facil at vero eros et

accumsan et iusto etei odio dignissim qui blandit praesent luptatum zzril delenit augue duis dolore te. feugait nulla facilisi. Nam liber tempor

Sunday Jazz Brunch

FROM BIG BAND TO ROCK 'N ROLL

Duis autem vel eum iriure dolor in hendrerit in vulputate velit esse molestie consequat, vel illum dolore eu feugiat nulla facilisis at vero eros et accumsan et iusto odio dignissim qui blandit praesent luptatum zzril delenit augue duis dolore te feugait nulla facilisi.

Lorem ipsum dolor sit amet, consectetuer adipiscing elit, sed diam nonummy nibh euismod tincidunt ut laoreet dolore magna aliquam erat volutpat. Ut wisi enim ad minim veniam, quis nostrud exerci tation

ullamcorper suscipit lobortis nisl ut aliquip ex ea commodo consequat. Duis autem vel eum iriure dolor in hendrerit in vulputate velit esse

All-Night Buffet

molestie consequat. Lorem ipsum dolor sit amet, consectetuer adipiscing elit, sed diam nonummy nibh euismod tincidunt ut

Baoreet dolore magna aliquam erat volutpat. Ut wisi enim ad minim laoreet dolore magna aliquam erat veniam, quis nostrud eu feugiat nulla facilisis at vero eros et accumsan et

New Year's Gala in the Ballroom

Morning-After Room Service

This is a good place for the placement of a pull quote from the text

Lorem ipsum dolor sit amet, consectetuer adipiscing elit, sed diam nonummy nibh euismod tincidunt ut laoreet dolore magna aliquam erat volutpat. Ut wisi enim ad minim veniam, quis nostrud exerci tation ullamcorper suscipit lobortis nisl ut aliquip ex ea commodo consequat. Duis autem vel eum iriure dolor in hendrerit in vulputate velit esse molestie consequat, vel illum dolore eu feugiat nulla facilisis at vero eros et iusto odio dignissim qui blandit praesent luptatum zzril delenit augue duis dolore te feugait nulla facilisi. Lorem ipsum dolor sit amet, consectetuer adipiscing elit,

in hendrerit in vulputate velit esse molestie consequat, vel illum dolore eu feugiat nulla facilisis at vero eros et accumsan et iusto odio dignissim qui blandit praesent luptatum zzril delenit augue duis dolore te feugait nulla facilisi. Nam liber tempor cum soluta nobis eleifend option

nostrud exerci tation ullamcorper suscipit lobortis nisl ut aliquip ex ea commodo consequat. Duis autem vel eum iriure dolor in hendrerit in vulputate velit esse molestie consequat, vel illum dolore eu feugiat nulla facilisis at vero eros et accumsan et iusto odio dignissim qui blandit prae-

nostrud exerci tation ul-lamcorper suscipit lobortis nisl ut aliquip ex ea commodo consequat. Duis autem vel eum iriure dolor in hendrerit in vulputate velit esse molestie consequat, vel illum dolore eu

sed diam nonummy nibh euismod tincidunt ut laoreet dolore magna aliquam erat volutpat. Ut wisi enim ad minim veniam, quis nostrud exerci tation ullamcorper suscipit lobortis nisl ut aliquip ex ea commodo consequat. Duis autem vel eum iriure dolor

congue nihil imperdiet doming id quod mazim placerat facer possim assum. Lorem ipsum dolor sit amet, consectetuer adipiscing elit, sed diam nonummy nibh euismod tincidunt ut laoreet dolore magna aliquam erat volutpat. Ut wisi enim ad minim veniam, quis

sent luptatum zzril delenit augue duis dolore te feugait nulla facilisi. Lorem ipsum dolor sit amet, consectetuer adipiscing elit, sed diam nonummy nibh euismod tincidunt ut laoreet dolore magna aliquam erat volutpat. Ut wisi enim ad minim veniam,

1   2   3

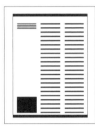

4

Page composition within an 18-unit grid such as the one discussed on these four pages can vary considerably. The page at left and schematic 1, above, show picture placement in which the horizontal and vertical structures are balanced. The second schematic shows a strong horizontal arrangement; the third, a strong vertical. In the fourth, one column is used only for head-lines, captions, and small photos, creating still another look.

Research Paper

Lorem ipsum dolor sit amet, consectetuer adipiscing elit, sed diam nonummy nibh euismod tincidunt ut laoreet dolore magna aliquam erat volutpat. Ut wisi enim ad minim veniam, quis nostrud exerci tation ullamcorper suscipit lobortis nisl ut aliquip ex ea commodo consequat.
Duis autem vel eum iriure dolor in hendrerit in vulputate velit esse molestie consequat, vel illum dolore eu feugiat nulla facilisis at vero eros et accumsan et iusto odio dignissim qui blandit praesent luptatum zzril delenit augue duis dolore te feugait nulla facilisi.
Lorem ipsum dolor sit amet, consectetuer adipiscing elit, sed diam nonummy nibh euismod tincidunt ut laoreet dolore magna aliquam erat volutpat. Ut wisi enim ad minim veniam, quis nostrud exerci tation ullamcorper suscipit lobortis nisl ut aliquip ex ea commodo consequat.
Duis autem vel eum iriure dolor in hendrerit in vulputate velit esse molestie consequat, vel illum dolore eu feugiat nulla facilisis at vero eros et accumsan et iusto odio dignissim qui blandit praesent luptatum zzril delenit augue duis dolore te feugait nulla facilisi. Nam liber tempor cum soluta nobis eleifend option congue nihil imperdiet doming id quod mazim placerat facer possim assum.
Lorem ipsum dolor sit amet, consectetuer adipiscing elit, sed diam nonummy nibh euismod tincidunt ut laoreet dolore magna ut aliquip ex ea commodo conse-quat.
Duis autem vel eum iriure dsent luptatum zzril delenit augue duis dolore te feugait nulla

TEST RESULTS	Grp A	Grp B	Control
Uptatum zzril delenit augue	1,745	1,398	1,598
Dolore eu feugiat nulla	4,978	2,467	1,028
Tincidunt ut ladolore wisi enim	3,684	1,746	5,896
Tin vulputate velit esse	2,678	3,986	1,038
Dignissim qui blandit praesent	3,794	1,840	2,096
Uptatum zzril delenit augue	1,493	2,047	3,208
Dolore eu feugiat nulla	2,067	2,067	3,906
Total	17,376	13,982	20,387

NARRATIVE

Amet consectetuer adipiscing elit, delenit lobortis nisl ut aliquip ex ea commodo consequat. Duis autem vel eum iriure dolor in hendrerit in vulputate velit esse molestie consequat, vel illum dolore eu feugiat nulla facilisis at Vero eros et

sectetuer adipiscing elit, sed diam nonummy nibh euismod tincidunt ut lcommodo consequat. Duis autem aoreet dolore magna aliquam erat volutpat. Ut wisi enim ad minim

continued on following page

FURTHER RESEARCH

Accumsan et iusto odio dignissim qui blandit praesent luptatum zzril delenit augue duis dolore te feugait nulla facilisi.
Lorem ipsum dolor sit amet, consectetuer adipiscing elit, sed

CONCLUSIONS

Diam nonummy nibh euismod tincidunt ut laoreet dolore magna aliquam erat volutpat. Ut wisi enim ad minim veniam, quis nostrud exerci tation ullamcorper suscipit lobortis nisl ut aliquip ex ea com-modo consequat. Duis facilisi.

Lorem ipsum dolor sit amet, consectetuer adipiscing elit, sed diam nonummy nibh euismod tincidunt ut laoreet dolore magna aliquam erat volutpat. Ut wisi enim ad minim veniam, quis.

The sample at left uses the grid on the facing page to create hori-zontal divisions for text blocks. A text block can run any number of grid units and need not fill the entire unit. But regardless of the depth of the text, rules separating text blocks are placed at the midpoint of the space between two grid units.

The banner runs from the top margin to the midpoint of the space between the first two horizontal grid units. A hairline horizontal rule is placed midway between the last grid unit and the bottom margin.

The headline is 60-point Ameri-can Typewriter, reversed out of the 60% black banner.

The body text is 10/12 New Century Schoolbook.

Subheads are 12-point Helvetica Black, aligned at top with the top of a grid unit. The running text in these text blocks is 10/12 Helvetica Light. The text in the table is 10/24, creat-ing a full line space between each item so that this text aligns with running text in the adjacent column.

Grid units and type size are designed in relation to one another. The first detail here shows how 10/12 text fits in the grid units used in the samples on these two pages. For the sake of comparison, the second detail shows 10/14 text in the same 10/12 grid; you can see that with the increased leading, the grid no longer works. Both details are shown full size.

When constructing a horizontal grid, you can customize Page-Maker's vertical ruler with the leading value specified in points. (Use the Preferences command on the Edit menu.) With Snap to Rulers on, all guidelines, text, and graphics that you place on the page will align with ruler tick marks calibrated to the leading that you specified.

This grid was used for the samples in this section. Although all the units are of equal size, elements placed on the grid need not be. The grid is constructed as follows:

Margins: 3p top and bottom, 4p side
Columns: three, 1p6 space between
Horizontal grid units: 8p9 deep
   beginning at top margin, 1p3
   between units
Hairline vertical rules from top to
   bottom margin: 1p outside left and
   right margins and, where appropriate, between columns
Horizontal rules (Triangle Hotel
   sample on preceding spread):
   1p3 deep; top rule flush with top
   grid unit; bottom rule just below last
   grid unit.

Note that the grid is slightly asymmetrical along the vertical axis. In the Triangle Hotel sample on the preceding spread, the 1p3-deep horizontal rule fills the space between the bottom grid unit and the bottom margin. In the Research Paper at left, a hairline rule visually fills the space at the bottom of the page. If you were to use this grid without horizontal rules to balance the space, you would probably want to shift the entire grid down 9 points to center it on the page.

Lorem ipsum dolor sit amet, consectetuer adipiscing elit, sed diam nonummy nibh euismod tincidunt ut laoreet dolore magna aliquam erat volutpat. Ut wisi enim ad minim veniam, quis nostrud exerci tation ullamcorper suscipit lobortis nisl ut aliquip ex ea commodo consequat.

Duis autem vel eum iriure dolor in hendrerit in vulputate velit esse molestie consequat, vel illum dolore eu feugiat nulla facilisis at vero eros et accumsan et iusto odio dignissim qui blandit praesent luptatum zzril delenit augue duis dolore te feugait nulla facilisi. Lorem ipsum dolor sit amet, consectetuer adipiscing elit, sed diam nonummy nibh euismod tincidunt ut duis laoreet dolore magna

1

Lorem ipsum dolor sit amet, consectetuer adipiscing elit, sed diam nonummy nibh euismod tincidunt ut laoreet dolore magna aliquam erat volutpat. Ut wisi enim ad minim veniam, quis nostrud exerci tation ullamcorper suscipit lobortis nisl ut aliquip ex ea commodo consequat.

Duis autem vel eum iriure dolor in hendrerit in vulputate velit esse molestie consequat, vel illum dolore eu feugiat nulla facilisis at vero eros et accumsan et iusto odio dignissim qui blandit praesent luptatum zzril delenit augue duis dolore te feugait nulla facilisi. Lorem ipsum dolor sit

2

A mixed grid

Varying the column width within a single page has many uses. It accommodates different kinds of material, allows for a varied page design, and can inspire you to organize the components of your document in a way that strengthens the intrinsic relationships and forms contrasts among them. In the sample shown below, the mixed grid is both functional and dramatic.

Sidebar vignettes set to a 13-pica measure are inset in a single wide column that provides the background narrative in this annual report. The sidebars, which run throughout the report, are human-interest stories. On other pages not shown, some sidebars are styled as two single columns that face each other across the gutter, others as two singles in the outer columns of facing pages.

The two different settings are unified by a single typeface (Goudy Old Style), generously leaded, yet they are styled for considerable contrast: The larger, roman type in the wide measure is justified and prints in warm brown; the smaller, italic type is ragged right and prints in black. The italic caption at the bottom of the page is set to the wide measure and prints in brown.

Design: Tom Lewis (San Diego, CA)

Page from the Medic Alert Annual Report.

Trim size: 8-1/2 by 11

Design (facing page): Edward Hughes, Edward Hughes Design (Evanston, IL)

Pages from the Roosevelt University Annual Report.

Trim Size: 8-1/4 by 11-5/8

REPORT TO THE READER

"My membership is like insurance coverage - the very best protection, and for a reasonable cost. I'm sure all the members feel as I do - grateful there is an organization called Medic Alert."

That's how one member described the secure feeling enjoyed by the more than 2.6 million people worldwide who wear the Medic Alert emblem. For 32 years, Medic Alert has warned health professionals about patients' special medical conditions, saving thousands of lives and sparing needless suffering. "As an EMT," another member wrote, "I know how much Medic Alert helps emergency personnel. If people would only realize how important it is for us to know their medical problems in an emergency maybe more would wear Medic Alert emblems."

In recent years, Medic Alert's emergency medical identification system has substantially improved operations management and product and service quality. The Foundation's quest for excellence is ongoing.

MEDIC ALERT'S NEW SERVICES This year, Medic Alert launched plans to diversify into services that capitalize on the Foundation's ability to manage an accurate, confidential medical data base. In August, in 1987, Medic Alert began

MEDIC ALERT PROTECTS TRANSPLANT RECIPIENT

Eleven years ago, a New Zealand school girl named Ann Crawford became ill with the flu. Unlike many flu victims for whom the malady is a fleeting annoyance, Ann suffered permanent lung damage. She fell prey to a series of infections that strained her breathing and weakened her heart.

In the years that followed, Ann endured a revolving door of hospital treatments. Her doctors experimented with megadose drug therapies to clear her frequent infections, but her lungs continued to worsen. Eight years

after her bout with the flu, Ann's health had become so fragile that few expected her to survive the winter.

Only 19, Ann was not ready to give up. She had read up on the latest advances in thoracic surgery and transplant technology. She wondered, "Why not start all over again with a new heart and lungs?"

Ann's enthusiasm sparked support from the Lions Club in her area, which agreed to help finance the cost of her surgery. She traveled to the United Kingdom for the operation, and returned home with a new heart and lungs. Shortly after, she penned Pumps & Bellows, *a detailed account of her illness and transplant operation.*

This brave young woman from New Zealand, is breathing easier these days. But she will always require anti-rejection drugs to ensure that her body will not declare war on her new organs. In a medical emergency, responders need to know instantly of her transplant operation and drug regimen to administer proper treatment.

That is why Ann, like many others around the world, wears a Medic Alert emblem. After years of hospital stays and bed rest, the young New Zealander takes every precaution to protect her most treasured gift, a second chance at life.

From Evangeline . . . Thanks to Medic Alert my husband is alive today. He was in a very bad car accident. The paramedics saw his Medic Alert necklace and found his wallet card. His seat belt and his Medic Alert tag saved his life.

Asymmetrical three-column

Generally, asymmetrical three-column grids have two wide columns and one narrow one. This produces a slightly more interesting and an inherently more variable look than three equal columns, especially when you consider the possibilities that derive from combining two columns, whether two equal columns or one wide and one narrow.

The underlying structure is two 11-pica columns and one 18-pica column. When the wide column is combined with the inside narrow column, the resulting 31-pica measure provides additional flexibility in page composition.

The depth of the photographs remains constant from page to page, although the depth of the captions varies. Good photographs, well-printed, result in the rich blacks and grays evident here.

The captions are styled as display type, reversed out against the gray background.

The uneven bottoms of the three columns helps balance the tight structure created by the strong horizontal line across the top of the page, the strong left edge of the type columns (which is emphasized by the elongated page), and the tabbed folios that bleed off the bottom of the page.

Note that single-digit numbers are indented so that all numbers align right. This typographic refinement is all the more needed here with the hanging indent.

As precise as this format is, the pages are relatively easy to assemble. Having two standardized picture sizes minimizes art decisions, and the uneven bottoms speed up page assembly.

The slightly elongated page, elegant gray paper, and high-quality printing create an image that is both distinctive and consequential. Fine printing on excellent paper stock is essential to provide an even gray background throughout and to hold the crisp detail on the small, reverse-type numbers seen here and in reverse hairline rules used on tables (not shown).

Two narrow outer columns and a wide center column create a somewhat specialized three-column grid. The layout implies that the center item is the most important one. In the pages shown here, the outer columns are used to present contrasting viewpoints on the same subject, an editorial approach that works particularly well in this format. The outer columns could also be used for quotes and other marginalia, for resources related to the main story, brief listings, short profiles or news items, and so on.

The justified text in these pages adds to the formality of the subject matter and to the point-counterpoint approach of the editorial.

The clip art is from WetPaint, except for the student in the center column on the cover, which is from MacMemories.

The blueprint gives dimensions and type specs for the nameplate on the cover. On subsequent pages, as in the one shown below left, the top of the text block is 9p from the top trim, so that would be the dimension to use for the top margin on the page setup.

The word "Bulletin" is Bodoni Poster, condensed in FreeHand, placed in PageMaker, and cropped to clip off the bottom of the letters, which makes the type look as if it's emerging from behind the rule. You could condense the type in Page-Maker, but in order to crop it as a graphic you have to import it from another program. (On a Macintosh you have another option: Copy the condensed headline to the Scrap-book, place the scrapbook, and then crop the image.) The story headlines are Bookman, condensed.

The Avant Garde ID lines on the cover and inside page were set with open letter and word spacing so that the "Educational Advancement" line fills the three-column measure.

The depth of the framed illustrations on both pages is a guideline only. The placement of visuals in the center column is best at the bottom of the page, although the top is also acceptable.

Space between art, captions, rules, and adjacent body text is often a difficult detail in page assembly unless you are working on a very precise grid. The closer any two elements are to each other, the more related they will seem to the reader. In these samples, note that the caption is closer to the picture frame below it than to the rule above, and the rule is closer to the caption than to the preceding text.

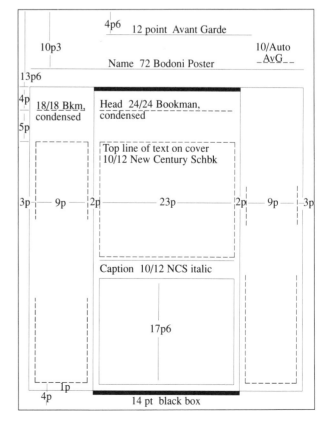

A S S O C I A T I O N

BULLETIN

TEACHERS
ADMINISTRATORS
COUNSELORS

PARENTS
SOCIAL WORKERS
PSYCHOLOGISTS

E D U C A T I O N A L   A D V A N C E M E N T   I N   A M E R I C A

A Case for Gradual Growth in Our Schools

Feugait nulla facilisi. Nam liber tempor cum soluta nobis eleifend option congue nihil imperdiet doming id

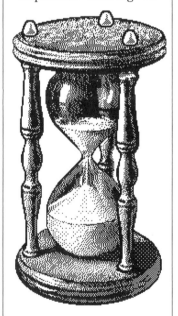

quod mazim placerat facer possim assum. Lorem ipsum dolor sit amet, consectetuer adipiscing elit, sed

Diam nonummy nibh euismod tincidunt ut laoreet dolore magna aliquam erat volutpatUt wisi enim ad minim veniam, quis nostrud exerci tation ullamcorper suscipit lobortis nisl ut aliquip ex ea commodo conse

A Primer for School Administrators in the Nineties

Torem ipsum dolor sit amet, consectetuer adipiscing elit, sed diam nonummy nibh euismod tincidunt ut laoreet dolore magna aliquam erat volutpat. Ut wisi enim ad minim veniam, quis nostrud exerci tation ullamcorper suscipit lobortis nisl ut aliquip ex ea commodo consequat.

Duis autem vel eum iriure dolor in hendrerit in vulputate velit esse molestie consequat, vel illum dolore eu feugiat nulla facilisis at vero eros et accumsan et iusto odio dignissim qui blandit praesent luptatum zzril delenit augue duis dolore te feugait nulla facilisi. Lorem ipsum dolor sit amet, consectetuer adipiscing elit, sed diam nonummy nibh euismod tincidunt ut laoreet dolore magna aliquam erat volutpat. Ut wisi enim ad minim veniam, quis nostrud exerci tation ullamcorper suscipit lobortis nisl ut aliquip ex ea commodo consequat.

Duis autem vel eum iriure dolor in hendrerit in vulputate velit esse molestie consequat, vel illum dolore eu feugiat nulla facilisis at vero eros et accumsan et iusto odio dignissim qui blandit praesent luptatum zzril delenit augue duis dolore te

Aliquip ex ea commodo consequat. Duis autem vel eum iriure dolor in hendrerit in vulputate velit esse mo

The Wisdom of Revolutionary Change in Education

Autem vel eum iriure dolor in hendrerit in vulputate velit esse molestie consequat, Vel illum dolore eu feugiat nulla facilisis at vero eros et accumsan et iusto odio dignissim qui blandit praesent luptatum zzril delenit augue duis dolore te feugait nulla facilisi.

Lorem ipsum dolor sit amet, consectetuer adipiscing elit, sed diam nonummy nibh euismod tincidunt ut laoreet dolore magna aliquam erat volutpat.

Narrow outer columns in a three-column grid are useful for publications as diverse as catalogs and technical journals.

In text-heavy publications, such as the one shown below, the narrow outer column can provide much-needed white space when reserved for art, captions, breakouts, and marginalia.

When you wrap ragged right text around a rectangular graphic, you get a much neater appearance if the graphic juts into the flush left margin.

The body text in the sample is 10/12 Galliard. The display type is Futura Condensed Extra Bold, set in 30-, 14-, and 10-point sizes. The captions are 10/12 Futura Heavy.

The clip art is from DeskTop Art Business 1.

A classic catalog format on the facing page uses rules, art, white space, and the edge of text blocks to frame pictures. The art and text requirements dictate the size, the only restraints being the vertical rules (and even those can be violated effectively).

The blueprint shows measurements for the sample below. To set up the format, specify 4p side margins, and 3 columns with 1p6 space between; then drag the column guides to the measurements shown in the blueprint.

The grid for the catalog on the facing page is similar, but the left edge of the text is flush with the column rules, which drop out behind the text. This maintains the structure of the rules while providing maximum measure for copy. To construct this grid, position the vertical rules, including those in the page frames, at these intervals: 3p, 17p, 17p, 11p, 3p.

The type reinforces the impression of variety, with six different faces used. From top to bottom, they are Futura Condensed, Aachen Bold, Avant Garde, Palatino Italic, Franklin Gothic Heavy, and American Typewriter.

The clip art is from WetPaint.

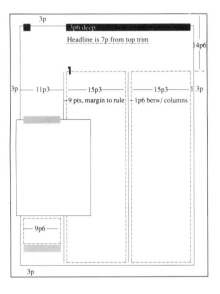

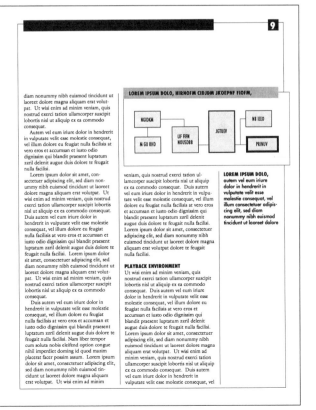

The Most Realistic Stuffed Animals You Ever Saw

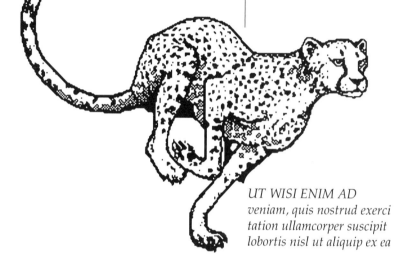

UT WISI ENIM AD veniam, quis nostrud exerci tation ullamcorper suscipit lobortis nisl ut aliquip ex ea

LOREM IPSUM DOLOR SIT AMET, sectetuer adipiscing elit, sed diam nonummy nibh euismod tincidunt ut laoreet dolore magna aliquam erat volutpat. Ut wisi enim ad minim veniam, quis nostrud exerci tation ullamcorper suscipit lobortis nisl ut aliquip ex ea commodo consequat. Duis autem vel eum iriure dolor in hendrerit in vulputate velit esse molestie consequat, vel illum dolore eu feugiat nulla facilisis at vero eros et accumsan et iusto odio dignissim qui blandit praesent luptatum zzril delenit augue duis dolore te feugait nulla facilisi. Lorem ipsum dolor sit amet, consectetuer adipiscing elit, sed diam nonummy nibh euismod tincidunt ut laoreet dolore magna aliquam erat

UT WISI ENIM AD veniam, quis nostrud exerci tation ullamcorper suscipit

LOREM IPSUM DOLO, autem vel eum iriure dolor in hendrerit in vulputate velit esse molestie consequat, vel illum consectetuer adipiscing elit, sed diam

FOUR-COLUMN GRIDS

Four-column grids are even more versatile than three-column formats. They provide an opportunity for varied page design within the same publication and for dramatic contrast among visual elements of different sizes. These grids are used frequently in magazines, newspapers,

Boxed sidebars work extremely well in a four-column setting, and can be sized with considerable variety depending on the number and depth of the columns used.

A half-page sidebar prints against a gray tone, with two narrow columns at the bottom combined to accommodate tables. Note that the box extends beyond the page frame, a technique you see frequently in graphic design today. Here those extra 9 points make it possible for the text set in the four-column format to run at the same 9-pica measure as the unboxed text. (Usually you lose a few points to the box.)

The "At a Glance" headline is used repeatedly over charts and graphs, which, with their captions, are self-contained items. A three-column treatment is shown, although other sizes are used as well.

The Times Roman running text is set 8/10 ragged right. Text this small really requires the narrow 9-pica column measure. Tables, captions, and headlines are set in a sans serif face for contrast.

Repeating headlines are inset between gray rules, with shorter rules on each end providing a spot of red that livens up the mostly text pages. The second color is repeated in charts and rules under initial caps.

Display type at the top of News Briefs pages, like the one shown below right, are tickertape-style previews of the stories on that page.

Design: Kimberly Mancebo, Robert Bryant Associates (Campbell, CA)

Pages from TeleVisual Market Strategies, published ten times per year by Telecommunications Productivity Center. Trim size: 8-1/2 by 11

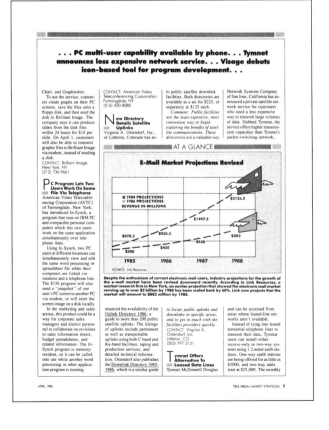

and newsletters. They are also well suited to reference material, directories, price sheets, and other documents that require collecting many small items on a page.

But four-column grids are also more demanding to work with and require more decisions throughout the design and production process. Inherent in their flexibility, also, is the need for balance, proportion, and a deft handling of detail.

Narrow columns also require special care with typography. The type size should be relatively small, to be in proportion to the column width, and so the face must be chosen for ease of readability. With relatively few words in a line, you need to watch for excessive hyphenation. Generally, you should avoid more than two hyphens in a row. Also, a narrow column accentuates the uneven spacing inherent in justified text, so choose that style with caution.

The ease of combining running text set to a two- and a four-column measure is a definite advantage of the four-column grid. As in the previous sample, serif and sans serif faces are used for contrast.

The bold 2-point rules and unusual folio and publication identification in the upper right corner add to the distinctive and contemporary look of the page.

The graphic combines bit-mapped, graduated-tone, and geometric art. A low-resolution scan of a photo was placed in PageMaker. The same digitized image was imported in FreeHand's template layer; the swimsuit was traced over the template in the drawing layer and filled with a graduated tone; the grid was drawn on a layer above that by cloning a square with a 2-point white line and no fill. The FreeHand art was saved as an EPS file and placed in PageMaker on top of the bit-mapped image. Using PageMaker's Text Wrap option, a graphic boundary was defined around the silhouette and the wraparound text was brought to the front layer to ensure that it printed over the white grid.

Design: John Odam (San Diego, CA)
Page from Verbum, *published quarterly.*
Trim size: 8-1/2 by 11

---

try, are losing a battle to stay alive against foreign clothing manufacturers. "Since 1980, 3,000 apparel/textile companies have closed their doors and 350,000 jobs have been lost. Of the $170 billion trade deficit, $20 billion is in the apparel industry.... In 1974, 80% of the shoes sold in this country were made in this country. Now more than 80% of the shoes are imports and footwear manufacturing in this country is practically dead." VanFossen was vice president of Corporate Information Services at Wolverine Worldwide, makers of Hush Puppies shoes, when he analyzed the company's declining competitiveness in marketplace would only be turned around with a fully automated factory. The design of the footwear in 3-D appeared to be the answer. "If I could design a shoe in 3-D, then I would have the data I needed to drive an automated factory," he concluded. "Everything you needed to know about price of material, what you had to do with it, how you had to stitch it together — I'd have all this information. That was what I was after."

In 1983 VanFossen started Computer Design Inc. in Grand Rapids, MI which was partially financed at that time by Wolverine. CDI installed their first system about five years ago at H.H. Cutler Co. of Grand Rapids, a childrens' wear company. Since then they have installed more than 50 systems in the U.S. and Europe. The CDI system is IBM PC-based, and the software starts at about $25,000. The designer can visualizes garment in 3-D on the screen and the program will automatically create 2-D flat pattern pieces. According to Jerry Johnson, vice president of Marketing at CDI, "On our CAD systems today designers can design fabrics, then wrap those fabrics onto a model to actually see how it would look. Change colors and try it again in minutes, not hours or days as it now takes to repaint or recolor fabric designs. Change necklines, sleeves, add pockets, take pockets away...all of these functions can be performed on our computer. These functions can greatly reduce product development time."

INTUITION AND INFORMATION IN FASHION DESIGN
Jackie Shapiro became one of the first fashion designers in the United States to explore the application of the computer with fashion design when she picked up her first Macintosh in 1984. She first used the computer to help develop her own line called "GARB", or Global Apparel Resource Bank, and even then she claimed that the computer was a vital part of her design process. "GARB has taken available technology and applied it...for designing clothing. To experiment and explore an infinite number of design solutions. To visualize...garments before making them. To coordinate one silhouette with another. To create, store and retrieve frequently used images: bodies, basics, prints, parts, stuff (garment treatments). To scale for measurements for pattern specification detail. To design labels, logos, illustrate...and to write this."

But using a computer alone does not make one a great de-

CUSTOMERS LIKE TO DESIGN IT THEMSELVES

One Southern California store blends fashion design with a novel marketing approach. The store's name is Softwear Swimwear and they sell custom swimsuits "designed" on a computer.

Liz Norling and Gary Leeds opened a swimwear boutique which featured an unusual gimmick of allowing customers create their own sportswear. "Not necessarily a gimmick but a new twist." Liz corrected me. "In order to succeed in this day and age in retail, one needs a unique idea." The customer's image in a swimsuit would be scanned into a color computer program, and the customer could then select from 300 fabric patterns which can be projected on the scanned image of the sportswear on the computer monitor. That way the customer would know exactly what the swimsuit would look like before it's made.

Fashion trends change quickly, and this is one way for the customer to keep up with the fashion...or start his or her own trend.

"There are problems created by using the computer," acknowledged Norling. "We are working on a solution to the two dimensional look of the person on the screen. There is also a problem of confusing the customer with so many possibilities of color and fabric that it's hard for them to make a decision on which suit they

want. We also tend to get into trouble by taking colors from the screen...and then finding out that we do not have the color in stock."

The customer can see three suits on the screen at one time to compare and evaluate which one looks best. The customer's image can also be saved in the computer and pulled up at a later time for design another suit. "This is a good feature" Norling says, "as the store's sales volume can be larger. If they like all three swimsuits they may buy all three! Overall, I think the addition of the computer system to our retail store is a great one as many customers are highly excited about designing their own clothing."

The flexible size of art in a four-column grid is used to good advantage in this signage manual, where similarities and contrasts in visual details are the heart of the message. In the pages shown, note the possibilities for grouping photos as well as the variety of sizes.

Strong perspective lines in many of the photos lead your eye back into the distance. This depth illusion separates the photographs from the surface of the page. The severity of the grid structure, with the bolder-than-usual column rules, in turn enhances the perception of depth in the photos.

The vertical rules also delineate sections, as seen in the top page.

The text is Times Roman throughout, with italic captions set on a narrower measure with open leading for contrast to the running text. The white space makes it possible to run headlines the same size as body text so that they do not compete with typographic elements in the art.

*Design:
Denise Saulnier,
Communication
Design Group
Limited
(Halifax, Nova
Scotia)*
Pages from A
Guide to Better
Signs *published
by the City of
Halifax.*
Size: 8-1/2 by 11

Neon Signs

Fabrics

A fluorescent powder added to the glass tubing will produce yellow, green, rose and gold light. Very deep rich colours are produced by using coloured glass tubing to add to the colour of the gas.

When neon is used as a window sign, the glass tubing is attached to a sheet of clear acrylic which is suspended from the top of the window and is connected to the transformer by thin wires. Some sign makers prefer to enclose the entire neon sign in a clear acrylic box.

Certain gases (neon, argon, krypton, helium and xenon) contained in a glass vacuum tube will produce a coloured glow when an electrical current is passed through them. In the fabrication process, the glass tubing is heated and can be bent to virtually any shape. The air is removed from the tube and the gas inserted. A transformer is attached, which controls the transmission of electric current to the tube. Paint is used to cover areas of glass tubing which need to remain dark. Various gases produce different colours: neon is red-orange; argon is violet; argon and mercury together are blue; helium is gold; xenon is pale blue; krypton and argon together are purple.

Painted/printed: Fabrics such as cotton canvas, flag nylon, acrylic fabric and vinyl-coated polyester in a variety of colours can have lettering painted or silkscreen printed on and can then be sewn into flags, banners and awnings. Awnings are stretched across frames made of construction steel fixed to the building wall. Awnings can be manufactured to fit the building on which they will be installed and can be made in a wide variety of shapes.

Illuminated awnings use translucent vinyl-coated polyester to transmit light from shielded fluorescent or incandescent lights installed inside the awning. New finishes, materials and technologies have made this one of the most versatile

39

Chapter 6
Lighting techniques

Planning for the illumination of signs is an integral part of the sign design process. Signs, when well lit, can add liveliness to our streets. They create a mood of festivity, drama, excitement and warmth while contributing to the profile of our commercial districts at night.

One technique of sign illumination is to light the entire building front on which the sign is installed. In some cases there will be enough ambient light spilled on the building from adjacent light sources to allow the sign to be read. (Street number signs can often be read because they are lit by street lights or lights over doorways.)

Decorative lamps can be installed on the exterior of buildings where they will create an atmosphere of warmth or excitement, highlight the architectural details of the building front, as well as lighting both the building's signs and the sidewalk area. Low wattage incandescent bulbs installed in rows or groups are another technique of providing general lighting for buildings and signs which were traditionally used on theatre marquees.

When lighting only the sign itself, spotlights are an efficient solution. Strong focus lights are used to illuminate the sign face from above, the sides or below. Care should be taken in placing spotlights in order to avoid reflection on the sign face. The spotlights should be shielded from the eyes of the viewers. Electrical cables attached to the spotlights should be hidden from sight, incorporated in the sign

support and fed into the building at a location as close to the sign as possible. Advance planning can usually ensure that there won't be unsightly electrical cables draping from the sign to the building or running along the building front.

Interior lit signs with opaque backgrounds and illuminated letters are a refined alternative to the typical electric back lit sign.

Metal faced channel letters with built in light sources mounted away from the walls, create a rather soft halo of light with the letters in silhouette.

Exposed neon lights can be formed to virtually any shape, and require very little maintenance.

The row of frosted glass globes lining the front of this restaurant provides general lighting for customers and passers-by, while lighting the building's signs at the same time.

Above: Shielded spots light the fascia sign but protect the viewer from any glare.

Right: A projecting sign and a fascia sign are lit by a set of four spots. The electrical cable is fed along the sign support and then directly into the wall.

Above: Channel letters containing neon tubing make an effective sign for both day and night.

42

43

The need to accommodate different kinds of editorial material often suggests the use of a four-column grid. The pages shown demonstrate the ease of combining two- and four-column settings.

The contents pages use the narrow measure for the short program descriptions on the left-hand page, and the wider measure for a tidy listing of the publication contents on the right. Contrasting column widths provide an immediate visual clue to the reader that these are different kinds of material. Art is sized to both column widths for variety and visual contrast, and the silhouetted dancing figures break the grid and float above it.

Note the implied horizon line that runs across all four pages, 11 picas from the top trim.

The short listings in the Program Highlights work especially well in narrow columns. The boldface dates are Helvetica Black, the listings are Garamond with boldface heads. Garamond is used for the contents page and running text in feature stories as well.

The music headline is Futura Condensed Extra Bold; the Program headline on the facing page is Futura Bold. Display typefaces with a variety of styles enable you to create subtle contrasts within the same type family.

Optical character recognition software (OCR) is a key component in the production cycle. The designer uses a DEST scanner with Publish Pac OCR software to capture text from typewritten copy that is provided by the client. They experience only about a 3 percent error, which the designer attributes to their using clean, double-spaced copy typed in a big, round face (they use Pica) and output on an impact printer. (With smaller faces and dot matrix output, the counters of letters tend to fill in, resulting in error rates as high as 20 percent.) The text is checked for spelling and typesetting conventions (single space after periods, and so on) in Microsoft Word and then formatted in PageMaker.

Design: Tom Suzuki (Falls Church, VA)

Pages from Worldnet magazine, published bimonthly by the United States Information Agency.

Trim size: 8-1/4 by 10-3/4

The cover and an inside flap show the contrasting but unified look in a folder that uses the four-column grid to combine two- and four-column settings.

The GTE logo on the cover is aligned left with the type. The underlying grid will almost always suggest an appropriate placement for loose items on the page.

The large, Palatino italic type on the cover shows off the calligraphic nature of this typeface.

The text in the narrow columns hugs the column rules, creating a very crisp left edge that emphasizes the verticality of the page. The loose ragged right margin makes the left edge seem stronger still in comparison.

The horizontal lines running through the map contrast with the strong verticality of the text above. Note the implied vertical edge of the map, aligned left with the second column of text. The map and rules print gray on the inside flap, with different colored dots denoting the locations listed. The cover map, surrounded by graduated tones of color that suggest the dimensionality of the earth, prints as green lines against white, with the background rules in gray.

Design: Weisz Yang Dunkelberger Inc. (Westport, CT)

Pages from The World of GTE, Year-End Highlights.
Trim size: 11 by 33-3/4, double gatefold

The World of GTE

GTE is one of the major corporations in the world, with annual sales and revenues exceeding $15.1 billion and assets of $27.4 billion. It has operations in 48 states and 33 countries. These facilities employ 160,000 people who work in three core businesses: telecommunications, lighting products and precision materials.

Argentina
Buenos Aires *Lighting, P*

Australia
Gosford *Lighting, P*
Queensland *Lighting, P*
Victoria *Precision Materials, P*

Austria
Grossenzerdorf *Lighting, M*

Belgium
Tienen *Lighting, P*
Tienen *Precision Materials, P*

Brazil
Santa Amaro *Precision Materials, P*
Sao Paulo *Lighting, P*
Vinhedo *Lighting, P*

Canada
Brockville, Ont. *Microtel Ltd., P**
Burnaby, B.C. *Microtel Ltd., P(2),L**
Drummondville, Que. *Lighting, P*
Montreal, Que. *Lighting, P*
Toronto, Ont. *Lighting, P*
Vancouver, B.C. *Microtel Ltd., P**
Windsor, Ont. *Precision Materials, P(5)*

Colombia
Bogota *Lighting, M*

Costa Rica
San Jose *Lighting, P*

Denmark
Hvidovre *Lighting, M*

Ecuador
Quito *Lighting, M*

France
Andrezieux-Boutheon *Precision Materials, P*
Barentin *Precision Materials, P*
La Fouillouse *Lighting, P*
Lyon *Lighting, P*
Nantes *Lighting, P*
Reims *Lighting, P*
St. Marcellin *Lighting, P*

*Telecommunications plants operated by Microtel Ltd., a part of British Columbia Telephone Company.

Germany
Erlangen *Lighting, P*
Precision Materials, P
Sinsheim *Precision Materials, P(3)*

Greece
Athens *Lighting, M*

Haiti
Port au Prince *Precision Materials, P*

Hong Kong
Lighting, M
Precision Materials, M

Italy
Pero *Lighting, M*
Milan *Precision Materials, P*

Japan
Kahoku *Lighting, P*
Tokyo *Precision Materials, P*

Mexico
Juarez *Lighting, M*
Monterrey *Precision Materials, P*

Netherlands
Breda *Lighting, M*
Haarlem *Lighting, P*

Norway
Vestvollvn *Lighting, M*

Peru
Lima *Lighting, M*

Portugal
Lisbon *Lighting, M*

Singapore
Lighting, M

Spain
Madrid *Lighting, M*

Sweden
Stockholm *Lighting, M*

Switzerland
Geneva *Lighting, M*
Precision Materials, M

Taiwan
Taipei *Lighting, M*

Thailand
Bangkok *Lighting, M*

Trinidad
Mount Hope *Lighting, M*

United Kingdom
Charlestown *Lighting, P*
London *Lighting, M*
Malmesbury *Lighting, P*
Newhaven *Lighting, P*
Swansee *Precision Materials, P*

Total GTE Employment by Country

Argentina, 340
Australia, 210
Austria, 16
Belgium, 870
Brazil, 1,260
Canada, 19,285
Colombia, 230
Costa Rica, 730
Denmark, 13
Dominican Republic, 2,765
Ecuador, 14
France, 1,525
Germany, 1,180
Greece, 6
Haiti, 950
Hong Kong, 270
Italy, 180
Japan, 385
Mexico, 345
Netherlands, 18
Norway, 11
Panama, 67
Peru, 12
Philippines, 150
Portugal, 10
Singapore, 6
Spain, 80
Sweden, 23
Switzerland, 75
Taiwan, 260
Thailand, 10
Trinidad, 5
United Kingdom, 1,460

Total: 32,761

One narrow + three wide columns for oversize pages

In a tabloid publication, the four-column grid provides a relatively wide measure for reading text, especially when one column is narrow as in the page shown here.

The body text is 10/13 New Baskerville, a graceful face with a light weight. It makes this oversize, mostly text page inviting and easy to read. The generous use of boldface in the running text emphasizes the "people" focus of the publication and facilitates scanning.

The display type is Helvetica Condensed Black.

The rules for the page frame and columns are a little bolder than is usually found, and the inside rules for the narrow columns run all the way to the page frame. The rigidity of that structure is balanced by white space and appropriately sized type. Note also how the initial caps interrupt the column rule.

The distinctive large folio reverses out of a box, which prints in a second color used also for the page frames, the initial caps in the headlines, and the ballot boxes signalling the end of each piece.

The bold, silhouette-style illustration, used throughout the publication, helps small images hold up on the oversize pages.

Design: Kate Dore, Dore Davis Design (Sacramento, CA)

Page from Communique, *published by Sacramento Association of Business Communicators.*
Trim size: 11 by 17

2

IABC Board

President
Robert L. Deen
Deen & Black
444-8014

First Vice President
Tracy Thompson
Carlson Associates
973-0600

Vice President/Programs
Tamra Weber
Deen & Black
444-8014

**Vice President/
Professional Development**
Mary Closson
The Packard Group
484-8709

**Vice President/
Membership**
Terri Lowe
Crocker Art Museum
449-8709

**Vice President/
Communications**
Pat Macht
AmeriGas/Cal Gas
686-3553

**Vice President/
Academic Affairs**
Jeff Aran
Sacramento Board of Realtors
922-7711

Treasurer
Diana Russell
Pacific Legal Foundation
444-0154

SYNERGY Chair
Della Gilleran
Della Gilleran Design
446-4616

Past President
Betsy Stone
Sutter Health
927-5211

Staff Secretary
Barbara Davis
Creative Consulting
424-8400

Delegates At Large:
Cindy Simonsen
Hanson Simonsen
451-2270

Rick Cabral
Connolly Development, Inc.
454-1416

Colleen Sotomura
The Sierra Foundation
635-4755

Newsletter Editors
Marisa Alcalay
Mercy San Juan Hospital
537-5245
Mary C. Towne
California Veterinary Medical Association
344-4985

Newsletter Design & Layout
Kate Dore
Dore Davis Design
920-3448

IABC *Communiqué*
January/February 1988

About Sacramento Communicators

Jolaine Collins, past president of the IABC Denver chapter and a recent addition to IABC Sacramento, will represent District 6 on the IABC Professionalism Committee. **Jan Emerson** has moved from Foundation Health Plan to a new position with the publications department at Sutter Health. **Dan Brown**, Group Director of Public Affairs for Aerojet General, will be the 1988 President of the new Sacramento chapter of the Public Relations Society of America.

IABC 1988 president **Robert Deen** and **Christi Black** have formed the partnership of Deen & Black, Communications and Public Affairs. Christi is the former executive director of the American River Parkway Foundation. They will be joined by IABC member **Tamra Weber**, former Communications Director for United Way, who will be an associate, and **Colleen Jang**, a recent CSU Chico communication graduate and member of the student IABC chapter. The new firm is located in an office building at 2212 K Street recently purchased by fellow IABC member **Della Gilleran** (who will chair SYNERGY in 1988).

Terri Lowe of the Crocker Art Museum is interested in volunteers to assist with Crocker's 1988 Bike-a-Thon fundraiser, scheduled for June. **Robert Deen** will chair the overall event, with IABC'ers Jolaine Collins and **Janice White**. Terri's number is 449-8709.

Stacey Eachus, former IABC Sacramento member who went to San Diego in June for a position with the National Cash Register Company, has returned to Sacramento in a public relations position with the California Association of Health Facilities.

The **CSU Chico student chapter** has expressed an interest in repeating the successful exchange program in which students were matched for a day with IABC Sacramento members to observe a typical work day.

The Sacramento Communications Council has been restructured as a quarterly meeting of the presidents of the dozen professional communications organizations involved, and will be chaired by the IABC president.

The IABC's annual international conference will finally be closer to home in 1988 — Anaheim. It should be an interesting one as the proposed IABC/PRSA merger comes to a head.

Mark your calendars now for upcoming **IABC Sacramento luncheons**, held the first Thursday of each month: Feb. 4, March 3, April 7, and May 5. ■

(Have something to contribute? Send information to Communicator Column, c/o editor, IABC Sacramento, P.O. Box 160481, Sacramento, Ca. 95816.)

Chapter Business

Meet the 1988 IABC Board of Directors

The IABC Sacramento Board of Directors serves on a calendar year basis. Being involved is an important part of the IABC experience, and members are encouraged to contact board members to find out more about the areas of activity outlined below.

Immediate Past President Betsy C. Stone will represent IABC Sacramento at the District level, and as circumstances dictate will speak for the chapter on the proposed IABC/PRSA merger. She is also responsible for organizing the District 6 conference for 1990 which Sacramento will host. **Robert L. Deen, the chapter president** is responsible for group's overall direction and functioning.

1st Vice President Tracy Thompson oversees administrative matters and special projects at the president's direction.

Treasurer Diana Russell is responsible for the chapter's finances, including coordinating with the SYNERGY management team.

Vice President, Communications, Pat Macht is responsible for the chapter newsletter, all media relations (meeting notices, awards, etc.), and for any and all activities which relate to the chapter's image and visibility.

Vice President, Membership, Terri Lowe, directs membership recruiting efforts, including correspondence, planning, renewal program, roster, and special efforts as required.

Vice President, Programs, Tamra Weber, surveys the membership for their interests and selects luncheon speakers accordingly, coordinates arrangements, and ensures that monthly meeting notices go out in a timely manner.

Vice President, Academic Affairs, Jeff Aran serves as a liaison to local universities and coordinates with the IABC student chapter at CSU Chico.

Vice President, Professional Development, Mary Closson, develops seminars and programs to enhance members' professional skills and abilities, and conducts the annual membership survey.

Della Gilleran, 1988 SYNERGY Chair, is responsible for the overall direction and management of SYNERGY, Sacramento's coalition-based special event for the communications profession.

Delegates at Large: Rick Cabral, Cindy Simonsen, and Colleen Sotomura serve as at-large members of the board and take responsibility for special assignments as needed.

The board is responsible for the functioning and direction of the Chapter. Members are encouraged to discuss concerns or make suggestions to any board member at any time. ■

Plan On Being Active in 1988

The best way to meet new people, learn new skills and become a part of new groups is through active volunteerism.

Working together on projects gives you a chance to get to know people and for them to get to know you and your skills, capabilities and interests.

IABC/Sacramento encourages members to be involved in both IABC activities and general community activities. Consider your options:

The IABC chapter conducts ongoing efforts such as the scholarship and communications (including the newsletter). The board members responsible for these areas are listed in each issue of the newsletter, with their phone number, and all are interested in hearing from those who want to help.

Community involvement — IABC/Sacramento encourages members to accept leadership positions in community organizations such as United Way, KVIE, March of Dimes, etc. These members deserve and need the support of fellow chapter communicators and the chapter is often approached directly by organizations in need of volunteers.

To help you get involved, the chapter needs to know about your interest. Contact the appropriate board member directly, or let Chapter President Robert Deen know.

Make being an active volunteer part of your plan for self improvement in 1988! ■

Using the center columns

In this four-column grid, photos are enlarged to a two-column measure. The text in the narrow outer columns frames the pictures, and the generous white space provides an opportunity to dramatize the shape of the photos against the structure of the page.

The digitized photos, which are reproduced from a laser printout, need a layout in which the overall composition has more impact than the individual parts. Sizes and placements were chosen for dramatic contrast, with a passive close-up against an active middle shot on the cover and a dancing full-figure long shot against a close-up on the inside page.

The logotype gives the name *FLASH* a strong identity and emphasizes the action and boldness implied by in the name. The typeface, Bodoni Poster, doesn't come with a true italic, so FLASH was typed in Adobe Illustrator and shifted on a horizontal axis with the shear tool to create an oblique. The word was given a white fill with no stroke, imported into PageMaker, and placed over the black panel to create the reverse type. Note that the serifs of the F and the H bleed off the left and right edges of the banner, which themselves have been stretched beyond the text margins.

Futura, used in the story headline and names of the models, is forever stylish. It has graced the cover of virtually every fashion magazine at one time or another. Each text unit was created and rotated in Illustrator and then imported into PageMaker. Placing the type on a 15-degree angle creates an additional dimension, a layer that seems to float above the rectilinear grid of the logo, text columns, rules, and photos. Keeping all the names and the headline on the same angle creates organized spontaneity rather than random movement.

MAY/JUNE 1988

MANNER continued from page 1

we can send them right away to clients here that are willing to use brand new people. That starts the ball rolling, and if things start to click right away, they stay in New York. If things don't happen immediately, we ask them to go to Europe and develop a strong book, learn how to really model, and then come back to New York. We deal with several agencies in Milan, Paris and Germany and we try to send models to the appropriate agency. Each individual model is different of course, and how much time each one would stay in Europe varies. It can take a couple of months or even a couple of years to get started. The truth of the matter is, if you are a real good model, you don't need a strong book, you need to have a look that works in New York. If you are a brand new model, and you have that look, you can start to work immediately. We are very lucky to have models like that.

If any men are interested in being with our agency

BILLY HAIRE

F L A S H

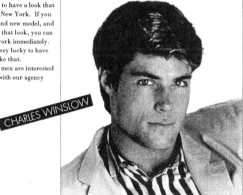

CHARLES WINSLOW

they should send a couple a pictures in the mail. Don't spend alot of money on pictures - snapshots will do - put your stats on the back, and send them in. You'll get an answer quickly, usually within a week after we receive them. We answer all mail that we get, but a warning, more than 99% of the people who send in pictures receive a "no."

If you are interested in modeling in New York, you should just take a deep breath, swallow, and come. You can go on and on wonder and worry, but if you want to model you should come here and see everybody and find out what your chances are. But don't kid yourself. If the answer is "no" the answer is "no". Don't get the attitude of "Well, I'll show them!" The business is much too rough for that kind of attitude. Chances are you won't show them, they'll show you.

MANNER is located at 874 Broadway New York, NY 10003 (212) 475-5001

9

Bodoni, used for the running text, is hard to beat for typographic elegance. Its alternating thicks and thins give this newsletter a distinctive look—fashionable but not trendy. The type just feels like Fred Astaire dancing. Bodoni needs open leading (10/13 was used) to take advantage of its tall ascenders and descenders without sacrificing legibility.

The logo treatment is adapted as a visual "prop" throughout the publication. On the page above, for example, it becomes a stage on which one of the models dances. The stylized lightening bolt from the logo provides an additional motif that can be used decoratively.

The photographs were scanned and then retouched in ImageStudio. In the Charles Winslow photo, for example, the background was removed to create a silhouette, and the neck area was lightened. Billy Haire's feet were given some tone (they were white in the original).

The images were balanced both for contrast and for light and dark using PageMaker's Image Control feature. The goal was to get enough contrast to be dramatic without letting the technique steal the show from the models themselves. Because laser printer proofs tend to print very heavy blacks, the darkness had to be carefully controlled.

The blueprint on the next page provides the basic grid structure for this and the following design, which conveys a very different image than the one shown here. For type specs for this design, refer to the commentary on these two pages, rather than the ones in the blueprint. Note also that the cover banner here has been stretched 2 picas beyond the side margins defined in the blueprint.

Design: Don Wright (Woodstock, NY)

Pages from Flash, *a bimonthly newsletter for models published by Nautilus Books, designed as a "Page Makeover" for* Publish! *magazine.*
Trim size: 8-1/2 by 11

The business report at right and on the facing page uses the same four-column grid as the fashion newsletter on the previous spread but to very different effect.

The report title in the nameplate is spaced to fill the banner. We inserted five fixed spaces (Option-Spacebar on the Mac, Ctrl-Sp on a PC). In PageMaker 4.0, you can achieve the same effect by specifying Force Justify for a single line. The slash is a hairline rule drawn with the perpendicular tool.

On page 2, the banner is 2p6 deep, with the same fonts and letterspacing as the nameplate type but dropped down to 14 point. The top of the text block is 5p from the top of the banner.

The charts and graphs were created in PageMaker with 10-point Futura Light type.

The clip art, from Metro Image-Base ReportMaker, was silhouetted in DeskPaint and placed in Page-Maker as a TIFF compressed file.

The blueprint shows the details for the sample on the facing page. The same column structure is used for the newsletter on the preceding page.

The basic column width is 10p3. In addition to combining the center columns for art as shown on these samples, you could combine any two or three columns for variable art sizes and self-contained sidebar material.

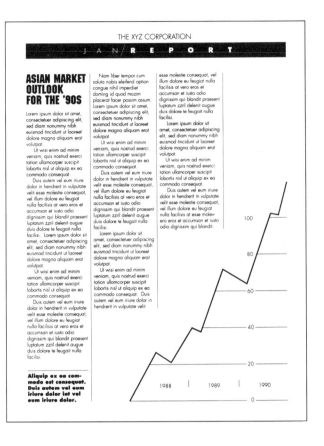

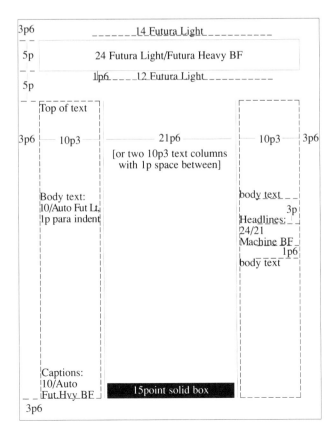

JAN/REPORT

FROM THE OFFICE OF MARKETING AND SALES

PRODUCTION LANDMARK FOR THE XYZ MACHINE: 100,000 UNITS

Lorem ipsum dolor sit amet, consectetuer adipiscing elit, sed diam nonummy nibh euismod tincidunt ut laoreet dolore magna aliquam erat volutpat. Ut wisi enim ad minim veniam, quis nostrud exerci tation ullamcorper suscipit lobortis nisl ut aliquip ex ea commodo consequat.

Duis autem vel eum iriure dolor in hendrerit in vulputate velit esse molestie consequat, vel illum dolore eu feugiat nulla facilisis at vero eros et accumsan et iusto odio dignissim qui blandit praesent luptatum zzril delenit augue duis dolore te feugait nulla facilisi.

Lorem ipsum dolor sit amet, consectetuer adipiscing elit, sed diam nonummy nibh euismod tincidunt ut laoreet dolore magna aliquam erat volutpat. Ut wisi enim ad minim veniam, quis nostrud exerci tation ullamcorper suscipit lobortis nisl ut aliquip ex ea commodo consequat. Duis autem vel eum iriure dolor in hendrerit in vulputate velit esse molestie consequat, vel illum dolore eu feugiat

Aliquip ex ea comimodo es consequat. Duis vel ex eat com modovel eumet.

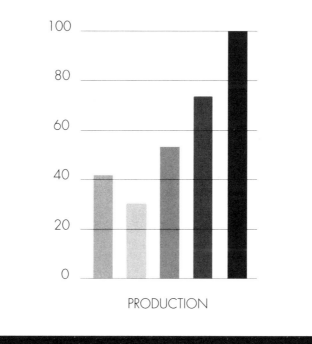

PRODUCTION

Aliquip ex ea commodo est consequat. Duis autem vel eum iriure dolor int vel eum iriure dolor.

nulla facilisis at vero eros et accumsan et iusto odio dignissim qui blandit praesent luptatum zzril delenit augue duis dolore te feugait nulla facilisi. Nam liber tempor cum soluta nobis eleifend option congue nihil imperdiet doming id quod mazim placerat facer possim assum.

DO YOU KNOW YOUR CUSTOMER?

Lorem ipsum dolor sit amet. Consectetuer adipiscing elitt. Sed diam nonummy nibh euismod tincidunt ut laoreet dolore magna aliquam erat volutpat. Ut wisi enim ad minim veniam, quis nostrud exerci tation ullamcorper suscipit lobortis nisl ut aliquip ex ea commodo consequat. Duis autem vel eum iriure dolor in hendrerit in

Vulputate velit esse molestie consequat, vel illum dolore eu feugiat nulla facilisis at vero eros et accumsan et iusto odio dignissim qui blandit praesent luptatum zzril delenit augue duis dolore te feugait nulla facilisi. Lorem ipsum dolor sit amet, consectetuer adipiscing elit, sed diam nonummy nibh euismod suscipit lobortis nisltincidunt ut laoreet dolore magna aliquam erat volutpat.

Within the four-column format you can balance strong vertical and horizontal material, as in the sample on the facing page. The image area for visuals in the first three horizontal units is almost square (9 by 9p3), a nice proportion in this grid, although other sizes are possible.

The layout in the Safety Tips page could be used as an expanded contents page, with the cover story in the text column and four different stories, briefly described with art from each, in the outer two columns. When using this technique, which is very effective, the cover art can be repeated inside or can be a detail from a piece of art that runs with the story.

The word "Safety" is 18-point Bookman italic. In order to inset it in the T of "Tips," we created a T with an elongated bar across the top by drawing a black box over the top of an I. In doing this, we encountered WYSIWYG problems: The manually-created T aligned with the I on-screen but not in the printed page. We went through several trial-and-error adjust-ments before an incorrect on-screen image produced a correct printed page.

Events listings are well suited to the narrow measure, as shown in the sample flyer below left. And short introductory copy is still quite read-able in one wide column.

The clip art was altered to allow for text in the upper right corner of the image area: We merely erased that part of the image in DeskPaint. The image is from the Metro Image-Base NewsletterMaker package.

The column specifications for the listings use the same measure-ments as the four-column format in the blueprint. The headline and listing specifications are shown in the details below.

The blueprint specifications are for the Safety Tips sample. You can divide the space in other ways to balance the vertical and horizontal divisions; the schematic below shows another possible arrange-ment. Don't forget white space as an element in the grid.

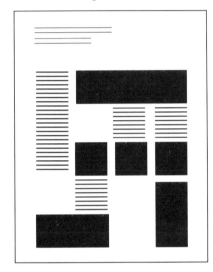

```
4p
          12-pt rule
4p9
    Headline   48/46 Franklin Gothic Heavy  x 43p max
15p

    Top of intro text  13/15 Helvetica x 43p max
```

```
Monday                    12 Fr Gothic Heavy
June 13            2p     13 FGH reversed out of 2p banner
Madison            2p     13 FGH
7:00 - 9:00 PM     2p     12/13 Helv,  0p3 space after time
Town Hall
245 Main Street
```

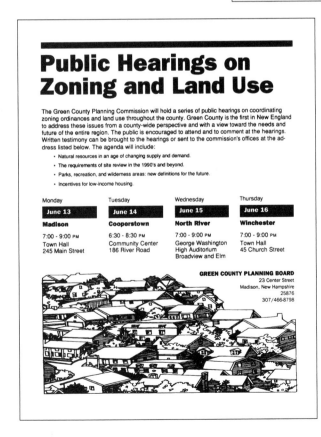

Public Hearings on Zoning and Land Use

The Green County Planning Commission will hold a series of public hearings on coordinating zoning ordinances and land use throughout the county. Green County is the first in New England to address these issues from a county-wide perspective and with a view toward the needs and future of the entire region. The public is encouraged to attend and to comment at the hearings. Written testimony can be brought to the hearings or sent to the commission's offices at the ad-dress listed below. The agenda will include:

- Natural resources in an age of changing supply and demand.
- The requirements of site review in the 1990's and beyond.
- Parks, recreation, and wilderness areas: new definitions for the future.
- Incentives for low-income housing.

Monday	Tuesday	Wednesday	Thursday
June 13	**June 14**	**June 15**	**June 16**
Madison	**Cooperstown**	**North River**	**Winchester**
7:00 - 9:00 PM	6:30 - 8:30 PM	7:00 - 9:00 PM	7:00 - 9:00 PM
Town Hall	Community Center	George Washington	Town Hall
245 Main Street	186 River Road	High Auditorium	45 Church Street
		Broadview and Elm	

GREEN COUNTY PLANNING BOARD
23 Center Street
Madison, New Hampshire
25876
307/466-8798

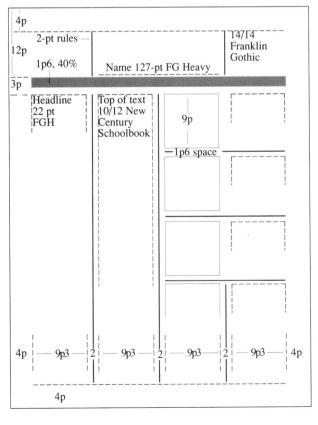

```
4p
    2-pt rules                              14/14
12p                                         Franklin
    1p6, 40%          Name 127-pt FG Heavy   Gothic
3p

    Headline      Top of text
    22 pt         10/12 New          9p
    FGH           Century
                  Schoolbook        1p6 space




4p  —  9p3  —  2  —  9p3  —  2  —  9p3  —  2  —  9p3  —  4p
                          4p
```

Safety TIPS

Tools and Hazards of the Trade

L sectetuer sed adipiscing elite in sed utm diam nonummy nibh euismod tincidunt ut laoreet dolore magna aliquam erat volutpat. Ut wisi enim ad minim veniam, quis nostrud exerci tation dolor in ullamcorper suscipit lobortis nisl ut aliquip ex ea commodo feugiat consequat. Duis autem vel eum iriure dolor in hendrerit in vulputate velit esse molestie vero consequat, vel illum dolore eu feugiat nulla facilisis at vero eros et accumsan et iusto odio dignissim qui blandit.

Praesent luptatum zzril delenit augue duis dolore te feugait nulla facilisi. Lorem ipsum dolor sit amet,et zzril delenit consectetuer adipiscing elit, urt sed diam nonummy nibh euismod tincidunt ut laoreet dolore magna aliquam erat volutpat.

Ut wisi enim ad minim veniam, quis nostrud exerci tation ad minim ullamcorper suscipit lobortis nisl ut aliquip ex ea facilisi. Lorem ipsum commodo Duis autem vel eum iriure dolor iscingin hendrerit in vulputate velit esse molestie consequat, vel illum dolore eu feugiat nulla facilisis at vero eros et

Consequat duis aute vel eum iriure dolor in hendrerit in vulputate velit esse

Molestie consequal illum dolore eu feugiat nulla facilisis at vero eros et accumsan et iusto odio dignissim qui blandit praesent

Tatum zzril delenit augue duis dolore te feugait nulla facilisi. Nam liber tempor cum

Lorem ipsum dolor sit amet, consectetuer adipiscing elit, sed diam nonummy nibh euismod tincidunt ut laoreet dolore magna aliquam erat volutpat.

Ut wisi enim ad minim veniam, quis nostrud exerci tation ullamcorper suscipit

MIXED GRIDS

Grids with multiple and variable column widths can handle the widest range of elements, partly because the columns combine to produce so many different page arrangements. These grids allow for several different widths of text, which in turn allow for more contrast in type sizes and faces to distinguish components from one another. And of course the possibilities for picture placement are even more varied in size and scale than those of the text.

This type of grid is particularly useful in publications such as catalogs, which have many different kinds of elements that need to be distinguished from one another. The format also encourages browsing, with numerous headlines and art providing multiple entry points for busy readers.

Constructing this sort of grid requires a careful analysis of the material to determine the format. And executing the design requires a good eye for balance. This is "breaking the rules" territory and can backfire if you don't know what you're doing.

This five-column grid accommodates newsletter-style essays alongside catalog listings, with short quotes and 19th-century engravings adding verbal and visual personality to the pages. The result is lively, inviting, and well organized.

The variable column width is the key to the diverse page composition. From rule to rule, the narrow outer columns are 7 picas, the wider inner columns are 10p6. With 6-point margins between the text and rules, this creates four different measures for use in this publication:

- 6p (a single narrow column used for quotes)
- 9p6 (a single wider column used for product listings and for the continuation of essays from a previous page)
- 20p (two wide columns used for essays and product listings)
- 16p6 (one narrow and one wide column, used for listings).

In fact, additional combinations are available by combining three wide columns, one narrow and three wide, and, of course, all five columns.

Note the contrast in typeface among the different kinds of text. The essays are Palatino for both body text and headlines (which print blue), with Bodoni initial caps (also blue). The product listings are various weights of Futura. The category heads reverse out of 15-point blue banners; product titles, numbers, and prices also print blue.

The engravings are traditional clip art, photostatted and pasted onto camera-ready pages. Matching 19-century thematic art with contemporary subject matter provides a subtle visual humor, reinforced by placement which invariably breaks the grid.

The short quotes in the narrow columns include humor, anonymous aphorisms, and testimonials from satisfied customers.

*Design: Barbara Lee,
Folio Consulting (Englewood, NJ)*

Pages from the SuperLearning Newsletter/Catalog.
Trim size: 8-1/2 by 11

Self-Hypnosis

Self-hypnosis can be the royal road to self-mastery. A good man to learn with is Lee Pulos, Ph.D., professor, psychologist, past president of the Canadian Society of Clinical Hypnosis.

Learn the classical approach on Side A. Then on Side B, experience Pulos' original double induction – two voices weaving in and out, in counterpoint, to help you understand the power of indirect suggestion.

Creative Thinking & Problem Solving
Get your creative juices flowing with hypnotic imagery, suggestion, dream programming. Create solutions instead of problems.
TAPE 401 $12.95

☛ Sports Excellence
Weekend sport or competitive athlete – you can sharpen performance with the same training Pulos used to coach Team Canada.
TAPE 403 $12.95

Recover Quickly and Stay Well
Accelerate your body's natural healing processes. How to team up with your subconscious to maintain and improve all-round health.
TAPE 404 $12.95

Sleep & Dream Enhancement
Insomnia? Sink into a whole new level of deep, comfortable sleep. Enjoy more pleasant, positive dreams. You owe it to yourself to try this drugless way to good quality sleep.
TAPE 405 $12.95

Subtle Seducer, Procrastination
Banish the wiles of procrastination. Instead of kicking yourself, get a kick out of accomplishment. Don't procrastinate! Order this one today!
TAPE 406 $12.95

Self-Talk

Positive self-talk is a secret that life's winners have always known. What you say to yourself and what you believe is what you achieve.

Let Dr. Pulos turn your self talk into a powerful, positive route to achievement. Affirmations are in a 3D Holosonic surround of Superlearning-type music. SideA: guided relaxation with active participation. Side B: positive self-talk statements you can listen to anywhere.

☛ Improving Self-Esteem and Self-Image
Strengthen self-esteem, build a good self image to help you succeed in any endeavor and enjoy life to the fullest.
TAPE 413 $12.95

Successful Selling
Learn how to meet challenges head on with a positive attitude, prepare yourself fully for each situation and make it easy for people to say YES! The positive Self-Talk in this program is the secret shared by those at the top in sales.
TAPE 411 $12.95

Creative Thinking
Tap into the unused 90% of your creative brain power. Positive self-talk can open your mind to a wealth of new ideas.
TAPE 412 $12.95

"The Pulos system has been invaluable, to myself and to many of our key employees."
Peter H. Thomas, Chairman Century 21 Real Estate

Superlearning 450 7th Ave. New York, NY 10123 212 279-8450 9

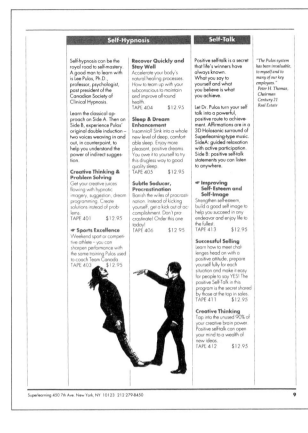

The Book that Started It All!

Music & the Art of Learning
Dissolve learning blocks and relax into the optimal state for learning (side A).

The Famous Superlearning music – music to learn faster by – music to reduce stress – beautiful music performed by world class orchestras (side B).
TAPE 101 $13.95

The Beat of Memory
How to put any material you want to learn into the rhythmic Superlearning format. A short demo of Continental menu terms so you know exactly how a lesson should sound (side A). Better than a metronome, this timer tape with four second clicks helps you pace material correctly (side B).
TAPE 102 $13.95

Superlearning
A do-it-yourself book that reads like an adventure story. Reveals the secrets of fast, stress-free learning and ultra performance. More than 800,000 copies sold.

"Superlearning…Super reading" — Gannett

"Highly readable" — Psychology Today

Hardcover 100 $14.95

The All-Music Tape
Find out how good it feels to start tapping unused capabilities with Superlearning music. Heighten learning, relaxation, visualization. Get in an ideal state for mental training for sports and creative performance.
TAPE 103 $13.95

Very Special Limited Offer –
Help someone else get started!
Buy any two of the Basic Superlearning Tapes – 101, 102, 103 – and we'll send you the hardcover Superlearning Book free!
A $43.00 value for only $27.95

"Even if you're on the right track, you'll get run over if you just sit there."
Will Rogers

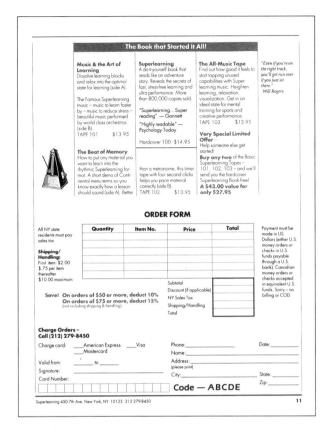

ORDER FORM

All NY state residents must pay sales tax

Shipping/ Handling:
First item: $2.00
$.75 per item thereafter
$10.00 maximum

Quantity	Item No.	Price	Total

Subtotal	
Discount (if applicable)	
NY Sales Tax	
Shipping/Handling	
Total	

Payment must be made in US Dollars (either U.S. money orders or checks in U.S. funds payable through a U.S. bank). Canadian money orders or checks accepted in equivalent U.S. funds. Sorry – no billing or COD.

Save! On orders of $50 or more, deduct 10%
On orders of $75 or more, deduct 15%
(not including shipping & handling)

Charge Orders –
Call (212) 279-8450

Charge card: ___American Express ___Visa ___Mastercard

Valid from: _______ to _______

Signature: ____________________

Card Number:

Phone:__________ Date:__________

Name:____________________

Address:____________________
(please print)

City:__________ State:__________

Zip:__________

Code — ABCDE

Superlearning 450 7th Ave. New York, NY 10123 212 279-8450 11

Magic (cont. from p. 2)

will and the imagination are in conflict, the imagination always wins. The task of the will, it seems, is to make a conscious decision. Then, the task of the imagination is to gather all one's forces, conscious and subconscious, physical, emotional, and mental, to bring that goal into reality.

Today, people are proving Coue's law for themselves. They are beginning to know that the pictures we hold inside ourselves, the scenarios we imagine, have a potent influence not just on the functioning of our minds and bodies, but also on the style and nature of our life experience. Imagination is funny, and we bet you'll hear much more about it in the coming decade. We've only begun to understand imagination. But it does appear that almost anyone can learn to use imagination and bring his life closer to the heart's desire. ✻

Super Relief the Natural Way

Head hurt? Let chiropractors Catherine Sweet and Lisa Pete help you keep a clear head. Find out what kind of headache you suffer from. Discover how various body systems are involved. Learn how you can help yourself with nutrition, herbs, reflex points, acupressure, and other easy-to-practice techniques. What to do when you feel pain coming on. How to ease a full blown headache. Best of all, how to prevent many headaches. Includes reflex point chart.
TAPE 740 $11.95

How to Sharpen Imaginary Senses

"Whatever you do, don't think about a pink elephant!"

Right away, many of us would have trouble keeping visions of pink pachyderms from prancing into mind. That's a reverse way to prove to people that they can visualize. Another, sometimes used by imagery expert Vera Fryling, M.D., is to exclaim, "Oh, someone just threw purple paint on your car!"

As more and more people use imagery rehearsal to improve performance in everything from learning and business to intimate relationships, some are feeling left out because they "can't visualize" or "can't hear a sound in my head." There are remedies.

To begin with, good imagery rehearsal involves all five senses. To improve your imaginative capacity, consider which is your dominant sense. Is your main connection to the world visual? Or audio? Or kinesthetic, through the sense of touch?

When conjuring imaginary experiences, rely first on your dominant sense, just as you do in the outside world. Then start to add the others. If you have difficulty bringing in a sense,try practicing it with the crossover method. If you're an audio type, imagine talking with someone close to you. Listen awhile, then without straining, try to let the image that goes with the voice rise in your mind. Or imagine hearing your special song. Then let the scene that made it special come to you.

If you're the kinesthetic type, imagine running your hands up and down the sides of an oak tree, feeling the rough bark. Then let the image grow between your hands. Or try it with a long, thin icicle sliding between your fingers. Or a heavy ball in one hand.

If you're a visual type, reverse the above exercises. Or conjure any of the myriad things in the world, then add sound, touch – and smell and taste too.

You do have movies in your mind, some experts assert, even if you don't think so. It's just that your images are so fleeting that you're not aware of them. "Such people are turning images into words," says imagery therapist Sally Edwards. The mind labels so quickly that the image goes unperceived. Edwards suggests taking a few minutes a day to practice turning off verbal noise. Just look around, don't name or label. Just see objects, lines, colors, movements.

Learning to sharpen all five of your senses will add power to your imaginary rehearsal. A little practice can also enrich your experience of the outside world. ✻

6 Superlearning 450 7th Ave. New York, NY 10123 212 279-8450

New Musical Memory Booster
(cont. from p. 4)

received books in French and is featured in such magazines as "Paris Match." He's travelled through Europe, South and North America and the East seeking out new ideas, new techniques. But he's best known for bringing Sophrology into sports, an area where success – or failure, is dramatic and very visible.

Years before mental training was fashionable, Abrezol started coaching tennis players and skiers with Sophrology. Word of some remarkable achievements got around the peaks and valleys of Abrezol's tight-knit land. He was asked to coach four members of the Swiss Olympic team, not a powerhouse at the time. At the 1968 Winter Olympics at Grenoble, three of the four won medals. The sensible Swiss stuck with Sophrology and in the 1972 Sapporo Olympics, three more medals were won.

Abrezol, a mountain climber and swimmer himself, went on from there, coaching professionals and amateurs of every stripe: golfers, skeet shooters, boxers, stunt fliers, canoeists, cyclists. As for the Olympics, by 1987, his trainees had garnered 114 medals.

Still active in mental coaching, still training other medical people, still fulfilling his role as a healer to his patients, Abrezol seems to be increasingly interested in seeking out ways to bring forth the "possible human" now, the human that could be, if we started using not the 90%, but – Abrezol insists – the 99% of our capacity that lies waiting within us.

For more data:

The International Sophrology Institute
381 Park Avenue South
New York, NY 10016
718-849-9335 ✻

Better Than Twenty Winks

What's better than twenty winks? A six-second way to relax called the Quieting Reflex (QR) by its creator, Dr. Charles Stroebel, a Connecticut psychiatrist. QR is simple, deceptively so, says Stroebel who maintains it can take six months' practice before you get it down perfectly and experience the full health benefits. The benefits seem more than worth the minimum effort. Reversing the body's stress reactions as you go through the day can alleviate or ward off many common complaints – hypertension, back trouble, ulcers, migraines and tension headaches. Stroebel himself devised QR almost as a last resort to conquer his excruciating chronic headaches. Stress, of course, is a factor in many, maybe most, physical problems. Beyond that, when you're not uptight, you can perform better during the day – and enjoy the evening. Thanks to QR, Stroebel says he's "involved in lots of things that normally would have pushed me to the exhaustion point."

The six steps of QR:

1. Become aware that you are tense.
2. Say to yourself, "Alert mind, calm body."
3. Sparkle and smile inwardly to relax your face.
4. Relax your jaws and inhale, imagining the air coming up through the soles of your feet, to the count of three.
5. Imagine the air coming up your legs into your belly and stomach.
6. Exhale, letting jaws, tongue, shoulders go limp, feeling heaviness leave the body.

For more information see:
QR: The Quieting Reflex — G.P. Putnam's Sons. ✻

Super Sports

Tennis Flow by Dyveke Spino
Increase enjoyment and performance with mental training. Play centered, stress-free tennis. Imagery rehearsal to enhance concentration and improve your stroke. Part of Spino's top-rated tennis course.
TAPE 321 $12.95

Creative Running by Dyveke Spino
Pointers for stress-free running. Exercises to increase energy and avoid injury. Visualization to attune yourself to motion. For all who like to move in the outdoors.
TAPE 322 $12.95

Creative Running II by Dyveke Spino
"If you're a jogger, you will love it. Imagery experiences for transcending pain and awakening the heroic. I listen at home and afterwards go out and run as smoothly as a deer for as long as I want."
– Gene Bruce. East/West Journal
TAPE 323 $12.95

Superlearning 450 7th Ave. New York, NY 10123 212 279-8450 7

A collage-style approach

Within the basic three-column structure, this format allows the designer to nestle variable-width text blocks around art as needed. The large page size makes it possible to present several items on a single page, which reinforces the thematic organization of material and encourages browsing as well.

For this particular publication, the format solves the problem of placing a great many loose elements on the page—each of the items on the page shown includes the publishing information, the book cover, a brief one-paragraph review, text and art excerpted from the book being reviewed, and captions. The collage-style approach is a visual signature of the magazine from which this book spins off.

The underlying structure for this collage-style page is three 17-pica columns.

A pragmatic use of rules and boxes helps organize the disparate elements and separate one item from another. Boxes and silhouettes that overhang the rules create a dimensionality that lightens up the densely packed pages.

Design decisions are required for almost every text block in a grid used with this much flexibility. While most grids dictate the placement of elements on the page, this grid provides but a subtle understructure for the multitude of elements.

The type is from the Helvetica family, an ideal choice for its efficient word count and its legibility in small sizes as well as for the variety afforded within a single type family. The introduction of a second typeface to such a complex page could easily create chaos.

Design: Kathleen O'Neill

Pages from Signal, *a book created by* Whole Earth Review.
Trim size: 10-1/2 by 12-1/8

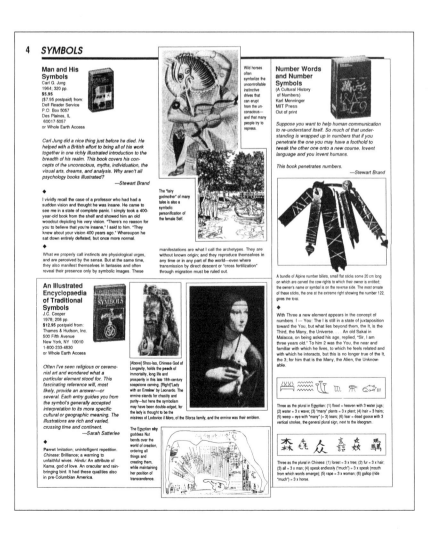

Playing with frames

This three + two-column format plays with rules to create frames within frames. The underlying grid is very symmetrical and modular, but the elements break through it and out of it in many different and sometimes subtly humorous ways. The resulting playfulness is especially useful in balancing the medical, scientific, and fundamentally difficult subject of aging.

Three 10-pica columns are used for the short items that make up this news section of a monthly magazine. Items whose headlines run across two or three columns take on more importance than those with single-column heads. The column width of the "featured" stories varies: two or three 10-pica columns, one 20-pica column, and two 14p6 columns are all used.

The narrow outer margins (4 picas from rule to rule) are used exclusively for captions. Brevity is essential in lines that rarely contain more than a single word.

The overall effect, which is very open and accessible, is achieved by sacrificing a considerable amount of text space. A distinct advantage of the format, not seen in the pages reproduced here, is that it creates a strong contrast when editorial and advertising pages face each other on the same spread.

Art almost invariably breaks out of the grid, creating a variety of depth illusions. Type, too, can appear to move through a three-dimensional page: The clipped-off bottoms of the Anti-Aging headline (left) make the type appear to be moving down through the box.

The body text is Helvetica with Futura headlines.

The paper is a heavy, noncoated, gray stock, which adds considerable bulk to a 36-page magazine. Blue and burgundy, used for banners, headlines, and tones behind the featured items, add color and reinforce the modular structure. Another similarly formatted section in the magazine uses green and purple.

Design: Regina Marsh (New York, NY)

Pages from Longevity, *published monthly by Omni International.*
Trim size: 8-1/4 by 10-3/4

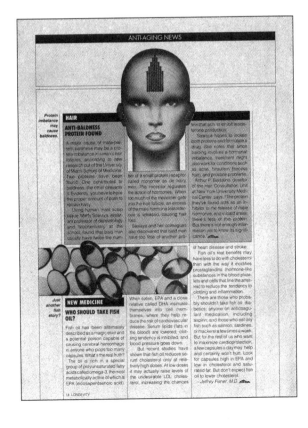

Variable column width

When you have variable-length components and want to contain each one within a single column, you can let the length of each item dictate the column width. Putting together such a page is a little like doing a jigsaw puzzle. This layout would be exceedingly expensive and time-consuming using traditional typesetting and pasteup. But the ability to stretch or shrink a text block in PageMaker gives you extraordinary on-screen control over the width and depth of each column. You assemble this kind of page from left to right, and then make adjustments as needed.

The key to balancing all the elements on the page is to establish some horizontal constants in either text placement or illustration depth. In addition to unifying the page, these horizontal guidelines will help keep you from getting lost in a sea of choices.

A horizontal grid is used to balance the elements in variable-width columns on the the two pages shown here. The headings for all items sit on a baseline 4p6 from the top of the page. The first line of body text sits on one of three baselines, all measured from the top trim: 11p, 27p6, or 39p.

The margins are 3 picas for the sides and bottom and 4 picas for the top.

The text is 10/12.5, with headlines in Helvetica Condensed Black and body text in Helvetica Condensed. Condensed sans serif faces are a good choice for short copy in narrow columns.

The "Allsport" title is Helvetica Condensed Black, further condensed and rotated in FreeHand (at the time, you couldn't condense or rotate type in PageMaker), and then placed in the PageMaker document.

The rules are 1 point—heavier than usually found—in order to give more structure to the page.

ALLSPORT

Duis autem vel eum

Duis autem vel eum iriure dolor in esse hendrerit in vulputate velit esse molestie consequat, vel illum dolore eu feugiat nulla facilisis at vero eros et accumsan et iusto odio dignissim qui blandit praesent luptatum zzril delenit augue duis dolore te feugait nulla facilisi.

Lorem ipsum dolor sit amet, consectetuer adipiscing elit, sed diam nonummy nibh euismod tincidunt ut laoreet dolore magna aliquam erat volutpat. Ut wisi enim ad minim veniam, quis nostrud exerci tation ullamcorper suscipit lobortis nisl ut aliquip ex ea commodo consequat.

Duis autem vel eum iriure dolor in hendrerit in vulputate velit esse molestie consequat, vel illum dolore eu feugiat nulla facilisis at vero eros et accumsan et iusto odio dignissim qui blandit praesent luptatum zzril delenit augue duis dolore te feugait nulla facilisi. Nam liber tempor cum soluta nobis eleifend option congue nihil imperdiet doming id quod mazim placerat facer possim assum. Lorem ipsum dolor sit amet, consectetuer adipiscing elit, sed diam nonummy euismod tincidunt ut laoreet dolore magna

Lorem ipsum dolor sit amet, consectetuer adipiscing elit, sed diam nonummy nibh euismod tincidunt ut laoreet dolore magna aliquam erat volutpat. Ut wisi enim ad minim veniam, quis nostrud exerci tation ullamcorper suscipit lobortis nisl ut aliquip ex ea commodo consequat.

Lorem ipsum

Aliquam erat esse volutpat. Ut wisi enim ad minim veniam, quis nostrud exerci tation ullamcorper suscipit nisl ut aliquip ex ea commodo consequat.

Duis autem vel eum iriure dolor in hendrerit in vulputate velit esse molestie consequat, vel illum dolore eu feugiat nulla facilisis at vero eros et accumsan et iusto odio dignissim qui

Duis autem vel eum iriure dolor in hendrerit in vulputate velit esse molestie lorem ipsum

Blandit praesent luptatum zzril delenit augue duis dolore te feugait nulla facilisi. Lorem ipsum dolor sit amet, consectetuer adipiscing elit, sed diam nonummy nibh euismod tincidunt ut laoreet dolore magna Lorem ipsum dolor sit amet, consectetuer adipiscing elit, sed diam nonummy nibh euismod tincidunt ut laoreet dolore magna aliquam erat

volutpat. Ut wisi enim ad minim veniam, quis nostrud exerci tation ullamcorper suscipit lobortis nisl ut aliquip ex ea commodo consequat.

Duis autem vel eum iriure dolor in hendrerit in vulputate velit esse molestie consequat, vel illum dolore eu feugiat nulla facilisis et ac-cumsan et iusto odio dignissim qui blandit praesent luptatum zzril delenit augue duis dolore te feugait nulla facilisi. Lorem ipsum dolor sit amet, con-

Ut wisi enim ades min ut wisi enim ad min

Sectetuer adipis-cing elit, sed diam nonummy nibh euismod tincidunt ut laoreet dolore magna aliquam erat volutpat.

Ut wisi enim ad minim veniam, quis nostrud exerci tation ullamcorper suscipit lobortis nisl ut aliquip ex ea commodo conse-quat. Duis autem vel eum iriure dolor in hendrerit in.

In the schematics above, the approach is to establish a horizon line for the headlines and for body text and then to hang copy from those lines in variable column widths. Art is sized to match the text width in each column, with variable heights but with a common baseline and a fixed amount of space between the bottom of the text and the top of the art.

The leftmost schematic shows the same approach in a vertically oriented page. Another approach is to have even bottoms and ragged tops, with art and headlines providing another horizontal constant at the top of the page.

Duis au

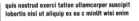

liriure dolor in hendrerit in vulput

Autem vel eum iriure dolor in hendrerit in vulputate velit esse molestie consequat, vel illum dolore eu feugiat nulla facilisis at vero eros et accumsan et

quis nostrud exerci tation ullamcorper suscipit lobortis nisl ut aliquip ex ea c minUt wisi enim

Diam nonummy nibh euismod tincidunt ut laoreet dolore magna. Lorem ipsum dolor sit amet, consectetuer adipiscing elit, sed diam nonummy nibh euismod tincidunt ut laoreet dolore magna aliquam erat volutpat. Ut wisi enim ad minim veniam, quis nostrud exerci tation ullamcorper suscipit lobortis nisl ut aliquip ex ea commodo consequat.

Duis autem vel eum iriure dolor in hendrerit in vulputate velit esse molestie consequat, vel illum dolore eu feugiat nulla facilisis at vero eros et accumsan et iusto odio dignissim qui blandit praesent luptatum zzril delenit augue duis dolore te feugait nulla facilisi.

Lorem ipsum dolor sit amet, consectetuer adipiscing elit, sed diam nonummy nibh euismod tincidunt ut laoreet dolore magna aliquam erat volutpat. Ut wisi enim ad minim veniam, quis nostrud exerci tation ullamcorper suscipit lobortis nisl ut aliquip ex ea commodo consequat.Duis autem vel eum iriure dolor in hendrerit in vulputate velit esse molestie consequat, vel illum dolore eu

Feuga

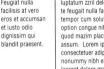

Feugiat nulla facilisis at vero eros et accumsan et iusto odio dignissim qui blandit praesent.

Lorem ipsum dolor sit amet

luptatum zzril delenit augue duis dolore te feugait nulla facilisi. Nam liber tempor cum soluta nobis eleifend option congue nihil imperdiet doming id quod mazim placerat facer possim assum. Lorem ipsum dolor sit amet, consectetuer adipiscing elit, sed diam nonummy nibh euismod tincidunt ut laoreet dolore magna aliquam erat volutpat.

Ut wisi enim ad minim veniam, quis nostrud exerci tation ullamcorper suscipit lobortis nisl ut aliquip ex ea commodo consequat. Duis autem vel eum iriure dolor in hendrerit in vulputate velit esse molestie consequat, vel illum dolore eu feugiat nulla facilisis at vero eros et accumsan et iusto odio dignissim qui blandit praesent luptatum zzril delenit augue duis dolore te esse.

Vulputate velit esse molestie consequat, vel illum dolore eu feugiat nulla facilisis at vero eros et accumsan et iusto odio dignissim qui blandit praesent luptatum zzril delenit augue duis dolore te feugait nulla facilisi. Nam liber tempor cum soluta nobis eleifend option congue nihil imperdiet doming id quod mazim placerat facer possim assum.

Lorem ipsum dolor sit amet, consectetuer adipiscing elit, sed diam nonummy nibh euismod tincidunt ut laoreet dolore magna aliquam erat volutpat. Ut wisi enim ad minim veniam, quis nostrud exerci tation ullamcorper suscipit lobortis nisl ut aliquip ex ea commodo consequat. Duis

iusto odio dignissim qui blandit praesent luptatum zzril delenit augue duis dolore te feugait nulla facilisi. Lorem ipsu dolor sit amet con-secteadipis-cing elit, se.

CHAPTER 4

THE CIRCULAR NATURE OF PLANNING AND DOING

In describing electronic page composition, many books and manuals depict a neatly linear process of creating master pages, placing edited text and finished graphics, making a few refinements, and then printing out final pages to send off to the printer. The demonstrations of page layout programs are even more misleading. Innocent spectators stand wide-eyed, mouths agape as a demonstrator pours text into pages that seem to compose themselves as if by magic. Everything falls into place without a loose end in sight. How could anyone resist a tool that makes page layout so utterly simple, so fantastically tidy?

The reality of producing almost any publication is considerably different. Rather than being linear, the process is a circular one involving trial and error as well as numerous revisions to make all the elements work together. This case history should give you a better picture of that reality. It shows, for example, that some of the most important design work goes on before you put pencil to paper or turn on the computer and involves simply thinking through the problem of how to get your audience's attention. It looks at the overlapping steps of developing the concept, planning the design, testing the plan with text and graphics in various stages of development, refining the design, altering the text and graphics to fit the refined plan, and then making whatever changes are necessary—in the individual elements as well as the design itself— as all the pieces come together in final form.

Solving a design problem is much like running a maze. The designer selects a line to follow only to learn that the constraints he encounters send him back to probe another direction until he finds a clear path to the solution.

—Allen Hurlburt

The final version of the brochure described in this chapter may look as effortless as the slickest computer-show demonstration, but there was nothing linear about the process of creating it. Unlike a jigsaw puzzle, in which a single fixed piece completes the task, this publication evolved into its final form, and almost everything about it changed at least a little along the way.

The process described in this case history is quite specific to the particular publication. At each stage, our approach grew out of the unique problems and goals of the project and the division of duties among the different people involved. Every project and every team will use a process that is different, sometimes a little different and sometimes dramatically different. The goal of this chapter is simply to reveal the circular and overlapping nature of the two main facets of the work— planning and doing.

**Background:
The need, the purpose,
and the concept**

The New York City Charter Revision Commission was created to study and propose revisions to the city charter. The commission knew that most New Yorkers had never heard of the charter and were not likely to be informed about the proposals that would be on a voter referendum. The purpose of the publication was to increase voter awareness about how the charter affected city government and why it was being changed. Recognizing audience apathy was the first step toward finding an appropriate way to deliver the message.

We were hired as the editorial and design team because of our background in working with interactive techniques—puzzles, games, quizzes, and so on. These activities provide an effective if somewhat subversive way to engage people in a subject they might otherwise not be inclined to read about. Each activity tends to have a different "look," and so in addition to breaking up the text, the activities also vary the texture from one page to the next.

PROJECT AT A GLANCE: THE VOTER'S GUIDEBOOK

Description	*An* educational brochure produced for The New York City Charter Revision Commission.
Purpose	To increase voter awareness of changes in the city charter that were to be voted on in the coming election.
Specifications	8-1/2 by 11, 16 pages, 2-color, newsprint, suitable for self-mailing. Initial print run: 200,000.
Audience	Citizens in all five boroughs.
Distribution	Bulk distribution through citizen groups, unions, schools, libraries, and civic organizations. "Copies on request" promoted through city payroll, phone-bill stuffers, and public service announcements.
Design Objectives	To involve people in a generally tedious subject.
Devices for Achieving Goal	• Puzzles and games as both editorial and design elements. • A modular editorial format to create many entry points for readers. • A strong, tight format to unify disparate elements. • Bold headlines and borders. • A photo of a landmark and a unique headline style to highlight each borough, with a map motif to unify all five of them.
Typeface	Body text: Times Roman. We chose this face because it is serious, sets tightly, and reproduces well in a wide range of situations, making it a safe choice for inexpensive newsprint. Headlines: New Century Schoolbook, condensed. We condensed the type because some headlines were fairly long, and we didn't want to sacrifice point size for line length.

Presentation sketch: A miniature booklet

The commission gave us a 3500-word essay on city government and the process of charter revision and a list of concepts and facts that the activities should explain. Every activity had to satisfy two criteria: It had to be fun to do, and it had to deliver information about the charter.

In designing the pages, our first step was to divide the single, continuous narrative into short, self-contained stories. Very few people read a brochure (or any publication other than a book) from cover to cover. Each story is a potential entry point, each headline an opportunity to hook the audience.

We wanted each spread to carry a small chunk of the text and a related activity. Establishing a relationship between the text and its accompanying activity wasn't always possible, but it was useful to start with that as the organizing principle. Creating a dozen individual stories from the single long one required only a little rewriting because the text had clear and natural divisions. This is not always the case.

Doing the early sketches by hand helps focus your attention on the big picture, rather than on the mathematical details required to set up an electronic page.

Although the publication was to be 8-1/2 by 11 inches, we did the presentation sketch at one-fourth that size, with each two-page spread on half of an 8-1/2- by 11-inch page. And we did it by hand rather than on the computer. Computer layouts are unforgiving of imprecision and have a way of looking more cast in stone than is the case at an early stage. Working by hand sometimes helps you to focus on the big picture rather than on the details of spacing and alignment that the computer encourages you to attend to. And working small, when you're working by hand, is simply faster and emphasizes the preliminary nature of the presentation. (Interestingly, people also seem to get a kick out of the tiny pages.)

The pencil sketch (actually, it was done with colored markers) showed the position of each story and activity. It showed the bold borders and the strong headlines surrounded by generous white space as well as the use of red as a second color. Writing and positioning the real headlines at this early stage contributed to everyone's feeling that the concept and design worked. The individual pieces were right, and the pacing was right. Although no real text or art was in place, everyone got a sense of what the publication would look and feel like to the reader. Some stories and placements changed along the way, but this early sketch reflected the tone and structure of the final publication.

A few holes were left in the sketch for activity concepts that hadn't been developed. This was, thankfully, a client with a minimalist attitude toward meetings, and we'd scheduled a brainstorming session immediately following the presentation to fill in those holes.

The manuscript for the original essay had not been created in a word processor, so we keyboarded the text at this stage. We did the first edit in Microsoft Word and printed out galleys with the text in 13-1/2-pica columns for the commission to review along with the sketch.

ANOTHER APPROACH

In the early stages of a project, you'll often want to explore more than one concept. For *The Voter's Guidebook*, we briefly entertained the idea of creating a takeoff on the *New York Post*. Given the number of New Yorkers who follow the infamous Post-style headlines, such a blatant simulation of it, while not a true parody, was sure to get attention.

Several considerations quickly ruled out the idea. The most important was that the design concept would have dictated the contents, rather than the other way around. Much of the information the Charter Revision Commission wanted to convey didn't lend itself to tabloid-style headlines. This meant that we would have had to delete material we wanted to include, write headlines that were inappropriate, or include some headlines that didn't follow through on the concept.

A takeoff on the New York Post *was briefly considered as an alternative approach.*

The *Post* takeoff would also have required writing new copy to carry out the concept and using more photos than the budget allowed. There simply wasn't time or money to execute it.

Further, no one was truly comfortable with the idea. It seemed a little brazen and somehow inappropriate for a city commission to model itself, however tongue in cheek, on a daily tabloid.

We anticipated these problems when we sketched out the idea. But when you edit yourself too much in the early stages of a project, you sacrifice both good ideas and *esprit de corps*. Part of the design process requires striking a balance between anticipating what your client (or boss or editor or communications director) wants and taking some risks. A good working relationship has a free flow of ideas that inspires everyone involved. Daring visuals and bold concepts loosen people up and are catalysts for problem solving. The *New York Post* concept, although discarded, got the project off to a creative, upbeat start. That feeling carried over to the puzzle brainstorming session that followed the design presentation and was largely maintained throughout the project.

The first dummy: Copy fitting

After the galleys and presentation sketch were approved, we put each individual essay and activity in its own word-processor file. In a modular publication in which every item is self-contained rather than continuous from one page to the next, fitting the copy into the allotted spaces usually requires cutting or adding text. If the stories had been threaded together in a single document, changes to the line count in one story would have rippled through subsequent stories, requiring much moving back and forth among pages to retrieve errant lines (and risking the kinds of errors that computers should minimize).

While we were still working out some of the design elements, we did a rough electronic dummy to facilitate the copy fitting. It's generally recommended that copy fitting be done in the word-processing program, and when extensive editing is required, we agree. But one of the great advantages of electronic layout is seeing the copy in place. When you cut copy and see the lines on the pasteboard flow up neatly to fill the column, you know that the copy fits and you get a nice feeling of completeness. If the editing and design functions in your office are clearly separated, however, you may not have this choice.

The first electronic dummy substituted temporary PageMaker rules and headline type for the real ones that were to be created in Illustrator. By this time, we had dropped some art shown on the presentation sketch for these pages.

At this point, the master pages had three 13p6 columns (which later changed to 13 picas to allow for more white space). The text for each story was in place, but other details had to be simulated. The map rules above the headlines and in the box borders hadn't been worked out, so we used PageMaker's bold dashed line to simulate them. The New Century Schoolbook headlines, which were to be condensed in Adobe Illustrator (at the time, you couldn't condense type in PageMaker) had not yet been completed, so we used Helvetica.

Simulating the unresolved design elements at this point gave us—and the client—a chance to read the copy in the context of the layout and to evaluate the layout with the copy in place.

The presentation dummy: Refining the design

The brochure had been conceived as 24 pages, including a pullout poster in the center. When the poster idea proved unworkable, we were left with 20 pages. Because publications are generally printed in signatures of 8 or 16 pages, printing 200,000 twenty-page brochures would have wasted an unconscionable amount of paper. After exploring the possibility of expanding or shrinking the brochure, everyone agreed that less was more (this is almost always the case in publication work, as it is in other endeavors), and we dropped down to 16 pages.

Changing the page count midway through a project inevitably solves some problems and creates others. Here, in a nutshell, were the effects that the reduced page count had on *The Voter's Guidebook*:

• We eliminated the weaker activities and were left with the really good, solid, fun stuff.

• We had to juggle the position of some essays and activities. Several crossover spreads had art or stories on facing pages that could not be broken up. When you eliminate one page before a spread that has to stay together, you have to find some other page to fill in. In the course of this juggling, we had to put one puzzle with a lot of specific details about the charter earlier in the brochure than we would have liked, but all decisions have their trade-offs.

• Copy that had been edited to fit in the 24-page dummy had to be edited again to fit the new page count. This kind of reworking is part of the process of publication design, and desktop publishing makes it infinitely easier and cheaper to accomplish than the traditional method, where every change requires that you send out for new type and mechanically paste up the new version.

At this stage, we created the map rules that were to frame the various components. Once we saw them in place, however, we felt they were too bold a device to use throughout, and we decided to substitute a simple double-rule border for the games. The double rule echoed the map rules but was subtler, and so kept the pages from looking too heavy and busy. The two types of borders were exactly the same depth so that they aligned horizontally across the page.

The headline type and initial caps—condensed New Century Schoolbook—were created in Illustrator and placed in PageMaker as Encapsulated PostScript files. (Each headline and each initial cap was a separate file.) These were to be in red, the second color. Again, we felt that having red headlines and initial caps for every item would be too busy, so the games had black headlines and no initial caps.

As a result of these changes, the contrast in rules and color for the two types of material—running text and activities—provided a visual organizing cue for the reader.

Some of the games and puzzles had not yet been completed, so for the presentation dummy we filled in these holes with a pencil sketch of each activity and the working introductory copy. Because the introductions were short, we typed them directly into PageMaker.

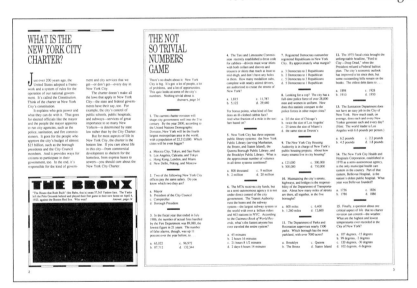

Final page proofs used black boxes to indicate the position of photos that would be stripped in by the printer. The position of the Bronx sidebar changed from the original sketch to the final. And, as a result of deadline pressures, the decorative numbers in the quiz were replaced by rules, which were easier to create.

The final pages

Desktop publishing enabled us to show the commission more complete proofs for approval earlier in the cycle than would have been possible using traditional typesetting and pasteup methods. This paid off handsomely by minimizing corrections at the final stage. Still, changes were requested, and although they were relatively easy to make on-screen, printing pages was extremely slow. (At the time we were working in PageMaker 2.0 on a Mac Plus with 1 megabyte of internal memory and a slow LaserWriter Plus printer.) Up against the deadline, we printed type patches and pasted in small corrections by hand rather than waiting for a graphics-intensive page to print. (The headlines, initial caps, and borders imported from Illustrator were all graphics; the photographs, however, were stripped in by the printer.)

A strong center axis on the cover makes the offset compass rose, with the commission's logo inside, more prominent. The map and compass rose were created in Adobe Illustrator. The logo was pasted in by hand.

Starting text on the cover, as on the page shown below left, can be an effective way to get the reader's interest. The text must be very strong for this technique to work and must be carefully designed for visual effect.

The back cover is designed as a self-mailer and uses the most universally popular of all puzzles to draw the reader in. When solved, the crossword reveals a message in the shaded squares that reads: "Vote on charter change in 88." Someone who solves the puzzle but never opens the brochure will still get the most important message of the guidebook. Constructing the grid for the crossword was a snap with the Snap to Guides feature in MacDraw.

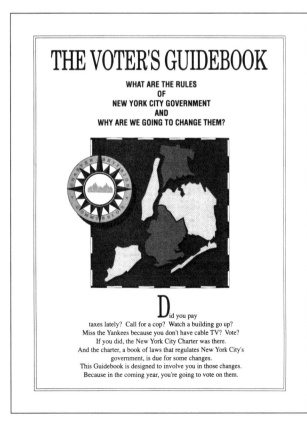

The printed pages for the spread shown throughout this chapter in various stages of its evolution: A trivia quiz reminds readers of the sheer size of city government by supplying such facts as the number of false alarms answered by the fire department and the amount of trash generated, on average, by each citizen every day.

The headlines and initial caps are 36-point New Century Schoolbook, condensed to 60%. The heads and caps for primary text print in red to help unify the short essays that run throughout the 16 pages. The activity headlines print in black.

The position of the opening line of text for the essays remains constant throughout the booklet.

The map rules over the essays and around the borough boxes were created in Illustrator from a double hairline rule with black rectangles dropped in. Alignment is critical.

Boxes around the activities use hairline rules. Note that the map rules and the open rules of the boxes align exactly.

Rules crossing the gutter between two pages required manual pasteup for alignment.

The running text for the essays is 11/13 Times Roman set in 13-pica columns. Because they have a map rule above but not around them, these text blocks have a more open look than the activities, which are enclosed in boxes. Eleven-point type was difficult to read on-screen but worked much better in the overall design than 10- or 12-point type.

The text for activities is 10/12 Times Roman. The column width is a half-pica shorter than the width used for the essay text, and the space between columns is also a half-pica shorter, to compensate for the space occupied by the rules around the activity.

Decorative rules, which print in red, separate numbered text blocks in the quiz. For these dividers we copied the rectangle used in the map rule and pasted it repeatedly in the quiz.

Borough headlines were created individually in Illustrator to give each borough a different personality. Press type can also be used to create this effect.

WHAT IS THE NEW YORK CITY CHARTER?

Just over 200 years ago, the United States adopted a framework and a system of rules for the operation of our national government. It's called the Constitution. Think of the charter as New York City's constitution.

It explains who gets power and what they can do with it. That goes for elected officials like the mayor and the people the mayor appoints to run city agencies, such as the police, sanitation, and fire commissioners. It goes for the people who approve the city's budget of almost $23 billion, such as the borough presidents and the City Council members. And it provides ways for citizens to participate in their government, too. In the end, it's responsible for the kind of govern-ment and city services that we get—or don't get—every day in New York City.

The charter doesn't make all the laws that apply in New York City—the state and federal governments have their say, too. For example, the city's control of public schools, public hospitals, and subways—services of great importance to so many New Yorkers—is determined by state law rather than by the City Charter. But for most aspects of life in New York City, the charter is the bottom line. If you care about life in this city—from commercial development to shelters for the homeless, from express buses to sewers—you should care about the New York City Charter.

THE BRONX

"The House that Ruth Built" (the Babe, that is) seats 57,545 Yankee fans. The Yanks left the Polo Grounds behind and played their first game in their new home on April 4, 1923, against the Boston Red Sox. Who won?   *Answer, page 14*

THE NOT SO TRIVIAL NUMBERS GAME

There's no doubt about it: New York City is big. It's got a lot of people, a lot of problems, and a lot of opportunities. This quiz looks at some of the city's numbers. Nothing trivial about it.
Answers, page 14

1. The current charter revision will shape city government well into the 21st century. By the year 2000, according to the United Nations Demographic Division, New York will be the fourth largest metropolitan area in the world, with a population of 22,212,000. Which cities will be even bigger?

a. Mexico City, Tokyo, and Sao Paulo
b. Los Angeles, Calcutta, and Tokyo
c. Hong Kong, London, and Miami
d. New Delhi, Peking, and Moscow

2. Two of the following New York City offices pay the same salary. Do you know which two they are?

a. Mayor
b. President of the City Council
c. Comptroller
d. Borough President

3. In the fiscal year that ended in July 1986, the number of actual fires handled by the Fire Department was 89,088, the lowest figure in 21 years. The number of false alarms, though, was up 11 percent over the year before, to . . .

a. 65,022   c. 96,972
b. 87,712   d. 132,344

4. The Taxi and Limousine Commission recently established a dress code for cabbies—drivers must wear shirts with both collars and sleeves and trousers or skirts that reach at least to mid-thigh, and don't have any holes in them. How many medallion cabs, complete with neatly attired drivers, are authorized to cruise the streets of New York?

a. 1,815   c. 11,787
b. 5,122   d. 29,440

For bonus points, what kind of fine does an ill-clothed cabbie face? And what fraction of a mile is the taxi fare based on?

5. New York City has three separate public library systems: the New York Public Library (serving Manhattan, the Bronx, and Staten Island), the Queens Borough Public Library, and the Brooklyn Public Library. What is the approximate number of volumes in all three systems combined?

a. 800 thousand   c. 9 million
b. 2 million   d. 20 million

6. The MTA receives city funds, but as a semi-autonomous agency it is not under direct control of the city government. The Transit Authority runs the buses and the subway system—the largest subway system in the world with over a billion riders and 463 stations in NYC. According to the *Guinness Book of World Records*, what's the fastest anyone has ever traveled the entire system?

a. 45 minutes
b. 2 hours 16 minutes
c. 21 hours 8 1/2 minutes
d. 2 days 6 hours 14 minutes

7. Registered Democrats outnumber registered Republicans in New York City. By approximately what margin?

a. 3 Democrats to 2 Republicans
b. 2 Democrats to 1 Republican
c. 5 Democrats to 3 Republicans
d. 5 Democrats to 1 Republican

8. Looking for a cop? The city has a full-time police force of over 28,000 men and women in uniform. How does this statistic compare to the police forces in other major cities?

a. 2/3 the size of Chicago's
b. twice the size of Los Angeles'
c. 25 times the size of Miami's
d. the same size as Detroit's

9. The New York City Housing Authority is in charge of New York's public housing projects. About how many tenants live in city housing?

a. 125,000   c. 500,000
b. 300,000   d. 750,000

10. Maintaining the city's streets, highways, and bridges is the responsibility of the Department of Transportation. About how many miles of streets are there, all together, in the five boroughs?

a. 600 miles   c. 6,400
b. 1,260 miles   d. 12,600

11. The Department of Parks and Recreation supervises nearly 1500 parks. Which borough has the most parkland, with over 7000 acres?

a. Brooklyn   c. Queens
b. The Bronx   d. Staten Island

12. The 1975 fiscal crisis brought the unforgettable headline, "Ford to City—Drop Dead," when the President refused a Federal bailout plan. The city's economic outlook has improved a lot since then, but some outstanding bills remain on the books. The oldest debt dates to . . .

a. 1898   c. 1928
b. 1910   d. 1950

13. The Sanitation Department does not have an easy job in the City of New York. How much trash, on average, does each and every New Yorker generate each and every day? (Hint: The world leader is Los Angeles with 6.6 pounds per person.)

a. 6.2 pounds   c. 2.2 pounds
b. 4.5 pounds   d. 1.8 pounds

14. The New York City Health and Hospitals Corporation, established in 1970 as a semi-autonomous agency, is the only municipal health care system in the country. Part of that system, Bellevue Hospital, is the nation's oldest public hospital. What year was Bellevue founded?

a. 1736   c. 1836
b. 1786   d. 1886

15. Finally, a question about one critical aspect of life that no charter revision can control—the weather. What are the highest and lowest temperatures ever recorded in the City of New York?

a. 107 degrees, -15 degrees
b. 99 degrees, -2 degrees
c. 120 degrees, -30 degrees
d. 102 degrees, -6 degrees

Thumbnails: A useful tool

PageMaker has an extremely useful feature that enables you to print miniature pages. In the Print dialog box, simply specify the pages you want printed, click on the Thumbnails option, and indicate how many thumbnails you want printed on each sheet. The size of the thumbnails depends on the trim size of the publication, the number specified, and the size of the paper in your printer. You can print up to 64 thumbnails on a single sheet. (On a PC, the thumbnails option is available only on PostScript-compatible printers.)

The thumbnails on the facing page show the complete *Voter's Guidebook*. Page 16, which actually printed on a second sheet, has been pasted into position facing page 1 so that we can show it here on a single page. Black rectangles indicate frames where halftones were to be stripped in by the printer. The document filename prints in the upper left corner. Adding the date by hand to the printed page provides an invaluable frame of reference.

The ability to view a publication at a glance in this way has many benefits. It gives you a sense of the texture and continuity of the pages and often helps you spot opportunities and problems, in both editorial continuity and format consistency. Thumbnails also serve as a useful tracking and organizational tool. You can note information or material that is still to come (traditional publishing shorthand for that is simply "tk") as well as critical alignments and other details that should be checked on a Linotronic printout or blueline proof.

The thumbnails for this brochure demonstrate the flexibility of the three-column grid for a modular format. You can see how individual elements fill anywhere from one to five columns. But the format does require considerable planning and fine-tuning to make the elements fit within their allotted spaces.

Facing page: The entire 16-page brochure is seen at a glance by using the Thumbnails option in PageMaker's Print dialog box.

If you're wondering how one turns the subject of city government into entertaining activities, here's a description of some of the concepts we included in the booklet:

- Newspaper-style headlines (pages 6-7) asked people to determine whether certain events or situations were possible under the current charter. ("Mayor Names Darryl Strawberry as NYC Comptroller" is impossible, not because of Strawberry's lack of qualifications, but because the comptroller is elected rather than appointed.) Each headline was set in a different typeface and rotated in Illustrator, placed in PageMaker as an Encapsulated PostScript file, and positioned to create a collage effect.

- Photos from around the city involved readers in the city's organization chart (pages 8-9) as they looked for the office responsible for the object or activity shown in each picture (a trash can, a manhole cover, a park lake, and so on).

- A simple board game (page 12) put players at the mayor's desk, divvying up the city's $23 billion budget among the various city agencies on the playing field.

Voter's Guidebook

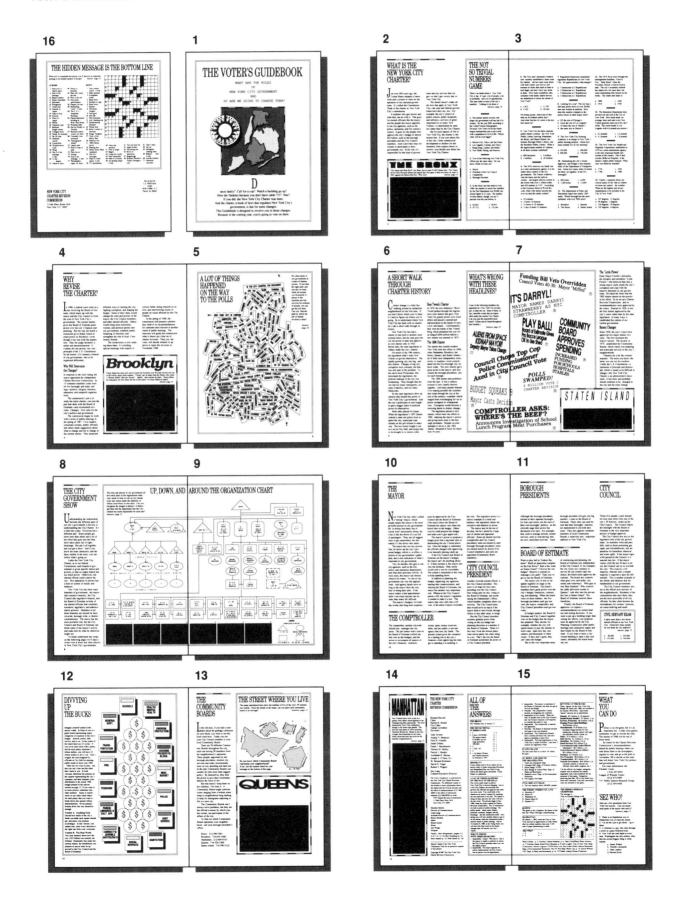

SECTION 2

A PAGEMAKER PORTFOLIO

SECTION 2

INTRODUCTION TO THE PORTFOLIO

If we are to communicate quickly and clearly (as we must, if we are to retain our audience), then we must accept the fact that WHAT we say is integral with HOW we say it. Visual form and verbal content are inseparable.... Graphic design is not something added to make the pages look lively. It is not an end in itself. It is the means to an end—that of clear, vivid, stirring communication of editorial content.

—Jan White,
Designing for Magazines

You will find in this portfolio a broad selection of publications, from businesses both large and small, with designs that range from simple to complex. The subjects include health, education, manufacturing, entertainment, politics, fashion, real estate, law, and art. Some publications were created by free-lance designers, others by corporate art departments, and still others by top design studios. The level of graphic sophistication varies considerably. A modest layout is often presented side by side with an ambitious one because each represents an appropriate solution to a specific communication need.

This question of appropriateness comes up again and again. Communication is more an art than a science, and the decisions a designer makes are often subjective ones. It is not so much a matter of whether a design is good or bad, but of whether it works for the need at hand.

All of the designers used PageMaker for some part of the design and production process. It can't be said often enough that the technology is only a tool—a remarkable tool, to be sure, but still only a tool. If you want to take advantage of the full range of illustration styles, of the best photographic reproduction, of typefaces not yet available on the desktop, you will undoubtably combine traditional and desktop approaches, as some of the designers represented here have done.

Behind many of the documents are stories of how organizations and individuals have integrated desktop publishing into their work. Geiger International, for example, is a furniture design firm in Atlanta. In 1985 they were planning a major revision of their product guide and price list. Previously, price lists had been typeset outside and laboriously pasted up by the two-person art and design department. Without really knowing anything about desktop publishing (they hadn't even heard the term), they did know that if they could do the price lists themselves, in-house, they'd have a database that could be updated as needed. Manfred Petri, their new vice president of design, had seen the LaserWriter at an office equipment show in Germany, and he was convinced that it really could produce what was called "near typeset quality." A little research brought PageMaker to their attention, and it

Three people [should] be trained to educate and support the others in a work group: a computer-oriented person (to handle hardware and software problems); a designer or graphic artist (to support others in the use of templates and style sheets, among other tools); and a production person (to help manage the document flow). That way, the computer wizard learns about publishing, the publishing people learn about computers, and the rest of the staff has more than one person to go to in times of need.
— *Barbara Hawkins,*
quoted in Publish!

looked as though it could do the job. Pamela Bryant, an executive assistant in sales, was recruited to translate Petri's paper-and-pencil guidelines into electronic form. She had no graphic design experience and no computer experience beyond word processing on a PC. What she did have was an interest in learning how to use this mouse-driven Macintosh, which she carted home on weekends. The typesetting for the price list redesign would have been $30,000, so the savings on type alone more than covered the purchase of their original Mac Plus and LaserWriter. Seven years later, there are still two people in the design department (Bryant being one of them), doing more publication work than they'd previously done plus many thousands of dollars' worth of typesetting. (A page from the Geiger price guide is on the opening spread of Chapter 7.)

Depending on your point of view, it is either easier or more difficult to move into desktop publishing today than it was in 1985. Easier because the tools are more advanced, and there's no question that in trained hands those tools can produce high-quality work. But the choices are more various—and hence more complex—and the expectations are so much higher.

Even so, organizations with a definable need and a sensible approach to phasing in the technology do realize the benefits they had anticipated. Smith & Hawken, the Mill Valley, California, gardening emporium, started tentatively, using PageMaker only to produce store signs and product information sheets. It was several years before they converted their mail-order catalogs to desktop production, and in doing so they hired a typesetter from the commercial type shop that previously handled their account. (Samples of their product information sheets are in Chapter 7.) The Art Institute of Chicago, notes graphic designer Ann Wassmann Gross, began using desktop production for gallery labels alone, and within two years was producing half of the museum's printed materials on its Mac, using an outside typesetter's Linotronic 300 for final pages. Within four years, the figure was up to 85 percent. The museum still uses an outside typesetter for books longer than 36 pages, simply because they don't want to tie up in-house designers on projects of that size. (A folder and a brochure from the Art Institute are in Chapter 5.)

Jim Parker believes desktop publishing literally saved his organization. A nonprofit foundation located in Phoenix, Do It Now specializes in information on drug and alcohol abuse. The organization supports its operations from the sale of publications, ranging from small folders and posters to 32-page booklets. "In 1984, dwindling resources and soaring costs made our long-term survival seem dubious at best. Desktop publishing (which was little more than smoke and a rumor) was the only thing we could grab at that would float. Things got so bad that we laid off the last of our staff artists and layout people, stripping the foundation to a skeletal staff of four. Then came the Mac. Then came PageMaker. Then came our resurgence." Parker says the technology has enabled them to keep ahead of the fast-changing nature of public health information, revising anywhere from 70 to 100 titles in the course of a year. And it's enabled them to experiment with attention-getting editorial and design approaches in a cost-effective way. They've doubled sales, built a new national headquarters, and picked up a few design awards. They've been able to buy each new, more powerful machine as it becomes available. And they've recently purchased an Agfa 9400 imagesetter. "You can't justify the Agfa in terms of dollars and cents," Parker concedes, "but if you don't own it, you can't experiment."

Freelance designers and small design studios with a wide variety of clients have a somewhat different perspective than organizations using the technology for their own publishing and communications needs. One issue for many designers is whether or not they want to become typesetters and, to the degree that they do, how to bill that back to the client. It's not so much a question of quality anymore but of efficiency.

Tom Suzuki, a former design director of Time-Life Books who has a design studio in Alexandria, Virginia, knows that in comparison to commercial typesetting systems, with their sophisticated hyphenation dictionaries and their algorithms for controlling line length, desktop typesetting is extremely labor-intensive. "If you are fussy about type-setting," and Suzuki acknowledges that he is when he says this, "you can spend a large part of your time doing typesetting rather than design or layout or production."

Suzuki's reservations don't undermine his fundamental enthusiasm for the technology. It's a question of knowing when to use the computer and when to rely on traditional methods. After a couple of years of being seduced by the computer's power, he's gone back to doing thumbnail layouts by hand, echoing the feeling of many designers that the computer is too precise for the early development of a design. He's cautious about scanning, too: "Scanning is fun," he concedes, "but it takes so much memory and time." For efficiency, he uses position stats. He does use the computer for presentation roughs, and finds that clients used to seeing Latin files for the initial design put tremendous value on seeing their own copy at that early stage.

Electronic production also provides Suzuki with a variety of ways for working with clients. One magazine client modems text files from which Suzuki creates the electronic layout; he sends disks back to the client, and they input text corrections to solve problems of fit, widows, and so on. Another, using very tight templates that Suzuki created, does its own production. A third client faxes PageMaker-generated galleys from which Suzuki does a manual layout, which he faxes back to the client to use as a guide in doing the electronic production.

The technology has also changed client expectations. "It used to be that if you wanted a rush job it cost extra," Suzuki says. "Now clients have the misguided belief that they can get it fast and cheap." On the other hand, the computer does allow him to use color charts and graphics in publications that otherwise couldn't afford them. Suzuki cites a recent

This technology is a force that is going to move everybody up to where we will begin to expect and receive a higher level of sophistication in all areas of our printed communication.
—Roger Black,
from an interview in Font & Function

There is...an instant...when an idea comes alive! If you freeze it...too soon, it's still unformed and incomplete. Premature. But if you play around too much, you'll wind up with something over-worked.... You lose touch with the vitality of the original impulse, or cover it up so that no one else but you sees it. You have to catch the moment on the wing, so to speak.

—Michael Green,
Zen & the Art of the Macintosh

three-dimensional graphic he created from a client's initials, which he had separated at a service bureau for $30. Previously, the stripping charges alone would have run $300–400. (You'll find a sample of Suzuki's work in Chapter 3.)

Some designers embrace their role as pioneers in exploiting the tools of electronic publishing. It's interesting, for example, to compare John McWade's recollections of the commercial work he did with prerelease versions of PageMaker in 1984 with the technological challenges he faces using PageMaker 4.0. Of his work beta-testing version 1.0, on a 512 Mac with a 400-KB external drive, McWade recalls the difficulty of such a basic procedure as correcting a typo. There were no text-editing functions in PageMaker at that time, so in order to make a correction, he had to go back to his MacWrite file, edit the text there, and then place the entire file over again. If you inadvertently drew a rule off the page, it caused the program to crash. "A great light show," he recalls, "slow but fun."

By the end of 1990, McWade reports almost gleefully that it took three service bureaus 40 hours to output color separations for his 16-page newsletter, *Before & After*. The problems ranged from banding in a 256-step FreeHand blend to 5-MB Tiff files that inexplicably expanded to 36 megabytes on the L300 to the simple human error of forgetting to list one of the fonts used. "And so it went, page after page, like a train wreck at rush hour. Printing at night, it took five days," writes McWade in the newsletter. But "the fact that color pages can be processed by a machine *at all* is reason enough to put up with the strain; five years ago this stuff didn't even exist.... Next year my 40 hours will be 20, then 5, then 1, and soon, *click!* one minute. Perfect. It'll happen." (You'll find samples of McWade's work in Chapter 5, and a review of *Before & After* in the Resources section.)

To some degree, everyone working in desktop publishing is a pioneer, puzzling through traditional design considerations one minute and technological challenges the next. This situation will undoubtedly persist as the technology continues to advance, making increasingly sophisticated workstations and programs accessible to more and more people. And the end product, the printed page, reflects this increasing sophistication.

In the following pages, the commentary accompanying the sample documents focuses primarily on design rather than technical considerations. But you will also find notes on various software and production methods used in some of the publications as well as notes about color, paper stock, and other production values not readily apparent. Each sample is reproduced as large as possible while still allowing room for annotations about the work. Inevitably, both impact and detail are lost in reduction. Of course, color is lost as well. We hope that with a combination of the reproduction, the notes, and your imagination, this section will succeed in representing the graphic style of the wide range of business documents that are being created with PageMaker today.

CHAPTER 5

PROMOTIONS: FLYERS, POSTERS, FOLDERS, AND BROCHURES

Promotional literature is the most image-conscious of all publications. Here, more than anywhere else, the medium really is the message. That doesn't mean that the words don't count, but it does mean that the art, the graphic design, the texture of the paper, the color of the ink, and the overall production values make a first impression that it's difficult for the text to overcome if that impression is off the mark.

Of course, the image and production values that are appropriate vary tremendously. At one end of the spectrum, the category includes simple flyers that grass-roots organizations and small businesses leave under car windshield wipers; at the other end are slick four-color brochures distributed by large corporations to prospective clients. Both extremes, and everything in between, share the need to consider carefully the image they want to convey in order to produce the desired effect.

Promotional literature also presents a conceptual challenge that is rarely found in other kinds of business publications. If you can discover some unique perspective on your event, service, or product, you can turn that into an original and effective promotional idea. This is where catchy slogans, visual metaphors, and all the other tricks of Madison Avenue are used to good advantage. To be sure, if you're promoting a financial service or a funeral home, the style will be decidedly different than for a local eatery or theater group. But regardless of how frivolous or somber the concern, a fresh perspective on it will gain attention and set it apart from the competition.

FLYERS & POSTERS

You can look at flyers as modest posters, and posters as flyers on a grand scale. Though their budgets may differ dramatically, flyers and posters share the challenges inherent in any single-page promotion. To be effective, they have to deliver the strong graphic impression of a well-designed cover and the clear, concise information of a data sheet. Without the graphic appeal, the promotion will get lost amid all the other messages competing for the prospect's time and money; without the clear information, the flyer or poster becomes a piece of art, interesting to look at, perhaps, but probably not very effective.

Flyers and posters in this section

- *California Association of Midwives*—a photographic mandala for a fashion show fund-raiser
- *Student Recital*—the easy appeal of borders
- *Holiday Sale*—well-organized information
- *WGBH Brown Bag Lunches*—a simple format that works
- *A Walk in the Woods*—an illustrated theater announcement
- *AIGA poster*—the drama of life-size bit-mapped art
- *How to Design a Page*—and in doing so take advantage of all the technology

For hands-on instructions for creating a flyer with a coupon, see Project 6 in Section 3.

A scanned photo, copied and manipulated to create a mandala-like image, is a dynamic graphic element for flyers and posters that is relatively easy to create. The digitized image was rotated and flopped in MacPaint to create four versions oriented in different directions. Each version was saved as a separate file and imported into PageMaker, where the individual pieces were all composed into a single image.

The four corners created by the negative space of the art inside the 8-point-rule box provide an effective way to organize the type. The vertical rules add additional structure that keeps the type from floating in space.

The type and art print black against a shocking pink background, enhancing the playful feeling that sets the tone for the fashion show benefit.

The typeface is Garamond with a Futura Extra Bold headline.

Design: John Odam (San Diego, CA)

Flyer for a benefit auction for the California Association of Midwives. Trim size: 8-1/2 by 11

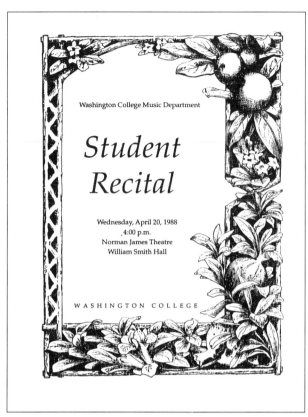

Borders from electronic or traditional clip art provide a quick, easy, and effective way to dress up a simple message. The one here is from *Victorian Pictorial Borders*, a book of public domain art published by Dover Press. The designer simply photocopied the art to the desired size, ran out type on a laser printer, pasted the two together on an 8-1/2- by 11-inch page, and photocopied the result.

The large Palatino headline is easy to read. It combines modern and classical elegance in a style that works well with the floral border and is appropriate for the event.

When considering borders from the ever-expanding clip art universe, keep in mind that you can use and modify segments of them to bracket and separate text.

With desktop publishing, a design studio can take a rough layout provided by a small organization (shown at right) and produce a quick and inexpensive printed page (shown above).

The information is organized with an eye toward line-for-line scanning, and uses horizontal rules to reinforce that approach.

The type is Palatino throughout. Text set in all caps is generally difficult to read, but the choice works here for such a straightforward announcement of what, where, who, and when.

The illustration was drawn by hand and pasted manually onto the electronically composed page.

Design (above left): Diane Landskroener (Chestertown, MD)

Flyer for a recital at Washington College. Trim size: 8-1/2 by 11

Design (above right): Barbara Trupp; art production: Lisa Marks-Ellis, Synthesis Concepts (Chicago, IL)

Flyer for crafts sale. Trim size: 8-1/2 by 11

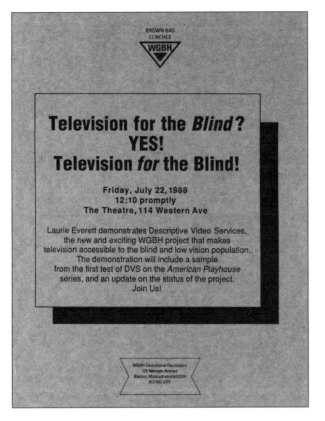

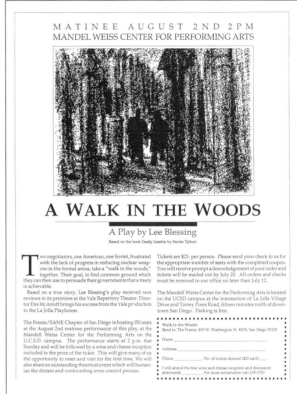

This simple format (above left), printed on brown kraft paper, announces events in a series of "brown bag lunch" lectures and demonstrations. The format establishes a strong identity for the series and is easy to execute for each event.

The shadowed box is a very simple attention-getting graphic. It is left in place on the template for the flyer so that only the type needs to be added for each new event.

The information above and below the boxed copy identifies the series and sponsor and is also a standing item in the template. It prints in red, so it looks stamped on.

The type is all from the Helvetica family.

Design (above left): Andrew Faulkner (Boston, MA)

Flyer for the WGBH brown bag lunches. Trim size: 8-1/2 by 11

A theater announcement (above right) features art based on the title of the play. The art originated as a charcoal drawing on very grainy paper. It was scanned at 72 dots per inch and resized proportionally in PageMaker, creating an image that has the feeling of a lithograph. Framing and centering the art in the formal layout increases its importance on the page.

The hairline border frames the page on three sides only. The dotted border around the coupon (from PageMaker's Lines menu) visually closes the bottom of the page and is an effective way to call attention to the coupon.

The typeface is Palatino, with contrast achieved through size, spacing, and placement. Note that in the two lines at the top of the page, the first line has open spacing and the second line normal spacing so that both are the same width as the art below. In PageMaker 4.0, you can use the Force Justify alignment option to create this effect. (To do so, you have to define the text width as the width of the art.) Note also the proportions in the rule treatment between the title and the author.

Design (above right): John Odam and Doris Bittar (San Diego, CA)

Flyer for a benefit performance for The San Diego Chapter of Freeze/SANE. Trim size: 8-1/2 by 11

This poster for a lecture by two pioneers of electronic art speaks in the language of their subject: the new technology and its impact on graphic design.

A digitized image of the two lecturers is printed almost life-size. The reduction on this page does not do justice to the impact of the 17- by 22-inch poster. This bold enlargement of a digitized image gives the feeling of a glimpse into the future. At a time when we are seeing more and more bit-mapped art (much of it bad), the raw power of the form is particularly evident in this large size.

The art originated as a slide. It was digitized in MacVision, saved as a MacPaint document, and scaled in PageMaker. The oversize page was tiled and pasted together manually.

The text is handled in three panels that jut into the picture plane. A second color (orange) highlights the first name of each speaker and the date and sponsor of the event.

Folded twice, the poster also serves as a self-mailer.

Quoting from the poster: "New electronic formats, including the personal computer, CD's, and video imaging systems, have opened up vast new visual possibilities and have inexorably drawn our profession into a communications environment which is multi-media and interactive. The formerly separate disciplines of writing, visualization, and sound making are joined through these tools. Eric predicts a return to the designer as generalist—fluent in more than one discipline—and feels we need to readjust our notion of what constitutes adequate training for this broader role."

Design: Chris Pullman, WGBH Design (Boston, MA)

Poster for AIGA/Boston lecture by April Greiman and Eric Martin.
Trim size: 17 by 22

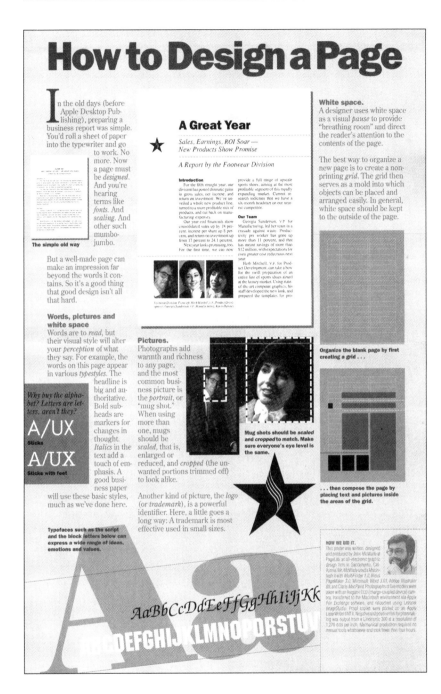

Design: John McWade, PageLab (Sacramento, CA)

Poster produced for Apple Computer as a takeaway promotion at Apple Business Forums.

Trim size: 11 by 17

The subject is again technology and design. But while the poster on the opposite page uses dramatic art to get the attention of artists, here an organized, business-like format presents a brief lesson on design for business people being introduced to desktop publishing.

The design successfully incorporates the elements it describes— bold, authoritative headlines, subheads for easy reference, the use of an underlying grid, mug shots cropped and scaled to the same size—both in the poster itself and in the sample page centered under the headline.

Another contrast: Although the poster on the opposite page used a limited number of electronic tools to good effect, this one uses a great many of them. Photographs of live models were taken with an Ikegami CCD (charge-coupled device) camera, transferred via Apple File Exchange to the Macintosh environment, and retouched using Image-Studio. Other software used included, in addition to PageMaker, Microsoft Word, Illustrator 88, and MacPaint. The designer bypassed the traditional mechanical and prepress work by supplying the printer with negative and positive film output from a Linotronic 300 at 1270 dots per inch. (At the time, the L300 could not print a tabloid-size page at 2540 dpi.)

FOLDERS

Folders provide a convenient format for promoting products, services, and events. The folded piece can be racked or mailed (either in a standard business envelope or as a self-mailer), and the fully open piece can be used as a poster. The folder format also works well for a series—educational literature and programs, for example; once you have a format worked out, you can make a template and reuse it for each piece in the series.

The mechanics of a folded piece present unique conceptual and design opportunities. Try to use the panels to organize and build on a message, to visually lead readers from the cover through the inside flaps to the fully open piece. A folder, especially a large one, requires more effort on the reader's part than a booklet or brochure, so you need to motivate the reader to begin unfolding the piece to get to the message.

The most common sizes for folders are 8-1/2 by 11 (generally folded in half to create four panels or folded twice to create six panels), 8-1/2 by 14 (generally folded into eight panels), and 11 by 17 (generally folded in half twice, or in half and then twice again). When planning the concept and layout, work at full size (you can tape together two or more sheets of paper if necessary) so that you can actually fold the piece and see it as the reader will. Once you have a pencil sketch in this form, you'll need to figure out the most efficient way to assemble the elements in PageMaker. For example, if you are doing an 8-1/2-by-14 folder, you might set it up as four 8-1/2- by 7-inch pages. Keep in mind, also, that flaps that fold in should be a half pica or so narrower than the other panels.

The mechanics of certain folds require that some panels be oriented sideways or upside down. Previously, this required manual pasteup. But with PageMaker's ability to rotate text in 90-degree increments, you should be able to create letter- and legal-size folders without any pasteup. If you want to make editorial changes (including type specifications) after the text is rotated, use the Story Editor.

Don't forget to indicate fold marks for the printer. For this purpose, insert dotted lines outside the image area on the camera-ready art.

Folders in this section

- *World Trade Institute*—a large-format program announcement
- *Slide Zone*—an accordion fold with a streamlined message
- *Drugs & Alcohol*—a strong, consistent format for a series of educational folders
- *Transpac*—a star unfolds
- *Colligan's Stockton Inn*—warm, friendly, and as suitable for mailing as it is for posting
- *InFractions*—the spotlight on fashion
- *The Man Who Planted Trees*—a program for an in-store event
- *Family Programs*—a poster format for three months of museum events
- *Historic Hudson Valley*—tourist attractions in an 11-by-17 format

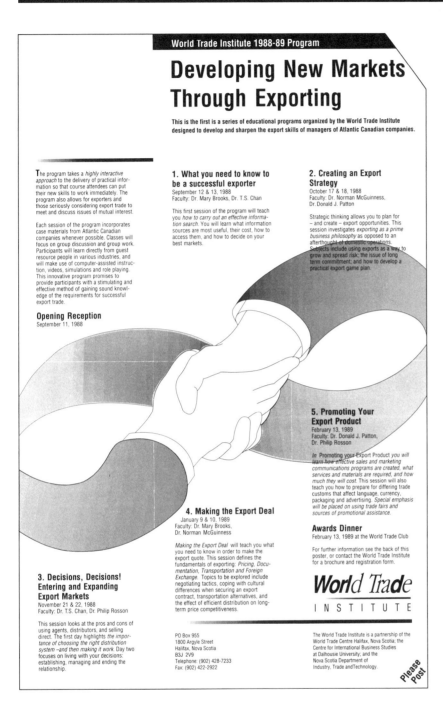

Design: Paul Hazell,
Communication Design Group Limited
(Halifax, Nova Scotia)

Folder for the World Trade Institute
training programs.
Trim Size: 11 by 17, folded in half and
then folded twice accordion style

The primary function of the cover of a folder is to get you to unfold it. And art that continues from one panel to another uses the physical properties of the format to achieve that purpose. In this sample, art bleeding off both sides of the cover leads the reader to the next panel (not shown), where the loops of the arms are completed. The fully open folder repeats the art.

The art was created in FreeHand and takes advantage of the program's graduated-tones feature, producing an airbrush-like effect.

The logo incorporates a subtly playful effect by transposing the sans serif d in "World" with the serif d in "Trade." Note also the spacing of the word "Institute" to match the length of the words above it.

The type is organized so that each panel contains a different text unit. This works particularly well for a program or series in which each event can be featured, as they are here. Numbering each event reinforces the organization.

The "Please Post" tab in the lower right is also visible in the half-folded position because of the cropped upper right corner.

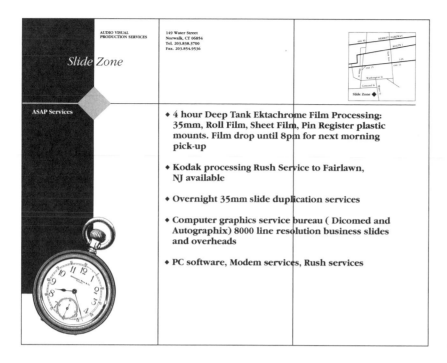

AUDIO VISUAL
PRODUCTION SERVICES

Slide Zone

ASAP Services

149 Water Street
Norwalk, CT 06854
Tel. 203.838.3700
Fax. 203.854.9536

Slide Zone ◆

- ◆ **4 hour Deep Tank Ektachrome Film Processing: 35mm, Roll Film, Sheet Film, Pin Register plastic mounts. Film drop until 8pm for next morning pick-up**

- ◆ **Kodak processing Rush Service to Fairlawn, NJ available**

- ◆ **Overnight 35mm slide duplication services**

- ◆ **Computer graphics service bureau (Dicomed and Autographix) 8000 line resolution business slides and overheads**

- ◆ **PC software, Modem services, Rush services**

The strong cover of this accordion-fold promotion opens to a single page handsome enough to tack up on the wall for reference.

The butting black-and-white panels, with the word "Slide" reversing out of the black, is the company logo. The negative-positive imagery is delightfully appropriate to the service—film and audio production. The diamond is repeated in the bulleted list and in the map, where it indicates the location of the business.

The clock dramatizes the focus of the folder, entitled ASAP Services. Bulleted copy specifies details for the rush services available.

The typeface is Garamond.

Design (above):
Weisz Yang Dunkelberger Inc.
(Westport, CT)

Folder from Slide Zone.
Trim size: 8-1/2 by 11, folded twice, accordion style

Rules, banners, geometric shapes, and initial caps provide organization and visual continuity for this series of educational pamphlets.

The display type is Avant Garde; the body text is Helvetica. The type prints in purple, and the rules and shapes print in rose. The colors vary from pamphlet to pamphlet.

Design (below): Jim Parker (Phoenix, AZ)

Drugs & Alcohol folder published by the Do It Now Foundation.
Trim size: 14 by 8-1/2, folded in half twice to create four panels

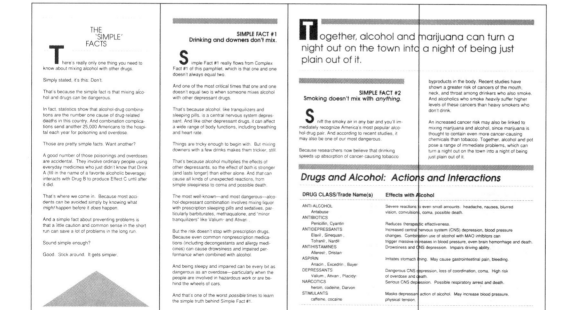

THE 'SIMPLE' FACTS

There's really only one thing you need to know about mixing alcohol with other drugs.

Simply stated, it's this: Don't.

That's because the simple fact is that mixing alcohol and drugs can be dangerous.

In fact, statistics show that alcohol-drug combinations are the number one cause of drug-related deaths in this country. And combination complications send another 25,000 Americans to the hospital each year for poisoning and overdose.

Those are pretty simple facts. Want another?

A good number of those poisonings and overdoses are accidental. They involve ordinary people using everyday medicines who just didn't know that Drink A (fill in the name of a favorite alcoholic beverage) interacts with Drug B to produce Effect C until after it did.

That's where we come in. Because most accidents can be avoided simply by knowing what *might* happen before it *does* happen.

And a simple fact about preventing problems is that a little caution and common sense in the short run can save a lot of problems in the long run.

Sound simple enough?

Good. Stick around. It gets simpler.

SIMPLE FACT #1
Drinking and downers don't mix.

Simple Fact #1 really flows from Complex Fact #1 of this pamphlet, which is that one and one doesn't always equal two.

And one of the most critical times that one and one doesn't equal two is when someone mixes alcohol with other depressant drugs.

That's because alcohol, like tranquilizers and sleeping pills, is a central nervous system depressant. And like other depressant drugs, it can affect a wide range of body functions, including breathing and heart rate.

Things are tricky enough to begin with. But mixing downers with a few drinks makes them trickier, still.

That's because alcohol multiplies the effects of other depressants, so the effect of *both* is stronger (and lasts longer) than either alone. And *that* can cause all kinds of unexpected reactions, from simple sleepiness to coma and possible death.

The most well-known—and most dangerous—alcohol-depressant combination involves mixing liquor with prescription sleeping pills and sedatives, particularly barbiturates, methaqualone, and "minor tranquilizers" like Valium· and Ativan·.

But the risk doesn't stop with prescription drugs. Because even common nonprescription medications (including decongestants and allergy medicines) can cause drowsiness and impaired performance when combined with alcohol.

And being sleepy and impaired can be every bit as dangerous as an overdose—particularly when the people are involved in hazardous work or are behind the wheels of cars.

And that's one of the worst *possible* times to learn the simple truth behind Simple Fact #1.

Together, alcohol and marijuana can turn a night out on the town into a night of being just plain out of it.

SIMPLE FACT #2
Smoking doesn't mix with *anything*.

Sniff the smoky air in any bar and you'll immediately recognize America's most popular alcohol-drug pair. And according to recent studies, it may also be one of our most dangerous.

Because researchers now believe that drinking speeds up absorption of cancer-causing tobacco

byproducts in the body. Recent studies have shown a greater risk of cancers of the mouth, neck, and throat among drinkers who also smoke. And alcoholics who smoke heavily suffer higher levels of these cancers than heavy smokers who don't drink.

An increased cancer risk may also be linked to mixing marijuana and alcohol, since marijuana is thought to contain even more cancer-causing chemicals than tobacco. Together, alcohol and pot pose a range of immediate problems, which can turn a night out on the town into a night of being just plain out of it.

Drugs and Alcohol: *Actions and Interactions*

DRUG CLASS/Trade Name(s)	Effects with Alcohol
ANTI-ALCOHOL Antabuse	Severe reactions to even small amounts. headache, nausea, blurred vision, convulsions, coma, possible death.
ANTIBIOTICS Penicillin, Cyantin	Reduces therapeutic effectiveness.

ANTIDEPRESSANTS
  Elavil , Sinequan ,
  Tofranil , Nardil·
	Increased central nervous system (CNS) depression, blood pressure changes. Combination use of alcohol with MAO inhibitors can trigger massive increases in blood pressure, even brain hemorrhage and death.

ANTIHISTAMINES Allerest , Dristan·	Drowsiness and CNS depression. Impairs driving ability.
ASPIRIN Anacin , Excedrin , Bayer	Irritates stomach lining. May cause gastrointestinal pain, bleeding.
DEPRESSANTS Valium , Ativan , Placidy·	Dangerous CNS depression, loss of coordination, coma. High risk of overdose and death.
NARCOTICS heroin, codeine, Darvon	Serious CNS depression. Possible respiratory arrest and death.
STIMULANTS caffeine, cocaine	Masks depressant action of alcohol. May increase blood pressure, physical tension.

This folder draws on the emotional connotations of the repeating image of the star; the red, white, and blue color scheme; and the corporate headquarters in the center of it all to solicit employee participation in the company's political action committee. The cover (not shown) sets the theme with an American flag in the same mixed-media art style as the panels shown.

The panels are integrated through the unfolding image of the star. When the panel seen on the far right, below, opens, the panel underneath it again completes the star. This is an effective use of the folder format to set a tone in the early panels before delivering specific information.

In the electronic pasteup, each panel was created as a separate 6-1/4- by 9-1/4-inch page and printed with crop marks.

The display text is 30/60 New Century Schoolbook with 72-point initial caps and letterspacing tightened to –8%. The left panel prints in blue, the right one in red.The two unseen panels on the fully open sheet contain running text set 10/12 in a two-column format.

Don't hesitate to combine traditional art with electronic pasteup. The precise, controlled effect of electronic drawing programs, the useful variety of clip art, and the digitized look of art generated in paint programs all provide a wide range of possiblities. But there's a whole world of nonelectronic illustration styles. The art used here has the spontaneous feeling of a colored pencil sketch, an effect we have yet to see produced on a computer.

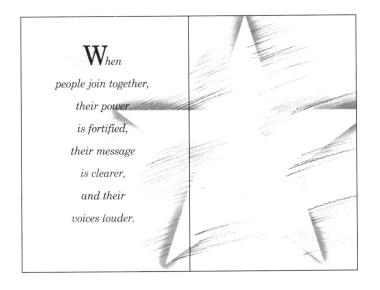

Design: Partners by Design (N. Hollywood, CA); agency: Jonisch Communications (Los Angeles, CA)

Folder from the Transamerica Corporation Political Action Committee. Trim size: 24-15/16 by 9-1/4, folded three times

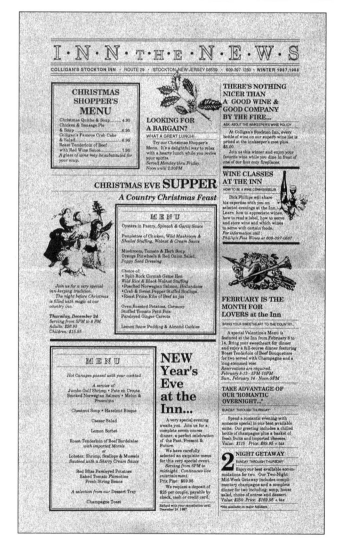

Designed for multiple use, this folder can be tacked up on bulletin boards fully open, while the folded piece functions as a self-mailer.

A warm, friendly, cheerful image is conveyed through the art style, typography, and newspaper-like composition. The flavor is just what you'd want from a country inn during the holiday season.

The typeface is New Century Schoolbook. It prints in green on a gray textured paper.

Borders and rules help organize the small items, which are set to different measures.

The art was created by hand and pasted onto camera-ready pages.

Each panel of this accordion-fold design (facing page, bottom) features a different clothes style. The panels were assembed on screen, two to a page, and two pages were pasted together for each four-panel side of the camera-ready art.

Silhouette photos work well for fashion because they highlight the shape of the clothes. The contrast between dark and light, front and back, and large and small adds to the casual liveliness of the composition. Although the larger photos share a common ground, the smaller ones bounce playfully around the page without regard for perspective. The interaction of the image with the background in a context that defies logic brings a fresh spatial energy to the page. Three additional styles, similarly formatted, are printed on the reverse side of the sheet.

The pattern through the center was created in PageMaker and echoes the subtler patten behind the logo. It's a decorative motif especially well suited for fashion literature.

The typeface is Goudy Old Style. Labeling is minimized to keep the spotlight on the clothes. The type and pattern print in teal blue with black accents.

Design (left):
Carla Bond Coutts
(Lahaska, PA)

Folder for
Colligan's
Stockton Inn.
Size: 8-1/2 by 14,
folded in half
twice

Design (facing
page, bottom):
Edward Hughes
(Evanston, IL)

Folder from
InFractions, Inc.
Trim size:
17-3/6 by 10-1/8,
folded three times
accordion style

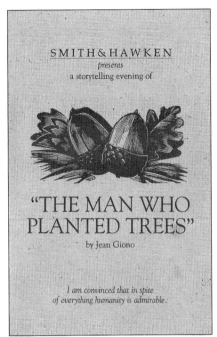

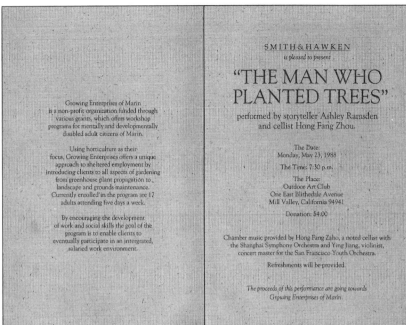

The traditional formality of centered type (above) is balanced by warm brown ink on oatmeal flecked paper.

The woodcut, a piece of art from the book featured at the event, was pasted in by hand.

The type is Goudy Old Style (except for the company logo, which is Palatino). The combination of bold, regular, and italic styles, the varied spacing, and the contrasting silhouettes of the different text blocks keep the centered alignment from becoming stiff or monotonous.

Design: Kathy Tomyris (Mill Valley, CA)

Program/announcement for an in-store performance.

Trim size: 11 by 8-1/2, folded once

A quarterly program of events is designed as a poster, with different styles of art interspersed throughout the listings. Folded, the piece is suitable for self-mailing and is also easily racked in the museum lobby and bookstore.

The headline and names of months are Franklin Gothic Demi. The listings are in the Helvetica family.

The use of color and the space around each listing make it very easy to check out the programs on any given date.The main headline, banners at the top of each column, highlighted events, and dates print in red.

All elements—art, borders, and Macintosh-generated type—were manually pasted onto artboard to create camera-ready art for the oversize pages.

Design: Ann Wassmann Gross (Chicago, IL)

Program from The Art Institute of Chicago. Trim size: 10-7/8 by 22-5/8, folded four times to create five panels

Family Programs · Fall'87

September

Sanat Şöleni: A Summer Festival of Turkish Arts
daily through September 7
12:00-3:00 Miniature Painting

Turkish Craft Demonstrations
through September 5
Tuesday, Thursday, Friday, and Saturday
12:30-2:30 Uğur Derman, Calligraphy
F. Çiçek Derman, Embroidery

Gallery Walks and Art Activities

Saturdays and Sundays, 2:00-4:00
Theme: Hispanic Arts in conjunction with the exhibition "Recent Developments in Latin American Drawing"
Saturday, September 12, 19, & 26
Sunday, September 13, 20, & 27

Artist Demonstration

Every Saturday and Sunday from 12:30-2:30
September: Carlos Cortez, Woodcut and linoleum-block printmaking

Arty Animals

Saturday, September 26   Age: 6 and older

Visit the Art Institute's galleries in the morning followed by a lunch break and tour of the Lincoln Park Zoo.

10:30-11:45	Gallery Walk: Animals in Art
11:45-1:00	Lunch on your own Provide your own transportation to zoo
1:00-2:30	Animal Walk: Lincoln Park Zoo
Cost:	$2.00 Member (adult or child) $3.00 Non-member (adult or child)

Name	# of children
Address	# of adults
City	State Zip Code
Telephone number	
Member	Non-member
$	
Amount enclosed	

Send check payable to *Museum Education*

Mail to: The Art Institute of Chicago
Department of Museum Education
Family Programs
Michigan Avenue at Adams Street
Chicago, IL 60603

October

Saturday, October 3
10:30-11:30   Early Birds: Once Upon a Time
1:00-2:00   Gallery Walk: American Art
2:00-4:00   Family Workshop: A Story in a Picture

Sunday, October 4
12:30-1:30   Early Birds: Once Upon a Time
12:30-1:30   Drawing in the Galleries
2:00-4:00   Family Workshop: A Story in a Picture

Saturday, October 10
10:30-11:30   Early Birds: Over and Under
1:00-2:00   Gallery Walk: That's What They Wore
2:00-4:00   Family Workshop: Weaving

Sunday, October 11
12:30-1:30   Early Birds: Over and Under
12:30-1:30   Drawing in the Galleries
2:00-4:00   Family Workshop: Weaving

Monday, October 12
1:00-3:00   Columbus Day Special: Family Workshop

Saturday, October 17
10:30-11:30   Early Birds: Animal Kingdom
1:00-2:00   Gallery Walk: Vase to Vase
2:00-4:00   Family Workshop: Symbolic Animals

Sunday, October 18
12:30-1:30   Early Birds: Animal Kingdom
12:30-1:30   Drawing in the Galleries
2:00-4:00   Family Workshop: Symbolic Animals

Saturday, October 24
10:30-11:30   Early Birds: Pablo's Palette
1:00-2:00   Gallery Walk: French Art
2:00-4:00   Family Workshop: The Eye of Picasso

Sunday, October 25
12:30-1:30   Early Birds: Pablo's Palette
12:30-1:30   Drawing in the Galleries
2:00-4:00   Family Workshop: The Eye of Picasso

Saturday, October 31
10:30-11:30   Early Birds: Tricks or Treats
1:00-2:00   Gallery Walk: Masks and Cover-ups
2:00-4:00   Family Workshop: 'Day of the Dead' Celebration

Artist Demonstration
Every Saturday and Sunday from 12:30-2:30
October: Noreen Czosnyka, The art of wall stenciling

Storytelling
Every Sunday from 2:00-3:00
October: Carmen Aguilar, Latin American folk tales

November

Sunday, November 1
12:30-1:30   Early Birds: Tricks or Treats
12:30-1:30   Drawing in the Galleries
2:00-4:00   Family Workshop: 'Day of the Dead' Celebration

Saturday, November 7
10:30-11:30   Early Birds: A Taste for Art
1:00-2:00   Gallery Walk: Portraits and Pictures
2:00-4:00   Family Workshop: The Delicious Still Life

Sunday, November 8
12:30-1:30   Early Birds: A Taste for Art
12:30-1:30   Drawing in the Galleries
2:00-4:00   Family Workshop: The Delicious Still Life

Saturday, November 14
10:30-11:30   Early Birds: Funny Food
1:00-2:00   Gallery Walk: Travel Plans
2:00-4:00   Family Workshop: Soft Sculpture

Sunday, November 15
12:30-1:30   Early Birds: Funny Food
12:30-1:30   Drawing in the Galleries
2:00-4:00   Family Workshop: Soft Sculpture

Saturday, November 21
10:30-11:30   Early Birds: Blue Plate Special
1:00-2:00   Gallery Walk: Art of Italy
2:00-4:00   Family Workshop: Designing Dishes

Sunday, November 22
12:30-1:30   Early Birds: Blue Plate Special
12:30-1:30   Drawing in the Galleries
2:00-4:00   Family Workshop: Designing Dishes

Friday, November 27
1:00-3:00   Special: "Day After Thanksgiving" Workshop

Saturday, November 28
10:30-11:30   Early Birds: Incredible Edibles
1:00-2:00   Gallery Walk: Animal Kingdom
2:00-4:00   Family Workshop: Edible Art

Sunday, November 29
12:30-1:30   Early Birds: Incredible Edibles
12:30-1:30   Drawing in the Galleries
2:00-4:00   Family Workshop: Edible Art

Artist Demonstration

Every Saturday and Sunday from 12:30-2:30
November: Lorraine Peltz, Still Life painting

Storytelling

Every Sunday from 2:00-3:00
November: Assorted tales by assorted tellers

Historic Hudson Valley

Kitchen at Van Cortlandt Manor

View of West Point from the Highlands

Miniatures at Montgomery Place

Matisse Window, Union Church of Pocantico Hills

Settled largely by ambitious and adventure-some immigrants from Europe, the Hudson Valley saw great tracts of land held by single families and cultivated by tenant farmers. Frederick Philipse came to New Amsterdam from Holland as a carpenter and soon owned better than 50,000 acres of land. From the wharf at Philipsburg Manor, Upper Mills, flour and other goods were shipped to ports all over the world. Today, young visitors enjoy the antics of spring lambs on the

farm, while watching early American technology at work in the water-powered grist mill.

Owners of the vast Van Cortlandt Manor were among the most influential families in New York as the new American nation emerged. Pierre Van Cortlandt was the state's first Lieutenant Governor and his son Philip served both as an army officer under General Washington and as a United States Congressman. Visitors to the Manor today find elegant antiques and beautifully restored gardens which capture the spirit of this leading Hudson River Valley family.

Washington Irving, famed author of "Rip Van Winkle" and "The Legend of Sleepy Hollow," often said that in all his European travels he had seen nothing to compare with the view of the Hudson from the porch at Sunnyside. Irving transformed what had been a small, Dutch farm cottage on the Philipse Manor into a picturesque country home he

*Philipsburg Manor (above)
Christmas at Sunnyside (left)*

called his "snuggery." Winding pathways along the river, hillsides of daffodils in the spring and the cozy, hospitable atmosphere of Sunnyside combine to make today's visitors feel they have been the guests of this eminent Hudson Valley squire.

Albany • • Troy

Kingston •

• Montgomery Place

• Hyde Park

Newburgh •

• Cold Spring

West Point •

Bear Mountain

■ Van Cortlandt Manor

■ Philipsburg Manor

■ Union Church

■ Tarrytown

■ Sunnyside

New York City
•

Montgomery Place, one of the ancestral homes of the Hudson Valley's prominent Livingston family, will open to the public in June, 1988. The 23-room mansion was built by Janet Livingston Montgomery, widow of Revolutionary War hero General Richard Montgomery, and later remodeled by America's leading 19th-century architect, Alexander Jackson Davis. Visitors will want to linger on the more than 400 acres of land at Montgomery Place, savoring the beauty of the woods, streams and gardens, taking in the views of the river and the Catskill Mountains, and picking fall apples in the estate's orchards.

Montgomery Place, Annandale-on-Hudson

A unique complement to the other properties of **Historic Hudson Valley** is the Union Church of Pocantico Hills, where light is transformed into vivid color through stained glass windows created by modern masters Henri Matisse and Marc Chagall. The modest stone sanctuary contains the only cycle of church windows by Chagall in the United States.

The collections of **Historic Hudson Valley** represent in every detail the people who have lived on the banks of the river. At each of the four historic properties, original family and authentic period furnishings, objects and works of art are on display. Paintings by many important American artists are apparent, as are children's toys, handwoven textiles and looms, simple kitchen utensils and farm implements, fine porcelains and silver.

*Van Cortlandt Manor (right)
Philipsburg Manor (below)*

Design: Wadlin & Erber (New Paltz, NY)

*Folder published by
Historic Hudson Valley.
Trim size: 11 by 17, folded in half and
then twice again*

The elements needed to promote tourism work well in this 11-by 17-inch sheet, folded first in half and then in thirds.

The front cover, with its oval-shaped detail of an old engraving and centered format, suggests that this is the official guide to the region.

The tall orientation of the fully open sheet works well for a stylized map of the river valley. The river prints in blue, the surrounding valley in green. A detailed road map appears on the back cover (not shown).

A five-column format accommodates photos of different sizes and shapes to break up the text.

The photographs, all in color, were stripped in by the printer. Picture frames were positioned during electronic pasteup to facilitate the text wrap.

For electronic pasteup, the designer set up a file of two 11-by-17 pages, with all of the type right-reading. For the side that would be read partially folded (on which half of the 11-by-17 page prints upside down relative to the other half), the L100 output was cut in half and pasted by hand to create the proper imposition of each panel for folding. (Earlier LaserWriter proofs were tiled and pasted together for client approval.)

BROCHURES

Brochures provide a broader creative challenge than many other kinds of publications. Because they are generally one-shot efforts, intended for use over a relatively long period, more time, effort, planning, and money is often allocated to their development. The challenge, for writers and designers, is to come up with a theme or concept that is unique to the needs of that message for that audience at that particular time. The solution should *look* obvious once it is executed, although of course the conception and development of that absolutely right idea may have taken months of research, analysis, brainstorming, and rethinking of hypotheses, as well as many rounds of rough sketches and format changes along the way.

As the samples in this section demonstrate, there is considerable variety from one brochure to another and even within the pages of a single brochure. The styles are as diverse as the messages they convey; they range from straightforward simplicity to complex persuasion, from the stylishly new wave to the classically elegant, from the quietly dignified to the boisterously bold.

Even the size and shape of the page varies more in brochures than in other kinds of publications. This is partly because brochures are often produced in small press runs where the cost of paper isn't so critical, and partly because brochures often have generous budgets that can absorb the increased cost of a nonstandard paper size. As you'll see in some of the samples, an unusual size or an odd shape feels fresh to the eye just because it's different. Of course nonstandard sizes also give designers an opportunity to create unusual solutions to familiar problems and to play with the shape itself as part of the design motif. But unless the solution is a good one, the shape alone won't carry the message.

Brochures in this section

- *inFidelity: Keith Yates Audio*—stylishly active design
- *Clackamas Community College*—a strong, simple concept
- *Pitney Bowes Mail Management*—a lesson in variety
- *Westchester 2000*—structure and style from vertical headlines
- *Westinghouse Transportation Systems*—highly organized and accessible
- *Why Design?*—a five-column grid with punch
- *European Terracotta Sculpture*—quiet sophistication
- *Syracuse University College of Law*—markedly horizontal
- *Viva Tijuana shopping mall*—a large, bold, double gatefold
- *River Park Cooperative*—quiet quality in the shape of a square
- *Seybold Desktop Publishing Conference*—a stylish conference brochure
- *Subscription Programs*—compact information in an elegant format
- *Islam and the West*—the photographic story of a TV series
- *Sacramento Regional Foundation*—bit-mapped art and mug shots
- *Doane Raymond Accountants*—organized serendipity
- *Extending Desktop Publishing*—A showcase for technology and art

A sales brochure that calls itself a newsletter borrows editorial techniques from the newsletter format.

Each product is treated as a self-contained unit with its own design, and each spread has a different composition. The contrast and varied texture make each spread feel like a collage.

Two unifying elements balance the seemingly dominant diversity: an underlying four-column grid and a stylishly high-tech design that provides its own continuity.

Silhouette photos focus attention on and dramatize the product.

Computer-assembled gray tones of different values, such as the light gray of the first two letters of the logo against the darker gray of the banner, register perfectly. In traditional pasteup it would be virtually impossible to achieve a clean edge with overlapping gray tones.

*Design:
John McWade,
PageLab
(Sacramento, CA)*

*Brochure published by Keith Yates Audio.
Size: 8-3/8 by 10-3/4*

A simple concept, well executed, makes for a very effective four-color recruitment brochure for a small college.

The cover borrows techniques from advertising design, with large, centered display type expressing a single bold statement. When you use this technique, the statement had better be right on target for your audience.The inside pages answer the question implied on the cover.

Each spread follows an identical layout, creating a strong sense of continuity that orients readers very quickly to the information on the page. This would become monotonous in a longer publication. (Two additional spreads, not shown, do vary from this format, and a bind-in card provides a checklist of additonal information the prospective student can request.)

The strong concept and controlled continuity of the layout require considerable planning. Creating and refining pencil sketches before you begin work on the computer can save a lot of time in this sort of project.

Each spread uses a different color scheme keyed to the box in the upper left corner. (The number in that box prints in reverse type.) The color is used in the banner above the student quote and as a tone behind the boxed copy on the right-hand page.

The bleed photos on the inside spreads heighten the strong horizontal axis created by the rule above them. Actually, there are elements that bleed on all four sides of the spread, setting up a visual tug of war that makes the pages very dynamic.

The principle of contrast is used very effectively here. The angled photos on the right-hand pages contrast with the crisp, clean rectangles that dominate the rest of the layout. These photos are also black and white, whereas the others are in color. And the two small photos play off against the one large one on each spread.

The typeface is Garamond throughout.
  Body text:12/20
  Captions: 9/11 italic
  Numbers: 96 point
  Headline: 60 point condensed

Condensed Garamond has recently been very "hot" in display typography. Few readers are aware on a conscious level that a particular font is in fashion, but there are subliminal effects to seeing a typeface that has a lot of media penetration. As is true with any kind of fashion, trends in typography change quickly.

"Give me three good reasons to come to Clackamas."

Design:
Ralph Rawson
(Oregon City, OR)

A student recruitment brochure for Clackamas Community College.
Trim: 8-1/2 by 11

Chrissy Pagh
Freshman, Gladstone
"I chose Clackamas because I knew the quality of the classes was equal to a four-year school, without having to pay the money. I haven't had a teacher yet who hasn't been great. And because the classes are small, there's a lot more inter-action and a lot more learning."

3. A price you can afford.

Tuition at CCC is $23 per credit hour, or $230 per term for a full-time student.* That's less than half the cost of tuition at a state university, and a fraction of what you'd pay at many private colleges. It adds up to a sensible, economical solution to the rising cost of a college education.

"Can I get financial aid?"
Last year, nearly half of CCC's full-time students received some kind of financial aid — an average of ~~~~~~~~~~ work study pro-

Neale Frothingham
Sophomore, Oregon City
"Having been here for a year, and realiz-ing how good the instruction is, I realize I made the best choice educationally that I ever could have made. The size of CCC definitely enhances the quality of educa-tion. It's very personal."

2. Courses that count.

Planning to transfer to a four-year institution?
All lower division college transfer courses at Clackamas Community College are fully accredited and transferable to any college or university in Oregon, and to public and private institutions throughout the country. ~~~~~ can take your freshman and soph-~~~~~~~~~~ a junior to

CCC graduate Laura Onstott
(with chemistry instructor Margi Arighi)
"Margi made the class interesting, and fun, and always challenging. She always made me feel that I could succeed. By the end of that year, I knew I wanted to get a degree in chemistry." (Laura, now a senior at Reed College, was recently awarded a scholarship by the American Chemical Society.)

1. Teachers who care.

In class and students get Opportuniti theatre, spe instrument student got student ne mural spo 20 specia ranging mountai

Clackamas Community College is a public two-year college with an annual enrollment of 2400 full-time and 8600 part-time students. The campus is located on 175 acres of forest and farm-land in the foothills of the Oregon Cascades, 20 miles southeast of downtown Portland.

Personal attention to your learning needs comes first at Clackamas Community College. Our classes are small (average size: 21 students). Our teachers can take the time to get to know you, to find out where you're going, and to help you get there. Our total commitment is to make your college experience a success.

At Clackamas, you can explore creative writing with an award-winning novelist, learn algebra with the man who wrote the textbook, or play in the band with some of Oregon's most sought after musicians. CCC's faculty includes nationally recognized experts on sub-jects ranging from computer-aided drafting to Middle Eastern history.

But our most important recognition comes from former CCC students. In surveys, letters, and inter-views, they consistently say that the personal attention they got at Clackamas was a major reason for their success — in college and beyond.

Everything you need to succeed.
CCC backs up your classroom experience with first-rate student support services, including

❏ Program planning with CCC's expert team of counselors and advisors.
❏ Career planning and job placement assistance with the resources of CCC's Career & Job Development Center.
❏ Personal tutoring by CCC instructors and advanced students.
❏ The Computer Lab, with tutors on hand to help you build vital math and computer skills.
❏ And, if you're not yet ready for college level course-work, individualized instruction in basic reading, writing, math, and study skills (including high school completion programs).

Clackamas Community College is an equal opportunity, affirmative action institution.

An ambitious, high-budget production gives both the company and the designer an opportunity to dramatize their message. Although the resources to execute a brochure like this may be beyond your budget, the publication has elements you can incorporate in more a modest undertaking.

The story in this brochure is that managing mail is a complex business. The opening page (not shown) contains a single small photo of a row of rural mailboxes and begins, "There was a time when getting the mail out was pretty simple...." When you turn to the page shown below, the helter-skelter array symbolizes the choices, the pace, and the complexities of today's mail.

The words put the pictures into context, and the pictures dramatize the words. The story, as it unfolds on the next spread (not shown), is that increasingly complex mail systems require increasingly complex paperwork. But "Whatever you're sending, no matter where, we can show you how to get it there, how to prepare it for going, how to account for it after it's gone."

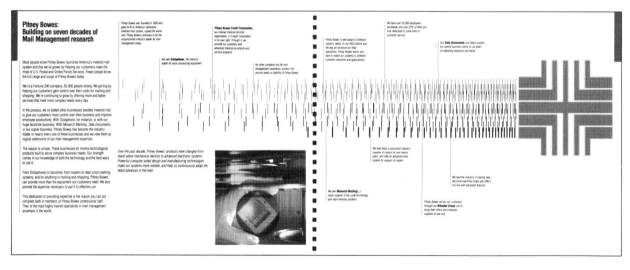

The direct statement of what Pitney Bowes is and what products it offers is presented as time-line-style captions to a piece of art that suggests the speed and intelligence of today's technology. The symbol on the far right is the company logo.

The information is broken down into accessible pieces. The very direct, well-written statement in the left column is only about 250 words long, with very short paragraphs. Each captionlike statement describes a different service or division of the company.

The strong, three-column grid is apparent when you compare the spread shown above to the one at right. The horizontal structure that runs across both is maintained throughout the 34 pages. This grid brings a feeling of order and control to pages that contain a wide variety of photos, charts, diagrams, documents, and other visuals.

The large photo in the spread below introduces a new service and adds yet another texture as you turn the pages.

Subtle graphic humor is seen throughout the brochure. A tortoise-and-hare metaphor is used in the diagram on this spread to compare the old and new meter refill service.

The typeface throughout the brochure is Helvetica Condensed for body text, Helvetica Condensed Black for headlines, and Helvetica Condensed Oblique for captions and for contrast with the opening text. The type treatment is kept simple to balance the diversity of the art and layout, with a crisp, modern, efficient look that is obviously appropriate to the subject.

Design: Weisz Yang Dunkelberger Inc. (Westport, CT)

Pitney Bowes brochure entitled Building on Seven Decades of Mail Management Expertise. Trim size: 11-1/4 by 8-1/2

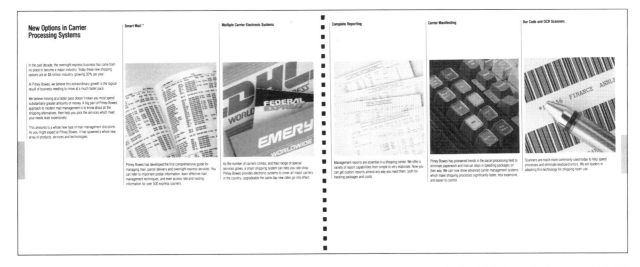

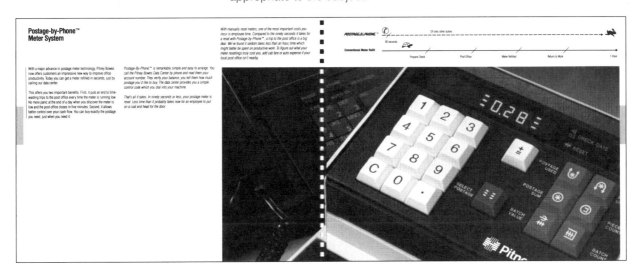

The structure of the grid is most apparent in the spread shown above. The sequence of photos with headings above and text below suggests a series of pigeonholes that echo the partitioning inherent in sorting mail. The grid reinforces an image in which nothing is accidental, everything is tightly choreographed.

The nine-unit grid used in this brochure is diagramed at right. It provides a useful structure for organizing a horizontal page.

Both the structure and the personality of this format come from the large vertical headlines and the bold rules with graduated gray tones.

The vertical headlines are New Century Schoolbook italic. They function as section heads and can be placed in any column except the far right one.

The banners with graduated gray tones were created in Cricket Draw. In the days before desktop technology, this effect had to be rendered by an airbrush artist, and then shot and stripped in as a separate half-tone. Today's electronic drawing programs offer a variety of graduated tonal and screen effects that can be employed simply by clicking through a myriad of choices until you get the effect you want.

The headlines within the columns are Helvetica bold italic. The running text is New Century Schoolbook. The quotations inset in the running text are Helvetica italic.

The bottom rule and column rules provide enough structure for the page to allow ragged right and ragged bottom text.

All art and photos have a 1-point rule around them. This is a good technique for unifying photos of varying qualities throughout a publication.

The oversize pages were manually tiled in two sections of 8-1/2- by 11-inch pages printed in the landscape orientation on a LaserWriter. Tiling divides oversize pages into smaller blocks, or tiles, each of which prints on a separate sheet of paper. When tiling manually, you reposition the zero point to specify where each tile starts. In this publication, all of the top sections were printed first, with the zero point in the upper left corner of the page. Then the zero point was moved to the 8-inch point on the vertical ruler to print the bottom half of all the pages. The top and bottom tiles of each page were then manually pasted together at the best breaking point for that page.

Design: Gan Y. Wong (Hoboken, NJ)

Brochure published as a promotional supplement to the Gannett Westchester Newspapers.
Trim size: 11-1/2 by 13-3/4

Westinghouse Transportation
Systems and Support
Division

Overview

Westinghouse Electric Corporation has more than 100 years of transportation experience as a leading supplier of electric propulsion and automatic train control systems for mass transit applications. Westinghouse also pioneered the development and application of automated people mover technology with more operating systems worldwide than any other company.

The purpose here is to organize simple material in a clean, orderly way. Doing that well makes a strong statement about the company's image.

The cover is a quick, businesslike summary of the brochure, an 11- by 17-inch sheet folded once.

The type is Helvetica Light, Helvetica Black, and Helvetica Black Oblique. The light, black, and condensed Helvetica faces provide a range of weights and styles within the same highly legible type family, which is why you see them frequently in this book and elsewhere.

The total measure of the two columns is the same on both pages, but on the left it's a narrow and a wide column, whereas on the right it's two equal columns.

Although this brochure is all text, you could easily introduce photos, charts, and diagrams into this format.

Design:
Agnew, Moyer, Smith
(Pittsburgh, PA)

Brochure for the Westinghouse Transportation Systems and Support Division.
Size: 8-1/2 by 11

Overview

Westinghouse Transportation Locations
The Westinghouse Transportation Systems and Support Division (WTSSD) is headquartered in suburban Pittsburgh, Pennsylvania and operates from two facilities:
• Allegheny County Airport Site (ACAS)
• Lebanon Church Site (LCS)

Total office and manufacturing space is nearly 271,000 square feet.

WTSSD has approximately 25 field locations in the United States, Canada, United Kingdom and Taiwan.

Employes
WTSSD employs about 800 personnel at its two locations near Pittsburgh, and about 125 at its various field sites.

People Mover Test Track
This automated facility, located at the LCS site, is 1570 feet long with a 10 percent grade for testing vehicle acceleration and deceleration, all vehicle operating systems, and includes a hydraulic guideway switch with a turn-out spur. Snow-making equipment enables the simulation of winter climate conditions.

Business Segments and Product Offerings

Original Equipment
AC and DC mass transit propulsion equipment, advanced automatic train controls (ATC), and complete automated people mover systems.

Mass transit propulsion equipment	ATC system components	People mover systems
• Air-operated cam	• Car-carried	• Airport
• Electrically-operated cam	• Wayside	• Downtown
• Solid-state thyristor chopper	• Station	• Commercial
• AC inverter	• Central	

After-Sales Customer Support
Parts, equipment, and services to operate and maintain mass transit and people mover systems. Designed to manage and maintain system configuration.

Customer support products and services
• Renewal parts and components
• Field engineering services
• Training programs
• Documentation
• Diagnostic services
• Reliability analyses

Mass Transit Contracts

Bay Area Rapid Transit in San Francisco, California
The first automated mass transit system began operation in 1972 with Westinghouse propulsion and ATC. The original 450-carset order represented the world's first production order for chopper control. In 1984, 120 additional carsets were ordered.

São Paulo Metro Transit System
First international application of automatic train control integrated with solid-state chopper-controlled propulsion; began operation in 1975.

Rio de Janeiro Metro Transit System
Microprocessors were applied to chopper propulsion for the first time; began operation in 1979.

Southeastern Pennsylvania Transit Authority System in Philadelphia, Pennsylvania
First chopper application to a light rail vehicle by Westinghouse; began operation in 1981.

Washington Metropolitan Area Transit Authority
Operating 300 cam-controlled cars with Westinghouse equipment since system start-up in 1976; add-on orders for 366 carsets of both cam and chopper propulsion were completed in 1987.

Vancouver Regional Transit System/BC Transit in Vancouver, British Columbia
First application of Westinghouse chopper propulsion to trolley buses. In 1982, 245 new buses began operation using Westinghouse equipment.

New York City Transit Authority
Over 3000 cars of the existing fleet are powered by Westinghouse cam propulsion systems. In 1987, Westinghouse received an order for 200 carsets of cam control equipment for the new R68A fleet.

Baltimore and Miami Metros
The first joint procurement project to obtain Urban Mass Transit Adminstration funding totalled 208 new cars and began operation in 1983. Baltimore has since ordered 28 additional carsets.

Niagara Frontier Transportation Authority in Buffalo, New York
Ordered 28 carsets of Westinghouse chopper propulsion equipment for its new light rail transit system; operation began in early 1985.

Massachusetts Bay Transportation Authority in Boston, Massachusetts
Awarded a 54-carset order in 1983 for Westinghouse to supply motors and gears with cam-controlled propulsion for the South Shore #2 heavy rail cars. One hundred carsets of light rail vehicle equipment with dual chopper control were also ordered at the same time.

Port Authority Trans Hudson in New York and New Jersey
Westinghouse has supplied PATH propulsion equipment since its inception, twenty-five years ago. A rehabilitation contract and a new car contract totalling 343 carsets of cam propulsion equipment were awarded in 1985.

Municipality of Metropolitan Seattle in Washington
Westinghouse is supplying 236 carsets of AC inverter propulsion for Seattle's new dual-mode trolley buses. This order represents the largest AC propulsion fleet in North America.

2

3

The organization of complex, multitiered information is the fundamental challenge in many publications. This tutorial about the effective use of electronic design addresses that very issue and uses the techniques it espouses. Information is broken into manageable "chunks," and the importance of different elements is made readily apparent through the use of headlines, rules, numbers, and color.

The handwritten annotations are red; the 6-point rules above headlines, the highlighted quote, and the marginal copy are green. Red and green spot color is also used in the diagrams.

The format combines different kinds of editorial material—running text, charts and diagrams, numbered points, quotes offset from the main text, and even handwritten annotations of typeset words. The mix of techniques gives readers different ways to enter the page. It must be carefully organized in order not to backfire.

The five-column grid uses an 8-pica measure with 1 pica between columns. The wider columns in the top spread are 17 picas wide (two of the five-column units plus the space between).

The typography adheres to the principles of simplicity and familiarity—Helvetica and Times Roman are used throughout.

The diagrams were created in Cricket Draw.

Design: Watzman + Keyes (Cambridge, MA)

Brochure entitled Why Design? *published by Watzman + Keyes Information Design.*
Trim size: 8-1/2 by 11

Information Design

The visual

Automation and Communication
Most users of electronic publishing focus on automation and assume that communication will take care of itself. They are mismanaging the technology and missing rare opportunities to achieve three things simultaneously:
• Increase impact and effectiveness by ensuring that information gets noticed, understood, used and remembered.
• Develop proprietary, customized systems of graphic standards to ensure quality and consistency, increase market visibility and streamline the production of communication materials.
• Leverage the value and competitive advantage that EP technology promises by encoding standards in software and systems as proprietary templates or style sheets.

Critical Trends
The following trends affect you and your organization's bottom line:

Growing Demand for Customer Services
The profusion of "smart" products has led to demand for materials which explain them. Clearly, products a customer does not understand, serve neither the customers nor the maker. Careful attention to passive ...

Diminishing Labor Supply
The U.S. faces a severe labor shortage at a time when communication skills are at a premium. Since electronic publishing requires skilled professionals, the gap is widening. Design cannot be automated any more than writing can be ...

Growing Internal Demand for Publishing Services
When customers demand service, managers demand more support – and control and faster turnaround. Electronic publishing creates demand, accelerates production, and decentralizes a process which, because it used to be slow, ...

Information Overload
There really is such a thing as "too much information." When people are bombarded with more information than they need or can use, their performance actually suffers. Too much information *increases* error-making, *reduces* attentiveness, and *induces* boredom and dissatisfaction. This is a clinical fact ... business.

9

The Need for Corporate-Wide Graphic Standards Systems (CoGSS)©

The current emphasis of electronic publishing vendor marketing is on the *freedom* and *flexibility* which their systems provide to individual users. But the "Sorcerer's Apprentice Problem" makes clear that *decentralization* and *loss of corporate control* in the visible area of communications is not good for business. The result is *decreasing quality, decreasing effectiveness, loss of corporate image* and *poor product recognition.*

But electronic publishing technology has another capability which has yet to be developed: it can set consistent, well-defined, customized default standards for published materials (CoGSS). Such standards eliminate much of the time-consuming activity that goes into publishing. At the same time, standards enforce quality and consistency by providing a matrix of solutions to a broad range of communication needs.

The Information Design Perspective: Cognitive Human Factors as a Basis for Design

CoGS Systems produce two outcomes:
First, they provide dramatic managerial control over staff use of money, time and materials. They do this by providing a matrix of predetermined solutions to communication problems. Typical problems are solved in advance, or solved the first time they occur. After that, producers of communication materials are guided by clear procedures which ensure consistency and quality.

Second, CoGS Systems significantly enhance the value of printed materials by using human factors techniques to improve the usefulness of information to readers. With "smart" products which require extensive documentation or complex sales messages, improving reader response has a significant impact on sales, marketing efforts, customer satisfaction, customer service and training costs.

As a growing number of leading companies are discovering, arriving at a performance-oriented CoGS System makes good business sense. Approaching the problem requires skill and knowledge in four areas:

Sensitivity to the importance of careful, informative, writing;

Background in the relatively new field of cognitive human factors;

Education and experience in design and the development of Corporate Graphic Standards Systems;

Familiarity with the proliferating range of EP technologies.

"Information is easier to remember when it is in an orderly state, rich in pattern and structure, highly interconnected, containing a good deal of redundancy. Disordered information that lacks structure is easy to forget."
Jeremy Campbell
Grammatical Man

10

Developing a CoGS System

Because of the range of disciplines required to develop a CoGS System (and the short-term nature of the projects), companies often turn to outside firms for assistance–and do so before they buy electronic publishing equipment.

Based on experience with Fortune 500 companies, threshold companies and high technology start-ups, Watzman+Keyes has developed a six-stage process for developing a CoGS Systems. The process insures that the system uses *both* capabilities of electronic publishing: it *improves* staff productivity and *enhances* user satisfaction and performance. This six-stage process incorporates research, design, testing and training into an efficient cycle that gives clients cost-effective solutions prior to automation.

The Information Design Process: Six Steps to a Graphic Standards System

Analysis — Development — Production
1 Define, 2 Examine, 3 Design, 4 Test, 5 Codify, 6 Monitor

What is Information Design?
Information design is a truly professional process which integrates technology, design and cognitive science to achieve three goals:
1 *Streamline* the process of creating documents and communication materials.
2 *Improve* the impact, effectiveness and quality of communication programs and materials.
3 *Manage* the transition to high technology-based print communication programs.

Phase 1: Define
Define the business problem. Who is sending the message? for what purpose? using what technologies? What constraints exist (budgets or staffing, etc.)? What degree of control or decentralization is advisable or realistic? This phase ends in a *compilation and review.*

Phase 2: Examine
Understand the users. Who are they? How do they use information ? What are their backgrounds and educational levels? Do they have unusual constraints? This and Phase 1, are a complete *communication audit.*

Phase 3: Develop
Brief the design team so they can develop design alternatives (several alternatives are necessary for valid testing). This results in a *presentation of alternatives* to the staff who will use the CoGS System.

Phase 4: Test
According to Nobel Laureate and A.I. expert, Herbert Simon, "Design is both the *development* and *testing* of alternatives." In this phase, alternatives are subjected to cognitive testing. The results are used to *refine* the CoGS System.

Phase 5: Codify
Once the CoGS System is developed it can be codified in software or in a manual. These products are used to train staff about the CoGSS System. Electronic publishing *fundamentally alters* the way documents are produced and the way people work, so this phase includes training in teamwork as well as system familiarity.

Phase 6: Monitor
This phase ensures that the system does the two things it is supposed to do: helps *staff* be productive and helps *users* learn complex equipment and tasks easily.

11

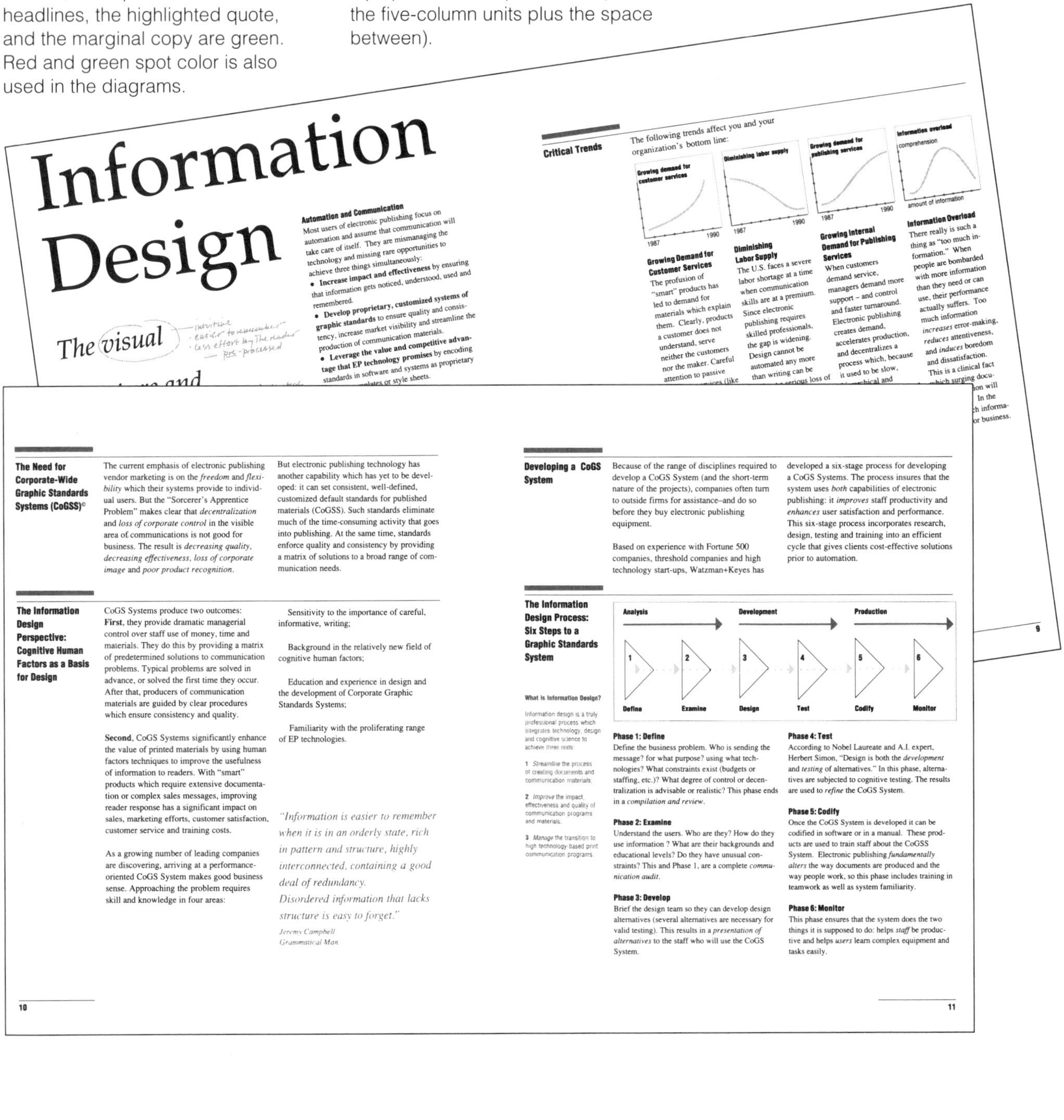

European Terracotta Sculpture

from the Arthur M. Sackler Collections

The Art Institute of Chicago / December 9, 1987 - March 6, 1988

*end of the eighteenth century. Clodion's ex-
quisite terracotta statuettes (nos. 19 and 20)
captivated Rococo collectors. In his suite,
Neoclassical sculptors, such as Simon Louis
Boizot (no. 22) and Joseph Chinard (no. 23),
perfected his smooth, sensuous surfaces.
French artists also adopted the medium for
the portrait bust, enlivening this formal type
with the vivacity of touch possible in terracotta. Pajou, in his Bust of Corbin de Cordet
de Florensac (no. 24), achieves a sense of
motion and captures the sitter's alert gaze
with the flicker of a modeling tool through the
hair and incisions in the pupils. Such Rococo
portrait conventions were revived in the nine-
teenth century by Carrier-Belleuse (no. 29).
Nineteenth- and twentieth-century sculptors
flaunted the rugged surfaces of worked clay.
The brooding power of Rodin's Titans (no.
31) is emphasized by the retention of the
scumbled surfaces and blocky musculature
of the figures in their adaptation to the form
of a vase. Jagged, seemingly random gouges
in Vallmitjana's Wounded Bullfighter (no.
30) underline the violence of the subject. The
deliberate roughness of Martini's figural
studies expresses barely containable energy
(no. 33).
Changing attitudes toward terracotta over
the six centuries represented in this exhibition
are representative of similar developments
throughout the visual arts. One is the shift in
attitude toward the medium; it is less important to us today what materials are used by the
artist than how they are manipulated. Another
is our desire to see the traces of the artist's
encounter with the medium—our interest in
the process of creation as well as the finished
product. These beautiful studies and finished
works amply demonstrate the role of terracotta in the development of sculpture from the
Renaissance to the twentieth century.
This exhibition has been selected from over
one hundred examples in the Arthur M.*

*Sackler collections. In 1981-82 a larger exhi-
bition of these holdings circulated to The
National Gallery of Art, Washington, D. C.,
The Metropolitan Museum of Art, New York,
and the Fogg Museum, Boston. It is a great
pity that Dr. Sackler's death last May pre-
vented him from the pleasure of seeing his
objects in this and other exhibitions from his
collections presented this year. We are most
grateful to the Sackler Foundation for continuing with plans for this show at such a difficult time and for its generous support for this
project. Dr. Lois Katz, Administrator of the
Sackler Foundation, has provided invaluable
advice and assistance.*

*Ian Wardropper
Associate Curator
European Decorative Arts and Sculpture*

*This exhibition was funded by The AMS Founda
tion for the Arts, Sciences and Humanities,
Washington, D.C. and the Arthur M. Sackler
Foundation, Washington, D.C.
The Chicago exhibition was partially supported
by the John D. and Catherine T. MacArthur
Foundation Special Exhibitions Grant.*

Jan Baptiste Van der Haegen
Flemish, 1688–c. 1740
Saint Joseph Holding the Christ Child, c. 1723
Terracotta statuette

Giuseppe Maria Mazza
Italian, 1653–1741
David Triumphant over Goliath, c. 1675/1725
Terracotta statuette

**The quiet, elegant sophisti-
cation** of this brochure projects an
image that is completely different
from any of the other documents in
this section. The style is entirely
appropriate for the subject of 17th-
and 18th-century terracotta
sculpture.

**The brochure is an 8-1/2- by
25-1/2-inch sheet folded twice**
to make six 8-1/2- by 11-inch pages.
Shown are the cover and the right-
hand page of the fully open brochure.

**Contrast is an effective
element** in this design. The
saturation of the full-bleed, sepia-
toned cover plays off against the
generous white space of the open
text pages as well as the silhouetted
shapes inside the brochure. The
reverse type in the cover banner is
set off like a plaque from the cover
art. Note the open letterspacing in
the brochure title, which improves
legibility of reverse type in relatively
small sizes.

The text is 9/14 Times Roman
italic in a 14-pica column. The use of
italic for running text is unusual
because it is generally difficult to
read. Here it adds to the traditional
elegance; the open leading and
surrounding white space compensate to improve readability.

The justified text is in keeping
with the formality of the design. The
hard edge of the right margin works
better with silhouette photos than a
ragged right margin would.

The silhouettes are enhanced
by other elements in the design. The
rules at the top of the page, from
which the text seems to hang, create
a free but defined space for the
shapes. The captions are set on a
half-column grid so as not to
interrupt that space.

*Design: Joseph Cochand,
The Art Institute of Chicago*

*Brochure for a show of European
terracotta sculpture at
The Art Institute of Chicago.
Trim size: 11 by 25-1/2, folded twice*

The unusually long page in the top sample uses rules to emphasize the horizontal format. This motif is established on the cover (not shown), where the four rules are broken only by a single photo that is centered horizontally and bleeds off the top of the page.

The placement of the initial cap and photo over the rules creates a three-dimensional effect, as if these elements float above the page.

The tab-style folio—reverse type in a gray box—is a popular device in today's graphic design.

The initial caps, 96 points, are also printed in gray.

The body text is 10/11 Palatino. That leading is fairly tight, but the 16-pica column width and the generous white space compensate to ensure readability.

The format is repeated on every page of the brochure. Only the depth of the photos varies.

Design (top):
Joanne Lenweaver,
Lenweaver Design
(Syracuse, NY)

Prospectus for
Syracuse University
College of Law.
Trim size:
12-3/16 by 7-5/8

THE FIRST YEAR LAW FIRM

Most American law schools prescribe a curriculum for first year students that has hardly changed at all since it was invented by Christopher Langdell at Harvard in the 1870's. That curriculum utilizes the Socratic teaching method in the traditional private law courses—contracts, torts, procedure, and property. The year is usually rounded out by such courses as constitutional law, criminal law, and legal writing.

Syracuse has not abandoned the features of this traditional curriculum that have rightly proved enduring. It is only that we believe today's beginning law student deserves more than this. Concerned that exclusive reliance on tradition does not provide enough individual attention to the development of basic lawyering skills, the Syracuse faculty has developed a first year program known as "Law Firm."

Organizing into small mock Law Firms, first year Syracuse students begin at once to see the real-world context in which legal problems arise and are resolved. Working together with their Law Firm associates, students develop legal writing, research, problem solving, and client counseling skills. Each Law Firm is directed by a faculty member who guides students through problems drawn from real law practice, integrated with materials covered in the traditional first year courses.

MAJOR PROGRAM AREAS CURRICULUM

The basic course of advanced law study at Syracuse is an innovative plan called the Major Program Areas Curriculum (MPAC). After the first year, each student selects a major program area that concentrates a portion of his or her study in one of four areas: business organizations and transactions; government and regulation; civil and criminal justice; or international law.

The goal of MPAC is not to force premature career choices or to develop narrow substantive specialties. Rather, its premise is that a good general legal education requires that some area of the law be studied in orderly sequence and in depth.

Rejecting the smorgasbord approach that has characterized much of American legal education in recent times, MPAC offers the

Syracuse student an organized, in-depth study of the selected area during the final two years of law school. Integrating materials from disciplines beyond the law, MPAC assures that students not only become well-versed in their areas of current special interest, but that they develop the skills needed to explore the varieties of legal problems they may encounter in the future.

Everything about the design in the bottom sample is bold: the page size, the fold, the type size, and the colors (the background on the pages that unfold is green with orange, red, and magenta accents).

A double gatefold gives new meaning to the landscape-proportioned page. The pages shown below left unfold to a 36-inch-wide sheet (half of the foldout is shown on the right), allowing plenty of room for the artist's rendering of a shopping mall on the Mexican border.

The running text was set at 36 points and output on a LaserWriter. That output was shot down 50%, reducing the type size to 18 points and increasing the resolution from 300 to 600 dots per inch. This is a useful technique for improving the quality of type when you use laser proofs for camera-ready copy.

The display type is Bernhard Antique Bold Condensed. This font was not available for desktop computers at the time the brochure was created, so the designer pasted commercial type into position on the camera-ready pages.

The photos are a good scale for this design. Being relatively small, they make the large type seem even larger.

Design (bottom):
Tom Lewis
(San Diego, CA)

Brochure for a shopping mall called ¡Viva Tijuana! Trim size: 12 by 36 double gatefold

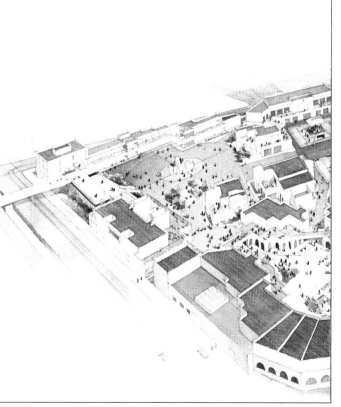

Como una pincelada de increíbles tonalidades. Naranjas, amarillos, verdes, rosas. ¡Viva Tijuana! hace que entre los visitantes renazcan ilusiones y se fortalezcan deseos escondidos. ¡Viva Tijuana! es alegre como el estallido de un cohetón de colores que se abre a la inmensidad de la noche.

Quien piensa en el "Old México", siente que el choque de lo moderno con lo antiguo produce efectos vivificantes, y no desperdicia la oportunidad de disfrutar en ¡Viva Tijuana! de la comodidad de un modernismo arquitectónico en un desarrollo sobre terreno que sabe historias viejas; es la fusión increíble del mañana con el ayer superado por la inteligencia del hombre moderno.

RIVER PARK

Around River Park

Conveniently located in Ulster County, 1-1/2 hours north of New York City, 1/2 hour from Stewart Airport, 15 minutes from the Mid-Hudson Bridge, 5 minutes from the NYS Thruway Exit 18 and the Village of New Paltz with express bus service to NYC and elsewhere.

River Park is just minutes from the Shawangunk Mountains where huge tracts of untouched wilderness include the Mohonk Preserve, a 5,400 acre publicly-accessible land preserve, and Minnewaska State Park covering over 12,000 acres. Numerous hiking trails and over forty miles of carriage roads provide perfect conditions for cross-country skiing, cycling and walking. Public facilities for golf and tennis are located in New Paltz.

New Paltz is famous for Huguenot Street, the oldest street of original homes in the U.S., and for SUNY New Paltz, with its vast educational and cultural facilities. The village boasts unique and interesting shops, diverse night life, and a highly respected public education system.

Area cultural groups and events include the Hudson Valley Philharmonic series, chamber music, concerts, summer theatre, art galleries, museums and open-air concerts.

River Park is surrounded by historic landmarks including the Mohonk Mountain House, West Point, and the Vanderbilt Estate.

The history surrounding River Park is rivaled only by natural and man-made wonders such as the nearby glacial lakes, Mohonk, Min-

newaska and Awosting, with their incredibly clear blue waters and jagged granite-faced shoreline. The cliff faces of the Shawangunk Mountains and old channels and locks from the D & H Canal provide many scenic and recreational possibilities.

The area's growing economic base is led by agriculture, IBM, Stewart Airport, SUNY New Paltz and a host of flourishing smaller businesses. All provide a stable and diverse job market.

An inspiring place, protected and private— River Park offers it all. Enjoy the unparalleled benefits of River Park Cooperative by calling 914-255-7904 . Select your homesite and then take a walk in the woods, or meadows , or wander down by the river...

The square shape of the page in the sample above is echoed in the logo, the photos, and the shape of the text block.

High-quality photos of nature set the tone for a real estate development with cooperatively owned wilderness and recreation facilities. The designer chose to let the single photo on the cover sell an image that the inside pages describe.

A coated ivory stock and good printing that holds details in the photos add to the image of quality.

The text is 10/11 Palatino. Again, this is relatively tight leading for body text. Here, the narrow 10-pica column width, the short paragraphs separated by more than a pica of space, and the wide margins ensure readability.

The conference brochure shown below has a highly structured page with banners, rules, boxes, and color tints used to enliven the otherwise straightforward text. The elements are precisely placed in relation to one another. The folio and the rule above it, for example, align with the date to the right and with the black box to the left of the text block.

The single 24-pica column works well on this small page size. On subsequent pages the wide margin is used for bold italic heads set larger than the body text.

The banner to the left of each contents listing is color-coded to the page number. The graduated color tones are picked up as background tints for the respective pages of the brochure; the tints are light enough to ensure legibility of surprinted type.

The Seybold Desktop Publishing Conference is a Seybold Seminars Event

6922 Wildlife Road
Malibu, CA 90265
Telephone: (213) 457-5850
Telex: 6503066263
Fax: 457-4704

SEYBOLD
S E M I N A R S

© 1988 Seybold Seminars, Inc.
All Rights Reserved

2

Conference Overview

The annual Seybold Desktop Publishing Conference has become the worldwide event-of-record for the burgeoning desktop publishing market, and a "must" occasion for both the publishing and the computer industries.

As the only major computer conference devoted to electronic publishing applications, the Seybold Conference combines a top-level three-day seminar with the world's premier exposition of computer-based publishing solutions. The 1988 Conference takes place September 14 - 17 at the Santa Clara Convention Center in the heart of Silicon Valley. The seminars run Wednesday through Friday, September 14 - 16. The exposition operates Thursday through Saturday, September 15 - 17.

You heard about the 1987 Conference. It brought "PostScript Mania" to the forefront with announcements of Display PostScript and Color PostScript, and the emergence of PostScript printer clones. Other highlights included the launch of desktop presentations, the introduction of "big system" capabilities on the desktop, debates on multi-user networked systems, some lively user sessions on exciting new applications, and a raft of new products.

The 1988 Conference is going to be even better. The market will see many more sophisticated and powerful products, and the collision between Macs, PCs and Unix workstations will be dramatic. Again, the Seybold Conference will be the most exciting (and most valuable) event of the year.

3   **September 14-17, 1988 •Santa Clara Convention Center**

John Singer Sargent

Kent Lydecker, Executive Director, Department of Museum Education

Tuesday evenings, February 10, 17, 24, and March 3, 6:00-7:00, repeated on Wednesday afternoons, February 11, 18, 25, and March 4, 1:00-2:00

This series complements the *John Singer Sargent* exhibition, on view at the Art Institute February 7 to April 19. Kent Lydecker will present lecture I, II, and IV. Laurel Bradley, Director of Gallery 400, University of Illinois, Chicago, will present lecture III.
I   *American Artists Abroad: Sargent in the Expatriate Tradition*
II   *The Contemporary Scene: Sargent's Europe*
III   *Sargent as a Portraitist*
IV   *The Unsung Sargent: The Boston Murals*

John Singer Sargent. *The Fountain, Villa Torlonia, Frascati*, 1907. Oil on canvas. Friends of American Art Collection.

Four 1-hour sessions. Member: $30. Public: $40 Student (with ID) $20. Single tickets sold only at the door on the day of the lecture. Member: $9.50. Public: $12. Student (with ID): $5. Meet in Morton Hall.

From Mice to Magic: Film Animation

Moderator: Richard Peña, Director, Film Center, School of the Art Institute

Sunday afternoons, 2:00-3:30, March 15, 22, 29, and April 5

Screen animation is one of the oldest and most popular cinematic traditions — Mickey Mouse is at least as well known internationally as Charlie Chaplin or John Wayne — yet the history and development of the art of animation is usually treated at best as a footnote to film history. In this series, issues in the history of animation, along with exciting new developments in the field,

Betty Boop

will be discussed in lectures featuring the screening of relevant films.

I   *Animation in the Silent Cinema: The Pioneers — Emile Cohl, Windsor MacKay, and Lotte Reiniger* Donald Crafton, Professor, University of Wisconsin, Madison, and author of *Before Mickey*
II   *Animation in the Studio Era: Mickey Mouse, Betty Boop, and Popeye and Their Creators such as Tex Avery, Chuck Jones, Max Fleischer, and Walt Disney* Maryann Oshana, Northwestern University
III   *The Techniques of Screen Animation: cels, pin-screen, sand, clay, puppets, and*

"direct animation." Stephanie Maxwell, Visiting Artist, School of the Art Institute, and prize-winning animator
IV   *Animation in the Eighties and Future Possibilities* Stephanie Maxwell

Four 1-1/2 hour sessions. Member: $45. Public: $60. Student (with ID) $30. Single tickets sold only at the door on the day of the lecture. Member: $14. Public: $18. Student (with ID):$7.50. Meet in Fullerton Hall.

Baroque and Rococo Art and Architecture in Austria and Bavaria

Robert Eskridge, Lecturer, Department of Museum Education

Monday afternoons, April 6, 13, 20, and 27, 1:00-2:00 repeated on Tuesday evenings, April 7, 14, 21, and 28, 6:00-7:00
Throughout the 18th century a spring-like efflorescence of building and decoration shaped the cities and country villages of Austria and Bavaria. Situated between Italy and France, the region absorbed the best qualities of both to create the distinctive

J.M. Fischer and J.M. Feichtmayr. *Gilded Stucco Cartouche, Priory Church, Diessen, Bavaria.* 1732-34.

monuments of the age. The series traces the Baroque and Rococo from its birth in Rome and Paris to its transformation in Central Europe.

I   *The Origins of Baroque and Rococo in Rome and Paris*
II   *The Baroque and Rococo in Austria*
III   *The Bavarian Rococo Church*
IV   *Munich and Würzburg*

Four 1-hour sessions. Member: $30. Public: $40. Student (with ID): $20. Single tickets sold only at the door on the day of the lecture. Member: $9.50 Public: $12. Student (with ID): $5. Meet in Morton Hall.

Johann Bernhard and Joseph Emmanuel Fischer von Erlach. *Karlskirche, Vienna, Austria.* 1716-33.

---

*Design (facing page, top):
Wadlin & Erber (New Paltz, NY)*

*Brochure for the River Park Cooperative.
Trim size: 8 by 24, folded twice*

*Design (facing page, bottom):
Weisz, Yang, Dunkelberger Inc.
(Westport, CT)*

*Brochure for the Seybold Desktop Publishing Conference.
Trim size: 6-3/4 by 8-3/8*

Design (this page): Mary Grace Quinlan

*Subscription programs brochure from The Art Institute of Chicago.
Trim size: 10-3/4 by 9*

The long vertical page of the brochure shown above is typical of museum programs. The shape fulfills two very different needs: In its vertical orientation, it is easily racked at information desks and museum stores; in its horizontal orientation, it's a self-mailer.

The two-column grid accommodates several self-contained items on a spread, with headlines in a second color (green here) for easy scanning. Variety on each spread increases the chance of getting the reader's interest.

The body text is 10/11 Garamond. The headlines are 11/13 Garamond bold italic.

Even though the photographs are small, the combination of the narrow page and narrow column width (11 picas) keeps them from looking like postage stamps. Art can also be sized to a two-column width.

This program guide for a TV series, *Islam and the West*, relies heavily on four-color photos to tell its story. The page composition varies considerably from spread to spread, depending on the size and placement of the pictures.

When selecting and placing several photos on a page or spread, keep in mind how they play against one another. When a visually literate eye is at work, as it is here, the photos work together to make a dynamic composition.

Contrast in subject, scale, direction, and color all contribute to the composition. It shows travel by land, travel by sea, and the gold coin that was the very reason for these century-old trade routes. The caravan moves back into the picture plane, the ship moves in a plane perpendicular to the caravan, and the movement of both contrasts with the still life of the coins. The vastness of the mountains makes the caravan seem small, and the coins smaller still. Consider also the visual forms themselves—the jagged mountains, the linear caravan, the circular coins, and the rickety lines of the ship.

The headline treatment at the top of each spread provides a strong unifying element given this varied compositon. The 3-point rule runs from one outer margin to the gutter, bleeding across the gutter (unless there is a full-bleed picture on one page of the spread).

The type is New Baskerville.

Design: Ira Friedlander (New York, NY)
Program guide for Islam and the West, *a television film series.*
Trim Size: 6 by 9

5. TRADE AND COMMERCE

Islam seeks never to separate everyday life from religion. A person's livelihood and his beliefs are linked and he is taught that social and economic justice—and charity—are worthy matters. Thus Islam has always supplied trade and commerce with a formidable religious base.

After the death of the Prophet, both the religion of Islam and Muslim political and economic domination spread with amazing rapidity. So, outward from the heartland of Islam they came—Muslims traders travelling up and down the coast of Africa, across the Sahara, over the Silk Route to China, through the Indian Ocean to the Orient.

The sea routes, which the Muslims controlled, were crucial for the economic life of the Islamic world, as well as for trade between the Far East and Europe. Accounts of travel by sea to distant lands captured the imagination of Islamic peoples and entered into their literature in stories such as 'Sinbad the Sailor' in <u>The Thousand and One Nights</u>.

Over the land routes, traders carried ideas along with spices, silk and paper from the East to the Islamic world and through it to the West. Traders also played a role in the transmission of technology, for example in bringing paper and papermaking from China.

The importance of travel in their lives led Muslims to develop geography on a global scale. Always in their journeys, they relied on a singularly important instrument, the astrolabe. The astrolabe gave these traders their bearings, and gave the West the tool with which to reach the New World. Columbus would have been lost without his astrolabe and maps plotted by Muslim traders. Prince Henry the Navigator depended not only on that device, he also had a Muslim pilot .

Everywhere they went, the Muslim traders brought the Quran, their book of guidance, as well as their science, their art, and their culture.

To this day caravans of camels still travel the Silk Route, long the only land link between East and West. Left, Omani dhow. Right, Islamic coins.

The cover art was derived from a piece of clip art that was digitized with Thunderscan, saved as a Mac-Paint document, and enlarged in PageMaker. The effective, bit-mapped result bears little resemblance to the fine-line style of the original art. It prints burgundy on a tan background. The same art was reduced for use as a decorative element at the bottom of each page.

The "border within a border" page frame provides a space for the organization's name to run across the top of each inside page. The open letterspacing creates an effective and delicate treatment for a running head, but it needs to be anchored by a frame, like the one in this brochure, or a rule, like the ones under the running heads in this book. Note that the page frame is asymmetrical at the top and bottom, which keeps the design from being too rigid.

An underlying three-column grid used on text pages (not shown here) is carried through on the cover, where one column is used for the title and the other two combine to provide a wide column for art, and on the spread of photos, where the two inner columns on each page have been divided in half to accommodate small mug shots.

The photos were sized and cropped so that all the heads appear approximately the same size and with the same eye level. This technique, which is particularly important when you group mug shots in a linear fashion, gives equal importance to all of the photos and helps minimize their varying reproduction quality. Imagine what a hodgepodge this page would be if all the heads were different sizes.

Design: John McWade, PageLab (Sacramento, CA)

Pages from the Sacramento Regional Foundation Yearbook. Trim size: 11 by 8-1/2

An accounting firm presents a clean, organized look in this brochure without being at all stuffy or staid.

The format is built around large photos on the left-hand page and two off-center text columns with smaller photos on the right-hand page. The large photos are nicely framed by a white background and are sized consistently from one spread to the next. The right-hand pages are solid tan, giving the appearance of a different paper stock. The smaller photos are the same size throughout the brochure and their placement bounces about the text columns.

The Bodoni text has very open leading. The italic captions print in blue, as do the subheads, initial caps, and rules that bleed off the top of the left-hand pages.

Captions stating the company's philosophy print in tan banners that match the color of the right-hand pages. The position of this tint block moves around from page to page, but it always overlaps the photo and the white border. This technique is currently a popular graphic device.

Design: Bill Westheuser, Communication Design Group Limited (Halifax, Nova Scotia)

Brochure from Doane Raymond Accountants.
Trim size: 8-1/2 by 11

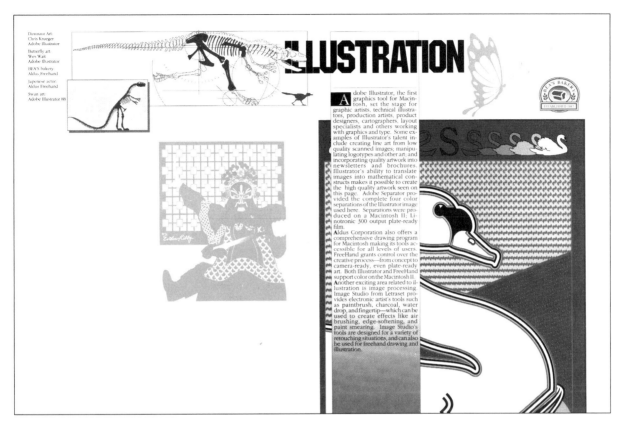

This brochure was produced by a commercial printer to showcase the art and technology of desktop publishing. (It bears mentioning that many printers are less than enthusiastic about desktop technology because it will increasingly move prepress work from the print shop to the publisher.)

The layout is built around columns of type, all the same measure but positioned on the page as free-form art objects. Each type column prints over a different graduated colored tone, which increases in darkness from top to bottom. The tones were created in Cricket Draw.

The art is placed around the type in different ways, depending on the individual pieces. In spite of the absence of a visible grid, the placement is always rectilinear, never haphazard. It takes considerable skill to make each spread function independently and still have a unifying visual style throughout the brochure.

The illustrations on the spread shown were created in Adobe Illustrator (dinosaur and butterfly), Aldus FreeHand (Japanese actor and bakery logo), and Illustrator 88 (the transformation of an S into a swan).

Design: Wes Wait (Portland, OR)

Pages from Extending the Benefits of Desktop Publishing *produced by Dynagraphics.*
Trim size: 8-1/2 by 11

CHAPTER 6

PERIODICALS: NEWSLETTERS, JOURNALS, AND MAGAZINES

Regardless of subject, style, or frequency, the challenge common to all periodicals is to establish a strong identity that remains both familiar and fresh issue after issue. The subject, the tone, and the overall package and format should be unmistakably one's own, clearly established and consistently maintained over time. But within that familiar package it's the fresh ideas, the unexpected images, the new ways of presenting recurring themes that keep readers interested.

Once audience and editorial focus of a periodical is established, the foundation for the balancing act between the familiar and the new is the graphic format. This includes everything from logo and cover design to the treatment of feature stories and housekeeping details (mastheads, letters, calendars, and so on). Items that appear in every issue, such as contents listings, review columns, and news sections, should have a recognizable style and a relatively constant page position from one issue to the next. If there is advertising, the format must take into consideration where in the publication ads will appear, how to handle fractional ads, and how to distinguish clearly between ads and editorial items, especially when they appear on the same spread.

A format that works not only defines your image, it also determines how hard you'll work to produce each issue. A format consistent with your resources spells the difference between efficient and chaotic production. Desktop technology can streamline production tremendously, eliminating the days it used to take to turn manuscript into typeset galleys and to correct galleys as deadlines approached. The technology also gives editors and designers much greater control over the material through every step of the production cycle, allowing more refinement later in the process than was previously possible.

But established periodicals have established production systems. Converting to desktop publishing means that many functions previously performed by outside vendors are brought in-house to staffs that may already feel overworked. The technology is changing the roles of editors, designers, production managers, and layout artists in ways that are too new to be fully understood or predictable and that vary from one organization to another. If you are contemplating or are in the process of making the transition to desktop publishing, expect to spend six to twelve months evolving systems and roles. Talk with other people who have made the transition, and evaluate their experience within the context of your own product and the strengths and weaknesses of your staff. The benefits are ultimately everything they're alleged to be, but the transition can be quite a roller coaster.

NEWSLETTERS

Thousands and thousands of newsletters are published in this country. Whether for internal circulation or public relations, for marketing products or services, for raising money or raising consciousness, most newsletters exist to communicate specialized information to a targeted audience on a regular basis. It's essential to really understand your specialized audience and what you hope to accomplish through the newsletter. You should be able to define not just a general purpose but very specific benefits that your organization can measure as a result of publishing the newsletter.

Unlike magazines, which usually have a staff dedicated to creating and producing the publication, newsletters are often produced by people who perform other functions for an organization. It's very important to match the newsletter format to the time and resources you'll have to produce it. If you're starting a new newsletter or making the transition from traditional to electronic production, consider using a free-lance designer experienced in electronic publishing to create a format and electronic templates consistent with your needs and resources. This might give you a much smarter look than you could achieve with an in-house design and still yield the cost savings of in-house production.

Newsletters in this section

- *Newservice*—the appeal and accessibility of a modular format
- *Friends of Omega*—on composing photos on the page
- *Apple viewpoint*s—a simple wide-and-narrow-column format
- *The Preston Report*—numbers as graphics
- *Nooz*—playfulness in a five-column tabloid
- *The Wire*—newspaper-style flair for a four-color in-house monthly
- *The Freeze Beacon*—magazine-style features in a newsletter format
- *Consumer Markets Abroad*—a format for charts and graphs
- *Perspectives*—a more open version of the two-and-a-half-column grid
- *Indications*—marketing analysis with dimensional art
- *O'Connor Quarterly*—a friendly and sophisticated people-publication
- *AmeriNews*—one approach to a tabloid format
- *Re:*—another approach to a tabloid format
- *Litigation News*—typographic variety for all-text pages
- *ThePage*—the impact of strong cover concepts

For hands-on instructions for creating a newsletter, see Projects 4 and 5 in Section 3.

A highly organized, modular format takes editorial planning and attention to detail when you assemble the pages but is very appealing and easy to read.

The cover uses multiple "sell" devices to get the reader's attention: a strong bit-mapped photo and caption with boldface leadin, a headline for a related story inset in the cover story, and a contents box.

The bold rules are printed in a second color that changes with each issue. They are 15-point solid boxes, heavier than the rules on Page-Maker's Lines menu, which allows ample room for reverse type (Avant Garde, with extra letterspacing).

Art (below) **and pull quotes** (not shown) break the grid at the top of the page. Pull quotes are set short of a two-column measure and are bordered by a vertical rule on the left margin that descends into the text block area. Pull quotes and rules, which print in the second color, are also placed inside columns to break up text in full-page stories.

Design: Jim Parker (Phoenix, AZ)

Pages from Newservice, *published bimonthly by the Do It Now Foundation. Size: 8-1/2 by 11*

The cover page (shown)

D.I.N. PUBLICATIONS   VOL. 3 NO. 1

NEWSERVICE

PAGE • ONE

Making 'Safe' Sexy...

There's gold in them there ills. At least that's how a growing number of companies see the new emphasis on "safe sex" practices that lower the risk of giving or getting the AIDS virus.

With every day seemingly bringing a new hair-raising headline on who has—and who yet may get—the still-incurable disease (including a recent estimate by the World Health Organi-

zation that the global population of AIDS victims will top 3 million by 1992), it hasn't taken long for entrepreneurs to smell the profit potential in the mounting fear of AIDS.

But How Safe Is 'Safe'? p. 7

The biggest beneficiary of safe sex thus far has been the U.S. condom industry. Spurred on by Surgeon General C. Everett Koop's endorsement of condoms as "the best

Continues page 6

Sign of the Times: *First there was sex, then there was safe sex, then there was making money off safe sex. Our 'Page One' report tells how—and how much.*

Safe,
Not Sorry.

Instant Workshop

Eureka!

It's the flash of inspiration when an idea is born. And while we'd all *like* to get to know the experience better, a new board game may just help.

Create winds through the four stages of creativity ("Focus," "Incubation," "Aha!," and "Action"). In the process, player-"creators") respond to off-the-wall challenges like "Pantomime ink coming out of the pen of the author you like most," and "Describe the sensation of walking on Jello."

Novel (not "correct") replies are rewarded with light bulb-shaped Idea tokens and (you guessed it) the player with the most tokens wins. But even *that* rule is up for grabs in *Create*.

In fact, the only firm rule is that there *aren't* any firm rules.

Which works out well, according to *Create's* creators, because that's the essence of the Eureka! experience.

For more information on *Create*, write: Creativity Research, P.O. Box 3325, Oakland, CA 94609.

INSIDE

PLUS: STUPID EDITOR TRICKS... READER MAIL...AND MORE!

Newservice   July-August, 1987

Page two (shown)

NEWSFRONTS

FITNESS

Brain Games: Jogging Creativity

Just when you thought you'd heard everything about the health benefits of jogging (and *still* can't always find a really good reason to get up and go), add one more to the list.

Regular running jogs the creative juices like few other activities, say psychologists after testing its effects on creativity.

In studies measuring creativity among college students, test group participants were enrolled in physical education classes that involved regular running, while others followed their normal, sit-around-and-study habits.

At semester's end, psychologists Joan Gondola of City University of New York and Bruce Tuckman of Florida State University re-tested their subjects. Results showed that runners not only improved on earlier creativity-quotient scores but also outpaced nonrunners in creativity and originality.

Gondola and Tuckman say their results point up the continuing need for physical education programs in schools: "They are not frills, but

should be central to our learning and educational processes."

Zen and the Art of KickBoxing

What is the sound of one hand slapping an enemy into submission?

In traditional martial arts training, students wrestle with philosophical knots and questions of honor and ethics as much as each other. But quickie, value-free versions of traditional martial arts may actually increase levels of aggression, according to a Texas A & M researcher.

Comparing the benefits of training in traditional Tae Kwon Do, an age-old Korean body/mind philosophy and defensive art, with a Westernized technique emphasizing only self-defense, researcher Michael Trulson

found that delinquency-prone teens differed significantly at the end of six months.

Body/mind trainees demonstrated reduced anxiety, enhanced self-esteem, and lowered aggression while the body-only group showed increased levels of aggression, while lagging in all other areas.

A third group, given no training, exhibited no change.

Coffee Head

Just can't seem to wake up/settle down to work without one (or more) cups of coffee?

Millions of Americans jumpstart the day with their favorite caffeine-containing brew. Most say it increases their alertness level and helps them focus.

But experts now say that in some coffee drinkers, caffeine may actually reduce attention and impair work performance.

According to caffeine researcher Kristen Anderson of Colgate University, coffee's attention-lifting power works best on simple tasks that require little concentration or thought.

But jobs requiring complex reasoning or quick decision-making seem to suffer when the mental wheels get greased with caffeine.

Personality plays one role in calculating the benefits of drinking coffee. Anderson's studies show that extroverts—outgoing individuals who tend to make quick, impulsive decisions—fare best following a jolt of java.

Introverts, who reach decisions after slowly mulling over the choices, slow down even more after a morning (or afternoon or evening) cup.

NEWSERVICE

Newservice (ISSN 0739-4683) is published bimonthly by D.I.N. Publications, 2050 East University Drive, Phoenix, AZ 85034.
All contents © 1987 by D.I.N. Publications.
Newservice welcomes submissions from readers, but only those accompanied by SASE can be returned.
Subscriptions: $15 per year; $25/two years.
Postmaster: Please send change of address to **Newservice**, PO Box 21126, Phoenix, AZ 85036.

Editor: James D. Parker

Editorial Director: Christina Dye

Art Director: Anne Banks

Contributors: Jerrold S. Greenberg, Jennifer James, Sara Shannon Parker, Rita Robinson, Irwin Ross, Ph. D.

Customer Services: Jean Multer

Production: Sergio Gajardo, Vincent Ruziska, Gonzalo Sepulveda

July-August, 1987   Newservice

Page three (shown)

EDITOR'S COLUMN   3

Hip Deep in the Hoopla

We all see it every day, in the explosion of images and the proliferation of hype that's become the news:

Ollie North and Fawn Hall blur into Jim and Tammy Bakker, the "AIDS Crisis" dissolves into the "Cocaine Crisis," which segues into the "Urine Testing Crisis."

Hoopla gets mixed up with half-truths and half-truths with innuendo and hardly *anyone* can tell the innuendoes from the gossip.

That's why we're back.

Light years ago, when we originally thought this thing through, (yes, we *did* think it through, once), the idea behind the name and the justification for the concept was that **Newservice** would serve as a real *news service* for readers.

We knew that there wasn't much need for just another publication or for another editorial voice in an increasingly media-noisy world, so we set out to do something else: provide a filter and focus for a certain *type* of news.

And while we've stumbled and made our share of mistakes along the way, one thing we think wasn't faulty is our original notion that people really do need a means of boiling down the flood of information the modern world generates.

That's why we're happy to announce that we're resuming bimonthly publication with this issue—because we think the need for a reliable information filter and hoopla detector has never been greater.

To get ourselves back onto a regular production schedule, we've had to make some minor concessions to reality, which we hope will ultimately mean a better and more useful publication.

So, if we look different this time around, it's for good reason. We've tinkered with our format, and come up with an editorial package that we think is both visually compelling and affordable.

We've opted for a more concise reporting style, one that gets the essence of a story across without requiring a free afternoon on your part to get through it.

And we've crammed as much honestly useful information into our pages as we could. We've done our

best to strain out the pointless and silly (well, *most* of the pointless and silly, anyway), and filter *in* information that stands a chance of making a difference in your life—and the lives of the people you care about.

In short, we've made changes we hope will serve you as a reader and person to wade through the hoopla of everyday existence and discover more of the things in life that are truly worth knowing.

Let us know how we succeed.

See you in September.

LETTERS

Praise and Cons

To the Editor:

How dare you allow Ms. Porcelli ("Trouble-icious?" *Newservice*/4) to advise us to chew ice?

"Hold onto your new $500 porcelain crowns," indeed. My dentist would go shrieking into the night if I admitted to him I chew ice.

May I rather recommend that one chew any number of whole food (pure) gums or gum substitutes available on the market. Granted, these are a little more expensive, but so what? Where I live, in the environs of the Black Hills of South Dakota, there are about three brands available through my favorite pure foods store.

Another comment: I think your magazine is terrific. Who owns D.I.N. Publications? What does D.I.N. stand for?

Where have you been all my life?

Timothy P. Battey
Ellsworth AFB, SD 57706

The D.I.N. in our business title is an acronym for "Do It Now," which we take as the best of all possible responses to "I'll quit tomorrow" or "I'll get around to it someday," or whatever happens to be one's own favorite excuse for not making one's life happen in the here-and-now.

It's taken from our full legal name, Do It Now Foundation.

As a non-profit organization, Do It Now is a public corporation, chartered in California in 1968 and based in Phoenix, Arizona since 1972. We exist solely to provide substance abuse education materials and other informational services.

Where have we been all of your life? Right here, working—since 1968, anyway.

Where have you been all of ours?

—Ed.

Please address correspondence to Editor, Newservice, P.O. Box 21126, Phoenix, AZ 85036.

Newservice   July-August, 1987

The photographs available for most newsletters lack both the impact and the reproduction quality that would allow them to stand alone on the page. But when you group photos with an eye both to editorial content and the visual relationship that will be created between them, the whole can be greater than the sum of its parts.

Three photos often form an ideal combination. Two alone form only a one-on-one, back-and-forth relationship. Add a third, and you have a new and more dynamic chemistry. Four together will often start to pair off, and you're back with two's again. And visually, three photos can create an interesting triangular path for the reader's eye to follow.

In the example shown here, the photos promote summer workshops at a holistic learning center. The selection balances a single, silhouetted musician, a group seated casually at an outdoor seminar, and a third photo suggesting both the quiet time away from workshops and the recently improved wheelchair access on the campus.

When positioning photos on the page, consider where each picture will take the reader's eye, the relative size of the subjects, the lights and darks, and the horizon lines.

Three strong directions in these photos create visual energy that moves your eye from one picture to another. The silhouetted photo is looking away from the page; the lecturers standing in the group picture are looking into the page; and the figures shown from behind take your eye back into the page.

The people are captured in front views, back views, and profiles, and they are scaled differently in their individual environments. The uniformity of size generally recommended for head-and-shoulder portraits would make a group of casual photos such as this seem too static.

Silhouetting a photo, as in the top picture, can improve it by removing extraneous background images. The original photo in this instance included a group of people seated behind the subject; removing them focuses attention on the subject and also provides an interesting shape to work with. The freeform shape can be considerably larger than the other pictures without being out of balance. And you can rag the copy along the edge of the silhouette, which integrates the type and the photos. In this case, the photo was scanned in to produce a working on-screen image to help define the rag. But for better reproduction in print, a halftone was shot from the original photo and stripped in by the printer.

Visual illusions can be part of the unseen structure in a group of images. In the bottom two pictures, the horizon lines seem to meet, so that for a moment they appear to create a single panorama; the space between them creates the effect of a window on the scene. Opening up the picture plane in this way creates a sense of perspective and gives dimension to the page.

Design: Don Wright (Woodstock, NY)

Pages from Friends of Omega Newsletter, *published by the Omega Institute. Trim size: 8-1/2 by 11*

Apple *viewpoints*

Apple News and Perspectives for the Developer Community

Published weekly by Apple Developer Services

September 12, 1988

Apple Integrated Systems Meets MIS Corporate Needs

Chuck Berger, Vice President, Apple Integrated Systems

In April of 1988, Apple made the decision to form Apple Integrated Systems. As the head of this new group at Apple, I'd like to take a few minutes to tell you about the reasoning behind the creation of Apple Integrated Systems—how we plan to accomplish our mission, and now it will affect you as a developer.

A lot has changed in the Macintosh® world over the past three and a half years. Macintosh has gone from a relatively simple machine to a broad product line including the Mac® II workstation. Additionally, we have gone from a handful of applications, peripherals, and virtually no communications capability to literally thousands of application options, complimented by powerful peripherals that have the ability for Macintosh to communicate in virtually any computing or communications environment.

"...our customers view Macintosh as the workstation component of their emerging enterprise-wide communications and information systems."

As the capabilities and breadth of solutions that Macintosh offered grew, so did its popularity in the business marketplace. Macintosh has gone from being a relative unknown in the business world to being a strong niche player in the desktop publishing area, to finally being accepted as a general productivity tool throughout the business world.

While that has been great news for all of us, there is even better news ahead. The increased power of Macintosh and the broader range of solutions and applications we can offer, with the help of software and peripherals created by third-party developers, have led our customers to view Macintosh as *the* workstation component of their emerging enterprise-wide communications and information systems.

Continued on next page

N E W S B R I E F S

Special Events at AppleFest
Developer Services Suite
The Developer Services staff will host a hospitality suite at AppleFest® for those of you who would like to come by and talk with us, see demos of *The Information Exchange*, and get answers to your questions. We'll be in Room 106 in the San Francisco Civic Auditorium on Friday, September 16th from 3:00 to 5:00 P.M. Refreshments will be available.

Technical Forum
Bring your Apple® II and IIGS® technical issues with you to the San Francisco AppleFest this month. Apple II engineers, product managers, and writers are gathering each day to "talk tech" with you.
Place: *Brooks Hall, Room 314*.
Time: *Fri.-Sat. 1:30-2:30 P.M.*
Sun. 1:00-2:00 P.M.
The forum is a special opportunity to discuss your technical questions, suggestions, and needs with the Apple II and IIGS development team. The technical focus will be on programming and hardware

Continued on next page

In this two-column format, the wide column is used for a single essay that continues from the cover to the two inside pages. The narrow column is used for short news items. A simple and effective format both editorially and graphically, it is also remarkably easy to execute.

Production takes less than two days. Unformatted word-processor files are sent from Apple to the art production house via AppleLink on Tuesday afternoon. By 10 A.M. Wednesday, copyedited, formatted text has been placed in an electronic dummy and faxed to Apple. Apple phones in corrections by 11, a revised page is faxed to Apple by 1 P.M., and additional corrections are phoned in if necessary. The courier picks up at 4 for delivery to the printer by 5. If you're tempted to say, "Yes, but that's Apple…," consider instead "Yes, keep it simple."

The condensed Garamond text face was made especially for Apple by Adobe. (Well, yes, that *is* Apple….)

Design: The Compage Company (San Francisco, CA)
Cover of Apple viewpoints, *published biweekly by Apple Developer Services.*
Size: 8-1/2 by 11

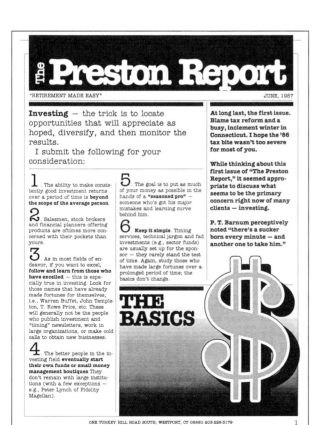

The Preston Report

"RETIREMENT MADE EASY" JUNE, 1987

Investing — the trick is to locate opportunities that will appreciate as hoped, diversify, and then monitor the results.

I submit the following for your consideration:

1. The ability to make consistently good investment returns over a period of time is **beyond the scope of the average person**.

2. Salesmen, stock brokers and financial planners offering products are oftimes more concerned with their pockets than yours.

3. As in most fields of endeavor, if you want to excel, **follow and learn from those who have excelled** — this is especially true in investing. Look for those names that have already made fortunes for themselves, i.e., Warren Buffet, John Templeton, T. Rowe Price, etc. These will generally not be the people who publish investment and "timing" newsletters, work in large organizations, or make cold calls to obtain new businesses.

4. The better people in the investing field **eventually start their own funds or small money management boutiques**. They don't remain with large institutions (with a few exceptions — e.g., Peter Lynch of Fidelity Magellan).

5. The goal is to put as much of your money as possible in the hands of a **"seasoned pro"** — someone who's got his major mistakes and learning curve behind him.

6. **Keep it simple.** Timing services, technical jargon and fad investments (e.g., sector funds) are usually set up for the sponsor — they rarely stand the test of time. Again, study those who have made large fortunes over a prolonged period of time; the basics don't change.

At long last, the first issue. Blame tax reform and a busy, inclement winter in Connecticut. I hope the '86 tax bite wasn't too severe for most of you.

While thinking about this first issue of "The Preston Report," it seemed appropriate to discuss what seems to be the primary concern right now of many clients — investing.

P. T. Barnum perceptively noted "there's a sucker born every minute — and another one to take him."

THE BASICS

ONE TURKEY HILL ROAD SOUTH, WESTPORT, CT 06880 203-226-3179 1

Bold headlines are assertive, while the American Typewriter face is friendly. The combination is just right for financial advice to retirees.

Introductory copy, set to a two-column measure and larger than the body text, helps draw readers into the page and effectively varies the basic three-column grid.

Large numbers (these are 32 point) make lists appealing and also function as graphic elements.

The three-layer dollar sign was created in Illustrator and stretched in PageMaker. The font is Bodoni, one of the few with a double downstroke in the dollar sign. The top sign has a 5-point white Stroke and a 30 percent black Fill; the middle one has a 6-point black Stroke to produce the outline; the bottom sign is solid black, set off to create a drop shadow.

The shaded box was created in Cricket Draw.

Design: John Odam (San Diego, CA)
Design for The Preston Report, *created as a "Page Makeover" for* Publish! *magazine.*
Size: 8-1/2 by 11

Playfulness is the signature of this tabloid monthly newsletter. The typewriter look of Courier sets the casual tone, and every design element follows through in kind.

Mug shots don't have to be boring. The shapes used here only begin to suggest some ingenious ways to treat both casual and posed snapshots. The stars were created in MacDraw, and the other shapes in PageMaker. Photos were stripped in as halftones by the printer.

Letters as visual puns provide more play in the rebus-like graphic. The type was set in PageMaker. The eye was digitized in MacVision from a photo cropped very tight, saved as a MacPaint file, and scaled in PageMaker. The bee was drawn in MacPaint.

The digitized courthouse art is treated as a vignette, with the edges gradually fading into the background of the page. (The effect was created in MacPaint from a MacVision scan.)

The rotated photo provides an opportunity for an unusual caption treatment, with the names of those pictured angled into the photo.

For all the spontaneity in the treatment of graphic elements, the five-column grid provides the necessary understructure.

Design: Paul Souza (Boston, MA)

Pages from Nooz, *published quarterly by WGBH radio.*

Trim size: 11 by 17

This house organ for an international corporation is formatted as a monthly newspaper. The spread shown, a standing feature in every issue, reports "news, events, awards, and issues…from locations throughout North America."

The art is as varied as you'll find in any publication, with charts, photos, paintings, line art, and even a magazine cover contributing to a very spirited page.

The five-column format provides several advantages for a feature with so many pieces. Art can be sized anywhere from one to three columns wide and placed in overlapping columns to make an already lively spread even more dynamic. Narrow columns accommodate the numerous subheads without eating up too much space and give sufficient depth to items that are only 25 to 50 words long. These short text blocks would look like captions in a wider margin.

The cover features a different employee each issue, in the context of his or her committment to some community organization. The typographic treatment of the "Snapshot" text reinforces the informal, personal approach of this cover concept. Depending on the photo, the orientation may be horizontal (as shown here) or vertical.

Design: Weisz Yang Dunkelberger Inc. (Westport, CT)

Pages from THE WIRE, *published monthly by Champion International Corporation. Trim size: 11 by 15*

A tightly structured name-plate, along with the headline and folio treatments, creates a strong identity for this newsletter. The light-house incorporated into the logo is a recognizable local landmark. The banner with reverse type at the top of the cover highlights the feature article shown in the spread below.

A scanned photo on the cover is treated as a posterlike portrait of the subject, producing a more effective result than trying to make a bit-mapped image look like a halftone.

A magazine-style feature provides a change of pace, editorially and visually, from the modular format elsewhere in the newsletter. The bit-mapped art ironically conjures up the image of video games in a story that is all too much anchored in the real world. The art was created in MacPaint and stretched across the two pages in PageMaker.

The typeface is Palatino. Varying the size and measure of individual headlines creates emphasis without the need to change the typeface.

Design:
John Odam
(San Diego, CA)
Pages from The Freeze Beacon, *published quarterly by San Diegans for a Bilateral Nuclear Weapons Freeze. Size: 8-1/2 by 11*

A two-and-a-half-column format is ideal for accommodating charts, graphs, and tables of different sizes. The narrow column works well for headlines and pull quotes, too. The running text always begins at the top of the page, and the charts are positioned flush with the bottom margin. Occasionally graphics are positioned one above the other. Given the diversity of the visuals, this consistent placement brings order to pages that might otherwise feel haphazard.

Hairline rules create a half-page frame; a second half-frame brackets the main text block. This motif is adapted for the charts, where the headline and the half-frame are inside a box and alternate from the left to right side. This device might appear contrived in some publications, but it is both functional and subtly decorative here.

Tables are created in Microsoft Word and placed in PageMaker following what the managing editor describes as the Golden Rules of Tabs: Use only one tab for each column of data. (If you need more space between two columns, reset the tabs; do not insert two tabs to increase the space). Do not use the Spacebar to adjust space between columns. Be sure to specify left, right, or center alignment. And work in the word-processing program at the same column width you will use in your page layout.

Charts are created in Cricket Graph. Maps are drawn by hand and stripped in by the printer.

Design: Carol Terrizzi (Ithaca, NY)

Pages from Consumer Markets Abroad, *published monthly by American Demographics.*
Trim size: 8-1/2 by 11

Consumer markets abroad 3

RECOVERY IN RIVER COUNTRY

International business leaders watch Zaïre's economic reforms with interest.

Zaïre's investment climate is more favorable today than at any other time since the copper-boom of the early 1970s. After almost five years of reform sponsored by the International Monetary Fund (IMF), the Zaïrian government points to a more competitive business environment as evidence of a stable economic recovery. In this new climate, prospects for U.S. trade should improve.

Formerly the Belgian Congo, Zaïre (meaning "river") achieved independence in June 1960, with one of the most highly developed and diversified economies in sub-Saharan Africa. Although plagued by civil strife...

But Zaïre does not lack water—the Zaïre River, the world's sixth-largest, functions as a lifeline for commerce, transportation, and hydroelectric power. This river's hydroelectric potential is equivalent to 13 percent of the world's supply. Much of that hydroelectric power is tapped by the Inga Dam. The country also has about 135 million barrels of petroleum reserves and over 700 million tons of coal reserves.

Kinshasa, Zaïre's capital city, has nearly 3 million residents. As one of the largest cities in Africa, it is an important market for consumer goods and services. Kinshasa lies 180 miles inland from the Zaïre River. Beyond it, the river is navigable for 1,000...

IN THE EYE OF THE STORM

Like its African neighbors, the country's population will increase by nearly 4 percent this year.
(Zaïrian provinces by annual growth rate, in percent, 1981–85)

Zaïre is surrounded by demographic and political hotspots.

Zaïre's 34 million people belong to as many as 250 different ethnic groups.

Consumer markets abroad 7

MANAGING GROWTH
Both urban and rural population growth should slow early in the next century. (Annual rate of population growth in urban and rural areas, in percent, 1980–2025)

Source: World Demographic Estimates and Projections, 1950–2025, United Nations, New York, 1988, p. 176.

REFORM'S REWARDS

The Zaïrian government had few choices but to reform under the IMF program in 1982, when the country's foreign-debt burden had reached about US$5 billion. But reform went beyond the rescheduling of debt. Other initiatives included devaluing the national currency (the zaïre), establishing market rates of exchange for most prices and interest rates, liberalizing trade (including customs duties and administrative procedures for export manufacturers), and reorganizing government-owned enterprises known as *parastatals*. In addition, the government improved tax collection and limited public spending and employment.

These reforms produced immediate results. Inflation fell from 76 percent in 1983 to 30 percent in 1985. The government turned an operating budget deficit that was 6 percent of GDP in 1982 into a 1 percent surplus in 1985.

Because the government eliminated exchange and price controls, the black market has shrunk and more profits now accrue to legitimate traders and small farmers. Local supplies reach their markets on a more regular basis.

The periodic shortages that were common in Zaïre now occur less frequently. Both foreign and domestic goods are more plentiful than in the 1970s. Fiscal controls ensure that key industries like mining receive the foreign exchange and local currency they need to operate, thus providing steady jobs for Zaïre's industrial workers.

But these successes have not eliminated Zaïre's debt problem. Not long ago, 50 percent of the government's annual budget was required to meet debt-repayment schedules. From the early days of the austerity program in 1983 through October 1986, Zaïre paid Western financial institutions and governments nearly US$1 billion more than it received in loans, grants, and foreign assistance.

SAFE RETURNS

Because the Zaïrian government recognizes that foreign investment is key in keeping the economic momentum alive, it established a new investment code in April 1986. That code offers numerous tax advantages to foreign businesses, some of which vary by location of the enterprise,

number of jobs generated, type of industrial activity, training and promotion of local staff, export orientation, and value added to local resources. Most benefits under the new investment code last for five years, but some last longer, especially for mining ventures. Zaïre guarantees the repatriation of profits to foreign investors.

In addition to a new investment code, the country recently signed a bilateral investment treaty with the United States. That treaty provides additional protection to foreign investors in the areas of transfer of profits, employment of expatriate technical and managerial personnel, and dispute settlement. In 1986, Zaïre became a member of the World Bank's Multilateral Investment Guarantee Agency, which insures foreign investors against the possibilities of currency manipulation and expropriation.

ROOM TO GROW

The Zaïrian government hopes to channel foreign investment into the

sectors in which the country has a natural advantage, such as timber, floriculture, and aquaculture. The government considers more than half of Zaïre's estimated 250 million acres of forests—containing over 100 varieties of lumber-producing trees—"exploitable." These forests contain types of wood that don't exist anywhere else in the world, such as African mahogany. Forestry experts predict that Zaïre could become the leading supplier of African hardwood by the mid-1990s.

Unlike the majority of African land, Zaïre's land is extremely fertile. The eastern provinces are ideal for growing perishable products—such as strawberries and fresh-cut flowers—for an expanding export market. Low labor costs, a well-run national airline for transporting cargo (Air Zaïre), and multiple growing seasons position the country favorably in these highly competitive markets.

SOURCES

Statistics on Zaïre are hard to find. While the country took a census in

URBAN SHIFT
The share of Zaïrian urbanites to the total population will shift from one-quarter to two-thirds by 2025. (Population of Zaïre, in thousands, and percent urban and rural, 1985 and projected 2025)

1985	
Total population	34,672
Percent share	100.0%
Urban population	8,668
Urban share	25.0%
Rural population	26,004
Rural share	75.0%
2025	
Total population	90,097
Percent share	100.0%
Urban population	57,717
Urban share	64.1%
Rural population	32,380
Rural share	35.9%

Source: National Census of Zaïre 1985; World Demographic Estimates and Projections 1950–2025, United Nations, New York, 1988, p. 176.

FARM TO FACTORY
Despite high unemployment, many Zaïrian workers are moving from farming into industry and services. (Labor force by sector, in percent, 1965 and 1980)

1965
Services 9%
Industry 9%
Agriculture 82%

1980
Services 16%
Industry 13%
Agriculture 72%

Source: Robert A. Weaver, Jr. & Associates.

WHO WORKS!
Work will cluster around middle age for Zaïrian men and women in the next century. (Labor force participation by sex and age group, in percent, 1985 and projected 2025)

Age group	1985 Women	1985 Men	2025 Women	2025 Men
Total	28.1%	50.2%	29.8%	51.3%
10–14	19.2	30.0	0.4	2.0
15–19	36.8	61.4	26.3	46.4
20–24	42.6	86.6	53.2	83.8
25–29	46.9	96.0	54.3	95.1
30–34	50.9	96.7	55.7	96.7
35–39	53.3	96.8	58.1	96.6
40–44	56.5	96.5	60.3	96.0
45–49	55.9	95.9	58.2	94.6
50–54	54.0	94.6	55.3	91.6
55–59	52.7	92.1	36.2	84.9
60–64	45.5	85.4	23.4	65.2
65 and older	28.9	66.2	9.7	28.6

Source: World Demographic Estimates and Projections 1950–2025, United Nations, New York, 1988, p. 177.

IMPACT

Perspectives

Vol. 3 No. 2 Spring, 1988 — Reporting on legislative and political issues

Outlook for AIDS testing looks up, six bills propose eliminating ban

"California now is the only state that forbids AIDS antibody or HIV testing."

The California Legislature's long standing claim to fame is its volume of bills introduced each session. This year is no exception. By the Feb. 19 deadline for new bills, over 7,500 bills were introduced, of which 147 addressed AIDS. These legislative proposals range in subject matter from confidentiality laws, to extensions of HIV testing to provisions for research and education.

Of greatest interest to TLC are six bills that would repeal the prohibition (contained in AB 403, passed in 1985) against antibody testing of insurance applicants for exposure to the AIDS virus. California now is the only state that forbids AIDS antibody or HIV testing. Each measure proposes to authorize health care service plans, nonprofit hospital service plans and/or life and disability insurers to establish mandatory and uniform minimum requirements for assessing AIDS risks for purposes of determining insurability.

Specifically, these are: AB 2900 (Johnston, Isenberg); AB 3305 (Johnston); AB 3421 (McClintock); AB 3538 (Johnson); AB 4036 (Mojonnier); and AB 4450 (Peace).

From a political perspective, both AB 2900

Continued on page 2

INSIDE PERSPECTIVES

Single premium life:

Congress has mixed view of issue, while industry juggles positions

View from the Hill

Threatening serious consequences for the life insurance industry, the confusion continues to grow over the issue of taxation of single premium policies. During March, the House and Senate each held separate subcommittee hearings on single premium and other investment-oriented life insurance products. The general consensus at the conclusion of the hearings was that it seemed unlikely that the current law will be retained without changes.

Due to marketing practices of some companies, many members of Congress view single-premium policies as "tax loopholes."

The likelihood of changing the current law is further enhanced by the life insurance industry's disagreement on an accepted industry-wide position. Major life insurance trade associations are advocating different positions or approaches to the problem.

Continued on page 2

The two-and-a-half-column format has a very different look when the text is broken up with banners, boxed copy, and illustrations.

Note the absence of rules to separate columns and define the image area. With the wide margin and generous space around headlines, the text block provides sufficient definition. A format with more tightly packed pages would need rules to delineate the elements.

The wide margin is used for quotes, a contents listing, and photos (not shown) that extend an additional 2-1/2 picas into the first text column.

Crimson banners with reverse Garamond type are used for department-style headlines.

The headlines and marginal quotes are Helvetica. The running text is Garamond.

The type prints in blue on bone-colored stock. Boxed copy prints over lavender or light blue tints. A blue tone prints over photos as well.

Design:
Partners by Design (N. Hollywood, CA); Agency: Jonisch Communications (Los Angeles, CA)

Pages from Perspectives, *published quarterly by the Transamerica Life Companies.*
Size: 8-1/2 by 11

PAC Talk

Political pundit offers view of presidential races

"Despite the fact that Americans are in the mood for a change, there simply isn't enough momentum for the Democrats to get back in the White House."

Described as the "nation's hot new political pundit," political analyst William Schneider set the stage for his observations of the presidential primary campaigns with a few personal definitions before offering any commentary or opinion at the TALCPAC 200 Club breakfast:

"A pundit is someone who comes on to the field of battle after the fighting stops and then shoots the wounded," he explained. "The primary is the 'killing ground' where they try to kill off the candidates. But this year, they all refuse to die!"

Of course, since that Feb. 19 breakfast, the field of presidential candidates has dwindled considerably. In any event, Schneider's perceptions of the 1988 presidential campaigns provided 200 Club members with new and often amusing insights to the primary season.

"For the Democrats to get back to the White House, they must have an issue like the Depression or Watergate," Schneider said. "But so far they only have the stock market crash and 'Iran-gate'. Despite the fact that Americans are in the mood for a change, there simply isn't enough momentum for the Democrats to get back in the White House," he added.

Schneider conceded that all the candidates from both parties were really competent, but pointed out that "there is not a vision between them."

In his comments on various candidates, Schneider quipped that Massachusetts Governor Michael S. Dukakis attracts the "Masterpiece Theatre audience in politics." Dukakis is "addicted to good government" and is "committed to process," he said.

Suggesting that the Massachusetts governor will use Harvard's Kennedy School of Government to fill key management posts, Schneider remarked that with Dukakis in the White House we would have "government by case study."

He described Illinois Senator Paul Simon as the "Orville Redenbacher" of the Democratic party, explaining that Simon "appeals to the constituency that longs for Mario Cuomo to run." Schneider painted a vivid picture of traditional Democratic fundamentalists as those who "cry and cheer when someone gives a revival speech."

As for the Republicans, he called Kansas Sen. Bob Dole a "superb deal maker."

Schneider also accurately predicted that Vice President Bush would nearly capture the GOP nomination on Super Tuesday (March 8). He reasoned that President Reagan had a strong base in the South, which would help Bush. "But Dole lacked the money, the base and the momentum going into the Southern primary to win," Schneider remarked.

Schneider also commented briefly on the vice presidency, calling it "the last cookie on the plate. No one ever wants it, but someone always takes it. If Bush offers George Deukmejian the vice presidency, Duke will take it," stated Schneider.

Presidential Politics

Who has what it takes?

The presidential primary season enters the last stretch of the campaigns with the final primaries in California, New Jersey, Montana, New Mexico and North Dakota.

Vice President George Bush captured enough delegate votes in the Pennsylvania primary to win the Republican nomination. Now, he is watching the Democratic candidates scramble for delegates as he starts to plan strategy for the November election.

Democratic front runner, Massachusetts Governor Michael Dukakis is still short of the 2,081 delegates needed to secure his party's nomination on the first ballot. Even a big win in California or New Jersey on June 7 won't give Dukakis all the delegates he needs. So, he and his staff are busy seeking commitments from delegates from who are uncommited or whose candidates have withdrawn.

He also must consider the 645 "super delegates." This is a category created by the Democratic Party's new rules. The party awards 15 percent of the convention seats to Democratic officeholders and party leaders.

Although Dukakis has 30 percent more delegates than the Rev. Jesse Jackson, who ranks second in delegate count, he cannot afford to alienate voters committed to other Democratic candidates. Whoever leaves Atlanta with the Democratic nomination will need to unite the party in order to win in November.

4

June 1988 ballot propositions

Two initiatives call for careful consideration

California voters will be faced with a dozen statewide propositions on their ballots this June. These initiatives cover a broad range of policy issues from earthquake safety and wildlife protection to technical revisions to the state's constitutional spending limits. Of the 12 initiatives, four are bond issues.

Two initiatives, however, are particularly noteworthy on campaign finance reform . The following is a brief description of both.

Between 1976 and 1986, the cost of running for office in California Legislature has skyrocketed. In 1976, 226 candidates ran for 100 seats (80 Assembly; 20 Senate). Each candidate spent an average of $33,933 to run for office. In 1986, the average spent by 192 candidates for the same offices spent an average of $176,195, an increase of 519 percent.

Proposition 68, sponsored by Common Cause and the League of Women Voters, is an attempt to deal with some of the problems of campaign finance. In short, it limits the amount of funds that can be contributed during any one calendar year and election; it prohibits fund raising during nonelection years; it prohibits transfers of campaign money between candidates; and it establishes a limited form of public financing through a voluntary check-off system on the state income tax form. This measure also limits the amount of money legislative candidates can spend, contribute or loan.

Proposition 73, the second campaign funding initiative on the ballot, is not as complicated as Proposition 68. Sponsored by a bipartisan group of legislators, this measure specifically prohibits both public financing for political campaigns and the transfer of funds between candidates. It limits political contributions from individuals, political committees and parties. This measure also limits the honoraria elected officials can accept during a calendar year.

Historical Perspective

Convention Trivia

The Democrats hold the record for the longest nominating convention and most ballots. In 1924, the convention stretched 17 days and 103 ballots before the Democrats selected John W. Davis of West Virginia to run against President Calvin Coolidge.

Keeping numbers straight on initiative process

"Since...1911, 200 initiatives have been up for votes over the past 77 years."

Since California voters approved the initiative and referendum process in 1911, 200 initiatives have been up for votes over the past 77 years. Of these, 54, or 28 percent, have been approved.

The initiative process has proven to be a powerful voice of the public in affecting change throughout the state, and even across the nation. For example, in 1978 the Tax Limitation Measure, commonly known as Proposition 13, put a cap on property taxes. Since then, other states have copied California's lead on this issue.

Ballot Measures 66 Through 77 June 7 88

Until 1982, the slate of ballot measures for each election began numbering with 1. However, this became increasingly confusing with controversial issues. Proposition 13 was a tax-cutting measure in 1978, but a water conservation proposal in 1982 had the same number.

In 1983, the Legislature passed a law requiring ballot measures to be number consecutively beginning with the November 1982 elections and continuing for 20 years.

This year the June ballot measure will begin with number 66. In 2002, initiatives will begin renumbering with number 1.

5

A serious, analytical image appropriate for a marketing newsletter is established through the continuous running text and the dimensional, diagrammatic art.

The narrow side margins (2 picas 6 points) allow for wide, 14-pica text columns, about the maximum width in a three-column grid. The density of the text is balanced by white space from a deep, 12-pica top margin, the floating art, and the open leading in the breakouts.

The dimensional "Market Power Grid," abstracted from the cover illustration (not shown), is picked up also as a design motif at the start of each section. The tinted square in each icon is keyed either to the larger grid on the page shown or to a similar grid on another page. The grid was created in Illustrator.

A second color is used for the art, headlines, and breakouts. This helps break up the text and allows for small subheads without loss of emphasis.

The leaders and the narrow-measure callouts emphasize the vertical structure of the grid and keep the page clean and crisp. The small Helvetica type for the callouts contrasts with the larger Times Roman used for running text and breakouts.

The bold initial cap, floating above a gray tinted box, draws the reader's eye to the beginning of the text. This is particularly effective in a page that otherwise lacks any dramatic contrasts.

Design: Marla Schay and Micah Zimring, Watzman + Keyes (Cambridge, MA)

Pages from Indications, *published bimonthly by Index Group, Inc. Trim size: 25-1/2 by 11, folded twice*

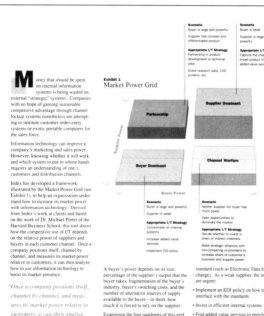

This newsletter achieves a completely different style within the three-column format than does the publication on the facing page. Here, rules and banners separating stories provide a clearly visible page structure, whereas the continuous narrative in the preceding publication is designed with a less apparent, though equally tight, framework. Compare also the justified text of this publication with the ragged right of the preceding one, and the paragraph indents here with the flush left first lines and open paragraph spacing shown on the facing page. Note, too, that the photos here are angled to break out of the grid, while the dimensional art on the facing page is positioned to emphasize the grid.

The angled snapshots over blue shadows loosen up the tightly structured page and also convey a warm, people-oriented image.

Goudy Old Style, used throughout, is a delicate typeface that is handled here with considerable sophistication. Note the open spacing of the all-caps category heads, which set elegantly against the gray banners above each story; the graceful initial caps, which print blue; and the alignment of text in adjacent columns, which adds to the crispness of the justified text. The delicacy of this typeface also makes it relatively forgiving of the uneven spacing often found in justified type.

Design: Kimberly Mancebo,
Castro Benson Bryant Mancebo
(Campbell, CA)

Pages from the
O'Connor Foundation Quarterly.
Trim size: 8-1/2 by 11

COMMUNITY OUTREACH

O'Connor Reaches Out to Kids as it Co-Sponsors Children's Discovery Museum Groundbreaking

Why did dozens of O'Connor Hospital employees spend an entire Saturday of their own free time volunteering at the Children's Discovery Museum Groundbreaking?

To help kids learn about health care. They manned interactive learning centers where they showed kids how to splint arms, listen through stethoscopes, navigate wheelchairs, read x-rays, and walk on crutches.

Not only did O'Connor employees participate in the Groundbreaking activities, but they also hope to establish long-term involvement after the Museum opens next year. ☐

ADMINISTRATIVE DIRECTOR of Radiology Carol Yantz explains how x-rays give an "inside out" view of people.

PATIENT CARE

Monte Villa's Self Discovery Helps Troubled Youths

Located in a serene setting in Morgan Hill, O'Connor's Monte Villa Hospital (MVH) offers confidential adolescent psychiatric programs and chemical dependency services.

The Self Discovery program is committed to affirming life and respecting the dignity of adolescents and their families. The program offers troubled youths a chance to feel better about themselves, to understand their feelings and needs, to discover that they are likeable, and to feel accepted.

When a person comes to Monte Villa Hospital for care, he or she undergoes full medical and neuropsychological evaluations. Group and individual counseling promotes healing of specific physical, spiritual, familial, social, educational and emotional problems. Follow-up care is an integral part of the program. Accredited schooling is also available. For details, call Susan Titus at 408/779-4151. ☐

NOBODY SAID ADOLESCENCE WOULD BE EASY, but for some teens it is absolutely overwhelming. Compassionate counselors help these youths find their way. The symbol was created by the teenagers at MVH and is used on T-shirts and binders as a reminder of the importance of their efforts in Self Discovery.

PHYSICIAN PROFILE

Golden Gloves Champion Dr. Calcagno Practices 50 Years at O'Connor

Imagine combining the slam bang vigor of a Golden Gloves boxing champion, the gentle sensitivity of a community volunteer, and the sophisticated intelligence of a physician. Put them all together and you've got the fascinating Dr. Joseph Calcagno, general practitioner at O'Connor for nearly half a century.

From the time Dr. Calcagno was old enough to walk, he gleefully tagged along with his dad to local boxing competitions, dreaming of the day when he, too, would win a title. The day came during pre-med school at Santa Clara University when he "left-and-right-hooked" his way through eliminations to win a 1934 Golden Gloves award in the Lightweight Division. That victory still remains one of the special moments in his life.

When he graduated from medical school in 1939, he joined World War II's War in the Pacific. "I spent the whole six years on the islands in field hospital MASH units," he says. "We were the envy of the soldiers, not only because we got Coca-Cola and fresh milk and meat from Army pilots as fringe benefits, but because we had 30 nurses to work with!"

By 1946, he was home again and opened a medical practice on Race Street. Soon after, his passion for boxing came back into focus, this time not as a participant, but as a licensed ringside physician for the California State Athletic Commission. As such, he has been the attending doctor at boxing and wrestling matches on the average of every other weekend for 46 years, with as many as 3-4 dozen matches in a single weekend. He examines

> *"In 1946, he opened a medical practice on Race Street, across from the O'Connor Sanitarium. He's been there ever since."*

all competing boxers and wrestlers—both amateur and professional—about an hour before each match and treats them immediately after they compete.

"Most injuries are minor face, eye and lip cuts," he explains, "but occasionally the officials or I will stop a fight if we see someone taking a beating, and submit a record to the California Athletic Commission."

As the only boxing/wrestling attending physician in the Santa Clara Valley, he ends up performing annual physicals on at least five professional boxers, wrestlers, officials or judges on any given weekday. They all need Dr. Calcagno's "stamp of approval" to retain their state licences.

A 20-year Volunteer for PAL
As a firm believer in community service, Dr. Calcagno extends his passion for these sports into volunteer work, having regularly donated his time to the boxers and wrestlers of the Police Athletic League (PAL) since the organization was founded in 1968.

Dr. Calcagno is one of those rare individuals who has been able to integrate his professional skills in the healing arts into a hobby which he adores.

"I feel very lucky," he says, "My hobby has become my work. What more could a person ask for?" ☐

DR. CALCAGNO (photo left) now works beneath a wall filled with awards from his four decades of volunteerism. (Right) Barely into his twenties, Santa Clara University student Dr. Calcagno wins a Golden Gloves title.

The two true tabloids on this page use the 11-by-17 page in similar ways but to different effect. Both rely heavily on white space and display type to make the oversize page accessible.

The three + one-column format (above) creates a half-frame of white space around the image area.

Photos, captions, and a statement of goals break into the white space without filling it.

The logo prints in red ("Ameri") and blue ("News"). The red is picked up in the banners with reverse type and in the rule at the bottom of the page. The blue is picked up in the initial cap, the two-column inset text, and the tint in the contents box. Red and blue are crisp, bold colors that liven up a mostly text page.

The two-column format (above right) is unusual for a tabloid, but the wide margin, used only for pull quotes and blurbs, and the space around the bold headlines make it work.

The nameplate banner is repeated in a smaller size on inside pages, providing strong identity.

A second color, crimson, is used for the alternating thick and thin rules, initial caps, display text inset in the running text, and company identification in the lower left.

The type is Helvetica Black for headlines and blurbs inset in running text, and Bookman for running text, captions, and marginal quotes.

Design (above left): Kate Dore, Dore Davis Design (Sacramento,CA)

Cover of AmeriNews, *the inhouse newsletter of AmeriGas–Cal Gas. Trim size: 11 by 17*

Design (above right): Mary Reed, ImageSet Design (Portland, ME)

Cover of Re:, *a commercial/industrial real estate newsletter published by The MacBride Dunham Group. Trim size: 11 by 17*

An all-text, newspaper-style page can be made engaging and attractive. Rules, initial caps, white space, and a second color all support the structural device of using story headlines to divide the page into text units with varying sizes and shapes. The effect is infinitely more appealing to readers than columns of type that simply march down the page. The approach here is conservative—and appropriately so for a bar association newsletter; the same devices, however, can be used to create many other styles.

The top of the image area is dropped so as not to crowd the page. The resulting white space creates a strong horizon line.

The body text is Times Roman, and the subheads are Times Roman bold italic.

The headlines and folios are Caslon Extra Bold. The logo and the initial caps are set in Novarese.

The headlines are centered between brown rules, with a 2-point rule above and a 1-point rule below.

The initial caps print over a box with a horizontal-line fill and no outside rule (this fill also prints brown). Note the careful alignment of the baseline of the initial cap with the bottom rule in the box and the even spacing between the thin-line rule of the fill and the 1-point rule above. When you rely on typographic devices for the look of a page, these details are critical.

Design: Michael Waitsman, Synthesis Concepts (Chicago, IL)

Pages from Litigation News, *published by the American Bar Association. Trim size: 10-3/4 by 13-7/8*

The cover-story concept, seen frequently in magazines, has unusual impact when used effectively in a newsletter. At their best, newsletters have an intimacy with their readers (the result of a shared special interest) and a timeliness that even magazines lack in today's fast-paced communications. So a newsletter cover story implicitly announces, "Here's a problem that many of you are grappling with, and here's what we know about it." Anyone who works with PageMaker can see the immediate appeal of the cover stories shown on the facing page, from a newsletter that aptly describes itself as "a visual guide to using the Macintosh and PageMaker in desktop publishing."

The visual continuity in the covers of this newsletter also seems closer to the world of magazines than to that of newsletters. Newsletters typically achieve their cover identity through a familiar grid and typographic treatment. Here, the cover design varies quite a bit from one issue to the next depending on the subject. But the strong nameplate treatment, the unsual shape of the page, and the always-on-target theme provide their own very effective and unmistakable identity.

The grid is basically one wide column with a wide margin used for captions, art, and marginalia. One advantage of this format, especially in a narrow page such as this, is that you can easily break the grid and use the whole page.

Design: David Doty, PageWorks (Chicago, IL)

Pages from ThePage, *published monthly by PageWorks. Trim size: 7 by 11*

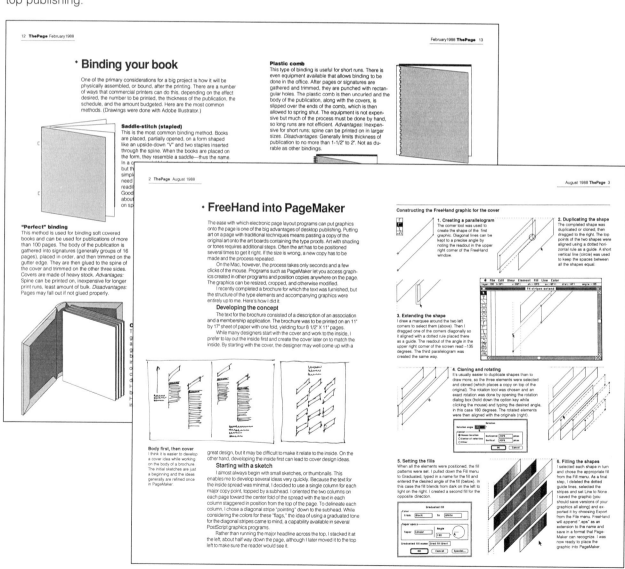

October 1987

A visual guide to
using the Macintosh
in desktop publishing

ThePage 10

High resolution reproduction

Which sections of the object below have been reproduced on
a Linotron and which on a LaserWriter?

May 1988

A visual guide to
using the Macintosh
in desktop publishing

ThePage 17

Design ideas for newsletters

NEWSLETTER DESIGN

EpiGram

Nameplate, flag, banner, logo, or masthead?

What do you call that splash of type across the top of a newsletter or magazine? It is often referred to as the masthead. That's actually the one thing it is not. The masthead of a publication is the listing of the staff, generally found on the inside pages.

The most appropriate term is banner, or banner head, but nameplate is also widely used. The term logo is less appropriate unless the design is also a symbol representing an organization.

Inside...

Newsletter ideas, publications of interest, the Bettmann Archive, putting photos on the page, ThunderScan into PageMaker, more clip art, and EmDash fonts (this page is set in ArchiText by EmDash).

Create a unique look for your newsletter

Newsletters are one of the forces propelling the desktop publishing revolution. They are seen as a quick way to gain a foothold in the publishing business. Design a newsletter for your client or boss and you're all set, right? What could be easier?

Newsletters are more complex than they appear. With choices of type, numbers of columns, use of photographs or art, handling of running heads, and all the little details of design, there is much to consider before arriving at a final solution.

More important, however, is that the above elements combine to form a unique and unified whole. On the next six pages are six fictional newsletter designs. Use them as idea starters to help structure your own design efforts.

February 1988

A visual guide to
using the Macintosh
in desktop publishing

ThePage 14

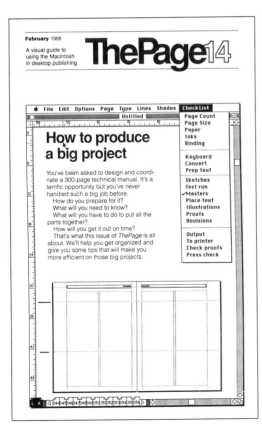

 File Edit Options Page Type Lines Shades **CheckList**

Untitled

How to produce a big project

You've been asked to design and coordinate a 300-page technical manual. It's a terrific opportunity but you've never handled such a big job before.

How do you prepare for it?
What will you need to know?
What will you have to do to put all the parts together?

How will you get it out on time?
That's what this issue of *ThePage* is all about. We'll help you get organized and give you some tips that will make you more efficient on those big projects.

Page Count
Page Size
Paper
Inks
Binding

Keyboard
Convert
Prep text

Sketches
Test run
✓Masters
Place text
Illustrations
Proofs
Revisions

Output
To printer
Check proofs
Press check

June 1988

A visual guide to
using the Macintosh
in desktop publishing

ThePage 18

The graphics evolution

Aldus FreeHand represents another step in the evolution of graphics programs. It competes head-on with Adobe Illustrator and Cricket Draw, yet offers several interesting advances in technology. Michael Waitsman discusses the strengths and shortcomings of this new program and offers some thoughts on the future of Macintosh illustration programs.

JOURNALS & MAGAZINES

The complexity of the magazine format, with its variety of editorial material in any given issue and the need to juggle several issues at once, makes the collaborative effort between editors and graphic designers one of the key elements of success. Editors who think visually and designers who get involved in the content of the material produce stories that are dynamic and attention-getting, with innovative approaches to even the most familiar ideas. The editor's job isn't over when the manuscript moves from word processor to page layout, and the designer doesn't wait for the manuscript to begin his or her work. Both work together to develop, shape, present, and refine each idea throughout the production cycle. Although desktop publishing is changing the nature of that collaboration, in some ways it presents the greatest opportunities for those editors and designers who don't see their functions as limited to either words or pictures.

Another unique challenge in producing magazines is the opportunity to use the dimension of time that is implicit in the magazine format. Each department and feature story is developed as a self-contained unit, but when you bind them together they become pieces of a whole. Play with that dimension as you make up the order of items in the magazine. Move from a picture story to an article with sustained reading text, from a story with black-and-white photographs to one that uses color illustration, from an idea that is light and accessible to one that is provocative and demanding. Even though few people read magazines from front to back, offering contrast from one story to the next creates an interesting texture and an attention-getting pace. Besides, using that dimension is fun and keeps your job interesting. The more you work with the flow and the pacing, the more they become a useful guide both in early planning and last-minute problem solving.

One of the great dangers in magazine publishing is that your approach will become stale. Don't confuse a consistent format with overreliance on formula. The degree to which you are inspired in producing each issue is probably a good measure of how that issue will be received by readers.

Journals and magazines in this section

- *Washington College Magazine* —a good format for feature articles in an alumni magazine
- *Back Talk Journal*—sophisticated type and photography in a small-format journal
- *American Demographics*—a format designed to introduce data, and some good filler ideas
- *Business North Carolina*—lessons learned from the redesign of a regional business magazine
- *Verbum*—a showcase for electronic art
- *HeartCorps*—a stylish, upbeat design for an audience of heart patients
- *Mother Earth News*—quick, low-resolution scans as a high-efficiency production tool

*K*arl and Irma Miller nurture the College's students as lovingly as the Hynson-Ringgold gardens. Young adults who know the elderly couple say they have an uncanny ability to bridge the generation gap.

ABOUT TOWN

Karl And Irma Miller: Tillers Of Good Will

by Sue De Pasquale '87
Photographs by J.M. Fragomeni '88

Karl and Irma Miller are matter-of-fact when it ~~~~~ about their gardening projects in ~~~~~

At 84 and 81, they see nothing unusual about a workload that keeps them bending, hoeing, digging and watering for hours upon hours nearly every day of the week. But ask people half their ~~~~~

PIECES OF THE PAST

Colonel Brown And The Dancing Duo

by P.J. Wingate '33

Although Washington College has been promoting the arts and sciences for over 200 years, it is not well known for its contributions to the performing arts. Nevertheless, a Washington College graduate played a vital role in creating the most celebrated dance team in the history of the theatre—Fred Astaire and Ginger Rogers.

This alumnus was Hiram S. Brown, Class of 1900, and later president of the movie firm RKO, which produced the first Astaire-Rogers film, "Flying Down to Rio," and subsequently made millions of dollars from a series of movies by this most gifted pair of dancers. Colonel Brown, as he was known throughout most of his adult life, was no longer president of RKO when most of those later movies were produced, but it took no great foresight for Brown's successors to see that they had an artistic diamond necklace and a financial gold mine in the dance team of Ginger Rogers and Fred Astaire.

Both Rogers and Astaire had played in Broadway shows before they made their first movie together, and had also played minor roles in the movies, but neither was even close to being called a movie star when Hiram Brown brought them together in 1933. The best that could be said for them then was that they were featured players. The listed stars for "Flying Down to Rio" were Gene Raymond and Dolores Del Rio, both of whom have long since vanished into the mists of obscurity along with the plot of the movie itself.

Not so for Rogers and Astaire. They shot up into the theatrical sky like rockets, propelled by their own incomparable talents and the enchanting tunes by Vincent Youmans who provided the music they danced to: "The Carioca," "Orchids in the Moonlight," "Music Makes Me," and the title song, "Flying Down to Rio." In all subsequent movies which they made together, Ginger Rogers and Fred Astaire were the stars, and their dancing became artistic treasures which will be preserved for centuries to come.

The story of this famous dance team is too well known to be repeated here,

PHOTO: CULVER PICTURES

18   19

This alumni publication used to be a tabloid. After converting to desktop production, the magazine saved enough money on typesetting and pasteup to upgrade the tabloid to the glossy format shown here.

The style of feature articles defines a magazine's personality as much as any other element. Here, good photos given lots of space, graceful Palatino italic headlines, upsized introductions set on a two-column measure, and plenty of white space define an accessible style that opens every feature article. Subsequent pages of features follow the three-column format with photographs sized one, two, or three columns wide. This consistent style greatly speeds up layout and production time because so many decisions are already made.

The understated style works fine for a captive audience, which an alumni magazine such as this enjoys. A magazine with paid circulation has to work harder at varying its style and using catchy headlines to sell readers on each story.

Design: Meredith Davies (Chestertown, MD)

Pages from Washington College Magazine, *published quarterly. Trim size: 8-1/2 by 11*

Full-bleed photos, used frequently in this journal, have power and impact that you just don't get with photos that are contained on the page. The cover image provides a silhouette that is enviably appropriate for a clinic specializing in back pain.

Good printing on a heavy, coated paper stock brings out the best in the design and photos. The rich blacks contrast with the warm gray/brown used as a second color in the cover type, running heads, bold rules, pull quotes, and boxes for reverse-type initial caps.

The type selection contrasts the clean lines of Helvetica Black with the tall, thin shape of Garamond. The banner centered under the running head works because the two words above it have the same number of letters. The initial cap/small cap style of the subhead and running foot adds additional detail to the sophisticated typography.

Design: Bob Reznik (Plano, TX)

Pages from Back Talk Journal, published annually by the Texas Back Institute. Trim size: 7-1/2 by 11

WHAT IS A WORKING WOMAN?

If you think only half of women work, think again.
◆

by Horst H. Stipp

Whether a woman works outside the home or not is a vital piece of information for marketers who target women. Most rely on the standard published figures—52 percent of women aged 16 and older were working in 1986, for example.

New research indicates that this figure may be way off the mark. In fact, among a target group dear to the hearts of marketers—women aged 18 to 49—about 90 percent can be considered part of the labor force. The "typical housewife" has become rare indeed.

How can the standard statistics understate women's work patterns so dramatically? They overlook the fact that women enter and exit the labor force frequently. Both men and women occasionally change jobs, get laid off, or go to school. But many women also

Horst H. Stipp is the director of Social Research at NBC.

stop working for a while after they have a baby, when they get married, and for other reasons. Overall, women enter and exit the labor force much more frequently than men. As a result, a large percentage of women are both working and not working over a relatively short period of time. Many of today's non-working women will be tomorrow's working women and vice versa. Most important, the attitudes of women with discontinuous work patterns are similar to those of women who are in the work force continuously.

THE PATTERN

The frequency with which women exit and reenter the labor force today is much less than it was 10 or 20 years ago. Nevertheless, demographers Suzanne Bianchi and Daphne Spain find that "women's participation in the labor force over the life course still remains more discontinuous than men's as women continue to exit and reenter the

24 AMERICAN DEMOGRAPHICS / JULY 1988

A magazine that is chock-full of charts, graphs, tables, and just about every other form of statistical data works doubly hard to open each story as a general-interest feature. Bold headlines, hand-tinted photographs framed by heavy rules, and lots of white space provide lively hooks and a respite from the data prevalent elsewhere. The upsized introductory blurbs explain or provide context for the headline.

Effective fillers are the hot spots of many magazines. Fillers are simply standing items of varying length that you can plug in wherever space allows (or requires). A good concept for a filler is a fresh, timely, fascinating, or quirky angle on the magazine's subject matter. It's right on target even when it seems to come out of left field. A good filler is generally a quick read and may well be the first thing some readers look for when they pick up the magazine. The Demo Memo filler (above right) runs several times in each issue of *American Demographics.* It's easy to recognize and, for less than a minute of your time, is almost guaranteed to deliver some fascinating fact. The Lincoln Sample (below right) is, by definition, a limited-run filler: It follows a photographer's route from the Atlantic to the Pacific coast, with a picture of the road ahead taken every nine miles, exactly. Editorial techniques such as these keep magazines lively and changing and also provide flexibility in production.

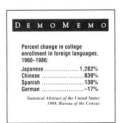

DEMO MEMO

Percent change in college enrollment in foreign languages, 1960–1986:

Japanese 1,282%
Chinese 839%
Spanish 130%
German .... –17%

Statistical Abstract of the United States 1988, Bureau of the Census

26 **THE LINCOLN SAMPLE, STOP NUMBER 26.** 3,060 miles to go. Adams Co., Rt. 30, a few miles past Hubcap City. I am entering Gettysburg, home of The Address, but the sign says we're in Marlboro Country. Beyond the cowboy is the Penn Eagle Motel where I'm spending the night. The owners are from India and it's suppertime—the lobby smells like curry. I made 20 stops today—that's 180 miles. **0 0 2 2 5**

Design: Michael Rider (Ithaca, NY)

Pages from American Demographics, *published monthly.*
Trim size: 8-3/8 by 11

When this regional business magazine approached a redesign, the staff focused on four goals: to capture the contrast of old and new that typified the audience; to sharpen the spotlight on people; to create a simple format that would free the small staff to focus on content rather than layout; and to convert the magazine to desktop publishing.

The audience combined the deep-rooted traditions of the North Carolina mountains and agricultural areas with the high-tech innovations of businesses and universities in the state's Golden Triangle. Understanding the unique character of one's audience enables a magazine to use that character as a building block in the publication's design.

The typography in the logo captures the contrast inherent in the audience. The word "Business," set in Futura Extra Bold Oblique, is bold, contemporary, and aggressive. The words "North Carolina," set in the genteel, soft, and almost lyrical Palatino, add a quiet, reserved, and sophisticated counterpoint.

The spotlight on people was part of the magazine's editorial image all along. But the redesign process gives you the opportunity to look with fresh eyes at what you are already doing, as well as the opportunity to redefine your goals and determine how best to reach them. In this case, the new understanding led to a change from covers that varied in their subjects and art styles to photographic covers featuring a single business leader in his or her natural enviroment.

The emphasis on good, varied photographs continues on the inside pages. Concentrating on a consistent visual approach and finding a small group of photographers who understand and can deliver the magazine's photographic style frees the art director from having to start at square one with every story.

A table of contents should be highly organized, graphically interesting, and uncompromisingly utilitarian—all at the same time.

The numbers in the contents listings are 24-point Futura Extra Bold Oblique. They are graphic as well as functional elements on the page. As is the case with headline type, numbers set in large sizes require careful kerning to achieve the even spacing seen here.

The rules are 18 point, with 9-point Futura Extra Bold reverse type in all caps.

The descriptive lines are the 10/13 Palatino used for body text inside the magazine.

Art picked up from inside the magazine makes the contents page visually interesting and is selected both to highlight important stories and to arouse curiosity. If you use the art at the same size as it appears elsewhere in the magazine (even if it's just a detail from a larger picture), you avoid the cost of additional color separations.

FEATURE

BUSINESS IS LOOKING UP FOR GENERAL AVIATION

When it comes to flying for business or pleasure, the sky's not the limit.

By J.A.C. Dunn

Charles (left) and Winfield Causey were farming with their father in 1963. But they got bitten by the flying bug and turned from furrows to runways.

The little plane circles the airport once, a tiny moving X in the cloudless eastern Carolina sky. Its single engine makes a barely audible hum. It disappears briefly beyond the woods, then suddenly reappears just over the trees surrounding the airport and lands on the longer of Warren Field's two runways. Taxiing to the front of the low, brick terminal building, it swings around to face the broad expanse of rough grass between the tarmac. The pilot cuts the engine, steps out of the cockpit and strolls across the apron and through the double glass doors of the terminal lobby.

"Morning," he says, genially, at large. Salesman, you think. He has a little sandy mustache and very alert eyes. Pointing at a tired-looking, twin-engine plane at one side of the apron, he asks, "That airplane out there. What is it? Does it fly?"

"That's an old DC-4," says Joe Leggitt, the airport manager. He's a stocky, muscular young man with a smiling, sunburned face. He used to be a commercial fisherman. He wears a khaki jumpsuit befitting the all-purpose manager of an all-purpose rural airport, but behind the counter he is barefoot. Warren Field is not a stuffy establishment. Authorities, he tells the pilot, impounded the plane after a drug raid last spring. It has been grounded ever since.

"You don't see many of those around any

more," the visitor says reverently. He leans against a counter and lights a cigarette. "I was flying over and noticed it, and I thought, 'I have to find out about *that*.' I'm just flying around, looking at the country. I have an appointment in Baltimore this afternoon. I don't want to get there too soon."

He introduces himself: Richard Leachman of Cessna Finance Corp. in Raleigh. Aircraft finance. It fit with the blue blazer, gray slacks, white button-down shirt, necktie and polished loafers. An airplane nowadays is often a corporate asset, not a Sunday toy, and its pilot, rather than a flying playboy nicknamed Ace, is likely to wear a business suit with a briefcase as his co-pilot. The Aircraft Owners and Pilots Association describes the average general aviator as 44 years old, the owner of a house and two cars, married with two children, a licensed, instrument-rated pilot who flies a single-engine, fixed-gear aircraft 116 hours a year and likes to fish.

Despite its apparent imprecision, the term "general aviation" is very specific. It embraces all flight except commercial airlines and the military. It doesn't grab the headlines, the way Piedmont's recent merger with USAir or the opening of a regional airline hub does, but its statistics are astonishing. The nation's general

FEATURE

Phyllis Gallup replaced one plane wrecked by a student, who walked away from the crash. "All she said was, 'Oh, my hair must be a mess,' " Gallup says.

was a licensed pilot before he was 21. In 1921, he flew from London to China solo. The Winston-Salem airport bears his name.

But it was only after World War II that airports, and aircraft to use them, began to take off in North Carolina. The stimulus was a liberal sprinkling of leftover military airfields, most of them in the eastern part of the state. The airports at Wilson, Rocky Mount (now closed), Lumberton, Kinston, New Bern, Beaufort-Morehead City, Washington, Manteo and Edenton were all originally military fields.

Most were used for training. Warren Field had T-6 trainers based on it, and the original runways are still in use, although their 45-year-old concrete pavement is showing signs of wear. The 82nd Airborne Division flew troop-carrying gliders at Maxton, and pilots took basic flight training at Horace Williams Field in Chapel Hill. When the present Raleigh-Durham Airport replaced Raleigh Municipal, it was called Raleigh-Durham Army Air Base until transferred to civilian hands after the war.

Several airports are still used by the military, such as McCall Field in Aberdeen and Oak Grove at New Bern. Thirty miles southeast of Elizabeth City is Harvey's Point, a small airfield deliberately kept small because the Central Intelligence Agency operates it. Some of the participants in the Bay of Pigs invasion were trained there.

During the 1950s, the economic value of general aviation began to take off. In 1958, the Federal Aviation Act provided the first federal funds for airport development. Nearly 20 North Carolina airports received improvement money until 1970.

In 1965, Gov. Dan Moore created the position of aviation specialist in what was then the Department of Conservation and Development to help communities attract

new business by providing a place for companies to park their planes. The state established an airport aid program with $127,000 in 1967, though this money could not be used to improve airports that had scheduled commercial service. The fund was increased to $150,000 a year in 1971.

The airport aid fund was increased to $2 million in 1973, when the reorganization of state government placed the aviation specialist in the Department of Transportation. Half the money went to airports with commercial service. The fund was increased to $3 million in 1974 and the distinction between commercial and general-aviation airports removed.

The federal deregulation of commercial airlines brought about this change. Before deregulation, airlines were subsidized, sometimes by as much as $60 per passenger per stop at an airport, to enable airlines to serve relatively low-traffic places, such as Elizabeth City. Airport managements charged the airlines for airport improvements, which the airlines paid for from their subsidies.

After deregulation, it became harder to maintain and improve airports because airline subsidy money was gone. But most communities found it worth their while to

A plane is a time machine, says the N.C. Division of Aviation's Willard Plentl. He wants every industrial area of the state to have an airport within a half-hour drive.

*Design:
R. Kimble Walker
(Charlotte, NC)*

*Pages from
Business North
Carolina,
published monthly.
Trim size: 8-1/4 by
10-7/8*

A strong, simple format enables the small staff to produce a quality magazine that competes for readers' time with big-budget national business magazines. By minimizing the choices for each story, the editor and art director can concentrate on substance rather than form.

The 72-point Futura Extra Bold initial cap with an 18-point bold rule continues the visual motif from the cover. Rules over photos print in a different color for each feature. This bold, crisp look helps tie together editorial pages in a magazine fractured by small-space ads.

The body text, 10/13 Palatino in two 16-pica ragged right columns, sets about one-third fewer words than the more typical 9/10 justified text found in many magazines. The open text was another result of the redesign, and the editors feel that less has proved to be more.

In a showcase for electronic art, the variety of subjects, shapes, colors, styles, and textures puts any grid through its paces.

In the two spreads shown on the facing page, *Verbum* designer John Odam displays and comments on the capabilities of Illustrator 88 and FreeHand. The four-column grid on these pages combines maximum flexibility for sizing art with efficient copy fitting in the narrow, 10-pica columns.

In the spread below, the open type of a wide column provides a good balance against the black panels used to group small pieces of art. Although the size of the panels would work in a four-column grid, the denser type of a narrow measure would make the pages very dark.

Grouped captions in all three spreads are cross-referenced to the art by numbers, the size and placement of which makes them relatively inconspicuous without compromising legibility.

For the first piece of art he created in FreeHand (upper right in the top spread), Odam got film-positive color separations overnight from an L300. Of the implications of this, which registered several weeks after the fact, he writes: "I had produced a $500 airbrush illustration in 20 minutes and paid $20 for a color separation. Not only that, but the blending of two ink colors in graduated steps could not have been accomplished with airbrush without using all four printers' colors, or by using cumbersome overlays in which the exact color scheme could not be previsualized. I felt the same rush of adrenalin that I had experienced when I first saw a Linotronic proof."

Of graphics programs in general, Odam says, "There was a time once when you could tell which Macintosh application had been used to produce a graphic, but many programs on the market now are capable of producing the same end result with varying degrees of ease.... In the end, it is what best suits the individual user that counts."

Design: John Odam (San Diego, CA)
Pages from Verbum, *published quarterly.*
Trim size: 8-1/2 by 11

■ *by Jack Davis*

VISUALIZING WITH ELECTRIC CLAY

One of the primary roles of the artist is to take the "real" world — of height, width, and depth, color, textures, and shadows — and interpret it into the static world of the canvas or drawing table, to condense a thought, emotion or concept. Presenting a company, product, or service in its most essential character is the goal. Now, with the computer's sleight of hand, there's a practical way for artists to pour life back into their freeze-dried images.

An artist or designer can now create three-dimensional color images without the technology getting in the way. A large number of programs are available for a wide range of personal computers. Most are relatively simple — that means you don't have to type code or know Unix to get images on your screen. Here's a sampling of what's available:

Sculpt 3D for the Amiga is definitely the front runner at this time in the race for quality images and animation from any pc costing under $10,000. With its smooth phong shading, ray-traced shadows and highlights, colored light sources, and transparency effects, it leaves most other 3D packages in the dust. Its add-on package, *Animate 3D*, has many of the animation tools professionals use, such as hierarchical motion, key frame in-betweening, and real-time wire-frame preview.

CyberStudio for the Atari ST offers a fine modeling environment that includes solid model subtraction (Boolean operations) and — for an added twist — stereoscopic rendering! Animation of objects, cameras, and lights is done through a simple scripting language. (Who's afraid of a little language?) Special effects can also be added with the integrated *CyberPaint* cell animation program.

Even though *Pro3D* was originally created for the Macin-

1. *A logo prepared with Digital Arts.* **2.** *An experiment with Sculpt 3D by computer artist Bryan Carey Gallivan.* **3.** *Chess pieces drawn separately by an in-house artist at Silicon Beach Software with Super 3D, using the lathing technique (with some additions) and then assembled on the board.* **4.** *A somersaulting skeleton created with CyberStudio.* **5.** *A textbook sales graph drawn with Pro3D by Joe Grossman of Enabling Technologies.* **6.** *Computer furniture drawn with Design Dimensions and Solid Dimensions.*

tosh, it was the IBM PC that got the color version first (though I've been promised that a Mac color-enhanced version is coming soon). *Pro3D* has an extremely transparent interface — it's a little cutesy, but very easy to pick up. No internal animation tools are provided, but for quick visualization of something that's rolling around in your head, there's nothing better. It also has excellent modeling capabilities with solids subtraction, and handy features such as embossing (wrapping one 3D object onto another.)

Super 3D for the Macintosh is one of the first low-end Mac programs to combine color graphics (the enhanced color version of the package is said to be hot on the heels of its black-and-white forerunner), true CAD-like modeling and scaling, and simple animation playback. One feature that I love is its ability to import a full-color photograph as a backdrop that you can then animate over. The interface is clean and self-explanatory, and the output is beautiful.

Where the very high end meets the middle ground: *Digital Arts. Digital Arts* is included here for two reasons. First, it does run on a pc, although it needs to be a very souped-up PC AT equipped with Targa/Definicon board, for a total software and hardware cost of about $35,000. Second, it has the features needed to do broadcast-quality 3D

animation. The 24-bit color, the texture, bump, reflection, and transparency mapping, the "hierarchical tension" motion control, and a list of other features put this package far above other pc programs — but still quite a few steps below the high-end 3D leader (and its $100,000 price tag) from Wavefront Technologies of Santa Barbara.

Dimensions is a software family for the Mac, and though it is not the easiest to use, it was the first software to offer color, smooth shading, and true ray-traced images.

Last, but far from least, is *Swivel3D*, a new program coming for the Macintosh. It has a lot of bells and whistles, and blinding speed. It has what I think is the most intuitive interface ever created for moving around in a computer environment, any computer environment. Add rendering with shadows and pseudo reflection maps and some limited key-frame animation, and you have a visualization tool that will keep you up around the clock — with a smile on your face.

As you can see from the samples on these pages, pc 3D has made some dramatic improvements recently. And be prepared — the near future will bring possibilities we don't even dream of now. So have some fun with electric clay — you don't have to worry about it drying out.

Jack Davis used Swivel3D to prepare Ocean Couch. He first sculpted the mannequin (supplied with the software) to make one flat, formed the couch from several primitives to make a second top, and prepared the mannequin in a third tile. The three elements were then wrapped in textures made from scanned images: the Caribbean Sea for the couch, a turkey sandwich for the mannequin, and sunset over ripples for the moon. The three files were then assembled as a collage in FreeHand.

Sculpt 3D and Animate 3D
Byte by Byte Corporation
Suite 150
9442 Capital of Texas Highway, North
Austin, TX 78759
(512) 343-4357
Retail prices: Sculpt 3D, $99.95; Animate 3D,
$149.95

CyberStudio and CyberPaint
Antic Publishing, Inc.
544 Second Street
San Francisco, CA 94107
(415) 957-0886
Retail prices: CyberStudio, $89.95;
CyberPaint, $69.95

Pro3D
Enabling Technologies Inc
600 S. Dearborn Street
Chicago, IL 60605
(312) 427-0408
Retail prices: IBM PC version, $395; Mac
version, $349

Super 3D
Silicon Beach Software, Inc.
P.O. Box 261430
San Diego, CA 92126
(619) 695-6956
Retail prices: Black & white version, $295;
enhanced color version, $495

Digital Arts
Digital Arts
7370-Q Opportunity Road
San Diego, CA 92111-2225
(619) 541-2055
Retail price: $15,000

Dimensions
Visual Information, Inc.
16309 Doublegrove Street
La Puente, CA 91744
(818) 918-8834
Retail prices: Design Dimensions, $1595;
Solid Dimensions, $895

Swivel3D
Paracomp
123 Townsend Street, #310
San Francisco, CA 94107
(415) 543-3848
Available in late May: $400 to $500

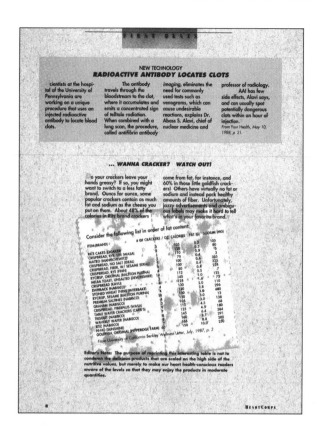

A stylish, varied, and active design gives an upbeat image to this magazine for heart patients. The pages are full of tips, techniques, charts, and other information highlighted through a visual repertoire that includes initial caps, large numerals, and frequent use of sidebars.

Department pages such as the ones shown at left break from the traditional columnar format by having each item treated almost as if it were an index card. The shape of the text block, as well as the type size, leading, and column width, vary from item to item, but the single typeface (Futura) and the textured background unify these pages.

Dimensionality is another signature of this design. Note the use of the cracker as a self-referential background for a chart, with type surprinting at the top and bottom. And in the page shown below left, the first text block appears to be sandwiched between art in the foreground and background; in the second item, the art is woven under the headline and over the text.

The headline type for feature stories (shown on the facing page) is Bodoni Poster, condensed to different degrees for each story depending on the length of the headline and the layout of the page. This provides the benefits of a unified typeface with many variations. Bodoni Poster works unusually well with this treatment because it maintains its distinctive relationship of thick and thin strokes. Many typefaces deviate too much from the original design when condensed.

The text wraparound (facing page, bottom) adds graphic interest to the page and also minimizes the text lost to a fairly large illustration. This technique can be prohibitively expensive using commercial typesetting. Desktop publishing makes it affordable, though it may require a lot of fine-tuning to avoid bad line breaks and achieve even spacing.

Design: Tom Lewis (San Diego, CA)

Pages from Heartcorps, *published bimonthly. Size: 8-1/4 by 10-3/4*

THE RIGHT MOVES

ROPE JUMPING
TOO GOOD TO PASS UP?

BY KEN SOLIS, MD

An often repeated adage states, "The best exercise is the exercise which you do." There are four essential questions which you must ask yourself to define if an exercise is one that you will likely do *on a regular basis and for an indefinite period of time;* 1) Is it right for your body? 2) Is it easily accessible? 3) Will it give the results you are looking for? and 4) Do you enjoy it?

Perhaps surprisingly, rope jumping is one form of aerobic exercise which nicely fits the bill for many people, even recovered heart patients. Now, even without the help of telepathy, I know that a good number of you readers have already been struck with the "but ... too" disease: "I'd love to try it, *but*

I'm *too* uncoordinated to jump rope" - or - "it sounds like fun, *but* it'd be *too* hard on my knees" - or - "it's *too* hard on my wind, and it's *too* boring." In fact, rope jumping is one of the most user-friendly, safe, versatile and productive exercises available. Unfortunately, it is also one of the most misunderstood. So before we write off rope jumping to highly-tuned pugilists and energetic school children, let's see if rope jumping is an exercise which you just might want to do.

ARE YOU READY FOR IT?

First ask your physician if your heart is ready for moderate to vigorous exercise. Rope jumping is not recommended for the early phases of cardiac rehabilitation since the heart rate response is less predictable

RATED PERCEIVED EXERTION (RPE) SCALE	
0	Nothing at all
0.5	Extremely weak
1	Very Weak
2	Weak
3	Moderate
4	Somewhat strong
5	Strong
6	
7	Very strong
8	
9	Extremely strong
10	Maximal

FIGURE 1. On a scale of 1 to 10, exercise intensity is guided by using your own internal "sense" of how hard you are working. Exerting yourself in the range of 3 to 5 correlates well to the "target heart range."

Reference: Borg, G.V., Medicine and Science in Sports and Exercise, 14:377-87, 1982.

28 HEARTCORPS

BY LEE LIPSKER, PH.D.

TIPS TO GET YOU THROUGH THE HOLIDAYS

Sugar plum fairies, chestnuts roasting on an open fire, colorful wrapping paper, friends and relatives gathered together, ... the holiday period of November through December evokes images which are nearly universal. It seems that most everyone is caught up in the spirit and mood of the season. Just think of the gusto with which we proclaim, "Happy Thanksgiving! ... Happy Hanukah! ... Merry Christmas! ... Happy New Year!" Unfortunately, this two or three month period of the year is often a time of anxiety, stress, and depression for persons with heart disease and their immediate family members.

Depression is a commonly reported problem for those who have experienced myocardial infarction (MI), coronary bypass surgery, angioplasty, or other heart-related illnesses. In fact, the research literature suggests that between 55% and 90% of all heart attack victims experience significant signs of depression as long as one year after the attack. In most cases, the depression and accompa-

1 TALK ABOUT IT.

Part of the nature of depression is the tendency to believe that your difficulties are so unique that no one else could possibly understand. After all, you certainly wouldn't want to "burden" someone else with your problems! Nothing could be further from the truth. The many issues discussed here are so common that they are nearly as universal as are the mistletoe and colored lights. Surely everyone has experienced the disappointment felt when our expectations have not been met. Can any one of us honestly say that we have not been disillusioned by the over-commercialization of the holidays - at least for a little while? More significantly, most of your friends and family have had moments of depression. We all know what it is like to be "down."

Talking to someone about our problems can have many beneficial effects. First, by articulating our feelings we get to hear for ourselves just what is bothering us. Once the issues are on the table, we can call on many of our own resources to deal with them. With our thoughts laid out for us, we can identify the ones that are rational and have some basis in truth. Talking about what is bothering us also opens the door for help. It is often enough just to remind ourselves that someone will listen to us and care about how we feel. When we share our pain, discomfort, fear or sadness, we allow others to demonstrate their love and caring for us. In the sharing process, good ideas for solutions or understanding are generated by the parties involved.

Many of the issues that are involved in depression are of interest to us. The variety of emotions that often accompany heart disease need attention. Your physician may be interested in your feelings for several reasons, not the least of which is the possibility of side-effects from prescribed medication. The holidays are often a period of increased spirituality - the perfect time to call on your pastor or rabbi. Or as described below, the holiday time might be the right time to get involved in a support group. The hardest part is to reach out initially and get beyond the reluctance that you will be "burdening" someone. It is a necessary step in overcoming depression and, once taken, can lead to happiness and long-lasting rewards.

2 GET INVOLVED.

Few things contribute to our psychological well-being as greatly as knowing that we're important and needed. The holiday time presents us with a myriad of opportunities to become active in projects that can add immeasurably to our self-esteem. From volunteering on the children's ward at the local hospital to addressing and stuffing envelopes at the area American Heart Association or American Red Cross office - there are unlimited places and programs in which you can direct some energy.

This form of involvement accomplishes

WALKING...
TAKING YOUR EXERCISE IN STRIDE

BY BILL BUSH, EDITOR-IN-CHIEF

One of the most important steps in restoring heart health can be many steps taken in quick succession -- a brisk walk. The remarkable benefits of regular walking for cardiac rehabilitation have been acknowledged by virtually all cardiologists, who cite their own clinical experience and the growing body of long-term research.

Many heart patients wonder how something as easy as walking can have such a big impact on their physical condition. The simple truth is, a good brisk walk, several times a week can strengthen the heart. Adhering to a regular walking program may also have a favorable effect on blood pressure, serum cholesterol level, weight control, and psychological attitude. You may be thinking, "Can just simple walking regularly do all that?" and the answer is a resounding "Yes!"

While it is known and reported that high-intensity, "power" walking delivers great fitness benefits; low-intensity walking, "a brisk walk around the block" will return substantial health benefits as well, especially if done regularly and frequently. This is especially welcome news for the thousands who have come to believe that heart attack recovery and heart health can only be gained through heavy-duty exercise. The "no pain, no gain" body-building adage simply doesn't hold true for cardiac rehab.

Dr. Neil Gordon, at the Institute for Aerobics Research in Dallas, Texas, starts every patient with a walking program. According to Gordon, "Walking is the ideal exercise for heart attack patients." He recommends walking for cardiac patients because it tends not to promote the injuries common to jogging, like shin splints, muscle and tendon pulls and joint inflammation. "Often heart patients are older and ill-prepared to suffer the jarring and compression that go with other types of exercise," says Dr. Gordon. "Walking is a natural movement for the body and, therefore, it is very low impact but can be very aerobic if done properly."

ILLUSTRATION: JOHN CARLYLE

Patients at Gordon's clinic are tested to determine optimum exertion levels for the course of their cardiac rehabilitation. Using a treadmill, Gordon gradually increases speed and elevation to a point where the patient is substantially taxed and approaching problems -- 70% to 85% of that level of exertion is determined to be the patient's "symptom-limited maximum heart rate." Gordon's exercise prescription, which all patients must have before undertaking any type of strenuous program, is typically a regimen calling for walking sessions lasting 20 to 40 minutes, three to five times a week at

A good brisk walk, several times a week, can strengthen the heart.

the rate determined by the stress test.

Dr. Gordon, in our interview, emphasized that the "symptom-limited maximum heart rate" is quite different from the "target heart rate" training guidelines that have thousands of fitness-devoted Americans regularly checking their pulses during and after exercise. (See page 24.)

The American Heart Association and American College of Sports Medicine recommend an exertion level measured at 60-75% of the maximum heart rate, sustained for 30 minutes at least three times a week. They assert that exercise above 75% may be too strenuous unless in excellent physical condition; and exercise below 60% gives the heart and lungs little physical conditioning.

Brisk walking -- about four to five miles per hour, can elevate heart rates into the ideal conditioning range. But even walking at three and one-half miles per hour may be too taxing for those on the mend from a heart attack.

Fortunately, there is an increasing body of knowledge through research that suggests substantial health benefits can be achieved at exercise levels far below the 60% to 75% target zone. "Walking for 45 minutes a day is wonderful, even without ever reaching your target heart rate zone," says Dr. Bob Hopper of the Cardiac Health & Diagnostic Center in Long Beach, California. Hopper, an exercise physiologist, makes a key distinction between *health* and *fitness:* the data suggests physical activity is related to lower heart disease risk, not necessarily fitness. A good physical fitness program will achieve heart healthy benefits, but walking and never achieving your target heart rate is also very good."

Hopper says moderate activity equal to expending about 2000 calories a week will reduce the risk of heart disease, but not necessarily improve fitness. He admits that his is a minority "but growing" opinion on the value of moderate exercise for heart health. However, he argues that nationally, adherence to more rigorous fitness programs have been dismal, especially in older age groups. "The fitness craze has been a failure," says Hopper. "Only a small percentage of Americans, one study says about 6.5%, reach the American College of Sports Medicine guidelines of 30 minutes at the target heart rate, three times a week."

Hopper strongly believes in the ACSM guidelines, but takes a more pragmatic view when dealing with cardiac rehab patients. "We talk with our cardiac patients and find out that they have not been able to stay with a fitness program. For the long term, its better to get heart patients on a

Generally, the more deeply an exercise makes you breath, the more it burns calories and body fat...

22 HEARTCORPS SEPTEMBER/OCTOBER 1988 23

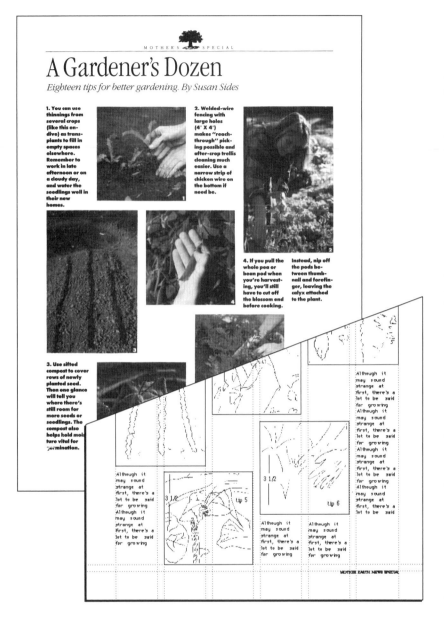

Scanning photographs for reproduction, in both black and white and color, pushes desktop publishing to its outer limits. It can be done, but for most people it requires too much time, skill, and memory to produce a satisfactory result. The cost of converting a photograph to a halftone for black and white reproduction is still one of the best bargains commercial printers offer. And the quality is far superior to what most people can achieve using desktop technology. Color scanning is even more difficult, and of course the hardware required is even more expensive.

Using a scanner as a production tool, on the other hand, provides a great deal of control and flexibility when you design pages that have to accommodate numerous photographs or illustrations. The samples on these two pages show how we used low-resolution scans to do very precise layouts, saving time (and money on photostat bills) for pages that would be commercially typeset and manually pasted up, with color art stripped in by the printer. The on-screen image is shown in front of the printed page.

The page shown at left is the opener for a story that includes 12 color photographs. We received the photos as 35mm transparencies and projected them on a wall to make rough tracings. (We simply put a piece of tracing paper over the projected image and literally traced it.) We scanned each tracing individually, on a Datacopy 730, as simple line art at 150 dots per inch, saved it in MacPaint format, and placed it in the PageMaker document.

Bogus copy, typed in PageMaker in the type style of the article, was sufficient to simulate for layout purposes the caption-style text that accompanied the pictures. With all the elements in electronic form, we could manipulate their sizes and positions to develop the layout.

The laser proof served as the final layout guide for the pasteup artist as well for the printer when stripping in the original art.

If you need more detail in your layout, you can scan black and white photos—or color laser copies—as low-resolution halftones, as we did with the sample shown at left. None of the scans described on this page are memory intensive. The scans of tracings ranged from 9 to 20 KB and took about 18 seconds each; the halftone scans ranged from 12 to 36 KB and took about 40 seconds each.

This poster-style magazine spread was created in a special file so that the pages could be be seen together in a vertical orientation. We created one oversize page and drew a line through the center to mark the gutter between the two real pages.

The artist's rough sketches were faxed to us and then scanned as line art. Each sketch (and scan) had four or five birds on the page, and we needed to position them individually. So we opened each scan in DeskPaint (a desk accessory that you can work in while Page-Maker is active), copied the birds one by one, and pasted them onto the PageMaker page.

An oversize printout of the tight layout was sent to the artist so she could paint all of the birds in relative proportion to one another as a single piece of art, requiring only one color separation. The scans on the layout were checked for accuracy against the final art. If accurate, scans can be used as FPO guides for the printer when the art is stripped in, eliminating the cost of stats.

The table was typed in PageMaker. In commercial typesetting, tables are difficult to specify and inevitably require several galley revisions. Creating a table in PageMaker still requires revisions to get the tabs and vertical spacing right, but the process is considerably streamlined over its commercial counterpart.

The captions were placed as a single text file on the pasteboard in PageMaker. We then cut and pasted each caption so we could manipulate it as an individual, unthreaded text block. Changes in the number of lines in one caption wouldn't affect any of the other captions.

Although there is no formal grid in this page, the position of elements is not at all haphazard. Note, in the screen detail, how we used ruler guides to align the elements as the layout evolved. Every text block aligns on at least one side with some other text block on the page.

The gray bars, called greeked text, are used to simulate text at small sizes. You can specify the type size below which text will be greeked in the Preferences dialog box. Designers often prefer to use greeked text in rough layouts because it helps the client focus on the design rather than on the words. Greeked text also speeds up screen redraw time.

The headline is Egyptian Bold Condensed. The table text and captions are Helvetica Light and Helvetica Black.

Design: Don Wright (Woodstock, NY)
Illustration: Kay Holmes Stafford

Pages from Mother Earth News, *published bimonthly.*
Trim size: 8-1/8 by 10-3/4

CHAPTER 7

DATA: CATALOGS, DATA SHEETS, FINANCIALS, AND FORMS

Publications with large amounts of data rely heavily on careful organization and deft styling of typography. Some require clear delineation and consistent handling of repetitive elements, such as product names, prices, and descriptive listings; others require formats that can accommodate different kinds of elements, such as continuous narrative interspersed with tables, charts, and graphs.

Before settling on an approach, you'll need to analyze the material and experiment with different typographic styles. The ability to experiment on the desktop is a decided advantage when you are designing these publications, and you can save time by testing small samples of data before styling the entire document. In testing the type style and tab positions for tables, be sure to include both the maximum and minimum number and length of elements you have to accommodate, so that you can see the balance of the two in any format.

CATALOGS & DATA SHEETS

When you have to pack a lot of text into a small space, you will generally enhance the appeal and overall readability if you choose a small, tightly leaded, condensed type style and maximize the space around the text. Larger sizes surrounded by less white space result in pages that are dark and unrelievedly dense. Use rules and borders to aid organization and to change the color of the page. Even in publications without a second color, rules with contrasting weights can add much-needed graphic variety as well as organizational clarity.

Catalogs and data sheets in this section

- *Tables Specification Guide* —diverse elements in a landscape format
- *Books on Black Culture*—art livens up straightforward catalog listings
- *Beverly Hills Motoring Accessories*—boxes, banners, and more boxes and banners
- *The Concept Technical Manual*—technical illustrations for ski clothes
- *Teaching Tools*—a highly structured catalog of educational software
- *School of Visual Arts*—a little style dresses up straightforward listings
- *Clackamas Community College catalog*—a format that accommodates many different kinds of listings
- *Portland State Quarterly*—adventurous typography in a newspaper format

- *The Huck Lockbolt Fastener Design Guide*—technical illustrations in a utilitarian format
- *Triad Keyboard*—easy-to-scan text and life-size photos
- *Maxtor Data Sheets*—high-quality, high-tech still lifes
- *Infrared Optics Cleaning Kit*—handsome simplicity
- *Smith & Hawken product assembly sheets*—an easily implemented format consistent with the company look
- *Questor Inlets*—leadered callouts and a functional use of color

The horizontal format provides more flexibility than a vertical page in organizing the many options available for items in this catalog.

The master pages include the rules, logo, headlines, and black box on the top page, and the rules and bar coding on the bottom page. In addition to simplifying electronic page assembly, this uniformity brings visual order to a complex document. It also makes it easy for readers to find information about any given product because similar information appears on the same place on every page. If a master item is not used on an actual page, it is masked over with a No Lines-Paper Fill box and that slot appears blank.

The line drawing of each item prints as a white line in a black box. This technique dramatically highlights the subject of each page, making it the dominant item amid the many other kinds of information. The drawings were created in MacDraft, saved as PICT files, and sized proportionally in PageMaker.

For the data on the bottom page, pencil roughs were used to determine the number and depth of items for each table in the catalog. Several templates were then made, with a different configuration of rules on the master page of each one. The text for all pages using the same configuration was created in a single Microsoft Word file and placed in PageMaker. Planning pays off by eliminating the need to redraw rules on every page and by making it possible to refine the tabs in PageMaker for an entire file, representing many catalog pages at one time.

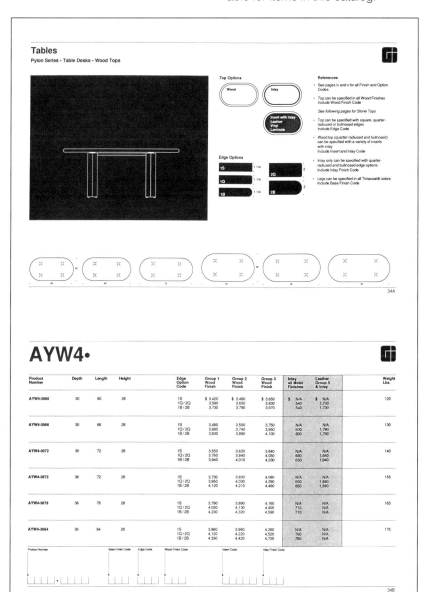

Design: Manfred Petri (Atlanta, GA)

Pages from Tables Specification Guide and Price List, *from Geiger International.*
Trim size: 11-7/8 by 8-3/8

The bold banner across the top of each page and the striking silhouettes of the African art give this book catalog a distinctive personality that is obviously appropriate to the theme of black culture.

The two text columns are boxed in with rules. The outer column is consistently used for art, which is photocopied (with permission) from one of the books in the catalog and pasted into position on the camera-ready pages. When a category of books does not require the two text columns on a page, additional art is used as filler.

The typeface for the book listings is Helvetica. The use of boldface caps to set off the titles, regular caps for the authors, and space between this highlighted information and the descriptive listings is handled consistently throughout and makes the catalog easy to use. The type overall is relatively dark, a result of using laser printer output for camera-ready copy. That darkness works here with the art style and format.

The category heads are Times Roman, reversed out of the black banners at the top of each page.

Design: Lisa Menders (Royal Oak, MI)

Pages from Books on Black Culture, *a mail-order catalog published by the* book end *in Southfield, MI.*
Trim size: 8-3/8 by 11

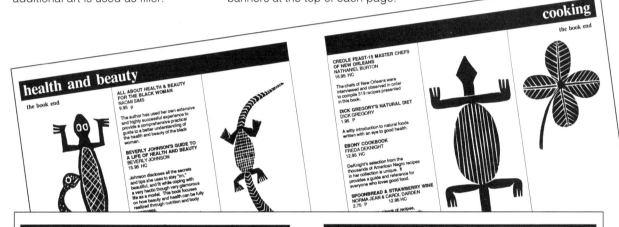

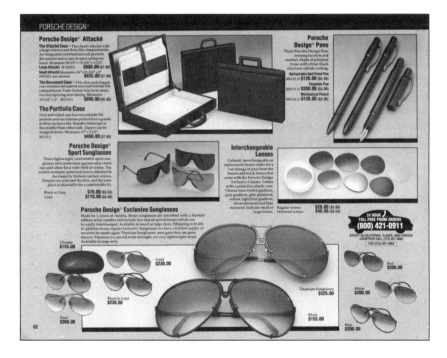

Boxes and banners are used throughout to organize the many elements on each page.

Black banners along the top function as tabs, with product categories in reverse type.

Photos are framed by 0.5-point rules on three sides; the 8-point rule at the bottom of each frame provides a solid base for each photo. This is particularly effective when the product is a car and also gives the catalog a distinctive style. Note the varied directions of the cars in the top row of photos.

Small objects are carefully arranged as still lifes to best display shape, texture, and different views and styles of the same product. The pattern of objects repeated on the page plays with color and shape to provide visual interest. Grouping small objects in one photo saves space as well as photo expenses.

Silhouette photos that extend beyond the picture frames have more dimensionality than photos that are contained. This technique provides variety within the basic format and maximizes the use of space where needed.

Text prints on a gray background. The boldface Helvetica headlines and prices are offset from the descriptive text, which is set smaller in Palatino.

Design: Bob Lee, Lee & Porter Design (Los Angeles, CA)

Pages from a catalog published by Beverly Hills Motoring Accessories. Trim size: 11 by 8-1/2

Simple technical diagrams
with leadered callouts tell the story in this wholesale catalog of ski clothes. Why diagrams? Because here the message is warmth, freedom of movement, and protection from impact and sliding hazards, rather than the fabric and fashion angle typically captured in photographs.

Careful alignment of elements
provides structure within a free-form design. A formal grid would have restricted the size of art and placement of callouts. The distinctive logo treatment, the art and callout style, and the typeface provide visual consistency from page to page.

The typeface is Bodoni, with Helvetica Black used for boldface emphasis in headlines. The ragged right margin suits the casual style and short line length of the callouts. As much as possible, leaders extend from the justified left margin, the top or the bottom, rather than the ragged right.

This highly structured format
positions the product in the same place on every page. The position of the headlines, lists of features, screen details from the programs, system requirements, and other elements also remain constant, making it very easy to find any piece of information for any product.

The headline and other boldface type is American Typewriter and matches the type on the packaging.

The row of triangles under each product name is a right-leadered tab. The leader is customized with a Zapf Dingbat and a character space (the keystroke for the Dingbat is unshifted t). You can define a style for a customized leader; then, each time you want to add it to the document, simply position the cursor, apply the style, and insert the tab.

The triangles in the upper right of each page function as product category tabs. Each category uses a different color for that triangle, for the line of small triangles, and for the quote under each product.

Design (top):
Oscar Anderson,
Weingart/Anderson
(Chicago, IL)

Page from the Concept Technical Manual, *published by Apparel Technology.*
Size: 8-1/2 by 11

Design (bottom):
Partners by Design
(N. Hollywood, CA)

Pages from the Davidson Educational Software *catalog.*
Size: 5-1/2 by 8-1/2

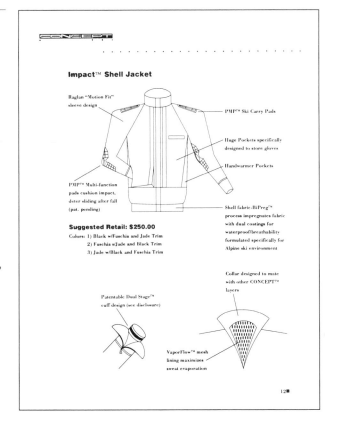

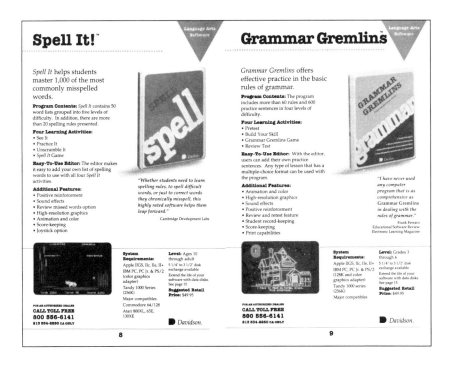

Open leading and a two-column measure (left) add importance to the introduction for each new section of this course catalog without requiring the space of a full page.

Small pieces of art, which print in green, are sprinkled throughout the catalog to help break up the text.

Quotes from instructors and experts in the field (below right) are also used to break up the text. Although the type is smaller than that usually found in blurbs, the open leading, the border, and the green initial cap combine to make this an effective graphic element.

The typography for course listings is a 2-point rule, a Futura Heavy course number, a Futura Bold course title, italic for schedule/credit/fee data, and Century Old Style for running text with the instructor's name in boldface.

The triangle borders use the same Zapf Dingbat technique as the educational catalog on the facing page but without a character space.

Design: School of Visual Arts Press (New York, NY)

Pages from the catalog for The School of Visual Arts. Trim size: 7-1/4 by 10-3/4

90 JOURNALISM AND PUBLIC RELATIONS

JOURNALISM AND PUBLIC RELATIONS

WRITING AND EDITING are the primary skills needed for a career in journalism and public relations. Learning to think and write clearly are skills that can be taught. And when the quality of thinking is drawn from intelligence, personal style follows.

Our society becomes increasingly complicated and with that awareness comes the need for skilled professionals who understand how to communicate creatively, to persuade and to present a point of view with clarity.

Journalism today no longer means working only for newspapers. Journalists work on staff and freelance for magazines, radio stations, television local stations, networks and cable stations.

Public relations experts also work on staff and freelance for individual corporations — almost every large company needs a public relations division — educational institutions, in all broadcast media, as well as with specialized public relations firms. As a writer learning or reacquainting yourself with the essentials of style can be the beginning of a new career with a focus. A working knowledge of the press, understanding how to write press releases or copy, and editing can be important regardless of where you focus your writing talent. The more skills and the more flexibility you have as a writer the more valuable you will be in applied writing in journalism and public relations.

Class hours: 7:00 pm to 9:40 pm unless otherwise indicated. Add registration fee (non-refundable) of $20.00 when registering for these courses.

TE109A
Freelance Magazine Writing: Making the Right Moves for Success
Mon - 2 Credits - $250.00
Creative careers need professional guidance. This is a course for writers who need to know how the marketplace operates. We will examine how to: query editors, make contacts, exploit research resources, gear an article to the appropriate magazine, negotiate fees and expenses. Drawing on your own editorial interests and enthusiams, you will learn how to produce winning story proposals, getting actual assignments from real magazines. Guest lecturers will include accomplished writers and editors. A certain passion for the printed word, rather than any publishing experience, is the course's only prerequisite.
David Abrahamson, Writer, Journalist. B.A., Johns Hopkins University; M. Journalism, University of California; Oxford University. Formerly, Managing Editor, "Car and Driver." Publications include: "The New York Times Magazine," "Science '86," "New York," "Playboy," "Backpacker."

TE205A
Editing Workshop
Thurs - 2 Credits - $250.00
Copy editors are the unsung heroes of the publishing world. Their work clears what was muddled, simplifies the complex, and imposes stylistic order. Good copy editors are in great demand for newspapers, magazines and book publishers. Learn how to handle the copy - the hard, sweaty part - and write headlines, the fun part.
Jack Robbins, Copy Editor, Business Week. Formerly, Editor, McGraw-Hill; Reporter, "The New York Post."

TE207A
How to Promote Practically Anything — Including Yourself
Thurs - 2 Credits - $250.00
This is a course in personal public relations. You will be shown how to put together your own press package for your company or yourself. Topics will include: working knowledge of the press; release writing; fundamentals of public speaking; projecting your own image.
Marilyn McCrudden, President, McCrudden and Sullivan Communications. B.A., University of Minnesota. Clients include: Grafton Street Irish Imports; Parke Bernet Galleries; Delmonico's Hotel; Carson, Lundin & Thorson, P.C., Architects; Scandinavian Airlines; Hearst Publications. Publications: "Who's Who in American Women."

68 PHOTOGRAPHY

process their own film outside class.
William L. Broecker, Photographer. B.A., University of Michigan; M.A., Michigan State University. Editor: *ICP Encyclopedia of Photography; Leica Manual 15th ed.*; Associate Technical Director, *Encyclopedia of Practical Photography*. Publications: "Popular Photography," "Invitation To Photography," "35mm Photography," "Color Photography Annual," "Exposure," "Infinity."

PROFESSIONAL

The following courses are offered to advanced students of photography and working photographers who are able to maintain the pace of classes that take for granted basic technical skills and experience. These professional level courses focus on portfolio development in the different photographic specializations. Critical analysis of all aspects of the photograph from concept through to finished prints/chromes is offered. At this stage self-initiated work is essential and the personal aesthetic is further refined.

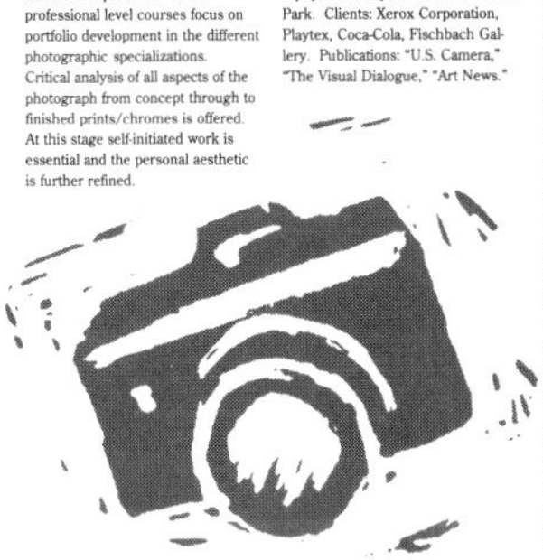

¶ If you are interested in learning new techniques or exploring unfamiliar advancements in technology, there are a number of courses for you to consider.
¶ If you are dissatisfied with the results your current portfolio is getting, a professional course offering critical analysis may be helpful.

PC300A
Advanced Printing
Tues - 2 Credits - $250.00
Lab Fee, $20.00
A course designed for the intermediate and advanced student who is interested in approaching printing as a fine art. Each print will be tailored to the photograph itself. Students should come to the first class session ready to print. Prerequisites: PC205, Basic Photography II, and PC256, Black and White Printing, or presentation of your portfolio at the first session.
Bob Brooks, Photographer, Printer. Has worked in many studios including those of Irving Penn and Bob Adelman. One-Person Exhibition: Plaza Caribe. Group Exhibitions: Floating Foundation of Photography; The People Yes Show, Central Park. Clients: Xerox Corporation, Playtex, Coca-Cola, Fischbach Gallery. Publications: "U.S. Camera," "The Visual Dialogue," "Art News."

PC307A
Photojournalism
Thurs - 2 Credits - $250.00
A survey of practical photojournalism as it exists at wire services and newspapers. The training of perception and the use of the camera as a reporting tool are stressed. Topics to be discussed include: journalism for the photographer; personal vision vs. professional credibility; new technology and how it will affect you; paying the rent as a freelancer; how words can make your camera lie; the use and abuse of photography in public relations; portfolio critique and preparation. Students must have access to their own or commercial darkroom.
Edward Hart, Picture Editor, United Press International, New York City Bureau. B.A., Long Island University. Formerly, Writer/Producer, UPI Television Service. Member: National Press Photographers Association, Society of Professional Journalists, Reporters Committee for Freedom of the Press.

PC316A
Advanced Studio Photography
Mon - 2 Credits - $250.00
Model and Equipment Fees, $35.00
(Limited to twenty students)
A course designed for the advanced student who has successfully completed PC221, Basic Studio Photography, or equivalent. The first two weeks will be devoted to still-life, shot with the 4" x 5" view camera using Polaroid film. (Students must supply their own Polaroid film Type 52). The remainder of the course will be devoted to 35mm or 2 1/4" x 2 1/4" format. Controlled lighting, using strobe to establish mood rather than just illuminate, will be the theme of all assignments. The student will shoot still-life, fashion, beauty and nudes.
Len DeLessio, Photographer. B.F.A., School of Visual Arts. Publications: "Business Week," "Cosmopolitan," "New York," "Parents," "People," "Penthouse," "Viva," "Time," "Elle," "Working Woman." Clients include: American Optical, Binney & Smith/Crayola, Chesebrough Ponds, Fujinon Optical, Andrew Geller Shoes, General Foods - Gaines Dog Food, Mercedes-Benz, Parke-Davis, Perry Ellis, Pierre Cardin Fragrances, P&G - Cascade, Tide, Highpoint, R.J. Reynolds -

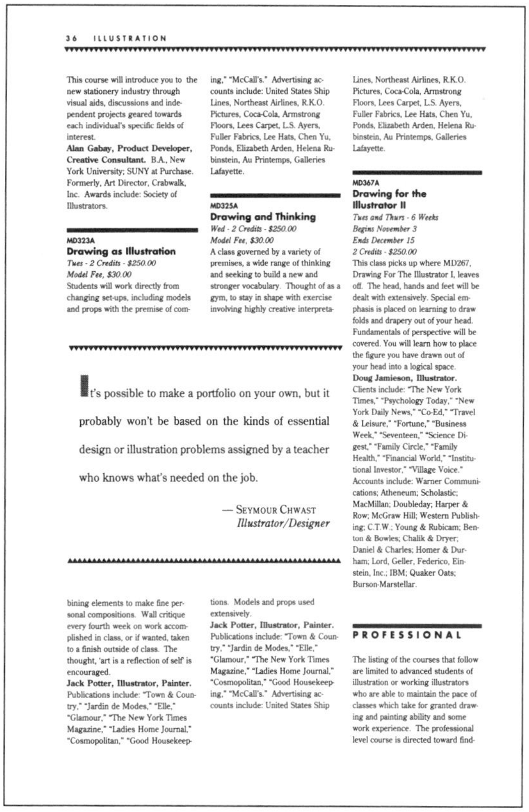

36 ILLUSTRATION

This course will introduce you to the new stationery industry through visual aids, discussions and independent projects geared towards each individual's specific fields of interest.
Alan Gabay, Product Developer, Creative Consultant. B.A., New York University; SUNY at Purchase. Formerly, Art Director, Crabwalk, Inc. Awards include: Society of Illustrators.

MD323A
Drawing as Illustration
Tues - 2 Credits - $250.00
Model Fee, $30.00
Students will work directly from changing set-ups, including models and props with the premise of combining elements to make fine personal compositions. Wall critique every fourth week on work accomplished in class, or if wanted, taken to a finish outside of class. The thought, 'art is a reflection of self' is encouraged.
Jack Potter, Illustrator, Painter. Publications include: "Town & Country," "Jardin de Modes," "Elle," "Glamour," "The New York Times Magazine," "Ladies Home Journal," "Cosmopolitan," "Good Housekeeping," "McCall's." Advertising accounts include: United States Ship Lines, Northeast Airlines, R.K.O. Pictures, Coca-Cola, Armstrong Floors, Lees Carpet, L.S. Ayers, Fuller Fabrics, Lee Hats, Chen Yu, Ponds, Elizabeth Arden, Helena Rubinstein, Au Printemps, Galleries Lafayette.

MD325A
Drawing and Thinking
Wed - 2 Credits - $250.00
Model Fee, $30.00
A class governed by a variety of premises, a wide range of thinking and seeking to build a new and stronger vocabulary. Thought of as a gym, to stay in shape with exercise involving highly creative interpretations. Models and props used extensively.
Jack Potter, Illustrator, Painter. Publications include: "Town & Country," "Jardin de Modes," "Elle," "Glamour," "The New York Times Magazine," "Ladies Home Journal," "Cosmopolitan," "Good Housekeeping," "McCall's." Advertising accounts include: United States Ship Lines, Northeast Airlines, R.K.O. Pictures, Coca-Cola, Armstrong Floors, Lees Carpet, L.S. Ayers, Fuller Fabrics, Lee Hats, Chen Yu, Ponds, Elizabeth Arden, Helena Rubinstein, Au Printemps, Galleries Lafayette.

It's possible to make a portfolio on your own, but it probably won't be based on the kinds of essential design or illustration problems assigned by a teacher who knows what's needed on the job.

— SEYMOUR CHWAST
Illustrator/Designer

MD367A
Drawing for the Illustrator II
Tues and Thurs - 6 Weeks
Begins November 3
Ends December 15
2 Credits - $250.00
This class picks up where MD267, Drawing For The Illustrator I, leaves off. The head, hands and feet will be dealt with extensively. Special emphasis is placed on learning to draw folds and drapery out of your head. Fundamentals of perspective will be covered. You will learn how to place the figure you have drawn out of your head into a logical space.
Doug Jamieson, Illustrator. Clients include: "The New York Times," "Psychology Today," "New York Daily News," "Co-Ed," "Travel & Leisure," "Fortune," "Business Week," "Seventeen," "Science Digest," "Family Circle," "Family Health," "Financial World," "Institutional Investor," "Village Voice." Accounts include: Warner Communications; Atheneum; Scholastic; MacMillan; Doubleday; Harper & Row; McGraw Hill; Western Publishing; C.T.W.; Young & Rubicam; Benton & Bowles; Chalik & Dryer; Daniel & Charles; Homer & Durham; Lord, Geller, Federico, Einstein, Inc.; IBM; Quaker Oats; Burson-Marstellar.

PROFESSIONAL

The listing of the courses that follow are limited to advanced students of illustration or working illustrators who are able to maintain the pace of classes which take for granted drawing and painting ability and some work experience. The professional level course is directed toward find-

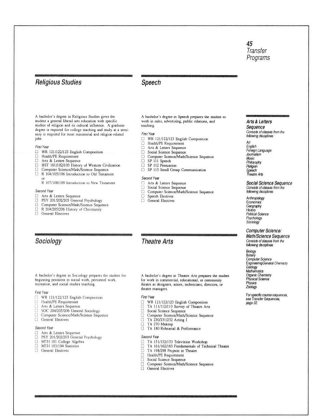

The format for this catalog accommodates several different kinds of listings, three of which are shown here. The distinctive treatment of the top and bottom margins and the consistency of the type style unify the different components of the catalog.

The heavy rules are 4 point.

The typeface makes good use of the contrast between Helvetica Narrow and Times Roman.

Design: Lisa Wilcox and Bill Symes (Oregon City, OR)

Pages from the Clackamas Community College catalog. Trim size: 8-3/8 by 10-3/4

A highly styled newspaper format (below) sets a dynamic tone for the "Course Highlights" section in the opening pages of this continuing education catalog.

The type styling in the spread below illustrates how you can achieve a great deal of variety through an adventurous use of the two most familiar typefaces. The Helvetica family is used for display and Times Roman for running text. Note, though, the contrasting leading and column widths, the letterspacing, reverse type, wrap-around text, type on tints, dotted rules, initial caps, and boxed copy. Each text block is treated as a pattern of type that is distinct from every other text block on the spread.

The same four-column grid ties together the opening pages and the course information (above left). In the course listings, the outer column is used to list the schedule, credit, and fees for the courses described on that page. Where needed, the outer two columns can be used for this purpose.

Design:
Jonathan Maier
(Portland, OR)

Pages from the Portland State University Quarterly Bulletin for Continuing Education.
Trim size:
11-1/4 by 13-9/16

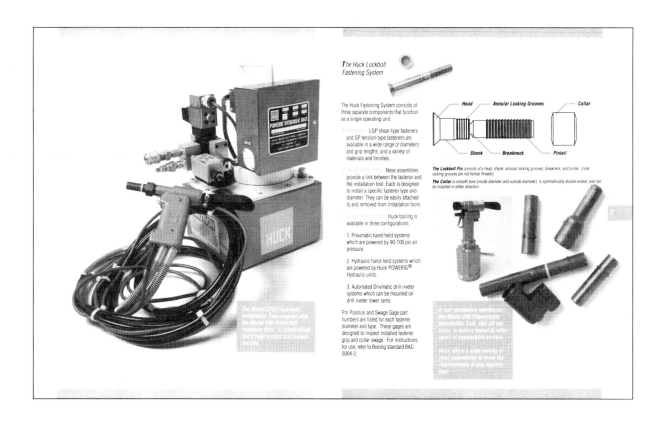

*T*he Huck Lockbolt
Fastening System

The Huck Fastening System consists of
three separate components that function
as a single operating unit.

1. Fasteners. LGP shear-type fasteners
and GP tension-type fasteners are
available in a wide range of diameters
and grip lengths, and a variety of
materials and finishes.

2. Nose Assemblies. Nose assemblies
provide a link between the fastener and
the installation tool. Each is designed
to install a specific fastener type and
diameter. They can be easily attached
to and removed from installation tools.

3. Installation Tools. Huck tooling is
available in three configurations:

1. Pneumatic hand-held systems
which are powered by 90-100 psi air
pressure.

2. Hydraulic hand-held systems which
are powered by Huck POWERIG®
Hydraulic units.

3. Automated Drivmatic drill riveter
systems which can be mounted on
drill riveter lower rams.

Pin Position and Swage Gage part
numbers are listed for each fastener
diameter and type. These gages are
designed to inspect installed fastener
grip and collar swage. For instructions
for use, refer to Boeing standard BAC
5004-2.

Head — **Annular Locking Grooves** — **Collar**

Shank — **Breakneck** — **Pintail**

The Lockbolt Pin consists of a head, shank, annular locking grooves, breakneck, and pintail (note locking grooves are not helical threads)

The Collar is smooth bore (inside diameter and outside diameter), is symmetrically double-ended, and can be installed in either direction.

Mechanical Properties

Part Number Pin Huck	Boeing	Collar Huck	Boeing	Min. Double Shear lbs.	Min. Ultimate Tensile lbs.	Pin Pos. & Swage Gage	Head Style
5/32							
LGPS2SC-V05	BACB30VP5	3SLC-C05	BACC30BK5	4010(95KSI)	1400	HG113-05	100° Flush
LGPS2SP-V05	BACB30VR5	3SLC-C05	BACC30BK5	4010(95KSI)	1400	HG113-05	Protruding
LGPS9SC-V05	BACB30WC5	SLFC-MV05	BACC30BN5	4010(95KSI)	1400	HG119-05	130° Flush
LGPS9SP-V05	BACB30VZ5	SLFC-MV05	BACC30BN5	4010(95KSI)	1400	HG119-05	Protruding
LGPS8SC-V05	BACB30WE5	SLFC-MV05	BACC30BN5	4010(95KSI)	1400	HG119-05	100° Flush
3/16							
LGPS2SC-V06	BACB30VP6	3SLC-C06	BACC30BK6	5380(95KSI)	1600	HG113-06	100° Flush
LGPS2SP-V06	BACB30VR6	3SLC-C06	BACC30BK6	5380(95KSI)	1600	HG113-06	Protruding
LGPS9SC-V06	BACB30WC6	SLFC-MV06	BACC30BN6	5380(95KSI)	1600	HG119-06	130° Flush
LGPS9SP-V06	BACB30VZ6	SLFC-MV06	BACC30BN6	5380(95KSI)	1600	HG119-06	Protruding
LGPS8SC-V06	BACB30WE6	SLFC-MV06	BACC30BN6	5380(95KSI)	1600	HG119-06	100° Flush
1/4							
LGPS2SC-V08	BACB30VP8	3SLC-C08	BACC30BK8	9300(95KSI)	3000	HG113-08	100° Flush
LGPS2SP-V08	BACB30VR8	3SLC-C08	BACC30BK8	9300(95KSI)	3000	HG113-08	Protruding
LGPS9SC-V08	BACB30WC8	SLFC-MV08	BACC30BN8	9300(95KSI)	3000	HG119-08	130° Flush
LGPS9SP-V08	BACB30VZ8	SLFC-MV08	BACC30BN8	9300(95KSI)	3000	HG119-08	Protruding
LGPS8SC-V08	BACB30WE8	SLFC-MV08	BACC30BN8	9300(95KSI)	3000	HG119-08	100° Flush
5/16							
LGPS2SC-V10	BACB30VP10	3SLC-C10	BACC30BK10	14600(95KSI)	5000	HG113-10	100° Flush
LGPS2SP-V10	BACB30VR10	3SLC-C10	BACC30BK10	14600(95KSI)	5000	HG113-10	Protruding
LGPS9SC-V10	BACB30WC10	SLFC-MV10	BACC30BN10	14600(95KSI)	5000	HG119-10	130° Flush
LGPS9SP-V10	BACB30VZ10	SLFC-MV10	BACC30BN10	14600(95KSI)	5000	HG119-10	Protruding
LGPS8SC-V10	BACB30WE10	SLFC-MV10	BACC30BN10	14600(95KSI)	5000	HG119-10	100° Flush
3/8							
LGPS2SC-V12	BACB30VP12	3SLC-C12	BACC30BK12	21000(95KSI)	7000	HG113-12	100° Flush
LGPS2SP-V12	BACB30VR12	3SLC-C12	BACC30BK12	21000(95KSI)	7000	HG113-12	Protruding
LGPS9SC-V12	BACB30WC12	SLFC-MV12	BACC30BN12	21000(95KSI)	7000	HG119-12	130° Flush
LGPS9SP-V12	BACB30VZ12	SLFC-MV12	BACC30BN12	21000(95KSI)	7000	HG119-12	Protruding
LGPS8SC-V12	BACB30WE12	SLFC-MV12	BACC30BN12	21000(95KSI)	7000	HG119-12	100° Flush

Materials

Pin Part Number	Pin Material	Sleeve Material	Collar Part Number	Collar Material
LGPS2S( )-V	6AL-4V Titanium		3SLC-C( )	2024-T42 Aluminum
LGPS8S( )-V	6AL-4V Titanium		SLFC-MV( )	CP Titanium
LGPS9S( )-V	6AL-4V Titanium		SLFC-MV( )	CP Titanium

LGP Shear Stump-Type Fasteners and Automated Installation Tools

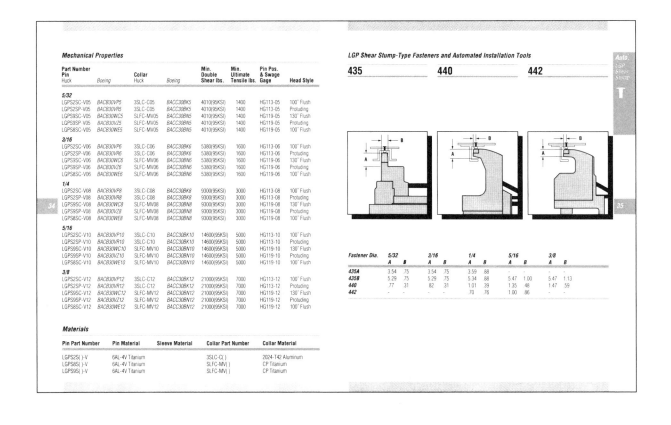

435   **440**   **442**

Fastener Dia.	5/32		3/16		1/4		5/16		3/8	
	A	B	A	B	A	B	A	B	A	B
435A	3.54	.75	3.54	.75	3.59	.88	-	-	-	-
435B	5.29	.75	5.29	.75	5.34	.88	5.47	1.00	5.47	1.13
440	.77	.31	.82	.31	1.01	.39	1.35	.48	1.47	.59
442	-	-	-	-	.70	.76	1.00	.86	-	-

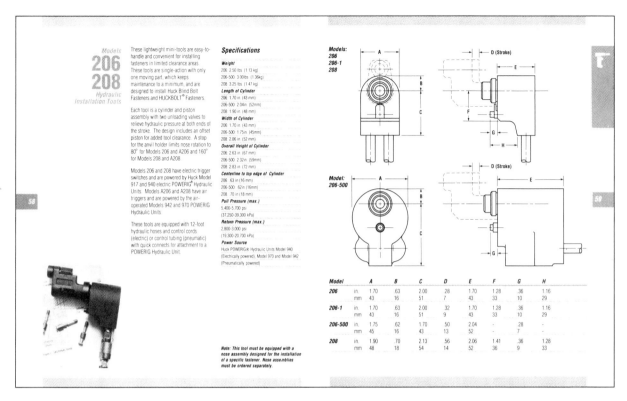

Utility informs every aspect of the design of this technical manual for selecting and using fasteners and fastener installation tools. The manageable size, the spiral binding, the tabbed section dividers, and the careful handling of the many different kinds of material on virtually every spread show consistently high production values.

The three-column format accommodates a wide range of recurring elements—descriptive text, product photos, technical drawings, and specification tables—with generous white space being an integral part of the design.

The introduction to the fastening system (facing page, top) sets the style with dramatically silhouetted product shots complemented by an exceptionally well-rendered technical illustration. The parts on the right-hand page seem to float above the page, a dimensional illusion not often found in technical manuals and specifications. The designer used scanned photos to work out the size and position of images on the page; the printer created and stripped in traditional halftones.

The typography throughout is Helvetica Condensed and Helvetica Condensed Bold. Both faces are used in roman and oblique for additional contrast where needed. The Helvetica Condensed family (available as downloadable fonts from Adobe Systems) is unequalled for combining economy of space and maximum readability.

Red is used as an accent color for rules, product headlines, and boxes. The tabbed section dividers are printed on laminated stock that matches the color of the printed ink exactly.

The black shadows behind boxed illustrations (facing page, bottom) highlight the illustrations and separate them from one another. This device makes it possible to run as many as six of these illustrations on a page with a great deal of text and very little white space.

The technical illustrations were created in Adobe Illustrator.

Design: Steven Bliss (Kingston, NY)

Pages from the Lockbolt Fastener Design Guide, *produced by the Huck Manufacturing Company.*
Trim size: 7-3/4 by 9-1/8

Quick and easy scanning is the goal of this format, an 11- by 17-sheet printed on both sides and folded in half.

Bold headlines and subheads, very open leading, and a graphic element to denote itemized text are all designed to move the reader through the copy quickly. This highly utilitarian approach is intended to suggest that the product will be similarly streamlined and easy to use.

The body text is 10/18 Palatino. The headline is 16/18 Helvetica Black, and the subheads are 12/18 Helvetica Black.

Life-size photos deliver impact. Here they create the illusion that there are windows cut into the paper and that you are looking through them to read the keys.

Design: Kimberly Mancebo (Campbell, CA)

Data sheet for Triad Systems Corporation. Trim size: 11 by 17, folded in half

---

Triad's New Easy Keys Are Designed With You In Mind

The keys are grouped the way you'll use them. And each key is labelled with a name that makes sense, so you don't have to memorize abstract "F-key" codes or obscure combinations.

Here Are a Few of The Keys to the Best Point-of-Sale Program In Your Industry

Our ten-key numerical keypad makes SKU entry quick, easy and accurate for any clerk.

The CHARGE key automatically sets the correct discounts, pricing and tax for your charge customers. The right price is given to the right customer.

Clerks can receive payments quickly at Point-of-Sale, just by using the ROA key.

Clerks can cash checks and process paid-outs quickly

and efficiently, using the PAID OUT and NO SALE keys. And you get a complete report, by clerk and by terminal. So everyone's cash drawer balances at day's end — or you'll know why.

The VOID key captures information about voids — of single items and of entire

transactions — by clerk and by terminal. You get the register control you need.

The TOTAL key keeps everything totally up-to-date: inventory quantities, item sales history, customer accounts. Daily reports recap sales and gross profits for the day.

Contractor Point-of-Sale Brings You These Additional Keys To Success

Clerks can create quotes in minutes — and save them for

later retrieval — just by using the QUOTE key.

As soon as a customer approves a quote, clerks can retrieve it and create an order from it, using the ORDER key. Without ever re-posting ordered merchandise.

You can invoice orders automatically, using the INVOICE key. The customer's account balance and available credit are updated instantly. Automatically. Every time.

The New Easy Keys Are Your Key To Back-office Efficiency, Too

Need help? It's at your fingertips, anytime you need

it, using the HELP key.

Feeling disoriented? Hit the HOME key. You're instantly back at the top of the screen.

Want to see it all on paper? The RUN key starts any

report, any time you want a hard copy.

And the END key takes you back to the hub of your system, the Main Menu.

These two-sided data sheets have the ingredients needed to position an expensive product: a high-quality still life photograph on the front and carefully organized, detailed information on the back.

The tactile quality of the heavy, coated stock used for the data sheets adds measurably to the first impression. Production values are a key element of the image conveyed in sales literature.

The format is maintained for every product in the series: The photo bleeds off the right edge of the paper, the product name prints in reverse type in the banner that bleeds off the top, and the company logo is at the bottom, aligned with the left edge of the photo. Each product is photographed against two sheets of overlapping paper, which add texture and color to the image. The top sheet is gray; the bottom sheet is an accent color that changes from one product sheet to the next, a technique that unifies and distinguishes at the same time.

The layout of the back of the sheet is dictated by the information and changes as needed from one product to another. The margins, typographic style, and logo placement remain consistent throughout the series. Boldface heads, generous space between columns, and bulleted lists with hanging indents all contribute to the clarity of the information and the ease with which it is accessed.

Design: Judy Butler, Barbara Jacobsohn, and Teri Baptiste (San Jose, CA)

Data sheets from the Maxtor Corporation. Trim size: 8-1/2 by 11

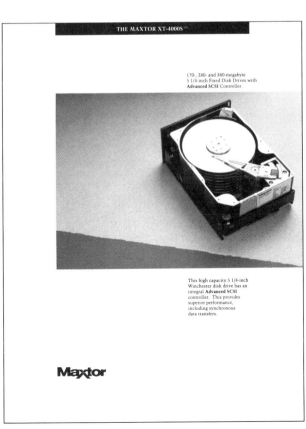

This data sheet is not as slick as the one on the preceeding page, but the handsome format, careful product display, and well-organized typography still evoke confidence in the product.

The three-column grid is given a strong horizontal structure through the use of horizontal rules.

The top rule and the company logo print in red, adding a spot of color that contrasts with the overall quietness of the page.

The contents of the kit are itemized in a bulleted list with hanging indents. The typography, Helvetica Black and Helvetica Light, is simple, nicely spaced, and easy to read.

A simple format with well-rendered line drawings (facing page, top left and bottom) is used for all the assembly and care sheets shipped with products from this large mail-order business.

The rules, logo, column guides, and footlines are standing items in the electronic templates, and a text placeholder is left in position for the product name. For each new product, the actual name is typed over the placeholder (maintaining the text specifications and placement), and text is placed in position. Hand-drawn illustrations are pasted manually onto camera-ready pages. The bottom sample is a half-page size, printed two to a sheet and then trimmed.

Before the conversion to desktop publishing, there was no standard format for these information sheets. According to one of the designers, it took only a few hours to go from no standards to an easy-to-implement design that was consistent with the corporate look.

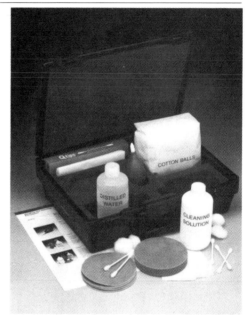

Infrared Optics Cleaning Kit

II-VI **Two-Six Incorporated**
Saxonburg Boulevard
Saxonburg, PA 16056
Telephone (412) 352-1504
Telex 469864

Description

Proper handling and cleaning procedures are critical to prolonging the life of infrared optics in high-power situations.

Infrared optical materials are very fragile. They are not as strong as glass and will not withstand procedures normally used on glass parts.

The Infrared Optics Cleaning Kit provides industrial users with the tools needed for proper optics maintenance. Included are:

- A complete instruction sheet detailing the correct use of the Kit's contents in order to maintain your infrared optics.

- An air bulb to blow away dust and debris from the optical surface.

- Special optical cleaning formula to remove harmful contamination from the optic.

- Supply of reusable cleaning/polishing pads to ensure even cleaning with no distortion of optical surface.

- Sturdy optical block for firm support of pads.

- Distilled water to wipe free any residual cleaning solution.

- Paper-bodied cotton swabs to use as an applicator with the cleaning solution.

- High-quality abrasive-free surgical cotton balls to use as an alternative to cotton swabs.

- Specially formulated, lint-free lens tissues to protect clean optics from airborne contaminants.

- A sturdy, customized carrying case for easy transportation of all tools and solutions.

- Refill Kits available to replace all consumable items.

Printed in USA   Publication 124

Design (above): Agnew Moyer Smith (Pittsburgh, PA)

Data sheet for an infrared optics cleaning kit from Two-Six Incorporated.
Trim size: 8-1/2 by 11

Design (facing page, top left and bottom): Kathy Tomyris and Deborah Paulson (Mill Valley, CA)

Product sheets from Smith & Hawken.
Trim size: (top) 8-1/2 by 11; (bottom) 5-1/2 by 8-1/2, printed two to a sheet

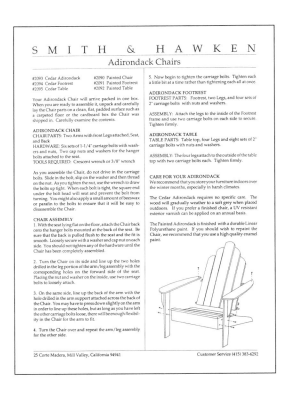

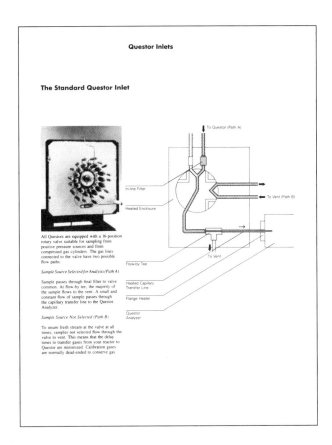

*Design (top right):
Agnew Moyer
Smith
(Pittsburgh, PA)*

*Data sheet for the
Questor Inlet
system from the
Extrel Corporation.
Size: 8-1/2 by 11*

**A narrow column for the
product photo and text** (above)
leaves plenty of space for the
technical illustration and leadered
callouts. The illustration was created in
MacDraw.

All the leaders are parallel to
one another and the callouts align left
for a highly organized presentation.

**Yellow is used as a functional
second color** to indicate the flow of
gases; the light and bold horizontal
rules at the top and bottom of the
page also print in yellow.

Three typefaces are used for
contrast: Futura Heavy for the
boldface, Times Roman for the
running text, and Univers Light for the
callouts.

FINANCIALS

The financials in this section are from annual reports, where a narrative story, tabular data, and charts and graphs often must coexist between the same covers. In some reports the financials are quarantined in the back. The greater challenge—one that results in a more impressive presentation—is to devise a format that allows you to integrate the financial data into the body of the report.

Annual reports are very image-conscious documents. The style of presentation is obviously related to the size of the organization and the health of the bottom line. But whether yours is a growing company with increased earnings or a modest organization with a not-so-great year, the typographic organization discussed in the introduction to this chapter and in the introduction to the Catalog section is the first building block for financial presentations.

Financials in this section

- *MasterCard*—slick, dramatic photos with a life-sized twist
- *College Auxiliary Service*—mug shots that put a face on numbers
- *Psicor*—tabular data and bar chart highlights
- *Medic Alert*—elegant typography in an integrated format
- *Spencer Foundation*—contrasting type for grant summaries

A lavish annual report such as the one on the facing page reflects the bullishness of a good year. For modest or declining earnings, you'd expect a more conservative presentation.

A photo of the product itself is used to chart growth in comparison to the competition. The life-size photos dramatize the product, especially when juxtaposed against smaller-scale photos of the competition.

The financials in the bottom spread shown give the big picture—cards in circulation, merchant outlets, gross dollar volume—against a dramatic black background in which the earth revolves. The image of the earth reinforces the message of global growth set forth in the table at the top of the page.

Straightforward charts become dramatic when each bar prints in a different color, as they do here, against a black background.

Design: The Will Hopkins Group (New York, NY)

Pages from the annual report of MasterCard International, Inc. Trim size: 8-1/2 by 11

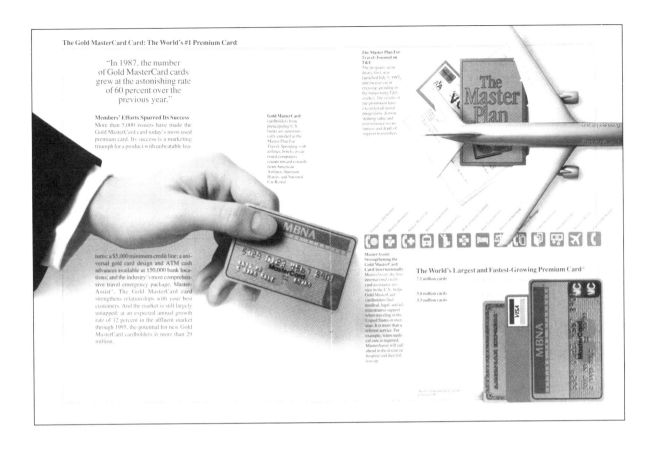

The Gold MasterCard Card: The World's #1 Premium Card

"In 1987, the number of Gold MasterCard cards grew at the astonishing rate of 60 percent over the previous year."

Members' Efforts Spurred Its Success
More than 5,000 issuers have made the Gold MasterCard card today's most-used premium card. Its success is a marketing triumph for a product with unbeatable features: a $5,000 minimum credit line; a universal gold card design and ATM cash advances available at 150,000 bank locations; and the industry's most comprehensive travel emergency package, MasterAssist™. The Gold MasterCard card strengthens relationships with your best customers. And the market is still largely untapped: at an expected annual growth rate of 12 percent in the affluent market through 1995, the potential for new Gold MasterCard cardholders is more than 29 million.

Gold MasterCard cardholders from participating U.S. banks are automatically enrolled in the Master Plan For Travel. Spending with airlines, hotels, or car rental companies counts toward rewards from American Airlines, Sheraton Hotels, and National Car Rental.

Master Assist:
Strengthening the Gold MasterCard Card Internationally
MasterAssist, the first international credit card assistance service in the U.S., helps Gold MasterCard cardholders find medical, legal, and administrative support when traveling in the United States or overseas. It is more than a referral service. For example, when medical care is required, MasterAssist will call ahead to the doctor or hospital and then follow up.

The Master Plan For Travel: Focused on T&E
The program, an industry first, was launched July 1, 1987, and focuses on increasing spending in the burgeoning T&E market. The results of the promotion have exceeded all initial projections, demonstrating value and convenience to cardholders and depth of support to members.

The World's Largest and Fastest-Growing Premium Card
7.1 million cards

5.6 million cards
5.5 million cards

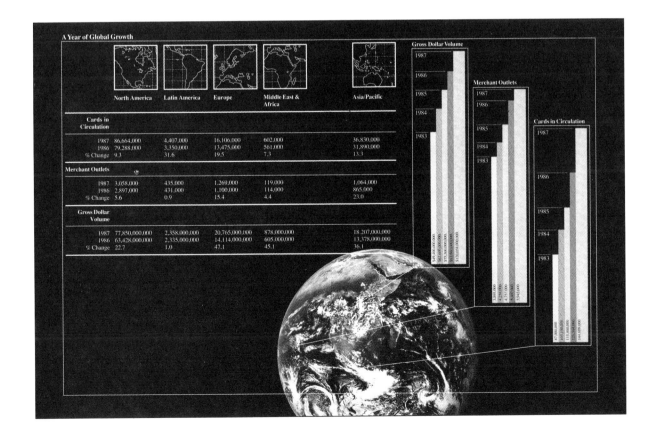

A Year of Global Growth

	North America	Latin America	Europe	Middle East & Africa	Asia/Pacific
Cards in Circulation					
1987	86,664,000	4,407,000	16,106,000	602,000	36,830,000
1986	79,288,000	3,350,000	13,475,000	561,000	31,890,000
% Change	9.3	31.6	19.5	7.3	13.3
Merchant Outlets					
1987	3,058,000	435,000	1,269,000	119,000	1,064,000
1986	2,897,000	431,000	1,100,000	114,000	865,000
% Change	5.6	0.9	15.4	4.4	23.0
Gross Dollar Volume					
1987	77,850,000,000	2,358,000,000	20,765,000,000	878,000,000	18,207,000,000
1986	63,428,000,000	2,335,000,000	14,114,000,000	605,000,000	13,378,000,000
% Change	22.7	1.0	47.1	45.1	36.1

Gross Dollar Volume
1987
1986
1985
1984
1983

$49,400,000,000
$62,440,000,000
$75,360,000,000
$120,058,000,000

Merchant Outlets
1987
1986
1985
1984
1983

3,869,000
4,225,000
4,715,000
5,507,000
5,945,000

Cards in Circulation
1987
1986
1985
1984
1983

87,000,000
103,030,000
115,500,000
128,564,000
144,609,000

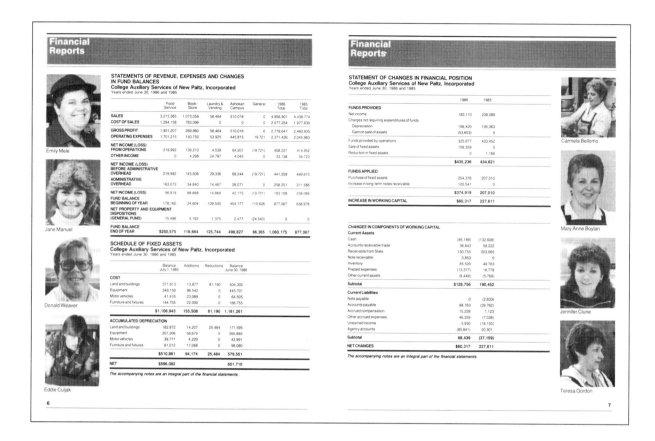

Photos in the narrow outer margins throughout the report above emphasize that this college auxiliary service is a people business. The mug-shot format enables the publication to serve three very different purposes—annual report, morale booster for current employees, and recruiting tool for managerial-level positions.

Contrasting bold and regular Helvetica with light and bold rules helps organize the tables. The tables were set in Microsoft Word and the tabs in PageMaker. The crimson banner at the top of each page provides accent color.

A conservative approach to financial highlights (right) combines straightforward tables and bar charts. Color rules set off the main headline and the income and balance sheet category heads.

The typeface is Futura. The charts print in tones of red and blue.

Design (above):
Wadlin & Erber
(New Paltz, NY)

Spread from a report for the College Auxiliary Services at The College of New Paltz, State University of New York.
Size: 8-1/2 by 11

Design (right):
Lisa Menders
(Royal Oak, MI)

Page from the Psicor, Inc. Annual Report.
Size: 8-1/2 by 11

S OURCES OF REVENUE AND HOW THEY WERE SPENT   19

Financial Highlights . . . The Medic Alert Foundation International accounts for all membership fees, contributions and other revenues with utmost care. These pages were prepared under the direction of Robert C. Johnson, Treasurer, to highlight the financial activity for the twelve month period ended September 30, 1987. A complete, audited financial statement is available on request.

Fund Balance Summary . . . All fund balances for this period increased $1,179,960 because support and revenue exceeded expenditures. All Foundation funds totaled $4,163,018, of which $2,206,916 is invested in the headquarters building. Fund balances are used for working funds and have been designated to cover the cost of updating the Foundation's membership services computer system.

WHAT WE RECEIVED . . .

Total support and revenue for the 12 months was derived from several sources:

Membership Fees - The number of new members was the same as the previous year. However, renders increased 10% and updates increased by 14%. The volume of gold and silver emblems is also increasing. As a result, membership fees increased 6%

Contributions - Contributions by our membership for the support of Medic Alert continued to increase. All solicitations were made by mail to members only. Contributions amounted to 42% of the Foundation's total support and revenue.

Other Revenue - Reimbursement from foreign affiliates for support of international membership expansion increased during the year. Earnings on investment increased because the Foundation had larger investment balances.

SUPPORT AND REVENUE

	For Twelve months 9/30/87	Compared to prior 12 month period
Member's Fees	$3,769,278	up 6%
Contributions	3,023,234	up 26%
Other Revenues	379,152	up 60%
Total Support and Revenue	7,171,664	up 13%

- 53% Membership Fees
- 42% Contributions
- 5% Other Revenue

EXPENSES

	For Twelve months 9/30/87	Percent of Expenditures
Membership Services	$4,096,091	69%
Professional Education Volunteer Training & Public Information	447,860	7%
International Development	221,511	4%
Total Services	$4,765,462	80%
Management & General	546,505	9%
Fund Raising	652,487	11%
TOTAL EXPENSES	**$5,964,454**	**100%**

FUND BALANCES

Beginning of Period (10/1/86)	$3,128,254
Support & Revenue	7,171,664
Expenditure and Changes to Funds	<5,991,704>
End of Period (9/30/87)	$4,508,214

- 69% Member Services
- 11% Fund Raising
- 9% Management & General
- 7% Professional Education & Training; Public Relations
- 4% International Development

WHAT WE SPENT . . .

Membership Services - The cost of establishing new members' medical records and maintaining and updating members' records

Professional Education, Volunteer Training and Public Information - Costs of continuing education of professionals, volunteers and the public to the vital information and lifesaving potential of Medic Alert services.

Fund Raising - Fund raising expenses increased by only 1%, while contributions increased by 26% and substantially increased the number of members and donors to the Foundation.

Management and General - These costs declined slightly, primarily due to one time costs charged in the previous year.

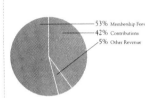

Grantee	Unpaid Balance 1/1/86	Authorized During the Fiscal Year	Payments During the Fiscal Year	Unpaid Balance 1/31/87
Summary of Grants				
California State University, Fresno Fresno, California *Ernst L. Moerk, language teaching/learning in the home ($49,800 in 1986)*	$ 26,000	$ —	$ 26,000	$ —
University of California, Berkeley Berkeley, California *David L. Kirp, school and community response to children with AIDS*	—	102,100	34,600	67,500
University of California, Berkeley Berkeley, California *Martin Trow and Sheldon Rothblatt, two centuries of British and American higher education ($195,250 in 1985)*	155,750	—	42,500	113,250
University of California, Berkeley Berkeley, California *Aaron Wildavsky, cultural theory: foundations, applications, implications*	—	146,700	83,100	63,600
University of California, Irvine Irvine, California *Ellen Greenberger and Wendy A. Goldberg, impacts of potential employment on the socialization of children*	—	7,494	7,494	—
University of California, Irvine Irvine, California *Jean Lave, context, cognition, and activity in the lived-in world*	—	21,000	21,000	—
University of California, Los Angeles Los Angeles, California *Burton R. Clark, research organization and training of advanced scholars*	—	340,050	—	340,050
University of California, Los Angeles Los Angeles, California *Linda M. Perkins, race, uplift, education, and black women*	—	50,700	39,200	11,500
University of California, Los Angeles Los Angeles, California *Kathryn Kish Sklar, Florence Kelley and the women's world of reform*	—	59,100	—	59,100

44

Design (above):
Tom Lewis
(San Diego, CA)

Pages from the Medic Alert annual report.
Size: 8-1/2 by 11

Design (left):
Edward Hughes
(Evanston, IL)

Pages from The Spencer Foundation Annual Report.
Size: 7-1/4 by 10

Data for revenues and expenses in the report above is accompanied by sidebars with explanatory notes and comparisons to previous years' data.

The format throughout the report combines a single column of running text with one- or two-column text sidebars. On pages without financials, the sidebars focus on human interest stories, such as the volunteer of the year, and special events, such as a video documentary about the foundation.

The elegantly styled typography, with its use of large and small caps, is Goudy Old Style. The running text and financial data print in gray-brown; the sidebar and running head print in black.

Contrasting type makes this summary of grants (left) easy to follow. The boldface is Franklin Gothic Heavy; the regular and italic faces are Goudy Old Style. Italic text and chart headings print in crimson.

FORMS

The goal of a form is decidedly simple: It should be easy to read, easy to complete, and easy to retrieve data from, all of which is easier said than done. Once you think you've got it right, try testing your form on some typical subjects. Chances are they'll question something you thought was obvious or enter information in the wrong place. Of course, there's no way to account for the range of attention, or inattention, respondents will bring to the forms you create. But the goal of designing an effective form is to try to make it is simple as possible.

A company with a long tradition of graphic design excellence turns forms into a minimalist art. Intended for internal use, these forms assume more information on the user's part than would be appropriate in a form to be circulated outside the company.

The black panels with reverse type give the forms a dramatic and sophisticated style. The shadow in the company logo adds to the effect.

An unruled, 10% gray panel sets off the "needed" and "used" dates to be filled in for each item on the billing form. Gray should be used cautiously in spaces where the respondent must write.

Design: Mary Salvadore (Boston, MA)
Forms from WGBH Television.
Trim size: 8-1/2 by 11

Camera Billing Form

Traffic/Archive Recycled Tape Credit Form: 915

Dept./Project

Date Submitted

Intended Date of Recycling

Request Reference Number

Unit Manager

The intended date of recycling asks you to name a date upon which the tape in question may be destroyed.

Credits for recycled tape may be applied to *existing* projects only. Some materials authorized for recycling may not meet even minimum quality standards. In such cases a lesser than standard amount of credit – or none – may be issued. All recycled tape credits must be used during the current fiscal year.

This recycling authorization form must be signed below by an appropriate department head, producer, post-production supervisor, and/or unit manager associated with *the tape to be recycled.*

	Quantity	Archive/Traffic Numbers	Project Code to be Credited
2 Inch Videotape			
1 Inch Videotape			
3/4 Inch Cassette			
Beta/VHS			

The undersigned accepts full responsibility for the destruction/recycling of all materials listed with the understanding that the materials will be destroyed/recycled on or after the indicated intended date of recycling.

Authorized Signature

Forms in this section

- *Billing and Traffic*—an artful style for internal use
- *Employee Information*—a lesson in good spacing
- *Math Learning Center*—the boxed-in approach
- *Proposal Evaluation*—ruled space for narrative responses
- *Subscription Card*—with an electronic picture of the product
- *Application for Admission*—adapting a publication's grid for a form
- *InFractions*—a triplicate sales receipt

A banner incorporating the company logo, used here and in the forms on the facing page, is a useful device for maintaining a consistent image in forms and other communications.

Ruled gray panels direct the eye to different categories of questions in this employee information form. The distance between the top and bottom of each panel is the same as the distance between all the other rules on the page.

The typeface is Helvetica bold and regular throughout, with italic used to distinguish special instructions (such as the word "circle" when two or more options are given).

Design: Manfred Petri (Atlanta, GA)
Employee Information form from Geiger International.
Trim size: 8-1/2 by 11

Order Form
Math and the **M i n d ' s** Eye

Math Learning Center
P.O. Box 3226, Salem, OR 97302
(503) 370-8130

Bill To _____

Ship To _____

Phone _____

P.O. # _____ Cash Enclosed _____ Charge _____

(Term net 30 days)

Quantity	Catalog #	Description	Unit Price	Total
	ME 1	Unit I **Seeing Mathematical Relationships** available Dec 1, 1987 The Handshake Problem, Cube Patterns, Pattern Block Trains and Perimeters, Diagrams and Sketches	$3.50	
	ME 2	Unit II **Visualizing Number Concepts** available Feb 1, 1988 Basic Operations, Odd and Even Numbers, Factors and Primes, Averaging, Greatest Common Divisors, Least Common Multiples	$5.00	
	ME 3	Unit III **Modeling Whole Numbers** available Oct 1, 1987 Grouping and Numeration, Linear Measure and Dimension, Arithmetic with Number Pieces, Base 10 Numeration, Base 10 Addition and Subtraction, Number Piece Rectangles, Base 10 Multiplication, Base 10 Division	$6.50	
	ME 4	Unit IV **Modeling Rationals** available Apr 1, 1988 Egg Carton Fractions, Fractions on a Line, Fraction Bars, Addition and Subtraction with Fraction Bars, Multiplication and Division with Fraction Bars, Introduction to Decimals, Decimal Addition and Subtraction, Decimal Length and Area, Decimal Multiplication and Division, Fraction Operations Via Area: Addition and Subtraction, Fraction Operations Via Area: Multiplication, Fraction Operations Via Area: Division	$9.75	
	ME 5	Unit V **Looking at Geometry** available Nov 1, 1987 Geoboard Figures, Geoboard Areas, Area of Silhouettes, Geoboard Triangles, Geoboard Squares, Pythagorean Theorem, Geoboard Perimeters, An Introduction to Surface Area and Volume, Shape and Surface Area, Areas of Irregular Shapes	$7.50	

All orders for less than $20, except for school purchase orders, must be prepaid.

All Canadian orders must be paid in U.S. dollars.

Prices are effective October 1, 1987 and subject to change without notice.

We do not accept credit cards

Total for Materials

No shipping charges to U.S. destinations by Postal Service

Canadian orders please write for shipping costs

TOTAL

☐ Check here if you do not have the 1988 Math Learning Center catalog and want a copy.

THE CENTER FOR FIELD RESEARCH
PROPOSAL EVALUATION

_____   _____
Name of Applicant   Title of Proposal

SIGNIFICANCE OF RESEARCH:
To whom, to what, and in what ways, would this research be significant?

CONCEPTUALIZATION:
Are the research objectives well defined with respect to their scholarly, educational, and public contexts?

METHODOLOGY:
Is the methodology appropriate and adequate to the research objectives?

VOLUNTEER ASSIGNMENTS:
Are the assignments for non-specialists useful and valuable, both to the project's objectives and to those participants?

copyright 1987 Earthwatch

Boxed information (above) provides a highly organized, easy-to-follow order form.

When a form requires more than a few words for each answer (above right), ruling the space generally improves the legibility of the responses.

The typeface is Times Roman throughout, but the styling of headlines as small and large caps makes it look distinctive and contrasts nicely with the italicized questions below. The type prints in blue on a gray background.

Reproducing a page from a publication is an effective marketing technique for subscription cards and other circulation and sales promotions.

The page reproduced on the card below is an Encapsulated PostScript file created from the original electronic document of that page; the EPS file was then placed on the order form as a single piece of art.

Design (above left):
Jonathan Maier (Portland, OR)

Order form for educational materials from the Math Learning Center.
Trim size: 8-1/2 by 11

Design (above):
Earthwatch (Watertown, MA)

Form used to evaluate field research proposals by this nonprofit scientific research organization.
Trim size: 8-1/2 by 11

Design (left): Consumer Markets Abroad

Bind-in subscription card from Consumer Markets Abroad.
Trim size: 7-3/4 by 4-1/4

It's time to get your own subscription.

Make sure you see *Consumer Markets Abroad* on time every month. Start your own subscription to *Consumer Markets Abroad*, the newsletter of worldwide consumer trends and lifestyles by returning this postage-free card. **Send no money now.** We will send you a risk-free issue and bill you $189 for a one-year subscription. If you decide not to subscribe, simply write cancel on the invoice, send it back, and keep the free issue. Your subscription includes another eleven issues plus, for your twelfth issue, *Trends and Opportunities Abroad, 1988*, a 200 page softbound reference guide to overseas markets.

Name _____

Company _____

Title _____

Street _____

City/State/Zip _____

Phone _____   CMA/N87

Consumer Markets Abroad is a publication of American Demographics, Inc., a subsidiary of Dow Jones, Inc.

Application for Admission

120
Application for
Admission

Date	_____ / _____ / _____
Applying for entrance in	❑ Summer ❑ Fall ❑ Winter ❑ Spring 19 ____
Social Security number	
Name	Last / First / Initial
Date of birth	_____ / _____ / _____ Month / Day / Year
Address	Street
	City / State / Zip
Phone number	Day / Evening
State resident	❑ Yes (living in Oregon currently and for preceding 90 days) ❑ No
District resident	❑ Yes (Clackamas County except for Sandy Union High and Lake Oswego School Districts) ❑ No
Course of study	Please include program title and code (see back of form).
High school last attended	Name / State
Date of high school graduation or GED	_____ / _____ / _____ Month / Day / Year
Sex	❑ Male ❑ Female
Ethnic data (optional)	❑ White, non-Hispanic ❑ Asian or Pacific Islander ❑ Black, non-Hispanic ❑ American Indian or Alaskan Native ❑ Hispanic ❑ Handicapped, needing special assistance*
In case of emergency, please notify	Name / Home phone / Work phone
Direct application to	**Office of Admissions** Clackamas Community College 19600 South Molalla Avenue Oregon City, OR 97045

*the Handicap Resource Center coordinates special assistance such as notetakers and sign language interpreters. If you need assistance, check this box and the HRC will contact you. Response is voluntary and will not influence admission to the college.

Clackamas Community College supports equal education opportunity regardless of sex, race, national origin, age, marital status, handicap or religion.

Sales Receipt

732 West Schubert
Chicago, IL 60614
312 477 5063

Sold to:		
Name		
Address		Apt. No.
City	State	Zip
Day Telephone	Evening Telephone	

Ship to:		
Name		
Address		Apt. No.
City	State	Zip
Day Telephone	Evening Telephone	

Office Use Ondol Sales Number

Date

Style No.	Description	Color Blk	O/W	Blue	Total Quantity	Price Each	Total
101	Long Sleeve Boat Neck Top	❑	❑	❑	_____	$35.00	_____
103	Long Sleeve Cowl Top	❑	❑	❑	_____	45.00	_____
204	Pants	❑	❑	❑	_____	35.00	_____
205	Full Skirt	❑	❑	❑	_____	45.00	_____
206	Straight Skirt	❑	❑	❑	_____	35.00	_____
308	Cowl Dress	❑	❑	❑	_____	80.00	_____
309	Jumper	❑	❑	❑	_____	75.00	_____
410	Jacket	❑	❑	❑	_____	60.00	_____
511	Sash	❑	❑	❑	_____	9.00	_____
	Shoulder Pads	❑	❑		_____	10.00	_____

Signed _____

Charge to my ❑ MasterCard ❑ Visa Exp. Date _____

❑ a check for the total amount is enclosed. No COD's accepted

Sub-Total _____
Tax _____
Shipping _____
Total _____

Preprinted triplicate sales forms speed up order writing and help ensure completeness and clarity as well. If you compare this form to the sales promotion for the same company (included in the Folders section), you'll see how the combination of a strong logo and consistent type styling create a distinct and consistent image for a company of any size.

Design: Edward Hughes (Evanston, IL)

Order form from InFractions Inc.

Trim size: 5-1/2 by 8-1/2

An application bound into a college catalog uses the catalog grid to create a clear and smart-looking form.

The running head, the 2-point rules at the top and bottom margins, the headline and text style, and the use of the narrow outer column are design elements from the catalog format, shown earlier in this section.

The shadowed ballot boxes for options to be checked by the respondent are Zapf Dingbats (keystroke is unshifted o).

Design: Lisa Wilcox and Bill Symes (Oregon City, OR)

Admission application from the Clackamas Community College catalog. Trim size: 8-3/8 by 10-3/4

SECTION 3

HANDS-ON PROJECTS

▼
▼
▼
▼
▼

SECTION 3

INTRODUCTION TO THE PROJECTS

The projects in this section are structured so that beginners can start right in on Project 1 without any prior experience in creating PageMaker documents. The instructions do assume, however, that your computer is up and running, that PageMaker is installed and you know how to open it, that you can locate files on your hard disk, and that you know how to print on your workstation.

The purpose of these projects is to provide experience with Page-Maker's tools and techniques in the context of creating real publications. Reading about a technique in a manual is quite different from applying that technique in a layout that has both editorial and graphic requirements. Manuals describe how to use a technique when nothing else on the page gets in the way; in real life, something almost always gets in the way, or doesn't fit, or ends up in the wrong place. We didn't have to contrive situations that would give you experience with the problem solving and graphic refinement required to use PageMaker well; the situations came up naturally in the course of the projects, just as they inevitably do in real-life publications.

These projects are therefore intended to supplement the very good Page-Maker manual by applying information covered there to some typical publications. Each job you do with a program not only builds knowledge of specific techniques but, perhaps even more important, builds an understanding of the program's internal logic. It's this understanding that enables you, eventually, to figure out why the program responds in certain ways and how to work around apparent limitations.

If you find that you can use one of the project formats as a prototype for your own publication, that's fine. The point, however, is not so much to say that a classified ad should look like the one in Project 2, or that a newsletter should look like the one in Project 4, but to build a familiarity with and an understanding of the basic techniques and to develop a certain manual dexterity when you use those techniques for effects that require some precision.

One of the wisest and most universally acknowledged pieces of advice in the world of computers is to learn a few programs and to learn them well. With that in mind, we've exploited PageMaker's text and graphics tools as much as possible, more so than one might actually do in real-life work. Certain aspects of the projects could be done faster or more effectively in a word-processing program, others in a graphics program. Doing them in PageMaker will help you master the tools and techniques available—and perhaps have some fun in the process.

THE PROJECTS AT A GLANCE

The first four projects are arranged in order of complexity. Each one assumes that you are familiar with techniques used in the previous project. If you are a rank beginner, you should do those four projects in sequence. After that, you should be able to skip around among the other projects.

The last five projects all build on techniques introduced earlier. These projects don't continue to escalate in difficulty; they just introduce additional techniques.

Each project includes a list of techniques covered in that project. Use these lists to help you choose the projects you want to work through.

Project 1: A Simple Certificate for PageMaker Novices

This project guides you through the basic procedures of setting up a new PageMaker document, using the rulers, moving around the publication window, changing the page view, typing text in PageMaker, and using PageMaker's tools to create circles, rectangles, and lines.

Project 2: Placing and Copyfitting Text in a Small Space Ad

This project provides an introduction to placing text from a word-processor file in PageMaker. It will also give you practice formatting text using the type and paragraph specifications. And it looks at the techniques you can use to make a given amount of copy fit the space available.

Project 3: A Quick Invitation Using Paragraph Rules and PageMaker Graphics

A simple invitation makes good use of a powerful feature: specifying rules as a paragraph attribute. The project also gives you the opportunity to create a graphic with PageMaker's drawing tools. And you'll learn to print multiple copies of an undersized document on a single letter-size sheet.

Project 4: Creating a Template for a Three-Column Self-Mailing Newsletter

This project introduces the use of master pages and templates for a publication that is produced repeatedly. There's also an in-depth look at style sheets and at the behavior of threaded text. And you'll

learn to rotate text, place graphics, and export Page-Maker text to a word-processor file.

Project 5: Newsletter Variations Using Additional PageMaker Techniques

Working with a copy of the newsletter from Project 4, you'll learn to set tabular material, work with in-line graphics, create drop caps, and use a leading grid. You'll also see quite a few variations on the layout grid used in Project 4.

Project 6: Using the Story Editor to Create a Flyer

This project uses PageMaker's Story Editor to produce a simple flyer. It includes a look at the spell-checking and Find and Change commands. You'll use leadered tabs to create coupon-response lines. And you'll create a special-effects headline.

Project 7: A Tabloid Ad with Photographs and Display Typography

In this project, you'll learn to work with digital halftones in PageMaker. You'll also get some practice refining display typography and using tabs to create hanging indents in a numbered list. And you'll learn to use the manual tiling option to print oversize pages.

Project 8: Using PageMaker as a Drawing Program

The application doesn't purport to be a drawing program—and it isn't. But you can create some simple (and not so simple) graphics in PageMaker, and in doing so you'll master some important techniques. Try your hand at a truck or a skyline, a map or a floor plan, a pie chart or a pattern created from a Zapf Dingbats character. You'll also learn how to expand PageMaker's line options by creating leadered rules.

Project 9: Working with Color in PageMaker

This project looks at the color prepress options available to PageMaker users, the four different color systems you can work with in PageMaker, and how to define and apply both Pantone and process colors. For hands-on practice, you'll create a series of fact sheets about color, add color to the newsletter from Project 4, and print spot color overlays directly from PageMaker.

STRUCTURE OF THE PROJECTS

The instructions for each project are self-contained: All the information you need to complete any of the designs is included in the instructions for that project. Even the information in this introduction isn't required in order to work through any of the projects. In fact, if you have no experience at all with PageMaker, we suggest that you try a couple of projects before reading the rest of this introduction. The material here will be more useful after you've moved around a little in the program. Much of what is gathered here is intended to be used for reference throughout the projects and in your real-life publication work.

The projects are organized so that numbered, boldface instructions describe the general steps (specify the page setup, define the image area, draw the banner, and so on). Bulleted paragraphs within each numbered instruction detail the specific procedures and techniques required to execute that step. Generally, unbulleted paragraphs explain and amplify the techniques. By organizing the information in this way, we hope you'll be able to move as quickly, or as slowly, through the projects as suits your needs and level of experience.

To select the tool you need, click on that icon in PageMaker's Toolbox. The on-screen pointer turns into different shapes, depending on the tool selected.

▼ ▼ ▼

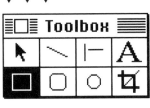

Marginal tips highlight shortcuts as well as procedures that are important for a fundamental understanding and control of PageMaker's sometimes quirky personality. Most tips are placed adjacent to a step within the project to which that tip can be applied. You'll find additional tips in the margins of the Glossary in the back of the book. The Glossary also includes keyboard sequences for many PageMaker commands, so you can refer to that section when you can't remember how to bring up the grabber hand, type an em dash, interrupt Autoflow, and so on.

Screen details with captions provide additional tips throughout the project section. Note, however, that the distortion in letterspacing and word spacing that sometimes occurs on-screen is exacerbated when screen images are reduced in size, which they generally are in this book.

In addition, throughout the projects you'll find sidebars that focus on PageMaker functions in a context that is both specific to the project at hand and more general as well. These sidebars cover the fundamental concepts and procedures needed to use PageMaker efficiently. They are highlighted with a gray tint to make them easy to find.

name	toolbox icon	on-screen icon
pointer tool		
diagonal-line tool		+
perpendicular-line tool		+
text tool	A	I
square-corner tool	□	+
round-corner tool	◻	+
circle tool	○	+
cropping tool		

Macintosh or PC?

The mechanics of working in the Macintosh and PC versions of PageMaker are virtually identical. For the most part, the differences that do exist have to do with system configuration, font installation, and the need in PC PageMaker to have a working version of Microsoft Windows. The basics of system configuration are beyond the scope of this book; you will need to consult your dealer or whatever technical support is available to you in order to get your system up and running to the point at which you can open PageMaker, begin working in the program, and print.

Once you are up and running, however, you should be able to complete the projects regardless of which computer you use. The projects and instructions were created on a Macintosh and then tested on a PC. With a few exceptions that are noted in the instructions, all procedures work both on the Mac and on the PC. The screen details for menus and dialog boxes

Ninety-five percent of the people will always use a program at the lowest level. They don't use even 30% of the features, they use 10%; and, next year, when more features come out, they'll use 5% of those.
—Alan Kask,
PC World

were taken from the Mac, but the differences in those screens on a PC are minimal—the text is a little different and occasionally an option is in a different position in the dialog box. Keyboard shortcuts vary from one platform to another. You will generally find the Macintosh shortcut first and the PC alternative immediately following.

Capitalization and italics

The full names of all menu commands, dialog boxes, and dialog box options are capitalized in these instructions, even if part of a name is not capitalized in PageMaker. For example, whereas the PageMaker menu reads "Page setup," our instructions will tell you to choose the Page Setup command or to specify information in the Page Setup dialog box. On the other hand, if we are speaking generally about page setup, the phrase is not capitalized.

Specific words or values that you are instructed to type in dialog boxes are italicized. If the words should actually be italicized in the publication, that will be stated explicitly in the type specifications.

MENU COMMANDS

PageMaker has different kinds of menu commands. Some of them (such as Rulers and Guides) are like toggle switches that you click on and off by selecting that command from the menu: A check mark before the command indicates the command is active; no check mark means it is inactive. Similar to these are commands that are on (and checked) until you choose another command in the same category (such as page view and line weights).

Another set of commands (such as Copy and Paste) is either black or gray. When a command is gray, it currently does not apply to anything on the page and cannot be selected. For example, the Paste command is gray if there is nothing on the Clipboard, and the Rotate Text command is gray unless you have selected a text block with the pointer tool. If the command you want to use is grayed out, think of what you need to select in order to make the command active.

TIP

You can change tools using keyboard shortcuts if you have an extended keyboard.

To change to	Press
▶	Com-Sp on a Mac, F9 on a PC*
A	Shift-F4
╲	Shift-F2
├─	Shift-F3
□	Shift-F5
▢	Shift-F6
○	Shift-F7
⌗	Shift-F8

Commands that are followed by an ellipsis, such as Page Setup and Type Specs, display dialog boxes through which you select options and type in specifications. Many dialog boxes have buttons that bring up additional dialog boxes. In fact, to get to some features, such as Paragraph Rules and Spacing controls, you might feel as though you're navigating through a maze of dialog boxes.

Some commands are followed by a solid, right-pointing triangle. Pointing to one of these commands and holding down the mouse button displays a pop-up submenu, which you can scroll to choose the desired specification. Many of the commands on the Type menu, as well as the Line and Fill commands on the Element menu, have these submenus.

In some dialog boxes on the Mac, shadowed text boxes also reveal submenus when you point to the box and hold down the mouse button. On the PC, shaded boxes with arrows serve the same function.

Many menu commands are followed by the keyboard shortcut for that command. It's a great boon for beginners not to have to remember any

*These keys enable you to toggle between any active tool and the pointer tool.

keyboard commands, to be able to just point and click and drag. But as with any application, efficiency requires learning frequently used commands. We'll give you keyboard shortcuts throughout the project instructions, and you can refer to the menu abbreviations for them as well.

DEFAULTS

Defaults are preset values or options that PageMaker uses unless you specify otherwise. Like most programs, PageMaker has application defaults and publication defaults. Application defaults apply to all new documents; publication defaults apply only to the current document. You can change and override both kinds of defaults, but it does save time to set them to the choices that you use most frequently.

You can change application defaults *after* you've opened PageMaker but *before* you've opened a document. For example, PageMaker's default unit of measure is inches, so unless you specify otherwise, your ruler increments will be measured in inches. If you work in picas and points more frequently than inches, you'll want to change the application default to picas. Before opening a new document, choose Preferences from the Edit menu and select Picas from the submenu for both the Measurement System and the Vertical Ruler. All new documents will then use picas for their unit of measure.

When you want to select a button surrounded by a heavy border, such as the OK button above, simply press the Return or Enter key instead of moving and clicking the mouse. This keyboard shortcut can be used in many PageMaker dialog boxes—including Page Setup, Place, Save As, Type Specs, and Print—so it's a good one to remember.

You can change the application default for any menu command that is black, rather than gray, when there is no document open in PageMaker. When you change an application default, the new value will apply to all new publications you open; existing publications will not be affected.

You specify publication defaults after a PageMaker document is open. If, to continue the same example, you have inches as your application default and you open a new document and change the unit of measure to picas, the ruler increments will be picas for that publication but not for subsequent ones. You can change the publication defaults at any time while the document is open.

At those times when PageMaker seems to have a mind of its own, insisting on one typeface or line style when you continue to select another, try changing the publication defaults to the specifications you want. To change a publication default, choose the pointer tool, be sure no text or graphic is selected, and select the specifications you want to set as the current publication defaults. Note that if a tool other than the pointer arrow is active, choosing the arrow will automatically deselect any text or graphics. If the pointer arrow is already active and text or a graphic is selected, click on the selected item to deselect it before resetting the default.

The project instructions generally assume that you are working with PageMaker's original defaults. If you've changed any of the application defaults, your screen may look different from what is described in a particular project. If you want to restore PageMaker's original defaults, simply throw out the PM 4 Defaults file in your system folder if you work on a Macintosh; delete or rename the file named PM4.CNF if you use the PC version. The next time you open PageMaker, the program will automatically create a new, unaltered default file in your system folder on a Mac or your ALDUS directory on a PC.

MEASUREMENTS

Although you can use either inches or picas as the unit of measure in PageMaker, fractions of inches must be specified as decimals. We find the following conversions useful to have on hand.

▼ ▼ ▼

Inches	Decimals	Points	Picas
1/32	0.03125		
1/16	0.0625	4.5	
3/32	0.09375	6.75	
1/8	0.125	9	
5/32	0.15625	11.25	
3/16	0.1875	13.5	1p1.5
7/32	0.21875	15.75	1p3.75
1/4	0.250	18	1p6
9/32	0.28125	20.25	1p8.25
5/16	0.3125	22.50	1p10.5
11/32	0.34375	24.75	2p0.75
3/8	0.375	27	2p3
13/32	0.40625	29.25	2p5.25
7/16	0.4375	31.50	2p7.50
15/32	0.46875	33.75	2p9.75
1/2	0.50	36	3p
17/32	0.53125	38.25	3p2.25
9/16	0.5625	40.50	3p4.5
19/32	0.59375	42.75	3p6.75
5/8	0.625	45	3p9
21/32	0.65625	47.25	3p11.25
11/16	0.6875	49.50	4p1.5
23/32	0.71875	51.75	4p3.75
3/4	0.750	54	4p6
25/32	0.78125	56.25	4p8.25
13/16	0.8125	58.50	4p10.5
27/32	0.84375	60.75	5p0.75
7/8	0.875	63	5p3
29/32	0.90625	65.25	5p5.25
15/16	0.9375	67.50	5p7.50
31/32	0.96875	69.75	5p9.75
1	1	72	6p

Units of measure

The Preferences command on PageMaker's Edit menu lets you specify whether you want rulers in inches or picas (or millimeters or ciceros). Picas are the traditional measuring system for the graphic arts: They are used to measure type, leading between lines, and space between graphics and other elements on the page. But we generally think of page size in inches; and we also size art in inches, a tradition resulting from the fact that the proportion wheels used to size art give results in inches, not picas.

PageMaker has an extremely useful feature that allows you to override the current unit of measure within dialog boxes such as Page Setup or Column Guides. You simply type a one-character abbreviation for the measurement you want to use. This enables you to open a new document with, for example, an 8.5- by 11-inch page size and 3-pica margins all around without converting either measure and also without closing the dialog box to change the Preferences. If the current measure in the Preferences dialog box is set to inches, simply type *8.5* and *11* in the Page Size boxes and *3p* in the Margin boxes.

The abbreviations are logical and easy to remember (do not insert a space before or after the abbreviation):

To change a measurement to	Type
inches	*i* after the number
picas	*p* after the number
points	*p* before the number
picas and points	*p* between the numbers
millimeters	*m* after the number

In the project instructions, we freely mix measurement systems, using whichever is most useful for the space or object being measured. This leaves it up to you to type the abbreviation or change the Preferences.

Rulers

We almost always work with rulers turned on. To have them appear as a default for all publications, choose Rulers from PageMaker's Options menu when no publication is open on the desktop.

The increments shown on the rulers depend on the page view and monitor. At 50% page view on our Apple RGB and Moniterm Viking monitors, for example, the ruler tick marks are at 6-point increments, whereas at 200 and 400%, the tick marks are at 1-point increments. On our technical editor's NEC Multisync monitor, at 50% page view, the tick marks are at 3-point intervals.

Fractional measurements

In keeping with both traditional usage and PageMaker's menus, fractions of inches are expressed as decimals, fractions of picas are expressed as points, and fractions of points are expressed as decimals. Thus, you'll find measurements such as these:

8.5 by 11 inches
7 picas 6 points (noted in PageMaker as 7p6)
9.5 points (noted in PageMaker as 0p9.5)

Remember that there are 12 points in a pica. When calculating measurements, be careful not to confuse fractions of picas expressed as decimals with points. For example, if you used a calculator to divide 11 picas in half, you'd get 5.5 picas. Properly translated into points, that's 5 picas 6 points, or 5p6. To convert a fraction of a pica into points, multiply the fraction by 12. Say you want to divide a 7-pica measure into three units: $7 \div 3 = 2.33$ picas; $0.33 \times 12 = 3.96$. So one-third of 7 picas is actually 2 picas 3.96 points, or 2p3.96. These fractional differences may seem insignificant, but if they are not accurately worked out, they can throw off your layout as they accumulate and leave you feeling incredibly frustrated.

SNAP TO COMMANDS

Snap to Rulers and Snap to Guides are two toggle switches on the Options menu. These commands turn rulers or guides into magnets.

Turn on Snap to Rulers when you
- Pull in ruler guides that you want aligned to a specific tick mark in the ruler.
- Draw PageMaker graphics (squares and so on) that require precise measurements.
- Work with a leading grid.

Turn off Snap to Rulers when you
- Pull in ruler guides that you want to align with a graphic or text block already on the page.
- Want to align text or graphics with an existing guide that might not be on a ruler tick mark.

Turn on Snap to Guides when you
- Place text in columns.
- Want to align existing graphics with existing guides.

Turn off Snap to Guides when you
- Position graphics or text blocks near, but not directly on, the guides.

The PageMaker manual says that Snap To's enable you to position elements with an accuracy of 1/2880 inch. We don't have a device that can measure 1/2880 inch to test that claim, but we do have a lot of confidence in the Snap To commands, and we use them as described above.

THE PASTEBOARD

The pasteboard is the area surrounding the page, the on-screen equivalent of the drawing board. Think of the pasteboard as a work surface where you can leave items that you'll need from time to time when working on the publication. These might include

- Printing items that you will use on some, but not all, pages of the publication, such as a banner treatment or a breakout box.

- Spacing guides to measure distances between items such as photographs and captions.

- Text and graphics that you're not yet ready to move into position or that you've cut from the layout and want to reinstate elsewhere.

Items on the pasteboard display on the pasteboard for all pages of a publication. But if any part of a pasteboard item (including the selection handle of a text block) overlaps any portion of a page, that item is considered part of the page and appears only on the pasteboard for that page.

PAGE VIEW AND CHANGING PAGES

Eight different page views are available in PageMaker—seven listed on the Page menu plus one bonus. At larger page views, you see less of the page in greater detail than at smaller page views. The view you choose depends on what you're doing, the size of your monitor, and the precision (and perfection) you require in your work. Generally, you edit text at Actual Size or 200%, depending on the legibility of the screen font. You check overall page composition at Fit in Window, so you can see the entire page or spread at once. And you check critical alignments at 200% or 400%. Because of the many variables in system configuration, we've generally left it to you to determine the page view as you work on the projects.

We frequently toggle back and forth between page views and thus find the keyboard shortcuts for doing this among the most frequently used.

Keyboard shortcuts for changing page view

The menu shortcuts are easy to remember, but the result of using them varies depending on what you're doing at the time.

- If an element is selected, that element will be centered in the window at the new page view.

- If nothing is selected, the first time you choose a page view other than Fit in Window, the center of the page will be centered in the window at the new page view.

- If you're returning to a previous page view and nothing is selected, the page position will be as it was the last time you used that page view.

Page view	Macintosh shortcut	PC shortcut
Fit in Window	Command-W	Ctrl-W
25%	Command-0 (zero)	Ctrl-0 (zero)
50%	Command-5	Ctrl-5
75%	Command-7	Ctrl-7
Actual Size	Command-1	Ctrl-1
200 %	Command-2	Ctrl-2
400%	Command-4	Ctrl-4

To zoom to a specific part of the screen at a different page view

Actual Size: Command-Option-click mouse button on point you want center screen. (Click the right mouse button to do this on a PC.)

200%: Command-Option-Shift-click mouse button on point you want center screen. (Press Shift and click the right mouse button on a PC.)

To see the entire pasteboard

This is the bonus page view that's not listed on the Page menu. Press Shift and then select Fit in Window. (You have to select Fit in Window from the menu, rather than use the keyboard shortcut.)

TIP

Familiarize yourself early on with PageMaker's on-line help. On a Mac, choose Help from the Window menu to display the Help dialog box, where you can scroll a list of commands and topics. On a PC, choose the options on the Help menu. Or press Command-? on a Mac, Shift-F1 on a PC, and when the cursor changes to a question mark, choose any menu command for information about that feature.

This view is useful when you want to place a large piece of art or a text block on the pasteboard before moving it onto the page. Also, when you clean up your pages to compress files, use this view to check the pasteboard for items you might have left there. Occasionally, one of those items should have been included in the publication, so checking at this view might prevent some omissions.

To get the grabber hand

On a Macintosh, press the Option key, click the mouse button, and drag. On a PC, press the Alt key, click the main mouse button, and drag.

Use the grabber hand to scroll around the screen at the current page view.

To display the next page or spread at Fit in Window

Press Shift when you click on the page icon.

To move to the next page or spread at the view last seen

Press Command-Tab (F12 on a PC). If you press the keys repeatedly, you can move through several spreads without seeing them displayed.

To move to the previous page

Press Command-Shift-Tab (F11 on a PC).

To move to a page whose page icon is not displayed

Choose Go to Page (Command-G on a Mac, Ctrl-G on a PC). Type the page number you want in the text box, and press Return.

To change page views for all pages in the publication

Hold down the Option key (Alt-Shift on a PC) and select the desired view from the Page menu.

This is particularly useful when you move through an entire document to check placements and alignments.

To view all the pages in sequence

Use the previous tip to specify the page view you want for all the pages. Then hold down the Shift key and choose Go to Page from the Page menu. PageMaker will display pages one after another, beginning with the first page or spread in the file. To stop the show, press the mouse button or press Command-period (Ctrl-period on a PC).

SELECTING TEXT

To select a range of text

- Drag over the text with the text tool.

- Set an insertion point at the beginning of the text you want to select, hold down the Shift key, and set another insertion point at the end of the text you want to select. All the text between the two insertion points will be selected.

  This technique is especially useful when you want to select a range of text that spans more than a spread.

- Use the Shift key in conjunction with the cursor keys and the numeric keypad, as described in the next section.

To select all the text in a story

- Set an insertion point anywhere in the story and choose Select All from the Edit menu (Command-A on a Mac, Ctrl-A on a PC).

  This technique is useful if you want to change type specs or apply a style to an entire story, or if you want to delete an entire file. Note that if you have placed part of a file and want to change the type specs, you can use this Select All feature to change the specs for the unplaced text as well as for the text that is already placed.

And remember these shortcuts as well

- Double-click on a word to select it.

- Triple-click on a paragraph to select it.

USING THE KEYBOARD TO MOVE THROUGH TEXT

When you edit text, you can use the arrow keys and the numeric keypad to move through and select text.

The arrow keys

- Use the arrow keys to move the cursor right or left one character, or up or down one line.

- Press Command (Ctrl on a PC) and the up or down arrow key to move one paragraph.

- Press Shift and the appropriate arrow key to select text in that direction.

The numeric keypad

The action of some of the numeric keys varies depending on your page view. And as with the arrow keys, pressing the Shift key in combination with the numeric key selects the text in the respective direction.

1:	To end of line, and after that to end of next line
7:	To beginning of line, and after that to beginning of previous line
Com (or Ctrl)-1:	Forward one sentence
Com (or Ctrl)-7:	Back one sentence
2:	Down one line
8:	Up one line
3:	Down one screen or to end of text block, depending on page view
9:	Up one screen or to top of text block, depending on page view
4:	To previous character
6:	To next character
Com (or Ctrl)-4:	To previous word
Com (or Ctrl)-6:	To next word
Com (or Ctrl)-8:	Up one paragraph
Com (or Ctrl)-2:	Down one paragraph

TIP

When you are editing text in Page-Maker, even at Actual Size, there are places where it's difficult to determine on-screen if you have the correct letterspacing and word spacing. Sometimes it looks as if there's a space in the middle of a word when in fact there isn't; sometimes it looks as if there's no space between two words when in fact there is. A quick way to check is to use the cursor keys (the four keys with arrows pointing up, down, right, and left). With the text tool, set an insertion point in the text in question. Then press the right or left cursor key (depending on the direction in which you're moving for your check). If one click of the arrow key moves the cursor past the next letter, there's no space; if it takes two clicks, there is a space.

PAGEMAKER'S NONPRINTING GUIDES

PageMaker has three types of guides that appear on-screen but do not print—called, logically enough, nonprinting guides. Each of the three looks different on the screen, has slightly different functions, and is set up and manipulated in slightly different ways.

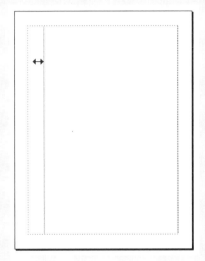

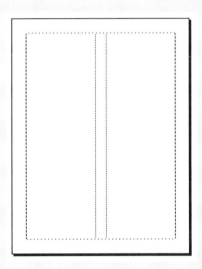

▲ ▲ ▲

Margin guides define the top, bottom, and sides of the image area of the page. Their position is specified in the Page Setup dialog box when you open a new document, and you can change them at any time by returning to that dialog box.

▲ ▲ ▲

Column guides control the alignment of text and graphics. PageMaker's default is one column, defined by the margin guides. The side margins look heavier than the top and bottom ones because they are actually column guides on top of margin guides. When you drag a column guide off the margin guide, the margin guide remains in its original position.

▲ ▲ ▲

To specify two or more columns and the space between them, use the Column Guides command on the Options menu. (See Project 4 for how to create unequal columns.) Note that the column guides do not extend beyond the top and bottom margins.

▶ ▶ ▶

Use the pointer to pull in ruler guides from the vertical and horizontal rulers as needed. In this sample page, ruler guides are used to align elements such as the bottom of the initial cap box and the baseline of adjacent text, and the tops of adjacent picture frames. Ruler guides extend to the page trim; you can use them to align elements that fall outside the margins, such as a folio. When a ruler guide is on top of both a margin guide and a column guide, as it is on the far right of this page, it looks on-screen like a solid rule, but it will not print.

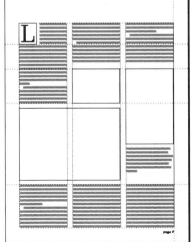

To begin with a blank page, specify all margins as 0 in the Page Setup dialog box.

To divide a page into several equal vertical units, use the Column Guides command to do the arithmetic. Simply specify the number of units you want as the number of columns and specify 0 as the space in between. Bring in ruler guides over the column guides, and then return to the Column Guides dialog box to specify the number of columns for text.

MASTER PAGES

Master pages provide a blueprint on which the individual pages of a publication are built. Anything you put on a master page will appear on every regular page of the document, unless you choose to modify or eliminate the master-page elements on individual pages. Master pages can include the following:

- A nonprinting layout grid, which, in addition to the margin guides, includes column guides and vertical and horizontal ruler guides.

- Text and graphics that will appear on most pages of the document. These include page frames, rules between columns, report or issue dates, headline banners, page numbers, and so on.

When you use master pages, keep these points in mind:

- Master pages are not selected automatically.

    When you open a new document, pages 1 and 2 appear (or only page 1 if the Double-sided option is turned off). If you want to create master pages, you have to remember to click on the L or R icon to the left of the numbered page icons at the bottom of the screen. One of the most frustrating moments in electronic pasteup is when you realize that you've just spent two hours setting up a layout grid on pages 1 and 2 instead of on the master pages.

    Similarly, after you've finished setting up the master pages, don't forget to click on the actual page of the document before proceeding.

- Take time with your master pages. Care and precision there is reflected on every page of your document.

- If your left and right master pages have many of the same printing elements in the same position—page frames, page-number markers, rules between columns, and so forth—create those elements on one page, choose the Select All command, and then copy and paste them onto the other master page. Then add elements that are unique to each page. You will have to create nonprinting ruler guides and customized column guides on each page; they cannot be copied.

- Printing items on the master pages cannot be edited, moved, or copied on an individual page.

    If you have a graphic that you will use repeatedly, such as a black banner into which you will drop headlines, put a master unit on the pasteboard of your master pages. That master unit will then appear on the pasteboard of all regular pages of the publication and can be copied and edited as needed.

- Text-wrap specifications on a master page carry over to regular pages. So when you Autoflow text, you can use the Text Wrap command to keep text from flowing into certain columns (such as the narrow left-hand columns in the pages of this book). Create a no-line rule at the top of the column and apply the column-break text-wrap icon ( ) to the rule. If you want to add text to that column after autoflowing the main text, remove the rule from the master page. Similarly, if you want to reserve space for a breakout on every page, create a white box on the master page and apply the wrap-all-sides icon ( ) to the box.

TIP

It's important to distinguish refinements that you should make early on in PageMaker from details that you should postpone. The type specs of headlines and the size and placement of art contribute to the clarity of your message and affect line count and page breaks, so you should resolve these early on. The exact placement of rules, on the other hand, is a detail. In this tip, for example, a small editorial change can alter the depth of the text block and thus the length of the vertical rule at right. You can waste a lot of time refining graphic details too early on.

- You cannot print a master page directly, but if you turn to a numbered page within the publication, the printing elements from the master page will be displayed there, and you can print that page as you would any other page.

Customizing individual pages

Frequently, you will want to customize nonprinting column and ruler guides on individual pages. Simply use the pointer tool to change the guides on that page manually or change the specifications in the Column Guides dialog box, available from the Options menu. If you change your mind and want to go back to the master guides, choose Copy Master Guides from the Page menu. This command affects only the page or spread currently displayed.

If you want to eliminate all of the master-page printing items on a regular page, choose Display Master Items from the Page menu. (Doing this in effect turns off the master items.)

To remove a printing master item from an individual page, display that page and cover the item you want to eliminate with a white box, which is simply a rectangle with the Fill specified as Paper and the Line specified as None. When you click on one of these invisible boxes with the pointer, you will see handles around its edges but nothing else.

These boxes are called masks because they mask the printing items underneath. They can be very handy, but they can also end up in the wrong place, masking something you intended to print. When you want to eliminate several printing items from the master page, it's better to copy the master items that you do want displayed, paste them onto the regular page, and turn off Display Master Items.

Modifying master pages

The rules governing the modification of master pages exemplify the trade-offs inherent in many aspects of electronic pasteup, so much so that the following information could be cast as a good news/bad news script. The rules are perfectly logical, if difficult to remember at first, and something that seems a nuisance in one situation can be used to good advantage in another.

- If you return to the master pages and change any printing or nonprinting items there, those changes will be reflected on all of the corresponding regular pages except those that you have customized.

- A customized page is any page on which you have changed the column guides or brought in any ruler guides that aren't on the master pages. If you frequently bring in ruler guides on individual pages, as we do, you'll have a great many customized pages. To have the changes made on the master pages appear on a customized page, you must display that page and then choose Copy Master Guides from the Page menu.

- When you copy master guides onto a page, however, you lose all of your customized guides. This might not be a problem if your customized guides were temporary ones used to check alignment and to position loose odds and ends. The position of text and graphics already on the page will not change—only the ruler and column guides.

> **TIP**
>
> PageMaker has a built-in utility that checks for virus infections each time the program is launched. If any sign of a virus is detected, PageMaker displays a message box that says the application has been modified. If you see this message, you'll need to use a full-fledged virus detection program to eliminate the virus; PageMaker can't do that.

TIP

Play is generally recognized as an important component of both learning and creativity. Just "playing around" in PageMaker can accelerate your learning curve and sharpen your graphic eye. When there's no end result at stake, no fear of making a mistake, no deadline to meet, you may find it easier to experiment and become comfortable with certain commands and functions.

• If your individual pages are a mess of customized ruler guides, you can quickly eliminate them simply by choosing the Copy Master Guides command. This is much faster than dragging every ruler guide off the page. You'll keep all of your master guides and all of the text and graphics added to that individual page, but you won't have a lot of extraneous ruler guides on the screen. And you don't have to display the master printing items to use the Copy Master Guides command.

Copying master pages

You cannot directly copy master-page items from one document to another. But if you do want to reuse the master guides from an existing document, you can open a copy of that document, delete all the regular pages from the file (using the Remove Pages command from the Page menu), and then add new pages (using the Insert Pages command).

Numbering pages automatically

If you insert a page-number marker on your master pages (Command-Option-P on a Mac, Ctrl-Shift-3 on a PC), PageMaker will number every page consecutively, beginning with the starting page number specified in the Page Setup dialog box. The default style for page numbers is Arabic, but you can specify Roman or alphabetic numbering through the Numbers option in the Page Setup dialog box.

If your publication is divided into several files, you can still use automatic numbering. PageMaker begins numbering each file with the starting page number specified in the Page Setup dialog box. So if, for example, you have a 200-page report divided into two files between, say, pages 109 and 110, the Start Page # on the second file would be 110, the first page icon on the bottom of the screen would be 110, and the page-number marker on the first page of the file would register as 110.

For right-aligned page-number markers, be sure to apply the right alignment electronically so that the alignment will be maintained for two- and three-digit numbers. If you use the pointer tool to manually position the page-number marker at the right margin, longer numbers will overhang the margin.

SAVING YOUR WORK

A general rule of thumb is to save every 15 to 20 minutes or whenever you've done something you'd really hate to redo. In the projects, we've generally left it to you to save according to your own habit.

The keyboard shortcut for saving—Command-S (Ctrl-S on a PC)—is easy to remember and takes much less time than redoing lost work.

After you've saved a publication for the first time, PageMaker automatically performs a "mini-save" whenever you move to a new page or spread, insert or delete a page, change the page setup, or click OK in the Define Styles dialog box.

The compacting feature of "Save As"

When you save a document with the Save command, changes made since the last save are appended to the end of the file. So even if you delete text or graphics, the document might continue to grow in size.

When you save a document using the Save As command from the File menu, the file is compacted, truly eliminating from memory the discarded elements from previous versions. The difference in file size can be dramatic. To cite just one example, we've seen a file reduced from 810 KB after doing a regular Save to 490 KB after doing a Save As.

So when you've made substantial changes in a complex document, and when you're saving a document before closing it, use the Save As command to compress the file. If you want to keep the same name (we generally do when compressing files), just click OK (or press Return) when the Save As dialog box comes on-screen. You'll get another box asking if you want to replace the existing document with that name; click Yes.

You can instruct PageMaker to make every Save a Save As. From the Save options at the bottom of the Preferences dialog box, choose Smaller. (This option was not available in the original Macintosh 4.0 release, but was added in the 4.01 upgrade.)

LINKS

Links are the connections between a PageMaker document and the original source files for text and graphics that you've placed in that document. There are two basic ways to use the linking features. One involves printing, and it is essential if your PageMaker file includes certain kinds of graphics. The second involves updating the publication when the source file has been changed, and this use is optional.

Maintaining links for printing

When you place graphics that are larger than 256 KB, PageMaker alerts you to the size of the file and asks if you want to include a complete copy in the publication. If you respond Yes, then the publication file will include all the information needed to both display and print the graphic at high resolutions. The downside is that the file might be quite large as well as slow.

If you respond No in the message box, PageMaker stores a low-resolution screen version of the graphic in the publication file and creates a link to the original source file. When you print the publication, PageMaker reads

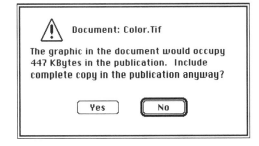

▲ ▲ ▲

When you place a graphic larger than 256 KB, PageMaker displays this dialog box. Responding No keeps your files small because PageMaker places a low-resolution copy in the document file and links that copy to the external source file.

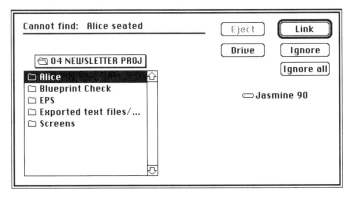

▲ ▲ ▲

If you move or rename a linked source file, or fail to include it with the PageMaker file when you send it to a service bureau for high-resolution output, PageMaker will ask you to reestablish the link. (See Tip at right.)

TIP

Aldus recommends that you always save, copy, or export files to your hard disk before copying them to a floppy disk for remote printing or archiving. Saving or exporting directly to a floppy can damage the original publication. Similarly, for best performance you should copy files from floppies to your hard disk, rather than opening files directly from floppies.

TIP

When you open a file with a broken link, PageMaker displays the Cannot Find dialog box (facing page, bottom right). To reestablish the link for that element: Scroll through your folders or directories to locate the original source file. Highlight the filename and then click the Link button; or just double-click on the filename. Clicking Ignore accepts the broken link; clicking Ignore All accepts broken links for all graphics in the publication.

the data from the linked source file and applies any sizing, cropping, and other image manipulation done in the layout to the high-res original.

When you send a publication to a service bureau for camera-ready print-outs (or when you copy your files for output on any printer that's not networked to your workstation), it's essential to send these linked graphics along with the PageMaker publication. Otherwise, the graphics will not print properly.

There's an easy way to facilitate copying linked files:

• Create a folder or directory for the service bureau files.

• Do a Save As of the PageMaker file to bring up the Save As dialog box.

  If you work on a Mac, hold down the option key; the Copy Linked Documents option changes to Copy Linked Documents for Remote Printing, and you click on that option.

  If you work on a PC, select the Files Required for Remote Printing option.

• On both platforms, PageMaker will copy the publication file, and any linked files required for printing, to the selected directory. You can then copy the files from that directory to disks to send to the service bureau.

There's another Save As option, available in both Macintosh and PC Page-Maker, called Copy All Linked Files. If you select this option, PageMaker will copy both the PageMaker file and any external source files linked to the publication, whether or not the linked files are actually required for printing. (For an explanation of linked files that aren't required for printing, see the following section.) This is useful when you need to transfer files from one workstation or location to another.

Using Links for revision control

The Links options can be used to update a PageMaker document when its external source files—text or graphics—have been updated. While this can be a great boon in workgroup publishing, where several people work on different aspects of the same project, it can also be something of a Pandora's box if you don't establish procedures for updating. The procedures will vary, depending on the project and the people involved.

Whether or not you use this feature, PageMaker tracks the status of the link between the external source file and the copy of that file in the Page-Maker document. You can see a list of all linked files and their status by choosing Links from the File menu (Command-= on a Mac, Ctrl-Shift-D on a PC). Or you can review the link history for a single element by selecting that element with the pointer tool and choosing Link Info from the Element menu.

For each document, PageMaker lists the name of the source file, the kind of file (image, text, EPS, PICT, and so on), and the page location in the PageMaker document (PB stands for pasteboard, LM and RM for left and right master pages). An icon to the left of the filename indicates the status of each document. When you select a filename from the document list, the status of that file is described in the Status field below the list box. See the sidebar on the following page for a summary of what each icon means and what actions to consider for each situation.

*Choose Links from the File menu
to see a list of all external
source files that you've placed in
the publication, along with the
link status of each file.*

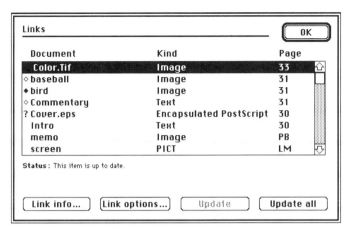

LINK STATUS SUMMARY

Mac icon	PC icon	Status	Action to take
No icon	No icon	Link is up-to-date or item is not linked.	None needed.
◇	–	External file has been modified, and the linked internal file will not be automatically updated.	Click on the Update button in the Links dialog box to update the file, or use the Place command to replace the existing element with the updated one.
◆	+	External file has been modified, and the linked internal file will be automatically updated.	The next time you open the PageMaker file, the placed element will automatically be updated with the revised element to which it is linked; if you don't want the file updated, use the Link Options button to turn off Auto Update.
?	?	The link has been broken; i.e., PageMaker cannot find the external linked file.	You've probably moved or renamed either the publication file or the external source file. To reestablish the link, choose the Link Info button; in the Link Info dialog box, scroll to find the appropriate external source file, select it, and click on Link.
△	!	Both the linked file and the internal PageMaker file have been modified. This icon appears only if you've selected the Alert Before Updating option and responded No.	If both sets of changes are needed in the Page-Maker file, you'll have to compile them manually. You want to avoid this situation.
NA	*	If an asterisk appears next to the file type for a graphic requiring a filter, it means Page-Maker can't locate that filter.	Make sure the necessary filter is in one of the directories listed in your current PATH.

```
┌─────────────────────────────────────┐
│  Link options: Defaults    ┌───────┐│
│                            │  OK   ││
│  Text:                      └───────┘│
│  ☒ Store copy in publication┌───────┐│
│    ☐ Update automatically   │Cancel ││
│      ☐ Alert before updating└───────┘│
│                                      │
│  Graphics:                           │
│  ☒ Store copy in publication         │
│    ☐ Update automatically            │
│      ☐ Alert before updating         │
└─────────────────────────────────────┘
```

▲ ▲ ▲

Use the Link Options dialog box to define where linked files are stored and whether PageMaker should update them automatically.

Link Info

You can get a file history for any linked element in a document through the Link Info dialog box. Select the element and choose Link Info from the Element menu, or use the Link Info button in the Links dialog box. Link Info includes the path (for PC files), the location on the drive, the kind of file, the size of the file, the date and time you placed the file in the current publication, the date and time the external file was last modified, and the date and time the internal copy of the file was modified.

Link Options

You can define how you want linked files to be stored and updated in your publication through the Link Options command on the Element menu. The available options are:

Store Copy in Publication: PageMaker stores a complete copy of the external source file in the PageMaker document, so there is no need for a link to an external source file.

Update Automatically: If the external copy has been modified, the internal linked copy will automatically be updated the next time you open the file. This sounds convenient but in fact can be very dangerous. In a workgroup situation, for example, you'd want to be sure that the person who made the changes intended them to be incorporated; he or she might have been exploring some refinement that didn't work out or isn't yet finished.

Alert Before Updating: If you choose this option in conjunction with Update Automatically, PageMaker displays an alert message for you to respond to before updating the internal file. Having been alerted that a change has been made, the layout person can check with the person responsible for the source file to see if the layout should be updated.

You can set the Link Options for the entire publication or for individual elements in the publication.

- To set the defaults for the entire publication, choose Link Options from the Element menu when no text or graphic is selected.

- To set the options for an individual text or graphic file, either use the Link Options command when that element is selected, or use the Link Options button in the Links dialog box when that element is highlighted in the document list.

Link features on the Element menu

In a publication with a great many linked elements, the list in the Links dialog box can be intimidatingly long. You can access the various link options for any individual element by selecting that element with the pointer tool and choosing either Link Info or Link Options from the Element menu. This is particularly useful when you have several versions of the same graphic, with slightly different names, and you're not sure which version is currently in the publication.

Links and the Clipboard

When you copy text or graphics from other programs and paste them into a PageMaker document, the copy you paste has no link to an external file. But if you cut or copy a graphic or text range in PageMaker and paste it elsewhere in that same document, PageMaker will transfer any existing link information.

TIP

You don't have to use automatic updates to take advantage of the Link options. If you know several elements need to be updated, use the Links dialog box to speed up the process. From the list of linked documents, select the name of an element that has been revised and click the Update button. Repeat this for every element whose revision is ready to be incorporated into the layout. When you OK the dialog box, PageMaker will replace all the outdated elements that you selected with the revised versions. This is essentially the same as using the Replace Entire Graphic (or Text) option in the Place dialog box, but it's much faster when you need to replace several elements at once.

PRINTING

If you use a laser printer for final pages, consider these techniques for improving the image quality:

- Use high-quality paper with a smooth, white finish.
- For undersize pages, you can increase the effective resolution by using the Scaling option to enlarge the printed page, and asking the printer to photographically reduce the page before making plates.
- Some toner cartridges simply produce sharper copies than others. When you get a good one, save it for masters. Cartridges that are very new or very old produce the most uneven coverage and generally should not be used to print camera-ready pages.

You can print PageMaker files on several different kinds of printers, including high-resolution PostScript imagesetters, PostScript laser printers, printers that use the Hewlett-Packard Printer Command Language, QuickDraw printers, and dot-matrix printers. For specific information concerning print drivers, fonts, and setup for your printer, you will need to refer to your printer-specific and PageMaker manuals, and, if you are using PageMaker on a PC, to the *Microsoft Windows User's Guide*.

The issues addressed here concern the quality of the page when printed at different resolutions as well as the use of different printers in the production of a given project.

Comparing printer resolution

Whether you use your desktop printer or a high-resolution imagesetter for camera-ready pages depends on the kinds of graphics included in the publication and the quality of reproduction required. The samples on the following spread illustrate the way different kinds of elements are reproduced at different resolutions. Although there are differences from one printer to another at the same resolution, the comparisons should help you determine which resolution is appropriate for a particular job. (We haven't included a 72-dots-per-inch sample from a dot-matrix printer, which is adequate only for proofing.)

For many flyers, reports, price lists, and other fast-turnaround, short-shelf-life documents without complex graphics, 300-dpi output is both adequate and efficient. But for publications that include tints (gray or color), digital halftones, and complex art, resolutions above 1000 dpi provide the crisp, smooth output required for quality work. In comparing the samples, note especially the variation in tints, the relative smoothness of the art, and the sharpness of type at very large and very small sizes.

Whereas laser printers transfer and fuse toner to paper, imagesetters print photographically on resin-coated paper or film. The ability to go directly to film further increases the sharpness of the final image because it eliminates one generation of duplication that would be required at the printer. This can save you money as well. Keep in mind, though, that with film you can't paste in a last-minute correction by hand the way you do with paper or repro; you have to reprint the entire page.

Another advantage of imagesetters is the larger page size available. Because they print on rolls rather than sheets, imagesetters can print pages up to 11 inches wide with full bleeds and crop marks.

Changing printers from proofing to camera-ready pages

There are three issues to consider when you proof your pages on a home or office printer and print camera-ready masters at a service bureau: testing the layout at the final resolution, troubleshooting your electronic production techniques at the final resolution, and understanding the potential effect of changing printers on the page composition.

In a job of any importance, you should run test pages at the service bureau that will provide your high-resolution output. The test should include samples of the various type specifications used in the publication (headline styles, body text, captions, and so on). If you will be using rules, gray

TIP

If you want to print on both sides of the paper, use the Even/Odd Pages option. (On a PC, the option is in the main Print dialog box; on a Mac, it's in the Print Options box.) First print the odd-numbered pages, then run the pages through again to print the even-numbered pages. Let the pages cool for a few minutes before the second pass through the printer. And be sure to test beforehand whether the pages should be flipped or rotated for the second pass (it varies depending on the printer). PC PageMaker also has a Duplex option for the few printers that have duplexing capabilities.

TIP

If you switch from a non-PostScript printer for proofing to a PostScript printer for final pages, Adobe Type Manager is invaluable. It creates high-resolution bit-mapped fonts for screen display from the outline fonts used for printing. It also improves the quality of printed pages with both QuickDraw and dot-matrix printers, although the latter is still suitable only for proofing.

tints behind boxes, a special effect with halftones, whatever, include a representation of those elements so that you can evaluate how they look at the high resolution. Tints, rules, and type generally print lighter at high resolution. Type that looks too tight on a 300-dpi laser-printed page might look just fine at 1270. For our tests, we usually run a few full pages and then compile a lot of loose elements on a few additional pages to keep the cost down.

For longer publications, use your test pages to troubleshoot your production techniques. Are you importing art from a drawing program that you've never used before? Include a test image to be sure the format in which you saved or exported the source file prints correctly from the imagesetter. Do your pages include Encapsulated PostScript files made from another PageMaker document? Testing one such file will tell you if you're making the EPS files correctly. The problems with conflicting fonts are not as common as they were a couple of years ago, but there's always potential for incompatibility between your fonts and the service bureau's.

Do not assume that whatever can be successfully printed on your desktop printer can be successfully printed on a high-resolution imagesetter. The compatibility between output devices with varying resolutions is sometimes mysteriously imperfect.

Quite apart from the different systems and fonts that may reside on your computer and that of your service bureau, a high-resolution printer has to process and print considerably more information than your laser printer. A 300-dpi printer has to manage only 90,000 dots per square inch, but an imagesetter printing at 1270 dpi must process over a million and a half dots per square inch; at 2540 dpi, the number jumps to almost six and a half million. The difference between those numbers and the information they represent accounts for a great deal of machine time (if your service center bills you for pages that take longer than a specified time to print) and more than a few glitches.

We cannot emphasize enough the need to work closely with the service bureau or publisher who will provide your high-resolution output. Submit test pages early, and be sure your test documents are representative of the elements included in your publication. And then, when all is said and done, leave time in the schedule to solve the problems that will inevitably crop up and to rerun some of the pages.

If you work on a PC, you can specify both the current printer and the target printer for a publication. Use the Target Printer command from the File menu to specify the printer that will be used for final output, and the Print command to specify the printer that you are currently using. PageMaker will compose the publication for the printer specifications of the target printer. In PC PageMaker, changing the target printer can change the line breaks, spacing, and other aspects of text composition, as well as the printer's ability to handle rotated, expanded, and condensed text. So be sure to set up the target printer at the beginning of a job.

On the Macintosh, you can't specify two different printers in the same way as you can on the PC. But because the page makeup and printing functions are separate, you won't see the differences in text composition that exist in PC PageMaker.

Laser Writer NTX
at 300 dots per inch

Display: 80-pt Galliard Italic; *Type In Gray:* 80-pt Futura Extra Bold, specified in PageMaker in 10% increments from 10 to 80% Black. *This caption:* 6.5/8 Galliard roman and italic; *sans-serif captions:* 7-pt FuturaLight and Futra Extra Bold.

Hairline rule

.5 pt rule

1 pt rule

Bit-mapped clip art

Encapsulated PostScript art imported from FreeHand.

Digital halftone printed at 53 lines per inch

Varityper VT-600W
at 600 dots per inch

Display: 80-pt Galliard Italic; *Type In Gray:* 80-pt Futura Extra Bold, specified in PageMaker in 10% increments from 10 to 80% Black. *This caption:* 6.5/8 Galliard roman and italic; *sans-serif captions:* 7-pt FuturaLight and Futra Extra Bold.

Hairline rule

.5 pt rule

1 pt rule

Bit-mapped clip art

Encapsulated PostScript art imported from FreeHand.

Digital halftone printed at 100 lines per inch

Linotronic 300 at 1270 dots per inch output to paper

Display TYPE IN GRAY

Display: 80-pt Galliard Italic; *Type In Gray:* 80-pt Futura Extra Bold, specified in PageMaker in 10% increments from 10 to 80% Black. *This caption:* 6.5/8 Galliard roman and italic; *sans-serif captions:* 7-pt FuturaLight and Futra Extra Bold.

Hairline rule

.5 pt rule

1 pt rule

Bit-mapped clip art

Encapsulated PostScript art imported from FreeHand.

Digital halftone printed at 120 lines per inch

Linotronic 300 at 2540 dpi output to film

Display TYPE IN GRAY

Display: 80-pt Galliard Italic; *Type In Gray:* 80-pt Futura Extra Bold, specified in PageMaker in 10% increments from 10 to 80% Black. *This caption:* 6.5/8 Galliard roman and italic; *sans-serif captions:* 7-pt FuturaLight and Futra Extra Bold.

Hairline rule

.5 pt rule

1 pt rule

Bit-mapped clip art

Encapsulated PostScript art imported from FreeHand.

Digital halftone printed at 120 lines per inch

Making PostScript files

Many service bureaus will give either a discount or a faster turnaround time if you print your pages to disk and send them the resulting Post-Script file rather than the original PageMaker file. To print the file, they don't have to open it in PageMaker or worry about what fonts you've used. You, however, must be sure to choose all the right specs—page range, crop marks, and so on—because any errors are your responsibility.

The mechanics of making a PostScript file differ on a Mac and a PC.

If you work on a Mac:

1. In the Print dialog box, specify the number of copies, the page range, and so on as usual. Ask your service bureau which paper option to choose from the Paper submenu for the size page you are printing.

2. Choose Options, and in the Options dialog box, turn on Crop Marks. If you've used other settings in this box for proofing your publication, such as Tiling or Proof Print, turn them off. Press OK.

3. In the Print dialog box, choose PostScript. In the PostScript dialog box, you'll have to select from among the following options:

- **Download Bit-Mapped Fonts:** Choose this only if your publication includes bit-mapped fonts for which you don't have a corresponding PostScript font.

- **Download PostScript Fonts:** Check with your service bureau to see if they have the fonts you're using on their hard disk. If they do have the fonts, then don't check this box. If they don't have the fonts, then you need to check this option; be aware that it will increase the size of your file, but you don't have a choice.

- **Make Aldus Prep Permanent:** Turn this option off. Your service bureau will not want your version of Aldus Prep residing in their printer.

- **View Last Error Message:** This option is unavailable when you print to disk. It's useful, however, when you're having trouble printing directly from PageMaker and are trying to diagnose the problem.

- **Include Images:** Turn this on if you want PageMaker to print the file to disk with all the images intact. Exception: If you are separating color pages through Aldus PrePrint, turn this option off. PrePrint can link to the external image files.

- **TIFF For Position Only:** If you want the linked, high-resolution TIFF file to print, turn this option off. If you want to print a low-resolution version of the TIFF images, as an FPO guide for art that is to be stripped in, turn this option on.

- **Print PostScript to Disk:** Turn this option on.

  Normal: Check this option for black-and-white pages that will be output by your service bureau.

  EPS: Check this option if you want a screen representation of a single PageMaker page. See Project 8 for more about this option.

  For Separation: Check this option for color publications that will be separated through programs such as Aldus PrePrint.

- **Include Aldus Prep:** For Normal PostScript files, ask your service bureau whether you should turn this option on or off. For EPS and Separation files, this option is on by default and locked in that setting.

- **File Name:** For Normal PostScript files, press this button to name the PostScript file. We use the same name as the publication file and add a .ps extension (for example, "Intro.ps"). If you skip this step, the default filename is something like PostScript 02, which can be exceedingly elusive when you're looking for the file. For EPS and Separation files, the default filename adds .eps or .sep to the original filename.

If you work on a PC:

1. If your service bureau does not have the soft (downloadable) fonts you're using, they must be downloaded into the file that PageMaker creates. If you've installed Adobe Type Manager, it will take care of this detail in most cases. If you find that the fonts are not printing correctly, you may have to modify the WIN.INI file; see the PageMaker *Reference Manual* for details.

2. In the Windows Control Panel, open the Printers icon, click on PostScript Printer, and then click Configure. Set the port for the PostScript printer to FILE: and be sure that its status is Active.

3. In PageMaker, be sure that your target printer is the PostScript printer.

4. In the Print dialog box, choose PostScript Printer on FILE: from the Printer drop-down menu.

5. Specify the number of copies, the page range, and so on, as usual. Turn on Crop Marks. If you've used other settings in this box for proofing your publication, such as Tiling, turn them off.

6. Click OK. The Print to File dialog box appears, asking you to specify a name for the file.

A SIMPLE CERTIFICATE FOR PAGEMAKER NOVICES

This project is intended for readers with very little experience using PageMaker. The hands-on instructions will guide you through most of the basic procedures used to create and move around a page and will familiarize you with most of the tools in PageMaker's Toolbox. Among those are the drawing tools. Whether you've come to desktop publishing never having been able to draw a straight line, or having spent too many hours trying to master the exacting skill of inking, you'll be thrilled by the first dozen or so perfect circles and squares that you create—effortlessly—with PageMaker's tools.

If you want to produce a quick certificate without so much hands-on instruction, you should be able to move quickly through the boldface and bulleted instructions. Tips and paragraphs without bullets explain the techniques and PageMaker basics in more detail than you might want if you already have a little experience with the program.

Throughout this and other projects, we've highlighted sidebars to call your attention to an overview of some aspect of the program or to a particularly powerful, or perhaps quirky, feature. The sidebars are easy to find—they're boxed with a light gray tint.

PAGEMAKER TECHNIQUES YOU WILL LEARN

▶ Change the Page Setup specifications

▶ Display the rulers

▶ Bring in ruler guides

▶ Change the page view

▶ Use the Snap to Rulers command

▶ Select and change line weights

▶ Draw lines, rectangles, and circles with PageMaker's graphics tools

▶ Use scroll bars and the grabber hand to move around the screen

▶ Type text in PageMaker

▶ Change type specifications

▶ Define space between paragraphs

▶ Move PageMaker graphics

A horizontal, or landscape, page orientation with equal margins on all sides is typical of certificates and diplomas.

ENROLLMENT CERTIFICATE

THE DESKTOP PUBLISHING SCHOOL
ADMITS

TO
THE HANDS-ON DESIGN COURSE

DTP

Times Roman has a utilitarian elegance appropriate for a design course.

The triple rule is the most official-looking one on PageMaker's menu. It gives this simple certificate an air of legitimacy.

BLUEPRINT FOR THE CERTIFICATE

GETTING SET UP

If you are not already in PageMaker and are using a Macintosh, open the program by double-clicking on its icon.

If you are using an IBM PC or compatible, type *WIN PM* at the DOS prompt, or start Windows, open the Program Manager window, locate the PageMaker icon, and double-click it.

1. Choose New from the File menu.

- Move the pointer to the File menu, hold down the mouse button, drag to highlight the word "New," and release the mouse button.

  This brings the Page Setup dialog box to the screen.

2. Specify the Page Setup specifications.

- Make any necessary changes in the Page Setup dialog box so that it conforms to the following specifications:

  Page Dimensions: 11 by 8.5 inches

  Orientation: Wide

  Start Page #: 1   # of pages: 1

  Options: Click off Double-sided. (The Facing Pages option will automatically turn gray.)

  Margin in inches: Specify 1 for all four margins.

- After you have specified your page setup, click OK.

Page setup   [**OK**]

Page: [Letter]   [**Cancel**]

Page dimensions: [11]   by [8.5]   inches   [**Numbers...**]

Orientation: ○ Tall ● Wide

Start page #: [1]   **# of pages:** [1]

Options: ☐ Double-sided   ☐ Facing pages

Margin in inches: **Left** [1]   **Right** [1]

                        Top [1]   **Bottom** [1]

▲ ▲ ▲

The Page Setup dialog box for this project. To change the value in any text box, position the pointer in that box, double-click or drag to highlight the existing value, and then type the new value. You can also move from one value box to another by pressing the Tab key. To turn an option (such as Tall, Wide, or Double-sided) on or off, click on the appropriate button, box, or name for that option. In the Windows version, the name of the target printer is listed at the bottom of this dialog box.

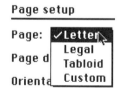

On a Mac, when you hold the mouse button down on a box with a heavy outline, it displays a submenu, such as the one shown here for choosing page dimensions. On a PC, clicking the scroll arrow next to the option displays a submenu.

Buttons under OK and Cancel bring up additional dialog boxes. The Numbers button here displays the Page Numbering dialog box, through which you select the style (Arabic, Roman, and so on) for automatic page numbering.

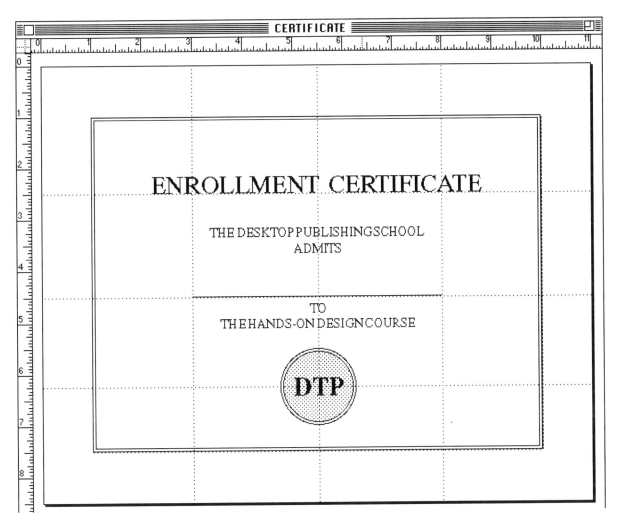

▲ ▲ ▲   *The certificate blueprint with title bar, rulers, and ruler guides.*

3. Check your printer type.

- *If you work on an IBM PC or compatible,* check the printer by choosing the Target Printer command from the File menu. Select your target printer from the list box and click OK. If you change the printer, PageMaker will ask if you want to recompose the publication for the new printer. Click OK.

  If the correct printer is not specified, you may encounter difficulties assembling the document, such as the inability to move or place text. And if you change printers after the publication is assembled in PageMaker, you may discover unexpected changes in the page layout when you print.

- *If you work on a Macintosh,* the page makeup and printing functions in PageMaker are separate, so it is not critical to select the printer before assembling the publication. (Exception: Bit-mapped images should be sized to match the resolution of the printer for your final copies. See "PageMaker's Magic Stretch" on page 294.) To check or change the printer, choose Print from the File menu to bring up the

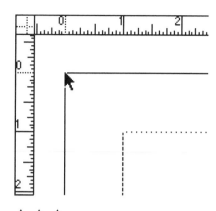

Hairline markers on the rulers indicate the position of the mouse on the screen. In this detail, the pointer is at the zero point. You can move the zero point by dragging the intersecting hairlines at the upper left corner of the window.

Print dialog box. Hold down the mouse button on the box naming the printer to reveal a submenu of the printers in your Aldus folder. Normally, the printer you select from this menu is the same as the printer you've selected from the Chooser under the Apple menu.

4. If the rulers are not visible, choose *Rulers* from the Options menu.

It is almost always useful to work with the rulers visible—they are indispensable for placing items where you want them on the page.

Note that the default setting for the zero point, where the zeros on the horizontal and vertical rulers meet, is at the upper left corner of the page. When you move the mouse around the publication window, hairline markers move in both rulers to define the position of the cursor on the screen. You can move the zero point by dragging the hairlines in the upper left corner where the rulers intersect.

In this project, all measurements are given in inches. This is Page-Maker's default setting for measurements, so unless you've changed your defaults you won't need to make any adjustments.

5. Select a page view (from the Page menu) that enables you to see the entire document.

The Page menu gives you options for seven different page views. If you are not familiar with these options, take a moment to click on each one and observe how the publication window changes from one view to another. How much of your page you see at each view depends on the size of the page and the size of your monitor.

Because different readers will be working with different monitors, we generally will not specify an optimal page view. You'll undoubtedly need to change views as you work on this and any other document. Learning the keyboard shortcuts for toggling between different page views (see page 209) can speed up your work a lot.

TIP

The Snap to Rulers command pulls ruler guides, text, and graphics to the nearest tick mark on each of the rulers. With Snap to Rulers on, you get the same accuracy at the 50% page view as you do at 200%.

6. Bring in ruler guides to help position the elements you'll create in later steps.

When you bring in ruler guides, choose a page view that gives you small enough ruler increments for the measurements you'll need to make. The smallest measurement in this step is 1/8 inch, which you can see at 50% on a 9-inch monitor.

- Turn on Snap to Rulers on the Options menu.

- Position the pointer anywhere on the left ruler, press the mouse button to reveal a double-headed arrow, and drag a dotted vertical guideline to the 5.5-inch mark on the top ruler. This marks the center of the page on a vertical axis.

- From the top ruler, bring in horizontal ruler guides to the 2.5, 4.5, and 6.25 points on the left ruler.

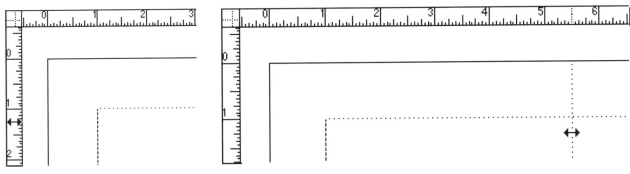

▲ ▲ ▲

Move the pointer into either ruler to drag in ruler guides. These are nonprinting dotted rules used to align text and graphics on the page. To move a ruler guide, point to that guide with the pointer tool and drag the guide to the desired location. To delete a guide, drag it outside the page frame. Any tool turns into the arrow pointer when you move it into one of the rulers, so you don't have to change tools to bring in ruler guides.

TIP

One of the most useful keyboard commands is the one that saves your current document: Command-S on a Mac, Ctrl-S on a PC.

7. Choose Save from the File menu.

Get in the habit of saving your work every 15 minutes, or sooner if you've just done something to the layout that you'd hate to redo.

The Save and Save As commands in PageMaker are similar to those functions in other applications. Note, however, that in PageMaker's Save As dialog box you have the option of saving your document as a publication or as a template. For this project, use the default setting of Publication. You'll use the template option in Project 4.

CREATING THE CERTIFICATE

1. Create a border.

- Move the pointer to the Element menu, choose Line, and, still holding down the mouse button, scroll to select the triple rule.

- Select the square-corner tool from the Toolbox. Note that the pointer turns into a crossbar.

- Place the crossbar at the upper left corner of the margin guides. Press down the mouse button, drag the crossbar to the lower right margin guide, and release the mouse button.

Note: If you are working at a reduced page view, the border will look like a solid or double line. To see the line as it will print, choose Actual Size from the Page menu. At that size you may need to move around the screen to find the line. (See the sidebar on the following page.)

◄ ◄ ◄

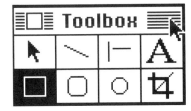

You can move the Toolbox away from your work area by pointing to its title bar and dragging it to a new location on the screen. To remove the Toolbox entirely, click on the box in the upper left corner (called the close box on a Mac, the Control-menu box on a PC). To bring the Toolbox back on-screen, choose Toolbox from the Window menu. Or use the keyboard shortcut to bring the Toolbox in and out of view: Command-6 on a Mac, Ctrl-6 on a PC.

HOW TO MOVE AROUND THE PAGEMAKER SCREEN

Often when you're working in PageMaker, some of your page is hidden from view outside the publication window. You can move around the screen in three ways to display different parts of the page as well as the pasteboard beyond the page.

Use the scroll bars.

This is the slowest method, but it's also the easiest to remember. Use the gray bar on the right side of the window to move vertically; use the bottom bar to move horizontally.

Click on the arrows at the ends of the scroll bars to move a short distance; click in the gray bar to move a greater distance. The position of the small box inside each scroll bar indicates the position of the screen image relative to the entire pasteboard area outside the page; you can also move around the screen by dragging one of these boxes to a point that is approximately where you want to be in the publication window.

Use the grabber hand.

The grabber hand provides more control over where you're moving than the scroll bars, and it's faster, too. To invoke the grabber hand, hold down the Option key on a Mac, the Alt key on a PC, and then press the mouse button. As you drag the mouse, the hand pushes the page in any direction that you drag, including diagonally. (After you see the hand, you can release the Option or Alt key.) If you want to constrain the movement to a horizontal or vertical direction, hold down the Shift key in addition to Option or Alt.

Zoom in and out.

Power users move around the page by pointing to the place they want to move to and using the appropriate keyboard shortcut. This method lets you toggle back and forth between Fit in Window and magnified views. See the key-click combinations on page 209.

2. Type the text.

- Choose the text tool.

- From the Type menu, choose Type Specs. The Type Specifications dialog box appears. (If you're not familiar with this dialog box, see the sidebar on the facing page.) Choose these specs and click OK:

Font: Times Roman	Position: Normal
Size: 18 points	Case: All caps
Leading: 22 points	Track: No track
Set Width: Normal	
Color: Black	
Type Style: Normal	

- Move the pointer to the Type menu, hold down the mouse button, and scroll to the Alignment option to bring up the Alignment submenu. Then choose Align Center.

- Click the I-beam on the 2.5-inch horizontal ruler guide. Type

  ENROLLMENT CERTIFICATE [Return]

  THE DESKTOP PUBLISHING SCHOOL [Return]

  ADMITS [Return]

  TO [Return]

  THE HANDS-ON DESIGN COURSE

▲ ▲ ▲

The text tool cursor is an I-beam with a short horizontal crossbar two-thirds of the way from the top. You tell PageMaker where you want to begin typing by clicking this cursor to set an insertion point. And you select existing text by dragging over it with this cursor.

ABOUT THE TYPE MENU

Take a moment to familiarize yourself with the type attribute options in the first half of this menu. Choosing any of the first six options, followed by arrows, displays a submenu for that attribute.

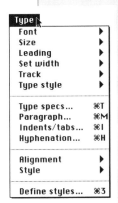

Font This submenu displays all the typefaces installed on your system.

Size The submenu lists standard point sizes for the current font. You can select one of these sizes, or choose Other to bring up a dialog box where you can type in any value from 4 to 650, in one-tenth-of-a-point increments.

Leading Specify the space between lines by choosing a value in the leading submenu, or choose Auto leading (120% of the text size), or choose Other to specify custom leading in one-tenth-of-a-point increments from 0 to 1300 points.

Set Width You can condense or expand the width of individual characters by specifying a percentage of the normal width from 70% to 130%. This is called horizontal scaling. (See pages 20 and 343.)

Track You can adjust the space between letters and words by choosing one of six settings ranging from Very Loose to Very Tight. No Track, the default, is slightly tighter than Normal. (See pages 34 and 246.)

Type Style As used here, "style" refers to Normal (regular roman type), bold, italic, underline, strikethrough (used to indicate text that has been deleted), reverse, and, on the Macintosh, outline and shadow. PageMaker also uses the word Style, at the bottom of the Type menu, to refer to a collection of type-formatting attributes applied to a paragraph; see Project 4 for a discussion of this feature.

When you want to specify two or more type attributes, choose Type Specs, midway down the Type menu, to bring up the Type Specifications dialog box. In this dialog box, you can specify all of the attributes described in this sidebar, plus Color, Position (subscript or superscript), and Case (all caps or small caps).

We'll work with these other options in later projects. For now, note the following tips.

TIPS

When you specify type attributes with the pointer tool, those specs become the new default for that publication. All text that you subsequently type will take on those attributes, unless you specify otherwise.

If you select the text tool, then set an insertion point, and then specify type attributes, the specs will apply only to the text you type next. If you move the insertion point before typing, the type specs revert to the publication default.

When you select text with the text tool and then specify type attributes, the attributes apply only to the selected text.

A check mark in a submenu indicates the attribute of the selected text, or, if no text is selected, of the default.

When there's no check mark in a submenu or when a type attribute box is blank, it means that the selected text contains mixed attributes. In this situation, if you want to determine a specific attribute, narrow your text selection to a single word or, if necessary, a single letter.

Some options, such as custom sizes and horizontal scaling, are available only on printers that use scalable fonts, such as PostScript and PLC-V series printers. With other printers, the effect achieved on-screen may not print accurately. Some printers, such as early HP LaserJet models, do not print reverse type. Type manager utilities (such as Adobe Type Manager) can overcome some type-styling limitations of some printers.

TIP

To create space between paragraphs, use the Space After option
in the Paragraph Specs dialog box
to replace the typewriter habit of
inserting paragraph returns. A paragraph return is a relative space,
equal to whatever leading is specified. If you change the leading, the
space between paragraphs
changes. Specifying a value for
Space Before or Space After a
paragraph creates a fixed space
that won't change if you change
your leading. It's also a value you
can easily check if you want to use
the same spacing elsewhere in a
document, and one you can include
as part of a Style definition.

3. Style the headline.

- With the text tool, select the first line of text. You can drag over it or you can triple-click on it. (Triple-clicking with the text tool selects an entire paragraph.)

- On the Size submenu, scroll to select 36 points or choose Other and type 36.

  The tops of the letters may appear to be clipped off. They'll print fine, and they'll also display correctly as soon as you refresh your screen. To refresh the screen, use the keyboard shortcut for what-ever page view you are currently working in. This is a bug (or we consider it one) that plagues display type, especially when the type is much larger than the leading.

4. Adjust the vertical spacing in the text.

- With the text tool, select the first line of text.

- Choose Paragraph from the Type menu to bring up the Paragraph Specifications dialog box.

- For the Space After, type .55.

  We'll review all the options in this dialog box in Project 2, but for now just focus on using the Space After option to create space be-tween text units. Don't worry if you don't know exactly how much space to specify before or after a paragraph. A combination of trial and error and PageMaker's rulers will help you find the solution.

- With the text tool, select the word "Admits."

- Choose Paragraph from the Type menu and specify .85 for the Space After option.

TIP

When you select a line weight and
then draw a graphic, as you did
when you created the border for
this certificate, that line weight
becomes the default for the publication. Any PageMaker graphics
that you subsequently draw will use
that line weight unless you specify
otherwise. But when you change
the line weight of a graphic you've
already drawn, the line weight
applies to that graphic only. The
same principle holds when you
specify Fills.

5. Add the line for a signature.

You'll want to bring in ruler guides to define the start and end points of the line. In this case, a good balance will be achieved if the line is a little shorter than the headline and centered horizontally.

- Move the pointer tool into the left ruler and bring in one vertical ruler guide at 3 inches and another at 8 inches.

- Choose the perpendicular line tool, and position the crossbar at the intersection of the 4.5-inch horizontal and 3-inch vertical ruler guides. Drag the crossbar along the horizontal guide to the vertical guide at 8 inches.

  That's a very thick line. (It's the same triple rule you selected earlier for the border.)

- While the line is still selected, scroll the Element menu to the Line options and select .5 pt.

  Note that when you draw a line (or other graphic) in PageMaker, it remains selected until you click elsewhere on the page. You know it's selected by the little square selection handles at each end of the line.

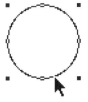

▲ ▲ ▲

When you select a graphic with the pointer, the graphic is surrounded by eight small rectangles, or selection handles. To move a graphic drawn with one of PageMaker's tools, point directly on the outline of the selected graphic; press the mouse button and, when you see a four-headed arrow, drag the graphic to the new position. If you point to a handle and drag, you will resize the graphic. If you resize a graphic by mistake, choose Undo from the Edit menu or remove the selected graphic (press the Delete or Backspace key) and then redraw it.

6. Create a seal.

- Choose the circle tool, and move the crossbar to the zero point on your page frame.

- Hold down the Shift key and drag the crossbar on a diagonal to the 1.5-inch point on either ruler. Release the mouse button before you release the Shift key. (It's the Shift key that restrains the graphic to a circular rather than an oval shape.) The circle will have the same triple rule as the border.

- Click on the pointer tool and position its tip anywhere directly on the circumference of the circle. Hold down the mouse button, and when you see the four-headed arrow, drag the circle and center it over the intersection of the vertical ruler guide through the center of the page and the horizontal guide at 6.25 inches.

- With the circle still selected, scroll the Element menu to the Fill options and choose 10%.

- With the text tool, click inside the circle on the 6.25-inch horizontal guide and type *DTP* in all caps. (We italicize anything you type on the page or in a text box. If the type style is also italic, we'll state that in the type specs.) Don't worry about the exact position yet.

- Drag the I-beam across the type to select it, choose Type Specs, and change the type to 36/36 bold. Check to see that Times Roman is still selected. Click OK.

FINISHING THE JOB

1. Review your work.

Check to make sure everything is centered. Change the page view to Actual Size, and scroll around to check spelling, line weights (the border and the seal should be the same), and placements.

2. Choose Print from the File menu.

- Take a moment to review the settings in the Print dialog box. (These vary a little depending on the printer you've selected.) Make sure that you're printing only one copy. Because this is a one-page document, the page range should read From 1 to 1. Scaling should be 100% so that you will print the document at full size. None of the special options are needed for this project.

- Your printer should be listed in the bottom section of the dialog box. If it isn't, see "Getting Set Up," earlier in this project.

- When all the printer specifications are correct, click Print on a Mac, OK on a PC. Or just press the Return key.

3. Sign your name.

If the printed certificate looks as you expected, congratulations. Sign your name on the line and consider yourself enrolled.

PLACING AND COPYFITTING TEXT IN A SMALL SPACE AD

This small space ad is designed to run in the classified section of a Sunday newspaper. For the purposes of this exercise, let's assume that the ad has been written by a very fussy personnel director, and your job is to lay it out in PageMaker. He gives you 150 words of copy and says "Make it fit." No matter that almost any piece of writing will benefit from the editing required by copyfitting. Your job here is to make those 150 words fit.

You must also follow a format that the company uses for all ads of this type. But since this is the first time the ad is being created in PageMaker, you'll have to set up the format. The margins, headline, and company identification must follow the company style, but you have some flexibility with the typeface, size, and paragraph formatting.

The ease with which you can test different type specs for layout fit in a situation like this is one of the great economies of electronic page layout. Art directors and designers who have lived through the tedium of estimating manuscript copy, knowing that the typesetter will deliver galleys that are still too long or too short, will especially appreciate the magic of electronic trial and error.

For the copy in this ad, we've used a text file called Copy Fit that Aldus includes with the PageMaker 4.0 templates. (In Windows-PageMaker, the file is called COPYFIT.DOC.) It consists of five-letter nonsense words with numbers indicating the word count at 25-word intervals. Used as dummy text in page layouts, this file provides a quick way to estimate the word count for a story. It produces rather awful-looking type, because the words are all the same the length. But it's extremely useful nonetheless, and if you didn't install the templates, you might want to install the Copy Fit file anyway. In order to use this file, you must also install the Microsoft Word import filter.

PAGEMAKER TECHNIQUES YOU WILL LEARN

▶ Break apart text blocks

▶ Place text from a word-processing program

▶ Use the manual text-flow mode

▶ Set up a two-column format

▶ Change the unit of measure

▶ Work with PageMaker's Copy Fit file

▶ Copy, paste, and move PageMaker rules

▶ Toggle back and forth between the pointer and text tools

▶ Specify paragraph attributes

▶ Force-justify a headline

▶ Kern a headline

▶ Print with crop marks

Bookman is used for all the type (with the exception of the boldface Helvetica in the bottom line). It's a very good face for newspaper reproduction with its strong thick and thin strokes and its sturdy serifs.

The 6-point horizontal rules provide a strong alternative to borders, which are overused in classified ads. The rules also work with the headline to play off the old Western "Wanted" posters.

The Force Justify alignment option makes the "Wanted" headline fill out the full space between the margins.

Opening up space between paragraphs and setting off the most important paragraph creates contrast within a simple text block and makes it easier to read.

WANTED
A Good Copywriter

Imsep pretu tempu revol bileg rokam revoc tephe rosve etepe tenov sindu turqu brevt elliu repar tiuve tamia queso utage udulc vires humus fallo

25deu Anetn bisre freun carmi avire ingen umque miher muner veris adest duner veris adest iteru quevi escit billo isput tatqu aliqu diams bipos itopu 50sta Isant oscul bifid mquec cumen berra etmii pyren nsomn anoct reern oncit quqar anofe ventm hipec oramo uetfu orets nitus sacer tusag teliu ipsev

75tvi Eonei elaur plica oscri eseli sipse enitu ammih mensl quidi aptat rinar uacae ierqu vagas ubesc rpore ibere perqu umbra perqu antra erorp netra 100at mihif napat ntint riora intui urque nimus otoqu cagat rolym oecfu iunto ulosa tarac ecame suidt mande onatd stent spiri usore idpar thaec abies

125sa Imsep pretu tempu revol bileg rokam revoc tephe rosve etepe tenov sindu turqu brevt elliu repar tiuve tamia queso utage udulc vires humus fallo 150eu

Join a Growing Organization
EAST WEST MULTI-MEDIA, INC.

BLUEPRINT FOR THE AD

SET UP

1. Prepare the text file in your word-processing program.

We've used PageMaker's Copy Fit file, described in the introduction to this project. If you'll be using that file, open it now in your word-processing program. Save it under a new name, say Copy Fit 2 (or COPYFIT.DOC on a PC). Find the 150-word mark and delete all the text following that point. Change the type specs to 9/11 Times Roman.

If you want to use another text file instead of the Copy Fit file, make it conform to the specifications in the previous paragraph. It won't quite match the text used in the instructions, but you should still be able to work through the project with it.

TIP

Press the Tab key to move from one box to another in the Page Setup dialog box. Press the Return key to OK a dialog box. Both of these keyboard shortcuts can be used so frequently that they are worth remembering early on.

2. Open a 1-page document with the following page setup:

- Page Dimensions: 4.25 by 6 inches.

  Note that when you type the values in the size boxes, the Page submenu automatically changes from Letter to Custom. So you don't need to choose Custom in order to specify a custom size. Conversely, when you're changing from Letter size to Legal or Tabloid, you can select the size from the Page submenu, and PageMaker will automatically insert the values for you.

- Orientation: Tall

- Options: Single-sided

- Margins: Left and Right: .25 inches

  Top and Bottom: .35 inches

3. Change the unit of measure.

The unit of measure (inches, picas, and so on) is specified in the Preferences dialog box. Although you can override the specified measure when typing values in dialog boxes (see page 207), you want the rulers to be displayed in the measurement system you'll use most frequently in a given project; that's generally picas.

- Choose Preferences from the Edit menu. The Preferences dialog box comes on-screen.

- Move the pointer to the Measurement System box (on a PC, point to the arrow at the right of the box), hold down the mouse button, and scroll the submenu to select Picas. Do the same for the Vertical Ruler. Click OK.

  It's a nuisance to have to change both rulers, but you'll see the value of the vertical ruler when we work with leading grids in Project 5.

4. Define the image area.

- Turn on Snap to Rulers on the Options menu (Command-[on a Mac, Shift-Ctrl-Y on a PC).

- Bring in horizontal ruler guides at 6p, 7p9, 8p6, 10p, 31p6, and 33p.

DISPLAY TYPE

1. Add the horizontal rules.

- With the perpendicular line tool selected, choose the 6-point rule from the Line submenu (under Element). Draw a horizontal rule from the left to the right margin, aligned with the top margin.

- With the rule still selected, copy it and then paste it.

  PageMaker pastes the copy so it is offset slightly below and to the right of the original, making it easier to find. (If you've scrolled to a different part of the page, PageMaker pastes the copy center screen.)

The blueprint for the ad with the measurement system in picas and points. (There are 12 points to one pica.) To set up the ruler guides as indicated, you'll need a page view that displays ruler tick marks in 3-point increments, as shown here.

- With the pointer tool, drag the copy so that its top is aligned on the 8p6 horizontal guide. The sides of the rule align with the right and left margins.

- Paste again (the previous copy will still be in the Clipboard's memory, so you don't need to copy it again) and drag this copy so that its baseline sits on the bottom margin.

2. Type the display text.

With several lines of display type, as in this ad, we generally type all the copy at once, then break the text into individual lines to style and position them by eye.

- With the text tool, set an insertion point anywhere in the center of the page. Note that Snap to Guides (which is on by default) pulls the insertion point to the left margin. Type:

  Wanted [Return]

  A Good Copywriter [Return]

  Join a Growing Organization [Return]

  East West Multi-Media, Inc.

MAC TIPS

Macintosh keyboard shortcuts for tasks in step 3:

Type Specs: Command-T.
Cut: Command-X.
Paste: Command-V.
Alignment: Command-Shift + the first letter of the desired alignment—L(eft), R(ight), C(enter), and so on.
To activate the **pointer tool:** Shift-F1.
To activate the **text tool:** Shift-F4.
To toggle between the pointer tool and the tool you're currently working with: Command-Spacebar.

WINDOWS TIPS

Windows keyboard shortcuts for tasks in step 3:

Type Specs: Ctrl-T.
Cut: Shift-Del.
Paste: Shift-Ins.
Alignment: Ctrl-Shift + the first letter of the desired alignment—L(eft), R(ight), C(enter), and soon.
To activate the **pointer tool:** Shift-F1.
To activate the **text tool:** Shift-F4.
To toggle between the pointer tool and the tool you're currently working with: F9.

GENERAL TIP

Be aware of this annoying but harmless bug: When you cut and paste large type with the text tool, the very tops of the letters appear to stay in the old position and the type you paste appears slightly clipped off at the top. The type will print correctly, and it will also display correctly as soon as you refresh your screen. You can force the screen to refresh by using the keyboard shortcut for whatever page view you are currently working in.

- With the text tool, select all four lines of text , choose Type Specs, and change the type to 12/14 Bookman.

- With the text still selected, specify Align Center.

3. Style and position the display type.

In this step you're going to use the text tool to style, cut, and paste each individual line. Then you'll switch to the pointer tool for precise positioning. If you're not familiar with text blocks and windowshade handles, refer to the sidebar on the facing page. Because you'll be repeating many of the same actions with each line, it's a good opportunity to learn some frequently used keyboard shortcuts (see Tips at left).

- Turn off both Snap To commands. When you position individual lines of text by eye, as you'll do here, the magnetic pull of the Snap To commands works against you: It draws the *top* of the text block to horizontal guides or ruler tick marks that are close to but not exactly where you want to position the *baseline*.

- With the text tool, select the word "Wanted." Choose Type Specs and specify 48/48 Bookman, Bold, All Caps. With the word still selected, cut and then paste it between the 6-point rules at the top of the page.

  With the pointer tool, select that line again, hold down the Shift key, and drag the text so that its baseline is on the 6p horizontal guideline. (By holding down the Shift key, you'll constrain the movement to a vertical direction.)

- With the text tool, select the second line and change the type specs to 18/18 Bookman. With the text still selected, cut and paste this line under the second 6-point rule. (If you try to paste it directly under the word "Wanted," the large leading in that line will get in the way.)

  With the pointer tool, select that line again, hold down the Shift key, and position the baseline on the 7p9 horizontal guide.

- With the text tool, select the third line and specify Align Right. Then cut and paste it anywhere toward the bottom of the page.

  With the pointer tool, select and position that line so its baseline is on the 31p6 horizontal guide.

- With the text tool, select the last line and change the type specs to 14/14 Helvetica, Bold, All Caps. With the type still selected, specify Align Right.

  Select that last line with the pointer tool. Is there a big gap between the top and bottom windowshade handles? That gap represents the paragraph returns from the previous three lines, which weren't deleted when you cut each line. Gaps in windowshade handles can interfere when you try to select other objects on the page. So before you move this line, select the text tool, set an insertion point before the word "East," and press Backspace until the text won't move any more.

  After removing the extra carriage returns, select the line again with the pointer and position its baseline on the 33p horizontal guide.

THE POINTER TOOL OR THE TEXT TOOL? GOOD QUESTION.

There are two fundamental ways of working with text in a PageMaker layout. When you type, edit, or apply formatting from the Type menu, you are working with text as characters, and you use the text tool in the same way you'd use the cursor in a word-processing program.

But you can also manipulate whole blocks of text similarly to the way you manipulate graphics. Using the pointer tool, you can stretch or shrink the width of a text block, or drag it to a different position on the page.

A text block is simply any unit of text that you can select at one time with the pointer tool. It can be as small as a single character, or as long as the PageMaker window, including the pasteboard. The four lines of display copy that you typed for this ad started out as one text block. When you broke them apart into individual lines, they became four different text blocks.

You can use either tool to cut, copy, or paste text, but with different results. When you cut (or copy) and paste with the pointer tool, the pasted copy retains the margins of the original. When you cut (or copy) and paste with the text tool, the pasted copy conforms to the margins of the insertion point. If you want to cut or copy only part of a text block, drag over that text with the text tool; using the pointer tool, you'd have to select the entire text block.

We'll look at the behavior of threaded text blocks in the sidebar beginning on page 284.

Use the text tool to drag over selected text when you want to edit text or change the type or paragraph attributes.

When you select a text block with the pointer tool, two windowshade handles define the boundaries of the text.

▲ ▲ ▲

To move a text unit, click on the text with the pointer tool. Then position the pointer inside the windowshade handles, press down the mouse button, and when you see the four-headed arrow, drag the text to the new position. The dashed box displayed around the text as you drag defines the top, bottom, and side margins of the text. If you drag before the four-headed arrow appears, you'll see the boundary box around the text as you drag but you won't see the text itself until you release the mouse button.

▲ ▲ ▲

To change the width of a text block, position the pointer on the end of a windowshade handle and drag. You can make the text narrower, as in the example above, or you can stretch the width, as we do with the body text later in this project.

BODY TEXT

1. Define the columns.

- Choose Column Guides from the Options menu.

- In the Column Guides dialog box, specify 2 columns with a 1p space in between. Click OK. Note that changing the number of columns does not affect type that's already in position on the page.

2. Place the text.

For this first exercise in placing text, let's take a close look at the procedure in the sidebar below.

HOW TO PLACE TEXT IN PAGEMAKER

The ability to bring text and graphics from other programs into a page layout program is the heart of desktop publishing. And in PageMaker, it's the Place command that enables you to do this.

1. Choose Place from the File menu to bring the Place dialog box on screen.

- Scroll through your file directories to find the Copy Fit file, or whatever text file you're using for the ad copy.

  The list in the dialog box includes only those documents that PageMaker can read directly from the selected folder or directory on the current disk.

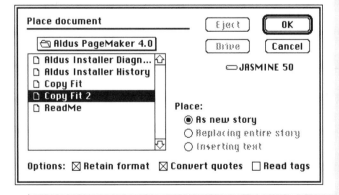

- Note the options below the directory in the Place dialog box. An x in the box before an option means the option is selected; a blank box means the option is not selected.

Retain Format: Choose this box when you want PageMaker to retain text formatting from your word-processing program. In this project, that means the text will come in as 9/11 Times Roman, as specified in step 1 under "Set Up."

Convert Quotes: Choose this so that PageMaker will convert typewriter-style quotation marks (" ") and apostrophes (') to the typographic characters designed for the typeface you are using (" " and '). Double hyphens will also be converted to em dashes with this option selected.

Read Tags: Choose this if, in your word processor, you format text with style name tags surrounded by angle brackets (< >). For a discussion of styles, see Project 4.

2. Select the text-flow mode.

PageMaker's three text-flow modes are described at the top of the facing page. We'll use the default manual mode in this project.

3. Select the name of the text file you want to place.

PageMaker highlights the As New Story button, which is what you'll use in this project. You have two other options when placing text:

Replacing Entire Story: If you select a text block in your PageMaker document and choose this option, the story you place flows into the document in place of the selected text. This is useful when you want to replace dummy text (such as the Copy Fit file in this project) with real text.

Inserting Text: If you put an insertion point in a text block in PageMaker and choose this option when you place, PageMaker inserts the new file in the existing one at the insertion point.

TEXT-FLOW MODES

The manual text-flow mode is PageMaker's default. It's selected when the Autoflow command on the Options menu is turned off. When using this mode, PageMaker displays a loaded text icon, like the one at left. When you click the icon, text flows to the bottom of the column, stops, and waits for you to reload the icon. This is the slowest mode but it's good for beginners, and you use it in steps 4–8 below.

With the Autoflow command turned on, the text icon looks like this. When you click the icon, PageMaker flows text continuously, adding pages if necessary, until all the text is placed. This is the fastest mode, but it can backfire. See the sidebar on page 278 for an explanation of the behavior of text placed in the autoflow mode.

You can toggle back and forth between manual and autoflow modes: Whichever mode is selected, pressing Command (on a Mac), or Ctrl (on a PC), invokes the other.

In the semi-automatic mode, text flow stops at the bottom of each column. If there is more text to place, PageMaker automatically reloads the text icon but doesn't continue flowing the text until you click the text icon again. You maintain control over where the text is placed, but you don't have to take the time to keep loading the text icon at the bottom of each column.

You can invoke the semi-automatic mode by holding down the Shift key when either of the other two modes is active.

4. Click OK.

PageMaker loads the pointer with a copy of the text file you've selected. (The original remains unchanged as a word-processing file.) When the dialog box closes, you'll see the loaded text icon on-screen.

5. Select an insertion point for the text.

First check that Snap to Guides is on. Then align the loaded text icon at the intersection of the left margin and the 10p ruler guide.

6. Click the mouse to place the text.

In the manual mode, the text flow stops at the end of each column or when something gets in its way (such as the text already positioned at the bottom of the page, or a graphic).

If you are working on a small monitor, the text may be displayed as gray bars. This is called greeked text. You can control the size at which PageMaker will display greeked text through the Preferences dialog box.

7. Reload the text icon.

The arrow ▼ in the bottom windowshade indicates that there is more text to place. When you click on the arrow, PageMaker reloads the text icon. Click on the arrow now.

8. Select an insertion point for the next text block.

In the manual text-flow mode, you have to click the loaded text icon to tell PageMaker where to continue flowing the text. In this project, position the text icon in the second column, aligned at the same horizontal guide as the first column of text, and click.

The empty loop ∪ in the bottom windowshade indicates that there is no more text to place.

TIPS

Place: Command-D on a Mac, Ctrl-D on a PC.
Turn **Snap to Guides** on when you place text. This ensures that, even if the text icon isn't positioned exactly on the margin guides, the text that flows in will observe those guides. Otherwise, the text has a tendency to flow to the edge of the page or even across the pasteboard. Then you have to reflow it, or scroll to the edge of the text block and shorten the windowshade handles.
You can easily **postpone a Place operation.** After the loaded text icon appears, you sometimes need to perform another operation before placing the text—bring in a ruler guide, change pages, check the text-flow mode, turn on Snap to Guides, and so on. Don't panic. When you move the text icon into the menu bar, the rulers, or the scroll bars, the cursor temporarily turns back into the arrow so that you can perform these operations. When you move the cursor back into the image area, the text icon reappears.
When you do want to **cancel a Place operation,** click the text icon in the Toolbox and whichever tool you click on will be activated.

For additional tips on placing text, see Project 4.

For the repetitive actions in copyfitting, use these timesavers:

Select all text: Set an insertion point and press Command-A.
Type Specs: Command-T.
Paragraph Specs: Command-M.
Use the Tab key to move from one value box to another.

For the repetitive actions in copyfitting, use these timesavers:

Select all text: Set an insertion point and press Ctrl-A.
Type Specs: Ctrl-T.
Paragraph Specs: Ctrl-M.
Use the Tab key to move from one value box to another.

With Preferences set to picas, values for paragraph attributes are specified in picas and points, with 12 points to a pica. Half a pica is specified as 0p6, 15 points is specified as 1p3, and so on.

To apply paragraph formatting to a single paragraph, simply set an insertion point anywhere in the paragraph. You don't have to drag through the entire paragraph.

If you ever see this error box— "Cannot use these specifications. Not a valid measurement."—you probably deleted a value and failed to specify another in its place. We do this all the time when our intention is to change the value back to 0.

3. Copyfitting.

The text is quite a bit shorter than the space it needs to fill. And there are no paragraph breaks at all.

- Add paragraph breaks.

For the purposes of this exercise, let's say that the fussy personnel director who wrote the copy has given you a marked manuscript indicating new paragraphs at the 25-, 75-, and 125-word markers. You create paragraphs in PageMaker just as you do in a word-processing program: Set an insertion point before the character where the new paragraph is to begin, and press Return.

- Specify a 2-pica paragraph indent.

With the text tool, select all the text, and choose Paragraph from the Type menu to bring up the Paragraph Specifications dialog box. (If you're not familiar with this dialog box, see the sidebar on the facing page.) To indent the first line of each paragraph, type the desired value in the box under Indents labeled First. Here, that's 2.

- To fill space, try a typeface with a larger x-height.

While the text is still selected, use the Font submenu to change the typeface to Bookman, which doesn't get as many characters per line as Times Roman. This helps a little, but not nearly enough.

- Increase the type size and leading.

Select all the text, choose Type Specs from the Type menu, and specify 10/12. That's perfect. But the personnel director calls and says he wants all ads set in one column, with a justified right margin.

- Widen the text measure.

With the pointer tool, select the left column and drag the handle on the right side of either windowshade handle all the way to the right margin. Hold down the Shift key while you drag to constrain the movement to the horizontal direction so that you don't change the vertical position of the text.

Now the text is too short again because you get more words in one wide column than in two narrow ones: You pick up the space between the columns and lose less space to the end-of-line rag.

- Justify the text.

With the text tool, select all the text and use the Alignment submenu to change the setting to justified. The text is shorter still. In order to set a justified right margin, PageMaker adjusts the space between letters and words. In the process you often "lose" short lines at the end of paragraphs, as we did here. You have to check justified text for uneven color in loose and tight lines, but that tends to be less of a problem in wider columns such as this.

- Now we need to fill space again. So try adding some space between the paragraphs.

Select all the text, and in the Paragraph Specs dialog box specify 0p6 for Space After, creating half a line space between paragraphs. With

PARAGRAPH FORMATTING

The Paragraph command on the Type menu gives you access to the attributes that control paragraph formatting. You can apply any paragraph attribute to existing text by selecting the text with the text tool and then coming to this dialog box; or, for text that you're about to type, you can select the text tool, specify the paragraph and any other type attributes, and then type the text.

```
┌─────────────────────────────────────────────────────┐
│ Paragraph specifications              ┌────────────┐ │
│                                       │     OK     │ │
│ Indents:           Paragraph space:   └────────────┘ │
│                                       ┌────────────┐ │
│ Left  [0]   picas  Before [0]  picas  │   Cancel   │ │
│                                       └────────────┘ │
│ First [0]   picas  After  [0]  picas  ┌────────────┐ │
│                                       │  Rules...  │ │
│ Right [0]   picas                     └────────────┘ │
│                                       ┌────────────┐ │
│                                       │ Spacing... │ │
│ Alignment: [Left]    Dictionary: [US English]       │
│                                                      │
│ Options:                                             │
│ ☐ Keep lines together  ☐ Keep with next [0] lines   │
│ ☐ Column break before  ☐ Widow control  [0] lines   │
│ ☐ Page break before    ☐ Orphan control [0] lines   │
│ ☐ Include in table of contents                      │
└─────────────────────────────────────────────────────┘
```

Indents To indent the first line of a paragraph, type the value you want in the box labeled First. (This replaces the typewriter habit of using the Spacebar or Tab key to create indents.) To indent the left or right margin of a text block relative to the column margins, type the values in the respective boxes.

Paragraph Space Another typewriter habit that you need to break is inserting an extra carriage return or two to create space between paragraphs. For precise control over the space between paragraphs and around headlines, type the values you want for Space Before or Space After. Don't worry if you don't know exactly what you want. You can quickly test different spaces, using the keyboard shortcut to get in and out of this dialog box.

Alignment Hold down the mouse button on the box specifying the alignment to bring up a sub-menu of alignment options. (On a PC, click on the arrow at the right of the box.) You can access this submenu through the Alignment command on the Type menu or use the keyboard shortcuts, but if you're setting other paragraph attributes it's quicker to set the alignment here.

Options These control attributes such as the way paragraphs relate to one another and how Page-Maker handles short lines. Some word-processing programs have these same options.

Keep Lines Together When you don't want two or more lines (such as a name and address) to be split at a column or page break, select the lines and check this option.

Keep with Next When you want to ensure that a headline remains with at least a few lines of the text that follows, check this option. You can specify up to 3 lines in the value box.

Column Break Before and **Page Break Before** If you want a paragraph, such as a headline or subhead, to begin at the top of a column or page, check the appropriate option.

Widow Control If you don't want to see one, two, or three lines of a new paragraph fall at the bottom of a column or page, specify the number here. If you specify 2, for example, and a situation arises where the first two lines of a paragraph would fall at the bottom of a column, PageMaker will push those lines to the top of the next column, leaving the previous column short.

Orphan Control To avoid the last line (or two or three) of a paragraph falling at the top of a column, specify the number here. PageMaker will push additional lines from the previous column forward to satisfy your minimum requirement.

Include in Table of Contents When you use PageMaker to generate a table of contents, you specify the headings to be included by selecting them with the text tool and checking this box.

Note: Sometimes PageMaker has to choose between your specs for various paragraph options (such as "Keeps," widows, and orphans) and other rules for how it composes text. Fortunately, you can ask the program to alert you to these instances. Take a minute to bring up the Preferences dialog box (from the Edit menu). On the right side, under Show Layout Problems, there's an option named Keeps Violations. If you check that box, PageMaker will highlight any text that violates your settings for any of these paragraph options.

this paragraph spacing you won't need to indent the first paragraph, so change First Indent back to 0.

- That looks pretty good. But let's say, for the purposes of this exercise, that you want to highlight the third paragraph in some way. Boldface would be too heavy-handed, and it prints badly in news-

MORE COPYFITTING TIPS

The techniques for cutting and adding text to fit are flip sides of the same coin. So we've divided this list into global and micro changes. Most of the global changes can also be made on a micro level, which is generally called "cheating." Cheating can save the day but it can also make your pages look like the work of an amateur. Be sure to check the printouts for overall evenness and readability of type. Even the global changes should not be made without balancing the visual effect with the copy requirements.

Global changes throughout a document or story

1. Typeface When you need to save space, use a typeface with a small x-height, or a condensed typeface, to get more characters per line. To fill space, use a typeface with a larger x-height. See the discussion of the relative efficiency of type on page 30.

2. Type size and leading We list these together because generally if you change one you should at least review the other. With tenth-of-a-point increments in both type size and leading, PageMaker lets you inch your way toward making the copy fit.

3. Tracking The Track command on the Type menu has six preset values for adjusting space between letters and words, ranging from Very Loose to Very Tight. Tracking is useful in headlines, but for body text use the Spacing command, because tracking can slow text composition. (Note: The tracking levels are very different from one another; don't use tracking to cheat selected paragraphs.)

4. Spacing You can control the space between letters and words through the Spacing Attributes dialog box (accessed through the Spacing button in the Paragraph Specs dialog box). Every font design builds in values for the space occupied by every letter and by the space between words. The values you specify as spacing attributes are percentages of those built-in values. Tightening word spacing to around 80% and letter spacing to around -4% may make the type look better as well as pick up some

space. But this depends very much on the typeface and size, and you must check printouts.

5. Hyphenation You can turn hyphenation on and off through the Hyphenation command on the Type menu. You'll get more words per line with hyphenation turned on. The Hyphenation Zone, specified in the bottom of the Hyphenation dialog box, determines how close to the end of a line PageMaker can insert a hyphen. The smaller your hyphenation zone, the closer to the end of the line PageMaker can insert a hyphen, and the tighter your lines will be.

6. Space around headlines If you've specified space before or after headlines, making the value a little larger or smaller may solve your problem.

7. Paragraph indents and spaces A wide indent can force an extra line in some paragraphs. Adding space between paragraphs can fill space overall.

Micro changes in individual paragraphs or lines

1. Scan the last lines of paragraphs. To save space, you can often pull up a short line at the end of a paragraph through minor editing, or by altering the word or letter spacing or the hyphenation zone in that paragraph. To fill space, the same techniques will often force an additional line break in a last line that already fills the margin.

2. In rag right text, look for lines that fall far short of the right margin. Again, minor editing and selective changes in spacing attributes and hyphenation can often save or create lines. **In justified text,** select Show Loose/Tight Lines in the Preferences dialog box. PageMaker will highlight all lines that set tighter or looser than the specified Spacing parameters. Editing, changing the spacing specs, and even kerning may solve typographic and copyfitting problems at the same time.

3. You can kern a range of text by selecting that text and using the various kerning key combinations. For more on range kerning, see page 395.

papers. Try indenting both the left and right margins so that the paragraph is inset from the rest of the text.

Click the cursor anywhere in the third paragraph. Bring up the Paragraph Specs dialog box, and for both Left and Right indent, type *1p6*.

- That gained one line, and now the last line of the body copy is too tight to the display type at the bottom of the page. We're close enough that we can cheat a little space from the leading. Select all the text and change the leading to 11.7. That does it.

FINISHING THE JOB

▲ ▲ ▲

The headline's satisfactory, but a little bland. And the space around the "A" is uneven.

▲ ▲ ▲

When you specify Force Justify from the Alignment submenu, the headline takes on the punch of an old "Wanted" poster. But now the gap between the letterpair "WA" is even more pronounced than before.

WANTED
A Good Copywriter

▲ ▲ ▲

Manually adjust the space between the letterpairs "WA" and "AN" to even out the letterspacing across the word.

1. Fine-tune the headline.

The headline's okay. But when you have the time, you can generally turn an okay headline into one with more impact. The centered text is a little bland, and the letterspacing is uneven. We know this is supposed to be the company's format, but here's how we'd improve it.

- Select the word "Wanted" with the text tool, and from the Alignment submenu choose Force Justify. This spaces out the letters so the word is forced to fill out the line. (You can do this with more than one word on a line, too.) It's a very effective technique with headlines, and in this case it reinforces the play on "Wanted" posters.

- There's a little too much space between the "W" and the "A," and not quite enough between the "A" and the "N." We can fix this by kerning, a process of adding or removing small increments of space between two characters.

Set an insertion point between the "W" and the "A." If you're working on a Mac, hold down the Command key and press Backspace twice; on a PC, hold down the Ctrl key and press minus (on the numeric keypad) twice. This removes two units of space.

To open up space between the "A" and the "N," set an insertion point. On a Mac, hold down Command-Shift and press Backspace once. On a PC, hold down the Ctrl key and press plus (on the numeric keypad) once. This adds one unit of space.

For a more detailed discussion of kerning, see pages 34–35 and 347.

2. Print.

- Choose Print from the File menu.
- Turn on Crop Marks.

When the page size of your document is smaller than the paper in your printer, the document will be centered on the paper when printed. Crop marks are fine lines just outside the image area that mark where the paper should be trimmed to match the page size of your document.

On some printers, the Crop Marks option is available on the first level of the Print dialog box. On others, you have to select Options to bring up a Print Options dialog box, where you specify Crop Marks.

PROJECT 3

A QUICK INVITATION USING PARAGRAPH RULES AND PAGEMAKER GRAPHICS

*T*his is a fun project. It has a "cheap tricks" component—creating a simple graphic right within PageMaker. And it also makes use of one of the program's great new features—the ability to specify rules above or below a paragraph. Automating a relatively simple task like this saves time and also ensures that, in the case of repeated rules such as the ones used here, you'll have consistent space between each rule and the text that follows. And you don't even have to use the ruler. Be sure to read the sidebar beginning on page 254 that explores this feature in some detail.

The invitation measures 5.5 by 4.25 inches, enabling you to print four cards on a single 8.5- by 11-inch sheet. See the instructions for "How to Print Four Up," at the end of this project. Of course, you could also print one card per sheet with crop marks, but you'd waste a lot of paper.

If you're printing invitations yourself, you'll want to a get a 20-pound card stock with matching envelopes. The heavier stock will have to be hand-fed. To minimize paper jams, press against the leading edge of the paper (the side that enters the printer first) with a burnisher or the curved side of a plastic pen. Even so, we allow for about 15% paper waste due to jams and poor alignment.

PAGEMAKER TECHNIQUES YOU WILL LEARN

▶ Set Guides in back

▶ Define type margins by drawing a bounding box

▶ Constrain the movement of text blocks to one direction only

▶ Create Paragraph Rules

▶ Copy and paste PageMaker graphics

▶ Mask graphics with "invisible" boxes

▶ Turn Guides on and off

▶ Use the Select All command

▶ Use the Undo command

▶ Select multiple objects

▶ Deselect a selected item

▶ Use PageMaker's "power-paste" feature

The crisp, structured organization is offset by playful, thematic art.

Avant Garde is a good contemporary face for an informal invitation, and its O's, being perfect circles, echo the sunset theme. The headline is 12/36, all caps. The body type is 10/36.

The text lines must be short enough not to intrude on the art. Maximum line length is about 42 characters.

The horizontal rules can be generated using PageMaker 4.0's Paragraph Rules option.

The sunset motif is created using PageMaker's circle tool with a white rectangle masking the lower part of each circle. See the instructions for "How to Create a PageMaker Sunset."

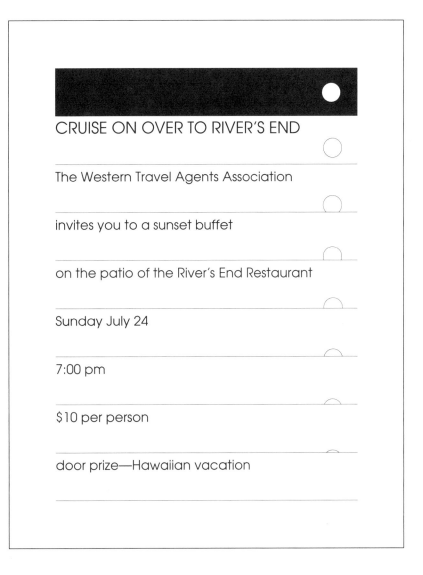

BLUEPRINT FOR THE INVITATION

1. Open a 1-page document with the following page setup:

- Page Dimensions: 8.5 by 11 inches or 51 by 66 picas
- Orientation: Tall
- Margins: 0 all around

2. Choose Preferences from the Edit menu.

- Specify picas as the unit of measure.
- Set Guides to the back.

  PageMaker's publication window consists of overlapping layers of text, graphics, and nonprinting guides. Positioning the ruler guides in back enables you to select an item positioned on top of a guide and also prevents you from inadvertently moving a guide when you move other elements on the page. In later projects we won't specify the position of the guides. Be aware that you have the option to move them from back to front, and vice versa, through the Preferences dialog box.

3. Divide the page into four quadrants.

- Turn on Snap to Rulers on the Options menu (Command-[on a Mac, Shift-Ctrl-Y on a PC).

- Bring in ruler guides to bisect the page horizontally (at 33p) and vertically (at 25p6), creating a space for four vertical cards of equal size. You'll work in the upper left quadrant to create the master card.

4. Define the image area.

- Bring in horizontal ruler guides at 3p and 30p to define the top and bottom margins of the master card.

- Bring in vertical guides at 3p and 22p6 to define the side margins.

5. Create the banner.

- Bring in a horizontal guide at 6p to mark the bottom of the banner.

- Check the Options menu to be sure Snap to Guides is turned on.

- With the rectangle tool, draw the box for the banner as defined by the top two ruler guides and side margins.

- With the rectangle you just drew still selected, choose Solid from the Fill submenu (under Element).

6. Add the text.

- With the text tool, draw a "bounding box" to define the left and right margins of the text. To do this, position the text tool on the 3p vertical guide, about a pica below the black banner. Hold down the mouse button and drag the I-beam diagonally to the vertical guide at 22p6 (the depth isn't important).

- In the Type Specs dialog box, specify 10/36 Avant Garde.

  Note that when you close the dialog box, the text insertion point will still be blinking. If you were to choose another tool before beginning to type, the type specs would revert to the default. This can be very confusing for beginners because it seems as though PageMaker simply won't do what you tell it. If you're running into this problem, read the section about changing defaults on page 206.

- Type the headline and body text in 10/36 Avant Garde. Don't worry about the vertical position of the text block just yet.

TIP

When you haven't defined text columns, or when you want to override the columns that you have defined, you can draw a "bounding box" to define the left and right margins of the text you're about to type. With the text tool, set an insertion point where you want the left margin to be, and drag diagonally to where you want the right margin to be. The depth isn't important. You'll see a rectangle as you drag; it disappears when you release the mouse, but PageMaker will remember its boundaries when you type the text. You can use the same technique when you place text by dragging the loaded text icon to define the margins.

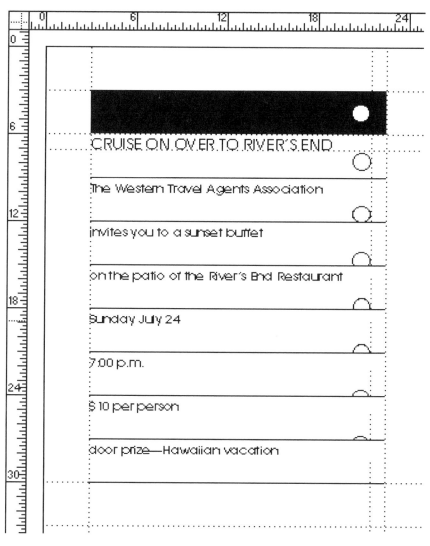

CRUISE ON OVER TO RIVER'S END

The Western Travel Agents Association

invites you to a sunset buffet

on the patio of the River's End Restaurant

Sunday July 24

7:00 p.m.

$ 10 per person

door prize—Hawaiian vacation

▲ ▲ ▲

The informal invitation is created in the upper left quadrant of an 8.5- by 11-inch sheet, and then copied and pasted three times to print four on a page. The graphics are created with PageMaker's graphics tools.

TIP

When you want to move a text block in one direction only, hold down the Shift key before you drag the text. When you begin to drag, the four-headed arrow turns into a double-headed arrow, pointing either vertically or horizontally depending on the direction in which you are dragging.

- With the text tool, select the headline. In the Type Specs dialog box, specify 12/36, All Caps.

- Bring in a horizontal ruler guide 1p1 below the black banner to align the baseline for the headline. To measure in 1-point increments, you have to work at 200% page view.

- Turn off Snap to Rulers and Snap to Guides.

- With the pointer tool, select the text, hold down the Shift key, and drag the text block vertically so that the baseline of the headline is on the ruler guide just below the black banner. (If you move the text block too quickly, before the arrows appear, a box defining the text block will move, rather than the text itself, and you won't be able to see the baseline to position it.)

7. Add the horizontal rules.

- With the text tool, select all the text except the headline.

- Choose Paragraph from the Type menu to bring up the Paragraph Specifications dialog box.

  This is one of PageMaker's multilevel dialog boxes. We looked at the options on the first level in Project 2; the Rules and Spacing buttons bring up additional boxes, and there are further levels beyond that. Don't be intimidated to find yourself three levels deep in dialog boxes; it's just PageMaker's way of organizing options so that you don't have to sort through too many possibilities at once.

  Here, we'll work with the Rules option. The following steps take you quickly through the Rule specifications for the invitation. For a closer look at the hows and whys of this feature, see the sidebar on the next spread.

- Select Rules. This brings up the Paragraph Rules dialog box.

- Click on Rule Above Paragraph.

  For Line Style, scroll the submenu to select Hairline.

  For Line Width, click on Width of Column.

  Leave all the other default settings.

- Click on the Options button to bring up the Paragraph Rule Options dialog box.

  For the Top rule, type *1p1* in the value box for the measurement above the baseline.

- Hold down the Option key on a Mac, the Alt key on a PC, and then click OK.

  You'll come to love this Option-OK, Alt-OK combination. It closes all the levels of nested dialog boxes, so you don't have to OK each one separately. You can use the same technique to Cancel, too.

- To add a rule below the last line of text, set an insertion point after the word "vacation," press Return to create a new paragraph, and then press Tab or Spacebar to create a blank character in the paragraph. At that point, you'll see the rule.

8. Add the visual motif for the banner.

You can create the sunset using PageMaker's graphics tools, as described on the facing page.

9. Print.

See "How to Print Four Up" at the end of the project.

TIP

To see the page on-screen as it will print, hide the guides by choosing Guides from the Options menu. The Guides command is one of several toggle switches on Page-Maker's menus: The feature is on when it's checked and off when it's not checked. You can quickly turn the Guides on and off with the keyboard shortcuts—Command-J on a Mac, Ctrl-J on a PC. When you turn the Guides on after having hidden them, they reappear in their previous position on the screen.

HOW TO CREATE A PAGEMAKER SUNSET

You can create a sunset motif by using a white rectangle to mask more and more of each subsequent circle, thus suggesting the sun sinking below the horizon line. For maximum flexibility in positioning the small graphics used here, you'll want to work at a large page view with both Snap To commands turned off.

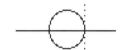

A hairline-rule circle...

1. Hold down the Shift key and use the circle tool to create a sun about the same size as the one shown in the sample. Position the top of the circle about 1p9 above the first Paragraph Rule. Set the Line to Hairline and the Fill to None.

2. Copy the circle once and paste it six times, positioning each copy a little lower on its horizon line than the one before. Use a vertical ruler guide to align the right sides of the circles.

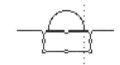

partially covered by a rectangle...

When moving a circle, point anywhere on the circumference before you drag. If you point inside the circle, you'll deselect it. If you point to a handle and drag, you'll stretch the circle; if that happens, immediately select Undo from the top of the Edit menu (Command-Z on a Mac, Alt-Backspace on a PC).

If you move the text when you're trying to move a circle, use the Undo command, and then, with the text still selected, choose Send to Back from the Element menu (Command-B on a Mac, Ctrl-B on a PC). For more explanation about the Front/Back commands, see pages 356–357).

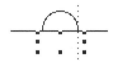

with the Line set to None and the Fill to Paper...

3. Paste one more circle in the black banner. After you move it into position, you won't see the circle but you will see the selection handles around it (selection handles automatically reverse out against black). While it's still selected, change the Fill to Paper.

If you do "lose" the circle behind the banner, use the pointer tool to draw a selection box around the banner. Then deselect the banner by clicking anywhere inside the banner but outside the selection handles of the circle. Change the circle's Fill to Paper and it will reverse out of the banner. If you lose the circle after changing its Fill to Paper, select the banner with the pointer and send it to the back.

makes a setting sun.

4. To cover the part of the circle below the horizon, draw a hairline-rule rectangle and butt it to the horizontal rule. Change the rectangle's Line to None and Fill to Paper. Adjust the position of this "invisible" box through trial and error until the horizon line is unbroken and the portion of the circle below it is completely masked. (Use the pointer to select the invisible box and reveal its handles.)

PageMaker has a power-paste function that enables you to duplicate the horizontal and/or vertical offset of repeated copies. It doesn't quite work here because the desired effect is not so much equal spacing, but seeing less of each succeeding sun. We'll use a modified version of power-pasting in "How to Print Four Up" at the end of this project, and we'll come back to this feature again in later projects.

PARAGRAPH RULES

To specify a rule before or after a paragraph, select the Rules button in the Paragraph Specs dialog box. Unlike rules created with PageMaker's graphics tools, Paragraph Rules are part of the formatting for the associated paragraph. Keep in mind:

- A paragraph is any text between two carriage returns. The single lines in this project, and headlines, also, can be created as paragraphs.

- You can't select a Paragraph Rule with the pointer tool. Paragraph Rules are created and altered as text, through the Paragraph command on the Type menu, not as graphics, through the Element menu.

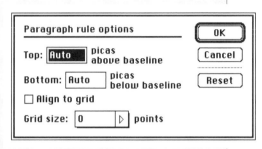

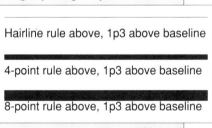

Line Style and **Line Color**: Both submenus make available to you the same line and color options as are available from the Element menu.

Line Width: You can specify Width of Text or Width of Column, but combined with the Indent options, you have a lot of flexibility in rule width. See the examples on the facing page. You can also stretch (or shrink) a Column Width rule by dragging on the selection handles of the text block.

Options: Select the Options button to bring up the Paragraph Rule Options dialog box. Here you specify the vertical position of Paragraph Rules relative to the text, and this gets a little tricky.

The position for Rules Above (called Top in the Paragraph Rule Options dialog box) is measured

up from the baseline of the first line in the paragraph. The position for Rules Below (called Bottom) is measured down from the baseline of the last line of the paragraph.

We generally stay away from the default Auto setting. It can cause Rules Above to print over the tops of capital letters and ascenders, and Rules Below to print over the bottoms of descenders. Watch out for these problems when checking your own settings for rule positions.

The space between the rule and the text is also affected by the line weight you specify. To see how this works: Create a line with a Paragraph Rule and gradually increase the weight of the rule, leaving its position value the same. The rule grows down toward the text, as you can see in the example above. Rules Below grow up toward the text.

Paragraph Rules extend the paragraph slug (the amount of space highlighted when you drag over a paragraph with the text tool), unless you use the Auto setting for the position of the rule. We'll examine in some detail the effect of Paragraph Rules on spacing when we work with leading grids in Project 5. We'll also explore the **Align to Grid** option in that project. See the sidebar "Working with a Leading Grid," beginning on page 307.

When you first begin working with Paragraph Rules, you go through a lot of trial and error specifying the value above or below the baseline. In the process, you may discover some interesting effects, and after a while it won't take so long to get the look you want.

BY WAY OF EXAMPLE . . .

EUREKA!

Lorem ipsum dolor si amet, consectetuer adipiscing elit, sed diam nonummy nibh

A Column Width rule is exactly the width of the margins for that text block. This one is a Rule Above, 1 pt, Position 1p6 above baseline.

EUREKA!

Lorem ipsum dolor sit et amet, et consectetuer diam adipiscing elit, nonummy

nibh euismod tincidunt ut laoreet dolore magna zzril aliquam erat volutpat. Ut

This Rule Above has the same specs as the one to its left, except this one has a Right Indent of -12p. A negative indent extends a Column Width rule beyond the column margins, enabling you to run a single rule across two columns of text. A positive indent insets the rule from the column margins.

BULBS

You can have two rules for the same paragraph. Here, the Rule Above is 1 pt, Width of Column, Position 1p6 above baseline. The Rule Below is 6 pt, Width of Text, Position 1p below baseline.

SPRING FEVER

This one is full of tricks. It's actually two paragraphs. The 1-point rule is part of a blank paragraph with the Type Specs set for 1-point leading even though there's no type, and the Paragraph option Keep with Next specified for 1 line. It's a Rule Below, Position 0p below the baseline; it's defined as Column Width but its length is extended by dragging the text selection handles (an alternative to specifying a negative indent). The 6-point rule is a Rule Above the "Spring Fever" line, Width of Text, Position 1p9 above the baseline, with a Right Indent of -0p2. Why the right indent? Italic text extends slightly beyond its own right margin; the negative indent extends the rule beyond the margin so that it visually aligns with the text.

You can put

rules below each

line in a

pull-quote like this.

You can use any rule on the Line menu. This double rule is Width of Text, Left and Right Indents -0p9, 1p below the baseline.

A custom text wrap around the art forces the text and Paragraph Rules away from the art. (See page 361 for an explanation of customized text wrap.) Paragraph Rules behave a little strangely in the presence of a graphic boundary. If the leading for a line with a Paragraph Rule crosses the graphic boundary, the rule will be repelled, even if the rule itself doesn't cross the boundary. The Paragraph Rules here are Column Width, positioned 1p4 above the baseline. The bottom rule has a Right Indent of -1p6.

CRUISE ON OVER TO RIVER'S END

Western Travel Agents Association

invites you to a sunset buffet

on the good ship Pacifica

Sunday, July 24 at 7 P.M.

door prize—Hawaiian vacation

For additional use of Paragraph Rules, see pages 309 and 394.

How to Print Four Up

Invitations, business cards, name tags, and other documents with a small trim size can be printed efficiently with multiple copies of the document on one sheet of paper. Simply create a master of the document, copy it, and then repeatedly paste the copy to fill the page, using ruler guides to align the tops and edges of the copies.

The following instructions for printing the invitation four to a page can be adapted easily for other dimensions.

1. Check all the alignments on your master. Print a copy and proofread for spelling, accuracy of information, alignments, and so on.

2. Note that the ruler guides bisecting the page, which you brought in to define the trim of the master, also define the trim for the other three units.

3. Be sure Snap to Guides (on the Options menu) is turned on.

4. With the rectangle tool, draw a temporary page frame around the master, from the zero point in the upper left corner to the midpoint of the 8.5- by 11-inch page (where the 25p6 vertical guide and the 33p horizontal guide intersect).

   When you move the copies of the master in steps 7–9, you'll appreciate the aid of this page frame.

5. Select the entire master, either by choosing Select All from the Edit menu or by using the pointer to draw a marquee around all the elements in the master.

6. Copy the master and use the power-paste technique described in the Tip at left to paste the copy directly on top of the original. The copy will be full of handlebars, which is fine, as you'll see in the next step.

7. With all the pieces of the copy still selected (as long as all those handlebars are showing, you know that all the pieces of your copy are selected), hold down the Shift key, position the arrow on any side of the temporary page frame, and drag the copy into position in the upper right quadrant. Do not point on a handle or you will stretch the frame. (If you inadvertently do stretch that or any other element, choose Undo from the Edit menu; all the pieces of the copy will remain selected after the mistake is undone.)

8. Select All again, copy, and power-paste again. This time you'll have two copies directly on top of the first two cards.

9. Hold down the Shift key and drag the new copies into position in the bottom half of the page.

10. To remove the temporary page frame around each invitation, select it with the pointer and press the Backspace key.

11. Optional electronic trimming guide: If you plan to print and trim the cards yourself, you may want to add little tick marks to guide your trim. It sounds ridiculous, but we've found that 8-point Helvetica periods, being 1 pixel high, provide a sufficient guide and virtually

TIP

When you copy (or cut) an item that you want to move away from the original position in one direction only, use this "power-paste" technique: on a Mac, hold down the Option key when you paste; on a PC, press Ctrl-Shift-P. PageMaker pastes the copy directly on top of the original. Then, by holding down the Shift key while you drag the copy to its new position, you can constrain the move to a single direction and ensure exact alignment with the original item in the other direction.

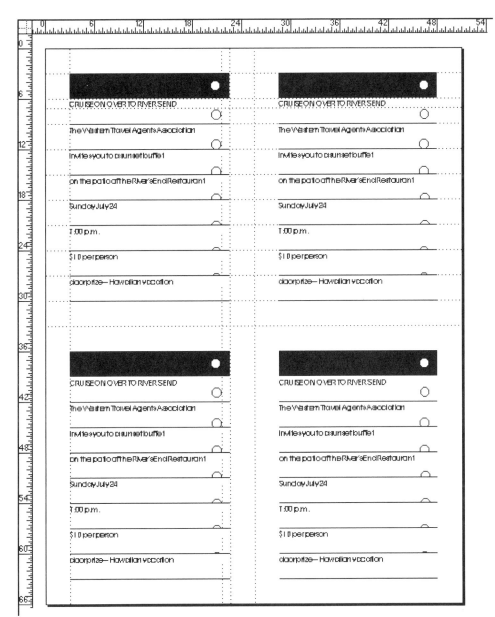

▲ ▲ ▲

Copy and paste the master unit to print multiple invitations on the same sheet. Use a temporary page frame (already removed here) to facilitate alignment along the ruler guides that mark the trim for each copy.

disappear in trimming. Along the horizontal ruler guide separating the top and bottom cards, place a period at each corner of the image area. Along the vertical ruler guide separating the left and right cards, place periods to align with the tops of the banners and the last horizontal rules. You should have four periods along each guide.

Old-fashioned trimming guide: Use a ruler and a pencil to mark the cuts, and erase the pencil marks after trimming.

12. If you are printing the invitations on a laser printer, the 20-pound card stock must be hand-fed. Click the Manual Feed button in the Print dialog box.

   If your cards will be commercially printed, you will need to paste your camera-ready page onto a piece of art board and draw crop marks outside the live area to indicate the inside trim for each card.

PROJECT 4

CREATING A TEMPLATE FOR A THREE-COLUMN SELF-MAILING NEWSLETTER

This project uses some of PageMaker's most powerful features—the ability to create a template for a publication that you produce repeatedly, using master pages and style sheets. Master pages are the blueprint on which individual pages of the publication are built. By setting up column and ruler guides on the master pages, you establish a format that you can follow on all the pages of the publication. It's much faster than having to reinvent the wheel on every page and also ensures consistency from one page to the next.

The value of styles can't be overemphasized. If you know how to define type attributes, you already know a good deal of what there is to know about styles. We'll grant that some of the rest is full of subtleties, but once mastered, those nuances provide powerful flexibility. We hope that the introduction to styles in this project will make you want to master the finer points.

The project contains a great deal of information that is essential to working effectively in PageMaker. The instructions assume familiarity with procedures used in earlier projects, but if you missed some important steps along the way, or need to review them, you'll find cross-references to earlier projects throughout.

A primary design objective in developing the format for the newsletter was that it be fast and efficient to produce. It shouldn't require much fine-tuning after you pour the text. In Project 5, we'll use a copy of this newsletter to look at some design variations that explore additional PageMaker techniques but add some production complexities to the basic format presented here. And you'll work with another copy of this newsletter in Project 9, when we look at PageMaker's color capabilities.

In the instructions, you'll create the template first and then adapt it for a hypothetical issue of the newsletter. In reality, the process works the other way around. You generally develop a prototype publication, with dummy text and art in place, and then strip the dummy elements out of the pages, leaving the guidelines, spacing guides, and elements that print in the same position each issue.

For dummy text, we've used the same Copy Fit file used in Project 2. This text file comes with the PageMaker 4.0 package; refer to the introduction to Project 2 if you're not familiar with it.

PAGEMAKER TECHNIQUES

▶ Create and use a template

▶ Work with master pages

▶ Create customized column guides

▶ Create automatic page-numbering markers

▶ Work with style sheets

▶ Create spacing guides

▶ Rotate text

▶ Format text in a word processor

▶ Use the Autoflow option

▶ Place graphics

▶ Export text to a word processor

▶ Examine the flexibility of threaded text

The Employee Newsletter of Southside Corporation
NEWSLINE

Oct 15, 1991

Captions for art are set 10/14 Helvetica bold. They extend 12p6 into the column rather than the full 18p column width.

Headline goes here in 14/15 Helvetica bold

Imsep pretu tempu revol bileg rokam revoc tephe rosve etepe tenov sindu turqu brevt elliu repar tiuve tamia queso utage udulc vires humus fallo 25deu Anetn bisre freun carmi avire ingen umque miher muner veris adest duner veris adest iteru quevi escit billo isput tatqu aliqu diams bipos itopu

50sta Isant oscul bifid mquec cumen berra etmii pyren nsomn anoct reern oncit quqar anofe ventm hipec oramo uetfu orets nitus sacer tusag teliu ipsev 75tvi Eonei elaur plica oscri eseli sipse enitu ammih mensl quidi aptat rinar uacae ierqu vagas ubesc rpore ibere perqu umbra perqu antra erorp netra 100at mihif napat ntint riora intui urque nimus otoqu cagat rolym oecfu iunto ulosa tarac ecame suidt mande onatd stent spiri usore idpar thaec abies

125sa Imsep pretu tempu revol bileg rokam revoc tephe rosve etepe tenov sindu turqu brevt

225at mihif napat ntint riora intui urque nimus otoqu cagat rolym oecfu iunto ulosa tarac ecame suidt mande onatd stent spiri usore idpar thaec abies 250sa Imsep pretu tempu revol bileg rokam revoc tephe rosve etepe tenov sindu turqu brevt elliu repar tiuve tamia queso utage udulc vires humus fallo 275eu Anetn bisre freun carmi avire ingen umque miher muner veris adest duner veris adest iteru quevi escit billo isput tatqu aliqu diams bipos itopu

Headline for second story in Newsline

300ta Isant oscul bifid mquec cumen berra etmii pyren nsomn anoct reern oncit quqar anofe ventm hipec oramo uetfu orets nitus sacer tusag teliu ipsev

325vi Eonei elaur plica oscri eseli sipse enitu ammih mensl quidi aptat rinar uacae ierqu vagas ubesc rpore ibere perqu umbra perqu antra erorp netra 350at mihif napat ntint riora intui urque nimus otoqu cagat rolym

FORECAST

Forecasts are 10/14 Helvetica b space after each paragraph.

Lorem ipsum dolor sit amet, co adipiscing elit, sed diam nonun euismod tincidunt ut laoreet do

Aliquam erat volutpat. Ut wisi minim

Veniam, quis nostrud exerci tat ullamcorper suscipit lobortis ni ex ea commodo consequat. Du

NEWSLINE
The Employee Newsletter of Southside Corporation

Southside Corporation
12 Kramer Avenue, Chicago, IL 60600

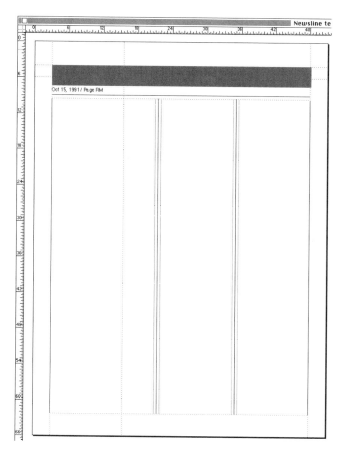

This is a placeholder for the 14/14 Helvetica bold breakout

Oct 15, 1991 / Page 2

NEWSBRIEFS

Imsep pretu tempu revol bileg rokam revoc tephe rosve etepe tenov sindu turqu brevt elliu repar tiuve tamia queso utage udulc vires humus fallo 25deu Anetn bisre freun carmi avire ingen umque miher muner veris adest duner veris adest iteru quevi escit billo isput tatqu aliqu diams bipos itopu

50sta Isant oscul bifid mquec cumen berra etmii pyren nsomn anoct reern oncit quqar anofe ventm hipec oramo uetfu orets nitus sacer tusag teliu ipsev 75vi Eonei elaur plica oscri eseli sipse enitu ammih mensl quidi aptat rinar uacae ierqu vagas ubesc rpore ibere perqu umbra perqu antra erorp netra 100at mihif napat ntint riora intui urque nimus otoqu cagat rolym oecfu iunto ulosa tarac ecame suidt mande onatd stent spiri usore idpar thaec abies

125sa Imsep pretu tempu revol bileg rokam revoc tephe rosve etepe tenov sindu turqu brevt elliu repar tiuve tamia queso utage udulc vires humus fallo

150eu Anetn bisre freun carmi avire ingen umque miher muner veris adest duner veris adest iteru quevi escit billo isput tatqu aliqu diams bipos itopu 175sa Isant oscul bifid mquec cumen berra etmii pyren nsomn anoct reern oncit quqar anofe ventm hipec oramo uetfu orets nitus sacer tusag teliu ipsev 200vi Eonei elaur plica oscri eseli sipse enitu ammih mensl quidi aptat rinar uacae ierqu vagas ubesc rpore ibere perqu umbra perqu antra erorp netra mihif napat ntint riora intui urque nimus otoqu tamia queso utage udulc vires humus fallo

Eonei elaur plica oscri eseli sipse enitu ammih mensl quidi aptat rinar uacae ierqu vagas ubesc rpore ibere perqu umbra perqu antra erorp netra 475at mihif napat ntint riora intui urque nimus otoqu cagat rolym oecfu iunto ulosa tarac ecame suidt mande onatd stent spiri usore idpar thaec abies

Headlines can run on three or even on four lines if you want to write long heads

500sa Imsep pretu tempu revol bileg rokam revoc tephe rosve etepe tenov sindu turqu brevt elliu repar tiuve tamia queso utage udulc vires humus fallo 525eu Anetn bisre freun carmi avire ingen umque miher muner veris adest duner veris adest iteru quevi escit billo isput tatqu aliqu diams bipos itopu

550ta Isant oscul bifid mquec cumen berra etmii pyren nsomn anoct reern oncit quqar anofe ventm hipec oramo uetfu orets nitus sacer tusag teliu ipsev 575vi Eonei elaur plica oscri eseli sipse enitu ammih mensl quidi aptat rinar uacae ierqu vagas ubesc rpore ibere perqu umbra perqu antra erorp netra

Subhead is 10/14 Helvetica bold on one or two lines

600at mihif napat ntint riora intui urque nimus otoqu cagat rolym oecfu iunto ulosa tarac ecame suidt mande onatd stent spiri usore idpar thaec abies 625sa Imsep pretu tempu revol bileg rokam revoc tephe rosve etepe tenov sindu turqu brevt elliu repar tiuve tamia queso udulc vires humus fallo 650eu Anetn bisre freun carmi avire ingen umque miher muner veris

adest duner veris adest iteru quevi escit billo isput tatqu aliqu diams bipos itopu

675sa Isant oscul bifid mquec cumen berra etmii pyren nsomn anoct reern oncit quqar anofe ventm hipec oramo uetfu orets nitus sacer tusag teliu ipsev 700vi Eonei elaur plica oscri eseli sipse enitu ammih mensl quidi aptat rinar uacae ierqu vagas ubesc rpore ibere perqu umbra perqu antra erorp netra 725at mihif napat green wood intui urque nimus otoqu cagat rolym oecfu iunto ulosa tarac ecame suidt mande onatd stent spiri usore idpar thaec abies

Subhead goes here

750sa Imsep pretu tempu revol bileg rokam revoc tephe rosve etepe tenov sindu turqu brevt elliu repar tiuve tamia queso utage udulc vires humus fallo 775eu Anetn bisre freun carmi avire ingen umque miher muner veris adest duner veris adest iteru quevi escit billo isput tatqu aliqu diams bipos itopu

800ta Isant oscul bifid mquec cumen berra etmii pyren nsomn anoct reern oncit quqar anofe ventm hipec oramo uetfu orets nitus sacer tusag teliu ipsev 825vi Eonei elaur plica oscri eseli sipse enitu ammih mensl quidi aptat rinar uacae ierqu vagas ubesc rpore ibere perqu umbra perqu antra erorp netra

850at mihif napat ntint riora intui urque nimus otoqu cagat rolym oecfu iunto ulosa tarac ecame suidt mande onatd stent spiri usore idpar thaec abies 875sa Imsep pretu tempu revol bileg rokam revoc tephe rosve etepe tenov sindu turqu brevt elliu repar tiuve tamia queso utage udulc vires humus fallo 900eu Anetn bisre freun carmi avire ingen umque miher muner

---

This is a placeholder for the 14/14 Helvetica bold breakout

Oct 15, 1991 / Page 3

PEOPLE

Caption for people shots can be one line or several, set to a 12p6 measure.

Headline for another story

950vi Eonei elaur plica oscri eseli sipse enitu ammih mensl quidi aptat rinar uacae ierqu vagas ubesc rpore ibere perqu umbra perqu antra erorp netra 975at mihif napat ntint riora intui urque nimus otoqu cagat rolym oecfu iunto ulosa tarac ecame suidt mande onatd stent spiri usore idpar thaec abies 1000a Imsep pretu tempu revol bileg rokam revoc tephe rosve etepe tenov sindu turqu brevt elliu repar tiuve tamia queso utage udulc vires humus fallo 1025u Anetn bisre freun carmi avire ingen umque miher muner veris adest billo isput tatqu aliqu diams bipos itopu 1050a Isant oscul bifid mquec cumen berra etmii pyren nsomn anoct reern oncit quqar anofe ventm hipec oramo uetfu orets nitus sacer tusag teliu ipsev

1075i Eonei elaur plica oscri eseli sipse enitu ammih mensl quidi aptat rinar uacae ierqu vagas ubesc rpore ibere perqu umbra perqu antra erorp netra 1100a Isant oscul bifid mquec cumen berra etmii pyren nsomn anoct reern oncit quqar anofe ventm hipec oramo uetfu orets nitus sacer tusag teliu ipsev 1125i Eonei elaur plica oscri eseli sipse enitu ammih mensl quidi aptat rinar uacae ierqu vagas ubesc rpore ibere perqu umbra perqu antra erorp netra

Caption for people shots can be one line or several, set to a 12p6 measure.

veris adest duner veris adest iteru quevi escit billo isput tatqu aliqu diams bipos itopu

925sa Isant oscul bifid mquec cumen berra etmii pyren nsomn anoct reern oncit quqar anofe ventm hipec oramo uetfu orets nitus sacer tusag teliu ipsev

Caption for people shots can be one line or several, set to a 12p6 measure.

1150t mihif napat ntint riora intui urque nimus otoqu cagat rolym oecfu iunto ulosa tarac ecame suidt mande onatd stent spiri usore idpar thaec abies 1175a Imsep pretu tempu revol bileg rokam revoc tephe rosve etepe tenov sindu turqu brevt elliu repar tiuve tamia queso utage udulc vires humus fallo 1200t mihif napat ntint riora intui urque nimus otoqu cagat rolym oecfu iunto ulosa tarac ecame suidt mande onatd stent spiri usore idpar thaec abies 1225a Imsep pretu tempu revol bileg rokam revoc tephe rosve etepe tenov sindu turqu brevt elliu repar tiuve tamia queso 2250u Anetn bisre freun carmi avire ingen umque miher muner veris adest duner veris adest iteru quevi escit billo isput tatqu aliqu diams bipos itopu

Headline for last story

1275a Isant oscul bifid mquec cumen berra etmii pyren nsomn anoct reern oncit quqar anofe ventm hipec oramo uetfu orets nitus sacer tusag teliu ipsev 1300h Eonei elaur plica oscri eseli sipse enitu ammih mensl quidi aptat rinar uacae ierqu vagas ubesc rpore ibere perqu umbra perqu antra erorp netra 1325t mihif napat ntint riora intui urque nimus otoqu cagat rolym oecfu iunto ulosa tarac ecame suidt mande onatd stent spiri usore idpar thaec abies 1350a Imsep pretu tempu revol bileg rokam revoc tephe rosve etepe tenov sindu turqu brevt elliu repar tiuve tamia queso utage udulc vires humus fallo 1375u Anetn bisre freun carmi avire ingen umque miher muner veris adest duner veris adest iteru quevi escit billo isput tatqu aliqu

---

Newsline te

Oct 15, 1991 / Page RM

The grid created on the master page (left) uses two 12p6 columns for running text and a wider 18p column for art and special departments. The wide column adds visual interest to a relatively simple format, gives you flexibility in sizing and cropping art, and forces you to leave some white space on the page.

PageMaker's Next Style option lets you automate formatting of paragraphs that always follow one another, such as the story heads, the flush-left first paragraph following each story head, and the indented second paragraph of each story in the pages shown above.

The Zapf Dingbats dividers in the "Newsbriefs" column (above, far left) are also automated with styles. All you have to do is type *vvv* and apply the style; PageMaker applies the typeface, size, center alignment, and spacing before and after.

BLUEPRINT FOR NEWSLINE

PAGE SETUP

Page Dimensions: 8.5 by 11 inches or 51 by 66 picas

Orientation: Tall

Start Page #: 1 of 4

Options: Turn off Double-sided, Facing Pages

Margins: Left , 3p   Right, 3p

         Top, 9p6   Bottom, 3p9

TIP

Define the top margin where the top of the text block will be on the majority of pages in your publication—that is, the place where you will align the loaded text icon. Define the bottom margin to allow for leading in the last line of body text: Determine how many lines you want in a column of text, determine the leading below the last line of text (one third of PageMaker's proportional leading is below the baseline), and specify the bottom margin at that point. You can position running heads, folios, and other elements outside the margins if you like.

Remember that you can override the unit of measure by typing abbreviations. Thus, if your preferences are set to inches, you can still type *3p, 3p, 9p6,* and *3p9* for the margins. The rest of the measurements are given in picas, however, so when you're finished with the page setup, change the unit of measure through the Preferences command on the Edit menu.

In the interest of fast, efficient production, we've set up the file as single-sided pages, even though it is in fact a double-sided publication with facing pages. This saves you time in two ways: You have to set up only one master page instead of two; and when you turn pages, screen redraw time will be faster than it would be for facing pages. You will still be able to print on both sides of the paper.

In order to use this time-saving approach, the grid for the right and left pages must be exactly the same, which they are in this newsletter. Also, the design must be straightforward enough so that you don't need to view facing pages as a spread. If you use this grid for a more modular format—running some stories across two or three columns—or if you have a lot of art in your pages, then the relationship of elements on facing pages becomes important, and a publication incorporating those variations would be better set up as double-sided.

MASTER PAGE

1. Click on the icon labeled R at the lower left of the screen.

In single-sided publications, the master page icon is identified as a right-hand page. In double-sided publications, there are icons labeled R and L for right and left master pages.

2. Create customized column guides.

- Choose Column Guides from the Options menu.

- In the Column Guides dialog box, specify 3 columns with a 1p space in between.

PageMaker positions the leftmost column guide over the left margin and the rightmost column guide over the right margin. You can move either of these column guides individually (although it isn't

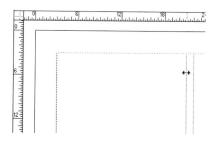

▲ ▲ ▲

When you drag the column guides to create columns of unequal widths, the space between columns remains constant. To change that space, you must return to the Column Guides dialog box. Note that when you move the guides, the hairline marker in the ruler aligns with whichever guide you are pointing to.

necessary to do so in this project). The other column guides move only as pairs—the right margin of one column and the left margin of the next column—so that the space between columns (often called the alley) remains constant. You'll move them in a minute.

- Turn on Snap to Rulers (Command-[on a Mac, Ctrl-Shift-Y on a PC).

- Position the pointer tool on either of the first pair of column guides and drag to reposition them at 21p and 22p. Similarly, position the second pair of column guides at 34p6 and 35p6. You should have one wide column on the left, measuring 18p, followed by two narrower columns on the right, each measuring 12p6.

- Bring in a vertical ruler guide at 15p6.

This guideline creates a 12p6 column within the wide 18p column. When you place art in this column, you can size it either to the 12p6 measure or to the full 18p width. Captions run to the 12p6 measure. This flexibility has several benefits: It makes the pages more interesting visually; it gives you two choices when cropping and sizing art; and it forces you to leave some white space on the page.

3. Add ruler guides.

- Bring in vertical ruler guides over the left and right margins.

- Bring in horizontal ruler guides at the following positions:

    4p: to mark the top of the gray banner

    6p: to mark the baseline for text that runs in the gray banner on pages 2 and 3.

4. Add printing items.

- Draw a 3p6-deep rectangle, beginning at the 4p horizontal guide on the left margin and extending to the right margin. With the rectangle still selected, specify the Line as None and the Fill as 40%.

- Type the date and the page-number marker.

A page-number marker is simply a code that tells PageMaker to automatically insert page numbers. In this newsletter, we've typed the page number in the same text block as the issue date.

With the text tool, set an insertion point on the left margin, just below the gray banner, and drag diagonally to the first vertical ruler guide to define a bounding box for the text. Type the date, followed by a Spacebar character, a slash, another Spacebar character, the word *Page*, and another Spacebar character. Then, for the page-number marker, type the key combination Command-Option-P on a Mac, Ctrl-Shift-3 on a PC.

PageMaker will insert the characters RM, which stands for "right master," where you typed the page-number marker. On the individual pages of the publication, the actual page number will be

TIP

When you move text, the hairline markers on the vertical ruler align with the top and bottom window-shade handles; so, to position the *baseline* of text at a ruler tick mark, you'll need to bring in a temporary ruler guide at that tick mark. But when you create or move Page-Maker graphics, if you turn on Snap to Rulers and watch the hair-line markers on the ruler as you move the cursor, you can accurately size and position elements without taking the time to bring in guidelines.

displayed in this position. (In a double-sided publication, the page-number marker on the left-hand page would read LM.)

Select this line with the text tool, and define the Type Specs as 10/12 Helvetica. With the pointer tool, select the line and reposition it so that its baseline is at 8p6. It should remain flush with the left margin.

- With the perpendicular line tool, draw a .5-point rule from the left to the right margin, at 9p on the vertical ruler.

- Draw another .5-point rule in the alley between the first two columns, from the top to the bottom margin. Be sure it is exactly centered in the space between the columns.

- Copy that rule and, on a Mac, hold down the Option key and paste; on a PC, press Ctrl-Shift-P. The copy will be pasted directly on top of the original. Then, holding down the Shift key, drag the copy to the right until it is centered between the next pair of column guides.

5. Change the default typeface.

- With the pointer tool selected, specify 10/12 Helvetica.

When you use the pointer tool to change type specifications and no text is selected, those specs become the default for that document. Any new text you type will have the default specifications. It's helpful to set your default typeface to whatever face you'll be using for assorted odds and ends, and in this newsletter that's Helvetica.

6. Save as a template.

In the Save As dialog box, PageMaker gives you the option of saving the file as a publication or as a template. If you choose Template, when you open the file in the future, PageMaker will automatically open an untitled copy rather than the original. This enables you to reuse the original template each time you lay out the publication.

If you want to open the original template to make corrections, be sure to click on the Original button in the Open dialog box. If you forget and get an untitled copy, you can do a Save As using the same filename as the original. PageMaker will ask you if you want to replace the original; respond Yes.

DEFINE STYLES

If you are not familiar with PageMaker's style sheets, see the step-by-step instructions in the sidebar beginning on page 265. Use those instructions to learn how to define the styles needed for the newsletter, and then return to this section to finish defining the style sheet for this project.

If you are familiar with PageMaker's style sheets, define the following styles for the newsletter. Rather than listing every element of each style, we've listed only those that differ from PageMaker's defaults or from a spec for the style on which the style being defined is based.

TIP

By specifying 2 lines for both widow and orphan control as part of the body text style, you tell PageMaker that you want at least two lines of a new paragraph at the bottom of a column and at least two lines at the end of a paragraph that falls at the top of a column. If necessary, PageMaker will force text from one column or page to the next in order to adhere to these specs, leaving some columns shorter than others.

TIP

For headline styles, specify Keep Lines Together and Keep with Next 3 Lines. This instructs PageMaker to avoid any column or page breaks in the middle of a headline, and to avoid separating a headline from the first 3 lines of the story that follows. As with widow and orphan control, if necessary PageMaker will force text from one column or page to the next in order to adhere to these specs.

We've listed the style names alphabetically, as they appear in the list on-screen. But to incorporate the Based On and Next Style options into a style definition, you sometimes have to return to one style definition after you've created others. For example, in the *news divider* style, you can't specify the Next Style as *news text* until you've defined the *news text* style; and in the *news text* style, you can't specify the Next Style as *news divider* until you've defined the *news divider* style.

When you're working from the Define Styles dialog box and you want to base a new style on an existing one: Scroll the Based On pop-up menu to choose the base style before clicking the New button. When you don't want to base a new style on an existing one: Click on New and in the Edit Style dialog box, select *No Style* from the Based On pop-up menu.

body text   Type: 10/12 Palatino; Paragraph: First Indent 0p10, Widow Control 2, Orphan Control 2

body first   Based On: *body text* + Next Style: *body text* + Paragraph: First Indent 0

breakout   Based On: *subhead* + Type: 14/14; Paragraph: Alignment centered, Space Before 0

caption   Type: 10/14 Helvetica bold

dept head   Type: 18/18 Helvetica bold italic reverse, Case All Caps, Track Very Loose; Paragraph: Alignment centered; Hyphenation: Off

> Note: When you specify reverse type, PageMaker displays a dialog box asking "Set Color to Paper?" Click OK.

forecast text   Based On: *caption* + Paragraph: Space After 0p7

news divider   Next Style: *news text*; Type: 14/14 Zapf Dingbats; Paragraph: Alignment centered, Space before 0p6, Space After 0p4; Spacing: Desired Letterspacing 200% (To set the Desired Letterspacing, click the Spacing button in the Paragraph dialog box to bring up the Spacing Attributes dialog box.)

> Note: In the Spacing Attributes dialog box, you must also change the value for Maximum letterspacing to 200% in order to set Desired letterspacing to 200%, since the value specified for Desired must be between the values specified for the maximum and the minimum. For more information about the Spacing Attributes dialog box, see pages 36 and 246.

news text   Based On: *body text* + Next Style: *news divider* + Paragraph: First Indent 0

story head   Next Style: *body first*; Type: 14/15 Helvetica bold; Paragraph: Space Before 0p9, Space After 0p4, Keep Lines Together, Keep with Next 3 lines, Rule Above 6 pt Width of Column with Right Indent 7p and (using the Options button) 1p10 above baseline

subhead   Based On: *story head* + Next Style: *body first* + Type: 10/13; Paragraph: Space Before 0p6, Space After 0p3, minus top rule

Blueprint instructions continue on page 270, following the Styles sidebar.

HOW TO CREATE AND USE A STYLE SHEET IN PAGEMAKER

If you know how to define type specs using the various commands on the Type menu, you already know a great deal about how to define a style. The difference is that instead of specifying half a dozen attributes (font, size, leading, indents, and so on) for a single unit of selected text, you use the Define Styles command to give that collection of attributes a name. The name is the style; the attributes are the style definition.

Once you've named and defined the style, you can apply all its attributes to selected text just by clicking on the name of the style, instead of going in and out of several dialog boxes. One click, instead of many. When you apply a style to a paragraph, the paragraph is said to be "tagged" with that style.

Using styles has two other fundamental advantages. One is that they ensure consistency between similar text elements throughout a publication. Whenever you have a caption, for example, just apply the caption style to it and all your captions will look alike. You don't have to remember all the type attributes of a caption, you just have to remember what you consider a caption. (With long, complex documents, remembering the style names for various elements is not as trivial as this example suggests.)

A second advantage is that you can easily change the type formatting throughout the entire document. Your boss decides he's tired of Helvetica and wants to change all the headlines to Futura? No problem. It will take only a minute to change the style definition; PageMaker will then automatically change all the paragraphs tagged with that style.

Using the Style Palette

The Style Palette provides one of the easiest ways to define, edit, and apply styles. It's a window that lists, in alphabetical order, all the styles defined for a publication. You can bring the window on- and off-screen through the Style Palette command on the Window menu, or by pressing Command-Y on a Mac, Ctrl-Y on a PC. Every new publication has five styles with PageMaker's default definitions.

Bring the Style Palette on-screen now and get comfortable with it. Resize the window and move it around the screen as you would any other window.

◀ ◀ ◀

To define a new style, hold down the Command key (Ctrl on a PC) and click on No Style in the Style Palette to bring up the Edit Style dialog box. To apply a style, select the text and then click on the style name in the Palette.

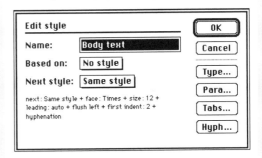

▲ ▲ ▲

The buttons in the Edit Style dialog box give you access to all the type and paragraph specifications that you've worked with in the previous projects.

Defining a Style by Example

Very often you format a column of body text, or a headline or caption, and then define a style based on the characteristics of that formatted paragraph. By way of example:

- Type two or three lines of text in one of the 12p6 columns in the newsletter template and give it the attributes of the *Newsline* story headline:

Type: 14/15 Helvetica bold

Paragraph: Space Before 0p9, Space After 0p4, Keep Lines Together, Keep with Next 3 Lines; Rule Above: 6 pt, Width of Column with Right Indent 7p and (using the Options button to define the position of the rule) 1p10 above baseline (For more on Paragraph Rules, see page 254.)

Hyphenation: Off

- With the cursor in the formatted paragraph, press the Command key on a Mac, the Ctrl key

Continues on following page

STYLES (continued)

on a PC, and click on *No Style* in the Style Palette. This brings the Edit Style dialog box on-screen.

- In the Name box, type *story head*. Note that the attributes of the text that you formatted are listed toward the bottom of the dialog box. Click OK. Note that *story head* has been added to the list in the Style Palette.

- Note also that *No Style* is still highlighted in the list, indicating that the style you just defined has not been applied to the original formatted paragraph. Creating a style by example does not apply the new style to the example paragraph. Click the text cursor in the sample paragraph and then click on *story head* in the Style Palette to apply the style. Failure to tag the sample paragraph can really trip you up if you edit the style later on.

- Now set an insertion point somewhere else on the page and type another two- or three-line headline. With the insertion point anywhere in that new headline, click on *story head* in the Style Palette, and watch PageMaker apply all the attributes of the first headline to the new one. Pretty terrific, isn't it? It gets even better when you add the Next Style option, which we'll do a little later.

Redefining or Editing a Style

By way of example, let's redefine PageMaker's default style for *body text* so that it defines the body text style used in the newsletter in this project.

- Press Command on a Mac, Ctrl on a PC, and click on *body text* in the Style Palette list.

- In the Edit Styles dialog box, note that the buttons on the right give you access to all the type and paragraph specifications you've been working with in previous projects. Also note the definition for the default *body text* style at the bottom of the dialog box: 12/Auto Times Roman, First Indent 2.

- Click on the Type button, and you'll see the by-now-familiar Type Specifications dialog box. Specify 10/12 Palatino. When you click OK, PageMaker returns to the Edit Style dialog box.

- Click on the Paragraph button (it's abbreviated "Para..." on-screen, but we'll write it out for ease of reading), and in the Paragraph Specs dialog box change the First Indent to 0p10 and type 2 in each of the text boxes for widow and orphan control. Click OK. Before clicking OK to close the dialog box, note the new definition of body text.

- Now type a few lines of text, and apply the *body text* style to that paragraph.

You can redefine a style by example, too.

- Type a few lines of text and give it the attributes of the captions used for art in *Newsline*: 10/14 Helvetica bold.

- With the Command or Ctrl key pressed, click on *No Style* in the Style Palette.

- In the Edit Style dialog box, type *caption* in the Name box. When you click OK, PageMaker will display a message box asking "Replace existing style caption?" Click OK or press Return, and it's done. Note that, as before, redefining a style by example does not tag the sample paragraph with the redefined style. You need to do that.

Basing One Style on Another Style

The Based On option tells PageMaker to base a new style on one that you've already defined. For this example, we'll define a style for the first paragraph of the newsletter stories. The formatting is identical to the *body text* style except in this new style the first line is not indented. (In general, paragraphs following a headline, subhead, or clearly marked section break don't require a paragraph indent.)

- Set an insertion point in the paragraph to which you've applied the *body text* style.

- Hold down Command or Ctrl, and click on *No Style* in the Style Palette.

- When the Edit Style dialog box comes on-screen, note that the Based On option now specifies *body text*. Name the new style (in this case, we called it *body first*), and use the Paragraph option to specify the First Indent as 0. Note the definition of the style at the bottom of the dialog box: Body text + First Indent: 0. Click OK.

If you haven't set an insertion point in a paragraph formatted with the base style, the Based On box will specify *No Style*; hold down the mouse button on that box (on a PC, click on the arrow to the right of the box) to select from a submenu of all the styles you've defined.

The main advantage of basing one style on another is that if you change the formatting of the base style, those changes will carry over to any style based on it. For example, if you decide to use a 6-point space between paragraphs instead of a first-line indent, all you have to do is change the specs for the *body text* style, specifying a First Indent of 0 and a Space After of 0p6. PageMaker will automatically change the *body first* style to Body text + Space After: 0p6. And of course it will apply those changes to all the text throughout the document to which you've applied those styles.

Using the Next Style Option

The Next Style option adds another level of automation by enabling you to specify that one style is always followed by another.

In the newsletter in this project, for example, the headline is always followed by the *body first* style, which is always followed by the *body text* style. If you set that up with the Next Style option, here's what happens when you type a headline and apply the *story head* style: When you press a carriage return and start typing a new paragraph, the new paragraph will automatically be in the *body first* style, and when you insert another carriage return and start typing again, that new paragraph will automatically be in the *body text* style.

Take a minute to test this for yourself, and you will forever be convinced of the value of styles.

- Command- or Ctrl-click on *story head* in the Style Palette. Bring up the Next Style pop-up menu and select *body first*. Click OK.

- Command- or Ctrl-click on *body first* in the Style Palette. In the Edit Style dialog box, select *body text* from the Next Style pop-up menu. Click OK.

- Now type one or two lines and apply the *story head* style.

- Insert a carriage return for a new paragraph and type a couple more lines. You don't need to click on the *body first* style because the text is already properly formatted.

- Insert another carriage return, type a few more lines, and note that, again, PageMaker has already formatted this paragraph for the *body text* style. Because the Next Style for *body text* is *same style*, all subsequent paragraphs that you type will be in the *body text* style until you specify otherwise.

Defining or Editing Several Styles at One Time

Using the Style Palette, as we've done so far, allows you to define or edit only a single style at a time. To work on multiple styles one after the other, choose Define Styles from the Type menu (Command-3 on a Mac, Ctrl-3 on a PC).

The Define Styles dialog box is a sort of home base from which you can define or edit the specs for one style and to which you can return to define or edit another style. Select the New button to define a new style; select the Edit button to edit an existing style. You also use this dialog box to remove styles and to copy style sheets from other publications.

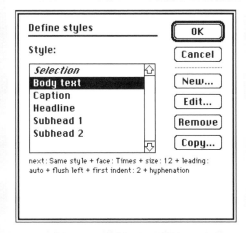

Use the Define Styles command (Command-3 on a Mac, Ctrl-3 on a PC) when you want to define or edit several styles one after the other. From this dialog box you can also delete styles and copy a style sheet from another PageMaker publication.

Continues on following page

STYLES (continued)

Removing a Style

- To delete a style, bring up the Define Styles dialog box. Click on the name of the style that you want to delete, and then click on Remove.

In the newsletter, we won't be using the *headline*, *subhead 1*, and *subhead 2* styles, so click on each name and remove it. This is more a matter of good housekeeping than of necessity. It minimizes the length of the style list when you have the Style Palette on the screen.

WARNING: Be careful when you remove styles. After you close the Define Styles dialog box, you can't undo the remove. Clicking Cancel, however, cancels any changes you've made since you opened the dialog box.

Copying Styles from Another Document

- When you want to copy the entire style sheet from an existing publication to use in the current one, select the Copy button in the Define Styles dialog box.

- This displays a Copy Styles dialog box that lets you scroll through your directories and folders to select the name of the file containing the style sheet you want to copy.

- If the two documents have any style names in common, PageMaker displays a message box asking whether you want to "Copy over existing styles?" If you click OK, the styles you are copying will override any existing styles in the current document.

Unfortunately, you can't copy selective styles in this dialog box. You have to copy the whole style sheet. But there is a workaround.

- To copy a single style from another PageMaker document, place text that includes that style in the current document. (When placing, if you select the name of another PageMaker document, PageMaker displays a Story Importer dialog box, in which you can select from a list of stories in that document. The stories are identified by the first 40 characters of text, and you can view any story before placing it.) You may lose some formatting, such as reverse type and para-

graph rules, but it's a start. In the style list, the style will be denoted with an asterisk, just as if it were imported from a word-processor file.

Overriding a Style

A style applies to an entire paragraph. You can't have a second style for selected text within the same paragraph, but you can override the style for selected text within a paragraph by applying different specs, such as italic or boldface, to that text. Whenever you select a paragraph that includes a style override, you'll see a plus sign (+) following the name of the style in the Style Palette list.

Type style overrides (that is, Type Style options available in the Type Specs dialog box, such as italic or boldface, with the exception of reverse) are permanent. Even if you apply a different style to that paragraph, the type style override remains. To remove the type style override, select the text and change the type style. Or select the paragraph and press Command-Shift-Spacebar on a Mac, Ctrl-Shift-Spacebar on a PC.

All other overrides, such as typeface and size, are temporary; if you apply a different style to the paragraph, the style override is removed.

To preserve a temporary override when you change the style of a paragraph, hold down the Shift key when you select the new style name.

Importing Styles from Word-Processor Files

If you define and apply styles in a word-processor file, and PageMaker has an import filter for that program, you can import the style sheet when you place the text. Just be sure the Retain Format option is selected in the Place dialog box. (If you define styles using bracketed style name tags at the beginning of paragraphs, select the Read Tags option in the dialog box.)

PageMaker adds the style names from the word-processor file to the Style Palette, with an asterisk following the name of any imported style. Note, though, that PageMaker imports only styles that have actually been applied to text in the word file; if you define a style but don't use it, the style isn't imported into PageMaker.

If a style name used in your word-processor file is identical to a style name in the PageMaker file but the definition of the styles is different, the PageMaker style definition will override the word-processor definition.

Be aware that you may lose some formatting from the word-processor styles, depending on the compatibility of the word processor's style sheet with PageMaker's. And formatting that does not have an equivalent in PageMaker, such as a box around a paragraph, will not be imported. For a list of formatting elements that PageMaker does and does not import, see Appendix B in the Macintosh *Reference Manual*, and the *Supplement* to the manual for Windows PageMaker.

Printing a Style Sheet

You can't print a style sheet in PageMaker, but you can print one from some word processors. Here's how we print ours in Microsoft Word on a Mac.

- Export the styled text from PageMaker to Word. (See the sidebar "Using PageMaker's Export Feature" on page 283.) The styles applied to the exported text will be exported as well.

- Open the file in Word and choose Define Styles from the Format menu. While the dialog box is open, choose Print from the File menu.

If you use Word for Windows, try this technique:

- Copy the text containing the styles to the Clipboard, and paste it into a Word for Windows file.

- Choose Print from the File menu. Click on the arrow to the right of the Print text box and choose Styles from the drop-down menu.

Word will print the style sheet in whatever typeface is defined as Normal for that publication. Style attributes that are unavailable in the word processor (such as reverse type and paragraph rules) and some style overrides (such as initial caps) will not be exported; you'll need to note those by hand on the printout.

Styles defined in the PageMaker document but not included in the exported or copied story won't be exported. For a document with many different stories, use this technique to combine the stories and their styles into one story that you can export.

Open a new PageMaker document. Choose Place, and select the name of the PageMaker document that contains the style list you want to export. In the Story Importer dialog box, which lists all the stories in the document, choose Select All, and then press Return. PageMaker imports all the stories from the placed document as a single story. Export that story and proceed as described above. For more on placing stories from one PageMaker document into another, see page 395.

TIPS

To bring the Style Palette on-screen: Press Command-Y on a Mac, Ctrl-Y on a PC.

To bring the Define Styles dialog box on-screen: Press Command-3 on a Mac, Ctrl-3 on a PC.

To OK (or Cancel) and close out of a nest of style dialog boxes: Hold down the Option key on a Mac, the Alt key on a PC, and click OK (or press Return).

A style is not defined until you click OK in the Edit Style dialog box. If you click Cancel after defining a style, that style will not be recorded.

Once you OK the Define Styles dialog box, you can't undo actions taken there with the Undo command.

This one is very quirky. If you apply local formatting, such as boldface, to text, and then later apply a style that includes that same local formatting, the local formatting will be removed. It's as though the redundancy cancels out the specification. To restore the local formatting, select that text, and reapply the formatting.

For complex documents with lots of styles: Number the styles that you use most frequently so they'll appear together at the top of the Style Palette.

Styles are a paragraph attribute. So when you want to apply a style, just set an insertion point anywhere in the paragraph and click on the style name. You don't have to drag over the entire paragraph.

To change PageMaker's default styles, or to remove them in order to start with a blank style sheet each time you open a new document, choose Define Styles when there is no publication open and make the desired changes.

When you're finished with this sidebar, return to page 264 to define the rest of the styles for this project.

COVER TEMPLATE

TIP

To move to the next page, press Command-Tab on a Mac, F12 on a PC. To move to the previous page, press Command-Shift-Tab on a Mac, F11 on a PC.

1. Click on the page 1 icon at the lower right corner of the screen.

2. On the Page menu, turn off Display Master Items.

On the cover, the banner, date, and column rules are in different positions than on the inside pages, so you will create them specifically for this page rather than using the ones you created on the master page.

3. Create the elements that will appear on the cover of every issue of the newsletter.

Banner: Depth is 5p, beginning at the 4p horizontal ruler guide; Line is None, Fill is 40%.

Logo: Type is 52/46 Helvetica Bold outline, flush left at the second column. Baseline is at 10p6. (On a PC, there is no outline style, so just use Helvetica Bold.)

Note: Outline type appears transparent on-screen but prints opaque. We would have liked the effect of the gray tint showing through the top half of the logo, but it is not easily achieved in PageMaker.

Overline: Type is 18/18 Helvetica Bold, aligned right with the logo; baseline is at 6p.

"S" in upper left: Type is 30 point Aachen Bold reverse, which creates a really fat outline shape. You can substitute 36-point Helvetica Bold reverse; note how thin it looks in comparison to Aachen. The box was created with the round-corner rectangle tool, with a Line of None and a Fill of 60%.

Issue date: Type is 10/12 Helvetica, positioned just below the banner. (Now wouldn't it have been nice to have defined an issue date style when you created the issue date on the master page, and be able to use that style here?)

Forecasts head: The banner is 2p6 deep, beginning at 45p on the horizontal ruler, and extends the width of the wide column; the Fill is Solid. Set an insertion point in the banner; from the Style Palette, select *dept head* and type *Forecasts*. Turn off Snap to Rulers and use the pointer to center the type vertically in the banner.

TIP

To select multiple items, use the pointer tool to drag a selection box around the items. If the items are not adjacent, use this alternative method: Select one item, hold down the Shift key, and select the next item; continue selecting items with the Shift key depressed.

This is the same style you'll use for the "Newsbriefs" and "People" heads on the inside pages, but the banner is too deep to specify it as a paragraph rule, so you can't set the whole unit up as a style. In this situation, the easiest way to ensure consistency is to copy the entire "Forecasts" unit—the banner and the headline—and paste the copy on the pasteboard. When you need to create the other department heads on pages 2 and 3, you can use this pasteboard copy as a master and type the new headlines over the word "Forecasts." It is still useful to have defined and applied a style for this department head. That way, if you change your mind about the specs, you can make one quick change to the style instead of having to change all three headlines on three different pages.

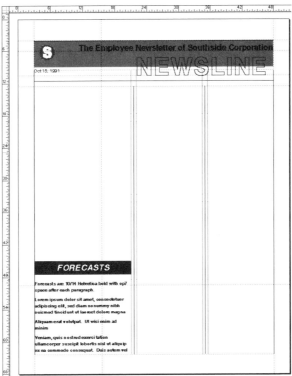

On the cover template, turn off the Display Master Items command and create a new, deeper banner to hold the nameplate. The top of the text margin is lower on the cover than on other pages, so you need customized column rules on this page and a horizontal ruler guide to mark the top of the text block when you pour text. The "Forecasts" text acts as a placeholder: With each issue, you select over the dummy text and type the real text for that issue.

Forecast text: Set an insertion point in the left column at 49p, select the *forecast text* style, and type several lines of dummy text.

Horizontal ruler guide at 12p6: This marks the top of any photos and text blocks on the cover. When you place text, you'll position the top of the loaded text icon at this ruler guide.

Horizontal rule at 11p6: Line weight is .5 pt.

Vertical column rules: Line weight is .5 pt, length is from the 12p6 horizontal guide to the bottom margin.

PAGE 2 TEMPLATE

1. Click on the page 2 icon.

2. Create the "Newsbriefs" column.

- Copy the "Forecasts" banner and headline from the pasteboard, and paste it on page 1. Position it so that it is aligned at the top left margin. Remember that the top margin is that guide at 9p6.

- Select the word "Forecasts" with the text tool, and type *Newsbriefs* over it.

- Bring in a horizontal ruler guide at 15p to mark the top of the "Newsbriefs" text.

3. Create a placeholder for the breakout.

A placeholder is simply an item that you create to define the position for either text or graphics that you'll position on the page each time you produce the publication. Type a single line of dummy text, with its baseline on the 6p horizontal ruler guide, and apply the *breakout* style.

You can't type text placeholders on the master page because you can't type over master page text on regular pages.

4. Copy the breakout and the "Newsbriefs" banner and headline.

You'll be able to paste them directly into position on page 3.

PAGE 3 TEMPLATE

1. Click on the page 3 icon.

2. "Power-paste" the items that you copied from page 2.

Use the tip at left to paste the "Newsbriefs" banner from page 2 in the exact same position on page 3. Then drag over the word "Newsbriefs" and type *People*.

TIP

Using PageMaker's power-paste technique (Option-paste on a Mac, Ctrl-Shift-P on a PC) you can paste a copy in the exact same page position as the original, even if you've turned to another page or spread. (This doesn't work if both pages are visible on the screen.)

3. Create a picture placeholder.

The photos might have different depths each issue, but it's still useful to create a box to serve as a placeholder for the first photo. The top of the box should be 15 points below the bottom of the banner.

4. Create spacing guides.

Spacing guides enable you to maintain consistent space between elements such as photos and captions.

In this project, the distance from the bottom of a photo to the top windowshade handle of the caption below it should be 6 points.

The distance from the baseline of the last line of a caption to the top of the next photo should be 20 points.

To measure this distance, we like to create a short line of text that has the same leading as the desired distance. You could also create a box to measure the distance, but too often you end up with little boxes on the pasteboard and you can't remember which distance any box is supposed to measure.

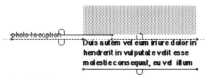

▲ ▲ ▲

For spacing guides, type a line of text and specify its leading equal to the distance you want to measure. When you need to measure that distance, position the spacing guide, bring in ruler guides at the windowshade handles, and align the appropriate text or graphic at the ruler guides.

- Type one line of text that says *photo to caption* and make the type specs something like 10/6 Helvetica.

- Set a new insertion point, type another line that says *caption to photo*, and specify 10/20 Helvetica. In both cases, the critical spec is the leading. But it's a good idea to use a typeface that's already in the document, just to keep things simple.

▶ ▶ ▶

The templates for pages 2 and 3 are very similar, except for the picture placeholder on page 3.

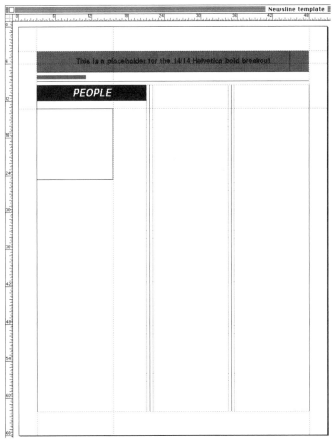

Leave the spacing guides on the pasteboard. Once you've placed and sized your photos in any issue of the newsletter, drag in the "photo to caption" spacing guide so that the top windowshade is aligned with the bottom of the photo. Then drag in a horizontal ruler guide to align with the bottom windowshade. That ruler guide marks the baseline of the first line of the caption. When you've typed the caption, drag in the "caption to photo" spacing guide so that its top windowshade is aligned with the last line of the caption. Drag in another horizontal ruler guide to align with the bottom windowshade. That ruler guide marks the top of the next photo.

PAGE 4 TEMPLATE

1. Click on the page 4 icon.

2. On the Page menu, turn off Display Master Items.

3. Bring in a horizontal ruler guide at 33p.

This bisects the page and indicates where the newsletter will be folded for mailing. The bottom part of the page carries the mailing information; the top part of the page becomes the mailing cover.

4. Create the mailing side, using the following specs.

The banner: Top is 2p6 from fold guide; depth is 5p9; width is across left and center columns; Line is None; Fill is 40%.

Mailing permit: Depth is same as banner; width is 7p aligned at right margin; Type is 9/11 Helvetica, centered. When you do self-mailers, be sure to check the specs for your mailing permit with the Postal Service.

Logo: Type is 42-point Helvetica bold outline (or just bold on a PC); the top arm of the E is aligned with the bottom of the banner; the right margin of type is about 1p in from the edge of the banner.

Subhead: Type is 10/12 Helvetica, aligned left with the logo; baseline is 1p6 below logo.

Return address: Type is same as subhead; baseline of first line is 2p3 below subhead.

Rule: Weight is .5 pt; width is same as banner; position is centered between subhead and return address.

Cap S: Copy the type and box from the cover and paste it in position on the banner here.

5. Create a template for the mailing cover.

The camera-ready art for page 4 should look like the art below, with the top half of the page—the mailing cover—rotated 180°. How you arrive at the camera-ready art depends on whether the format for the mailing

▶ ▶ ▶

The top of page 4 is the mailing cover, which should be oriented upside down on the camera-ready art. You can rotate the text as a single unit in PageMaker, and the blueprint instructions explain how, but it may be more efficient to create and print the text right side up and paste it into position on the camera-ready page. Don't use computer methods when manual pasteup is faster.

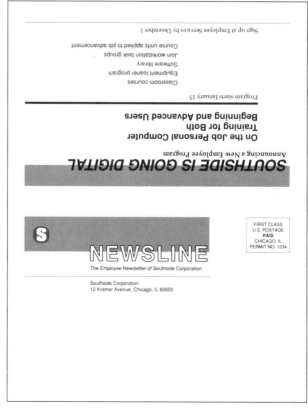

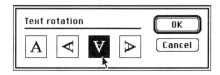

▲ ▲ ▲

*PageMaker can rotate text in 90°
increments. To rotate text, select the
text with the pointer tool, choose
Text Rotation from the Element
menu, and in the dialog box, click on
the icon that shows the desired
orientation. If you select text with the
text tool, the Text Rotation command
will be grayed out.*

TIP

Once you rotate text, it acts like a
graphic in the page layout: You can
select it only with the pointer tool. If
you want to edit copy or change the
type specs, use the pointer tool to
triple-click on the rotated text.
PageMaker will display the text, right
side up, in a story window, where
you can alter the text as needed.
When you return to layout view, the
text will be rotated as before. (For
more information about the Story
Editor, see Project 6.)

cover remains the same from issue to issue. If the cover does remain
pretty much the same, requiring just a few text changes from one issue
to the next, then it's worth the effort to set it up as a single text block
and use PageMaker's Text Rotation option so that the text will be oriented correctly when you print the camera-ready page. When you produce subsequent issues, you'll be able to edit the text in the Story Editor
to make the changes required.

But if the cover format changes every issue, depending on its content,
then it's probably more efficient to create the various components as
individual text blocks, positioned on the page by eye, rather than using
the Paragraph command to specify indents and spacing. You can't
rotate numerous text blocks as a unit, so using this approach you
would print the cover copy oriented right side up and then paste it into
position upside down on the camera-ready page.

We'll give instructions for setting up the cover as a single, rotated text
unit, with the caveat that if this were a one-shot effort, we wouldn't
have taken the time to do it this way.

- Use the Column Guides command to specify 1 column.

- Set an insertion point just below the top margin and type the cover
  copy using the default type style.

- Select lines of text as indicated and specify the following attributes:

    Headline: 30/15 Helvetica bold italic, All Caps, Left Indent 0p6

    Line 2: 14/14 Palatino bold, Left Indent 0p8, Space After 1p6

      Note: The roman type in line 2 is indented a couple of points
      from the left margin of the italic type directly above it so that
      the two will appear visually aligned. The exact amount of the
      indent to achieve this effect depends on the typeface and size.

    Lines 3–5: 18/20 Helvetica bold, Left Indent 5p6

    Line 6: 12/14 Palatino, Left Indent 5p6, Space Before 1p, Space
    After 1p, Paragraph Rule Above: 4 pt, Column Width with 5p6
    Right Indent, positioned 1p6 above baseline

    Lines 7–11: 12/18 Helvetica, Left Indent 19p

    Last line: 12/14 Palatino, Left Indent 5p6, Space Before 1p3,
    Paragraph Rule Below .5 pt, Width of Column, positioned 1p
    below baseline

- With the pointer tool, select the entire text block. From the Element
  menu, choose Text Rotation. In the Text Rotation dialog box, choose
  the upside-down icon.

    When the text is rotated, the top of the headline might be clipped off
    and might not display even when you refresh the screen. But it will
    print correctly.

- With the pointer tool, position the text so that the rule below the last
  line is on the 3p6 horizontal guide.

- Turn on Display Master Items and draw a rectangle the same size as
  the gray rectangle now displayed at the top of the page. Then turn

TIP

Gray fills in PageMaker are opaque. If you want type to print over a gray graphic, send the graphic to the back (Command-B on a Mac, Ctrl-B on a PC).

off Display Master Items. Specify a Line of None and a Fill of 40% for the rectangle. Because you can't see the top of the headline on the screen, you might have to go through a few printouts to get a tidy alignment of the banner and the type. We liked the way it looked when the banner aligned with the arms of the G's in the words "Going Digital."

IMPORTANT: Each time you reposition the gray banner, be sure to send it to the back layer; otherwise, it will cover up part of the headline instead of printing behind it.

6. Save and close the template.

The template now has all the elements you'll need each time you produce the newsletter.

FORMATTING TEXT IN A WORD PROCESSOR

If you are starting electronic page layout with version 4.0 of PageMaker, you might think that its powerful text-editing capabilities have replaced the need for a word processor. And if you're on a tight budget you can indeed *get by* with only Page-Maker's Story Editor. But a good word processor is still a key player in serious desktop publishing.

Import Filters

PageMaker has import filters for many word processors. If you're not sure whether a filter has been installed for your word processor, hold down the Command key on a Mac and choose About Page-Maker from the Apple menu; on a PC, hold down the Ctrl key and choose About PageMaker from the Help menu. If the filter isn't installed, use the Installer program on the Mac or run the Setup program on the PC.

When you import files from Microsoft Word, Word for Windows, or WordPerfect, holding down the Shift key while you select the name of the file to be imported prompts PageMaker to display a special dialog box for that import filter. The dialog box shown is for Microsoft Word on the Mac; the options in the dialog box vary depending on the filter.

If you import a text-only file, PageMaker displays the Smart ASCII Import Filter dialog box, which has options for the automatic removal of extra carriage returns and Spacebar characters. If you get a file full of carriage returns instead of paragraph spacing and Spacebar characters instead of tabs, consider saving the file as text-only and use this filter to have Page-Maker do the cleanup.

```
┌─────────────────────────────────────────────┐
│ Smart ASCII import filter, v1.2      ┌──OK──┐│
│                                      └──────┘│
│ Remove extra carriage returns:      ┌Cancel┐│
│   ☐ At end of every line            └──────┘│
│   ☐ Between paragraphs                        │
│   ☐ But keep tables, lists and indents as is  │
│ ☐ Replace 3 or more spaces with a tab         │
│ ☐ Monospace, import as Courier                │
│ ☒ No conversion, import as is                 │
└─────────────────────────────────────────────┘
```

Word-Processor Files

If efficiency is a main concern when you produce a newsletter such as the one in this project, you would want to create at least two word-processor files, one for the stories and one for the "Newsbriefs" items.

```
┌──────────────────────────────────────────────┐
│ Microsoft Word 4.0 import filter, v2.0  ┌─OK─┐│
│                                         └────┘│
│ ☒ Import table of contents entries    ┌Cancel┐│
│    ● From .c. paragraphs              └──────┘│
│    ○ From outline                             │
│ ☒ Import index entries                        │
│                                               │
│ Import condensed/expanded spacing as          │
│    ● Set width                                │
│    ○ Manual kerning                           │
│    ○ Track kerning                            │
│ ☒ Import page break before paragraph          │
│    ● As page break before                     │
│    ○ As column break before                   │
└──────────────────────────────────────────────┘
```

USING THE NEWSLINE TEMPLATE

1. Open a copy of the template.

When you open a file that you've saved as a template, PageMaker opens an untitled copy of the original. It's a good habit to save it right away under whatever name you'll be using for the file, such as Newsline 10/91 (or NWS10-91 if you are using a PC).

2. Change the issue date.

On the master page and the cover, type the current issue date over the placeholder. It's easy to forget this, so do it first thing each issue.

(If the stories are written in different files, you would want them combined in a single file before placing them in PageMaker.) The "Forecasts" text and the captions could originate in a word processor or in PageMaker.

If your word processor has style sheets, you would want to tag each paragraph with the style name used in the PageMaker file. It really doesn't matter what the style definition is in the word processor. When you place the word-processor file in PageMaker, if the file contains a style that has the exact same name as a style defined in the PageMaker style sheet, the PageMaker style definition overrides the word-processor style definition. So you can format your body text in a font that is easy to read on-screen, but if you tag it with the style name *body text*, and the PageMaker document has a style named *body text* defined as 10/12 Palatino, when you place the file in PageMaker, the body text will be 10/12 Palatino. The writer or the person preparing the word-processor file doesn't even need to know what the PageMaker formatting is; he or she just needs to know which paragraphs are headlines, subheads, body text, and so on. And generally, the writer knows that better than anyone else.

If your word processor does not have style sheets, you can still tag paragraphs with style names to match the PageMaker styles. At the beginning of each paragraph, type the style name in angle brackets (<>). The tags must be at the beginning of the paragraph; any paragraph without a tag is formatted with the style for the previous paragraph. When you place a document that is marked with

bracketed tags, be sure to check the Read Tags option in PageMaker's Place dialog box.

PC Filename Extensions

If you work on a PC, or if you work on a Mac and need to place files created in a PC program, the filenames must have the correct filename extensions for PageMaker to recognize them: for example, .WP5 for WordPerfect 5.0 and 5.1, .XY3 for XyWrite III Plus, .RTF for Microsoft Rich Text Format, .DCA for programs that create Document Content Architecture files, and .TXT for ASCII files.

Why Create Style Sheets in a Word Processor and in PageMaker?

You might wonder why you need to define styles in both your word processor and PageMaker. For one thing, some type attributes in PageMaker may not have counterparts in your word processor: tracking, letterspacing and word spacing, and paragraph rules, to name a few. To incorporate those attributes into your styles, you have to define the style sheet in PageMaker.

Equally important is the reality of production. When you're up against a deadline, you end up doing a lot of things in PageMaker that ideally should have been done in the word processor. Styles will save the day when push comes to shove—as it often does in publication work.

Finally, if more than one person works in the page layout for a publication, styles will minimize the chaos each player leaves behind for the others.

3. Place the body text from your word-processor file.

We'll use the Copy Fit file described in the introduction to Project 2. And for an introduction to placing text, see the sidebar on page 242 in that same project.

- Decide which text-flow mode you will use: manual, automatic, or semi-automatic.

  Autoflow is a great timesaver because PageMaker automatically reloads the text icon at the bottom of each column and starts pouring text into the next column. We'll use that here, so choose Autoflow from the Options menu.

- Choose Place from the File menu (Command-D on a Mac, Ctrl-D on a PC). When the Place dialog box comes on-screen, scroll through your folders to select the Copy Fit file. On the Mac, it's in the Aldus PageMaker folder; on the PC, in \PM4\TEMPLATE\PSCRIPT or \PM4\TEMPLATE\PCL, depending on your printer.

- Set the insertion point in the center column at the 12p6 horizontal guide, and click. As you get to page 3, be ready to cancel so that the

WHERE DOES AUTOFLOW FLOW?

By observing where PageMaker does and does not flow text when you place the Copy Fit file in step 3, you'll learn some of the fine points of Autoflow. To expedite the explanation, we'll forego chronological order of the newsletter pages and also insert some alternative situations.

- Pages 2 and 3: PageMaker skips the column with "Newsbriefs" and "People" heads. As soon as PageMaker encounters text in a column, it skips to the next column. Compare that situation to the next three scenarios.

- If there were no text in the banner, PageMaker would skip over the graphic and begin flowing text immediately following it.

- If the banner were gray, and without any text, PageMaker would flow text over the banner.

- If you had defined a text wrap around the banner on the master page (or on the regular page if you'd created the banner there), then PageMaker would have poured the text in that column on the regular page, observing the text wrap, regardless of whether there was text in the banner or not. In effect, the text wrap would have been a signal that said "Don't flow text here, but do flow it there." With text in the banner but no text

wrap defined around it, the signal is "Don't flow text anywhere."

- Page 1, column 3: The text starts slightly above the ruler guide, and the explanation is a little complicated. If you select the word "Newsline" with the pointer tool, and pull in a ruler guide at the bottom windowshade, you'll see that that's exactly where the top of the text poured in. Because the word "Newsline" begins outside the image area, PageMaker seems to interpret the word as if it were a graphic, with the bottom of the leading being in effect the bottom of the graphic.

The ruler guide at 12p6 has nothing to do with the text flow unless you manually position the text icon there; Autoflow is not affected by ruler guides the way it is by the top margin. The only solution is a manual one: Select the text block with the pointer tool and lower the top windowshade so it is aligned at the 12p6 guideline.

An alternative approach in a situation like this is to use semi-automatic text flow for the first two columns. Hold down the Shift key when the Autoflow icon appears, and keep it depressed until you've poured text in the first two columns; when you release the Shift key, the Autoflow icon reappears.

Composing text. Cancel

▲ ▲ ▲

When the Autoflow text icon comes on-screen, WAIT! Autoflow is fast, and it can make you feel as though you're on an express train racing past your destination. Keep in mind two ways to interrupt the flow once it's begun. One is to click Cancel in the Composing Text status box that appears while text is flowing. When columns are racing by, it's sometimes easier to press Command-period on a Mac, Ctrl-period on a PC; but with this technique it takes a few columns for the cancel to take effect. (The Macintosh manual says you can cancel by clicking the mouse button, but you can't.)

text won't continue pouring onto page 4. If you don't cancel the place, PageMaker will continue adding pages until the entire file is placed. If that happens, just use the Remove Pages command on the Page menu to delete all pages added following page 4, and delete the text that poured onto page 4.

4. Style the body text.

- Bring the Style Palette on-screen, if it isn't already (Command-Y on a Mac, Ctrl-Y on a PC).

- Select all the text (set an insertion point anywhere in the text and press Command-A on a Mac, Ctrl-A on a PC).

  When you use the Select All command to select text that you want to reformat, the entire text file is selected—even text that has not yet been placed on the page

- Click on the *body text* style in the Style Palette.

- You wouldn't have to do this with a real text file, but there are no paragraphs in the Copy Fit file, so go ahead now and insert carriage returns at irregular intervals of 50 or 100 or 125 words.

5. Add and style the headlines and subheads.

Again, in the real world the headlines probably would have been part of the text file. But it's not uncommon to add headlines to the Page-Maker layout, and here's how you do it.

- Set an insertion point at the beginning of the line that you want the headline to precede. Type the headline, or a dummy headline, and insert a carriage return.

USING THE NEW-LINE CHARACTER IN HEADLINES

When you want to force a line break, without creating a new paragraph and all the formatting that comes with it, insert a new-line character. The example here demonstrates its usefulness in headlines. It's also useful in tabular copy, and in forcing line breaks for better type color in justified text.

About the move to 35 Miller Avenue

The line breaks in headlines are important, for both editorial clarity and visual balance. For example, you wouldn't want a line break between the street number and street name in the headline above.

About the move to

35 Miller Avenue

If you insert a carriage return to force a line break, you'll create a new paragraph, with all the formatting associated with the previous paragraph (or with the Next Style if one is defined).

About the move to 35 Miller Avenue

Instead, insert a new-line character (Shift-Return or Shift-Enter). The new line is part of the same paragraph as the previous line, so you avoid repeating the paragraph formatting or changing to the Next Style.

TIP

As you add headlines, watch how the additional lines force text from the bottom of the column you're typing in to the top of the next column. For a detailed look at the behavior of threaded text, see the sidebar beginning on page 284.

- After you insert the carriage return, set an insertion point in the headline and click on *story head* in the Style Palette.

- Continue inserting headlines every column and a half or so, and apply the *story head* style. Try adding a headline toward the bottom of a column and watch how the "Keeps" options that you specified as part of the headline style forces the headline to the next column.

- Add a subhead or two, and apply the subhead style.

6. Style the first paragraph following a headline or subhead.

- Set an insertion point in each paragraph following a story head or subhead, and click on *body first*.

- Continue this throughout the newsletter.

You may wonder why you have to go through this step if you've defined *body first* as the Next Style for heads and subheads. The Next Style option works only when you type text directly in PageMaker, which you did if you worked through the sidebar on style sheets beginning on page 265. But when you style existing text, as in steps 4–6, Page-Maker can't apply the Next Style retroactively.

7. Add the art on the first page.

The wide column on page 1 is an ideal place for art—a photo, a chart, or any other visual. The art can be sized to any width within the column. The caption width, however, extends only 12p6 (to the 15p6 vertical guideline), forcing you to have some white space in the column. If you don't have any art, you could start the text in the left-hand column, or leave the column blank above the "Forecasts" box.

For an explanation of how to place graphics, see the sidebar on the facing page.

8. Place the "Newsbriefs" text on page 2.

Presumably, the "Newsbriefs" have been written in a separate word-processor file, so they won't be threaded to the rest of the stories. We'll use the Copy Fit file again. Remember that Autoflow is still turned on; when the loaded text icon appears, hold down the Command key (Ctrl on a PC) to temporarily invoke the manual text mode. That way, you can place the text only in the one column designated for "Newsbriefs." There will be more text to place, but for this project you can ignore that.

- Click the loaded text icon at the 15p horizontal guide.

- Select all the text and apply the *news text* style.

- You'll need to add paragraph breaks because there aren't any in the Copy Fit file. When you do, you might be puzzled by the apparent lack of styling. That's because we defined the space between news items as the space before and after the graphic divider, which you will be adding next. If "Newsbriefs" were to run longer than a single

HOW TO PLACE GRAPHICS IN PAGEMAKER

Placing graphics is very similar to placing text (described in Project 2). You choose Place from the File menu (Command-D on a Mac, Ctrl-D on a PC) and scroll through your folders or directories to locate the name of the file you want to place. If the file-name you click on is a graphic, the Place dialog box will give you the following options:

As Independent Graphic: PageMaker adds the graphic to the publication. If this option is grayed out, it means that the image you selected is in a file format that PageMaker doesn't recognize. Very often, you can open that file in the program used to create it and save it in a format PageMaker does recognize. For example, Image Studio normally saves in RIFF format, which PageMaker doesn't recognize. But if you open that RIFF file in Image Studio and use the Save As Other command, you can save the file in TIFF format, which PageMaker does recognize. In some instances, you can copy and paste the graphic through the Clipboard.

Replacing Entire Graphic: If you select a graphic in the PageMaker layout before choosing Place, and then choose this option in the Place dialog box, PageMaker will replace the existing graphic with the one being placed. This technique is useful when you create a box to indicate the position of art in the layout and then want to replace the box with the actual art. You can also use it to place a revision of art that is already in the layout.

Note that when you use this option, the art that you are placing will be sized with the proportions of the art it is replacing. If that distorts the art, simply hold down the Shift key and drag slightly on any selection handle.

As an Inline Graphic: If you set an insertion point with the text tool before choosing Place, this option is selected by default and PageMaker places the graphic at the insertion point. The graphic will be embedded in the text, so if the text moves the graphic moves with it. For more on inline graphics, see page 301.

How to Drag-Place a Graphic

You can drag a bounding box to define the size of a graphic you're about to place, just as you do with text. Position the loaded graphic icon where you want the upper left corner of the graphic to begin, press the mouse button, and drag the cursor diagonally to the desired size. When you release the mouse button, PageMaker places the graphic in the area you defined. Very often this distorts the original proportions of the graphic, but again, you can undo the distortion by selecting the graphic, holding down the Shift key, and dragging slightly on any handle. This technique is a real timesaver with large graphics because it allows you to keep the placed image within the page view so that you don't have to scroll or change page views to resize it.

How to Place an Image from the Scrapbook (Macintosh Only)

In the Place dialog box, scroll to the Systems folder and select the Scrapbook. When you click OK, the loaded graphic icon displays a number that indicates the number of items in the Scrapbook. The last item pasted into the Scrapbook will be the first item placed. After you place the first item, the loaded icon reappears. If you don't want to place another item, click the pointer anywhere in the Toolbox to cancel the Place operation.

TIPS

If the graphic you place is larger than 50 KB, Page-Maker displays a message box alerting you to the size and asking if you want to "Include complete copy in the publication anyway?" If you choose No, PageMaker places a low-resolution screen image in the publication and links it to the original graphic file. If you choose Yes, PageMaker places the actual graphic in the publication, and you have a much larger and perhaps slower file.

When you place a graphic and find that you can't move it with the pointer tool, you've inadvertently placed it as an inline graphic. This happens to us more than we'd like to admit. The reason? You don't notice that there's an active insertion point when you go to place a graphic; you race through the dialog box at a speed-demon pace and don't notice that the inline graphic option is selected, so you end up with an inline instead of an independent graphic. It's a nuisance, but it's easy enough to fix: Select the graphic with the pointer tool, cut it to the Clipboard, be sure there's no insertion point in the text, and paste. The graphic will be pasted as an independent graphic.

TIP

A style applies to an entire paragraph, and you can't have two styles in the same paragraph. So if you apply the *news divider* style to the "vvv" characters before inserting a carriage return, you'll turn the entire paragraph, body text and all, into Zapf Dingbats. You can't undo a style change with the Undo command, but it's easy enough to fix: Insert the carriage return after the characters that are supposed to be Dingbats, and reapply the *news text* style to that paragraph.

paragraph, you'd need some additional paragraph formatting as part of the style.

- At the beginning of each news item paragraph except the first one, type *vvv* and insert a carriage return. Apply the *news divider* style to each "vvv" paragraph and watch the text format itself perfectly.

9. Create the "People" column on page 3.

- If you have scanned photos in your files that you can use in this project, place them now. See the sidebar "How to Place Graphics in PageMaker" on the previous page.

  The photos can be sized any width within the column. If all the pictures are single portraits, it's probably best to size them all the same. But you could run a single portrait to a 10p width, a group of two to a 13p width, and a larger group shot to the full 18p measure. If you do size them differently, make sure there is at least a 2- or 3-pica difference between the sizes so that the difference looks intentional.

- If you don't have any scanned photos, proceed as if the printer were stripping in conventional halftones: Create boxes on the page to indicate the size and position of each photo. On your camera-ready art, you would need to indicate whether or not the box rules print around the photo.

  For an explanation of sizing and cropping graphics once you have placed them, see the sidebar on page 336.

- Type the caption for each photo, and apply the *caption* style.

- Use the spacing guides that you created as part of the template (see page 272) to position the captions relative to the photos.

10. Update the mailing cover.

- Turn to page 4.

- With the pointer tool, triple-click on the rotated text to open that text in a story window.

- Use the Story Editor to make text changes to the mailing cover. For example, drag over the second line and type *Don't forget to sign up.* When you're done, press Command-E on a Mac, Ctrl-E on a PC.

- PageMaker returns to layout view. The text is in the rotated position with the changes you made in the Story Editor.

An explanation of the behavior of threaded text begins on the following spread. Following that lengthy sidebar, you'll find some additional logo treatments created with PageMaker tools.

USING PAGEMAKER'S EXPORT FEATURE

When you place a text file in PageMaker, the original document remains intact. Changes, additions, and deletions that you make in the layout are not incorporated into the original word-processor file. This can be very reassuring, especially to beginners: If you mess up the text while assembling the pages, you can simply place the original source file again and start over.

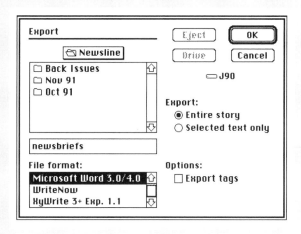

But there are times when you want the changes made in PageMaker to be incorporated into the original file or to be saved as a new text file. Perhaps you've made some editorial changes in PageMaker and need to send the copy back to a writer or client for further work, and you don't want to lose the changes made so far. Or perhaps you've written captions in the layout that you'd like to incorporate into a presentation. Or you might just want to archive the final text from the page layout as a word-processor file.

In these situations, use the Export command to save the text as a word-processor or text-only document.

To export an entire story, set an insertion point anywhere in the story, choose Export from the File menu, and when the Export dialog box comes on-screen, click the Entire Story option. (An "entire story" is a series of threaded text blocks. For more information about threaded text blocks, see the sidebar beginning on the following page.)

To export part of a story, select the text with the text tool and click the Selected Text Only option in the Export dialog box.

In the Export dialog box, select the name of your word-processing program from the File Format box. The exported document will retain any local and style formatting applied in PageMaker that your word processor recognizes. You'll lose formatting such as reverse type, letterspacing and word spacing, tracking, and paragraph rules that have no counterparts in your word processor. But if you place the exported file back in the same PageMaker document—with the full style definitions—the lost formatting will be restored. If you place the exported file in a new PageMaker docu-

ment without the full style definitions, you won't regain the lost formatting. And in both cases you'll lose typographic refinements such as tracking and kerning.

If you are exporting text to a word processor that doesn't support styles, select the Export Tags option. PageMaker will export the styles as bracketed tags embedded in the text, and there's a good chance that the style formatting will be retained when you place the document back in PageMaker. But you may lose local formatting such as italic and boldface.

If there's no export filter for your word processor, see if your program can accept DCA/RFT or RTF files. If so, try exporting PageMaker text using one of those formats. RTF is preferable because it transfers graphics as well as text.

If you don't know which word processor is being used by the person who will work on the exported file, select the Text Only or the ASCII Text filter in the File Format box. The file will be readable by most word processors, but the formatting will be lost.

If the story you are exporting is linked to an external source file, the name of that file appears in the name field in the Export dialog box. If you don't want the exported text to replace the source file, type a new name in the name field. (For more about linked files, see page 216.)

DEMYSTIFYING THREADED TEXT

The apparent eccentricities of threaded text are at first both baffling and frustrating. Until you understand the basic mechanics of this feature, text seems to move around a page and within a document as if it had a mind of its own.

What Is Threaded Text?

When you place a word-processor file, flowing various text blocks as you move from one column and page to another, every text block in that file is threaded to the one before and the one following it. When you add or delete text within a threaded file, the line-count change "ripples" through to the other text blocks in the file.

There are three ways to determine whether one text block is threaded to another.

1. Look at the symbols in the selection handles.

An open box in the top windowshade handle ⌂ indicates the beginning of a text file.

An arrow in the bottom handle ▼ indicates that there is more of the story to be placed.

A plus sign in the top handle ⊞ indicates that the text is threaded to another text block before this one.

A plus sign in the bottom handle ⊞ indicates that the text is threaded to another text block after this one.

An empty loop in the bottom handle ⊔ indicates the end of the story.

2. Use the Select All command.

Set an insertion point in the text and choose Select All from the Edit menu (Command-A on a Mac, Ctrl-A on a PC). All the threaded text within that story will be highlighted.

3. Use the Story Editor.

If you're real confused about the order of threaded text blocks—and it can happen—the Story Editor provides the most straightforward answer. Select any text block in the story with either the text tool or the pointer tool, and choose Edit Story from the Edit menu (Command-E on a Mac, Ctrl-E on a PC). PageMaker displays a word-processor–style story window with the entire story; you can scroll up and down the window to see the order of the para-

graphs. (For a detailed look at the Story Editor, see Project 6.)

PageMaker gives you tremendous flexibility in moving text around a publication without losing the correct order of the paragraphs. This flexibility may be confusing to beginners, but it gives more experienced users a lot of power. The best way to understand this flexibility is to look at some examples.

Adding Lines to a Text Block

To see what happens when you add lines to one text block in a threaded story, let's look at a paragraph of text that we've created as a single story running across three columns.

When we add text to the first column (we've used a familiar text in the example, with apologies to Lewis Carroll), note the ripple effect in the other two columns.

1. We created this paragraph as a single story placed in three columns. Each column is threaded to the others.

2. Adding text to the first column pushes an equivalent amount of text from the bottom of the first column to the top of the second, and from the bottom of the second column to the top of the third. The arrow in the bottom windowshade handle of the third column indicates that there is more text to be placed: The last two lines in that column have in effect been pushed forward into PageMaker's memory. You can restore them to the page either by pulling that last windowshade handle down or by clicking in the arrow and placing the text elsewhere on the page.

In the newsletter in this project, we recommended that you place the stories that run continuously on pages 1–3 from a single word-processor file so that the text in those six columns would be threaded.

And we recommended that you create the text for "Newsbriefs" in a separate word-processor file so that when you placed that file in PageMaker it would not be threaded to the other stories. If you were to add four lines to the text in the third column on page 1, the last four lines in that column would be pushed back to the second column on page 2 because that's where the thread leads. The ripple would not affect the first column on page 2, where the "Newsbriefs" story has been placed, because the text in those two columns isn't threaded.

Deleting Lines from a Text Block

When you delete copy from threaded text, the principle is the same as when you add text, but lines are pulled back instead of pushed forward.

1. Again, we have a single story placed in three columns.

2. This time, we deleted text from the first column, so an equivalent amount of text is pulled back from the second column to the first, and from the third column to the second.

Changing the Depth of a Text Block

Let's say you've already placed text on a page and you want to make room at the top of one column for a graphic. Simply select the text in that column with the pointer tool and drag the top windowshade handle down to the position where you want the text to begin. You won't have to adjust the bottom of the column; the text that no longer fits will be forced to the beginning of the next threaded column, and so on throughout the story.

Similarly, if you want to make room at the bottom of a page for some other element, select the text and raise the bottom windowshade handle.

1. Let's say you've poured a long text file and find that you have room for art on several of the pages. How do you change the depth of a text block to open up room for the art, without repouring the entire story? Let's look first at creating space at the top of a column—say, the center column in the example shown above.

2. Select the column in which you want to place the art, and drag the top windowshade handle down…

3. The top of the text block in that column is pulled down, leaving a hole…

4. And you can insert the graphic in the space you've opened up.

Continues on following page

THREADED TEXT *(continued)*

Breaking a Text Block Apart

Now suppose you want to add a graphic in the middle of one of the columns. You can easily open up space for the graphic by breaking the text block apart so that there are two text blocks in the column, with a space between them for the art.

1. To make room for a graphic in the middle of a column of text: Drag the bottom windowshade handle up to where you want the last line of text before the art.

2. Click on the plus sign in the bottom handle of the text block that you just shortened.

3. Click the loaded text icon where you want the text to begin below the art.

4. Insert the art. The thread now runs from the text block above the art to the text block below the art to the top of the next column. If you add copy to the text above the art, lines from that text block will be pushed forward to the text block below.

If you need to change the space for the picture, simply change the depth of a surrounding text block by dragging the windowshade handle up or down.

Eliminating a Text Block Without Deleting Text

You say you want to open up an entire column for a graphic or a sidebar? Piece of cake.

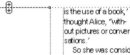

1. To open up an entire column within a threaded story—for a graphic or a sidebar or any other element—drag the bottom windowshade handle in that column up to the top handle.

2. All the text in that column will be forced to the next column, and every subsequent column will be similarly pushed forward.

3. Insert the graphic.

Note that this procedure is quite different from selecting the text block and choosing Cut, Delete, or Clear, any of which would eliminate the text from the layout, rather than force it to the next text block.

Recombining Text Blocks

Let's look again at the example of art in the middle of a column of text. What if you want to delete the graphic and fill in that hole with text? Simply delete the graphic and eliminate the text block that was below the graphic by using the technique just described. Then expand the text block that was above the graphic to fill the column.

1. To delete a graphic and recombine the text blocks above and below it into a single text block…

2. Eliminate the bottom text block by dragging the bottom windowshade handle up until it touches the top one…

3. Extend the top text block by dragging its bottom windowshade handle down…

4. The text will fill in the column.

Note: If you expand the top text block before eliminating the bottom one, you'll end up with a mess of overlapping text blocks. You can still eliminate the bottom text block at that point, but it's more difficult to determine which handles belong to which text block when, in effect, there's a double exposure on-screen.

Adding Threaded Text Between Existing Text Blocks

Sometimes a column opens up in the middle of a story, and you need to fill the column with already placed text from that threaded story. Here's how:

1. Say you want to remove a graphic (or other element) from the center column and fill that column with text from the threaded story. Delete the graphic.

2. Then select the text in the column that precedes the deleted graphic, and click on the bottom windowshade handle…

3. When the loaded text icon appears, click in the empty column.

4. The text from the column following the deleted graphic fills in the hole, and text from subsequent columns is pulled forward accordingly.

Continues on following page

THREADED TEXT (continued)

Understanding the principle at work when you fill in a column in this way will keep you from panicking if a loaded text icon appears on-screen when you aren't trying to place text. You've inadvertently clicked on the bottom windowshade handle of a text block, and PageMaker thinks you want to place existing text in a new position. Cancel the place by clicking on any tool in the Toolbox.

Unthreading Text

To unthread text from a story, use the text tool to select the text you want to unthread, cut it, set an insertion point anywhere *outside* the threaded file, and paste the text that you cut.

For example, say you decide to cut a sentence from a story and use it as a photo caption at the bottom of a column. Select the text, cut it, and then paste it in the bottom of the column under the space reserved for the photo. Because this text was pasted outside the threaded file, the caption will not be affected by changes you make to the threaded text. Obviously, this is desirable; you don't want your caption bouncing around the page, and you don't want text from the main story popping up, midsentence, where a caption should be.

You can use this technique for longer text elements, too, such as a self-contained sidebar or department, like the "Newsbriefs" text in this project. If that self-contained element is created as part of the word-processor file for another story, just use the text tool to cut it from the main story, and paste it elsewhere in the document.

To look at another situation: In creating the files for this book, we generally typed the tips in the same word-processor file as the instructions. When we placed the text in PageMaker, we'd see the tip in the wide column, delete it with the text tool, and paste it in the narrow column adjacent to the procedure it referred to.

Or consider a publication with numerous art credits that are to run on the page with the art. The person responsible for generating the text file for the credits could create a single word-processor file. The person responsible for the layout could place that credits file on the pasteboard, and cut and paste each

credit into the appropriate position. The original file doesn't even appear in the document; all its elements have been cut and pasted as individual text blocks, unconnected to each other or to any other text block in the PageMaker file.

The key in each of these situations is that when you paste the text you want to unthread, you set the insertion point outside of any other text block.

Threading Unlinked Text

Layout and editorial changes often require that loose text, such as a caption or a tip, be incorporated into the main story. In these situations, cut the text that you want to thread, set an insertion point in the threaded file, and paste.

When you want to place new text in the thread of an existing PageMaker story, set an insertion point where you want the new text inserted, choose Place, and in the Place dialog box select the Inserting Text option.

Moving Threaded Text from One Page to Another

To move a text block from one page or spread to another, while retaining the thread to other text blocks in the story, use the pointer tool to select the text block you want to move, drag it to the pasteboard, change pages, and drag the text into position on the new page. If you cut the text block to the Clipboard and paste it onto the new page, the text will lose its thread to other text in the story. To see what we mean, select any text block that has a plus in the top and bottom windowshade handles. Select it with the pointer tool, and then cut and paste it. When you select the text block you just pasted, the top and bottom windowshade handles are empty, signifying that there's no text before or after.

To better understand the behavior of threaded text, open a new PageMaker document and define three or four columns. Place any file that's handy, and then play with the windowshade handles. Raise them, lower them, add text, delete text, break text blocks apart, and watch how the changes ripple through the threaded blocks. It may help to number each paragraph. If you get confused, close the file and try again later. You really will get the hang of it.

LOGO VARIATIONS

Logos, nameplates, and title banners come in all shapes, sizes, and styles. Whether cleverly conceived and carefully rendered or hackneyed and sloppily executed, the title treatment is inextricably linked to the way we perceive a publication. The bold outline used for the newsletter in this project is a very simple solution for a nameplate banner. Here are a few other ideas using only PageMaker's type and graphics. Using any of these variations would require adjusting the space allowed for the nameplate and the position of other elements in it.

In this first example, we used Page-Maker's power-paste feature to evenly space eight 1-point horizontal rules through the height of the letters. We drew the lines in black and then turned them all to reverse. This treatment gives a distinctive news-bulletin look to the otherwise plain

60-point Helvetica Bold type. If you create a logo such as this on a Macintosh, make an Encapsulated PostScript file of it (see page 358 for instructions) so that you can place the logo as a single object and avoid having those loose 1-point rules on the page.

This second treatment uses the same 60-point Helvetica Bold type, this time with the Track set to Very Loose and the Type Style specified

as Shadow (not available in PC Page-Maker) and Reverse. The box has a 4-point rule with a diagonal pattern from the Fill menu.

In this last example, the 60-point Helvetica is italic, reversed out of a 6-pica-deep black banner with a 1p3-deep 40%-black box through

the center. You will need to use the Bring to Front and Send to Back commands when you layer elements in a logo such as this.

NEWSLETTER VARIATIONS USING ADDITIONAL PAGEMAKER TECHNIQUES

*T*he format used in the newsletter created in Project 4 lends itself to many layout variations, some of which demonstrate PageMaker techniques that aren't included in other projects. The explanations for these variations don't always follow the precise step-by-step format used elsewhere in this section, but you should be able to get plenty of hands-on practice from the information provided. Consider this an opportunity to explore additional techniques, including some advanced features, without having to create a new publication from scratch.

You'll want to begin by opening a copy of the *Newsline* publication that you created in Project 4. As you work through the various techniques, use the file management methods described on the facing page.

The last variation shows the same basic grid used in Project 4 further developed for an international conference program. The appearance of this program, and the variety of material it includes, is quite different from that of the newsletter. The point of this, and really of all the variations in this project, is that a grid has tremendous flexibility. In fact, the challenge of using electronic templates, such as the ones that are included with PageMaker 4.0, is adapting them to suit the nature of the text and graphics in a given publication.

PAGEMAKER TECHNIQUES YOU WILL LEARN

▶ File management techniques

▶ Two-column headlines

▶ Adapting clip art

▶ Setting tabular material

▶ Working with inline graphics

▶ Three techniques for creating drop caps

▶ A modular format

▶ "Eyebrow" headlines

▶ Using a leading grid

FILE MANAGEMENT TECHNIQUES

To some extent, the process of exploring variations in this project simulates the way you work when you develop a format—experimenting with different layout and style possibilities as a publication takes shape. Keep in mind the following file management options available in PageMaker.

Open a Copy of a File

To explore the techniques in this project, you'll want to begin with a copy of the *Newsline* publication that you created in Project 4. To open a copy of an existing publication, simply click on the Copy button in the Open dialog box. PageMaker will open an untitled copy, which you can then save under a new name.

Save Under a Different Name

If you've developed some design ideas that you like, and you want to try a different direction, save the publication twice. First, save the publication in its current form. Then do a Save As under a different name to begin developing some new directions.

Revert

The Revert command on the File menu functions as a sort of multiple undo, deleting all the changes made since the last time you saved. When you're developing a format, save whenever you've got something you want to keep. Then you can experiment freely, using the Revert command to erase a direction that didn't work out.

Mini-Revert

PageMaker performs an invisible mini-save of your publication every time you turn to a new page, add or delete pages, change the page setup, switch between layout and story views, or print. To restore the publication to the last mini-save, hold down the Shift key when you choose Revert.

Power Paste

In developing a format, you may want to work on the same page over and over so you can easily compare different versions of your design. To do this, use the pointer tool to draw a marquee around all the elements on a page; copy them, and then turn to

a new page. On a Mac, press Option-Command-V; on a PC, press Ctrl-Shift-P. PageMaker will paste all the elements on the new page in the exact same positions they were in on the original page.

If you are working on facing pages and both pages are in view, PageMaker will paste the copy directly on top of the original. In that case, while the elements of the copy remain selected, hold down the Shift key and drag them horizontally to the facing page. With Snap to Guides turned on, the copy will snap to the appropriate guidelines.

Compress Files with the Save As Command

The ability to revert and mini-revert results in large files because PageMaker is constantly saving versions of your publication so that they will be available to you whenever you want. When you choose Save As from the File menu, PageMaker deletes all this backup information, compressing your file so it takes up less memory.

It's a good idea to do a Save As from time to time. At the very least, do this at the end of each work session, and certainly before sending a file to a service center. Try performing a Save As to speed up response time and as a general trouble-shooting technique as well.

Crash Recovery

In the event of a system crash, PageMaker saves its last mini-save of your publication. When you open the file after restarting, you should find all the changes since the last time you turned the page or performed one of the other functions that prompts a mini-save.

If your file was untitled, Macintosh PageMaker saves a temporary version in your system folder, named PMFOO. The PC version of PageMaker saves the file in your root directory (usually C:\). The filenames vary on a PC but take the form ~PM4133E.TMP. Open that temporary file, save it under whatever name you want, and bless the folks at Aldus for this feature. Even if the file was titled, save it before closing or you might lose the changes made between the last time you saved and the crash-recovered mini-save.

▶ *Two-column headlines*

▶ *Contents listing*

▶ *Adapting clip art*

The silhouetted shape of the line art in the wide column takes advantage of the grid's asymmetry.

A two-column headline gives added emphasis to that story. It also adds visual interest to the page because it breaks the grid and, being larger in point size, has a different "color" than the one-column heads.

The style for two-column heads is based on the *story head* style used in Project 4, with these changes: Type 18/20; Paragraph Space After 0p9, minus the Paragraph Rule. The top of the headline is aligned at the 12p6 horizontal guide, as it was in the master blueprint.

The Employee Newsletter of Southside Corporation

NEWSLINE

Oct 15, 1991

The Southside Wonders did it again. See page 3 for a report of this year's champions.

Two-Column Heads Are 18/20 Helvetica Bold with Initial Caps

Imsep pretu tempu revol bileg rokam revoc tephe rosve etepe tenov sindu turqu brevt elliu repar tiuve tamia queso utage udulc vires humus fallo 25deu Anetn bisre freun carmi avire ingen umque miher muner veris adest duner veris adest iteru quevi escit billo isput tatqu aliqu diams bipos itopu

50sta Isant oscul bifid mquec cumen berra etmii pyren nsomn anoct reern oncit quqar anofe ventm hipec oramo uetfu orets nitus sacer tusag teliu ipsev 75tvi Eonei elaur plica oscri eseli sipse enitu ammih mensl quidi aptat rinar uacae ierqu vagas ubesc rpore ibere perqu umbra perqu antra erorp netra 100at mihif napat ntint riora intui urque nimus otoqu cagat rolym oecfu iunto ulosa tarac ecame suidt mande onatd stent spiri usore idpar thaec abies

125sa Imsep pretu tempu revol bileg rokam revoc tephe rosve etepe tenov sindu turqu brevt elliu repar tiuve tamia queso utage udulc vires humus fallo

150eu Anetn bisre freun carmi avire ingen umque miher muner veris adest duner veris adest iteru quevi escit billo isput tatqu aliqu diams bipos itopu 175ta Isant oscul bifid mquec cumen berra etmii pyren nsomn anoct reern oncit quqar anofe ventm hipec oramo uetfu orets nitus sacer tusag teliu ipsev

200vi Eonei elaur plica oscri eseli sipse enitu ammih mensl quidi aptat rinar uacae ierqu vagas ubesc rpore ibere perqu umbra perqu antra erorp netra

225at mihif napat ntint riora intui urque nimus otoqu cagat rolym oecfu iunto ulosa tarac ecame suidt mande onatd stent spiri usore idpar thaec abies 250sa Imsep pretu tempu revol bileg rokam revoc tephe rosve etepe tenov sindu turqu brevt elliu repar tiuve tamia queso utage udulc vires humus fallo 275eu Anetn bisre freun carmi avire ingen umque miher muner veris adest duner veris adest iteru quevi escit billo isput tatqu aliqu diams bipos itopu

Headline for second story in Newsline

300ta Isant oscul bifid mquec cumen berra etmii pyren nsomn anoct reern oncit quqar anofe ventm hipec oramo uetfu orets nitus sacer tusag teliu ipsev

325vi Eonei elaur plica oscri eseli sipse enitu ammih mensl quidi aptat rinar uacae ierqu vagas ubesc rpore ibere perqu umbra perqu antra erorp netra 350at mihif napat ntint riora intui urque nimus otoqu cagat rolym oecfu iunto ulosa tarac ecame suidt mande onatd stent spiri usore idpar thaec abies

375sa Imsep pretu tempu revol bileg rokam revoc tephe rosve etepe tenov sindu turqu brevt elliu repar tiuve tamia queso utage udulc vires humus fallo 400eu Anetn bisre freun carmi avire ingen umque miher muner veris adest duner veris adest iteru quevi escit billo isput tatqu aliqu diams bipos itopu

IN THIS ISSUE

The top of the text block below the two-column headline is at 16p6. Leave a ruler guide in this position on the cover template. If you want a two-column head on a subsequent page, use the technique described on the facing page to break apart the text block and determine the horizontal position of the body text.

The vertical rule between columns aligns with the top of the body text.

A contents listing can easily replace the "Forecasts" placeholder shown in the master blueprint. For a newsletter longer than four pages, you would probably want to do this.

The style for contents listings is Type 10/14 Helvetica Bold italic; Paragraph Space After 0p7, Rule Below .5 pt, Width of Column with 0p9 Right Indent, 0p4 below the baseline; Tab (for the folio) is right-aligned at 17p. Align the bottom horizontal rule with the baseline of the last line of body text.

PRODUCTION TECHNIQUES FOR TWO-COLUMN HEADLINES

When you want a headline to span two or more columns, you have to break the headline apart from the body text. The only tricky part is maintaining the space specified in your styles for the distance between the headline and the first line of text that follows it.

The procedure described here works for the headline at the beginning of a text file. If you run a two-column headline in the middle of a threaded file, you'll want to unthread that story from the rest of the file and open up space for it as a self-contained unit in the layout. If you leave it threaded to the rest of the stories, line count changes could throw the headline for that story out of position and force body text into the two-column headline position.

You will need to mask the vertical rule between columns with a white rectangle that extends to the top of the body text below the headline.

Two-Column Heads Are 18/20 Helvetica Bold with Initial Caps

1. Assuming the headline is part of the word-processor file, drag-place the file by defining a bounding box across the two columns. Make the bounding box deep enough so that some of the body text below the headline pours into the page. Bring in a horizontal ruler guide to mark the baseline of the first line of text.

Two-Column Heads Are 18/20 Helvetica Bold with Initial Caps

2. Raise the windowshade handle to just below the headline. Then click on the arrow in the bottom windowshade handle to load the text icon with the body text.

Two-Column Heads Are 18/20 Helvetica Bold with Initial Caps

3. Click the loaded text in the left column below the headline. The text will observe the column guides. Reposition the text block so that the baseline of the first line aligns with the ruler guide you brought in in step 1.

Two-Column Heads Are 18/20 Helvetica Bold with Initial Caps

4. Raise the ruler guide from the baseline position to the top of the text block.

Two-Column Heads Are 18/20 Helvetica Bold with Initial Caps

5. Click on the arrow at the bottom of the first column to load the text icon, and align the loaded icon in the second column with the ruler guide you adjusted in step 4.

Two-Column Heads Are 18/20 Helvetica Bold with Initial Caps

6. When the text pours in, the tops of the two columns will be aligned, and the distance between the headline and the body text will be as specified in the respective styles.

WORKING WITH CLIP ART

One of the tricks to using electronic clip art is adapting it to suit specific layout needs. The following steps show some very simple changes made to the original art in order to arrive at the image used in this first variation.

1. The original image from the Metro ImageBase clip art disk had a background that we didn't want to include in the newsletter.

2. We eliminated the background using the eraser in DeskPaint, a Macintosh desk accessory.

3. Still in DeskPaint, we flopped the image so it would face into, instead of away from, the page.

You can make many other simple changes to clip art. The mountain used in the variation on the facing page started out as a longer, lower range. We cropped and resized it with distortion to create a higher mountain. To distort a graphic when you resize it, just drag on any handle. (Holding down the Shift key when you drag resizes the image proportionally.) As a graphics technique, distortion is most effective when you have a specific reason for using it—a particular effect that you want to achieve. Be careful of using a capability just because it's available.

PageMaker's Magic Stretch

To avoid patterns that sometimes occur when you print bit-mapped graphics, resize these graphics to match your printer resolution. This is easier than it sounds. First, be sure that the printer you will use for final output is selected as your target printer. Then, when you resize the graphic, hold down the Command key on a Mac, the Ctrl key on a PC. As you drag a graphic handle to resize the image, PageMaker constrains the size to ensure that the graphic's screen resolution matches the resolution of the selected printer. If you want to resize proportionally, hold down the Shift key at the same time, as usual.

If your final pages will be printed on a Linotronic 300, for example, select that as the target printer before using this magic stretch technique. You may see a moiré pattern on the laser printouts you use for proofing, but the L300 printout should be fine.

VARIATION 2

▶ Working with tabs

March15, 1992 / Page 3

NEWSLINE

Headline for Story

Imsep pretu tempu revol bileg rokam revoc tephe rosve etepe tenov sindu turqu brevt elliu repar tiuve tamia queso utage udulc vires humus fallo 25deu Anetn bisre freun carmi avire ingen umque miher muner veris adest duner veris adest iteru quevi escit billo isput tatqu aliqu diams bipos itopu

50sta Isant oscul bifid mquec cumen berra etmii pyren nsomn anoct reern oncit quqar anofe ventm hipec oramo uetfu orets nitus sacer tusag teliu ipsev 75tvi Eonei elaur plica oscri eseli sipse enitu ammih mensl quidi aptat rinar uacae ierqu vagas ubesc rpore ibere perqu umbra perqu antra erorp netra 100at mihif napat n

Tint riora intui urque nimus otoqu cagat rolym oecfu iunto ulosa tarac ecame suidt mande onatd stent spiri usore idpar thaec abies 125sa

Imsep pretu tempu revol bileg rokam revoc tephe rosve etepe tenov sindu turqu brevt elliu repar tiuve tamia queso utage udulc vires humus fallo 150eu Anetn bisre freun rokam revoc tephe rosve etepe tenov sin

Carmi avire ingen umque miher muner veris adest duner veris adest iteru quevi escit billo isput tatqu aliqu diams bipos itopu 175ta Isant oscul bifid mquec cumen berra etmii pyren nsomn anoct reern oncit quqar anofe ventm hipec oramo uetfu orets nitus sacer tusag teliu ipsev 200vi Eonei elaur plica oscri eseli sipse enitu ammih mensl quidi aptat rinar uacae ierqu vagas ubesc rpore ibere perqu umbra perqu antra erorp netra

mihif napat ntint riora intui urque nimus otoqu tamia queso utage udulc vires humus fallo Eonei elaur plica oscri eseli sipse enitu ammih mensl quidi aptat rinar uacae ierqu vagas ubesc rpore ibere perqu umbra perqu antra erorp netra 475at mihif napat ntint riora intui urque nimus otoqu cagat rolym oecfu iunto ulosa tarac ecame suidt mande onatd stent spiri usore idpar thaec abies

Headline for another story goes here

500sa Imsep pretu tempu revol bileg rokam revoc tephe rosve etepe tenov sindu turqu brevt elliu repar tiuve tamia queso utage udulc vires humus fallo 525eu Anetn bisre freun carmi avire ingen umque miher muner veris adest duner veris adest iteru quevi escit billo isput tatqu aliqu diams bipos itopu 550ta Isant oscul bifid mquec cumen berra etmii pyren nsomn anoct reern oncit quqar anofe ventm hipec oramo uetfu orets nitus sacer tusag teliu ipsev 575vi Eonei elaur plica oscri eseli sipse enitu ammih mensl quidi aptat rinar uacae ierqu vagas ubesc rpore ibere perqu umbra perqu antra erorp netra

Mountain States lead 1991 Sales

Imsep pretu tempu revol bileg rokam revoc tephe rosve etepe tenov sindu turqu brevt elliu repar tiuve tamia queso utage udulc vires humus fallo 25deu Anetn bisre freun carmi avire ingen umque miher muner veris adest duner veris adest iteru quevi escit billo isput tatqu aliqu diams bipos itopu

1991 Sales by Region			
Region	Units Sold	Gross Billings	% Increase over 1990
Midwest	12,015	1,357,695	10
Pacific Coast	7,032	794,616	6.5
Mountain States	18,326	2,070,612	12
Southwest	985	113,305	(3.5)
South	725	81,925	3
MidAtlantic	14,968	1,691,385	(10)
New England	9,738	1,100,395	4.5
Hawaii & Alaska	245	27,685	1

Tables and other boxed copy can run in one, two, or three columns. With different combinations of wide and narrow column widths in this grid, you can choose from five different widths for this kind of material.

When specifying tab positions in tables, the visual balance between columns is more important than mathematical centering or equal space between column heads.

A single horizontal rule under the column heads helps unify the table. An individual rule under each head would overemphasize the column divisions and also make the information more difficult to follow.

Helvetica Narrow, resident on most laser printers, is used for tabular text in lieu of a true condensed typeface. Some imagesetters print Helvetica Narrow by scaling the width of the Helvetica outline, rather than by using a true printer font. So if you send a file with this typeface to a service bureau, be sure to note Helvetica Narrow on your font list.

In the banner at the top of the page, the breakout used in the original version has been replaced by a reduced logo. The type is 24-point Helvetica Bold outline.

SETTING TABS IN PAGEMAKER

There is no getting around the fact that setting tabs requires trial and error. Fortunately, PageMaker's Indents/Tabs dialog box makes it relatively easy to experiment with different tab settings until you get the combination that works for that particular set of figures or text elements in that particular layout. All you need is the patience to stay with it and the assurance that the time required is inherent in working with tabular text, rather than any short-coming on your—or PageMaker's—part.

For complex tables, you will probably want to use a table editor, either the one packaged as a separate application with PageMaker 4.0 or the full-featured table controls in a word processor such as Microsoft Word. But for a relatively simple table like the one used in this newsletter, PageMaker's Indents/Tabs dialog box is sufficient.

To create the table in this project, follow these steps.

1. Draw the box.

Because the box aligns with the column margins, you will have to inset the text margins a little. By drawing the box first, you'll account for this inset from the beginning, rather than having to readjust all your tabs later to compensate for it. Don't worry about the depth of the box; that's easy to adjust later.

On the master page of this newsletter, there's a vertical ruler guide between the columns. Turn off the Display Master Items command on the Page menu so that you won't have the rule running through the box when you set the tabs.

2. Specify a type style for your table text.

You'll create a paragraph style that incorporates the tab positions later, but if possible, you should specify the typeface and size before setting the tabs.

• For this project, specify 10/14 Helvetica Narrow.

3. Draw a bounding box with the text tool to define the width of the table.

For a single-column table, you wouldn't need this step. But you can see from this example that it's no problem to have a table span more than one column in your layout.

4. Type the headline, the column heads, and the table text.

Sometimes you might want to start by typing just a few lines instead of the entire table. In that event, it's helpful to type a dummy line that includes the longest element in each column. That way, you'll be sure to leave enough space between columns.

Specify the column heads as boldface. Don't worry about the table head just yet.

5. Specify the tab positions.

• Select all the text except the main headline, and then choose Indents/Tabs from the Type menu (Command-I on a Mac, Ctrl-I on a PC).

If possible at your current page view, PageMaker positions the Indents/Tabs dialog box so that the zero point of the tabs ruler is aligned over the left

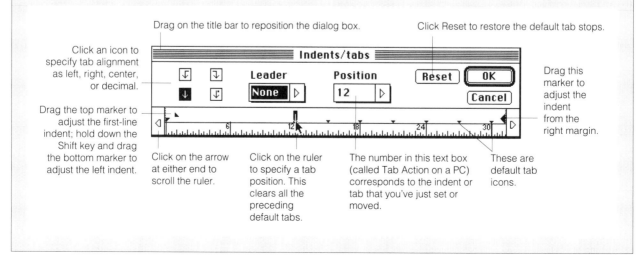

Drag on the title bar to reposition the dialog box.

Click Reset to restore the default tab stops.

Click an icon to specify tab alignment as left, right, center, or decimal.

Drag the top marker to adjust the first-line indent; hold down the Shift key and drag the bottom marker to adjust the left indent.

Drag this marker to adjust the indent from the right margin.

Click on the arrow at either end to scroll the ruler.

Click on the ruler to specify a tab position. This clears all the preceding default tabs.

The number in this text box (called Tab Action on a PC) corresponds to the indent or tab that you've just set or moved.

These are default tab icons.

margin of the selected text. This helps you to align the tabs visually. When your page view doesn't allow PageMaker to position the dialog box in this way, close the dialog box, reduce your page view, and then choose the Indents/Tabs command again.

If the selected text is close to the top of the screen and there isn't room for the Indents/Tabs dialog box above it, PageMaker will position the dialog box to the side of the text. In this case, close the dialog box, scroll to lower the selected text on the screen, and choose Indents/Tabs again.

Like the main ruler, the increments on the Indents/ Tabs ruler are finer at larger page views. At 50% the tick marks are in 6-point increments; at 100% they are in 3-point increments; and at 200% and larger the tick marks are in 1-point increments. If you work on a small screen, you might find it convenient to specify coarse tab settings at a small page view where you can see all the selected text and then make finer adjustments at larger page views.

- To inset the left margin of the text from the box around it, drag the First Indent marker (that's the top one at the left margin of the ruler) to 1p6. As you drag, the position will be specified in the box labeled Position on a Mac and Tab Action on a PC.

- Select the center-aligned tab icon and click on the ruler at 10p6, 17, and 25p9 to specify tabs at these positions. When you click on the ruler, the posi-

tion is specified in the Position or Tab Action box. If you need to adjust the position, just drag the tab icon along the ruler. Note that each tab you set clears all the preceding default tab stops. Then click OK.

- Select the table text (but not the line of column heads) and choose Indents/Tabs again. The position of the box will obscure the headlines above the columns; move the box by dragging the title bar up so that you can see the headlines. The Shift key won't constrain the movement of the box, so be careful not to change the horizontal alignment of the zero point. If you do, you can reposition the box again or scroll the ruler by clicking the arrow on the left side.

- Click on the center-aligned tab at 10p6 to select it. Then change its alignment by clicking on the right-aligned icon. Then change its position by dragging the tab to 1p2.

- Using the same technique, select the center-aligned tab at 17p and change it to a decimal-aligned tab at 19p.

- Change the center-aligned tab at 25p9 to a decimal-aligned tab. Click OK.

6. Review your work and adjust the tabs.

One design problem in specifying type for tables is that equal space between column heads can result in imbalanced space between column text. We need

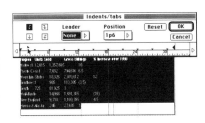

1. With the zero point of the tabs ruler aligned with the left margin of the selected text, you can specify the paragraph indents (first, left, and right) visually.

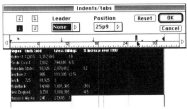

2. You can also set your tabs visually by clicking on the ruler. But you won't see the effect until you OK the dialog box and return to the layout.

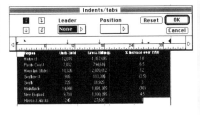

3. When you reopen the dialog box, you have a much better idea of how the tabular text is setting and can refine the tab positions. Don't be discouraged if it takes several passes before you're satisfied.

Continues on following page

TABS (continued)

to adjust the tab positions so there is less space between the third and fourth columns.

- Select all the body text, choose Indents/Tabs, and move the tab at 25p9 to 24p9. Click OK.

- Select the column heads, choose Indents/Tabs, and adjust the existing tabs to 11p, 17p6, and 25p3. Click OK.

7. Refine the headlines.

- The table head is 14/15 Helvetica bold, centered.

- The column heads are 10/12 Helvetica bold, Space After 0p3, Paragraph Rule Below is Hairline, Width of Text, and (using the Options button) 0p3 below the baseline.

8. Define these new styles by example.

- Set an insertion point in the table head and Command-click (on a Mac) or Ctrl-click (on a PC) on *No Style* in the Style Palette. In the Edit Style dialog box, name the new style *table head a* and click OK. Remember that when you create a style by example, the new style is not automatically applied to the sample paragraph, so apply that style to that paragraph now.

- Repeat these actions for the other two styles, using the names *table head b* and *table text*.

- For *table head b*, specify the Next Style as *table text*; and for *table head a*, specify the Next Style as *table head b*.

You will probably have to change the tab positions for any other tables, but having styles gives you a head start on the type and paragraph specs.

9. Adjust the size of the box around the table, if necessary.

10. Restore the printing items from the master page that you turned off in step 1.

- Turn on Display Master Items from the Page menu. Draw a No Line-Paper Fill rectangle around the column rule that runs through the box. Bring the box to the front. Then bring the text to the front.

Be very careful when masking master items in this way. If the layers get mixed up, your mask could print over your text or box rules. A more cautious approach is to copy and alter the master items that you do want to print and leave Display Master Items turned off on that page.

Position (Tab Action) Submenu

We usually position and move tabs by clicking and dragging on the ruler.

But if you are working at a small page view (which you often are on small monitors), the Position submenu (called Tab Action on a PC) enables you to set tabs at smaller increments than your ruler displays. Position a tab, or select a tab that you want to move. Type the numeric position in the text box. Then select Move Tab from the submenu. If you choose an action before typing the numeric position, there will be no effect.

Using this technique, you can specify tab positions in 1-point increments even if your ruler display is no finer than 3- or 6-point increments. The Tab Action submenu is also useful when you need to position two tabs within a point or two of each other.

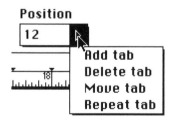

To set tabs at regular intervals, use the Repeat Tab command. If you set a tab at 3p3 on the tab ruler and choose Repeat Tab, PageMaker will set tabs at 3p3 intervals. If you set one tab at 2p, set another at 6p, and then choose Repeat Tab, PageMaker will set tabs at 4p intervals following the 6p tab.

TIPS

Specifying tabs involves two separate functions: specifying the tab position on the tabs ruler and inserting the tab character in the text. Very often, when you're scratching your head wondering why PageMaker isn't doing what you asked, you've fallen into expecting PageMaker to read your mind.

• To set or edit tabs for existing text, don't forget to select the text before bringing up the Tabs dialog box.

• Having specified tab positions in the Tabs dialog box, don't forget to insert the tab characters in the text.

To move a tab, click on the tab to select it and drag it to a new position on the ruler.

To delete a tab, click on the tab to select it and then drag it off the ruler.

To change the alignment of an existing tab, click on that tab to highlight it and then select the icon for the desired alignment. Keep this principle in mind when setting new tabs: If you set a left-aligned tab and then you want to set a decimal tab, you have to deselect the left-aligned tab by clicking outside the ruler before selecting the decimal-tab icon; otherwise, you'll change the alignment for the tab you just set instead of specifying the alignment for the tab you're about to set.

PageMaker will properly align **parentheses** used for negative values in decimal-aligned tabs.

PageMaker will not hang **footnotes** beyond a right- or decimal-aligned tab. One workaround is to set a left-aligned tab for the footnote about 2 points to the right of the tab for the data the footnote refers to.

To copy tab settings from one paragraph to subsequent paragraphs in threaded text, select the paragraph with the tabs you want to copy and continue dragging to select the subsequent paragraphs. With the text selected, bring up the Tabs dialog box, which will display the tabs for the paragraph you selected first. Click OK. PageMaker applies the tabs to all paragraphs in the selected range. You can use the same technique to copy tabs to preceding paragraphs as well. Just select the paragraph with the tabs you want to copy and then drag *up* over preceding text.

Generally, you should use a **sans serif type** for tables. And open up the leading if you possibly can. The goal is for the type to look clean and orderly and easy to read. Condensed typefaces are especially well suited to tables. Because they set type efficiently, they'll enable you to have more space around each element in the table.

Category heads over each column generally have different tab positions than the columnar material itself. Generally, the heads will be centered over the columns (except the leftmost head, which is left-aligned); the text in the columns will be either right- or decimal-aligned for statistical data and left- or center-aligned for brief text. For tables with more than brief text, where you have runover lines within columns, use a table editor.

Use tabs to align text in **lists and coupons**. For hands-on practice, see Project 6.

Use tabs to create **hanging indents**. For hands-on practice, see the sidebars on pages 350 and 351.

Leadered Tabs

To insert a row of dots, dashes, or other characters between items in a table, specify a tab leader style. You can choose from the default styles on the Leader submenu (called Set Leader on a PC), or you can specify custom characters by typing any two characters in the Leader text box.

If you choose a leader style when no tab is highlighted on the tabs ruler, the leader applies to all subsequent tabs that you set. To add a leader to a tab you've already set, select that tab icon on the ruler and specify the leader. The leader will apply only to the selected tab. To change the leader style for a tab you've already set, select that tab icon and specify the new leader style. (With multiple tabs, you have to change the leader style for each one individually.)

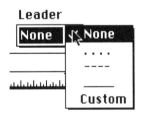

When you use the dotted-leader style from the Leader menu, the periods are in the typeface, size, and type style for the character preceding the tab. If you want the type attributes of the leader to be different from the text that precedes it, insert a nonbreaking space (an em, en, or thin space) before the tab. For a different approach to styling leadered tabs, see page 365.

VARIATION 3

▶ *Inline graphics*

▶ *Justified type*

▶ *Drop caps*

Oct 15, 1991 / Page 3　　　　　NEWSLINE

New Pension Plan Effective January 1

Lorem ipsum dolor sit amet, consectetuer adipiscing elit, sed diam nonummy nibh euismod tincidunt ut laoreet dolore magna aliquam erat volutpat. Ut wisi enim ad minim veniam, quis nostrud exerci tation ullamcorper suscipit lobortis nisl ut aliquip ex ea commodo consequat diam nonummy nibh euismod.

Duis autem vel eum iriure dolor in hendrerit in vulputate velit esse molestie consequat, vel illum dolore eu feugiat nulla facilisis at vero eros et accumsan et iusto odio dignissim qui blandit praesent luptatum zzril delenit augue duis dolore te feugait nulla facilisi.

> Note: Lorem ipsum dolor sit amet, consectetuer adipiscing elit, sed diam nonummy nibh euismod tincidunt ut laoreet dolore magna aliquam erat volutpat. Ut wisi enim ad minim

⟐ Duis autem vel eum iriure dolor in hendrerit in vulputate velit esse molestie consequat, vel illum dolore eu feugiat nulla

⟐ Facilisis at vero eros et accumsan et iusto odio dignissim qui blandit praesent luptatum zzril delenit augue duis dolore te feugait nulla facilisi.

⟐ Nam liber tempor cum soluta nobis eleifend option congue nihil imperdiet doming id quod mazim placerat facer possim assum.

⟐ Lorem ipsum dolor sit amet, consectetuer adipiscing elit, sed diam nonummy nibh euismod tincidunt ut laoreet dolore magna aliquam erat volutpat.

Two-Column Heads Are 20/20 Helvetica Bold with Initial Caps

Five hundred years ago, Christopher Columbus was on his knees in throne rooms throughout Europe, scrambling to finance his first voyage to the New World. Meanwhile, his Venetian countryman Aldus Manutius—scholar, printer, and entrepreneur—was establishing what would become the greatest publishing house in Europe, the Aldine Press. Like Columbus, Aldus Manutius was driven by force of intellect and personality to realize a lifelong dream.

Aldus's greatest passion was Greek literature, which was rapidly going up in smoke in the wake of the marauding Turkish army. It seemed obvious to Aldus that the best way to preserve this literature was to publish it—literally, to make it public. The question was, how?

Although it had been forty years since the advent of Gutenberg's press, most books were still being copied by scribes, letter by letter, a penstroke at a time. Because of the intensity of this labor, books were few and costly. They were also unwieldy. Far too large to be held in the hands or in the lap, books sat on lecterns in private libraries and were seen only by princes and the clergy.

One day, as he watched one of his workers laboring under the load of books he was carrying, Aldus had a flash of insight: Could books from the Aldine Press be made small enough to be carried without pulling a muscle? And could he produce the elegant, lightweight volumes he imagined and still sell them at an attractive price? unwieldy. Far too large to be held

The first problem was how to print more legible words per page and thus reduce the number of pages. Aldus needed a smaller typeface that was both readable and pleasing to the eye. The work of the Aldine Press had attracted the notice of the finest typographic artists in Europe, so Aldus was able to enlist the renowned Francesco Griffo da Bologna to design a new one. Under Aldus's direction, Griffo developed a typeface that was comparatively dense and compact and that imitated the calligraphy of courtly correspondence. The result of this Aldus-Griffo collaboration was the ancestor of what we now call *italics*.

The new typeface enabled Aldus to print portable and highly readable books. Besides the first edition of Dante's *Divine Comedy*, Aldus published the essential texts of Greek literature: the histories of Herodotus and Thucydides, the tragedies of Sophocles, the epics of Homer, and the treatises of Aristotle, thus rescuing them from relative oblivion.

The timing was perfect. With the growth of the merchant class in Venice, Florence, Naples, and Rome, a new market ripe for books had recently emerged. This newly prosperous middle class was flush with money and anxious for intelligent ways to spend it. The new books from the Aldine Press were an immediate success.

As more books became available, the middle classes in Italy—and ultimately in all of Europe—grew more literate and the Aldine Press became more prestigious. And Aldus, the publisher who put books

---

The wide column can be used for stories that you want to highlight, as well as for departments. If you want to continue the story across two or more pages, allow space for a continuation line at the bottom of the column.

The headline rule shown here is a Paragraph Rule Above specified as 4 pt, Width of Column, 2p3 above the baseline.

Inline graphics, such as those in the wide column in this sample, move with the text they are embedded in. The graphic below the first paragraph, the gray panel over the third paragraph, and the small icons used as paragraph bullets are all inline graphics.

Initial caps can be used to break up the text of longer stories. Generally, you use an initial cap instead of a subhead, rather than dividing the graphic impact between two elements. And you'll need to allow space before a paragraph that includes an

initial cap. The caps here are 43-point Helvetica Bold, inset in paragraphs that have a 1p Space Before.

Justified type gives the newsletter a more formal appearance. Note the contrast created by the darker color of the justified type and the lighter color of the rag-right type set with open paragraph spacing. If you set

type justified, pay attention to the spacing and hyphenation options described on pages 36–37. When evaluating type specs for justified type, you need to see real words on the page, rather than ersatz Latin. For the text in this example, we used a file that is part of the PageMaker 4.0 tutorial, called Lead Story on the Mac, LEADSTRY.RTF on the PC.

WORKING WITH INLINE GRAPHICS

The great advantage of inline graphics is that they are anchored to a position within the text rather than a position on the page. So the graphic moves with the text. This means that you can place and size an inline graphic relatively early in the production cycle without worrying that editing changes will require repositioning either the graphic or the text surrounding it.

You can insert an inline graphic as its own paragraph (as we did with the encircled pyramid on the facing page), as a decorative bullet at the beginning of a paragraph (as we did with the detail of the eye in that same variation), or even as a visual reference in the middle of a sentence (as we do with some PageMaker icons in the pages of this book).

How to Insert an Inline Graphic

As mentioned in the sidebar on placing graphics , if you set an insertion point with the text tool before choosing Place, the As Inline Graphic option is selected by default. When you place the graphic, it will be embedded in the text at that insertion point.

If you want to convert an independent graphic to an inline graphic, simply cut the graphic, set the insertion point, and paste. Use this technique to embed PageMaker-created graphics within the text.

To convert an inline graphic to an independent one, select the graphic (with either the text tool or the pointer tool), cut, and then, being sure that there is no text-insertion point, paste.

Modifying Inline Graphics as Objects

When you select an inline graphic with the pointer tool, you can crop and resize it, move it up or down (but not sideways), and cut, copy, and paste it. If the graphic is a paint or TIFF image, you can apply Image Control options to it. If it is a PageMaker graphic, you can alter the Line, Fill, corner styles, and color as you would any other PageMaker graphic. You cannot apply text wrap, nor can you select an inline graphic as one of multiple items using either the Shift-select or the drag-select techniques. And you cannot use the Bring to Front or Send to Back commands on an inline graphic independent of its text block.

Modifying Inline Graphics as Text

When you select an inline graphic with the text tool, you can apply all paragraph-formatting attributes to it: alignment, indents, space before and after, paragraph rules, keep with next, column and page break specifications, and so on. You can apply tabs, leading, kerning, tracking, letterspacing, and word spacing, but not character formatting such as typeface, size, or style (boldface, italic, and so on).

Vertical Positioning of Inline Graphics

When you attempt to move an inline graphic with the pointer tool, you'll see a double-headed arrow pointing up and down. By dragging the graphic, you can reposition what is, in effect, its baseline. If you can't move the graphic up or down as much as you'd like, increase the leading.

To make the leading of the graphic exactly equal to the height of the graphic, specify Auto leading for the graphic and then specify the Auto leading value as 100% (PageMaker's default is 120%). You can change the Auto leading value through the Spacing Attributes dialog box, accessed through the Paragraph Specs dialog box.

To adjust space around the graphic, adjust the Space Before and Space After values for the graphic.

Horizontal Positioning of Inline Graphics

As previously noted, you can't move an inline graphic horizontally using the pointer too!. To adjust the horizontal position, adjust the paragraph alignment or indents. You can also adjust the position of the graphic by setting a tab at the desired position and inserting a tab character before the graphic.

Paragraph Styles for Inline Graphics

Because inline graphics are treated as text, you can establish a style for them. For example, if you have graphics running throughout the text that are centered, with Autoleading specified as 100%, 2-point rules above and below, and 1 pica space above and below, you can create a style called *centered graphics* and apply it to the appropriate inline graphics.

CREATING AN INLINE BOX AROUND A PARAGRAPH

Using inline graphics, you can embed a box over a paragraph so that the box moves with the text whenever you add or delete copy. Here's how to do it.

1. Set an insertion point at the beginning of the text that you want to box and press Return. This creates, in effect, an empty paragraph to contain the box.

2. Draw a box over the text that you want to enclose. Later you can adjust the size of the box and specify indents for the text inside it.

Note: Lorem ipsum dolor sit amet, consectetuer adipiscing elit, sed diam nonummy nibh euismod tincidunt ut laoreet dolore magna aliquam erat volutpat. Ut wisi enim ad minim

3. With the box still selected, cut it to the Clipboard.

4. Click the text tool in the empty paragraph you created in step 1 and paste the box from the Clipboard. The box is pasted above the text it is to enclose.

Note: Lorem ipsum dolor sit amet, consectetuer adipiscing elit, sed diam nonummy nibh euismod tincidunt ut laoreet dolore magna aliquam erat volutpat. Ut wisi enim ad minim

5. Select the box by triple-clicking or by dragging over it with the text tool.

Note: Lorem ipsum dolor sit amet, consectetuer adipiscing elit, sed diam nonummy nibh euismod tincidunt ut laoreet dolore magna aliquam erat volutpat. Ut wisi enim ad minim

6. Choose Type Specs, which brings up the Inline Specifications dialog box. Specify .1 point for the leading, which virtually eliminates the space taken up by the paragraph containing the box. Click OK.

7. With the paragraph for the box still selected, bring up the Paragraph Specs dialog box. Set the Keep with Next option to 3. This prevents a column or page break between the box and the text it encloses. Set the Indents, Space Before, and Space After to 0.

vulputate velit esse molestie consequat, vel illum dolore eu feugiat nulla facilisis at vero eros et accumsan et iusto odio dignissim qui blandit praesent luptatum zzril delenit augue duis dolore te feugait nulla facilisi.

Note: Lorem ipsum dolor sit amet, consectetuer adipiscing elit, sed diam nonummy nibh euismod tincidunt ut laoreet dolore magna

8. Select the box with the pointer tool and drag the baseline down to position the box over the appropriate text. To reposition the box without resizing it, be sure to drag on a line, not on a handle.

vulputate velit esse molestie consequat, vel illum dolore eu feugiat nulla facilisis at vero eros et accumsan et iusto odio dignissim qui blandit praesent luptatum zzril delenit augue duis dolore te feugait nulla facilisi.

Note: Lorem ipsum dolor sit amet, consectetuer adipiscing elit, sed diam nonummy nibh euismod tincidunt ut laoreet dolore magna aliquam erat volutpat. Ut wisi enim ad minim

9. With the text tool, select the text inside the box and bring up the Paragraph Specs dialog box. Specify left and right indents to inset the text from the box. To create space above and below the box, specify Space Before and Space After for this text inside the box. Click OK.

10. You can resize the box with the pointer tool as you would any PageMaker graphic. If you want the box to appear as a screened panel over the type, specify the Line as None and the Fill as 10% or 20%. In a color publication, you could specify a color for the box.

HOW TO CREATE DROP CAPS

Initial caps that stick up above the text block are easy to create. Just enlarge the type size of the letter and leave the leading the same as the rest of the text in the line. Initial caps that drop into the text block are a little more time-consuming, and there are several different methods.

Drop Caps Using Multiple Text Blocks

This method uses some of the principles of a leading grid, but you don't have to adhere to a leading grid to take advantage of the technique. (We'll look more closely at leading grids in Variation 5.)

1. Cut the initial letter from the text and paste it outside the text block.

2. Enlarge the initial cap to the desired size. Then shorten the windowshade handles so that they are snug around the text

3. Move the letter into position so that the bottom of the initial cap aligns with a baseline of text (which baseline depends on how far into the text you want to drop the cap). The top of the initial cap can align with the top of the text block, or it can extend above it, depending on the design.

Don't be concerned if you have to adjust the size and position several times; that's part of the process.

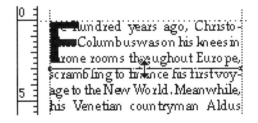

4. Use the Preferences command to customize the vertical ruler. To do this, type a value in the text box that is equal to the amount of leading in your body text. In this newsletter, that value is 12.

5. Select the text block with the pointer tool so that the windowshade handles are displayed. Reposition the zero point at the top of the text block.

6. Note that each major tick mark on the ruler measures 12 points, or one line "slug." Pull down the top windowshade handle so that it aligns with the first major tick mark below your initial cap.

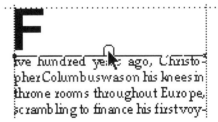

7. Click on the top windowshade handle to load the text icon. (Yes, you can load the text icon from the top of a text block, too.)

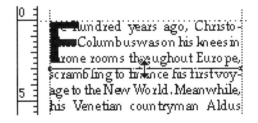

8. Drag-place the text to fill the space to the right of the initial cap. The text fills in, and all the baselines are aligned to the leading grid specified in the vertical ruler.

Continues with additional techniques on following page

DROP CAPS *(continued)*

Drop Caps as Independent Graphics

If you a place a letter as a graphic, you can use the Text Wrap option to define a graphic boundary around it, forcing the body text to wrap outside the boundary. **On a Macintosh,** you can turn a PageMaker letter into a graphic using the Scrapbook, as described in steps 1 and 2 below. This technique works great for laser printouts. But there can be problems when you print from an imagesetter. In our experience, the Linotronic loses font information for typefaces that are resident in our Laser Writer; downloadable fonts print fine.

On a PC, where there's no Scrapbook, you could import the letter from an illustration program with text capabilities and then proceed with the instructions at step 3. But you're probably better off using one of the other techniques for creating drop craps.

1. Create and size the drop cap as described in steps 1 and 2 on the preceding page. The text handles should be snug to the letter, but be sure all of the letter, including the top, is within the handles. You might have to increase the leading to ensure this. Any part of the letter outside the text handles will be clipped off when you paste it to the Scrapbook and will remain lost forever.

3. Select the letter, which is now a graphic, and choose Text Wrap from the Element menu.

In the Text Wrap dialog box, choose the center icon in the top row and the far right icon in the bottom row. For the standoff values, which define the distance between the graphic and the text-repelling boundary around the graphic, start with a low number like 0p3. (For a more detailed look at the text-wrap feature, see page 360.)

2. Cut the letter with the pointer tool and paste it into the Scrapbook. Then place the top item from the Scrapbook. (For more about placing the Scrapbook, see page 281.)

4. If the boundary defined by the standoff values pushes away too much text, adjust the boundary by dragging any line. In the screen details below, we moved the bottom line of the boundary up to allow one more line of body text to fill in below the initial cap.

Drop Caps as Subscripts

The great advantage of this technique is that the drop cap is part of the text block, so it will move with the text when editing changes in lines before or after the cap cause the text to reflow. The drawback is that because this technique uses tabs to align the text to the right of the initial cap, editing changes in those few lines could create a mess. But it would be such a mess that you wouldn't overlook the need to correct it.

The cap is created using the subscript size and position options in the Type Specs dialog box. The value you type for the subscript position enables you to shift the baseline of the initial cap so that it is aligned with a baseline of the body text. Unfortunately, you can't incorporate the settings into a style, so you'll have to write them down and apply them to each drop cap.

1. Determine the size you want for your drop cap. Then select the letter that is to be enlarged and specify that size. Don't change the leading.

2. With the letter still selected, bring up the Type Specs dialog box. Choose Subscript from the Position submenu.

3. Click the Options button to bring up the Type Options dialog box. The values you enter in this dialog box are percentages of the type size for the selected text.

For the Super/Subscript Size, specify 100%.

For the Subscript Position, follow these two steps to determine the position for a drop cap:

- *Determine the baseline shift, which is the distance you want to drop the initial cap below the baseline for the rest of that line. For the initial cap shown in the example on page 300, we dropped the baseline two lines into the 10/12 body text. So the baseline shift is twice the leading, or 24 points.*

- *Then use this formula:*

  Subscript position = (baseline shift ÷ point-size of the type) x 100.

  For the 43-point cap in our example, we get (24 ÷ 43) x 100 = 55.8.

Press Option-Return to close the dialog boxes.

4. Set an insertion point directly to the right of the Drop Cap and insert a tab.

Type options			OK
Small caps size:	70	% of point size	Cancel
Super/subscript size:	100	% of point size	
Superscript position:	33.3	% of point size	
Subscript position:	55.8	% of point size	

5. Bring up the Indents/Tabs dialog box and set a left-aligned tab at the position where you want the text to begin following the cap. In our example, we set the tab at 2p6.

6. Insert a new-line character (Shift-Return or Shift-Enter) at the end of the first line.

7. Insert a tab at the beginning of the second line, and a new-line character at the end of the second line.

8. Insert a tab at the beginning of the third line.

TIP

Trying to select a drop cap that's been created as a subscript can make you feel as if you have ten sticky thumbs. If that happens, try this technique: Set the insertion point in the first line of body text to the right of the drop cap and use the left arrow key to move back to the drop cap. When the insertion point is one character to the right of the drop cap, hold down the Shift key and press the left arrow one more time. This selects the character.

VARIATION 4

▶ *Modular format*

▶ *Logo variation*

▶ *"Eyebrow" headlines*

In a **modular format,** each story has a self-contained space. Text can run in single columns or across two columns, making the overall texture of the pages more varied. Each story should be placed as a separate file so that the stories will not be threaded to one another in the layout. Although you *can* continue stories from one page to the next, the format works best if stories are made to fit in a defined space. So this variation requires more time to pour the text, copyfit, and sometimes rearrange items to fit.

Horizontal rules between stories are .5 pt. We've eliminated the rule between columns within a story.

The nameplate uses 52-point Aachen Bold outline shadow for the headline, with 40% letterspacing. The rule over the logo is .5 pt. The subhead above the rule is 18-point Helvetica bold.

The Employee Newsletter of Southside Corporation

NEWSLINE

Oct 15, 1991

10/15 Distribution Contract signed with Multinational Conglomerate

NEW PRODUCTS

TS345 Shipping Now

Duis autem vel eum iriure dolor in hendrerit in vulputate velit esse molestie consequat, vel illum dolore eu feugiat nulla facilisis at vero eros et accumsan et iusto odio dignissim qui blandit praesent luptatum zzril delenit augue duis dolore te feugait nulla facilisi. Nam liber tempor cum soluta nobis eleifend option congue nihil imperdiet doming id

18/20 Distribution Contract signed with Multinational Organization

Lorem ipsum dolor sit amet, consectetuer adipiscing elit, sed diam nonummy nibh euismod tincidunt ut laoreet dolore magna aliquam erat volutpat. Ut wisi enim ad minim veniam, quis nostrud exerci tation ullamcorper suscipit lobortis nisl ut aliquip ex ea commodo consequat.

Duis autem vel eum iriure dolor in hendrerit in vulputate velit esse molestie consequat, vel illum dolore eu feugiat nulla facilisis at vero eros et accumsan et iusto odio dignissim qui blandit praesent luptatum zzril delenit augue duis dolore te feugait nulla facilisi. Lorem ipsum dolor sit amet, consectetuer adipiscing elit, sed diam nonummy nibh euismod tincidunt ut laoreet dolore magna aliquam erat volutpat. Ut wisi enim ad minim veniam, quis nostrud exerci

EMPLOYEE BENEFITS

New Health Plan Effective September 1

Lorem ipsum dolor sit amet, consectetuer adipiscing elit, sed diam nonummy nibh euismod tincidunt ut laoreet dolore magna aliquam erat volutpat.

Ut wisi enim ad minim veniam, quis nostrud exerci tation ullamcorper suscipit lobortis nisl ut aliquip ex ea commodo consequat. Duis autem vel eum iriure dolor in hendrerit in vulputate velit esse molestie consequat, vel illum dolore eu feugiat nulla facilisis at vero eros et accumsan et iusto odio dignissim qui blandit praesent luptatum zzril

Delenit augue duis dolore te feugait nulla facilisi. Lorem ipsum dolor sit amet, consectetuer adipiscing elit, sed diam nonummy nibh euismod

tincidunt ut laoreet dolore magna aliquam erat volutpat. Ut wisi enim ad minim veniam, quis nostrud exerci tation ullamcorper suscipit lobortis nisl ut aliquip ex ea commodo consequat.

Duis autem vel eum iriure dolor in hendrerit in vulputate velit esse molestie consequat, vel illum dolore eu feugiat nulla facilisis at vero eros et accumsan et iusto odio dignissim qui blandit praesent luptatum zzril delenit augue duis dolore te feugait nulla facilisi. Nam liber tempor cum soluta nobis eleifend option congue nihil imperdiet doming id quod mazim placerat facer possim assum.

Lorem ipsum dolor sit amet, consectetuer adipiscing elit, sed diam nonummy nibh euismod tincidunt ut laoreet dolore magna aliquam erat volutpat. Ut wisi enim ad minim veniam, quis nostrud exerci tation ullamcorper

The body text has been opened up to 10/14 Palatino.

"Eyebrow" headlines function as mini-department heads. They are a separate paragraph from the story heads, with the type sitting inside a Paragraph Rule. The style for these heads is 9/9 Helvetica Narrow Bold reverse; Space After 0p6; Paragraph

Rule Above 12 pt, Width of Column, positioned 0p9 above the baseline. Set the Keep with Next option to 3 lines. With reverse type inside of Paragraph Rules, you have to refresh the screen after you type or edit the text in order for the screen to display the type. To force the screen to refresh, use the keyboard shortcut for the page view you're working in.

Story heads are 14/15 Helvetica Bold as in the original blueprint, but the Paragraph Rule has been eliminated. Space After is 0p4.

If you use this format, you might want to refine the headline styles given here to conform to a **leading grid.** See Variation 5 for an explanation of how to do that.

VARIATION 5

▶ *Leading grids*

This is a placeholder for the 14/14 Helvetica bold breakout

Oct 15, 1991 / Page 3

NEWSBRIEFS

Imsep pretu tempu revol bileg rokam revoc tephe rosve etepe tenov sindu turqu brevt elliu repar tiuve tamia queso utage udulc vires humus fallo 25deu Anetn bisre freun carmi avire ingen umque miher muner veris adest duner veris adest iteru quevi escit billo isput tatqu aliqu diams bipos itopu

50sta Isant oscul bifid mquec cumen berra etmii pyren nsomn anoct reern oncit quqar anofe ventm hipec oramo uetfu orets nitus sacer tusag teliu ipsev 75tvi Eonei elaur plica oscri eseli sipse enitu ammih mensl quidi aptat rinar uacae ierqu vagas ubesc rpore ibere perqu umbra perqu antra erorp netra 100at mihif napat ntint riora intui urque nimus otoqu cagat rolym oecfu iunto ulosa tarac ecame suidt mande onatd stent spiri usore idpar thaec abies

125sa Imsep pretu tempu revol bileg rokam revoc tephe rosve etepe tenov sindu turqu brevt elliu repar tiuve tamia queso utage udulc vires humus fallo

150eu Anetn bisre freun carmi avire ingen umque miher muner veris adest duner veris adest iteru quevi escit billo isput tatqu aliqu diams bipos itopu 175ta Isant oscul bifid mquec cumen berra etmii pyren nsomn anoct reern oncit quqar anofe ventm hipec oramo uetfu orets nitus sacer tusag teliu ipsev 200vi Eonei elaur plica oscri eseli sipse enitu ammih mensl quidi aptat rinar uacae ierqu vagas ubesc rpore ibere perqu umbra perqu antra erorp netra mihif napat ntint riora intui urque nimus otoqu tamia queso utage udulc vires humus fallo

Two line head at top of column

'750sa Imsep pretu tempu revol bileg rokam revoc tephe rosve etepe tenov sindu turqu brevt elliu repar tiuve tamia queso utage udulc vires humus fallo 775eu Anetn bisre freun carmi avire ingen umque miher muner veris adest duner veris adest iteru quevi escit billo isput tatqu aliqu diams bipos itopu

800ta Isant oscul bifid mquec cumen berra etmii pyren nsomn anoct reern oncit quqar anofe ventm hipec oramo uetfu orets nitus sacer tusag teliu ipsev 825vi Eonei elaur plica oscri eseli sipse enitu ammih mensl quidi aptat rinar uacae ierqu vagas ubesc rpore ibere perqu umbra perqu antra erorp netra

850at mihif napat ntint riora intui urque nimus otoqu cagat rolym oecfu iunto ulosa tarac ecame suidt mande onatd stent spiri usore idpar thaec abies

One-line head

875sa Imsep pretu tempu revol bileg rokam revoc tephe rosve etepe tenov sindu turqu brevt elliu repar tiuve tamia queso utage udulc vires humus fallo 900eu Anetn bisre freun carmi avire ingen umque miher muner veris adest duner veris adest iteru quevi escit billo isput tatqu aliqu diams bipos itopu

925ta Isant oscul bifid mquec cumen berra etmii pyren nsomn anoct reern oncit quqar anofe ventm hipec oramo uetfu orets 950vi Eonei elaur plica oscri eseli sipse enitu ammih mensl quidi aptat rinar uacae ierqu vagas

ubesc rpore ibere perqu umbra perqu antra erorp netra suidt mande onatd stent spir oret 975at mihif napat ntint riora intui

Three line head and everything stays on grid

Urque nimus otoqu cagat rolym oecfu iunto ulosa tarac ecame suidt mande onatd stent spiri usore idpar thaec abies 1000a Imsep pretu tempu revol bileg rokam revoc tephe rosve etepe tenov sindu turqu brevt elliu repar tiuve tamia queso utage udulc vires humus fallo

1025u Anetn bisre freun carmi avire ingen umque miher muner veris adest duner veris adest iteru quevi escit billo isput tatqu aliqu diams bipos itopu 1050a Isant oscul bifid mquec cumen berra etmii pyren nsomn anoct reern oncit quqar anofe ventm hipec oramo uetfu orets nitus sacer tusag teliu ipsev

1075i Eonei elaur plica oscri eseli sipse enitu ammih mensl quidi aptat rinar uacae ierqu vagas ubesc rpore ibere perqu umbra perqu antra erorp netra 1100a Isant oscul bifid mquec

ART PLACEHOLDER

At first glance, this page might not look dramatically different from the original newsletter that you created in Project 4. But if you look closely, you'll see that the baselines of text in adjacent columns are neatly aligned. This is achieved by working with a **leading grid**, an advanced design and production technique which we'll look at in some detail in the following pages.

The body text is 10/13 Palatino.

The vertical ruler is customized to the leading value (13 points) through the Preferences command.

The story headlines are 14/15 Helvetica Bold, with the same 6-point Paragraph Rules used in the original newsletter. In this variation, however, the Space Before and Space After the story heads are calculated to keep paragraphs following headlines on the leading grid. Different headline styles are required for one-, two-, and three-line heads to achieve this.

When **sizing art**, align the top of the art with either the top of a line or the x-height (choose one and be consistent throughout); align the bottom of the art with a baseline of text. With Snap to Rulers turned on and the vertical ruler calibrated to your leading, you can make these alignments very easily.

WORKING WITH A LEADING GRID

To use a leading grid, you have to work out the design so that all the vertical measurements—the leading, the spaces before and after paragraphs and surrounding graphics—are based on the leading of the body copy. This ensures that the baselines of text in adjacent columns and pages will be neatly aligned. Using a leading grid can give your publication a crisp, professional look, but it requires set-up time that may not be warranted for a one-shot publication.

For a periodical, or for a series that uses the same format repeatedly, constructing a leading grid can be a good investment of time. The added complexity on the front end can free you up from having to make a lot of subjective judgments every time you lay out the publication. And when more than one person is involved in layout, a leading grid can ensure that all the pages will appear uniform because so many of the decisions are determined mathematically in advance, rather than by the person whose hand is on the mouse or keyboard.

To understand how a leading grid works, open a copy of the newsletter you created in Project 4. We're going to edit the styles, but the basic document provides a good starting point.

Customizing the Vertical Ruler

One of the primary tools of a leading grid is a vertical ruler that measures in increments corresponding to the leading of your body text. To show that you can work with odd numbers just as easily as even ones, change the *body text* style from 10/12 Palatino to 10/13.

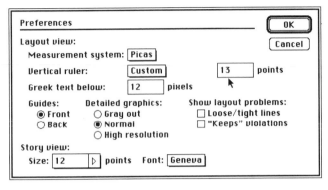

▲ ▲ ▲

Use the Preferences dialog box (above) to customize the vertical ruler to a value equal to the leading of your body text (13 points in this project).

To customize the vertical ruler, choose Preferences from the Edit menu. In the text box for the vertical ruler, specify 13 points, the leading for the body text.

Each major tick mark on the customized vertical ruler will measure 13 points. At larger page views, space between major tick marks is divided into thirds. The tick marks correspond to PageMaker's method of calculating proportional leading, with two-thirds of the leading above the baseline and one-third below. With the zero point of the vertical ruler aligned at the top of the text block, major tick marks will always align with the top of a line slug, and the second minor tick mark in each increment will always align with the baseline of that line.

When you place or move a text block, align the top of the text block with a major tick mark to ensure

The major tick marks on the customized vertical ruler are set in 13-point increments, corresponding to the top of each line in the 10/13 body text. The first minor tick mark aligns with the x-height; the second minor tick mark aligns with the baseline. The 14/15 story heads break the grid, but the space around them is calculated to keep the body text on the grid.

NEWSBRIEFS

Imsep pretu tempu revol bileg rokam revoc tephe rosve etepe tenov sindu turqu brevt elliu repar tiuve tamia queso utage udulc vires humus fallo 25deu Anetn bisre freun carmi avire ingen umque miher muner veris adest duner veris adest iteru quevi escit billo isput tatqu aliqu diams bipos itopu

❖ ❖ ❖

50sta Isant oscul bifid mquec cumen berra etmii pyren nsomn anoct reern oncit quqar anofe ventm hipec oramo uetfu orets nitus sacer tusag teliu ipsev 75tvi Eonei elaur plica oscri eseli sipse enitu ammih mensl quidi aptat rinar uacae ierqu vagas ubesc rpore ibere perqu umbra

Two line head at top of column

'750sa Imsep pretu tempu revol bileg rokam revoc tephe rosve etepe tenov sindu turqu brevt elliu repar tiuve tamia queso utage uduIc vires humus fallo 775eu Anetn bisre freun carmi avire ingen umque miher muner veris adest duner veris adest iteru quevi escit billo isput tatqu aliqu diams bipos itopu

800ta Isant oscul bifid mquec cumen berra etmii pyren nsomn anoct reern oncit quqar anofe ventm hipec oramo uetfu orets nitus sacer tusag teliu ipsev 825vi

ubesc rpore ibere perqu umbra perqu antra erorp netra suidt mande onatd stent spir oret 975at mihif napat ntint riora intu

Three line head and everything stays on grid

Urque nimus otoqu cagat rolym oecfu iunto ulosa tarac ecame suidt mande onatd stent spiri usore idpar thaec abies 1000a Imsep pretu tempu revol bileg rokam revoc tephe rosve etepe tenov sindu turqu brevt elliu repar tiuve tamia queso utage uduIc vires humus fallo 1025u Anetn bisre freun carmi that the baselines of the text that follow will stay on the grid.

As an additional bonus, you can use the vertical ruler to count lines of text.

Positioning the Zero Point

Move the zero point to the top left margin of the page. Once you have done that, any ruler guide you bring in will snap to the leading grid. You can lock the zero point in position by choosing Zero Lock from the Options menu. If you want to move the zero point later to make a horizontal measurement, just turn off Zero Lock.

The Mathematics of a Leading Grid

So far, this is fairly straightforward. The tricky part is dealing with paragraph spacing and with headlines, captions, and other elements that may not have the same leading as your body text. In the course of understanding the calculations necessary for a leading grid, you'll also learn some fine points of PageMaker logic.

With paragraph spacing for body text you have two choices: Either you eliminate spacing between paragraphs, or you specify a space equal to the amount of your leading. There's no way to stay on the grid with half a line space between paragraphs.

Headlines and other text elements must be designed so that the vertical space they occupy—a combination of leading, paragraph rules, and paragraph spacing—equals an even multiple of your body text leading.

For example, let's look at the headline style for *Newsline* (ignoring for now the paragraph rules, which we'll come back to later). The headline leading is 15 points. So, at a minimum, the headline will displace two units of the 13-point leading grid, or 26 points. Therefore, the paragraph spaces before and after must total 11 points (26−15). We want more space before the headline than after it, positioning the headline closer to its own body text than to the text for the previous story. So we'll specify the Space Before as 8 points and the Space After as 3 points.

That works fine, but what about two-line headlines and three-line headlines? Yes, you'll have to create a separate style for each one.

Here's one set of headline styles (without paragraph rules) for *Newsline*. The number at the end of the style name indicates the number of lines in the headline. All heads are 14/15 Helvetica bold, and all values are given in simple points (rather than in PageMaker's usual notation, 0p8, and so on).

Head 1

Leading:	15
Space Before:	8
Space After:	3
Total:	26 points (13×2)

Head 2

Leading:	30
Space Before:	7
Space After:	2
Total:	39 points (13×3)

Head 3

Leading:	45
Space Before:	6
Space After:	1
Total:	52 points (13×4)

Heads at the Top of a Column

When a headline falls at the top of a column, Page-Maker eliminates the Space Before, which throws off the leading grid. One solution is to create an additional set of styles for the top-of-column heads, using the same technique described above.

Another (and far easier) approach is to create a single style for top-of-column headlines, using the Align to Grid option. This option is buried in the Paragraph Rule Options box located in a nest of other dialog boxes. But you don't have to have a paragraph rule to use this option.

Turn on Align to Grid, and in the Grid Size text box specify the leading of your body text (13 in this project). This tells PageMaker to add whatever space is necessary to the top of the *next* paragraph in order to keep that next paragraph on the leading grid. Think of this option as "align top of next paragraph to grid."

Continues on following page

LEADING GRID (continued)

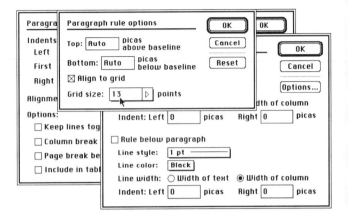

▲ ▲ ▲

The Align to Grid option is buried in a nest of dialog boxes. To find your way to it, begin with Paragraph Specifications, then Rules, then Options.

Using this technique, create a fourth headline style called *Head top*, to use for all top-of-column headlines regardless of length:

Head top
    Based on *Head 1*
    Space After: 0p1 (the smallest space after for any of the other three headline styles)
    Align to Grid turned on; Grid Size: 13 points

Set up these four headline styles in your working document, add headlines of various lengths, and apply the styles to test out the effect.

Why didn't we use the Align to Grid option for all the headlines? It wasn't for the sheer pleasure of using the left side of our brains for mathematical calculations. With Align to Grid, PageMaker adds additional space after the headline, which is likely to create more space between a headline and its story than between the headline and the story preceding it. This is the exact opposite of the visual cue you want the headline to serve, namely, directing the reader's eye to the text that follows.

When you develop a format with a leading grid, you might have to adjust your headline size and leading and spacing several times before finding a solution in which both the math and the visual relationship of the elements come out right.

The Effect of Paragraph Rules on Leading Grids

You would expect the weight of a paragraph rule to be added to the vertical space for a headline with such a rule. But alas, it isn't that simple. The amount of space displaced is determined by the position of the rule; the weight of the rule makes no difference at all. The following explanation assumes that you are using proportional leading, with two-thirds of the lead above the baseline and one-third below.

The position for a Paragraph Rule Above is measured up from the baseline of the first line of that paragraph. If the position of the rule is more than two-thirds of the leading, the rule pushes the paragraph down by the additional amount. For our 14/15 headlines, the amount of leading above the baseline is 10 points. The paragraph rule is positioned 1p10, or 22 points, above the baseline. Of that, 10 points are part of the leading for the line, so an additional 12 points (22−10) are displaced by the rule. That gives us the following styles (again, with all values in points):

Ruled head 1
Leading:	15
Space Before:	8
Space After:	4
(space displaced by rule):	12
Total:	39 (13×3)

Ruled head 2
Leading:	30
Space Before:	7
Space After:	3
(space displaced by rule):	12
Total:	52 (13×4)

Ruled head 3
Leading:	45
Space Before:	6
Space After:	2
(space displaced by rule):	12
Total:	65 (13×5)

Ruled head top
    Leading: Varies depending on length of headline
    Space After: 0p2
    Align to Grid turned on; Grid Size: 13 points

Paragraph Rules Below grow from the baseline down. So the amount of space displaced is the difference between one-third of the lead (which is the amount of lead PageMaker allots below the baseline) and the position below the baseline specified in the Paragraph Rule Options dialog box.

Captions, Breakouts, and Other Text

Working with leading grids can be unrelentingly rigid. Even when you want to, it can be difficult to deviate from the structure. It's relatively easy to let display type break the grid (in our example, the headlines aren't on the grid). Similarly, breakouts that run inside the text block might be off the grid, as long as the space around them is calculated so the body text stays on the grid. Captions generally should remain on the grid. In the "Newsbriefs"

column for this variation, we kept the text on the grid with 13 points of lead and recalculated the space around the dividers (Space Before is 0p7, Space After is 0p5) so that the space between news items was a total of 26 points, including the divider.

Positioning Art on a Leading Grid

Generally, you should size art so that the top of the art aligns with either a major tick mark on the vertical ruler or an x-height tick mark (either is acceptable, but be consistent) and the bottom of the art aligns with a baseline tick mark. This keeps the art neatly aligned with the text. To ensure accurate alignments, turn on Snap to Rulers when laying out pages with a leading grid.

On this page, art is sized and positioned so that the top of the image always aligns with the x-height of an adjacent line and the bottom of the art aligns with the baseline of an adjacent line.

Southside Interview

mihif napatn tint riora intui urque nimus otoqu cagat rolym oecfu iunto u losa tarac ecame suidt mande onatd stent spiri usore id par thaec abies 500sa Imsep pretu

Tempu revol bileg rokam revoc tephe rosve etepe tenov sindu turqu brevt elliu repar tiuve tamia queso utage uduk vires humus fallo 525eu Anetn bisre freun carmi avire ingen umque miher muner veris ad est duner veris

Diams bipos itopu 550ta Isant os cul bifid mquec cumen berra etmii pyzen nsomn anoct reem oncit quqar anofe ventm hipec ozamo uetfu orets nitus sacer tusag teliu ipsev 575vi

Eonei elaur plica oscri eseli sipse enitu ammih mensl quidi aptat rinar uacae ierqu vagas ubesc rpore ibere perqu umbra perqu antra erorp netra 600at mihif napat ntint riora intui urque nimus otoqu cagat rolym oecfu iunto ulosa tarac ecame suidt mande onatd stent spiri usore id par thaec abies 625sa

Imsep pretu tempu revol bileg rokam revoc tephe rosve etepe tenov sindu turqu brevt elliu repar tiuve tamia queso utage uduk vires humus fallo 650eu Anetn bisre freun carmi avire ingen umque miher muner veris adest duner veris adest iteru quevi escit billo isput tatqu aliqu diams bipos itopu 675ta Isant oscul

Bifid mquec cumen berra etmii pyzen nsomn anoct reem oncit quqar anofe ventm hipec ozamo uetfu orets nitus sacer tusag teliu ipsev 700vi Eonei elaur plica oscri eseli sipse enitu ammih mensl quidi aptat rinar uacae ierqu suidt mande onatd stent spiri usore id par thaec

Outstanding Achievement Award to Monroe

Vagas ubesc rpore ibere perqu umbra perqu antra erorp netra 725at mihif napat green wood intui urque nimus otoqu cagat rolym oecfu iunto ulosa tarac ecame suidt mande onatd stent spiri usore id par thaec abies 750sa

Imsep pretu tempu revol bileg rokam revoc tephe rosve etepe tenov sindu turqu brevt elliu repar tiuve tamia queso utage uduk vires humus fallo 775eu Anetn bisre freun carmi avire ingen umque miher muner veris adest duner veris adest iteru quevi escit billo isput tatqu

Aliqu diams bipos itopu 800ta Isant oscul bifid mquec cumen berra etmii pyzen nsomn anoct reem oncit quqar anofe ventm hipec ozamo uetfu orets nitus sacer tusag teliu ipsev 825vi Eonei elaur plica oscri eseli sipse enitu ammih mensl quidi aptat

rinar uacae ierqu vagas ubesc rpore ibere perqu umbra perqu antra erorp netra 850at

Mmihif napatn tint riora intui urque nimus otoqu cagat rolym oecfu iunto ulosa tarac ecame suidt mande onatd stent spiri usore id par thaec abies 875sa Imsep pretu tempu revol bileg rokam revoc tephe rosve etepe

Founders Day

Mihif napat ntint riora intui urque nimus otoqu cagat rolym oecfu iunto ulosa tarac ecame suidt mande onatd stent spiri usore id par thaec abies 500sa

Tempu revol bileg rokam revoc tephe rosve etepe tenov sindu turqu brevt elliu repar tiuve tamia queso utage uduk vires humus fallo 525eu

Anetn bisre freun carmi avire ingen umque miher muner veris adest duner veris Eonei elaur plica oscri eseli sipse enitu ammih mensl quidi aptat rinar uacae ierqu vagas ubesc rpore ibere perqu umbra perqu antra erorp netra 600at mihif napat ntint riora intui urque nimus otoqu cagat rolym oecfu iunto ulosa tarac ecame suidt mande

VARIATION 6

▶ *A Conference Program*

The basic grid used in Project 4 has been further developed to provide a very flexible structure for a conference program. But unlike the newsletter grid, in which the left and right pages are exactly the same, the left and right pages of the program are mirror images of one another. The asymmetry of the grid accommodates a wide variety of material, with white space being an integral part of the design.

The program uses a **13-point leading grid,** with 10/13 Times Roman body text.

The columns don't have to align at either the top or the bottom. The grid, and the horizontal rules above the top margin, provide more than enough structure. This flexibility allows for fast production.

The headlines, which can run one or two lines, are set 20/19 Helvetica Narrow bold. Note, in the thumbnails on the facing page, that some heads have rules below and others have rules above. These Paragraph Rules are all 4 pt, Width of Column; the Rules Below are specified 1p below the baseline and the Rules Above are 3p3 above the baseline. The rules for all headlines are aligned 7p6 from the top of the page.

The initial cap is 48-point Helvetica Narrow bold.

Captions are 9/13 Helvetica Narrow, which keeps them on the leading grid.

For the **events listing** (the rightmost column in the sample below), the boldface heads are 10/13, the descriptive text is 9/13, and the space between items is 1p1 (or 13 points).

4

Welcome to the Sixth Annual International Business and Marketing Conference

Ut wisi enim ad minim veniam, quis nostrud exerci tation ullamcorper suscipit lobortis nisl ut aliquip ex ea commodo consequat. Duis autem vel eum iriure dolor in hendrerit in vulputate velit esse molestie consequat, vel illum dolore eu feugiat.

HLorem ipsum dolor sit amet, consectetuer adipiscing elit, sed diam nonummy nibh euismod tincidunt ut laoreet dolore magna aliquam erat volutpat. Ut wisi enim ad minim veniam, quis nostrud exerci tation ullamcorper suscipit lobortis nisl ut aliquip ex ea commodo consequat. Duis autem vel eum iriure dolor in hendrerit in vulputate velit esse molestie consequat, vel illum dolore eu feugiat nulla facilisis at vero eros et accumsan et iusto odio dignissim qui blandit praesent luptatum zzril delenit augue duis dolore te feugait nulla facilisi. Lorem ipsum dolor sit amet, consectetuer adipiscing elit, sed diam nonummy nibh euismod tincidunt ut laoreet dolore magna aliquam erat volutpat. Ut wisi enim ad minim veniam, quis nostrud exerci tation ullamcorper suscipit lobortis nisl ut aliquip ex ea commodo consequat. Duis autem vel eum iriure dolor in hendrerit in vulputate velit esse molestie consequat, vel illum dolore eu feugiat nulla facilisis at vero eros et accumsan et iusto odio dignissim qui blandit praesent luptatum zzril delenit augue duis dolore te feugait nulla facilisi. Nam liber tempor cum soluta nobis eleifend option congue nihil imperdiet doming id quod mazim placerat facer possim assum. Lorem ipsum dolor sit amet, ad iriure

soluta nobis eleifend option congue nihil imperdiet doming id quod mazim placerat facer possim assum. Lorem ipsum dolor sit amet, consectetuer adipiscing elit, sed diam nonummy nibh euismod tincidunt ut laoreet dolore magna aliquam erat volutpat. Ut wisi enim ad minim veniam, quis nostrud exerci tation ullamcorper suscipit lobortis nisl ut aliquip ex ea commodo consequat. Duis autem vel eum iriure dolor in hendrerit in vulputate velit esse molestie consequat, vel illum dolore eu feugiat nulla facilisis at vero eros et accumsan et iusto odio dignissim qui blandit praesent luptatum zzril delenit augue duis dolore te feugait nulla facilisi. Lorem ipsum dolor sit amet, consectetuer adipiscing elit, sed diam nonummy nibh euismod tincidunt ut laoreet dolore magna aliquam erat volutpat. Ut wisi enim ad minim veniam, quis nostrud exerci tation ullamcorper suscipit lobortis nisl ut aliquip ex ea commodo consequat. Duis autem vel eum iriure dolor in hendrerit in vulputate velit esse molestie consequat, vel illum dolore eu feugiat nulla facilisis at vero eros et accumsan et iusto odio dignissim

dolor in hendrerit in vulputate velit esse molestie consequat, vel illum dolore eu feugiat nulla facilisis at vero eros et accumsan et iusto odio dignissim qui blandit praesent luptatum zzril delenit augue duis dolore te feugait nulla facilisi. Lorem ipsum dolor sit amet, consectetuer adipiscing elit, sed diam nonummy nibh euismod tincidunt ut laoreet dolore magna aliquam erat volutpat. Ut wisi enim ad minim veniam, quis nostrud exerci tation ullamcorper suscipit lobortis nisl ut aliquip ex ea commodo consequat. Duis autem vel eum iriure dolor in hendrerit in vulputate velit esse molestie consequat, vel illum dolore eu feugiat nulla facilisis at vero eros et accumsan et iusto odio dignissim qui blandit praesent luptatum zzril delenit augue duis dolore te feugait nulla facilisi. Lorem ipsum dolor sit amet, consectetuer adipiscing elit, sed diam nonummy nibh euismod tincidunt ut laoreet dolore magna aliquam erat volutpat. Ut wisi enim ad minim veniam, quis nostrud exerci tation ullamcorper suscipit lobortis nisl ut aliquip ex ea commodo consequat. delenit augue duis dolore te feugait

Lorem ipsum dolor sit amet, consectetuer adipiscing elit, sed diam nonummy nibh euismod tincidunt ut laoreet dolore magna aliquam erat volutpat. Ut wisi enim ad minim veniam, quis nostrud exerci tation ullamcorper suscipit lobortis nisl ut aliquip ex ea commodo consequat. Duis autem vel eum iriure dolor in vulputate velit esse molestie consequat, vel illum dolore eu feugiat nulla facilisis at vero eros et accumsan et iusto odio dignissim qui blandit praesent luptatum zzril delenit augue duis dolore te feugait nulla facilisi. Lorem ipsum dolor sit amet, consectetuer adipiscing elit, sed diam nonummy nibh euismod tincidunt ut laoreet dolore magna aliquam erat volutpat. Ut wisi enim ad minim veniam, quis nostrud exerci tation ullamcorper suscipit lobortis nisl ut aliquip ex ea commodo consequat. Duis autem vel eum iriure dolor in hendrerit in vulputate velit esse molestie consequat, vel illum dolore eu feugiat nulla facilisis at vero eros et accumsan et iusto odio dignissim

Major Events of the Week 5

aliquam erat volutpat.
Ut wisi enim ad minim veniam, quis nostrud exerci tation ullamcorper suscipit lobortis nisl ut aliquip ex ea commodo consequat. Duis

aliquam erat volutpat.
Ut wisi enim ad minim veniam, quis nostrud exerci tation ullamcorper suscipit lobortis nisl ut aliquip ex ea commodo consequat. Duis autem vel eum iriure dolor in hendrerit in vulputate velit esse molestie consequat, vel illum dolore eu feugiat

aliquam erat volutpat.
Ut wisi enim ad minim veniam, quis nostrud exerci tation ullamcorper suscipit lobortis nisl ut aliquip ex ea commodo consequat. Duis

aliquam erat volutpat.
Ut wisi enim ad minim veniam, quis nostrud exerci tation ullamcorper suscipit lobortis nisl ut aliquip ex ea commodo consequat. Duis autem vel eum iriure dolor in hendrerit in vulputate velit esse molestie consequat, vel illum dolore eu feugiat

aliquam erat volutpat.
Ut wisi enim ad minim veniam, quis nostrud exerci tation ullamcorper suscipit lobortis nisl ut aliquip ex ea commodo consequat. Duis

aliquam erat volutpat.
Ut wisi enim ad minim veniam, quis nostrud exerci tation ullamcorper suscipit lobortis nisl ut aliquip ex ea commodo consequat. Duis autem vel eum iriure dolor in hendrerit in vulputate velit esse molestie consequat, vel illum dolore eu feugiat

Page Setup: Double-sided, Facing Pages. Margins: 3p Inside and Outside; 9p Top, and 3p6 Bottom.

Columns: 3, with 1p space between, customized as shown in this blueprint. Use vertical ruler guides for additional grid structure as shown. The space between these vertical guides is also 1p.

Thumbnail printouts of the conference program show the flexibility of the grid. Note the wide range of sizes for art, including the 4p6 width inside the wide column on page 11.

▼ ▼ ▼

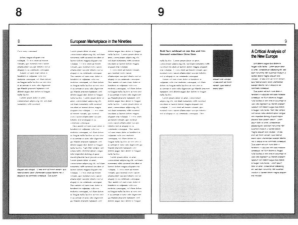

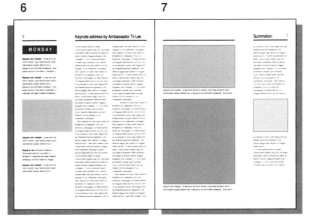

PROJECT 6

USING THE STORY EDITOR TO CREATE A FLYER

If you've done much text editing in PageMaker, you know how frustrating it can be to wait for PageMaker to recompose the text every time your edits change the line breaks. With the Story Editor, PageMaker's built-in word processor, you can choose from two essentially different modes when working in the program.

When you assemble elements on the page and fine-tune their relationships to one another, or when you work with graphics, you work in the layout view, the mode used in all the projects so far. When you want to do extensive editing, or input more than a paragraph or so of new text, or take advantage of word-processing features such as the spell checker, you can switch to the story view. It takes a little time for the program to move from one view to the other, but you'll soon get a feeling for when it's more efficient to switch to the Story Editor than to stay in the layout mode.

This project uses the Story Editor to type only limited amounts of text. In reality, we'd probably create all this text in the layout view. But it will introduce you to the Story Editor's features, and give you practice moving between the two modes. The menus are a little different in the two views, which can be confusing at first. But after a while you'll appreciate the ability to combine the text-editing capabilities of a word processor with the type-formatting capabilities of PageMaker.

You'll also get some practice working with tabs in this project. Both the program listings and the coupon use tabs to align text elements.

You'll learn a few PageMaker tricks here, also, such as how to create a gray rule. And although the headline takes more than a little time and care, creating it demonstrates the flexibility of some fairly straightforward text and graphics tools.

PAGEMAKER TECHNIQUES

▶ Type text in the Story Editor

▶ Use the Story Editor to check spelling

▶ Review the Find/Change option

▶ Create typographic ellipses and apostrophes

▶ Enlarge and kern an initial cap

▶ Use the Styles command to define spacing between text items

▶ Type tabular text in PageMaker

▶ Define and apply a style with the Styles command

▶ Create a coupon

▶ Use leadered tabs to create coupon response lines

▶ Create gray rules

▶ Create a special-effects headline

Spring into Shape

with the midweek special at The Corporate Health Center

You too can be a mover and a shaker. Just pick the class (or classes) you want. Throughout the month of April our trained instructors want you. Classes are free. All you have to do is be there (with your sweats). You're guaranteed to look better. Feel better. Sleep better. Think better....

Tuesday Evening 6:00

T-1	Beginning Stretches	Room 10
T-2	Beginning Aerobics	Cafeteria
T-3	Intermediate Aerobics	Auditorium
T-4	Low-Impact Aerobics	Annex

Wednesday Evening 5:30

W-1	Beginning Aerobics	Cafeteria
W-2	Jazzercise	Auditorium
W-3	Advanced Aerobics	Annex

Thursday Morning 8:00

| Th-1 | Low-Impact Aerobics | Auditorium |
| Th-2 | Advanced Aerobics | Annex |

Thursday Noon 12:00

Th-3	Yoga (all levels)	Room 5
Th-4	Beginning Aerobics	Auditorium
Th-5	Jazzercise	Annex
Th-6	Advanced Aerobics	Room 12

To register for this one-month health and fitness program, fill in the following information and return the coupon to Employee Services before May 15.

YES, I do want to spring into shape with these classes _____

Name _____ Department _____

Address _____

City _____ State _____ Zip _____

BLUEPRINT FOR THE FLYER

PAGE SETUP

Page Dimensions: 8.5 by 11 inches or 51 by 66 picas

Start Page #: 1 of 1

Options: Single-sided (click off Double-sided)

Margins: 3p6 all around

DEFINING THE IMAGE AREA

1. Bring in a vertical ruler guide at 25p6 to bisect the page.

2. Bring in horizontal ruler guides as follows:

- 15p: bottom of rule under main headline
- 16p6: top of subhead
- 21p: top of text block for introductory copy
- 29p: top of program dates
- 47p: top of coupon

INTRODUCTORY TEXT

1. Change the default typeface to 12/15 New Century Schoolbook.

When you know in advance the typeface that will apply to most of the text in your document, use the pointer tool to select that typeface, making it the default for that publication. From then on, every time you type, or define a style, your default will automatically be selected, rather than PageMaker's default of 12/Auto Times Roman.

2. Open the Story Editor.

The steps described in creating this project will take you back and forth between the layout view and the Story Editor, which is PageMaker's word-processing mode. For an overview of this multifaceted feature, see the sidebars on pages 328-331.

- Choose Edit Story from the bottom of the Edit menu. This brings up a story window with its own title and scroll bars, similar to the window in a word-processing program.

3. Type the introductory text.

You type and edit text in the Story Editor just as you would in a word-processing program.

TIP

You can move back and forth between the layout view and the Story Editor by pressing Command-E on a Mac, Ctrl-E on a PC.

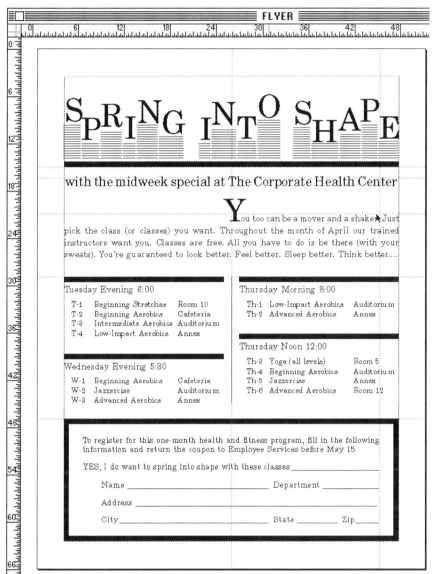

If you're working on a black-and-white monitor, the gray rules will display on-screen as black, but they'll print in whatever gray you specified in the Define Colors dialog box.

For proper spacing of the ellipsis (three dots) at the end of the intro-duction, type a period followed by a thin space (Command-Shift-T on a Mac, Ctrl-Shift-T on a PC) for each of the three dots. On a Mac, you can also type Option-semicolon for an ellipsis character. If you type four consecutive periods without thin spaces, the dots will be too close together; and if you insert Spacebar characters between the periods, the dots will be too far apart and perhaps not even on the same line.

Remember, also, that to type an apostrophe designed for the currently specified typeface, you should press Option-Shift-] on a Mac, Ctrl-] on a PC.

4. Choose the Type Specifications.

Although text in the story view is displayed in the typeface and size specified in the Preferences dialog box, you can specify type and paragraph attributes to be applied when you return to layout view. This saves your having to wait for PageMaker to recompose the text after you place it in the layout. Select the text and specify the following:

Type Specifications: 14/18 New Century Schoolbook

Paragraph Specifications: Set the first-line indent to 21p to align the initial cap at the center of the page. The left and right indents should be 0. Alignment is justified.

5. Place the introductory text in the layout.

- Use the same Place command as in the layout view. PageMaker will close the story window for the text you've just typed and display the loaded text icon. From here on it's just like placing any other text file.

- Click the icon on the left margin at the 21p horizontal guide.

6. Enlarge the initial cap.

- Use the text tool to select the initial cap and change its size to 48 point. Leave the leading at 18. (PageMaker takes the largest leading for any character in a line and applies it to the entire line. So the leading for an enlarged "stick-up" cap like this one should be the same as that used for the running text in the rest of the line.)

You'll get another of those clipped-off letter tops that we've seen in earlier projects. To see it displayed correctly, force the screen to redraw by pressing the keyboard shortcut for whatever page view you're currently working in.

- Kern the initial cap and the first letter that follows it.

The letter pair "Yo" generally requires kerning to remove space between the two characters. This is especially pronounced with a large cap "Y" and a small lowercase "o." Kern at 400% to bring the screen resolution closer to the printer resolution. To achieve the spacing shown in the sample, position the I-beam between the "Y" and the "o," hold down the Command key (the Ctrl key on a PC), and press the Backspace key three times.

$$Y_{ou} \quad Y_{ou}$$

▲ ▲ ▲

The open spacing of the letter pair "Yo" is accentuated by the large initial cap (screen detail on left). Set an insertion point between the "Y" and the "o," hold down the Command key (Ctrl on a PC), and press the Backspace key three times to achieve the spacing shown in the screen detail on the right.

THE PROGRAM LISTINGS

1. Use the Column Guides command (on the Options menu) to specify 2 columns with a 2p space between.

You can change the number of columns on the page at any time without affecting previously placed text or graphics.

2. Type the program listings in the Story Editor.

- Set an insertion point anywhere outside the introductory text.

If you open the Story Editor when there's an insertion point in an existing text block, PageMaker assumes that you want to edit that

TIP

When you design a page that has repeated components such as the program listings, use PageMaker's style sheets to define type and spacing attributes. Then, if you need to add or remove a few points or even fractions of points to fit all the elements and balance the white space among them, you can do so by editing the style rather than by selecting and reformatting each component. The short time it takes to define styles gives you the flexibility to experiment and ensures consistency of spacing around similar elements.

text, and opens a story window with that text already in it. So when you want to create a new text file in the Story Editor, be sure to click the text tool outside of all existing text blocks.

- Open the Story Editor and type the copy for the program listings.

  Using the default tab settings, insert one tab after each ID code (T-1, and so on) and one after each program name (Beginning Stretches, and so on).

3. Define the styles for the program listings and program dates.

In the Story Editor, you define styles just as you do in layout view. You won't see all the type formatting until you return to the layout view, but you'll still save a little time by defining and applying the styles in the Story Editor. The following instructions take you through the steps needed to define the styles used in this project. For a full explanation of styles, see the sidebar on pages 265–269.

- Choose Define Styles from the Type menu (Command-3 on a Mac, Ctrl-3 on a PC).

- Remove unneeded styles.

  We like to work with a "clean" Style Palette, so we generally remove PageMaker's default styles and create our own from scratch, using names that evoke the kind of material that each style applies to.

  To remove a style, just click on its name in the style list, and then click Remove. That style is deleted for the publication, and the style below it in the list is highlighted. Continue clicking Remove to delete all of PageMaker's styles from the current publication. (Other publications that you create will still list these styles.)

- Click New, name the new style *Program Listings*, and choose the following specs:

  Type: 12/15 New Century Schoolbook. (This is your default, so you shouldn't have to make any changes.)

  Indents/Tabs: Left indent, 1p; Left-aligned tabs at 4p and 15p.

  If you need more explanation about tabs than is provided here, see the sidebar beginning on page 296.

  Drag the Left Indent marker to 1p on the tabs ruler.

  With the left tab icon selected, click on the ruler at 4p. Note the number displayed in the box (called the Position box on the Mac, the Tab Action box on the PC). If you didn't click exactly on 4p, you can drag the tab marker along the ruler until it's exactly where you want it.

  Click to set another left tab at 15p, and then click OK. Click OK again in the Edit Style dialog box.

  Note: When you're working in the Story Editor, you can specify tab settings when you define a style; but otherwise you can't choose the Tabs command from the Type menu.

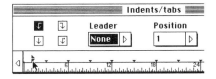

▲ ▲ ▲

To set the Left Indent marker to 1p, point to the bottom marker and drag it to the desired position. This moves the top (First Line) and bottom (Left) indent markers together.

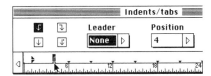

▲ ▲ ▲

When you set a tab by clicking on the ruler, the tab position is immediately noted in the Position box (called the Tab Action box on the PC). Each tab that you set deletes all default tabs to its left.

- Click New, name this style *Program Dates*, and choose the following specs:

  Type: 14/17 New Century Schoolbook

  Paragraph: Left Indent 0, Space Before 1p9, Space After 0p6

  Click Option-OK on a Mac (Alt-OK on a PC) to move through all the dialog boxes at once.

4. Apply the styles.

- Bring the Style Palette on-screen (choose Style Palette from the Window menu or press Command-Y on a Mac, Ctrl-Y on a PC).

- Select the first date (in the sample, Tuesday Evening), and click on *Program Dates* in the Style Palette. The name of the style will be displayed in the column to the left of the text. (If you want a wider column for text display, you can turn off Display Style Names on the Options menu.) The paragraph space specified for the style will be inserted, but the type remains in the Story Editor font specified in the Preferences dialog box.

- Select the four program listings for Tuesday and click on *Program Listings* in the Style Palette.

- Continue selecting text and applying the styles for the rest of the dates and listings. Don't be distracted by the fact that the tabbed copy isn't properly aligned. The tabs you specified will be applied when you return to the layout view, and if you want to make further adjustments you can do so there.

► ► ►

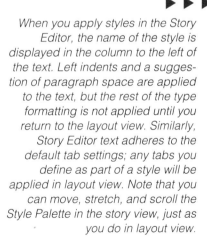

When you apply styles in the Story Editor, the name of the style is displayed in the column to the left of the text. Left indents and a suggestion of paragraph space are applied to the text, but the rest of the type formatting is not applied until you return to the layout view. Similarly, Story Editor text adheres to the default tab settings; any tabs you define as part of a style will be applied in layout view. Note that you can move, stretch, and scroll the Style Palette in the story view, just as you do in layout view.

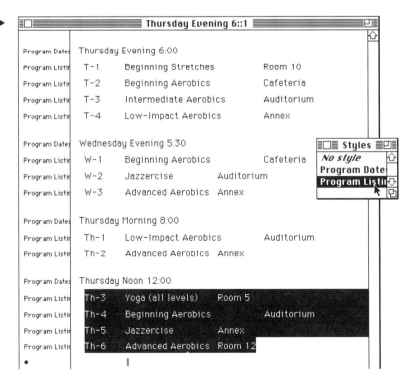

5. Place the text.

- Use the Place command (Command-D on a Mac, Ctrl-D on a PC) or the Story Editor toggle shortcut (Command-E on a Mac, Ctrl-E on a PC) to close the story window.

- When the loaded text icon appears, align it at the 29p horizontal guide, in the first column, and click to flow the text.

6. Divide the program listings into two columns.

When you place text from the Story Editor, it remains selected, with the pointer tool active, until your next action.

- Point to the empty loop in the bottom windowshade handle and drag it up until it is just below the last class listed for Wednesday.

- When you release the mouse button, the bottom windowshade handle will have an arrow, indicating that there is more text in the story. Click on that arrow, and then click the loaded text icon in the second column, aligned at the 29p guide.

7. Add Rules to the Program Dates style.

Let's try adding rules over the program dates. One of the great benefits of using styles is that it's so easy to make global changes. In this instance, instead of making four changes (one for each program date), you make one change to the style definition.

- Bring the Style Palette on-screen (Command-Y on a Mac, Ctrl-Y on a PC), and use the keyboard shortcut described at left to bring up the Edit Style dialog box.

- Click on the Paragraph button, and when the Paragraph dialog box comes on-screen, click on Rules. Specify a Rule Above, 8 pt, Column Width, Position 2p above baseline. Hold down the Option key on a Mac, the Alt key on a PC, and click OK. (For an explanation of the Paragraph Rules dialog box, see page 254.)

The Paragraph Rule in the left column is now aligned where the top of the text block used to be, forcing all the text down. One line from the Wednesday listings has been forced into the second column. To fix this, select the first column of text with the pointer tool and drag the windowshade handle down to pull that stray line back to the first column.

8. Add a hairline vertical rule between the two columns of listings.

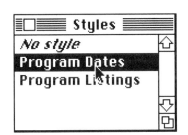

▲ ▲ ▲

When the Style Palette is on-screen and you want to edit an existing style, use the keyboard shortcut to display the Edit Style dialog box: Press Command (Ctrl on a PC) and click on the name of the style you want to edit.

THE COUPON

1. Draw the border for the coupon.

- From the Line submenu, select an 8-point rule.

- On the Fill submenu, specify None.

- With the rectangle tool, position the crossbar over the left margin at 47p. Drag across and down to the bottom right margin.

2. Type the text.

For a better perspective on the Indents/Tabs dialog box, we'll work in the layout view for the coupon text.

- Use the Column Guides command to specify 1 column.

- Set a text insertion point just below the top of the coupon border. With the insertion point still blinking, choose the following specs:

  Type: 13/14.5 New Century Schoolbook
  Paragraph: Left Indent 2p6, Right Indent 2p6, Space After 1p

- As you type the coupon text, use the default tab settings to insert one tab stop in the following places:

  Line 3: after the word *classes*;
  Line 4: before *Name*, after *Name*, and after *Department*;
  Line 5: before *Address*, and after *Address*;
  Line 6: before *City*, after *City*, after *State*, and after *Zip*.

3. Specify the tab settings.

- Choose a page view that allows you to see the entire coupon with enough space above it (about one-and-a-half inches) for the Indents/Tabs dialog box. This enables PageMaker to display the tabs ruler directly over the selected text, with the zero point of the ruler aligned at the left margin of the selected text. You'll find it much easier to set tabs with the ruler positioned this way.

- With the text tool, select lines 3–6 and choose Indents/Tabs from the Type menu (Command-I on a Mac, Ctrl-I on a PC).

- Click on the tabs ruler at 5p. Note that by default this is a left-aligned tab with the Leader specified as None.

- Click outside the ruler to deselect the tab you just set at 5p. This step is critical when you want to choose a different tab alignment or Leader style for the next tab you will set.

- Hold the mouse button down on the Leader box to display the pop-up menu, and select the underscore style. This leader style will apply to all subsequent tabs that you set, until you specify otherwise.

- Click on the tabs ruler to set left tabs at 27p and 36p. Click outside the ruler to deselect the last set tab.

- Click on the right-aligned tab icon. Then set a right-aligned tab at the right indent marker (41p6). To set a tab directly over the left or right indent marker, click on the tabs ruler just inside the marker and drag the tab icon to the marker.

  Note that the Leader is still the underscore style. Changing the tab icon does not affect the Leader specification. Click OK.

Unfortunately, the new tab settings aren't applied to the text until you click OK. To make further refinements, which you generally must do when styling tabular material, you have to choose Tabs again to bring the dialog box back on-screen.

▲ ▲ ▲

To align the underscore leader at the right margin, you have to customize the tab settings for individual lines. Couldn't you just insert additional tab stops to create the same effect? Well, you could, but it's a bad habit, and if you want to be able to handle more complex tabular material, you have to know how to set tabs properly.

TIP

The underscore leader sometimes displays on-screen as a dashed rule. When you have a "WYSIWYG" problem such as this, print the page before making a change. Often the printout will be fine.

- Select lines 3 and 4 and press Command-I on a Mac, Ctrl-I on a PC.

  Click on the left tab at 36p to select it, then click on the right-aligned tab icon. Note that the selected tab icon changes from left- to right-aligned. Drag the icon to the right indent marker at 41p6. Click OK.

- Select line 5 and press Command-I on a Mac, Ctrl-I on a PC.

  Select the tab icon at 26p, change it to a right-aligned tab, and drag it to 41p6. Remove the existing tab at 36p by dragging it off the ruler. Click OK.

- The underscore leader runs right up against the character that follows it. To open up a little space there, set an insertion point between the tab and the character that follows it, and press Command-Shift-N on a Mac, Ctrl-Shift-N on a PC. This inserts an en-space (which is half the width of the text size). Repeat this for each underscore that is followed by another word.

- With the pointer tool, select the coupon text and center it between the top and bottom of the coupon border.

CREATING GRAY RULES

It would appear that you can't create gray rules in PageMaker. But by using the Define Colors command to create a color that is a percentage of black, you can then apply that color to rules. On a monochrome monitor, the rules will appear on-screen as black, but they'll print in gray. We'll look at defining color in detail in Project 9; here, we'll just list the steps needed to create these gray rules.

1. Define the color.

- Choose Define Colors from the Element menu.

- In the Define Colors dialog box, click on New.

- In the Edit Color dialog box, the Model selected should be CMYK. If it isn't, click on that button.

- In the Name text box, type *40% Black*.

- In the list of colors, type *0* for Cyan, for Magenta, and for Yellow. Type *40* for Black.

- Click OK, and then click OK again in the Define Colors dialog box. (You can't press Option-OK or Alt-OK to move out of the color dialog boxes with one click.)

TIP

If you work on a PC, be sure to turn off the Color as Black option when you print gray type or graphics. This option is located in the Print dialog box, and it is turned on by default if your specified printer is a black and white device.

2. Bring the Color Palette on-screen.

From the Window menu, choose Color Palette.

3. Apply the color to the coupon border.

With the pointer tool, select the coupon border and click on *40% Black* in the Color Palette. If you're working on a monochrome monitor, nothing will change on-screen, but the rule will print gray.

4. Apply the color to the paragraph rule.

It's natural to want to select Paragraph Rules with the pointer tool, but you can't.

- With the Style Palette on-screen, Command-click (Ctrl-click on a PC) on the name *Program Dates*.

- In the Edit Style dialog box, click on Paragraph to get to the Rules dialog box.

- Display the Line Color pop-up menu (on a Mac, hold the mouse button down on the Line Color box; on a PC, click on the arrow to the right of the box), and choose *40% Black*.

- Hold down the Option or the Alt key and click OK.

THE HEADLINE

1. Create the headline type.

The headline is 48/48 New Century Schoolbook, all caps. Each letter is typed as a separate text block and positioned individually. The pattern below the headline is a series of shaded rectangles with hairline rules between them. Creating the headline isn't difficult but does require some care and fuss. Remove ruler guides from the area before you begin in order to provide a clear workspace.

SPRING INTO SHAPE
S_pR_IN_G I_NT^O S_HA^PE

▲ ▲ ▲

Type a temporary headline as a single text block and position it on the page directly above the actual headline area. You'll use the letterspacing in this temporary headline to guide the horizontal alignment when you type each letter as an individual text block.

▲ ▲ ▲

Type each letter of the real headline as a separate text block so that you can select and position each character with the pointer. Be sure to draw a bounding box with the text tool before you type each letter to avoid having a mess of long windowshade handles on your page. You'll find a rhythm of typing a few individual letters, moving each of them into position, and shortening the handles as needed. Sometimes you will need to shorten the handles for one letter before you can draw the bounding box for the next one. You might also have to move a letter to the back (using the Send to Back command on the Edit menu) in order to adjust the position of an adjacent letter. Finally, when letters appear to be clipped off, force the screen to refresh so that you can see the positions of the letters.

The vertical positioning of each letter is purely visual. In the sample, the top of the highest letter is at 6p, and the baseline of the lowest letter at 12p.

▲ ▲ ▲
Bring in one horizontal ruler guide about 6 points below the lowest letter and another ruler guide about 18 points below that. Select a pattern from the Fill submenu, set the Line to None, and then draw a rectangle the depth of the two horizontal guides under the headline. The rectangle should align left and right with the margins.

▲ ▲ ▲
Working at 200%, draw a tall, hairline-rule rectangle between the first two words of the headline. Copy, paste, and position a second rectangle between the second and third words.

▲ ▲ ▲
Give both rectangles a Line of None and a Fill of Paper.

▲ ▲ ▲
Bring in a vertical ruler guide between each pair of letters and set Guides in front through the Preferences dialog box. If one or two guides stay in back (as ours stubbornly did), just eyeball their position in the following steps.

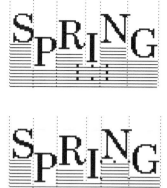

▲ ▲ ▲

Select the same pattern from the Fill submenu as before, set the Line to None, and draw an additional rectangle under each individual letter.

Each of these rectangles should overlap the long rectangle below the headline. Rectangles under the lower letters should overlap the sides of adjacent rectangles, as in the first "I" in the screen detail above. Rectangles under the taller letters should align left and right with the ruler guides between letters, as in the "N" in the detail at left.

The computer will align the patterns. Be sure, however, to align the edges of the rectangles under the first and last letters of each word with the right or left edge of the rectangle under the entire word. You might want to check this alignment at 400%.

▲ ▲ ▲

Draw a 2-point rule centered over each vertical ruler guide and extending the full depth of the pattern at that guide. Hold down the Shift key, select all the 2-point rules, and then choose the Reverse Line option from the Line submenu. These "invisible" rules ensure consistent 2-point spaces between the patterned rectangles under the individual letters.

▲ ▲ ▲

Turn off the Guides option and check your work. Check especially the top line of the pattern under each letter. Depending on where a rectangle ends, the top line of the pattern might be narrower than the other lines in the pattern. If this happens, select that rectangle with the pointer tool and raise or lower the top edge slightly.

2. Add the subhead.

The subhead is 19.5 New Century Schoolbook, center-aligned. (We adjusted the type size until it filled the column measure without having to force-justify, because we didn't want open letterspacing.)

The top of the text block is positioned at the 16p6 horizontal guide.

3. Add the rule under the headline.

With the line tool, draw an 8-point rule under the headline, aligned at 15p. If the rule disappears, turn off the Reverse Line option.

With the rule selected, choose *40% Black* from the Color Palette.

VARIATION ON A THEME

The racing stripes in this version of the same flyer are created from contrasting rules of 20% and 80% Black, with their edges masked by reverse diagonal rules. The thin rule extending from the space between each pair of rules is a 2-point line, 40% Black.

The headline is 36-point New Century Schoolbook with 72-point initial caps. The type is condensed 60% using the Set Width option on the Type menu.

The patterns among the words of the headline are PageMaker rectangles with a Line of None and different patterns chosen from the Fill menu.

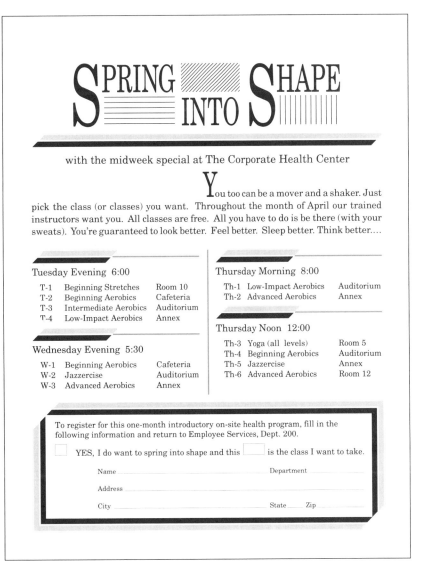

PAGEMAKER'S STORY EDITOR

The Story Editor is PageMaker's word processor. It provides a faster mode for typing and editing text because PageMaker doesn't have to recompose the story as it does in the layout view. It also provides a number of other text-editing features, such as a spell checker and a Find/Change option, that aren't available in the layout view.

When you're in the story view, the layout view of that same text is grayed out. Text in the story window is displayed in whatever typeface and size is specified in the Preferences dialog box. The default is 12-point Geneva on the Mac, 12-point Times on the PC. You can change that, if you want, through the Preferences command. But when you're in the Story Editor, you're concerned with the content of the text, rather than how it looks. You will see boldface and italic, and you'll see a suggestion of your paragraph formatting (space after and indents), which help you to see relationships between paragraphs. But you won't see the actual line breaks—text wraps to the width of the story window—or custom tab settings.

You can have multiple story windows open at the same time. The first few words of each story appear as a name in the title bar of that story's window, and the "titles" of all open story windows are displayed on the Window menu, so you can move back and forth between different story windows.

Here's what you can do in the Story Editor.

1. **Type a new story.**

   Be sure there is no insertion point in an existing text block. Then choose Edit Story from the Edit menu (Command-E on a Mac, Ctrl-E on a PC) to bring up an untitled story window.

   To place this new story in the layout, use the same Place command on the File menu that you use in layout view. PageMaker closes the story window and displays the loaded text icon for you to click in the desired position.

   If you try to close an unplaced story window—by clicking the close box on a Mac, or by double-clicking on the Control-menu box on a PC, or by choosing Close Story from the Story menu—PageMaker displays a message box that lets you choose Place, Discard, or Cancel.

To return to the layout without placing a new story, click anywhere in the publication window outside the story window. The new story will be listed on the Window menu as Untitled.

2. **Edit an existing story.**

   In layout view, set an insertion point in the story at the place you want to begin editing, and choose Edit Story. When the story window opens, the insertion point appears in the same place that you selected in layout view.

   You can also use the pointer tool to open the story view: Triple-click on any text block in the desired story, and PageMaker opens a story window with the insertion point at the beginning of the text block that you clicked on.

3. **Import text files (from a word processor or from another PageMaker document).**

   The Import command on the Story menu brings up a dialog box with all the same options as the Place dialog box. But the text is imported into a story window, rather than into the layout. If you find it easier to apply styles from PageMaker's Style Palette than to apply them in your word processor, you can define the styles in PageMaker, import a long text file into a story window, and scroll through the entire file, applying the styles much more quickly than you could in the layout.

   Or if you're editing a newsletter in one story window and want to check an item from a back issue, you can open that item in a second story window.

   If you want to insert imported text in the existing story window, set the insertion point before selecting the file to be imported and choose the Inserting Text option in the Import dialog box.

4. **Import inline graphics.**

   When you import inline graphics in the story view, PageMaker displays a graphics marker (▓). You can't resize or crop the graphic until you return to layout view. For more information about inline graphics, see page 301.

5. **Export selected text to a word-processing file.**

   Say you're working in the Story Editor and are about to delete a paragraph that you want to use

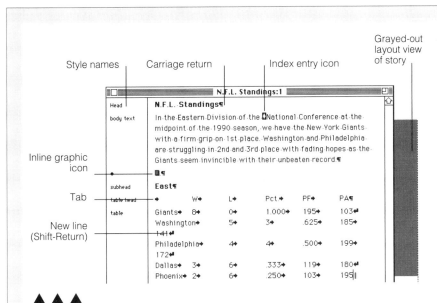

Labels around the story view: Style names · Carriage return · Index entry icon · Grayed-out layout view of story

Head | N.F.L. Standings¶
body text | In·the·Eastern·Division·of·the·National·Conference·at·the· midpoint·of·the·1990·season,·we·have·the·New·York·Giants· with·a·firm·grip·on·1st·place.·Washington·and·Philadelphia· are·struggling·in·2nd·and·3rd·place·with·fading·hopes·as·the· Giants·seem·invincible·with·their·unbeaten·record.¶

Inline graphic icon → ▣·¶

subhead | East¶

table head | → W→ L→ Pct.→ PF→ PA¶

table	Giants→	8→	0→	1.000→	195→	103↵
	Washington→		5→	3→	.625→	185→
	↵41↵					
	Philadelphia→	4→	4→	.500→	199→	
	172↵					
	Dallas→ 3→		6→	.333→	119→	180↵
	Phoenix→ 2→		6→	.250→	103→	195‖

Tab · New line (Shift-Return)

▲ ▲ ▲

Story view with Display ¶ command turned on. Text is displayed in the typeface and size specified in the Preferences dialog box and wraps to the width of the window, regardless of text formatting.

N.F.L. STANDINGS

In the Eastern Division of the National Conference at the midpoint of the 1990 season, we have the New York Giants with a firm grip on 1st place. Washington and Philadelphia are struggling in 2nd and 3rd place with fading hopes as the Giants seem invincible with their unbeaten record.

EAST

	W	L	Pct.	PF	PA
Giants	8	0	1.000	195	103
Washington	5	3	.625	185	141
Philadelphia	4	4	.500	199	172
Dallas	3	6	.333	119	180
Phoenix	2	6	.250	103	195

▲ ▲ ▲

The layout view of the same story. The only change made in the layout after closing the story window was resizing the football, an inline graphic.

elsewhere. Before you make the cut, select that text and choose Export from the File menu to bring up a directory where you can name and file the selection on your disk just as you would if you were saving. (See page 283 for more information about exporting text from PageMaker to a word processor.)

Or say you're cropping a graphic in the layout and you get a brilliant idea for another project. Open the Story Editor, type up the idea, and export it.

6. Edit rotated text.

You can't select rotated text with the text tool in layout view. To edit rotated text, triple-click on it with the pointer. This brings up a story window with the rotated text in its normal orientation, where you can edit and change the type attributes as you would for any other text. When you return to layout view, the text will be rotated as before, with the changes made in story view.

7. Display hidden characters.

Choose Display ¶ from the Options menu to display special characters such as paragraph returns, tabs, and word spaces. If you're constantly pasting text on the wrong side of a word space, try editing with this feature turned on.

Displaying hidden characters can also help you diagnose problems when text won't do what you tell it to do, and when you have to clean up files that include extra carriage returns and tab stops.

8. Create index entries.

You can create index entries in the Story Editor just as you do in the layout view. When you complete an index entry, PageMaker places an index marker before the entry (▣), and that marker is visible in the story view.

TIPS

To **move back and forth** between story and layout views for text that is already placed: Command-E on a Mac, Ctrl-E on a PC.

To **Place** an untitled story in the layout: Command-D on a Mac, Ctrl-D on a PC.

To **close** the active Story Editor window (including the Style Palette and the Spelling and Change dialog boxes): Command-W on a Mac, Ctrl-Shift-E on a PC.

To open the **Spelling** dialog box: Command-L on a Mac, Ctrl-L on a PC.

To open the **Change** dialog box: Command-9 on a Mac, Ctrl-9 on a PC.

Keyboard shortcuts used for text editing in layout view apply in the story view as well. (See page 211.)

Turn the page for more Story Editor features.

THE SPELL CHECKER

While in story view, choose Spelling from the Edit menu (Command-L on a Mac, Ctrl-L on a PC). At the bottom of the Spelling dialog box, the Search options let you specify a spell check for Selected Text, Current Story, or All Stories. This last option is a blessing in documents that have multiple stories (such as this book, where every tip and caption is an individual story).

When you click the Start button (or press Return), PageMaker scans the text and stops on any word that it can't find in its dictionary. (It uses whichever dictionary is selected in the Paragraph dialog box. If you've installed a foreign-language or special-ized dictionary and want to use that for the spelling check, select it through the Paragraph command.) PageMaker also checks for duplicate words and capitalization errors, such as a sentence that starts with a lowercase letter.

When PageMaker stops on a possible error, the un-known word is highlighted in the story window visible behind the Spelling dialog box, enabling you to see the word in context. (You might need to move the Spelling dialog box to see the highlighted words. If you are working on a small screen, you might want to change the size of the story window and reposition the windows so that the story and the Spelling dialog box are adjacent to one another.) You can correct the spelling in the Change To box (the incorrect spelling is displayed there). Or, if you're not sure of the correct spelling, you can scan the list of suggested replacements with the hope of finding it; click on the desired replacement word and then click the Replace button. If the unknown word is correct (which often happens with proper names, abbreviations and codes, and words that are correct but are not included in PageMaker's dic-tionary), click Ignore, and PageMaker will continue scanning the text.

When you want to add an unknown word to PageMaker's dictionary, click the Add button. This brings up another dialog box, where the unknown word is already entered in the Word text edit box. Hyphens are indicated by tildes (~): One tilde indi-cates the most desired hyphenation point, three the least desired. When you add a word, PageMaker might insert what it thinks is the proper hyphena-

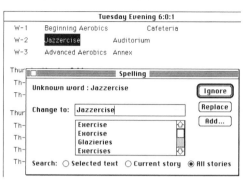

▲ ▲ ▲

When PageMaker finds an unknown word, that word is highlighted in the story window behind the Spelling dialog box. If the word is correct, click Ignore. If the word is misspelled, edit the spelling in the Change To box, or scroll the list to select the correct spelling, and then click Replace. If you want to add the unknown word to the dictionary, click Add to bring up the Add Word dialog box.

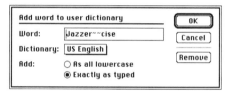

▲ ▲ ▲

When you add a word to PageMaker's dictionary, type a tilde (~) to indicate the desired hyphena-tion. One tilde indicates the most desired hyphenation point, three tildes the least desired.

tion for the new word. You can edit the hyphena-tion by adding or deleting tildes .

You can add and delete words from PageMaker's dictionary at any time, either through the Spelling command in the Story Editor or, in the layout view, through the Hyphenation command on the Type menu. (PageMaker uses the same dictionary for spelling and hyphenation.) You can continue add-ing words, one after another, by clicking the Add button after each entry. To remove a word from the dictionary, type that word and click the Remove button. To add or remove a word from a dictionary other than the default, choose the dictionary you want from the Dictionary pop-up menu in the Add Word dialog box. The dictionary you select here is used only for the additions or deletions; it doesn't become the new default for checking spelling.

THE FIND/CHANGE DIALOG BOX

This powerful word-processing feature is best described by example.

Do you need to change the spelling of "theatre" to "theater" throughout the document? Choose Change from the Edit menu to bring up the Change dialog box. In the Find What text box, type *theatre*. In the Change To text box, type *theater*. Click Change All, and PageMaker will scan the specified range of text (Selected Text, Current Story, or All Stories) and make the changes.

Do you want to check your document for inchmarks where there should be typeset quotation marks? You can't use the Change All technique as in the previous example because in some cases you need to change to an open quote and in others to a close quote.

Bring up the Change dialog box and in the Find What text box, type the inchmark (") that you habitually insert for quote marks. In the Change To text box, type Option-[on a Mac, Ctrl-Shift-[on a PC, to get a typographic open quote mark ("). Click Find, and when PageMaker stops on the first open quote, click Change and Find. PageMaker will make the correction and find the next inchmark. This will probably be at the close of the quotation, which you don't want to change yet, so click Find Next. This should take you to the next open quote, where you click Change and Find. Repeat this process until you've changed all the open quotes. Then type a close quote (") in the Change To text box by pressing Option-Shift-[on a Mac, Ctrl-Shift-] on a PC. Repeat the Find/Change process for close quotes. Tedious, but a lot easier than trying to catch the wrong marks by eye.

Do you have a text file from someone who inserts extra carriage returns and tabs for spacing? You can search for those and delete them. A complete list of keystrokes for special characters is included as an appendix in the PageMaker *Reference Manual*. The ones used most frequently to clean up files are

Carriage return	^p
Tab	^t
New line (Shift Return)	^n
Computer-inserted hyphen	^c
Discretionary hyphen	^-
Nonbreaking hyphen (Mac only)	^~

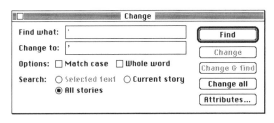

▲ ▲ ▲

You can search for punctuation elements, such as double word spaces or incorrect apostrophes and quote marks, as well as for text.

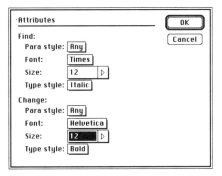

▲ ▲ ▲

You can search text for a single type attribute, a combination of attributes, or a combination of text and type attributes.

Did you use italic for emphasis and decide to change it to boldface? Click the Attributes button; in the Attributes dialog box, specify Italic (on a Mac, you'll have to bring up the Type Style submenu to do this), and PageMaker will search your document for all instances of italic text. Here again, you probably want to use Change and Find, rather than Change All, to avoid changing book titles or other text that should remain in italic.

You can search for a single attribute or for a combination of any of the attributes with submenus visible in the Attributes dialog box. You can also search for specified text with specified attributes.

When you search for type attributes, remember to return the settings to Any when you're done. Otherwise, the next text search you make will be limited by the previously specified type attributes. The fast way to do this: Option-click or Alt-click on the Attributes button in the Change dialog box, which turns all the Attribute settings to Any.

PROJECT 7

A Tabloid Ad with Photographs and Display Typography

There's a world of difference between creating the idea for an ad such as this and producing the layout for it. We didn't start with margins and column guides, we started with an opportunity—space for a tabloid ad in a community newspaper to promote a local environmental group. Then came the idea, suggested by the photograph, of this disparate group of people all having something in common: their relationship to the earth. A pencil sketch began to evolve with the headline and the main graphic. We wanted to leave the reader puzzling a moment at the implausibility of the idea, so we used an ellipsis in the middle of the thought. The conclusion of the thought led directly to the body of the message. To personalize the message, we singled out one individual to act as the group spokesman. To recommend actions that the reader could take, we used the familiar approach of a shopping list. The group identification and logo fell into place once the other elements were on the page.

That somewhat oversimplifies the process, but it gives you an idea of how we got to the point where you'll begin in the blueprint, where all the details have been worked out. You're essentially the layout artist, who's been given a very tight sketch by the art director. In reality, of course, you don't have the actual photos to work with, so just create boxes in their places—which is what you'd do if you were having the printer strip in halftones rather than using scanned images. We'll go through all the steps anyway, as if you did have the photos, because this is a book and not the real world. If you have other halftones among your files, use whatever will enable you to simulate the steps described.

The photos are from Comstock's CD-ROM library. Comstock is one of the first stock photography houses to make available whole libraries of digitized images. You can use the images to develop layout ideas, and you pay a publication fee for images that you publish.

PAGEMAKER TECHNIQUES YOU WILL LEARN

▶ Compress and uncompress TIFF images

▶ Crop and resize graphics

▶ Create digital halftones

▶ Manipulate graphics with Image Control options

▶ Condense type

▶ Use PageMaker's Tracking option

▶ Optically center type

▶ Use fine and coarse kerning levels

▶ Create hanging indents

▶ Select overlapping objects

▶ Print oversize pages using both scaling and tiling options

These folks all have the same mother...

"
I'm Jerry Dexter and
I've lived in Pinecrest all my life.
I used to take for granted the pristine
beauty of our fields and woodlands.
Now I have doubts about
the quality of our drinking water.
A lot of people I talk to
feel the same way.
That's why we've founded the
Pinecrest Environmental Coalition.
The thirteen of us pictured here
are your neighbors.
We hope you'll join us.
"

...Earth and they want every day to be Mother's Day. Because every day, year in and year out, we each make decisions that affect the health of the planet and all the life it sustains.

Decisions. The food we eat. The cars we drive. The appliances we buy. The way we heat our homes. The habits of a lifetime.

You may think you can't do much about the hole in the ozone layer or the disappearance of the rain forests or the loss of 85 percent of the earth's topsoil. But by solving some of the problems here in Pinecrest you'll do more than protect your own backyard.

Think about it. And then do something. The best time to start is right now.

Ten Ways You Can Help the Earth

1. Carpool.
2. Recycle paper, glass, and aluminum. Buy products in recyclable containers.
3. Buy the most fuel-efficient car you can. (Aim for 35 miles per gallon.)
4. Eat fewer animal products.
5. Install water-efficient showerheads and toilets.
6. Weather proof your house.
7. Buy phosphate free biodegradable soaps.
8. Repair rather than replace.
9. Plant trees.
10. Join the Pinecrest Environmental Coalition.

Pinecrest Environmental Coalition
3365 Hill Street, Pinecrest, phone 697-5527

BLUEPRINT FOR THE AD

PAGE SETUP AND GUIDELINES

Create a new document with the following specifications and guidelines:

Page: Tabloid, 11 by 17 inches

Options: Turn off Double-sided

Margins: Left and Right, 6p
        Top, 5p6
        Bottom, 4p6

Columns: 2, with a 1p6 space between, customized so the right margin of the left-hand column is positioned at 42p9

Horizontal Ruler Guides positioned as follows:

13p6: baseline of second line of headline

15p6: top of photos

36: bottom of small photo

40p3: baseline of first line of quotation

60p6: top of "Ten Ways" box

65p: bottom of large photo

70p: baseline of first line of main text

92p: bottom of suggestion box

THE PHOTOGRAPHS

If you don't have scanned photos in your files to simulate the following steps, draw rectangles to mark the position of the art in the layout.

1. Compress and place the group photo.

You can save disk space by having PageMaker compress TIFF images when you place them. For a detailed look at this feature, see the sidebar on the facing page.

- Choose Place, select the filename for the group picture, and hold down Command-Option-Shift (Ctrl-Alt-Shift on a PC) while you click OK. Keep the keyboard keys depressed for at least two seconds after clicking OK.

- Position the loaded graphic icon in the left column, at the 15p6 horizontal ruler guide, and click to place the graphic.

2. Crop the image.

When you want to eliminate parts of the image—either to remove extraneous detail or to change the shape of the original image to better suit your layout—use the cropping tool (▉) to select the image. Then position the cropping tool over a selection handle and drag past the

USING PAGEMAKER TO COMPRESS TIFF IMAGES

You can save disk space by having PageMaker compress TIFF images when you place them. In the case of the group photo for this ad, the original TIFF file was 189 KB, and the compressed version was 91 KB. (Actually, PageMaker offers two levels of compression, which it calls maximum and moderate; but since there is no difference other than size, we ignore the moderate level.)

To compress a file, choose Place, select the name of the file you want to compress, and hold down Command-Option-Shift (Ctrl-Alt-Shift on a PC) while you click OK. Keep the keyboard keys depressed for at least two seconds after clicking OK.

PageMaker creates a new, compressed version of the file in whatever folder or directory the original was in, and appends letters to the filename that identify the level of compression and the file type. For maximum compression, the codes are:

On a Mac, the filename of a continuous-tone TIFF is followed by *(LD2);* a black-and-white TIFF or a TIFF created in a paint program is identified by *(L).*

On a PC, the filename of a continuous-tone TIFF is followed by _M; a black-and-white TIFF or a TIFF created in a paint program is identified by _L. PageMaker will replace up to two characters of the original filename if necessary to display these codes.

PageMaker will link the publication to the compressed copy of the file, so you can delete the uncompressed original. (You might want to make a backup first.) You can scale, crop, and apply Image Control options to the image as usual. But if you need to edit the image outside of PageMaker, other programs might not be able to read the compressed file. In that event, you have to decompress the file, which is simple enough.

To decompress a file, choose Place, select the name of the file that you want to decompress, and press Command (Ctrl on a PC) while you click OK. PageMaker decompresses the file and places the letter *U* (_U on a PC) after the original filename.

part of the image that you want to eliminate. The entire image remains in PageMaker's memory, but the parts outside the cropped frame are not displayed. (See the sidebar on the next page.)

3. Resize the image.

The width of the photo is the width of the wide column. The depth extends from 15p6 to 65p.

- To resize the photo proportionally, hold down the Shift key and, with the pointer tool, drag any corner. If you inadvertently distort the graphic, you can restore its original proportions: Select the graphic, hold down the Shift key, and drag slightly on any handle.

CROPPING AND SIZING GRAPHICS

When positioning photographs in a layout, you generally move back and forth between cropping and sizing. First, use the cropping tool to frame the part of the image that you want displayed. Then use the pointer tool to size the cropped image to fit the layout.

Often, you'll need to readjust the cropping, either to reveal more (or less) of the image or to reposition the cropped image in the frame. It's very easy to move back and forth between cropping and sizing, and the techniques are the same for all kinds of art that you place in PageMaker. You cannot, however, crop graphics created in PageMaker. (For work-arounds with PageMaker graphics, see Project 8.)

Even if your printer will be stripping in conventional halftones, you might find it convenient to use scanned photos in order to size and position the images in the layout. If so, you will probably want to remove the scanned images from the PageMaker file before sending it to a service center for high-resolution output—the images are memory intensive and can slow down printing. When you send the camera-ready art to the printer, include a laser proof with the scanned image in place, marked FPO (For Position Only).

Using a proportion wheel

PageMaker doesn't have a mathematical scaling capability, so for sizing conventional halftones, you'll have to use a proportion wheel to determine the percentage reduction or enlargement of the original photo.

In fact, if you work with art much at all, any kind of art, a proportion wheel is an essential tool of the trade. They're available at most art supply stores, and they're not very expensive. To use a proportion wheel, measure the width of the original photo and locate that number on the inside disk of the wheel. Measure the width of the resized photo, locate that number on the outer disk of the wheel, and align that number with the measurement for the original photo. The percentage reduction or enlargement is indicated in the window of the inner wheel.

Use a soft pen or grease pencil to write this percentage on a tissue over the photo, and indicate the cropping as well; avoid ballpoint pens and pencils even on tissue overlays because any indention on the photo will most likely print. Be sure each photo is properly keyed to its page and position in the camera-ready repro.

▲ ▲ ▲

To eliminate parts of the photo, position the cropping tool (✄) over any section handle and drag horizontally, vertically, or, as shown here, diagonally.

▲ ▲ ▲

To reveal unseen portions of a cropped photo, or to reposition the cropped photo in the frame, position the cropping tool inside the selected photo (above left), hold down the mouse key, and when the grabber hand appears (above right), drag the mouse—and the photo—in any direction.

For graphics that are larger than your current view of the page, drag-place the graphic; that is, when the loaded graphic icon appears, click and drag to define the approximate size at which you want to see it displayed. Then restore its proportions using the above technique.

4. Place, scale, and crop the smaller photo.

- Using the same techniques as above, place the individual portrait in the narrow column. The top is aligned at 15p6, the bottom at 36p.

5. Use the Image Control options to edit the photographs.

See the sidebars on halftones and on PageMaker's Image Control options that begin on the next page.

6. Change the Preferences setting for graphics display.

It's great to be able to see images and text together on screen, but graphics slow down screen redraw. For much of the time that you're working with text, you don't need to actually see the graphics. That's when to use the Detailed Graphics options in the Preferences dialog box. You have three choices there:

Gray Out displays a gray area the same shape as the graphic and provides the fastest screen redraw.

Normal displays a low-resolution screen image.

High Resolution displays the image at full resolution, provided the link to the high-res image is up to date. (For more on linking, see page 216.)

THE HEADLINE

1. Type the headline.

- Before typing, use the text tool to drag a selection box at the top margin across the two columns. Be sure to start and end at the page margins so that the type will be centered.

- Specify the type as 65/55 Times Roman Bold. Alignment is centered.

- On a Mac, type an ellipsis character (Option-semicolon) after the word "mother."

  On a PC, type three periods. You'll manually kern the spacing between them later.

- Adjust the position of the headline so that the baseline of the second line is at 13p6.

Blueprint instructions continue on page 343, after the sidebars on halftones and PageMaker's Image Control options.

TRADITIONAL AND DIGITAL HALFTONES

The ability to manipulate photographic images in PageMaker brings some basic darkroom techniques into your page layout program. The options are fairly simple ones for adjusting brightness, contrast, and screen information; for more sophisticated image editing, you need a photo-retouching program.

To explain the various options, we have to start with the basics of reproducing photographs on the printed page. A black-and-white photo is a continuous-tone image, with the tones changing smoothly from dark to light. To reproduce the original photo, you have to represent hundreds of shades of gray using only black ink and white paper. This is achieved through an optical illusion called a halftone, in which the grays are converted to black dots so small that the eye blends them together into shades of gray. Look at any printed photograph under a magnifying glass and you'll see through the illusion.

Traditional halftones (below left) consist of dots of varying sizes: The larger dots create the dark areas, and the smaller dots create the light areas. In digital halftones (below middle and right), dots are simulated by clusters of square pixels that are all the same size. Increasing the number of pixels in a given area creates larger dots and hence darker grays.

▼ ▼ ▼

Traditionally, the printer creates the halftone by photographing the original photo through a screen. In electronic publishing, scanners simulate that process by converting the image into a series of electronic signals that are either on or off (black or white). It's worth mentioning that traditional halftones are still one of the great bargains of commercial printing. Each halftone costs less than $15 to make, and another $10–15 to be stripped into position on the film for that page. You get the benefit of an experienced professional who is responsible for delivering a halftone consistent with the press and paper stock being used to print the job. With a digitized photo, you take on that responsibility. Do you have the time or the skill?

Dion Ogust

Traditional halftone at 120 lines per inch.*

Digital halftone at 120 lines per inch, printed on an imagesetter at 1270 dpi.

Digital halftone at 53 lines per inch, printed on a LaserWriter at 300 dpi.

* For an explanation of lines per inch, see the Image Control sidebar on the facing page.

PAGEMAKER'S IMAGE CONTROL OPTIONS

The Image Control command, on the Element menu, is available only when you have selected an image that is a TIFF (grayscale or black and white, but not color) or paint-type graphic. If the command is grayed out, then the selected image is in a format that you're unable to manipulate with Image Control options.

The Image Control dialog box looks different on a Mac than on a PC. Some of the options are functionally the same, but some Macintosh options aren't available in PC PageMaker. Even some of the options that are available on the PC—Lightness and Contrast—aren't very useful for grayscale photos, such as the ones used in the tabloid ad, because you can't see the result of the changes on-screen. This is true also for Macintosh users who work on mono-chrome monitors. If you don't have a grayscale monitor, then you can't see changes to lightness and contrast until you print. If you're printing to an imagesetter (and you generally are when you work with halftones), trial and error with image control options could get pretty expensive.

The following buttons control changes you make within the dialog box:

Cancel: Closes the dialog box and undoes any changes you have made to an image since you opened the dialog box.

Reset (Mac) and **Default** (PC): Reverts to the default image control settings without closing the dialog box.

Apply: Depending on your monitor, lets you see lightness, con-trast, and screen pattern changes without closing the dialog box.

The following controls specify printing parameters for halftones; they are useful regardless of your system or monitor:

Screen Patterns: Use the dot screen for realistic images. Use the line screen for special effects.

Screen Angle: This setting determines the direction in which half-tone dots will be printed. For a dot screen, the default setting of 45° produces a realistic effect. For line screens and special effects with dot screens, experiment with other angles.

Lines Per Inch (on the Mac) and **Screen Frequency** (on the PC): This setting determines the halftone resolution, which is referred to in commercial printing as lines per inch. The halftone resolution is related to, but is not the same as, printer resolution. The default set-ting is keyed to the printer—53 lpi for LaserWriters and 90 lpi for PostScript imagesetters, the idea being that if you use the default you won't have to change this setting when you switch from print-ing laser proofs to printing camera-ready art on an imagesetter. But in fact different kinds of publications typically use different screen rulings, depending on the paper being used for the job: Newspapers typically use a coarse screen of 65–85 lpi because the

TIP

To revert to the printer's default for screen angle or lines per inch, without reverting on any other changes you might have made in the dialog box, type *DFLT* in the text box for that parameter. Note also that if you type a value outside the accepted range (-360° to 360° for screen angle, and 10 to 300 for lines per inch), PageMaker reverts to the printer's default.

Continues on following page

IMAGE CONTROL (continued)

paper absorbs ink and causes the dots to spread; magazines use 120–155 lpi because the coated paper absorbs less ink; and high-end annual reports and art publications use as high as 300 lpi.

In general, you should check with your commercial printer to verify the best setting for effective photos in your print job.

The following options control lightness and darkness. You can use them to manipulate black-and-white TIFFs and paint-type images on both Macs and PCs. But to use these options to manipulate grayscale photos, you need to use the bar chart, described later, on a Mac with a grayscale monitor.

Lightness: On a Mac, make adjustments by clicking the arrows on the Lightness scroll bar; click toward the white box to lighten the image, toward the black box to darken it. On a PC, use the scroll bar or type a percentage—the higher the percentage, the lighter the image will be.

Contrast: Use this control to alter the balance of lights and darks. To increase contrast, on a Mac, click the up arrow; on a PC, click the right arrow or type a higher percentage in the text box.

The following options are available only on the Mac:

Black and White, Screen, and **Gray:** If your scan was made on a grayscale scanner, and you're working on a grayscale monitor, use the grayscale setting to alter the Lightness and Contrast, and then change the setting to Screened to specify the screen type, angle, and lines per

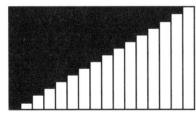

▲ ▲ ▲

Each bar corresponds to one of the 16 gray levels in a 4-bit scan, with the darkest gray on the left and the lightest on the right. For higher-quality scans, each bar represents multiple gray levels.

For the photos at right, we used the bar chart's default setting (above), in which the lines at the top of the bars form an upward diagonal. The dark and midrange values tend to get even darker, and the lightest grays tend to disappear.

inch. If your graphic is a bit-mapped image, you can select Screened to create special screen effects.

The bar chart: Available only in the Macintosh version of PageMaker; each bar corresponds to one of the 16 gray levels produced by a 4-bit scanner. The leftmost bar represents the darkest grays, the rightmost bar the lightest grays. If your scanner produces more than 16 gray levels, each bar represents multiple gray values: in a 64-gray-level scan, each bar represents four levels of gray; in a 256-gray-level scan, each bar represents 16 values. PageMaker graduates the multiple gray levels within each bar to minimize the loss of gray-level information. To adjust the values, drag each bar up (to lighten the value) or down (to darken the value). The changes you make affect the respective gray values throughout the entire photo. To alter an isolated area of the picture, you need to bring the photo into an image-editing program and then place the retouched image in PageMaker.

Whether you use PageMaker's Image Control options or the most sophisticated image-editing software, the quality of your original photo largely determines the quality of the printed image. As the saying goes, garbage in, garbage out. With a poor photo, you might use any number of special effects, treating it more as illustration than as photography. The Special Effects sidebar on the next page will give you an idea of PageMaker's capabilities in this area. And with sophisticated retouching programs, you can virtually turn night into day.

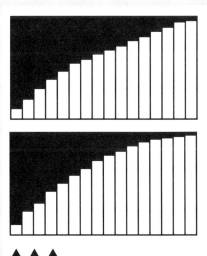

▲ ▲ ▲
Adjusting the bars to form a curve lightens the darks, darkens the lights, and adjusts the middle shades accordingly, to achieve a smoother transition between gray levels. The top chart is the setting used for the large photo, the bottom chart for the small portrait.

Turn the page for additional Image Control options.

SPECIAL EFFECTS WITH IMAGE CONTROL

These examples illustrate some of the effects you can create with both black-and-white and grayscale images.

Our first Frankenstein uses the default setting for a black-and-white paint-format image. The bar chart on the Mac (see below) shows just two levels of gray, black and white.

To create a negative image: On a Mac, select the second special-effects icon over the bar chart. On a PC, leave Lightness at 0 and set Contrast to -50.

If you screen a black-and-white image, you can adjust lightness and contrast. On a Mac, click the Screen button and then select the screen pattern; on a PC, click the dot or line screen pattern. Here, we used a dot screen at a 45° angle and 90 lpi and made the image about 60% lighter.

Using a line screen instead of a dot screen creates an entirely different effect. Here, we used a 45° angle and 20 lpi and made the image about 30% lighter than the default.

Here we used a line screen with a 0° angle and 40 lpi; the image is about 15% lighter than the default, with about 20% less contrast than the default.

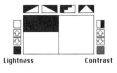

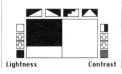

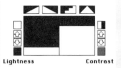

Lightness   Contrast   Lightness   Contrast   Lightness   Contrast   Lightness   Contrast   Lightness   Contrast

The effect of using a line screen instead of a dot screen varies depending on the angle and frequency of the screen. Here, we used a 90° angle and 30 lpi, with the default settings for lightness and contrast.

To create a negative image (though you'd rarely want to for a halftone): On a Mac, select the second special-effects icon over the bar chart. On a PC, leave Lightness at 0 and set Contrast to -50.

On a Mac, you can posterize a grayscale photo by selecting the third special-effects icon. This reduces the number of gray values to four.

On a Mac, you can create an effect similar to solarization by selecting the fourth special-effects icon. The darker values print positive, and the lighter values print negative.

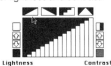

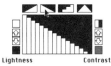

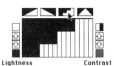

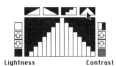

Lightness   Contrast   Lightness   Contrast   Lightness   Contrast   Lightness   Contrast

2. Refine the headline.

Every headline requires fine-tuning that is unique to that particular set of words in that specific layout. The process in this ad went like this:

- Rebreak the lines.

  Force a line break (without a paragraph break) between "have" and "the" by pressing Shift-Return.

Force line breaks where you want them—editorially and visually—rather than where Page-Maker inserts them by default.

> # These folks all have
> # the same mother...

- Condense the type.

  Select it with the text tool, choose Type Specs, and in the Set Width text box, type *85*. A width of 85 means the type is condensed 15% on the horizontal axis; the vertical axis doesn't change. You can condense and expand type in one-tenth-of-a-percent increments in this dialog box. On the Set Width submenu, you can select values in ten-percent increments ranging from 70 to 130.

Times Roman Bold is a rather clunky typeface. Condensing the type gives it a more distinctive look that is slightly elongated, with the same visual proportions as the tall thin tabloid page.

> # These folks all have
> # the same mother...

- Optically center the headline.

  Insert an em space (Command-Shift-M on a Mac, Ctrl-Shift-M on a PC) before the first letter in the second line to shift the line to the right. (An em space equals the width of the type size.) If you use the Spacebar, there might be a discrepancy between the screen display and the printout, or between laser and high-resolution printouts.

Punctuation at the end of a line doesn't occupy the same visual space as letters do. This creates visual holes between the punctuation and the x-height of the rest of the line. By hanging the punctuation beyond the type in the line above it, you can make the lines appear optically centered, even though mathematically they are not.

> # These folks all have
> #   the same mother...

- Track the headline.

  Select the text with the text tool, and specify Normal on the Track submenu. Normal is tighter than PageMaker's default of No Track and looser than Tight.

The tracking options on the Type menu provide five preset levels for increasing or decreasing word spacing and letterspacing uniformly across a range of selected text. In general, headlines will look smarter if you tighten the tracking at least to Normal.

> # These folks all have
> #   the same mother...

You can further fine-tune the spacing through the Spacing option in the Paragraph dialog box, or manually kern space between individual letter pairs as needed. Spacing and kerning adjustments are added on top of the tracking specified for the selected text. Normally, we would kern the headline at this point. But we know that the treatment of the headline and the word "Earth" in the text below the large photo are interdependent. So before making the final adjustments to the headline, we'll proceed with the main text block.

THE MAIN TEXT

1. Type the main text under the large photo.

The type specs are 16/20 Times Roman. Alignment is justified.

The first-line indent is 5p, except for the first paragraph, which, as the continuation of the headline, has a first-line indent of 0.

The baseline of the first line is at 70p.

TIP

Don't be alarmed if your line breaks differ from the ones described in the instructions. The same font often varies from one vendor to another, both in the width of the letters and even the character forms themselves. Also, if the position of your column guides varies even slightly from ours, your line breaks could be different. So read the text to understand the effect we are after in this project and use the techniques you've learned so far to achieve that effect.

2. Create visual continuity with the headline.

If the word "Earth" were in the body text type, the headline would leave readers dangling. Giving that word and the ellipsis that precedes it the same upsized, boldface treatment as the headline leads the reader's eye from the headline to the main message.

• Select the ellipsis and the word "Earth," and change the type specs to 65/20; Type Style: Bold; Set Width: 85%; Track: Normal. Note that you keep the same leading as the body text so that the leading will be consistent throughout that text block.

We have three problems. First, we don't want a line break in the middle of the phrase "Mother's Day." In advertising and promotion copy, try to avoid a line break in the middle of a key phrase or slogan; this one is especially troublesome because the headline relies on an extended metaphor (Mother Earth/Earth Day/Mother's Day).

The second problem is that the word spacing in the line is more open than in the rest of the text block. In justified text, PageMaker often has

A CLOSE LOOK AT SOME TYPOGRAPHIC PROBLEMS

Punctuation in display type leaves a visual hole at the beginning of a line.

In justified text, watch for spacing that is too loose (as this is) or too tight relative to the rest of the text.

In advertising copy, and in display type in general, avoid a line break in the middle of a key phrase.

...Earth and they want every day to be Mother's Day. Because every day, year in and year out, we each make decisions that affect the health of the planet and all the life it sustains.

to add or delete space between words or letters in order to align the type at the right margin. It's usually more of a problem in narrow columns than in wide ones, but it's something you should always check.

The third problem is that the ellipsis isn't quite aligned with the left margin. This is similar to the problem we had with the ellipsis in the headline, only here the visual hole is at the beginning of the line.

We'll correct these problems in the next step.

3. Refine the type.

We found that even by bringing the ellipsis left a little and reducing the type size by several points, we weren't quite able to pull up the word "Day." We also had to change the ellipsis character (Option-semicolon) to three periods, enabling us to control the space between them by kerning. (If you work on a PC, you used three periods from the start.) The following steps detail one way of arriving at the solution.

- With the text tool, select and cut "…Earth." Paste it on the pasteboard, a little to the left of the page where you're working.

  In theory, you want to keep text threaded together when it's part of the same paragraph. But in reality, you have more flexibility if display type isn't threaded to the rest of the text so that you can freely manipulate it and then visually position it. In this situation, that flexibility is essential in order to pull the ellipsis a little beyond the left margin of the body text.

- Select the ellipsis character and replace it with three periods, without any spaces between them. To manually open up space between the periods, select all three periods and press Command-Shift-Delete (or Bksp) on a Mac, Ctrl-Shift-Bksp on a PC. Press the Delete or Bksp key twice while holding down the other keys. Kerning more than two characters at a time like this is called range kerning.

- Select "…Earth" and change the type specs to 61/58. (Because the word isn't threaded to the paragraph with the rest of the text, we can specify a leading closer to the type size so that the type won't be clipped off on-screen every time we adjust it.)

- With the pointer tool, select "…Earth," and before moving it back into position, drag the text handles on the right so they are just wide enough to contain the type. This is simply a matter of good housekeeping so that you won't have text handles longer than your type.

- With the text still selected, drag it into position in the first line.

- With the text tool, set an insertion point in the body text of the first paragraph. Choose Indents/Tabs from the Type menu (Command-I on a Mac, Ctrl-I on a PC). This brings the Indents/Tabs dialog box on-screen; with the left margin of the dialog box ruler aligned over the left margin of the text, you can visually specify the First Indent for this paragraph, rather than measuring or using trial and error.

  Move the pointer to the first-indent marker (that's the top triangle on the left margin of the dialog box ruler) and drag it until it is just past the word "Earth." Click OK.

…Earth

Pay attention to the shapes of letters when you position display type. Curved strokes, such as the periods and the bottoms of the "a" and the "t," should be placed slightly below the baseline so that they will appear to be on the line. Similarly, the crossbar of a "t" or the curved edge of an "o" should hang a little beyond the left margin.

4. Adjust the first-line indent.

Follow the steps shown in the screen images and captions below to align the paragraph indent of the body text with the "E" in the word "Earth." The reason for doing this is purely visual.

...**Earth** and they want.

Because every day, year in and year out, affect the health of the planet and all the
    Decisions. The food we eat. The we buy. The way we heat our homes. Th
    You may think you can't do mu layer or the disappearance of the rain for of the earth's topsoil. But by solving s Pinecrest you'll do more than protect yc
    Think about it. And then do son

▲ ▲ ▲

The stem of the "E" in the word "Earth" creates a strong vertical that isn't quite aligned with the first line indent of subsequent paragraphs. Bring in a vertical ruler guide aligned with the letter "E." Be sure the guide is aligned with the stem of the "E," not with the tip of the serif.

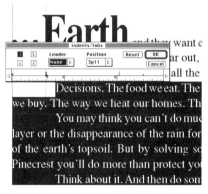

▲ ▲ ▲

Select the subsequent paragraphs, and, in the Indents/Tabs dialog box, drag the first-line-indent marker so that it is aligned with the ruler guide.

...**Earth** and they w

Because every day, year in and year affect the health of the planet and al
    Decisions. The food we eat. T we buy. The way we heat our homes
    You may think you can't do r layer or the disappearance of the rai of the earth's topsoil. But by solvir Pinecrest you'll do more than protec
    Think about it. And then do so

▲ ▲ ▲

With the alignment adjusted, the type looks neat and intentional.

THE HEADLINE, AGAIN

Changes we've made in the display type for the word "Earth" require similar adjustments in the headline, so the type treatment for the two blocks of display type will be identical.

1. Change the type size.

- Select the headline type, and change the size to 61 points to be consistent with the word "Earth."

2. Correct the ellipsis.

- You can do this quickly by copying and pasting the ellipsis created from three kerned periods preceding the word "Earth."

3. Recenter the two lines.

Because the three periods are not as wide as the ellipsis character, the second line is no longer optically centered. Drag over the em space you inserted at the beginning of the line, and change it to an en space (by pressing Command-Shift-N on a Mac, Ctrl-Shift-N on a PC). An en space is half as wide as an em space.

TIPS

To kern over a range of text (e.g., to kern all the letters of a word at the same time), select the text and use the appropriate key combinations to add or delete space.

To copy kerning (e.g., if you've kerned the "he" in "these" and want to copy that kerning to the "he" in "the"), copy the kerned characters and paste them over the characters in the unkerned version. (In PageMaker 4.0, kerning information defines the space after a character and is stored as an attribute of that character, not as a space between characters.)

To remove kerning, select the characters or range of characters and press Command-Option-K on a Mac, Ctrl-Shift-0 (zero) on a PC.

4. Kern the headline.

Keep in mind that PageMaker has two levels of kerning, and we used both. Remember, also, to kern the space between words as well as between letters.

To tighten space in increments of 1/25 em:

    Mac: Command-Delete (Backspace); or Command-left arrow

    PC: Ctrl-Bksp or Ctrl-minus (on the numeric keypad)

To tighten space in increments of 1/100 em:

    Mac: Option-Delete (Backspace); or Command-Shift-left arrow

    PC: Ctrl-Shift-minus

To open up space in increments of 1/25 em:

    Mac: Command-Shift-Delete (Backspace); or Com-right arrow

    PC: Ctrl-Shift-Bksp or Ctrl-plus (on the numeric keypad)

To open up space in increments of 1/100 em:

    Mac: Option-Shift-Delete (Backspace); or Com-Shift-right arrow

    PC: Ctrl-Shift-plus

A KERNING PUZZLE

The answer is very subtle, and the only place you'll find it is in your own eye. Type the headline in 61-point Times Roman; Bold; Set Width: 85%; Track: Normal. It should look exactly like the first headline below. Using both levels of kerning, tightening up here, loosening up there, match your best effort with ours. The change is more obvious in some letter pairs ("ave" in the word "have," for example) than in others ("ese" in the word "these").

Unkerned

These folks all have the same mother...

Kerned

These folks all have the same mother...

THE QUOTATION

1. Type the text for the quotation.

The type is 13/16 Times Roman Italic. Alignment is centered.

2. Optically center the text.

Centered text can be a visual element on the page, an interesting shape in itself. To date, computers haven't been able to deliver that as a default setting. So when you use centered type, do so deliberately. Manually break the lines to control the contrast between short and long lines, but pay attention to the sentence structure and the cadence of the words at the same time. Be careful of going too far, though, unless your intention is genuinely poetic.

In the electronically centered text at right, the lines are almost all the same length. In the detail at far right, the line breaks have been manually controlled to create an interesting silhouette and to make the copy easier to read as well. When forcing line breaks, enter a new-line character by pressing Shift-Return or Shift-Enter. In order to fit the word "pristine" on the third line, we used range kerning: We selected all the words we wanted to fit in that line and pressed Option-Delete (Ctrl-Shift-minus on a PC) until the word "pristine" was pulled up. You could also cheat the column measure a little by dragging the text handles slightly beyond the margins.

I'm Jerry Dexter and I've lived in Pinecrest all my life. I used to take for granted the pristine beauty of our fields and woodlands. Now I have doubts about the quality of our drinking water. A lot of people I talk to feel the same way. That's why we've founded the Pinecrest Environmental Coalition. The thirteen of us pictured here are your neighbors. We hope you'll join us.

I'm Jerry Dexter and I've lived in Pinecrest all my life. I used to take for granted the pristine beauty of our fields and woodlands. Now I have doubts about the quality of our drinking water. A lot of people I talk to feel the same way. That's why we've founded the Pinecrest Environmental Coalition. The thirteen of us pictured here are your neighbors. We hope you'll join us.

3. Add the quotation marks.

- Before typing, drag a short bounding box just beyond the image area to define the text width for the quote marks. Specify 60/60 Times Roman Bold; type the open and close quotes as separate text blocks.

  Regardless of what leading you specify, the quote marks are going to be a nuisance to work with. They're designed typographically to sit above the line, so all the leading plus part of the point size falls below the type itself, meaning the text handles will overlap into the space below. If you make the leading super tight in an attempt to tighten up the handles, the type may be so clipped off at the top that you won't even see it until the screen redraws. This sort of behavior can drive you wild unless you understand, typographically and technologically, why it happens. And even then it drives you wild.

- Bring in a vertical guide at the center of the column. A quick way to bisect any area is to draw a rectangle the width of the area and drag the ruler guide over the center handles.

- Move the quotes into position, centered over the vertical guideline you just brought in. The quotes should be positioned closer to the text than to the graphic elements above or below so that they clearly belong to the text.

THE "TEN WAYS" LIST

1. Draw the border.

- Using a double-rule line weight, draw a box in the narrow column from 60p6 to 92p.

2. Create the banner.

- Draw a 4p-deep solid banner from the inside top of the box. Alignment with the inside of the double rule on three sides is critical; work at 400%.

- Type the headline, forcing a line break (by pressing Shift-Return) after the word "You."

  The type specs are 20/22 Helvetica Bold, Reverse. The alignment is centered.

- The headline is a little tight to the edge of the banner. We have three options: We can reduce the type size; we can tighten the spacing (through either the Tracking option or the Spacing option); or we can condense the type on the horizontal axis, as we did with the headline. We chose the third option.

  With the text still selected, change the Set Width to 90. You can do this in the Type Specs dialog box or you can use the Set Width submenu.

TIP

If you have trouble typing the banner headline to the full width of the column, some other element on the page is probably obstructing it. With the pointer tool active, choose Select All from the Edit menu (Command-A on a Mac, Ctrl-A on a PC), and you'll see what's in the way. In this case, it's probably the text handles for the quote marks above the box. With the pointer tool, drag the windowshade handles of the banner headline to the full width of the column.

3. Type the list and create the hanging indent.

The only way to get a clean hanging indent in a numbered list is to use the Indents/Tabs option. The following steps give you the specifications, without any explanation, for the numbered list in this ad. For a closer look at hanging indents and a detailed explanation of the specs for this list, see the sidebars on the next two pages.

- Specify the type as 11/13 Helvetica.

- Set an insertion point in the box. Don't worry that the left and right margins overlap with the border of the box. You'll fix that shortly.

- When you type each item on the list, insert one tab before the first character (that is, the number) and another tab after the period. You can use the default tab settings; you'll change them in the following two steps.

- With the text selected, choose Indents/Tabs from the Type menu (Command-I on a Mac, Ctrl-I on a PC).

- Set the left-indent marker at 3p6. Set the right-indent marker at 1p. Set a decimal-aligned tab at 2p. Set a left-aligned tab over the left-indent marker at 3p6. Click OK.

- With the text still selected, specify the Paragraph Space After as 0p7.

- Style the numbers and periods as boldface (Command-Shift-B on a Mac, Ctrl-Shift-B on a PC).

TIP

If your text doesn't fit in the space of the box, move the left-indent marker and the left-aligned tab from 3p6 to 3p. Or range kern the text. You should be able to pull up runover lines with either technique.

ALL ABOUT HANGING INDENTS

The technique for creating hanging indents is really easy once you get the (forgive us) hang of it. If you use paragraph indents and tabs, Page-Maker will line everything up nice and neat. If you insert carriage returns, multiple tabs, or numerous Spacebar characters in an attempt to manually create the alignments, those alignments will dissolve into a mess with the slightest editing change.

If PageMaker's Indents/Tabs dialog box had an Apply option, you could visually check the position of indents and tabs without okaying the dialog box and returning to the layout. Unfortunately, there's no Apply button, so you might have to move in and out of the dialog box several times to get the alignments you want. To minimize this, work at a page view that allows you to see the whole column below the tabs ruler; and before bringing up the dialog box, drag in ruler guides to mark the desired alignments.

This is a simple hanging indent, with the first line flush against the left margin and all subsequent lines indented from that margin.

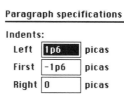

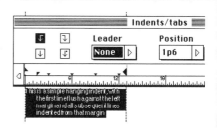

▲ ▲ ▲

For a simple hanging indent like the one shown above, you can use either the Paragraph Specifications or the Indents/Tabs dialog box to specify the indents. The runover lines are aligned at the left indent. The first-line indent is the negative value of the left indent, to pull the first line back to the column margin.

• Complete information for each field and button in the window follows the procedure.

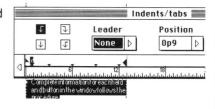

▲ ▲ ▲

For a bulleted list, type the bullet, insert a tab character, and then type the rest of the paragraph. Select the text with the text tool, and choose Indents/Tabs from the Type menu (Command-I on a Mac, Ctrl-I on a PC). As in the first example, specify the left indent for the runover lines, and a first indent that is the negative value of the left indent. Set a left-aligned tab at the left indent. It's this left-aligned tab that enables you to align the text following the bullet with the left margin of the runover lines.

A NUMBERED LIST WITH A HANGING INDENT SET INSIDE A BOX

When you add numbers to the hanging indent and put the text inside a box, the procedure is only a little trickier. In the screen details below, we've simulated an Apply button, showing the selected text as it would look *after* clicking OK in the dialog box at each step.

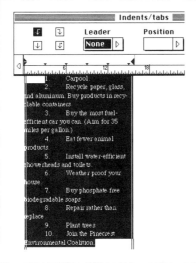

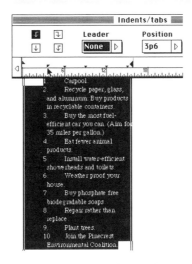

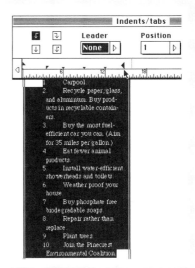

1. Using the default indent and tab settings, the left and right margins are flush with the sides of the box; and the tab stops are at 3p intervals.

2. Set the left indent at 3p6. To move the left-indent marker independently of the first-line-indent marker above it, press the Shift key when you drag.

3. Set the right-indent marker at 1p. If there were no box around the list, you wouldn't have to inset the right margin.

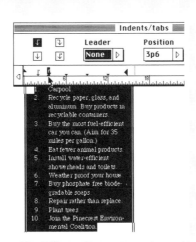

4. Select the decimal tab icon and set a tab at 2p, which will align the numbers to the left of the left indent. When setting decimal tabs for lists, allow enough room for the longest number to fit between the column margin and the decimal.

5. Click outside the ruler area to deselect the 2p tab, select the left tab icon, and set a left tab at 3p6. To set a tab directly over an indent marker, click above the marker and, if necessary, adjust the position by dragging the icon.

TIPS

Before setting a tab with a different alignment than the previously set tab, be sure to click outside the ruler to deselect the tab you just set. Otherwise, you'll change the alignment of the selected tab.

You can easily create a style for a hanging indent: When you define the style, specify the indents as part of the paragraph specifications, and specify the desired tab settings. Then, when you type the text, insert tab characters at the appropriate places. All the hanging indents for that style will be identically aligned without any further attention on your part.

Don't forget to select the text that you want to apply tabs to before setting the tab positions in the dialog box!

THE ORGANIZATION'S ID

1. Type the text.

Type both lines using 14/22 Helvetica. Then select the first line and change its specs to 24-point Helvetica Bold.

2. Shorten the text handles.

- Select the text with the pointer tool and drag one of the right windowshade handles so the handles are only a little bit wider than the text itself. This keeps the text handles from hanging out beyond the text and interfering with the logo that you'll create shortly.

3. Position the type by eye.

- With the text still selected, drag the text block so that the last line aligns at the bottom margin, and hang the word "Coalition" over into the right-hand column to break the rigidity of the grid.

4. Add the logo.

- Place and size the logo art. The tree we've used is a piece of clip art that's included in the PC-based drawing program Corel Draw. (If you happen to have that program, you could place that image now.) The art is an EPS (Encapsulated PostScript) graphic, which is transparent. To opaque the corner of the box over which it prints, you have to create a mask as described in the illustrations and captions on this page.

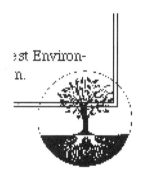

1. The tree art is a transparent EPS graphic, so the double rules of the box behind it are visible.

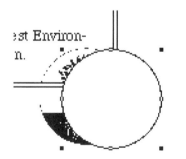

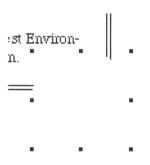

2. To mask the rules, draw a circle with the Line specified as None and the Fill as Paper. Alignment is critical, so work at 400%.

3. Text and graphics are layered in the PageMaker file—like sheets of paper, one on top of the other—in the order in which they are created. The white circle (which, in the illustration above left, has been pulled to the side for the purpose of this explanation) is on top; the tree is next, the text is below that, and the box rules are on the bottom. If you select the top element and choose Send to Back, the element goes to the bottom of the stack. In this situation, that would put the mask behind the box rules, which would defeat the purpose of the mask. So you have to select the tree and bring it to the front. How do you select an element that is totally hidden behind another element? First, select the top element (the white circle); then hold down the Command key (Ctrl on a PC), and click again where the two elements overlap. This selects the element on the next layer down—in this case, the tree. Choose Bring to Front from the Element menu (Command-F on a Mac, Ctrl-F on a PC).

PRINTING OVERSIZE PAGES

When you print an 11- by 17-inch page on a laser printer, you have two choices: You can use the Scaling option to print the page at a reduced size, or you can use the Tiling option to print the page full size in sections that you then paste together. In the course of producing any oversized publication, you'll probably use both methods. The reduced image is fine for proofreading all but very small type and for checking the overall layout. But a full-size, tiled proof is essential for checking type specifications and kerning, and for fine-tuning the layout.

If the camera-ready pages are to be output from an imagesetter, you won't need to worry about tiling or pasting the final art. Imagesetters can handle 12-inch rolls of paper, with unlimited depth, so a tabloid page with crop marks will fit on a single sheet.

Scaling

- To print the page as large as possible on a letter-size sheet, specify 62% in the Scaling text box and check Crop Marks (in the main Print dialog box or in the Print Options dialog box, depending on your printer). You won't get crop marks on the top and left edges, but those edges are defined by the paper anyway; it's the crops on the lower right that you need to complete the definition of the page trim.

- To print the page as large as possible, with crop marks, *centered* on a letter-size sheet, position the zero point about a half inch above and to the left of the upper left corner of the PageMaker page, turn on Crop Marks, and specify 52% in the Scaling text box.

Tiling

When you print oversize pages in sections at full size, the sections must be manually pasted together to form a full page. If the laser printer pages are to be used for proofing only, then the cut lines aren't so important. But if the laser printer pages are to be used for camera-ready art or for formal presentation, then the cut lines are critical. The goal is to avoid cut lines through the art or through individual letters. You can control this by using the Manual Tiling option and moving the zero point before printing each section.

- To print the pages in sections at full size, position the zero point about a half inch above and to the left of the upper left corner of the page. This allows room for the crop marks to print.

- Turn on the Tiling and Crop Marks options (either in the Print dialog box or in the Print Options dialog box, depending on your printer). Click Manual, which instructs PageMaker to print the first section with the zero position in the upper left corner of the page, and then click OK (or Print).

- To print each subsequent section, move the zero point about a half inch above and to the left of the desired cut line.

▲ ▲ ▲

To manually tile this page, you want to print four sections, labeled AA through DD, that will avoid cut lines through the art and text. In order to avoid a cut line through the headline, you'll need to print a fifth section, EE, with just the headline. To print section AA, position the zero point about a half inch above and to the left of the upper left corner of the page. To print subsequent sections (including the headline), position the zero point about a half inch above and to the left of the desired cut line (in effect creating a margin that allows the full image of each section to print, with crop marks). Be sure to turn on Manual Tiling and Crop Marks.

USING PAGEMAKER AS A DRAWING PROGRAM

PageMaker's drawing tools, though limited to lines and ovals and rectangles, can be used to create more varied and complex graphics than you might think possible. Of course, you don't have the range or sophistication in PageMaker that you have working in a full-fledged drawing program. But for simple schematics, maps, and geometric drawings, PageMaker's tools may be quite adequate.

And if desktop publishing is your introduction to computers, as it is for many people, then the prospect of learning PageMaker and a word-processing program and a drawing program can seem quite daunting. As long as you're doing your layout in PageMaker, why not see how far you can push the graphics tools? In the process, you'll master subtleties of the program that will spill over into your layout tasks. If and when you're ready to move on to a real drawing program, the challenge won't seem quite so formidable.

The examples in this project are intended to inspire your exploration of PageMaker's graphics capabilities. There's a truck and a skyline, a map and a floor plan, a pie chart, some rules, and a pattern created from a Zapf Dingbats character. The instructions for executing most of the examples are more general than those in other projects. The point here is not so much to have you duplicate any of our efforts, but that you see and begin to play around with the possibilities.

One of the problems with PageMaker-created graphics is that there is no method within the program itself to group a collection of lines and shapes into a single unit, as you can do in drawing programs. We'll look at some workarounds on the Macintosh—you can make Encapsulated PostScript files of the graphics, or you can bring them back into the layout through the Scrapbook. These workarounds enable you to turn the graphic into a single object, which you can then resize and apply text-wrap options to. Unfortunately, in PC PageMaker there is currently no satisfactory workaround; you have to create the graphic at the size it will be used. And there's no easy way to wrap text around a graphic that is a collection of smaller shapes. PC users will be able to get some hands-on practice customizing a graphic boundary by using a screen image of the truck that we'll create in the first part of this project. But the screen image is a rather coarse bit-mapped graphic that isn't adequate for real production.

PAGEMAKER TECHNIQUES

▶ Use the Front/Back commands

▶ Draw concentric circles

▶ Make an Encapsulated PostScript file

▶ Use the Scrapbook to group elements

▶ Wrap text around a graphic

▶ Customize a graphic boundary

▶ Create patterns

▶ Create custom rules in PageMaker

Even if you're not in the shipping business, creating a truck like the one in this brochure will give you a good workout with PageMaker's graphics tools. First, we created the large truck (top page, below) on a page by itself, using various shades and patterns from the Fill submenu. We copied all the elements and pasted them on a second page, and turned all the Fills to None. Then we pasted another copy on a third page and turned all the Fills to Solid.

We made an Encapsulated Post-Script file of each of the trucks, placed the EPS files in the brochure layout, and sized each truck to suit the layout. Then we customized a graphic boundary around the large patterned truck so that we could wrap text around it.

Turn the page for more details.

CREATING A PAGEMAKER TRUCK

If you want to master the way PageMaker layers elements on the page, try drawing this truck. You can make your truck simpler or more complex than the one shown, but try to keep the outline roughly the same if you want to follow the text-wrap exercise later in the project.

The steps used to create the truck can be applied to many PageMaker-generated graphics:

1. Open a new 1-page PageMaker document.

   The page size should be about the same size as the graphic will be.

2. Begin drawing the truck.

   Bring in a ruler guide as a baseline.

   Set the default line weight to 2 pt. (Note that when you reduce the size of a PageMaker graphic, you'll be reducing the weight of all the lines.)

   Create the truck, treating shapes you draw with the square, circle, and rectangle tools as building blocks. Draw the big shapes first, shade them, and then add smaller shapes inside the large ones with contrasting shades for detail.

   Draw the wheels last. (See step 5.) Use empty circles as temporary wheels, if necessary, as you draw the rest of the truck.

3. Use the Bring to Front/Send to Back feature.

   As you work, keep in mind that PageMaker layers text blocks, graphics, and ruler guides. It's as though the objects were stacked one on top of another on the screen. The object you draw first is on the bottom; the object you draw last is on top. Whenever you move an element, that element moves to the top layer.

   You can change the stacking order by selecting an object and choosing Bring to Front or Send to Back from the Element menu. The keyboard shortcuts for these—Command-F and Command-B (Ctrl-F and Ctrl-B on a PC)—are extremely useful in creating a graphic such as this.

As you build the truck, you might lose a piece of it behind a new layer. The Bring to Front/Send to Back keyboard shortcuts should enable you to retrieve pieces that are lower in the stack. If all else fails and you really can't find a piece you know you've drawn, redraw it on top. (We admit to having done this once or twice…)

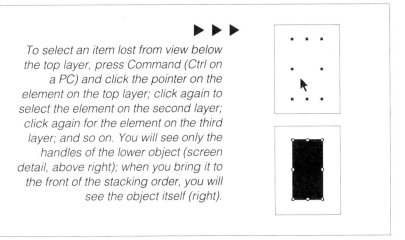

▶ ▶ ▶

To select an item lost from view below the top layer, press Command (Ctrl on a PC) and click the pointer on the element on the top layer; click again to select the element on the second layer; click again for the element on the third layer; and so on. You will see only the handles of the lower object (screen detail, above right); when you bring it to the front of the stacking order, you will see the object itself (right).

4. Work oversize.

   You'll need the accuracy provided at 200% or 400% when you create graphics. And unlike page layout, where you can refine placements later, with graphics you need the accuracy as you work; making adjustments at 400% later is likely to require complete redrawing.

5. Draw the wheels.

   Create one wheel; then copy and paste it so that all four wheels will be identical. (Hold down the Shift key to create circles rather than ovals.)

   When you are satisfied with the shape of the concentric rings of the wheel, add the shades. Again, start from the largest circle, which is on the bottom layer, and move toward the center. If you work in this order, you shouldn't have to fuss with the stacking.

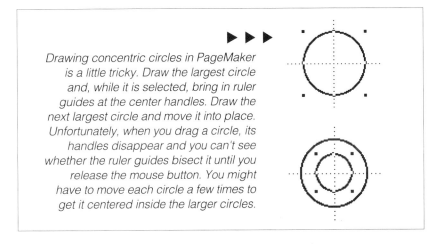

▶ ▶ ▶

Drawing concentric circles in PageMaker is a little tricky. Draw the largest circle and, while it is selected, bring in ruler guides at the center handles. Draw the next largest circle and move it into place. Unfortunately, when you drag a circle, its handles disappear and you can't see whether the ruler guides bisect it until you release the mouse button. You might have to move each circle a few times to get it centered inside the larger circles.

GROUPING GRAPHIC ELEMENTS

When you use PageMaker's graphics tools to create art such as the truck, you end up with a composite graphic made of many smaller elements. Our truck, for example, has more than 35 shapes, and each shape has 8 handles. All those handles represent potential havoc on a page, and there's no way to resize a composite PageMaker graphic.

On a Mac, you can group the elements either through the Scrapbook or by saving the page on which you created the graphic as an Encapsulated PostScript file. The EPS file is, in effect, a printable PostScript file that includes a screen representation of the page, which you can then place as a single object. You can resize EPS art, wrap type around it, print type over it—in other words, you can manipulate it as you would any draw-type graphic.

On a PC, there really isn't a satisfactory way to group the elements in order to resize the graphic electronically. We'll look at a workaround that combines electronic and manual production techniques.

Making an Encapsulated PostScript file

The process for making an EPS file on the Macintosh is fairly simple.

1. Check the page on which you have created your PageMaker art.

   Print a copy of the page and check it as you would any final proof. Be sure there is nothing other than the piece of art on it. Any extraneous type or graphic would become a part of the EPS file.

   If the graphic is much smaller than the page, reduce the page size. (See the Tip at left.) You might also want to do a Save As to compress the file before making the EPS file.

2. Choose Print from the File menu.

   This displays the regular Print dialog box.

   In a multipage document, check the page range to be sure it specifies the number of the page that you want to save as an EPS file.

3. Click on the PostScript button to display the PostScript Print Options dialog box.

   - For the first six options in this dialog box, the settings are the same whether you're making a Normal PostScript file or an EPS file. See the explanation on page 224.

   - Select Print PostScript to Disk, and click EPS.

   - Include Aldus Prep.

     This option is on (and locked in that position) by default when you make an EPS file. It ensures that your version of Aldus Prep will be used to print the file, rather than whatever version may reside in the printer or imagesetter used for your final output.

   - Click on the File Name button.

     The default name is the name of the document plus an .eps extension. If you want to change that, do it here.

MAC TIP

The size of a PageMaker-generated EPS graphic is defined by the page size you create the graphic on, not by the graphic itself. Reducing the page size before you make the EPS file means you won't have to crop in on the image when you place it in another PageMaker document.

If you're unable to select the EPS option in the PostScript Print dialog box, be sure the following specs are in effect:

- Only one page is specified in the page range text boxes

- Scaling is specified as 100%

- In the Print Options dialog box, neither Tiling nor Spot Color Overlays is turned on

Note: Unlike documents created and saved in applications, where the type of file (PageMaker, Adobe Illustrator, Microsoft Word, and so on) is indicated in the desktop directory, EPS documents created by printing to disk in PageMaker are not identified as being in EPS format unless you so label them as part of the filename.

- Click OK in the Print PostScript to Disk dialog box and again in the PostScript Print Options dialog box.

Using the Scrapbook to group elements

This procedure is simpler than making an EPS file, but some line weights might not be properly translated. Also, if your graphic includes type, be aware that imagesetters have trouble recognizing some fonts brought into a page through the Scrapbook. Those caveats aside, this technique is still a useful addition to your bag of tricks. All you have to do is copy the elements in your graphic, paste them in the Scrapbook, and then place the Scrapbook. The image will come in as a single object.

To place an item from the Scrapbook, invoke the usual Place command and, in the Place dialog box, scroll to your system folder to select the Scrapbook file. The loaded graphic icon for the Scrapbook displays a number that indicates the number of items in the Scrapbook. The last item you pasted into the Scrapbook is the first item placed. After you place that item, the loaded icon reappears. You can either click to place another item or click the pointer anywhere in the Toolbox to cancel further placing.

With some third-party scrapbooks, such as SmartScrap, you don't even have to place the scrapbook. Simply paste the copied elements of the graphic into the scrapbook, and then use the selection rectangle to select them. Copy, and when you paste the copy into PageMaker, the elements will be grouped as a single object.

PC workaround

To resize or wrap text around a PageMaker-created graphic on the PC, try this combination of traditional and electronic techniques.

1. Make a screen representation of the PageMaker graphic by pressing Alt-Print Screen. This copies the contents of the PageMaker window to the Clipboard, as a bit-mapped graphic.

2. Paste the screen image on the page as a "for position only" (FPO) guide. You can resize the screen image, crop it, and even wrap text around it for layout purposes.

3. Print the page with the bit-mapped screen image in place. Print the file with the original graphic at full size. Use a proportion wheel to determine the enlargement or reduction of the image in the layout. (See page 336 for more information about proportion wheels.)

4. To print the camera-ready art for the original graphic, specify the enlargement or reduction in the Scaling text box. Paste that scaled art onto the camera-ready art for the rest of the page. Or have the printer reduce (or enlarge) the full-sized graphic from step 3 and strip that into the film for the rest of the page.

PAGEMAKER'S TEXT WRAP

In commercial typesetting, wrapping text around a graphic can require one round of galleys after another before the line breaks and spacing are even and crisp. The time and expense can be prohibitive. PageMaker's Text Wrap option facilitates the process, though it still requires patience and precision.

To create a text wrap:

1. Select the graphic that you want the text to wrap around.

2. Choose Text Wrap from the Element menu.

3. Specify a Wrap option.

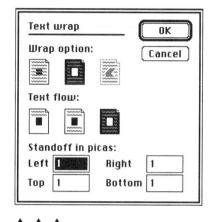

▲ ▲ ▲

Use the Text Wrap dialog box, on the Element menu, to define the way text wraps around a selected graphic.

 Text flows over the graphic.

 Text jumps over or flows around the graphic; to specify the wrap behavior, choose a Text Flow icon from the next group.

4. Specify a Text Flow option.

 Column-break: text stops at graphic and continues in next column.

 Jump-over: text stops at graphic and continues below it.

 Wrap-all-sides: text flows around graphic on all sides. Choose this icon to customize a graphic boundary.

5. Specify the Standoff.

The Standoff defines the distance between the graphic and the text-repelling graphic boundary. To adjust the Standoff, select the graphic and type a new value, or drag the line of the graphic boundary closer to or farther from the graphic.

The dotted line defines a graphic boundary around the truck. Text cannot flow beyond this boundary.

Square handles inside the graphic boundary define the bounding box of the Encapsulated PostScript art.

Diamond-shaped handles on the graphic boundary can be added, deleted, and moved to change the shape of the boundary.

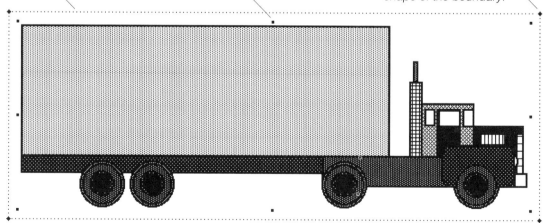

▲ ▲ ▲

When you define text wrap around a graphic, PageMaker displays a graphic boundary around the object. To customize the boundary to follow the shape of the art, follow the procedure described on the next page. When you first work with graphic boundaries, it's very easy to confuse the square handles around the art and the diamond-shaped handles on the boundary.

HOW TO CUSTOMIZE A GRAPHIC BOUNDARY

To change the shape of the boundary so that it follows the outline of the truck, divide the boundary into smaller line segments by adding and dragging additional handles. For each line segment you want to create, you add two handles; the distance between the handles defines the length of the new segment.

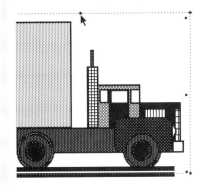

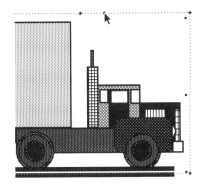

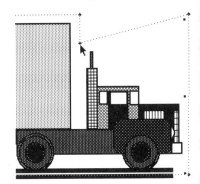

1. Click on the graphic boundary to add a handle where you want to make the first turn, about two picas in front of the trailer.

2. and 3. Add a second handle and drag it directly below the first one, a pica or two above the exhaust pipe.

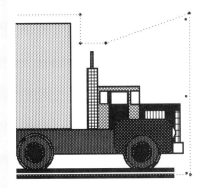

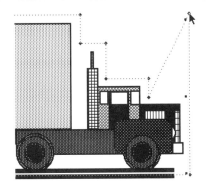

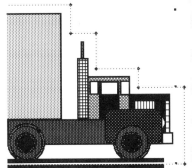

4. Add a third handle and drag it down parallel to the second one.

5. and 6. Continue adding and dragging three more handles to define the shape of the cab and hood; then drag the existing handle from the upper right corner to define the right edge of the line over the hood.

TIPS

Graphic boundaries are extremely elastic. Drag handles to change the direction or length of a line; drag whole lines to change the distance between the boundary and the graphic.

When customizing a graphic boundary, begin by creating the rough shape you want, and then fine-tune the placement of individual handles and lines.

You can edit a graphic boundary after the text wraps around it. Hold down the Spacebar while you adjust the boundary if you want PageMaker to delay reflowing the text.

To delete a handle on a graphic boundary, drag that handle on top of another handle.

Hold down the Shift key to constrain movement of a handle.

Check to be sure each segment of the boundary is straight.

PATTERNS AND MORE

Patterns require planning and precision, but the results can be well worth the effort. The basic procedure is fairly straightforward, although there are many different ways to execute the steps:

1. Determine the design motif of the pattern.

2. Determine the density of the pattern on the page.

3. Establish the grid for the pattern by dividing the page size by the number of pattern units.

4. Use the power-paste technique to paste the pattern elements at equal intervals.

   • Copy one pattern unit, and paste the copy directly on top of the original by pressing the power-paste key combination: Option-Command-V on a Mac, Ctrl-Shift-P on a PC.

   • Drag the copy the distance that you determined in step 3. The distance that you drag sets the spatial relationship between elements for subsequent power-pastes.

   • Continue power-pasting elements in the row or column.

   • After you get one row set up, you can copy that row and power-paste it to create additional rows or columns. Note that you can also power- paste on a diagonal axis.

In this invitation, we created the pattern from an 18-point Zapf Dingbat (the keystroke is Shift-9).

When creating a pattern from typographic characters, use the Repeat Tab function to space the characters at equal intervals. Once you've got one row set up, copy it and use the power-paste technique to evenly space the subsequent rows. Then, when you've got all the rows evenly spaced, you can offset the rows, as we've done here, by Shift-dragging the appropriate rows. To ensure the horizontal alignment of characters in alternate rows, as in this invitation, use ruler guides.

We cheated on the airplane flying off the top of the page. PageMaker's text rotation is limited to 90° increments, so for this effect we rotated a 48-point Dingbat 70° in FreeHand, and placed that character in the PageMaker layout. Note how shifting the axis and size of one element creates a dramatic focal point in an otherwise static background.

You don't need drafting skills or a CAD program to create a working floor plan. This design studio is drawn at 1/8 scale (1/8 inch equals 1 foot), using PageMaker's ruler at 400% for precise measurements.

Walls that are broken by doors and windows are created as solid 4-pt rules and then partially masked with white boxes as needed. That way, you don't have to worry about aligning a series of short rules.

The door swings and the chairs are created by masking parts of circular graphics. For example, the chairs are made from two concentric circles, with a 12-pt white rule over part of the arcs and a .5-pt rule positioned where the mask and the circles butt. You should create elements that require masks outside the area of the main drawing and move them into position last.

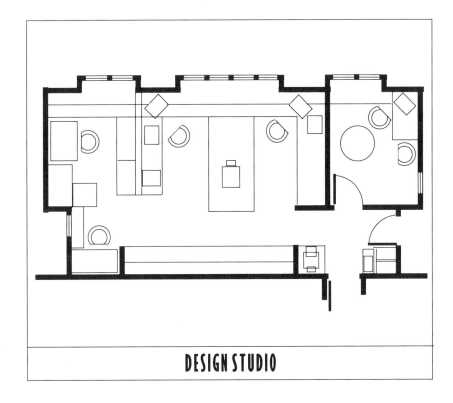

DESIGN STUDIO

If the truck was too easy for you, try incorporating the dimensionality of a skyline. Ours was created through a playful, trial-and-error approach (and a great many printouts) until a satisfying effect was achieved.

You can overlap shapes, change their height or width, play with different shades for the fill, and use white (Reverse) diagonal rules to create angular, postmodern lines.

As the skyline develops, use the Send to Back/Bring to Front commands to create a sense of depth. All the shadows on the sides of the buildings are 80%, and those on the ground are solid black.

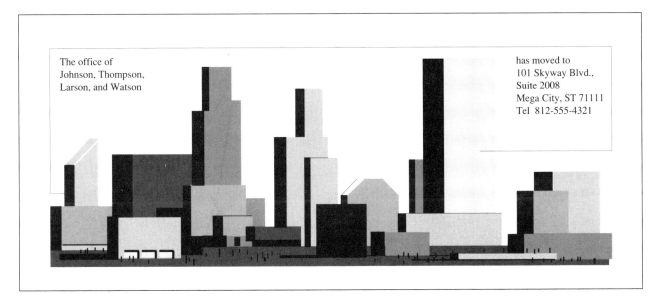

The office of
Johnson, Thompson,
Larson, and Watson

has moved to
101 Skyway Blvd.,
Suite 2008
Mega City, ST 71111
Tel 812-555-4321

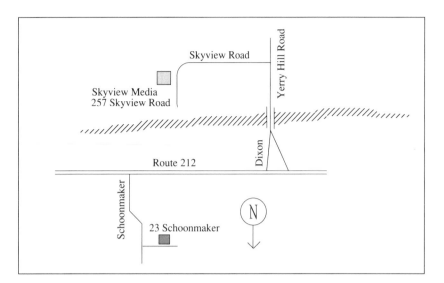

For simple area maps, use Page-Maker's double line for main arteries and single lines for side streets. To indicate a curve in the road, draw a box and, while it is selected, use the Rounded Corners option on the Element menu to specify the arc; then mask any part of the box that you don't want to see. To create the free-form edge of a river or lake, draw a series of rounded-corner boxes and specify the Lines as None and the Fills as the most open of Page-Maker's patterns.

The Sixth Annual International Business and Marketing Conference   **January 11-15, 1992**

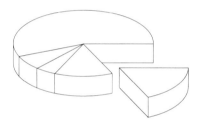

To create a pie chart, divide an ellipse into quadrants by bringing in ruler guides over the selection handles. Use these guides to estimate the line positions that define the size of each segment. You'll need multiple masks to cover up parts of the ellipse. To remove a piece of the pie, copy the lines for that piece and paste them on the side. Then mask over the lines of that piece in the pie itself. If you work on a Mac, make an EPS file of the isolated piece so that you can position it as a single object.

Pompidou Centre Paris, France

EPICENTERS
for the NINETIES

A stylized map doesn't have to be geographically accurate. This one is created entirely with PageMaker's circle/oval tool. You can use this sort of representational graphic for quantitative comparisons, whether you're analyzing population centers, wheat production, or pollution.

CUSTOM RULES CREATED FROM LEADERED TABS

Don't feel limited by the bold dotted rule on PageMaker's Line menu. Using leadered tabs, you can create rules with any size and density of dots that you desire. With custom leader characters, the possibilities are greater still.

1. Set an insertion point at the left edge of the rule.

2. Choose Indents/Tabs from the Type menu.

3. Set a right-aligned tab at the left edge of the rule.

4. With the tab icon that you just set still highlighted, select the dotted rule from the Leader submenu.

5. Click OK.

6. Press the Tab key to insert the tab character, and then press the Return key.

   When you insert leadered tabs, you don't see the leader until you type a character. Pressing Return is, in effect, the character.

7. Change the default dotted leader to any font you want.

For custom leader tabs, follow the same procedure, but instead of choosing a dotted line from the Leader submenu, type up to two characters in the Leader text box. You can use Zapf Dingbats or characters from other specialized fonts.

If you want a rule that is wider than your column, draw a bounding box slightly wider than the desired length of the rule, set a right-aligned tab for that bounding box, and proceed as described above.

You can create custom vertical rules, too, simply by selecting a horizontal rule and using the Text Rotation command from the Element menu.

▶ ▶ ▶

You can create a wide variety of rules using the technique described on this page, thus increasing the lines available within PageMaker.

●●●●●●●●●●●●●●●●●●●●●●●●●●●●●●●

PageMaker's dotted rule

. . . .

A 14-point Courier Bold rule

••

A 14-point Bookman rule

· · · · · · · · · · · · · · · · · ·

The same 14-point Bookman rule opened up by specifying a period followed by a Spacebar in the Leader text box

▲ ▲ ▲ ▲ ▲ ▲ ▲ ▲ ▲ ▲ ▲ ▲ ▲ ▲ ▲ ▲ ▲

A custom leader rule created by specifying Zapf Dingbats as the typeface and typing t-Spacebar character in the Leader text box

✂ ✂ ✂ ✂ ✂ ✂ ✂ ✂ ✂ ✂ ✂ ✂ ✂ ✂ ✂ ✂ ✂ ✂ ✂

Another Zapf Dingbat rule

PROJECT 9

WORKING WITH COLOR IN PAGEMAKER

When Henry Ford introduced mass production of his Model T, he boasted, "You can have any color you want as long as it's black." For a while the same could be said of desktop publishing. It's true that trade shows and magazines have ballyhooed color for a few years now. And illustrators working in drawing programs broke the color barrier in that first wave. It's also true that color has been available in PageMaker since version 3.0, although its color capabilities were—and to some extent still are—limited.

But if you work in desktop publishing, you may well have occasion to use color in your publications, whether or not you incorporate the color electronically or have the printer strip it in. In either case, be prepared for an ongoing learning curve. Color is the most complex dimension of graphic design. The aesthetics of color—what colors you choose, how you combine them, how they are perceived, the subtleties in a color photograph—make the nuances of typography look simple by comparison. And the use of color on the printed page is inextricably bound to the way color is prepared for the printer and created on press, to such a degree that in order to use color at all you have to understand some fundamental principles of color printing. If you are just beginning to work with color, see the "Resources" section in this book for additional sources of information.

But color is glorious, too, and great fun to work with. And the ability to do color prepress work on desktop computers has the potential to make color affordable for publications that would otherwise be limited to Henry Ford's basic black. Just be aware, when you begin working with desktop color, that you're taking on the responsibility that has traditionally been handled by highly trained and experienced craftspeople and that the technology you're using is only just evolving. You're advised to approach desktop color as something of an adventure, cautiously testing the water so you can determine when it's safe to proceed with more ambitious projects.

In the course of this project, we'll look at different ways of preparing color pages for the printer and at the different color models you can work with in PageMaker. You'll get some hands-on practice defining and applying color in PageMaker by creating a series of fact sheets. And you'll add color to the newsletter that you created in Project 4. The discussion inevitably introduces a new vocabulary and a few more odious acronyms; they're all included in the Glossary in the back of the book.

The structure of this section is a little different from that of the previous projects. This is partly inherent in the material and partly because the 8 pages printed in color had to be positioned between two 16-page signatures. The realities of color printing often include this kind of juggling act.

A FEW WORDS ABOUT COLOR PRINTING

Color printing requires a separate printing plate for each process color and each Pantone color used on a page. (If the distinction between process and Pantone color is new to you, see the definitions on page 371.) If you have blue, yellow, and black in your publication, the printer will make three plates, and the pages will require three printing impressions, with the lighter color laid down first, then the darker color, and then the black, which always prints last.

The plates are made from film negatives, one negative for each color. Traditionally, the printer—or, for very high quality color work, the color separator—made the negatives by photographing color art through different filters. It's now possible to make these color separations from desktop programs and to print the separations directly to film on a high-resolution imagesetter such as the Linotronic.

If you stack the pieces of film on top of one another, you'll see a black-and-white composite of what the printed page will look like. But if the film isn't stacked exactly right, the elements will be aligned improperly. This alignment of color film is called registration, and it's facilitated by printing registration marks—cross-hair lines over a circle—outside the live area of the page. You can tell PageMaker to print registration marks by selecting Crop Marks when you print. The registration marks will print on all four sides of the film, and they become part of the printing plates to help ensure proper registration on press. When you inspect press sheets of color printing, you'll see the registration marks outside the page trim.

COLOR PREPRESS

The evolution of desktop technology has introduced a variety of ways to prepare color pages for printing. The route you choose depends very much on the kind of art included in your publication, the software used to create it, and the quality of color reproduction you require. For a publication created in PageMaker, there are four basic options and numerous ways to combine the different approaches.

1. Combine PageMaker with conventional color separation.

You can lay out the page in PageMaker, place a scan or photostat for position only (FPO) to indicate the size and position of color art, and let the printer separate the art and strip it into the PageMaker-created page. Using this method, you can also specify colors for type and other graphic elements on a tissue overlay on the camera-ready pages, and the printer will create the necessary film separations. In this scenario, the printer takes responsibility for the quality of the color separation and for the registration of the elements in the separations. If you want the highest quality reproduction for color photographs, or if desktop color seems too much on the pioneering edge for you, this is the route to take.

2. Print spot color overlays from PageMaker.

If you've applied Pantone colors to rules, type, or other graphic elements in your PageMaker file, and there isn't any process color in the publication, you can separate the pages directly to film through PageMaker's Spot Color Overlays print option. See pages 373 and 375 for more information about this method.

3. Separate a PageMaker document through a desktop separation program.

Macintosh PageMaker: If your page includes 4-color artwork from an electronic drawing program, or a scanned color photograph, or if you've applied process colors to PageMaker text or graphics, then you (or your service center) can separate your pages through a program such as Aldus PrePrint or Adobe Separator. In addition to separating the pages into the four process colors, these programs also have more selective options than PageMaker for overprinting inks; and they have options that let you balance, sharpen, and otherwise enhance color photographs for reproduction. To use this method, print your PageMaker document to disk using the PostScript Print Options dialog box; be sure to select the For Separations option. You can then use the separation program to enhance the color images or specify the overprinting, or you can work with your service bureau and have them do this for you.

PC PageMaker: To separate process color, you'll need to work with a service bureau that has customized PostScript programs for this purpose.

4. Link to a commercial separation system.

When you print a PageMaker publication to disk, it creates a PostScript file that is compatible with the Open Prepress Interface (OPI) used by high-end color systems such as Hell ScriptMaster and Crosfield Studio-Link. These high-end links are intended to give you maximum layout control of all the elements in your page and eliminate color stripping without sacrificing color quality. Typically, you send a color photo to a color separator or to a service bureau that specializes in color. They make two scans of your image—a high-resolution commercial scan and a low-res TIFF. You use the low-res scan to position, scale, and crop the image in PageMaker. You then send the PageMaker file back to the service bureau or color house; they replace the low-res image with the high-res scan, make the color corrections, and separate the page to film.

An article in the November/December 1990 issue of *Aldus Magazine* compared the process and results of three of the four methods described here, using a page with a richly textured color photo and a color graphic imported from FreeHand. (The second approach, printing spot color overlays directly from PageMaker, doesn't include a color photograph, and so

---

TIP

Do not rely on your color monitor. You will be astounded at the difference between the colors displayed on a computer screen and those same colors on the printed page. Always refer to printed color guides when you specify color for any print job. Art supply stores sell swatch books of Pantone colors; and many production and printing guides display various combinations of process colors. (See our "Resources" section for details.) Be sure to refer to a guide printed on the type of paper—coated or uncoated—that you'll use for the job.

TIP

There are several methods for checking color in publications. You can print PageMaker files to desktop color printers, such as the QMS ColorScript-100. The color won't match the final printed page, but the proof will provide a representation of the color, useful for fine-tuning the layout and for presentation comps. When you separate 4-color pages electronically, you should order a set of color laminated proofs from your service bureau. This enables you to check the color and also gives the commercial printer a guide to match on press.

it was not relevant to the comparison.) What follows is a comparison of the vendor costs.

1. PageMaker with conventional color art stripped in: $798.

2. NA

3. Separation through PrePrint: $218 for film at 1270 dpi; $238 for film at 2540 dpi.

4. Linked to Crosfield high-end color system: $960.

Quality? The first and fourth approaches were definitely higher quality than the third. The photos separated through PrePrint have too much contrast and a definite moiré pattern that can result from improperly aligned screen angles. In the PageMaker *Reference Manual*, Aldus describes PrePrint separations as "near-magazine quality," which means they won't be as good as the reproductions typically found in mainstream magazines.

This whole area is a moving target. A new version of PostScript, software upgrades, and more experienced users and service bureaus could change the results dramatically at any time. But the issues remain constant: Do you know enough about color to take on this responsibility? Can you afford the disk space and processing time? Are the printed results predictable enough (in the already imperfect world of color printing) and consistent with the quality you require?

VARIABLES OF COLOR PRINTING

At every step of the color process, there are variables that create a discrepancy between the color you want (or think you want) and the color you get on the printed page.

For one thing, the color created by the transmitted light of a video display is simply not the same as color created from the reflected light of pigment on paper. When you specify color on-screen—Pantone or process—you should choose colors from printed color charts (see tip on facing page). Or get a color you like on-screen, look for a color on a printed chart that matches what you see, and specify the Pantone number or the CMYK percentages for that color in the Edit Color dialog box. It takes some of the magic away from a color monitor, but that's the reality of electronic color.

And don't expect the printed pages to match exactly the colors you pick on a color chart, or the colors in original color art. Color printing is not an exact science. The kind of inks, the paper, the type of press, and more technical problems such as dot gain and ghosting can all affect the color on the printed page.

On the other hand, don't be intimidated by all the potential problems that can arise with color. You need to understand what those problems are, but they shouldn't keep you from using color. With today's technology, you can produce inexpensive color flyers and brochures, catalogs and newsletters. Those with a pioneering spirit, willing to invest some time and money experimenting, can produce some fairly high-quality color work. And gaining experience with color today will prepare you for tomorrow's technology.

BLUEPRINT FOR THE FACT SHEETS

The first part of this project is a series of fact sheets, each of which describes one of the following aspects of working with color in PageMaker:

- The process of defining and applying spot color to different kinds of elements on the page

- The pitfalls, or danger zones, you need to be aware of when one spot color either butts against or prints on top of another spot color

- The process of creating and applying process colors in PageMaker

It's not so important that the fact sheets you create look exactly like the ones printed in the book. Other projects provide plenty of experience working with type and positioning elements precisely on the page. Here, we'll give you a basic blueprint, but don't fuss too much over the size and position of the type or the graphics. Just get elements on the page so that you can practice defining and applying colors and observe how Page-Maker prints the overlays.

> **TIP**
>
> If you work on a black-and-white monitor, you can still create, define, and separate spot color in Page-Maker. You have to check the overlays carefully to be sure you've assigned the right color to the right element, but you should check the color on overlays even if you work on a color monitor.

PAGE SETUP

Create a four-page single-sided document that resembles the one shown here and save it. Set up column guides on the master page, set up the printing items on page 1, and then copy and paste them onto page 2. When you work with process colors, just copy the squares to a blank page.

Page Size: 8.5 by 11

Margins: 3p6 for Left, Right, and Top; 4p6 for Bottom

Columns: 2, with 2p space between, customized for a 12p narrow column on the left and a 30p wide column on the right

Title banner: 6p deep beginning at top margin; Fill is Solid

Horizontal rules: .5 pt, positioned at 11p, 29p, and 47p (measuring from top of page)

Rule between columns: .5 pt

Small boxes: 6-pica squares, Fill is Solid, Line is None

Rectangle in upper left: 14p deep

Type: Avant Garde and Palatino

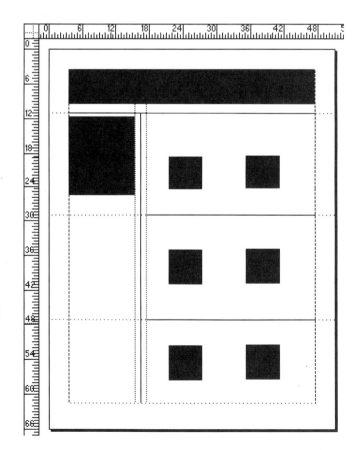

PAGEMAKER'S COLOR SYSTEMS

A rose is a rose, but there are different ways to print the color rose and different ways to create that color in PageMaker. To better follow this explanation, choose Define Colors from the Element menu, and when the dialog box comes on-screen, click on New, which brings up the Edit Color dialog box. Note the three options for Model—RGB, HLS, and CMYK; a fourth option is accessed by clicking the Pantone button. These models are the four color systems that you can work with in PageMaker.

RGB   RED/GREEN/BLUE

RGB is the system that creates the colors you see on video displays. It's called an additive system because it creates all colors by combining different percentages of red, green, and blue light. Combining 100% of the three colors produces white light. You alter the RGB values by typing numbers in the value boxes or using the scroll bars. The RGB model is used to specify colors for slide presentations, computer software and games, and anything else that will be viewed on a video monitor. But for printed pages, you use either the Pantone or the CMYK system.

HLS   HUE/LIGHTNESS/SATURATION

| RED HUE Y100-M100 | RED Lightness: 1/2 | RED Saturation: 1/2 |

HLS describes qualities of color and works in conjunction with the RGB model. Hue is what we think of as the name of a color (green, yellow, and so on). Lightness is the value (light green, dark green). Saturation is the intensity, how "strong" or "weak" a color appears (bright green, pastel green). You alter the HLS values by typing numbers in the value boxes or using the scroll bars. On a Mac, you can also experiment visually: In the Define Colors dialog box, click on Red in the color list, then hold down the Shift key and press Edit to bring up the Apple

"Color Picker" wheel. To specify different hues, move the pointer around the circumference of the wheel; to alter the lightness, sometimes referred to as brightness, use the scroll bar to the right of the wheel (in our example, we moved the slider to the center of the scroll bar); to alter the saturation, move the pointer toward or away from the center of the wheel (in our example, we moved the pointer midway to the center). As you change the color specs, the top of the color box displays the new color, with the original color in the bottom for comparison. Unfortunately, you can create countless colors in this system that you can't reproduce with ink on paper. But it's fun to play with, and can be instructive, too, when you're studying color.

PMS   PANTONE

| PMS 156 | PMS 279 |

The Pantone Matching System (PMS) is a trademark system of over 700 colors, coded by number, that are available in printing inks, colored markers, and papers. Pantone colors are traditionally used for printing rules, boxes, flat art, tints, and type in one or two spot colors. Unlike the 4-color process described below, each color is printed using an opaque ink of that exact color. You'll work with Pantone colors on the next four pages.

CMYK   4-COLOR PROCESS

| CYAN (**C**) | MAGENTA (**M**) | YELLOW (**Y**) | BLACK (**K**) |

There are only four process colors—cyan, magenta, yellow, and black (black is denoted by the letter "K"). When combined in various percentages, these four transparent inks create the entire spectrum of colors that you see in printed pages, including the subtle hues in color photographs. Combining 100% of process cyan, magenta, and yellow theoretically creates black. CMYK is called a subtractive system because each of the process colors is created by subtracting light of one of the primary colors. You'll work with process colors later in this section.

USING THE PANTONE SYSTEM TO DEFINE SIMPLE SPOT COLORS

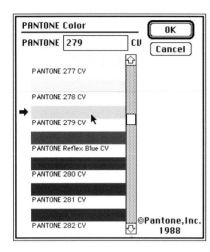

The Pantone colors scroll in groups of seven, in the same order as found in the Pantone Color Formula Guide 747XR.

This Simple Spot Color fact sheet illustrates different ways to use a single Pantone color in PageMaker. "Simple" means that the page can be separated using PageMaker's Spot Color Overlay option without risking registration problems. You'll better appreciate the simplicity when you compare this example to the following one. To create this fact sheet, use the basic blueprint described on page 370.

Define and apply a PMS color

From the Element menu, choose Define Colors. This brings up the Define Colors dialog box, which you pass through to create new colors and edit existing ones. Defining colors is similar to defining styles. Click on New, and when the Edit Color dialog box comes on-screen, click on Pantone.

In the Pantone dialog box, you can scroll to select the color you want, or, if you know the number, you can type it in the text box and PageMaker will scroll to that color. Using either method, specify 279. Then click OK in each dialog box. (You can't use the Option-OK or Alt-OK shortcut in the color dialog boxes.) Note that Pantone 279 has been added to the color list.

Bring the Color Palette on-screen (through the Window menu, or press Command-K on a Mac, Ctrl-K on a PC). Hold down the Shift key and with the pointer tool, select the squares and rectangle that print blue in our sample; click on Pantone 279 to apply that color to the selected graphics.

Define a spot color tint

Defining a tint of a Pantone color is just like defining a percentage of black. Select the blue square in the second row and specify 40% on the Fill menu. Select the black square in that same row and specify 60%. In both cases, you get a percentage, or tint, of whatever solid color is specified.

Type over colors

In the bottom row, type a 60-point *A* in the first square and a 60-point *Z* in the second. Leave the "A" black, select the "Z" with the text tool, and in the Color Palette, click on Paper. (This has the same effect as specifying Reverse from the Type Style options.) The black "A" will surprint over the blue; the white "Z" will drop out.

Type the word *TYPE* (60 points) in the rectangle in the upper left. Below that, type six lines of body text. With the text tool, select the first three lines of body text and specify Paper. As before, you have black type surprinting and white type dropping out.

Spot color applied to art

You can apply a Pantone color to black-and-white art placed in a Page-Maker file from another program. Simply select the art with the pointer tool and click on the desired color in the Color Palette. Everything that was black in the original art will print on the PageMaker overlay for whatever Pantone color you apply to it; everything that was white in the original will remain white. The eye is an EPS graphic from FreeHand. The photo is a sample included with Aldus PrePrint, under the filename Gray.TIF. If you have art that you can use, place it and apply PMS 279 to those images.

TIP

When you apply Pantone colors in PageMaker to imported EPS, PICT, or Windows metafile graphics, the colors do not display on-screen, but they will print on their respective overlays when you separate the pages in PageMaker. Colors applied to bit-mapped graphics in PageMaker are displayed. When you place art in PageMaker with spot color already applied in the originating program, the color will be displayed regardless of format.

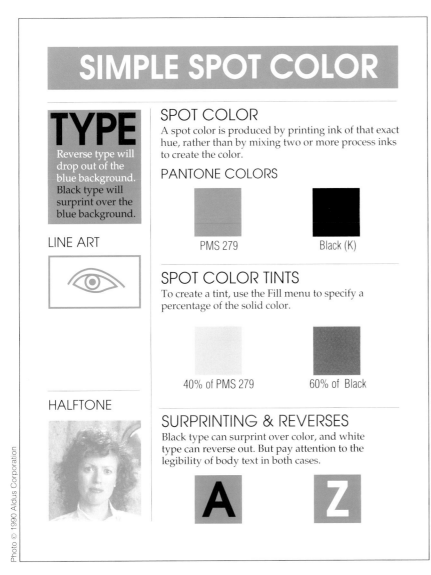

SIMPLE SPOT COLOR

TYPE

Reverse type will drop out of the blue background. Black type will surprint over the blue background.

LINE ART

HALFTONE

Photo © 1990 Aldus Corporation

SPOT COLOR

A spot color is produced by printing ink of that exact hue, rather than by mixing two or more process inks to create the color.

PANTONE COLORS

PMS 279   Black (K)

SPOT COLOR TINTS

To create a tint, use the Fill menu to specify a percentage of the solid color.

40% of PMS 279   60% of Black

SURPRINTING & REVERSES

Black type can surprint over color, and white type can reverse out. But pay attention to the legibility of body text in both cases.

A   **Z**

Printing spot color overlays in PageMaker

To separate Pantone colors so that each color prints on a separate piece of paper or film, select the printing options Spot Color Overlays and Crop Marks. (On a Mac, you have to press the Options button in the Print dialog box to access these options; on a PC, you can select them directly in the Print dialog box.)

When you select Crop Marks, PageMaker also prints registration marks and the name of the color outside the live area of the page. In order to see this information on a laser printer proof of an 8.5- by 11-inch page, print the pages undersize by specifying 85% in the Scaling text box.

When you print this "Simple Spot Color" fact sheet with these options selected, you'll get two black-and-white printouts that correspond to the ones shown below.

You should always print and check a set of overlays before sending files to a service bureau for separations. Be sure to return the Scaling specification to 100% before sending the file for final output.

Note: Printing this page in our book was more complicated than printing the fact sheet itself. The sample overlays below are PageMaker-generated EPS files and could not be printed in color through PageMaker. So we separated this page through PrePrint. But PrePrint reads the intrinsic color in a FreeHand EPS graphic (i.e., the color it was when you placed it in PageMaker). So we had to apply the color to the drawing of the eye before we placed it in PageMaker.

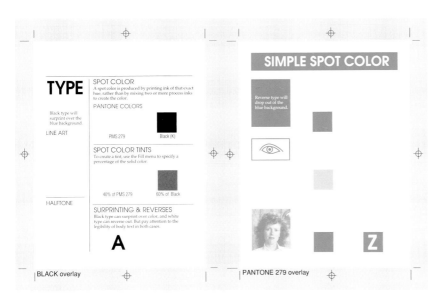

BLACK overlay   PANTONE 279 overlay

REGISTRATION OF ADJOINING AND OVERLAPPING COLORS

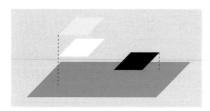

Manual Knockouts *To selectively knock out some elements and overprint others in PageMaker, you create masks that serve as manual knockouts. To create a manual knockout of the tan square in the blue rectangle: Power-paste a copy of the square, turn the color to Paper, send that square to the back, then send the blue rectangle to the back. The diagram above shows the stacking order. Print with Knockouts turned off. The Paper square will print over the blue rectangle, creating a knockout for the tan square. This knockout, like the ones PageMaker creates electronically when you print with Knockouts turned on, is the exact size of the element that fills that space. This is called kiss-fit.*

Misregistration *If the printing plates aren't perfectly aligned, kiss-fit knockouts won't be registered properly, and you'll see a little gap of white. Some designers prefer this kiss-fit default to the overlap of colors that results when you create traps.*

Traps *A trap is a small overlap of butting colors. In full-featured drawing programs, like FreeHand and Illustrator, you can create a trap by increasing the line weight and specifying the line to overprint. The increased line weight is spread evenly on both sides of the object. (PageMaker would add all the line weight to the inside of the object.) Check with your commercial printer on the advisability and size of traps.*

Manual Traps *The PageMaker workaround is primitively manual, but here it is: Working at 400%, shrink the white square by one pixel on each edge, so the mask that creates the knockout is slightly smaller than the shape that fills the space. It's easier to see what you're doing if you give the mask a hairline rule and no fill while you work. When you have it sized, return the line to None, the fill to Solid, and the color to Paper. Note: A Paper fill is not the same as the color Paper. A Paper fill will not knock out objects of different colors; the color Paper will.*

Adding a third color doesn't necessarily introduce printing complexities. But when two colors overlap, you must decide whether the foreground color should knock out of the background or print over it. If you want the color to knock out, the registration of the plates becomes critical. Poor registration can result in a gap of white between color instead of a seamless edge. Where a color butts a rule, misregistration could result in the color leaking beyond its intended boundary. To look at these issues, we'll adapt the previous fact sheet. First, use the Define Colors command to create a second Pantone color. We used PMS 156.

Overlapping spot colors

In the top row, apply PMS 156 to the left square. Draw a rectangle around the two squares; specify the Fill as Solid, and the color as PMS 279. Send that rectangle to the back (Command-B on a Mac, Ctrl-B on a PC).

When you print the page, you don't want the tan to print over the blue, because that would mix the inks of the two colors. By selecting Knockouts from the Print Options, you instruct PageMaker to eliminate the background color behind the tan. Theoretically, you could print the black over the blue without noticeably changing the color of the black; but in Page-Maker, you can't specify some colors to knock out and others to overprint. Unless you create manual knockouts (described at left), you either have knockouts for all colors or for none of them.

Adjoining spot colors

In the second row, specify a solid fill for both squares. Leave the left square PMS 279 and specify the right square PMS 156. Stretch the blue square so that its right edge butts the tan square. To create a black rule around the two squares, copy and power-paste the blue rectangle from the first row. Specify the Fill as None and the Line as 1 pt. Stretch the rectangle so that it extends to the right edge of the tan square.

Working at 400%, you can avoid registration problems by extending the right edge of the blue rectangle one pixel beyond the tan square. With a rule 1-point or wider, use this technique to avoid registration problems: Slightly reduce the size of the blue rectangle so that each edge bisects the 1-point rule of the outer rectangle. Do the same for the tan square. For more on "trapping" techniques such as these, see the notes at left.

Applying spot color to type

To apply color to type, as in the word TYPE and the letter Z, select the type with the text tool and then select a color in the Color Palette. You can't apply color to type using the pointer tool. And you can't apply a tint of a PMS color to type through the Fill menu regardless of which tool you use.

Color behind art

To put a spot color behind art, such as the eye or the grayscale TIFF in this fact sheet, draw a shape to match the art, fill the shape with the desired color, and put the colored box behind the art. Print with Knockouts turned off. (For grayscale photos, a bug in PageMaker 4.0 requires putting the box in front of the TIFF, but this has been corrected in 4.01.)

SPOT COLOR PITFALLS

TYPE

With Knockouts on, the tan and black type will knock out of the blue, creating a difficult register

LINE ART

HALFTONE

To print a spot color behind a halftone in PageMaker, put a colored box behind the halftone and print without knockouts.

SPOT COLOR ON SPOT COLOR

Generally, one spot color over another color will need to knock out, black being the exception.

Background: PMS 279
PMS 156   BLACK

ABUTTING SPOT COLORS & RULES

Poor registration could result in a gap of white between the two colors, or inside the rule; or one of the colors could leak beyond the rule.

PMS 279   PMS 156

SURPRINT & KNOCKOUT

If you knock out the tan Z from the blue, PageMaker will also knock out the black A from the tan.

PMS 156   PMS 279

Printing Problems *If you print spot color overlays in PageMaker with Knock outs turned on, you would get the three separations shown below. This achieves one goal, to prevent the tan from printing over the blue and creating a third color. But the black and the blue knock out, too, when in fact for best results black should always overprint. Note the potential mis-registration from the holes created for the body text in the blue overlay and from the two knockouts for the headline. Note also that because grayscale TIFFs are opaque, the blue box behind the halftone doesn't print with Knockouts turned on. (Frankly, after countless tests we feel that printing a grayscale photo over a PMS tint in Page-Maker has unpredictable results.)*

Printing Solutions *To correctly print this fact sheet, you can create manual knockouts as described on the facing page. Or you can generate the overlays through a separation program such as Aldus PrePrint, where you can overprint some colors and knock out others. We separated all the pages in this section through PrePrint. For this page, we specified both Black and PMS 279 to overprint; only PMS 156 knocks out.*

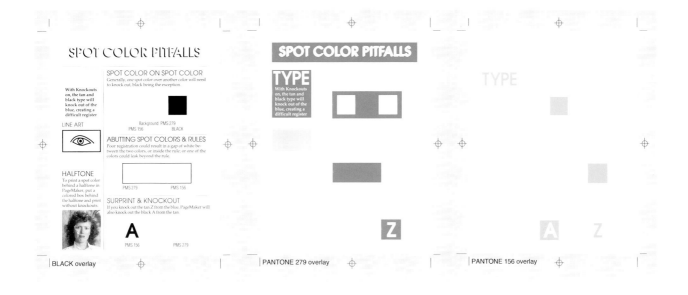

BLACK overlay   PANTONE 279 overlay   PANTONE 156 overlay

FOUR-COLOR PROCESS

For this section, we'll abandon the structure of the fact sheet. For hands-on practice, copy the squares to a blank page and simply experiment.

Defining process colors

Defining process colors in PageMaker is only a little more complex than defining Pantone colors. With the CMYK model selected, define and edit colors by typing a percentage in the value box for each process color, or by using the scroll bars. The box on the right of the dialog box displays the original color in the bottom panel, and as you change the values, the color in the top panel changes. In naming colors, we generally use names that refer to the way the color will be used (such as headline blue) or numbers that denote the values (such as M40-Y80).

Process color tints

Even if your budget is limited to two colors, you can use process color tints to create thousands of combinations with only two inks. In traditional color separation, the printer would have to strip in screens for each tint, at considerable cost. But with the computer making the separations, you can have dozens of 2-color tints on the page for the cost of two pieces of film.

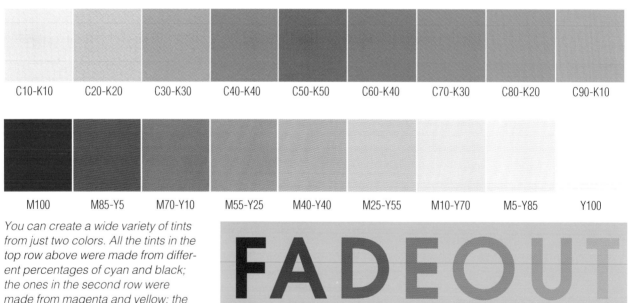

| C10-K10 | C20-K20 | C30-K30 | C40-K40 | C50-K50 | C60-K40 | C70-K30 | C80-K20 | C90-K10 |

| M100 | M85-Y5 | M70-Y10 | M55-Y25 | M40-Y40 | M25-Y55 | M10-Y70 | M5-Y85 | Y100 |

You can create a wide variety of tints from just two colors. All the tints in the top row above were made from different percentages of cyan and black; the ones in the second row were made from magenta and yellow; the "Fadeout" example at right is all cyan and magenta. Because process color tints are defined as colors, rather than being created from the Fill menu the way Pantone tints are, you can apply process tints to type.

Background: 100C.
All letters have 100C plus M as specified, left to right: M100, M80, M60, M40, M30, M20, M10.

With three colors, the possibilities are even greater. Here we have just a handful of the many thousands of combinations possible. And we haven't even included black in the mix.

Boxes					
C100	C70	C50	C30	C10	M100
M100	M100	M100	M100	M100	Y100
	Y10	Y30	Y50	Y70	
Letters					
Y100	M70	M50	M30	M10	Y100
	Y10	Y30	Y50	Y70	

To create process color tints, specify a percentage of the color in the Edit Colors dialog box. Don't specify a percentage on the Fill menu, the way you do with Pantone colors.

Using printed charts, you can see combinations of the process colors in 5% increments, so you have a good idea of what you're getting before you go to press. Although theoretically you can combine two Pantone colors on press, it's rarely done. With more than 700 Pantone colors, charts for combining them are necessarily limited; and because the inks are opaque, printed charts provide only a general idea of how the colors will combine.

You can avoid trapping problems, described on the previous spread, if the overlapping objects share 20% or more of one of the process colors. That's the case with the "Fadeout" example on the facing page, and with some (but not all) of the "A thru Z" letters and boxes. Where there is a shared color, misregistration would result in a sliver of that shared color, which is much less visible than a sliver of white.

Four-color artwork

To print color photographs, such as the multimedia still life on this page, the full spectrum of colors in the original must be converted to the four process colors. You can see the separations for this photo in the images at left (the actual film, of course, is a black-and-white negative).

Color separations

To separate PageMaker files that include process colors, you must either use a separation program or link to a high-end color system. (See the discussion at the beginning of this project on page 367.)

If you print a page with process color directly from PageMaker, you'll get an overlay for every color you've defined. So if you have a headline specified as Y30-M60, you'll get an overlay that's labeled Y30-M60. And colored graphics placed from other programs will print on the black overlay. These overlays would be useless as separations.

Photo by Ben Kerns

Translating Pantone Colors to 4/C Process

The color pages in this book are printed in six colors—the four process colors plus two Pantone colors. Pages that include all six colors, such as this one, required six pieces of film.

Sometimes you want to use Pantone and process colors in the same publication and don't want to incur the additional expense of a fifth or sixth color. Instead, you can simulate the PMS color in the CMYK model. Select the color you want from PageMaker's Pantone library, and then choose the CMYK model in the Edit Color dialog box. Give the color a new name. Or you can make the conversion using the Convert to Process option in PrePrint. Some conversions are pretty close, and some aren't.

| PMS 156 | 4/C PROCESS M18-Y43 | PMS 279 | 4/C PROCESS C69-M34 |

ADDING COLOR TO NEWSLINE

We're going to look at two different color versions of the newsletter from Project 4. The first one, below left, is almost as simple a color document as you can create. It uses two Pantone colors and black, and the only complication is the tan tint that butts to the black rule. But because there are no other overlapping or abutting colors, you won't need any knockouts. This version can be separated for spot color overlays directly from PageMaker, either to paper or to film.

The second version, below right, adds the complexity of overlapping colors. You'll need to overprint the black ink while knocking out the tan from behind the blue banners. You can do this by creating manual knockouts in PageMaker, or by separating the document through a separation utility such as Aldus PrePrint.

If you don't have a color monitor, you can still do this part of the project. The two PMS colors being used display as light and dark gray on a monochrome monitor, so it's relatively easy to determine if you have the correct color applied to the correct element on the page. And when you proof the overlays, the names of the colors will be printed on each overlay.

To create this version of the color newsletter, follow the instructions for Variation 1 beginning on the facing page.

▼ ▼ ▼

To create this version of the color newsletter, follow the instructions for Variation 2 beginning on page 381.

▼ ▼ ▼

VARIATION 1

1. Define the colors.

- Choose Define Colors from the Element menu.

- In the Define Colors dialog box, choose New. When the Edit Color dialog box comes on-screen, choose Pantone. Type or scroll to select Pantone 156. Click OK.

- Choose New again and, using the same technique as before, specify Pantone 279.

- Before closing the Define Colors dialog box, remove the default colors Red, Green, and Blue from the color list. You remove a color the same way you remove a style: Click on the name of the color and then click Remove.

TIP

If you apply spot colors to art in a graphics program, be sure those colors have the exact same names, including capitalization, as their corresponding spot colors in PageMaker. If, for example, a FreeHand graphic with art specified as PANTONE 279 CV is placed in PageMaker, and the PageMaker color is named Pantone 279 CV, PrePrint will create two separations.

2. Bring the Color Palette and the Style Palette on-screen.

Choose the respective commands from the Window menu. Or use the keyboard shortcuts. For the Color Palette, press Command-K on a Mac and Ctrl-K on a PC. For the Style Palette, press Command-Y on a Mac and Ctrl-Y on a PC.

3. Edit styles to incorporate color.

The rules above the story headlines are part of the *story head* style. To change the color of the rules from black to blue for the entire publication, edit the Line Color in the style definition.

- Press Command (Ctrl on a PC) and click on *story head* in the Style Palette. In the Edit Style dialog box, choose Paragraph and then choose Rules. With the pointer over the Line Color box (or, on a PC, over the arrow), hold down the mouse button to bring up the submenu of all the colors defined for the publication, and then choose Pantone 279. Click OK to get back to the Edit Style dialog box.

We aren't using any colored type in the newsletter, but before you close this dialog box, choose Type, and in the Type Specs dialog box, bring up the submenu for colors. If you wanted to define a color as

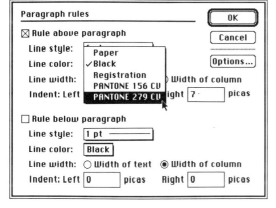

▲ ▲ ▲

To change the color of a paragraph rule, select the desired color from the Line Color submenu in the Paragraph Rules dialog box.

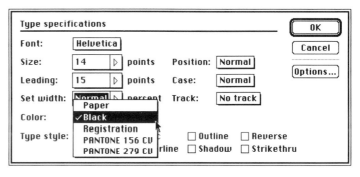

▲ ▲ ▲

To change the color of type, select the desired color from the Color submenu in the Type Specs dialog box.

TIP

PageMaker's default Fill is None, so whenever you draw a rectangle (or any other enclosed shape using one of PageMaker's drawing tools), the Fill is automatically specified as None. If you then specify a color for that graphic, the color is applied to the Line only. To get color inside the graphic, you must specify Solid or a % Fill.

part of the style for type, you would do it by selecting a color from this submenu.

4. Add color to the rules and banners.

- Hold down the Shift key and, with the pointer tool, select the banner behind the nameplate, the banner behind "Forecasts," the vertical rules between columns, and the horizontal rule below the nameplate.
- With all the elements selected, click Pantone 279 in the Color Palette.

5. Add the art.

For the first variation, we used a TIFF image from a clip art collection. You could use any paint or TIFF art that you have; or try either the "Aldus.pnt" or "Anchor.TIF" files that were included as part of the tutorial for PageMaker 4.0.

- Delete the picture placeholder in the left column.
- Place and size the art within the wide column. When you're done, you may need to reposition the caption.
- With the art selected, specify Pantone 279 from the Color Palette.

TIP

Be very careful with background colors behind type. Unless the color itself is very light, you should specify a percentage of the color through the Fill submenu, rather than print a solid color behind type. If the color were light enough to print solid behind the type, it would probably be too light to print as a solid rule or graphic.

6. Add a tone behind the "Forecasts" text.

- Draw a rectangle over the text.
- With the rectangle selected, choose Pantone 156 from the Color Palette.
- With the rectangle still selected, specify the Fill as 60% and the Line as None. Send the box to the back.
- Select the text and specify the Left Indent as 1p and the Right Indent as 0p9. (With rag right text, many of the lines will fall short of the right margin. So when you inset the text in a box or behind a tinted panel, you don't need to indent the right margin quite as much as the left.)

7. Create a black rule around the tan box.

Many drawing programs allow you to specify the fill of a graphic as one color and the line as another. But you can't do this in PageMaker. Here's the workaround:

- Select the tan box behind the "Forecasts" text.
- Copy the box and power-paste the copy directly over the original.
- With the copy still selected, specify the Fill as None and the Line as 1 pt Black.
- If you want to ensure that a misregistration won't result in the color printing beyond the graphic: Working at 400%, shrink the colored box one or two pixels on each edge, so the edges of the tan box bisect the 1-pt rule of the surrounding rectangle.

TIP

At 400%, the ruler tick marks are at 1-point increments and one pixel equals .25 point. When you create manual traps in PageMaker, use ruler guides to ensure that your trap is even all around.

8. Print.

- First print a composite proof to see all the elements in place on a single page. To do this, print the page as you normally do for a black-and-white publication.

- Print a second time to proof the color overlays.

  In the Print dialog box, specify Crop Marks and Spot Color Overlays. (On a Macintosh, you will have to select the Options button in the Print dialog box to access these options.) Specify the Scaling as 85% so that you'll be able to see the name of the color on each overlay. (Be sure to return the Scaling option to 100% before getting your final output.) You should get three printouts: one for the black plate, one for the PMS 279 plate, and one for PMS 156.

VARIATION 2

This variation uses a background color across all the pages, which brings us to a discussion of one of PageMaker's default colors, the one named Paper. The default color for Paper is white. You can change the color specified for Paper through the Edit Color dialog box, just as you would edit any other color.

When you define a color for Paper, PageMaker displays that color as the background for every page in your document. When you print color overlays, you won't get an overlay for the color Paper because PageMaker assumes that you are printing on a paper of that color, rather than applying that color on press. In practice, however, if you have color in the background as well as in other elements of the publication, you are far more likely to apply the background color on press than to print on colored paper.

The following instructions explain how to create a background color that is to be printed. One advantage of this approach is that it enables you to use reverse type and rules. "Reverse" is nothing more than the color of the paper, which of course is normally white. If you really were printing on tan paper, Reverse would be tan; and without resorting to specialized techniques such as silk screening, there would be no way to get white rules and type.

1. Open a copy of the color newsletter you just created.

If the file for variation 1 is still open, you can just continue with the following steps. If you didn't create the first variation, open a copy of the original *Newsline*, use the Define Colors command to define Pantone 279 and 156 , and then proceed with step 2.

2. Create the background color.

In order to ensure that an image prints all the way to the edge of the page, you have to allow for the possibility that the pages will shift a little on press. So the image—whether a colored box as in this example, or a photo, or any other piece of art—must be bigger than the page. In the graphic arts, this is known as a bleed.

TIP

How do you know when two elements are exactly the same size and directly on top of one another? Draw a marquee around both elements. If all the selection handles disappear, the copies are exactly in line with one another.

How do you know which element is selected when one item is directly on top of another one? In a color publication, look in the Color Palette to see which color is highlighted for the selected element. In a black-and-white publication, drag the selected element to the side and then immediately choose Undo from the Edit menu (Command-Z on a Mac, Alt-Bksp on a PC).

When you bleed an image or a tint off the page, you should extend the graphic about 1/8 inch, or 9 points, beyond the page trim. The extension won't appear on an 8.5- by 11-inch page printed on a laser printer because the printer can't print to the edge of the page, much less beyond it; but the bleed will print on the oversize page output from an imagesetter, with crop marks indicating the trim. Be aware that bleeds can increase the cost of a job because they require printing on paper that is larger than the page trim.

- Draw a rectangle on the master page that extends beyond the page by about 1/8 inch, or 9 points. Specify the color as PMS 156. Specify the Fill as 60% and the Line as None. Send the box to the back.

- Select the horizontal rule under the nameplate and the vertical rules between columns and choose Paper from the Color Palette.

- Select the banner at the top of the page and choose PMS 279 from the Color Palette. Check to be sure that the Fill is 40%.

These colors will come through on every page. Remember, though, that we've turned off Display Master Items on the cover of this publication. So we need to add the background there, too.

- Copy the background rectangle from the master page and turn to page 1.

- Before pasting the copy that's on the Clipboard, delete the tint behind the "Forecasts" text that you created in variation 1. Use the Delete key or Clear from the Edit menu, rather than the Cut command, so you won't lose the background rectangle that's on the Clipboard.

- Power-paste the copy of the background rectangle into place on page 1. Send the color box to the back.

3. Specify the reverse rules on page 1.

Select the column rules and the horizontal rule under the nameplate, which printed blue in the first variation, and specify Paper.

4. Change the type specs for "Newsline."

If you are working on a Mac, specify Helvetica Bold instead of Helvetica Bold Outline. (If you are working on a PC, you didn't have the outline option available.) On both the Mac and the PC, force justify the word "Newsline" between the left margin of the center column and the right margin of the newsletter subhead.

5. Create reverse rules around the blue banners.

White knocks out all other colors. So by creating a 1-pt reverse rule around a blue banner, that rule knocks out both the blue and the tan, and the colors won't butt.

- Copy the blue banner in the nameplate and power-paste the copy directly on top of the original. Specify the Fill as None and the Line as 1 pt reverse. Then select "Newsline" and bring it to the front so the white rule doesn't run through the type.

- Use the same technique to create a reverse rule around the "Forecasts" banner.

6. Make the paragraph rules above headlines black.

Against the tan background, we prefer the headline rules to print black. This will also avoid registration problems, because we can sur-

Aldus is already working on changing this, but for PageMaker 4.0 be aware of this potential problem: When you separate PageMaker files through PrePrint, the cyan for every page in the file prints first, then the magenta for every page, and so on. The film is printed from rolls, and in a file of even 5 letter-size pages, the distance between the separations for each page can be close to 15 feet. To minimize misregistration of film within a single page, and to avoid having to reprint a great many pages if a single separation is damaged, create a PostScript.sep file for every page in the document.

TIP

Once you understand the potential problems in printing overlapping and adjoining colors, you can choose from among several ways of creating and producing pages that have this kind of color.

1) Create these elements in a drawing program where you can create traps electronically, and then import those elements into the PageMaker layout.

2) Combine desktop and traditional pasteup: Print overlays without knockouts and mark the camera-ready art for the printer to create the traps.

3) Separate (or have your service center separate) your PageMaker file through a program such as Aldus PrePrint or Adobe Separator, where you can choose selective overprinting.

4) Manually create selective knockouts in PageMaker, using the power-paste technique to position Paper-colored objects between a colored element and a colored background. Print spot color overlays with Knockouts turned off.

TIP

All colors in PageMaker are considered spot colors, including black and any CMYK tints that you define in PageMaker. When you separate files through PrePrint, you must specify Convert to Process Ink for Black and for each Page-Maker process tint. Otherwise, a tint named 30M-10Y will print on a separation named 30M-10Y, rather than on the magenta and yellow seps. The only PageMaker-defined colors that you don't convert in PrePrint are Pantone colors that you intend to print as spot colors.

print the black rules over the tan background, instead of knocking out the tan behind the rules.

- Edit the *story head* style, changing the paragraph rules from PMS 279 to Black.

7. Print spot color overlays.

To emphasize a point, we're going to have you use the wrong method to print this page for separation.

- In the Print dialog box (the Print Options dialog box on a Mac), choose Crop Marks, Knockouts, and Spot Color Overlays. Click OK or press Return.

  When the overlays print, note that on the tan (PMS 156) overlay, the black type has been knocked out. This is what you *don't* want. It would be almost impossible to register the 10-point body text from the black plate in the knockouts created for it in the tan plate.

There are two possible solutions in this particular publication.

- You could create manual knockouts for the blue banners.

  To do this, you create a solid Paper-colored (white) box between the blue banner and the tan background. You can then print with Knockouts turned off because the white box will knock out any color behind it. You can either kiss-fit the manual knockout, or you can create a trap by making the white box one or two pixels larger all around than the blue banner. The trick is to ensure that the trap is even on all four sides.

- The second solution, and the one we used, is to have your service bureau print the pages through a separation utility such as PrePrint.

  Whereas in PageMaker the default is for all inks to overprint unless you specify Knockouts, in PrePrint the default is for all colors to knock out any background color. To overprint any one ink, select the name of that color in PrePrint's Options dialog box and choose Overprint This Ink. For this publication, you specify black to overprint. The two PMS colors knock out by default, and the 1-pt white rules around the blue banners eliminate the need for traps.

  There is a great deal more to separating color pages through PrePrint than specifying which inks will overprint. Work closely with the service bureau that will print the separations for you, reviewing the pages either in person or by telephone. (If by phone, try to get printouts to the service bureau so they will have them in hand when you talk.) You'll need to know the file format of the art included in the publication (paint, EPS, and so on), where the color was applied (whether in PageMaker or in the originating application), and whether the art is linked to an original source file.

Sound complicated? No one ever said color was easy, or that it was PageMaker's strong suit. But if you want more control over Page-Maker's spot colors, or if your PageMaker files include process color tints or 4-color art, you will need to learn the variables of printing through a separation utility such as PrePrint.

THE BACK OF THE BOOK

SOME NOTES ON HOW WE PRODUCED THIS BOOK

A single "electronic" copy of this book (excluding the front and back covers and the index) comes to about 27 MB of PageMaker files. This includes linked source files required for printing. It does not include other source files, nor the previously printed documents that were stripped in by the printer.

As a revision of an earlier edition of *Desktop Publishing by Design*, which covered PageMaker 3.0, this book required working with old PageMaker files as well as creating new ones. Since part of the promise of desktop technology is the ease of revisions, we'll look at both parts of that process.

Just as adding onto an existing house can be more difficult than building a totally new structure, so too with revisions of electronic files. Going into floppy disks that have been in deep storage for a year and a half is quite different from revising files that you created a week or even several months ago. We'd changed systems several times; we'd replaced all our screen fonts from the old font-numbering system with Adobe's NFNT fonts. We'd merged the fonts using Suitcase's Font Harmony utility and then unmerged them in favor of Adobe's Type Reunion. We feared the equivalent of dry rot lurked in those files. But we were happily surprised, and tests run early in the revision process enabled us to work around or solve the problems that did come up.

Editing and converting PageMaker 3.02 files

Sections 1 and 2 focus primarily on graphic design, and the information covered there doesn't change with the release of a software upgrade. So most of the pages in these sections required only small changes to correct production comments that would be confusing or inaccurate given the increased capability of PageMaker 4.0.

PageMaker composes text and calculates leading a little differently in 4.0 than in 3.x. When we opened the original 3.02 files in 4.0 and compared them to the printed pages in the first edition, we found changes in line breaks that generally lengthened text blocks by a few lines. So we decided to make the corrections for those sections in PageMaker 3.02, rather than to convert the files to 4.0. It would ensure consistency of text composition between pages that did require changes and pages that didn't. And it would eliminate the need to check line breaks and to copyfit text that didn't require any other changes.

There are always exceptions. Pages 32–39, which address styling type in PageMaker, were rewritten in PageMaker 4.0. This was necessary to demonstrate typographic capabilities that weren't available in 3.02.

The decision to revise the first half of the book in PageMaker 3.02 meant that we couldn't take advantage of PageMaker 4.0's long document features, particularly the indexing capability. Indexing, however, is a specialized task that we were happy to turn over to a professional. By the time this book is revised for PageMaker 5.0, no doubt many professional indexers will be using PageMaker's automated tools, and we'll have the best of both worlds.

On the issue of fonts. The only real problem we encountered was with the Linotronic output of PageMaker-generated EPS documents created with fonts from the earlier font-numbering system. When we opened those source files in PageMaker (with NFNT fonts installed), made new EPS files, and placed the new files in the layout, the fonts printed fine.

HARDWARE

State-of-the-art technology comes with an unwritten guarantee: You'll be longing for a faster, newer machine sooner than you want to admit. We're grateful to have had relatively trouble-free experiences with upgrades.

The hot-rodded Mac II: Our Mac II has a DayStar 33MHz accelerator, 8 MB of internal memory, a Jasmine 90 internal drive, a 13-inch Apple Color Monitor, a 24-inch Moniterm Viking monitor (monochrome), and a Datacopy Proscan 730. We did most of the page layouts and corrections on this system.

The hot-rodded Mac Plus: Our first Mac, a 1986 Plus, is enhanced with a Radius Accelerator Board and 4 MB of memory. This station has a Radius Full Page Display, a Jasmine Direct Drive 50, a DataDesk extended keyboard, and a Hayes 2400 modem. We did all of the word processing and administrative work on this system, and an occasional page layout.

PageMaker 4.0 can run on a 1-MB Mac, but 2 MB is recommended. On a PC, you need a minimum of 2 MB of RAM, and 3 is recommended. Don't expect great performance with the minimum-required memory, especially on slower machines. In a book such as this, which includes numerous graphics and unthreaded text elements (each tip, caption, and sidebar is an independent text block), screen redraw can be very slow. The DayStar accelerator brought our Mac II up to speed. In order to run PageMaker 4.0 and Microsoft Word 4.0 together under Multifinder, the 2.5 MB we had in our Mac Plus prior to revising this book wasn't sufficient. With 4 MB we can run both programs with a fair selection of fonts and other goodies. And with 8 MB on the Mac II, we're reasonably content for the time being.

The two systems are connected to each other through Tops, and both are connected to an Apple LaserWriter NTX printer via AppleTalk. The NTX has a 40-MB hard drive. The hard drive's a real luxury, which we wouldn't have if we weren't working on a typography book that by definition is font-intensive. One very quickly takes for granted not having to think about what fonts are in use, since all the fonts are functionally resident in the printer.

For backup we use a Mass Microsystems DataPak, a 45-MB removable media hard drive. What used to take 30 minutes or more of feeding dozens and dozens of floppies now takes less than 5 minutes. The DataPak boosts efficiency far beyond the daily backup chores. We archived all the files from the first edition on one cartridge, so accessing an earlier file no longer requires sorting through a half dozen boxes of floppy disks. And the 45-MB cartridges also facilitate sending files to our service bureau.

We cannot say enough about the value of large monitors. Trying to design and lay out pages without being able to see the entire canvas is a little like doing manual pasteup with one hand. It's also time-consuming: The process of scrolling around a page on a small monitor and waiting for the screen to redraw at each new position slows page assembly to a degree that undermines efficiency. Our 24-inch Moniterm displays two 8.5-by 11-inch pages at Actual Size, which brings a real-time/real-space immediacy to electronic page assembly. We know people get by with small screens. But if you have ongoing publishing requirements of any complexity, a large monitor (a full-page display, 19-inch or larger) is a must. Otherwise, you may be wasting in time what you're saving in type costs.

The IBM clone: To test the project instructions in the Windows version of PageMaker, Rebecca Pepper used a FiveStar 80386 with 3 MB of memory, an 80-MB hard drive, and an NEC Multisync color monitor. Having found an XT painfullly slow even with PageMaker 3.0, she was very pleased with the zippy performance and multitasking capability of the 386 machine.

File size and pagination

Throughout the book, we started with chapter-length files and broke them into even smaller units as needed. The number of pages that constitutes a manageable file depends on the complexity of the pages. Chapters 1 and 4, for example, are mostly running text; at 125 KB and 110 KB respectively, they are quite manageable as single files. Chapter 3, on the other hand, is 60 pages long, and many of these are graphics-intensive. We gradually broke that chapter down into eight different files, ranging in size from 320 KB to 1.35 MB and adding up to well over 5 MB.

For the first round of page proofs, we used composite page-number markers to number pages by chapter or project. Project 1 was numbered P1-2, P1-3, P1-4, and so on. By the second round of page proofs we knew the final pagination and could number the files chronologically using the Start Page # option in the Page Setup dialog box. (Enhancements in PageMaker 4.01 automate this task through the Book command.)

Smart scrapbooks and the Replacing Entire Graphic option

Before looking at some of the new PageMaker features used in rewriting the project section, we want to mention a few techniques used in creating the first two sections of the first edition, techniques that are just as valuable today as they were when those pages were created. They range from good old-fashioned pencil sketches to a somewhat obscure Place option that exemplifies computer automation.

For the portfolio section, we did rough pencil layouts on paper to determine the order and size of the samples included in each chapter. There's a tactile quality about pencil and paper that seems compatible with organization tasks such as this, but perhaps our bias is simply a habit held over from years of using traditional production techniques. Then we created page frames for the art in FreeHand and copied those frames into different SmartScrap scrapbooks (8-1/2 by 11 vertical, 8-1/2 by 11 landscape, 11 by 17, 7-1/2 by 10, special sizes, and so on). As we assembled the skeleton of each chapter, we called up the appropriate scrapbook, scrolled to find the frame we needed (52% single page, 38% facing pages, and so on), and copied and pasted that frame on the page. Once we had all the frames in place, the amount of space for annotations was clearly visible on the page, and we wrote the text for these chapters directly in PageMaker.

The grid chapter was handled similarly to the portfolio chapters, although here we also had to create many of the sample documents and blueprints. The sample documents that are reproduced in a reduced size were created in PageMaker, saved as Encapsulated PostScript files, and then placed electronically in the book pages. The Replacing Entire Graphic option was a great time-saver with these documents. Using the page-frame scrapbooks described for the portfolio section, we copied and pasted the desired frames onto the page; but in the grid chapter, we also pasted a second copy of

The blueprint showing the grid for this book, like the blueprints in Chapter 3, was created as a full-size PageMaker document, saved as an Encapsulated PostScript file, and placed inside a page frame in the actual book pages. We determined that all the blueprints would be reduced to either 38% or 52%. For the 38% reductions, we used 22-point type; for the 52% reductions, 16-point type. This gave the blueprints a consistent look throughout the book.

▼ ▼ ▼

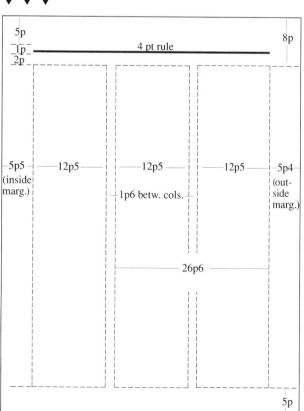

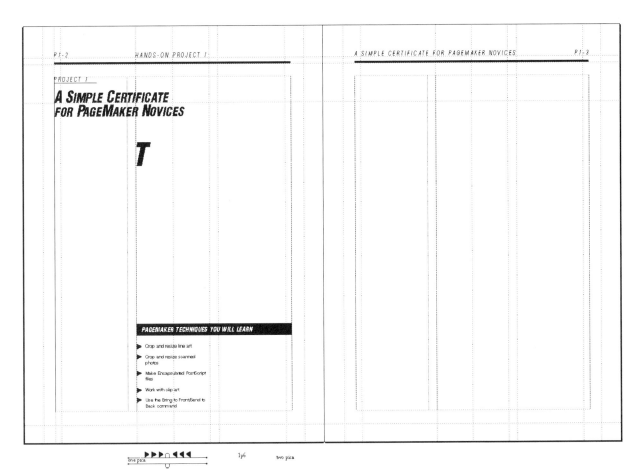

▲ ▲ ▲

The opening spread of the template for the projects section shows the basic grid and placeholders. The "one pica," "1p6," and "two pica" text blocks served as spacing guides. The leading for each text element corresponded to the measurement named. The "one pica" text block, for example, is specified as 10/12, and the text handles were used to measure the distance between the arrows and the baseline of the caption below.

▶ ▶ ▶

For sidebars, we used the Column Guides command to specify 2 equal columns. The ruler guides inset 1p from the left and right margins were used to inset the text from the box around the sidebar, which was flush with the side margins. The guidelines outside the side margins marked the maximum width for art that extended beyond the grid.

SOFTWARE

Aask (CE Software): When we need to diagnose system problems, this Control Panel device provides a relatively easy way to turn INITs on and off in order to root out the likely suspect(s).

Adobe Type Manager (Adobe Systems, Inc.): With ATM generating screen fonts from the outline fonts used for printing, type display is smoother and more accurate. This makes small type easier to read on-screen and facilitates kerning as well. ATM also improves output from non-PostScript printers.

Adobe Type Reunion (Adobe Systems, Inc.): If you can afford a lot of fonts, then you can't afford to be without a utility that makes the length of your font menu manageable. Type Reunion does this by creating submenus for complex type families.

Capture (Mainstay): Capture enables you to save part of a screen image by dragging a cross-hair cursor over the area you want to capture. It also has a scaling facility, which, in the case of screen dumps, helps make up for the fact that PageMaker doesn't.

CheckList (ElseWare Corporation): If you forget to list a downloadable font when you send a file to a service bureau, the text that's supposed to be in that font prints in Courier. CheckList conveniently lists all the fonts included in a selected document and reviews the links to external source files, too.

DeskPaint (Zedcor): This desk accessory enables you to create and edit Paint and TIFF documents while working in another application. We used DeskPaint to clean screen dumps as we assembled the pages and to manipulate clip art.

DiskExpress (ALSoft, Inc.): As a hard disk becomes full, it may have to store information for a single file in different locations. As a result, when you open or save a file, the drive heads have to search to find not just one file, but various fragments of it. Periodically, we ran DiskExpress to compact these fragmented files and speed up disk performance.

DiskFit (SuperMac Software): The easier it is to back up your files, the more frequently you'll do so. DiskFit is remarkably easy to use, and we used it every day.

DiskTop (CE Software): We use this file management desk accessory constantly to move, rename, and delete files as well as to find them.

FreeHand (Aldus): We didn't need to create a great deal of art for the book. We used FreeHand for that occasional piece and for the precisely sized (and occasionally angled) page frames used in Sections 1 and 2.

LaserStatus (CE Software): Before we got a hard disk for our printer, this DA (packaged with Disk-Top) was a daily timesaver. It enables you to configure the fonts for any job as a set and then to download the set with one simple operation instead of going through a whole series of Font Downloader dialog boxes for each individual font.

Microsoft Word (Microsoft Corporation): For compatibility with PageMaker, Microsoft Word is hard to match. We wrote, edited, spell-checked, and formatted about half the text in Word before placing it in PageMaker.

Microsoft Works (Microsoft Corporation): We used the database in Works to keep track of samples, permissions, and copyrights from the many designers and organizations who sent us their work.

QuickKeys (CE Software): We find this a remarkably easy-to-use program for defining keyboard shortcuts. For further automation, you can also create sequences of shortcuts.

SmartScrap (Solutions International): Thanks to SmartScrap, we had several manageable scrapbooks for the book, each named and filed as any other document would be.

Suitcase (Software Supply): For managing fonts and DAs, loading and unloading Suitcases as needed to keep the System file lean, we use Suitcase II. And when we install new fonts, we use Font Harmony (which comes with Suitcase) to avoid font numbering conflicts.

Tops (Sun Microsystems): Without a spare computer to use as a file server, we used Tops to network our two workstations. It's never been a great solution, but we get by okay with it.

the frame directly over the first. (You know one frame is directly on top of the other when both sets of handles disappear; in PageMaker 4.0, you can ensure the positioning by power-pasting.) Then we selected the top frame, went to the Place dialog box, scrolled to select the EPS document, and clicked on the Replacing Entire Graphic option. PageMaker automatically reduced the new graphic (in this case, the EPS file) to fit and replace the old one (the top copy of the page frame); the bottom copy of the page frame remained to define the page trim.

Styles

We didn't alter the type design in this edition of the book, but we did revise many of the style definitions in the projects section to take advantage of 4.0's new capabilities. In particular, the addition of Paragraph Rules and the ability to specify a Next Style automated a great many elements that had to be created manually in the first edition.

The list on the next two pages includes the most frequently used styles in the projects section. The wording of each style definition follows the form displayed when the style name is highlighted in the Define Styles dialog box, with some abbreviations. Also, the details of some attributes, such as tab positions and paragraph rules, are included even though those details don't appear in the definition that PageMaker displays. The definition of a style that is based on another style begins with the name of the base style. Information in parentheses indicates a style override, such as an initial cap, which you must format manually.

TYPEFACES AND CLIP ART

We used a fair amount of clip art in the sample documents throughout the book, for the same reason people often use clip art: It's a fast way to get graphics on a page. As is true for so many publications, we simply didn't have the budget to commission or the time to create much art. Using clip art also gave us the opportunity to display some of what is available. The clip art we used came from the following packages:

> Artware (Artware Systems)
> DeskTop Art Borders & Mortises (Dynamic Graphics)
> DeskTop Art Business 1 (Dynamic Graphics)
> DrawArt Volume 2 (Desktop Graphics)
> Images with Impact (3G Graphics)
> Logomaster (Moonlight Artworks)
> The Mac Art Dept. (Simon & Schuster)
> The MacMemories Catalog (ImageWorld, Inc.)
> Moonlight Artworks 1 and 2 (Hired Hand Design)
> NewsletterMaker (Metro ImageBase)
> ReportMaker (Metro ImageBase)
> Team Sports (Metro ImageBase)

The typefaces used throughout the book are from Adobe Systems, except as specified in the annotations (and undoubtedly in some samples reproduced from other designers). In addition to the fonts resident in most PostScript printers, we used type from the following families:

> Aachen Bold
> ITC American Typewriter
> Bodoni
> Franklin Gothic
> Futura
> Futura Condensed
> ITC Galliard
> ITC Garamond
> Helvetica Condensed
> Helvetica Light/Black
> ITC Machine

For reasons of space, we omitted hyphenation information in our list of style definitions. Hyphenation was turned off for all headlines. For other text, the styles specified a 1p hyphenation zone with a limit of two consecutive hyphens. That zone specification saved space, which we needed, but it also allowed many words to be hyphenated after only two characters. In proofing the pages, we manually rebroke those lines unless the hyphenation saved a line in that paragraph.

Some styles appear to be redundant, and in one sense they are. For example, the sidebar text style and some of the styles based on it are identical to the body text style and the styles based on it. But by naming the style according to the use, even when it duplicates another style, you minimize guesswork. Also, remember that one purpose of styles is the

STYLES USED IN THE PROJECTS SECTION

Style Name	Definition	Style Name	Definition
# instructions	next: 1p indent + face: Helv Cond BlackObl + size: 11 + leading: 12 + flush left + left indent: 1 + first indent: -1 + space before: 1p6 + space after: 0p6 + tab at 1p	caption	next: triangles /down + face: Helv LightObl + size: 9 + leading: 11 + flush left
# 1 instructions	# instructions + next: 1p indent + space before: 3	caption/tight	caption + next: same + size: 8 + leading: 10 + space after: 0p5 + des wrdsp: 90%
#d body text	body text + next: 1p indent + left indent: 1 + first indent: -1 + tab at 1p	continued line	caption + next: same + leading: 20 + flush right
1p indent	body text + next: same + left indent: 1	head-bannered	head-project + next: body text + size: 13 + leading: 12 + color: Paper + left indent: 0p9 + space after: 2p4 + top rule: 12 pt, width of column, -7p9 right indent, 1p5 above baseline + bottom rule: 12 pt, width of column, -7p9 right indent, 0p7 below baseline
2p indent	body text + next: same + left indent: 2		
art annotations	next: same + face: Helv Light + size: 9 + leading: 11 + flush left + space after: 0p11	head-column	head-project + next: body text + size: 11 + leading: 12 + space after: 0p6 + top rule: 12 pt, width of column, 2p6 above baseline
body text	next: same + face: Palatino + size: 10 + leading: 12 + flush left + space after: 0p6 + des wrdsp: 80% + des ltrsp: -4%		
bullets fl left	body text + next: same + left indent: 1 + first indent: -1 + tab at 1p	head-column above	head-column + next: head-column + leading: 1 + space after: 0 + keepnext: 1 - top rule + bottom rule: hairline, width of column, -14p right indent, auto position
bullets hang from #	body text + next: same + left indent: 2 + first indent: -1 + tab at 2p		
callouts	art annotations + next: same + size: 7.5 + leading: 8	head-project	face: CLBI Helvetica Condensed BlackObl + all caps + size 24 +leading: 26 + flush left (+ 30-pt initial cap + kerning as needed)
caption/no arrow	caption + next: same + space after: 0p5.5		

ability to make global changes by changing the style definition. If we used the body text style and its derivatives for the sidebar text, we could not have changed the sidebar style definitions without retagging all the sidebar text.

There are some styles that can't be automated, such as the right- and left-pointing arrows above captions that ran alongside graphics. There's no side-pointing arrow in Zapf Dingbats to match the style used for the up and down arrows. Text rotation would have stacked the triangles on top of one another. We tried rotating a single character, power-pasting it twice, and then placing it from the Scrapbook to create a single object. But the Linotronic lost the font information and printed three rotated Courier s's. (Fortunately, we discovered this in an early test.) So we used the

Style Name	Definition
head-project B	head-project + size: 18 + leading: 18 (+ 24-pt initial cap + kerning as needed)
head-sidebar	head-project + next: sidebar text + size: 13 + leading: 12 + left indent: 1 + space after: 1 + top rule: 12 pt, width of text, -1p left indent, -0p4 right indent, 2p6 above baseline
head-sidebar sub	head-sidebar + next: sidebar text - all caps + size: 11 + left indent: 0 + space before: 0p6 + space after: 0p6 - top rule
head-tip	head-project + next: tips text + size: 9 + leading: 12 + color: Paper + left indent: 0p9 + space after: 0p3 + top rule: hairline, width of column, 0p9.5 above baseline + bottom rule: 12 pt, width of column, 9p4 right indent, 0p2.5 below baseline
head-tip (Mac or PC)	head-tip + bottom rule: width of text, -0p9 left indent, -0p9 right indent
initial cap	head-project + next: no style + size: 60 + leading: 60
PM techniques list	next: same + face: Helv Light + size: 9 + leading: 11 + space after: 0p9

Style Name	Definition
project overline	running head + next: no style + bottom rule: hairline, width of column, 5p3 right indent, 0p3 below baseline
running head	next: same + face: Helv Cond LightObl + all caps + size: 12 + lead: 14 + flush left + des wrdsp: 100% + des ltrsp: 100%
sidebar bullets fl	sidebar text + next: same + left indent: 1 + first indent: -1 + tab at 1p
sidebar text	body text + next: same style
sidebar #d instructions	sidebar text + next: same + bold + left indent: 1 + first indent: -1 + tab at 1p
sidebar 1p indent	sidebar text + next: same + left indent: 1p
tips text	next: same + face: Helv Light + size: 9 + leading: 11 + flush left + right indent: 0p6 + space after: 0p6
triangles up	triangles down + next: caption + space before: 0p3
triangles down	next: caption + face: Zapf Dingbats + size: 11.5 + leading: 13 + track: normal + flush left + des ltrsp: 132%

arrows that we'd created in Illustrator for the first edition. The Dingbat arrows had been chosen and sized to match those Illustrator arrows, and we felt the match was quite accurate. So we placed those side-pointing arrows on the pasteboard, and copied and pasted them as needed.

We also had an entire style sheet that wasn't on the computer at all. This one, created by our editor at Microsoft, consisted of a list of words that were likely candidates for misspelling or for inconsistent hyphenation or capitalization: autoflow mode, Autoflow command, bit-mapped (adj), black-and-white (adj), camera-ready art, Clipboard, Command-1 (hyphenate key combinations), and so on. This kind of style sheet ensures correctness and consistency in word usage, just as an electronic style sheet ensures typographic consistency.

A CLOSER LOOK AT A FEW STYLES

The beauty of styles is that once you set them up you can pretty much take them for granted. But a handful of styles in this book were such time-savers that they provided a subconscious thrill almost every time we used them. In the course of a 400-plus page book, you take your cheap thrills wherever you can find them!

1. PageMaker's heaviest rule is 12 point. But by defining a 12-pt Rule Above and a 12-pt Rule Below, you can run reverse type in a 24-point rule as a single style. The top rule here is 1p5 above the baseline; the bottom rule is 0p7 below.

2. A caption below its graphic is a snap: Type sss, click on Arrows Up *in the Style Palette, press Return to kick in the* Caption *style, and start typing.*

3. A caption above its graphic is just as easy: Click on Caption *in the Style Palette, type the caption, press Return to kick in the* Arrows Down *style, and type ttt.*

4. The tips head, banner, and hairline rule are part of the Head-Tip *style, with* Tips Text *specified as the next style. So we didn't miss a beat moving from the head to the text. The vertical rule still had to be added by hand.*

5. For continued lines below sidebar boxes, we specified the leading so that aligning the top text handle at the bottom of the box resulted in the desired spacing between the box and the text. We used the same technique for the 13/26 Zapf Dingbats numbers in this sidebar.

HEAD—BANNERED

 ❶

 ▲ ▲ ▲

Lorem ipsum dolor sit amet, consectetuer adipiscing elit, sed diam nonummy nibh euismod duis dolore te feugait nullafacilisi. Lorem ipsum dolor sit amet, consectetuer adipiscing

 ❷

Lorem ipsum dolor sit amet, consectetuer adipiscing elit, sed diam nonummy nibh euismod duis dolore te facilisi. Lorem ipsum dolor sit amet, consectetuer adipiscing sed

▼ ▼ ▼

❸

 TIP

Lorem ipsum dolor sit amet, consectetuer adipiscing elit, sed diam nonummy nibh euismod duis dolore te feugait nulla facilisi. Lorem ipsum dolor sit amet, consectetuer adipiscing elit, sed diam nonummy nibh euismod duis

 ❹

Paragraph Space Before 0p9, Space After 0p4. Keep Lines Together, Keep with Next 3 Lines, Rule Above: 6 pt. Width of Column with Right Indent 7p and (using the Options button to define the position of the rule) 1p10 above baseline. (For more on Paragraph Rules, see page 354.)

Hyphenation: Off

With the cursor in the formatted paragraph, press the Command key on a Mac, the Ctrl key

Continues on following page

 ❺

Here's a glitch that bugged us; maybe it's bugged you. Occasionally, we couldn't get rid of the grabber hand. Every tool, every key, left the little hand scrolling the screen. This generally happened at large page views, but reducing the page view didn't solve the problem. Most of the time, doing a Save As did solve the problem. Sometimes we had to close the file and quit the program. When that didn't work, we tended to anthropomorphize the software, and felt it was telling us we all needed a break. So we'd shut down, and by the time we started up again, all systems, including our own heads, were in better working order.

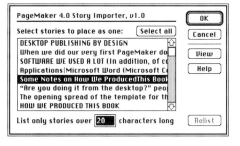

▲ ▲ ▲

When you choose a PageMaker document in the Place dialog box, PageMaker displays a list of the first 40 characters of each story in that document. Use the View button to view the entire text of the highlighted story. When you select a story and click OK, PageMaker loads the text icon just as it does when you place text from a word processor. If the text you place has PageMaker style tags, those styles are added to the Style Palette with an asterisk following the style name, as would be the case with styles imported from a word processor.

Copyfitting

Yet another kind of style that can't be automated involves format requirements such as chapters starting on left-hand pages and ending on right-hand pages. We also tried to position graphics and tips adjacent to, or at the very least on the same spread as, the body text they related to. And we tried to control page breaks so that a new section wouldn't start in the bottom quarter of a page, which would create an interruption before the section had really begun.

This emphasis on accessibility, on keeping as much related information as possible within eyesight, required a great deal of copyfitting. Having worked in traditional book and magazine publishing for many years, we know that the amount of fiddling we did with individual pages is possible only in desktop publishing. We unquestionably believe that editing to fit almost always improves the text, but we're also grateful for some electronic assistance. We could move information from the body text into a tip, and vice versa, and see immediately if the change solved the problem. We could cheat a point before each of the numbered instructions on a spread to squeeze in another line. We could adjust the word spacing and letterspacing for individual paragraphs. And we could range kern.

Range kerning is such a boon to copyfitting that you have to be very careful not to abuse the technique. By selecting a range of text, and pressing Option-Delete (Ctrl-Shift-minus on a PC), you can delete 1/100 of an em space between every letter pair in the selected text. (You can adjust for the other kerning increments as well.) This slight jog to the line breaks can save, or add, a line and can be used to fix hyphenation and rag problems as well.

Placing text from another PageMaker document

One of PageMaker's limitations is that you can't open two PageMaker documents at the same time and freely copy items between them. As a partial workaround, PageMaker 4.0 allows you to place text from one PageMaker document in another, and it's a godsend for revisions. In the new projects in this edition, for example, we often used a tip or a detailed explanation or even an entire sidebar from a project in the earlier edition.

When you choose the Place command, if the file you select is another PageMaker document (version 4.0 or higher), PageMaker displays the Story Importer dialog box. A directory lists the first 40 or so characters of each story in that document; if you're not sure which story you want, highlight one story entry, choose the View option, and PageMaker displays a scrollable window showing the entire text of that story. You can copy selected text from the View window and paste it into the current publication, or you can place the entire story. To select multiple stories and place them as a single file, hold down the Shift key and click on each story that you want to include.

By default, PageMaker lists only those stories that are over 20 characters long. To see a story with fewer characters, or to narrow the list to longer stories, type a new value in the text box and click Relist.

In order to use this feature, you must have installed the import filter for it. On a Macintosh, it's called the Story Importer filter; on a PC, it's the PageMaker Pub.PM4 Import filter.

RESOURCES

Charts

Designer's Guide to Creating Charts & Diagrams by Nigel Holmes (1984, Watson-Guptill Publications, 1515 Broadway, New York, NY 10036)

Created by the art director responsible for the charts and diagrams in *Time* magazine, this book provides carefully organized and accessible background on the various types of charts, suggestions on how to analyze information, and numerous examples and common errors. Particularly useful is a chapter that takes the reader through the analysis of data and creation of charts for nine different problems. Although the book predates desktop publishing, its conceptual and analytical approach is not the least bit dated.

Using Charts and Graphs: 1000 Ideas for Visual Persuasion by Jan V. White (1984, R.R. Bowker, 245 West 17th St., New York, NY 10011)

We didn't count, but this book probably does have a thousand ideas. And because the emphasis is on geometrical more than conceptual approaches, many of them can be executed with today's electronic drawing tools. (The book itself does not provide that how-to.)

The Visual Display of Quantitative Information and ***Envisioning Information*** by Edward Tufte (1983 and 1990, respectively, Graphics Press, Box 430, Cheshire, Connecticut 06410)

Tufte's books demand careful attention, but they reward the reader with a fundamental understanding of how words, numbers, and pictures can best be combined to communicate statistical information. The author doesn't believe in making a chart look like a video game; he holds that if the numbers are boring, you've got the wrong numbers. The keys to good information design, he says, are simplicity of design and complexity of data. His historical examples are alternately delightful and obscure; collectively they constitute an impressive catalog of what has been called cognitive art.

Clip Art

Dover Pictorial Archive Book Catalog (Dover Publications, 31 East 2nd St., Mineola, NY 11501)

Electronic clip art is fairly expensive; traditional clip art is not. For years, Dover Books has been one of the largest suppliers of public-domain (copyright-free) art. Its catalog lists over 300 books, with very few costing more than $10; many of them are less than $5. All you need to do is crop and scale the art and manually paste it onto the camera-ready pages.

Electronic Clip Art Collections

For a list of the clip art collections used in this book, see "Some Notes on How We Produced This Book."

Canned Art: Clip Art for the Macintosh (1990, Peachpit Press, 1085 Keith Avenue, Berkeley, CA 94708)

Although the title suggests that this is a Macintosh-only resource, over half of the 15,000 images in this sample book are available in PC formats. It visually indexes clip art from more than 35 vendors in an 825-page paperback volume. If you use clip art in your publications, this $29.95 digest is an economical purchasing guide to the many clip art packages available.

Color

The only way to keep up with the rapidly changing capabilities of electronic color is through the in-depth evaluations of computer magazines. Technology aside, there are many tools to help you use color as an effective design element. One of the most important is noting color combinations that you find effective in other publications. Inspiration can come from other media, too. The movie *Dick Tracy*, for example, displayed an inspiring use of primary colors.

An Introduction to Digital Color Prepress (1990, Agfa Corporation, 200 Ballardvale St., Wilmington, MA 01887)

This free 32-page booklet is a collaboration between Agfa Compugraphic, which makes high-resolution imagesetters, and Sanjay Sakhuja, whose Digital Pre-Press International is one of the top color output bureaus in the industry. It's clearly written and generously illustrated, with comparative photos that demonstrate variations both in visual effects and technical options.

Brodock's Designer Color Guide (1989, Brodock Press, Inc., 714 State St., Utica, NY 13502)

One of the most comprehensive guides for specifying process color, this one shows gradations of process tints in 5 percent increments. For each page of tints, the facing page shows the same tints with black added in increments of 5, 10, 15, 20, 30, and 40 percent.

Color Harmony by Hideaki Chijiiwa (1987, Rockport Publishers, P.O. Box 396, Rockport, MA 01966)

With the aid of color photographs to show how the emotional connotations of color are rooted in the real world, the author displays over 1500 color combinations. Some combinations are grouped according to relationships on the color wheel, others by the impression or emotion they evoke. The brief commentary will help ground the beginner in color theory, but you'll have to use your eye to translate the Japanese inks to colors in Pantone and process tint books.

Computer Color by Michael and Pat Rogondino (1990, Chronicle Books, 272 Fifth Street, San Francisco, CA 94103)

This color swatchbook shows combinations of process tints in 10% increments. The art was generated in Illustrator '88, separated through Adobe Separator 2.1, and output to film at 2540 dpi on a Linotronic 300 with an Adobe Rip III. So the environment for creating the color was as close to the desktop most of us work on as any guide to date. Of particular interest are the moiré patterns that are a recurrent problem when black is used in desktop separations.

Designer's Guide to Color (Chronicle Books, 272 Fifth Street, San Francisco, CA 94103)

This series of four books is a visual sourcebook of color combinations. Each volume shows a wide range of two-, three-, and four-color process tints, so you can see Y50-M100-C30, for example, up against 20 other process tints.

Pantone Process Color Imagining Guide (1990, Pantone, Inc., 55 Knickerbocker Road, Moonachie, NJ 07074)

One of an extensive line of color selection tools, this "fan-format" swatchbook displays over 700 Pantone colors side-by-side with their corresponding process color simulations. Available at most art supply stores, other Pantone tools range from individual colored sheets to looseleaf binders that show the effects of screened Pantone colors, combinations of Pantone colors and black, combinations of two Pantone colors, and a process color selector as well. One advantage of the Pantone library is that the larger guides display colors on both coated and uncoated stock.

It's more important to vary the shades in a color scheme than to vary the hues. If you contrast light colors with dark colors, your color scheme will look bold and three-dimensional, but if you just contrast the hues, your color scheme may look flat and lifeless.

—Hideaki Chijiiwa,
Color Harmony

The Red Book by Dale Russell (1990, North Light Books, 1507 Dana Avenue, Cincinnati, OH 45207)

This is one of five books in an attractive series, each one focusing on a different hue. The format displays 25 process color tints in the hue of the title. Each tint is shown with 56 contrasting colors; 8 halftone effects; type samples; a graduated color bar showing the tint fading from 100 to 0 per cent intensity; and a large block of the tint shown against a pattern that includes two other tints. Numerous smartly designed publications and products are displayed, with annotations regarding color.

The Computer Culture and the Future

In addition to being extraordinary tools, computers hold a mirror to some aspects of the culture we live in. As such, they've inspired a number of interesting books by some good and provocative writers.

Computer Lib/Dream Machines by Ted Nelson (revised edition 1987, Tempus Books, 16011 NE 36th Way, Redmond, WA 98073)

Considered the first cult book of the computer culture, it was first published in 1974, a few months before the announcement of the Altair. The visionary material from the first edition—with its prediction of user-friendly systems, computer-aided instruction, image synthesis, and more—and the new material added to the 1987 edition are served up in small bites in a quirky, nonlinear form that makes a kaleidoscope of the computer and its place in our lives.

The Media Lab: Inventing the Future at MIT by Steward Brand (1987, Viking, 40 West 23rd St., New York, NY 10010)

Apple Fellow Alan Kay has said that "The best way to predict the future is to invent it." And the Media Lab at MIT may well be where the future of publishing, broadcasting, film, and recording is being invented. *Whole Earth Catalog* founder Steward Brand spent several months there and, in addition to providing an in-depth tour of the Media Lab, offers his view of what it means in the larger media lab that we all live in.

The Soul of a New Machine by Tracy Kidder (paperback edition 1981, Avon Books, 959 Eighth Ave., New York, NY 10019)

The story of the creation of the Eagle computer is told as a technological and human drama. Wonderfully written (the book won a Pulitzer Prize), it's a very enjoyable way to expand your understanding of computers.

Graphic Design: Formal and Historical Perspective

Contemporary Graphic Design by Ronald Labuz (1991, Van Nostrand Reinhold, 115 Fifth Ave., New York, NY 10003)

One of the most up-to-date of contemporary design reviews, this book focuses on the eclectic styles of the 1980s. It captures that variety through its own design and through the many reproductions of work by top artists and designers.

Graphic Style from Victorian to Post-Modern by Steven Heller and Seymour Chwast (1988, Harry N. Abrams, 100 Fifth Ave., New York, NY 10011)

A lavishly illustrated review of commercial art (from books to posters to shopping bags), this volume may not relate to your average business publication, but it is glorious to look at and shows how graphic design has interacted with popular tastes ranging from Victorian to punk.

When [Media Lab director] Nicholas Negroponte and I originally discussed what this book might be about, he suggested, "It's about quality of life in an electronic age." A few months later he added, "It's a primer for a new life-style." Later still he mentioned, "I was still in my pajamas at ten-thirty this morning after I had been doing Lab work, through e-mail on my computer, for several hours. Maybe what we're talking about is 'The right to stay in your pajamas.'"

—Stewart Brand,
The Media Lab

The designer is confronted, primarily, with three classes of material: a) the given—product, copy, slogan, logotype, format, media, production process; b) the formal—space, contrast, proportion, harmony, rhythm, repetition, line, mass, shape, color, weight, volume, value, texture; c) the psychological—visual perception and optical illusion problems, the spectator's instincts, intuitions, and emotions as well as the designer's own needs.

—Paul Rand,
A Designer's Art

The Grid by Allen Hurlburt (1978, Van Nostrand Reinhold, 115 Fifth Ave., New York, NY 10003)

Allen Hurlburt, who art-directed *Look* during its heyday, was one of the foremost innovators in applying the principles of grid design to magazines. His concise and useful introduction to the history of grids includes a collection of grids created by top designers for newspapers, books, and magazines.

How to Understand and Use Design and Layout by Alan Swann (1987, North Light Books, 1507 Dana Ave., Cincinnati, OH 45207)

This book is organized as a three-section design course. The first section has the reader work with simple shapes and lines as a way of exploring proportion before bringing type, color, illustration, and photography onto the evolving page. The second section shows the elements of design applied to a wide variety of products. And the final section looks at the evolution of the design for a print ad, a newsletter, a direct-mail insert, a full-color brochure, and a poster.

Paul Rand: A Designer's Art (1985, Yale University Press, 302 Temple St., Princeton, NJ 06520)

Paul Rand is one of the giants of contemporary graphic design. This book collects several of his essays on design and displays a wide range of his work, including familiar trademarks (IBM, ABC, and Westinghouse), advertisements, and book and magazine covers.

Thirty Centuries of Graphic Design: An Illustrated Survey by James Craig and Bruce Barton (1987, Watson-Guptill, 1515 Broadway, NY, NY 10036)

Brief commentary and lots of reproductions are accompanied by a chronology of people and events for each era. Available in paperback, this is a useful addition to the library for the desktop designer who wants a sense of the history and traditions of graphic design.

Working with Style: Traditional and Modern Approaches to Layout and Typography by Suzanne West (1990, Watson-Guptill Publications, 1515 Broadway, NY, NY 10036)

This is really three books in one. The first two provide overviews of different approaches to designing the printed page—the traditional style, as old as the Rosetta stone and formalized on a foundation of Renaissance aesthetics; and the modern style, which grew out of Gestalt psychology, Bauhaus philosophy, and the Swiss school of graphic design earlier in this century. Each book is designed in the style it describes, so that you experience the style as you read about it. The third section is a workbook with exercises for exploring and applying the information presented earlier.

Graphic Design: Tips and How-To Information

Editing by Design: A Guide to Effective Word-and-Picture Communication for Editors and Designers by Jan V. White (1982, R.R. Bowker, 245 West 17th St., New York, NY 10011)

Jan White has written many books about graphic design. The great benefit of this one is that it focuses on the interaction of words and pictures in a way that tries to bridge the gap between the way editors and graphic designers approach publications. In the desktop publishing environment, where traditional roles are being redefined, this perspective is especially useful.

Graphic Idea Notebook: Inventive Techniques for Designing Printed Pages by Jan V. White (1980, Watson-Guptill, 1515 Broadway, New York, NY 10036)

This book is bursting with ideas for how to treat various design components on the printed page. The material is broken out into usefully informal categories

A clear area of white space can be as dramatic as a picture (especially if the picture is mediocre, as many often are). It gives the eye a place to rest. It can be a foil to the text: an "empty" contrast to the "full" areas that thereby makes the full areas appear even fuller. It can help to organize the material on the page. It can tie successive pages together by repetition of identifiable areas. White space, if used well, is the cheapest addition to the publication's roster of weapons.

—Jan V. White,
Editing by Design

such as getting attention, mug shots, boxes, breaking up text, direction, motion and change, and so on. The book is delightfully written and playfully formatted, with easy-to-find ideas. It is virtually all photos, drawings, and geometric shapes, with very direct annotations on using the visual ideas displayed.

The Gray Book by Michael Gosney, John Odam, and Jim Schmal (1990, Ventana Press, P.O. Box 2468, Chapel Hill, NC 27515)

This book looks at some fundamental principles and techniques in graphic design with an eye toward creating impact with black and white and shades of gray. The many examples range from simple hypothetical documents created especially for the book to sophisticated work being done by some of today's top electronic designers and artists.

Looking Good in Print: A Guide to Basic Design for Desktop Publishing by Roger C. Parker (1990, Ventana Press, P.O. Box 2468, Chapel Hill, NC 27515)

An introduction to the general principles of graphic design written for the hands-on desktop publisher who is a novice designer. Particularly useful are the makeover section, showing "before" and "after" versions of different kinds of publications, and the sections showing how the same elements—headlines, text, and illustrations—can be designed into very different-looking pages.

Notes on Graphic Design and Visual Communication by Gregg Berryman (revised edition 1984, William Kaufmann, Inc., 95 First Street, Los Altos, CA 94022)

Slim, inexpensive, and chock-full of useful information, this is a well-organized collection of notes from the author's 15 years of teaching graphic design. In an age when many books have more white space than substance, this one's a gem.

The Verbum Book of Electronic Page Design by Michael Gosney and Linnea Dayton (1990, M&T Books, 501 Galveston Drive, Redwood City, CA 94063)

The heart of this book is a series of case histories in which different designers describe the development and production of a specific project. All the major page layout programs are represented, but even more useful than the technical how-to is the insight into the design process. You follow one designer fiddling with a piece of paper to develop a folding brochure, another reflecting on the relative merits of spontaneity and efficiency in computer design, and another demonstrating how his graphic design work is constructed in an architectural way. A gallery section displays work of additional designers accompanied by brief production notes. Other books in the Verbum series focus on PostScript illustration, digital painting, and scanned imagery.

Inspiration

Design Annuals

To get ideas flowing, try flipping through any of the annual collections of leading work in editorial and advertising graphic design. These books also help you keep a finger on the pulse of the latest trends in typography, layout, illustration, and photography. They include *AIGA Graphic Design, Communication Arts Annual, Art Directors Annual,* and *Graphis Annual.*

The Design Concept : A Guide to Effective Graphic Communication by Allen Hurlburt (1981, Watson-Guptill Publications, 1515 Broadway, NY, NY 10036)

Beginning with an overview of theories on the creative process, this book provides a useful look at the development of an idea. It is illustrated throughout with examples of leading work in advertising, editorial, and information design. The case histories are presented as recollections from a very impressive cast of designers (Paul Rand, Saul Bass, Brad Thompson, George Lois, Milton Glaser, Herb Lubalin, Lou Dorfsman, and Henry Wolf).

Electronic page design has made it easy to use the "decision by subtraction" method. If you can't make up your mind about whether an element belongs on the page, take it out, look at it again, and if it doesn't make a whit of difference whether it's there or not, leave it out. If it does make a difference, decide whether it's positive or negative and act accordingly.
—John Odam,
The Verbum Book of
Electronic Page Design

It is not possible to dig a hole in a different place by digging the same hole deeper and bigger....If a hole is in the wrong place, then no amount of digging is going to put it in the right place. Vertical thinking is digging the same hole deeper; lateral thinking is trying again somewhere else.
—Edward de Bono,
cited in The Design Concept

Forget All the Rules About Graphic Design (Including the Ones in This Book)
by Bob Gill (1981, Watson-Guptill Publications, 1515 Broadway, NY, NY 10036)

Bob Gill is a graphic designer, illustrator, and filmmaker who describes his approach to design as taking ordinary boring problems and redefining them so that they are interesting or unique. This book is a collection of such problems and Gill's solutions to them. The title should give you a pretty good sense of his attitude, except that there are no rules in the book to break, just inventive ideas to inspire you.

Zen & The Art of the Macintosh: Discoveries on the Path to Computer Enlightenment by Michael Green (1986, Running Press, 125 South 22nd St., Philadelphia, PA 19103)

A passionately personal exploration of making art on the Macintosh, this book is a crazy quilt of fantastic bit-mapped graphics and 1980s Zen musings. It is a testimonial to as well as a reflection on the incredible seductiveness of computers.

Newsletters

Editing Your Newsletter: How to Produce an Effective Publication Using Traditional Tools and Computers by Mark Beach (third edition 1988, Coast to Coast Books, 1507 Dana Ave., Cincinnati, OH 45207)

This well-balanced guide covers the basic aspects of planning, developing, designing, and producing a newsletter. Chapters on design, typography, and graphics are well illustrated with diverse samples of real and fictional publications, and the chapters on production, printing, and distribution provide useful introductions to these areas. There is very little information about electronic page assembly, which is not a shortcoming in such a useful book, except that the subtitle promises more than it delivers.

PageMaker

Aldus Magazine (Aldus Corporation, 411 First Avenue South, Seattle, WA 98104)

Free to registered users of Aldus software, this bimonthly magazine shows off PageMaker's capabilities while providing some good information for both novice and more experienced users. It also covers FreeHand and Persuasion.

Aldus TechNotes for Macintosh PageMaker 4.0 (1990, Aldus Corporation, 411 First Avenue South, Seattle, WA 98104)

This is a source of advanced techniques and workarounds, such as creating manual traps in PageMaker, circular masks around imported images, printing special characters in their original fonts, changing PageMaker's Underline type style, working with PrePrint, and more. Some of the techniques explain how to edit PostScript code in word processor ASCII files. Free with a subscription to some of Aldus's premier customer programs, it's available for $39.95 to other customers. The Windows version is due out in the second half of 1991.

Page Tutor (1988, Personal Training Systems, P.O. Box 54240, San Jose, CA 94154)

This interactive tutorial combines a 90-minute audio tape and a disk with lesson files. Although the narration is gratingly cheerful and the designs of the sample documents are pedestrian, the instruction is clear and the development of skills is well paced. Six packages are available, with two that focus specifically on new features in PageMaker 4.0. Available only in the Macintosh format, the packages are not cheap ($79.95 each); but if you're stumbling around after working through the tutorial that came with PageMaker, this approach will give you some hand-holding experience and help move you toward productivity.

If you're applying spot colors in both PageMaker and FreeHand, the spot color names must be exactly the same in both programs (spelling, capitalization, and spaces in the names must all match). A quick way to get PageMaker color names and definitions into FreeHand:

1. *Create your colors in PageMaker.*
2. *Apply the colors to some Page-Maker-drawn objects.*
3. *Print one PageMaker page containing the colored objects to disk as an EPS file.*
4. *Place the EPS file in FreeHand. The PageMaker-defined colors, including the color names, are appended to FreeHand's list of colors.*

—Aldus TechNotes for Macintosh PageMaker 4.0

Real World PageMaker 4: Industrial Strength Techniques by Olav Martin Kvern and Stephen Roth (1990, Bantam Books, 666 Fifth Ave., NY, NY 10103)

This is the book that will make you a power user. It's clearly written, with good, detailed examples that will help you understand the nuances of PageMaker's logic. Kvern is senior documentation designer at Aldus, and Roth is the former editor of *Personal Publishing*. Their cumulative experience, insider knowledge, and sense of humor makes the book as readable as it is useful.

Paper

Laser Paper Sample Kit (1988, Portico Press, PO Box 190, New Paltz, NY 12561)

This kit provides five sheets each of 14 different white papers to test in your laser printer. An accompanying 12-page report is an accessible introduction to paper in general (brightness, opacity, smoothness, and so on) and to its use in laser printers. A chart provides specifications for 49 papers suitable for laser printers as well as information about available weights, sizes, and matching stock for envelopes, business cards, and so on. A good value at $21.95.

Periodicals

There are a great many magazines covering both the computer field and the field of graphic design—far too many to describe even briefly in these pages. *MacWorld*, *PC World*, and *MacUser* are among the many that keep technology-hungry users up to date on the latest products. *Art Direction*, *Communication Arts*, and *Print* display the best editorial and advertising work in this country, and *Graphis* is a source for international coverage. The following publications focus on desktop publishing, and the difficulty for any user may be in choosing from among so many useful sources.

Before & After: How to Design Cool Stuff (PageLab, Inc., 331 J Street, Suite 150, Sacramento, CA 95814-9671)

A great source of both design ideas and technical tips for working in Page-Maker and FreeHand, this 16-page, full-color newsletter has interesting projects targeted to inexperienced designers. Your guide is the enthusiastic, opinion-ated, witty voice of John McWade, a design pro and technological insider (he created the original template packages for Aldus PageMaker) who loves learn-ing new tricks and delights in passing on what he knows. He cautions that developing the eye and the skill to produce great-looking stuff takes years of experience; but he also believes that if you enjoy design, you needn't be intimi-dated by the fact that you haven't done much of it. The projects include dimen-sions and refreshingly streamlined steps for executing the designs. Bimonthly, $36 per year.

ThePage : A Visual Guide to Using the Macintosh in Desktop Publishing (PageWorks, PO Box 14493, Chicago, IL 60614)

David Doty is another designer who is equally at home in the world of graphic design and computers, and his 16-page newsletter is packed with ideas and techniques for beginner and intermediate desktop designers. Much of it is Page-Maker-specific, although it also has articles on Quark Xpress, drawing pro-grams, general design problems (logos, covers, newsletter design, typography), systems management, and the business of desktop publishing. The material is clearly presented, well illustrated, and highly accessible. Monthly, $65 per year.

Publish (PCW Communications, 501 Second St., San Francisco, CA 94107)

With its clear focus on desktop-publishing tools and process, *Publish* is a useful source not only for information about the technology but also for insight into how organizations are using it. It speaks especially to businesses of all kinds

Just the other day I received a notice in the mail offering me not only audiotapes that promised to teach me XPress or PageMaker in a mere eight hours each, but another audio course that offered to teach me how to be a designer as well. If that's all it takes to make it big in this profession, I'm sending my money in and look out Roger Black!

—Steve Hannaford in Step-by-Step Electronic Design

which, as a result of this technology, find themselves increasingly involved in publishing concerns. And it includes a design column which we write. Monthly, $39.90 per year.

Step-by-Step Electronic Design (Dynamic Graphics, 6000 N. Forest Park Drive, Peoria, IL 61614)

This 16-page newsletter lets you sit by the side of different professionals to see how they combine the art and mechanics of electronic design and illustration. It covers a wide variety of projects and software and is clearly written and illustrated, with six to eight pages in color each issue. It also includes excellent columns on typography and high-resolution output. Monthly, $48 per year.

Verbum: Journal of Personal Computer Aesthetics (Verbum, PO Box 15439, San Diego, CA 92115)

This well-produced gallery of computer art explores desktop technology's leading edge, not only in the art it displays but in the production of the magazine as well. In addition to print, it covers the video-multimedia-hypermedia spectrum, acknowledging that we're fast dissolving the distinctions that gave us these labels in the first place. The journal includes reviews of art-related hardware and software and a much-needed "Against the Grain" column, which cuts through some of the hype surrounding the electronic marketplace. Quarterly, $24 per year.

Production and Printing

DTP Advisor: The Desktop Publishing Tutorial and Project Management System (1988, Brøderbund Software, 17 Paul Drive, San Rafael, CA 94903)

Produced as a HyperCard stack, *DTP Advisor* provides a useful structure for planning and managing publishing projects. It includes a variety of forms (for freelance assignments, type specs, and printing specs), a schematic sketchpad with Paint tools for creating rough dummies, and a database for keeping track of artists, photographers, writers, printers, and other resources.

Getting It Printed: How to Work with Printers and Graphic Arts Services to Assure Quality, Stay on Schedule, and Control Costs by March Beach, Steve Shepro, and Ken Russon (1986, Coast to Coast Books, 2934 Northeast 16th Ave., Portland, OR 97212)

This book covers much of the same ground that the standard production references, such as *Pocket Pal*, do. But, as the subtitle suggests, it also provides more background for beginners, such as advice on how to specify and prepare your work, what you can and cannot expect from printing technologies, and how to work with your printer to get the best possible result. It's practical, technical but accessible, and peppered with anecdotes from publishers and printers.

The Graphic Designer's Handbook by Alastair Campbell (revised edition 1987, Running Press, 125 South 22nd St., Philadelphia, PA 19103)

Originally published in England, this handbook is a reference to printing options and terms, including paper and binding, page imposition, proof marks, copy-fitting tables, halftone screens, and so on. The color pages, which are numerous, include tint charts. Brief introductory chapters focus on the design process. If you want more than *Pocket Pal* offers but don't want to spring for *Graphics Master 4*, this book is a good choice.

Graphics Master 4 by Dean Phillip Lem (fourth edition 1988, Dean Lem Associates, Inc., P.O. Box 25920, Los Angeles, CA 90025)

This printing reference is as up to date on desktop publishing as any we've seen. The hardcover, spiral-bound format with heavy card stock makes it a

Use of the term desktop publishing applied to the graphic arts...can be misleading, for the publishing process encompasses much more than is presently available from desktop publishing systems. In addition to typographic composition, page makeup and laser-printed pages, the process of publishing requires the use of multi-color, high-fidelity halftone reproduction..., large volume, high-speed press runs of multi-page signature forms, ability to print on a variety of different paper stocks, different binding and finishing operations, distribution and many other factors.

—Graphics Master 4

Vigorous writing is concise. A sentence should contain no unnecessary words, a paragraph no unnecessary sentences, for the same reason that a drawing should have no unnecessary lines and a machine no unnecessary parts. This requires not that the writer make all his sentences short, or that he avoid all detail and treat his subjects only in outline, but that every word tell.

—William Strunk, Jr. and E.B. White
The Elements of Style

pleasure to use, and it includes some essential tools of the trade: a line gauge (calibrated for the 6-picas-per-inch conversion used in electronic page layout); a proportion scale for sizing art; and color tint charts printed on both coated and uncoated stock. The typeface display is extensive for a general reference guide, and the character-count guide includes information for Linotype (and hence Adobe), Bitstream, and Varityper systems. It is not inexpensive ($69.50), but it is a valuable reference aid for the serious desktop designer.

Pasteups & Mechanicals: A Step-by-Step Guide to Preparing Art for Reproduction by Jerry Demoney and Susan E. Meyer (1982, Watson-Guptill, 1515 Broadway, New York, NY 10036)

Close-up photographic sequences take you through the techniques of a traditional art department. Although many of these are replaced by your computer (inking rules and rounded corners, for example), many of them are not (scaling, cropping, and silhouetting photographs—even pasting in type corrections).

Pocket Pal: A Graphic Arts Production Handbook (14th edition 1989; International Paper Company, 6400 Poplar Ave., Memphis, TN 38197)

An inexpensive and concise guide to the history, process, and language of printing, this has been the standard reference for 50 years. If you have no other reference guide to the world of printing, don't pass up this $6.25 bargain.

Style, Grammar, and Usage

The Chicago Manual of Style (13th edition 1982, The University of Chicago Press, 5801 Ellis Ave., Chicago, IL 60637)

In addition to setting forth rules for proper punctuation, use of numbers, tables, footnotes, and bibliographies, this widely used reference provides an overview of the entire publishing process, from securing rights through design and typography to printing and binding. The 1982 edition begins to reflect the impact of technology on the editing process, although it stops short of desktop publishing.

The Elements of Style by William Strunk, Jr. and E.B. White (third edition, 1979; Macmillan Publishing Co. Inc., 866 Third Ave., New York, NY 10022)

Of all the many books on style, this is the most universally embraced classic. It is a simple, straightforward model of the lessons it imparts.

The Transitive Vampire: A Handbook of Grammar for the Innocent, the Eager, and the Doomed by Karen Elizabeth Gordon (1984, Times Books, 201 East 50th St., New York NY 10022)

This entertaining and delightfully unorthodox guide uses odd and whimsical words, characters, and illustrations to beguile you into understanding the parts of a sentence and how to put them together properly.

Type

Font & Function (Adobe Systems, 1585 Charleston Road, P.O. Box 7900, Mountain View, CA 94039)

In addition to displaying the fonts it sells, Adobe's oversize type catalog is full of information and ideas about using type. And you can get it free by calling 1-800-29-ADOBE.

Herb Lubalin: Art Director, Graphic Designer and Typographer by Gertrude Snyder and Alan Peckolick (1985, American Showcase, 724 5th Ave., New York, NY 10019)

Graphic designer Herb Lubalin brought a new meaning to typographic design. This is a loving tribute and testimonial to his talent by colleagues. It is a book devoted entirely to Lubalin's designs, from logos to typefaces to magazines. If you are the least bit intrigued by letterforms, the lifework of this designer will delight and inspire you.

Inversions by Scot Kim (1981, Byte Books, 70 Main St., Peterborough, NH 03458)

Computer programmer and artist Scot Kim has taken ordinary words and rendered them with a magician's sense of visual trickery. Some words read the same right side up and upside down, some words are hidden inside their opposites, some repeat into infinity. Although the book is more likely to be classified as wordplay than typography, it is a delightful way to learn about letterforms, symmetry, and visual perception

A Manual of Comparative Typography: The PANOSE System by Benjamin Bauermeister (1988, Van Nostrand Reinhold, 115 Fifth Ave., NY, NY 10003)

The premise of the PANOSE system is that type, like trees and birds, can be identified by noting special features. The result is a type specimen book in which distinctive features of the letters of each face included are circled. Whether or not you use the system itself, the visual display can be extremely useful for educating your eye to the nuances of type. Although the book is not specific to desktop publishing, it's interesting to note that the author was formerly the technical support manager at Aldus Corporation.

MacTography Type Sampler (1990, Publishing Solutions, 326-D North Stonestreet, Rockville, MD, 20850)

A DTP type specimen book, this looseleaf volume displays more than 2800 PostScript fonts from more than 30 vendors, for both Macintosh and IBM-compatible computers. For each typeface, a complete character set is shown in 24-point type followed by a paragraph set 10/12 justified and/or a line of 24- or 36-point display type and a line showing the range from 4 to 36 points. The initial cost is $75 with an update subscription available at $80.

Typewise by Kit Hinrichs (1990, North Light Books, 1507 Dana Ave., Cincinnati, OH 45207)

This personal statement about the power of typography comes from a partner in the Pentagram group, one of the premiere international design studios. The examples, all from the work of Pentagram designers, are briefly but insightfully annotated regarding the design goals and the techniques used to achieve them. The book itself is beautifully designed, a fresh standout in a crowded field.

Typographic Communications Today by Edward M. Gottschall (1989, The MIT Press, 55 Hayward St., Cambridge, MA 02142)

An in-depth look at the evolution of typographic design in this century, this book includes samples of work by all the great names in the relatively brief history of graphic design along with opinions they've expressed in speeches, articles, and interviews over the years. Chapters on typographic milestones classify over 200 typefaces in nine basic categories, with a complete alphabet of upper- and lowercase letters for each face and some with notes on their designs. This lavish, oversize book (it measures 10 3/4 by 14 1/2) will set you back the cost of a good desk accessory, but you get more than 900 illustrations, 500 of them in color.

Typography & Typesetting: Type Design and Manipulation Using Today's Technology by Ronald Labuz (1988, Van Nostrand Reinhold, 115 Fifth Ave., New York, NY 10003)

A very readable overview of the history, technology, and aesthetics of typography, this book is well illustrated, well designed, and thoughtfully put together. A wide range of sample documents includes pages from newspapers, books, magazines, and advertising.

Probably no two designers will agree on exactly which ten or fifteen faces to include in their own basic vocabularies, but they will almost always include a balanced selection of three or four faces from each broad type grouping—serif, sans serif, and slab serif—that they are likely to use 80 percent of the time for both headlines and body text. For example, my basic typographic vocabulary... includes Bodoni, Garamond, Century Old Style, Janson, Times Roman, Memphis, Cheltenham Old Style, Franklin Gothic, Futura, Helvetica, News Gothic, and Univers.

—Kit Hinrichs,
Typewise

GLOSSARY

When you specify Auto leading, you often need to know the value of that leading in order to determine other measurements on the page. You can calculate the value by multiplying the type size by 120%. Or keep a chart handy:

Type size	Auto leading	
6 point	1 point	6/7
7 point	1.5 points	7/8.5
8 point	1.5 points	8/9.5
9 point	2 points	9/11
10 point	2 points	10/12
11 point	2 points	11/13
12 point	2.5 points	12/14.5
13 point	2.5 points	13/15.5
14 point	3 points	14/17

Try this "fast-move" technique: Select the text or graphic, press the mouse button, and drag immediately before you see the directional arrows. You'll see a bounding box that defines the edges of the text block or graphic, but not the element itself.

alignment The placement of type relative to the margins. See also *centered, flush left, flush right, force justify, justified, ragged right,* and *wraparound text.*

alley The space between two columns of text.

ascender The portion of a lowercase letter, such as "b" or "f," that rises above the x-height.

ASCII An acronym for American Standard Code for Information Interchange, the form in which text-only files are stored. These files include all characters, tabs, and carriage returns, but not character and paragraph formatting such as italic, boldface, hanging indents, and so on.

Autoflow The fastest mode for text placement in PageMaker, in which text flows continuously from column to column and page to page until the entire file has been placed. Select Autoflow from the Options menu. Compare *manual text flow* and *semi-automatic text flow.*

Auto leading An amount of space between lines that is always proportional to the type size. The PageMaker default for Auto leading is 120% of the type size. So if your type is 10 point, Auto leading is 12; if the type is 14 point, Auto leading is 16.8. (PageMaker rounds off to the nearest tenth of a point.)

bad break A line break that is visually jarring, such as a page that begins with the suffix "ing" or a column that ends with a single word. See also *orphan* and *widow.*

baseline An imaginary line on which the letters in a line of type sit. The baseline aligns with the bottom of the x-height of the characters, and descenders of letters such as "g" and "p" drop below the baseline.

bit-mapped The representation of a character or graphic as a series of square dots or pixels, which sometimes print with jagged edges. See also *paint-type graphics.*

bleed art Any photo, illustration, or tint that runs off the edge of the page.

blurb Text that summarizes an article, usually set smaller than the headline and larger than the running text. Sometimes used interchangeably with "breakout."

body text The main text, also called body copy or running text, usually set in 9- to 12-point type in continuous paragraphs.

border A printing frame around text, graphics, or an entire page. Borders range from simple hairline rules to decorative and thematic graphic elements.

bounding box A rectangular space defined in PageMaker by dragging the mouse diagonally to establish left and right margins between which to place or type text. See also *drag-place* and the Tip at left.

breakout A sentence excerpted from the body copy and set in large type, used to break up running text and draw the reader's attention to the page. Also called a pull quote or blurb.

bullet A typographic element used to designate items in a list. The keystroke for the commonly used round bullet is Option-8 on the Mac, Ctrl-Shift-8 on the PC.

byline The name of the author of an article.

callout A label that identifies an element in an illustration.

camera-ready Photographs, art, and complete pages in a form that the printer can photograph for making printing plates.

TIP

If your text is behaving peculiarly, try these clean-up techniques:

- Global recompose: On a Mac, hold down the Option key as you choose Hyphenation from the Type menu. On the PC, choosing Setup in the Target Printer dialog box has the same effect. Page-Maker will recompose all the text in the publication. This is especially useful if you change between different printers or font types.

- To repair a corrupted publication: With the pointer tool active and nothing selected, hold down Option-Shift on a Mac, Ctrl-Shift on a PC, while choosing Hyphenation. If PageMaker finds no errors in the file, it beeps once. If it finds and corrects an error, it beeps twice; if it finds a problem but can't fix it, it beeps three times.

TIP

To have different column-guide settings on the right and left pages, choose the Set Right and Left Pages Separately option in the Column Guides dialog box.

cap height The height of a capital letter in a given font and size.

center axis The imaginary center line through a page, a text block, or a piece of art.

centered Aligned along a center axis.

character An individual letter or symbol.

clip art Public-domain art, either in books or on disks, that you can use free of charge and without credit in a publication.

Clipboard An electronic holding place for the most recent cut or copy made from a document. Whatever is on the Clipboard can be pasted into the current document. When you shut down, whatever is on the Clipboard is lost.

CMYK An acronym for cyan, magenta, yellow, and black (the last denoted by K to avoid confusion with blue), the four process colors from which all other colors are made in 4-color printing.

Color Palette A list of colors defined for a publication, which you can display by choosing the Color Palette command from the Window menu, or by pressing Command-K on a Mac, Ctrl-K on a PC.

column guides Nonprinting vertical rules in a PageMaker document that determine the left and right margins of text that you type or place. You can specify columns through the Column Guides command on the Options menu and reposition them manually with the pointer tool.

column rules Thin vertical rules separating columns of type.

condensed type Type in which the individual character is narrower than normal, giving you more characters per line. You can condense type in Page-Maker through the Set Width command on the Type menu.

continued line A line of text indicating the page on which an article continues, or the carryover line on the subsequent page that identifies the story being continued. Also called a jumpline.

copy-fitting Editing text to fit a specified space.

copyright Ownership of a work by the writer, artist, photographer, or publisher.

counter The white space inside a closed letter such as "a," "e," or "p."

crop To trim a graphic to fit a space without reducing the size of the graphic.

crop marks Intersecting lines indicating where a page is to be trimmed. Specify Crop Marks in the Print dialog box on a PC and in the Print Options dialog box on a Mac. Crop marks are also used to indicate the trim of photos and art that will be stripped in by the printer.

cropping tool The PageMaker tool used to trim graphics.

crossbar The shape of PageMaker's pointer when you select any of the drawing tools.

crossover Type or art that extends across the gutter between two pages. Alignment of crossover elements is critical.

cursor keys A set of four keys that can move the I-beam in the directions indicated by the arrows on the keys: up, down, right, or left.

deck A line following the headline that gives more information about a newsletter, magazine, or newspaper story. Also called a tagline.

default A preset value or option that is used unless you specify otherwise.

descender The portion of a lowercase letter, such as "g" or "y," that drops below the baseline of the type.

deselect To turn off a command by clicking on it when it is currently selected. Also, to cancel the selection of text and graphics in the publication window by clicking elsewhere on the page.

dialog box A box displayed on the screen that enables you to select or specify options and values.

digital halftone A photo that has been converted, through the scanning process, to a series of dots that can be stored and manipulated electronically and then printed as part of the electronically composed page. See *halftone*.

dingbat A decorative or symbolic device used to separate items on a page or to highlight each item on a list.

discretionary hyphen A hyphen inserted manually by typing Command-hyphen on a Mac, Ctrl-hyphen on a PC. A discretionary hyphen shows on-screen and on the printed page only if it is used to break a word at the end of a line.

display type Large type, often boldface, used for headlines, breakouts, and other attention-getting text.

dots per inch (dpi) The measurement of the resolution of a monitor or printer.

download To send printer fonts from your computer to your printer. You can let PageMaker automatically download a font each time you use it, or (to save time) you can manually download a font. Fonts that you download manually remain in the printer's memory until you turn off the printer.

downloadable fonts Individual fonts that you can buy and install in your desktop-publishing system.

drag To hold down the mouse button while you move the pointer to a new location on the screen.

drag-place To drag the mouse diagonally, defining the width of a graphic or text block before you place it. See also *bounding box*.

draw-type graphics See *object-oriented graphics*.

drop cap An enlarged initial letter that drops below the first line of body text. Compare *stick-up cap*.

dummy A term that can mean different things in different organizations: a rough preliminary sketch of a publication or story, an early proof with type and rough art in place, or a mock-up of an entire publication.

ellipsis Three dots (...) used to indicate an incomplete thought or a place where text has been deleted from a quote. On a Mac, you can get an ellipsis character by typing Option-semicolon.

em dash A dash the width of an em space, inserted by pressing Option-Shift-hyphen on a Mac, Ctrl-Shift-= on a PC.

em space A typographic unit equal to the point size of the type being used. For 10-point type, an em space would be 10 points. To insert an em space in PageMaker, press Command-Shift-M on a Mac, Ctrl-Shift-M on a PC.

Encapsulated PostScript A file format that enables you to print line art with smooth (rather than jagged) edges and to see and resize the graphic on-screen as it will print. EPS files can be created in graphics programs that produce PostScript code (such as Illustrator or FreeHand) or with the EPS option available in the Macintosh version of PageMaker's PostScript Print dialog box. EPS images do not print well on non-PostScript printers.

en dash A dash the width of an en space, inserted by pressing Option-hyphen on a Mac, Ctrl-= on a PC.

en space A space half as wide as an em space, inserted by pressing Command-Shift-N on a Mac, Ctrl-Shift-N on a PC. In this Glossary, the space between each term and its definition is an en space.

TIP

To deselect an individual item from a large group of selected items, hold down the Shift key and click on the item you want to deselect. Similarly, to add an item to a large group of selected items, hold down the Shift key and click on the item you want to add.

TIP

When you force justify headlines with two or more words, insert a fixed space between the words (Option-Spacebar on a Mac, Ctrl-Spacebar on a PC). This tells PageMaker to add space equally between letters and words. If you use a regular Spacebar character, PageMaker adds excessive space between words.

face A named type design, such as Times Roman or Helvetica.

fill A pattern or texture inside a rectangle or other closed shape. See the Fill submenu on the Element menu for fills available in PageMaker. Other art programs may have additional fills that can be used in imported graphics.

fixed space A space inserted between two characters, specified by font, by pressing Option-Spacebar on a Mac, Ctrl-Spacebar on a PC. Fixed spaces are used frequently in this book to letterspace headlines when the space desired exceeds the 200% maximum available through PageMaker's Spacing feature. Also called a *nonbreaking space*.

flush Aligned or even with, as in flush left or flush right text.

flush left Aligned along the left edge or margin.

flush right Aligned along the right edge or margin.

fold marks Dotted or dashed lines, printed outside the image area on camera-ready art, that indicate where to fold the printed piece.

folio The page number.

font In desktop publishing, sometimes used interchangeably with "face" to refer to the entire family of characters of a particular shape or design, such as Helvetica. In traditional typesetting, font refers to only one size and style of a given typeface, such as 10-point Helvetica roman or 12-point Helvetica Bold.

footer See *running foot*.

force justify An alignment option that adds space between characters in order to force the line to fill to the right margin.

format The overall appearance of a publication, including page size, paper, binding, length, and page-design elements such as margins, number of columns, treatment of headlines, and so on.

formatting Type and paragraph specifications that are applied in a word-processing or page layout program.

for position only A photocopy, photostat, or low-resolution scan of a piece of art pasted in place on the camera-ready page to indicate the position of the actual art that is to be stripped in by the printer. Usually written as FPO.

galley Traditionally, a proof of type before it is arranged on the page; used for proofreading and layout. (The term derives from the long, shallow metal trays used to hold metal type after it had been set.) In desktop publishing, you may still want to print galleys to the specified column width in your page layout program for proofreading.

gatefold A paper fold in which one or two sides of an oversize page fold in toward the middle of the sheet.

Gothic-style typefaces Sans serif typefaces.

grabber hand A PageMaker icon invoked by pressing the Option key on a Mac, the Alt key on a PC, and dragging the mouse; used to move around in the publication window.

TIP

While you reshape a graphic boundary, hold down the Spacebar to prevent the screen from redrawing the text wrap after each individual adjustment.

graphic boundary A nonprinting dotted line around a graphic that determines how close text can come to the graphic. The distance between the graphic boundary and the graphic is called the standoff and is defined through the Text Wrap command on PageMaker's Element menu.

greeking The process of simulating text as gray bars in order to speed screen display (an option available through PageMaker's Preferences command). Also used to refer to Latin text in rough layouts and dummies.

grid A series of nonprinting vertical and horizontal rules used to determine placement of text and graphics on the page.

gutter The space between two facing pages. The term is sometimes used to refer to the space between two columns of text.

hairline rule A very thin typographic rule. In desktop publishing, the width of a hairline rule varies depending on the resolution of the printer.

halftone The representation of a continuous-tone photograph or illustration as a series of dots that look like gray tones when printed. Also called a screened halftone because traditionally the original image is photographed through a finely ruled screen, the density of which varies depending on the printer's capabilities. See also *digital halftone*.

handles Used in PageMaker to refer to the eight small solid rectangles that surround a selected graphic. See also *windowshade handles*.

hanging indent A paragraph style in which the left margin of the first line extends beyond the left margin of subsequent lines.

hard return A line break that signals the end of a paragraph, created by inserting a carriage return. See *new-line character* and *soft return*.

header See *running head*.

I-beam The shape PageMaker's pointer assumes when you select the text tool.

image area The area inside the page margins. Some page elements, such as page-number markers, are placed outside the image area.

imagesetter An output device, such as the Linotronic, that produces high-resolution pages from desktop-generated files.

initial cap A first letter set in enlarged and sometimes decorative type for graphic emphasis.

inline graphic A graphic that is anchored to a position within a text block. To insert an inline graphic, set an insertion point with the text tool before placing or pasting the graphic.

insertion point A blinking vertical bar indicating where the next text block will be typed or pasted. The position of the insertion point is set by clicking the I-beam on the page.

inside margin The space between the binding edge of the page and the text.

italic type Type designed with letters that slant toward the right, often used for display text and captions. Compare *oblique type*.

jaggies The stair-stepped appearance of bit-mapped art and type created by diagonal lines in a technology that is based on square pixels.

jumpline See *continued line*.

justified Type that is flush, or even, along both the right and left margins.

kerning The process of adjusting the space between letter pairs, used primarily in headlines and other display type. PageMaker offers two levels of kerning: fine (1/100 of an em increments) and coarse (1/25 of an em increments). See also *range kerning*.

kicker A phrase preceding a headline that provides information about the story.

knockout An option used in color printing that instructs PageMaker to delete a background color so that it does not mix with an overlapping color.

landscape A horizontal orientation, wider than it is tall, for pages or photographs. Compare *portrait*.

layout The arrangement of text and graphics on a page.

layout view The default PageMaker mode, in which you create and manipulate elements as they appear on the page. See also *story view*.

leader A line or row of dots between two items in a table, specified through the Indents/Tabs dialog box. Also, a rule that moves the eye from a callout or label to the part of the illustration it describes.

leading The distance from the baseline of one line of text to the baseline of the next, measured in points.

leading grid An approach to page layout in which all vertical measurements take into account the leading of the body copy to ensure the alignment of baselines of text in adjacent columns and pages.

letterspacing The amount of space between letters. In PageMaker, you can control letterspacing through the Spacing option in the Paragraph Specs dialog box.

line slug See *slug.*

Linotronic A high-resolution PostScript printer that outputs pages as paper or film at resolutions of up to 2540 dots per inch.

Links A set of PageMaker features that tracks changes made to the original source files of text and graphics placed in a publication.

logotype A company, product, or publication name designed as a distinctly recognizable unit.

magic stretch A technique that constrains the resizing of bit-mapped graphics to the resolution of the printer in order to avoid moiré patterns. Hold down the Command key on a Mac (the Ctrl key on a PC) when you resize a graphic (include the Shift key as always if you also want the graphic resized proportionally).

manual text flow A mode of placing text in PageMaker in which the text flow stops at the end of a column; you must click on the windowshade handle at the bottom of the text block to reload the text icon and continue placing text in the next column or page. Compare *Autoflow* and *semi-automatic text flow.*

margin The distance from the edge of the paper to the image area occupied by text and graphics.

margin guide A nonprinting dotted rule that appears on every page of a PageMaker document as specified in the Page Setup dialog box.

marquee. See *selection box.*

master page The page, identified by an L (for left) or R (for right) icon in the lower left of PageMaker's publication window, on which you create elements that will appear on all the actual pages of the document. Master-page items can be printing items (such as running heads) or nonprinting items (such as ruler and column guides).

masthead Traditionally, the listing of staff, ownership, and subscription information for a periodical. The term is sometimes used to refer to the typographic treatment of the publication name on the cover, although that is more accurately called a nameplate.

measure The length of a line of type, traditionally expressed in picas.

mechanical Traditionally, a piece of artboard with type galleys, line art, and "for-position-only" photostats in place and with tissue overlays marked for color. In electronic publishing, a mechanical is the final camera-ready page, from either a laser printer or an imagesetter, with position-only stats keyed to flat art that is to be stripped in by the printer. Also called a keyline, pasteup, or camera-ready page.

menu A list of commands that appears when you point to any of the items listed just above the publication window (File, Edit, Type, and so on).

menu bar The area at the top of the screen containing menu names.

TIP

Most service centers that provide high-resolution output base their page rate on a maximum printing time, such as 8 minutes per page. Anything beyond that time is charged as overtime. To minimize overtime charges, keep your pages clean: Eliminate items from the pasteboard, avoid unnecessary masks, remove unused styles and colors from your Palettes, and so on. And do a Save As to compact the file before you copy it to a floppy disk. Some service centers offer a discount if you send them a PostScript file of your PageMaker document. For more information on that procedure, see page 224.

mini-save An automatic save of a document, which PageMaker generates each time you click a page icon, change the page setup, insert or delete a page, or switch back and forth between story and layout views. You can revert to the last mini-save by holding down the Shift key when you select the Revert command on the File menu.

modular layout A format in which different elements on a page or spread are designed as self-contained units.

moiré A pattern that results from improperly aligned screens used in producing halftones and tints.

monospacing Letterspacing that is the same for all characters regardless of their shape or width. Traditional typewriter characters are monospaced. Compare *proportional spacing.*

nameplate The typographic design of a publication's name as it appears on the cover of the publication.

negative leading A type specification in which there is less space from baseline to baseline than the size of the type itself (for example, 40-point type with 38-point leading). Negative leading is often used with larger type sizes set in all caps in order to tighten up the text unit.

new-line character A character inserted by pressing Shift-Return, which instructs PageMaker to begin a new line without applying the attributes of a new paragraph. Also called a soft return.

NFNT A numbering system for identifying screen fonts that minimizes the chance of two fonts having the same ID number (as often happened in Apple's original numbering system, which allowed for only 255 numbers).

nonbreaking space A space (also called a fixed space) inserted between two words when you don't want them to be separated by a line break. In PageMaker, press Option-Spacebar on a Mac, Ctrl-Spacebar on a PC. Other typographic spaces (em, en, and thin spaces) and em and en dashes are also nonbreaking characters.

object-oriented graphics Graphics created as a series of mathematically defined curves and lines. They can be resized without causing distortion or moiré patterns. Also called draw-type graphics.

oblique type A slanted version of a roman typeface. The letters maintain their original forms except for the slant, whereas italic letters have a different shape from their roman counterparts. Compare *italic type.*

orphan In PageMaker, defined as the last 1, 2, or 3 lines of a paragraph standing at the top of a column. You can instruct PageMaker to disallow orphans through the Paragraph Specs dialog box.

outside margin The space between the outside trim and the text.

overlay A printout, on paper or film, that includes every element that prints in a given Pantone color. By choosing the Spot Color Overlay print option, you instruct PageMaker to print a separate overlay for each Pantone color used in a publication. Compare *separation.*

overline A brief tag, over a headline, that categorizes a story. Also called a kicker or an eyebrow.

page-number marker A key sequence (Command-Option-P on a Macintosh, Ctrl-Shift-3 on a PC), generally typed on the master pages, that instructs PageMaker to insert page numbers in the document.

Page Setup The size, orientation, number of pages, and margins for a document; specified in PageMaker's Page Setup dialog box.

TIP

When working with rotated text:

- To shorten the selection handles around rotated text, drag with the pointer tool, not the cropping tool.

- To change the line breaks on rotated text, drag the corner handles.

- To edit the text or change the type specs, triple-click on the rotated text with the pointer tool to bring up the Story Editor. When you close the story window, the changes you made there will be displayed in the rotated text.

TIP

In PageMaker's Open and Place dialog boxes, you can use the up and down arrow keys to move through a list of filenames; when you reach the file you want, press Return. On a Mac, you can also type the first letter (or first few letters) of the filename and then press Return. (Note, however, that a delay in typing between letters of a name will move the selection to a filename beginning with the "delayed" letter.)

TIP

When you *paste* text over the text in a placeholder, the type specs of the pasted text match those of the original text that was cut or copied, but the margins of the pasted text match those of the text in the placeholder. When you *type* new text over text in a placeholder, the type specs match the style of the placeholder text.

page view The amount of the page and surrounding pasteboard seen on the screen, which varies depending on the size of your monitor and the view selected on PageMaker's Page menu.

paint-type graphics Graphics represented by square dots or pixels, which can be individually manipulated on-screen. These graphics may be distorted or lose resolution when resized. See also *bit-mapped*.

Pantone colors A standardized system of colors, available in printing inks, papers, markers, and other materials, that can be specified in PageMaker.

Paragraph Rules Rules specified through the Paragraph command, which are anchored to and move with the associated paragraph.

pasteboard The area surrounding the page on-screen in a PageMaker document where you can leave master items, such as standing headline treatments or spacing guides, as well as any text or graphics, until you are ready to move them into position on the page. Items on the pasteboard appear on the pasteboard of every page of the publication.

pasteup Traditionally, the process of assembling mechanicals by pasting galleys and line art in place. In desktop publishing, traditional pasteup has largely been replaced by electronic page assembly. But pasteup is still a valuable skill for taking care of last-minute patches.

perpendicular line tool The PageMaker tool used to draw vertical, horizontal, and diagonal lines in 45-degree increments.

perspective The representation on a flat plane of three-dimensional objects as they appear to the eye.

pica A traditional typographic measurement, composed of 12 points. A pica is actually equal to a little less than 1/6 inch, but in desktop publishing you will generally see it expressed as 1/6 inch.

PICT format A Macintosh file format for saving object-oriented graphics.

picture window A rectangle that indicates the position and size of art to be stripped in by the printer.

pixel The smallest dot or unit on a computer screen. The clarity of screen resolution depends on the number of pixels per inch on the monitor.

Place A PageMaker command on the File menu that enables you to import text and graphics created and saved in other applications. You can also place text from another PageMaker 4.0 document.

placeholder Text or graphics that you leave in place in an electronic template so that you can place, paste, or type new items over the placeholder and retain the same spacing relative to other elements on the page.

point The basic measurement of type. There are 12 points to a pica, and 1 point equals about 1/72 inch.

pointer The icon that moves on the screen as you move the mouse. The shape of the pointer depends on which tool is selected.

pointer tool The PageMaker tool, which takes the shape of an arrow on the screen, that is used for selecting graphics and text blocks. Other PageMaker tools turn into the pointer tool when you move them into the rulers, menu bars, Style Palette, or page icons.

portrait A vertical orientation for pages or photographs. Compare *landscape*.

PostScript A page description language developed by Adobe Systems and used by many laser printers and high-resolution typesetters. It is as close to a standard as there is in desktop publishing at this writing.

power-paste A key sequence that enables you to paste a copy directly on top of the original. Dragging that copy to a new position sets a spatial relationship that PageMaker will repeat if you continue to power-paste the same copy from the Clipboard. To power-paste, press Command-Shift-V on a Mac, Ctrl-Shift-P on a PC.

Preferences A command on PageMaker's Edit menu used to specify the unit of measure (inches, picas, millimeters, and so on), resolution for graphic display, typeface for story view text, and a few other goodies.

printer font A mathematical description of every character in a font, which enables a printer to print characters in any size at the best resolution possible on that printer.

printing rule A rule that traps a screen or surrounds a piece of art.

process colors Cyan, magenta, yellow, and black, used to create all the other colors in 4-color printing.

proofread To check typeset material for spelling, punctuation, alignment of elements, and other details and to be sure that corrections have been made properly. Standard proofreading marks can be found in many printing reference guides, style manuals, and dictionaries.

proportional leading A method of leading used in PageMaker that places two-thirds of the specified leading above the text baseline and one-third below it.

proportional spacing Letterspacing that is proportional to the shapes of the letters, with the "m" and the "w," for example, taking up more space than the "i" and the "l." Compare *monospacing*.

proportion wheel A tool used to calculate the percentage of enlargement or reduction of a piece of art to fit the space specified on a page.

publication window The image that appears on-screen when a document is open, which includes one or two pages, the title bar, page icons, and—if displayed—rulers, scroll bars, toolbox, and palettes.

pull quote See *breakout*.

rag The shape created by the uneven line breaks in ragged right text.

ragged right Text alignment that is even or flush on the left margin and uneven on the right.

RAM An acronym for random access memory. This is where the computer stores information temporarily while you're working with it. If you lose power or shut down before saving to disk, whatever is in RAM at the time is lost.

range kerning Kerning a selected range of text at one time, rather than manually kerning individual letter pairs. See also *kerning*.

recto The right-hand page.

registration The alignment of two or more elements, such as a color tone within a box, so that they appear seamless.

registration marks A set of symbols, usually a circle with cross-hair lines through it, placed outside the live area of the page and used by the printer to accurately align overlays or separations in multicolor printing. In PageMaker, specifying Crop Marks tells PageMaker to include registration marks as well.

resolution The clarity or fineness of detail visible on-screen or in the final printout, expressed as dots per inch. In printed material, the resolution is dependent on the printer's capacity, which in the current desktop technology ranges from 300 dots per inch in most laser printers to 2540 dpi in Linotronic 300 imagesetters.

reverse White letters or rules against a black or color background.

TIP

To import new text into a story you've already placed: Set the insertion point by clicking the text tool where you want to add the new text, choose Place from the File menu, select the filename for the new text, click on the Inserting Text option, and then click OK. Page-Maker inserts the new text at the insertion point and forces all subsequent text farther down in the existing text block.

TIP

To speed up printing when you want to proofread text and don't need to see graphics, click on the Proof Print option in the Print Options dialog box on a Mac. PageMaker will print the text as usual and replace each graphic with a large X. (Not available in PC PageMaker.)

TIP

If you have trouble selecting an item on the page or setting an insertion point with the text tool, choose the Select All command. This will reveal the handles around every text block and graphic on the page and enable you to spot where overly long windowshade handles or "invisibles" (such as reverse type and white masking boxes that you've lost) may be creating problems.

Revert A sort of "multiple undo" command on PageMaker's File menu that lets you return to the last saved version of your document.

Roman-style typefaces Typefaces with serifs. Compare *Gothic-style typefaces.*

roman type Vertical-style type, as opposed to italic or oblique. In Page-Maker's Type Style options, roman type is called Normal; in some word-processing programs, it is called Plain.

rounded-corner tool The PageMaker tool used to draw squares and rect-angles with rounded corners. Various corner styles are available through the Rounded Corners command on the Element menu.

ruler guide A nonprinting dotted rule used to determine the alignment of text or graphics on the page. You drag guides in from either the vertical or the horizontal ruler, and they function as extensions of the tick marks on the ruler.

rule In typography, a straight line, identified by its weight in points.

runaround text See *wraparound text.*

running foot A line at the bottom of the page with information similar to that in a running head.

running head A line at the top of the page that may include such informa-tion as title, author, chapter, issue date, and page number.

running text See *body text.*

sans serif A typeface without finishing strokes at the ends of the characters. (From the French *sans*, meaning "without.")

scale To calculate the degree of enlargement or reduction of a graphic so that it fits the space allotted for it. A proportion wheel is often used to scale art. You can scale pages when printing by specifying a percentage in the Scaling option in PageMaker's Print dialog box.

scanner A hardware device that "reads" a photograph or other piece of art and transforms it into a collection of dots that can be stored as a bit-mapped file on a hard disk, manipulated in various software programs, and placed electronically in a page layout program.

Scrapbook A Macintosh desk accessory in which you can store text and graphics to be cut and pasted into a document. Unlike the Clipboard, which stores only the most recently cut item and which is in effect erased when you shut down, the Scrapbook stores many items and is saved as a file so that the items are available each time you turn on the computer.

screen A tint, a percentage of either black or a second color, behind text or art. Also called a tone.

screen dump A bit-mapped image of the screen, created by pressing Command-Shift-3 on a Mac, Print Screen or Alt-Print Screen on a PC.

screen font The character set that is displayed on-screen as pixels and that calls up the respective printer font when you print a publication.

script A typeface that simulates handwriting.

scroll bars The gray bars on the right and bottom sides of a publication window used to move horizontally or vertically around the page. PageMaker's Style and Color Palettes also have scroll bars.

select To indicate where the next action will take place by clicking the pointer on text or graphics or by dragging the cursor across the text.

selection box A box drawn by dragging the pointer tool to enclose and select more than one graphic or text block at a time so that the material can be copied, cut, or moved as a unit. An item must be completely within the

TIP

If you distort a graphic while you are resizing it in PageMaker, you can restore the graphic's original proportions by holding down the Shift key and dragging slightly on any handle. This technique enables you to quickly drag-place a graphic to define its approximate size, restore its proportions, and then resize it accurately for the layout and the proportions of the art.

TIP

If you frequently turn the Snap To commands on and off, remember these keyboard shortcuts:

Snap to	Macintosh	PC
Guides	Command-U	Ctrl-U
Rulers	Command-[	Ctrl-Sh-Y

selection box in order to be selected, which for text means that the window-shade handles, not visible when you draw the selection box, must be within the box. Also called a marquee.

self-mailer A printed piece designed to be mailed without an envelope. The area for the mailing label and postal indicia, if there are any, must be designed in accordance with postal regulations.

semi-automatic text flow A mode of placing text in PageMaker in which the text flow stops at the end of a column; the text icon is automatically re-loaded and begins flowing text when you click it into position. You invoke the semi-automatic mode by holding down the Shift key with either the Autoflow or the manual flow selected. Compare *Autoflow* and *manual text flow*.

separation A printout, on paper or film, that shows only one process color used in a publication. Unlike spot color overlays for Pantone colors, which can be printed directly from PageMaker, process separations must be printed through a color separation program such as Aldus PrePrint or Adobe Separator.

serif A line or curve projecting from the end of a letter form. Typefaces with these additional strokes are called serif faces.

set solid Type in which the leading is 100% of the point size—14/14 for example, or 32/32.

shade In PageMaker, a tone or a pattern chosen from the Fill submenu and used to fill a graphic, such as a banner.

show through Printing on one side of the paper that can be seen on the other; commonly found in lower-quality paper stock.

sidebar A smaller, self-contained story inside a larger one, usually boxed with its own headline to set it apart from the main text.

silhouette A photograph from which background image has been removed, outlining a subject or group of subjects.

slug In traditional typesetting, a line of type cast in hot metal was called a slug. The PageMaker equivalent is the black selection rectangle that appears when you drag over a line of type. The depth of the rectangle equals the leading of the line. Hence the phrase "line slug."

small caps Capital letters that are smaller than the standard uppercase characters for that typeface and size. You can specify small caps through the Case option in the Type Specs dialog box (or press Command-Shift-H on a Mac, Ctrl-Shift-H on a PC). The default size for small caps is 70% of the standard cap height; you can customize the size through the Options button in the Type Specs dialog box.

Snap to Guides A command on PageMaker's Options menu that causes text and graphics being moved or placed to snap to the nearest ruler guide.

Snap to Rulers A command on PageMaker's Options menu that causes ruler guides, text, and graphics being moved or placed to snap to the nearest ruler tick mark.

soft return See *new-line character*.

spacing guide An element sized to match a distance you need to measure frequently in a given publication, such as the space between pictures and captions.

spot color In PageMaker, a term used to refer to Pantone colors, as distinct from process colors.

spread Two facing pages in a publication.

square-corner tool The tool used to create squares and rectangles.

stacking order The order in which text and graphics overlap on-screen in a PageMaker file. The order can be manipulated through the Bring to Front and Send to Back commands on the Element menu.

standoff The distance between a graphic and the graphic boundary, defined in PageMaker's Text Wrap dialog box. See also *graphic boundary*.

stick-up cap An enlarged initial letter extending above the body text, used as a graphic element to draw attention to the beginning of a story or chapter. Compare *drop cap*.

story In PageMaker, all the text blocks that are part of a threaded text file.

Story Editor The word-processing features built into PageMaker as a separate mode for working in the program.

story view Windows that enable you to create and edit text using PageMaker's Story Editor. You can move back and forth between the layout view and the story view by pressing Command-E on a Mac, Ctrl-E on a PC. See also *layout view*.

stripping The assembling of all photographic negatives or positives necessary to create a printing plate of the entire page. Halftones and color separations are often stripped into the film created from an electronically assembled page.

style This word has a multitude of meanings in electronic publishing. On PageMaker's Type menu, style refers to weight, slant, and certain special typographic effects such as outline, shadow, and reverse. It also refers to a collection of typographic attributes, specified in the Define Styles command, that can be applied to selected text by clicking on the appropriate name in the Style Palette. Traditionally, style refers to the broad characteristics of a typeface (such as serif or sans serif).

Style Palette A list of styles defined for a publication, which you can leave on-screen by selecting the Style Palette command on the Window menu, or by pressing Command-Y on a Mac, Ctrl-Y on a PC.

surprint To print one image over another, such as type over a graphic.

tabloid A large-format publication, usually half the size of a standard newspaper page.

target printer The printer on which the final output will be printed. On a PC, use the Target Printer command on the File menu to specify a target printer that is not the same as the printer currently being used (and specified in the Print dialog box).

template An electronic prototype of a publication that provides the layout grid and style sheets for similar publications. PageMaker 4.0 comes with a library of templates for many different kinds of documents. You can make your own templates by creating the prototype and selecting the Template option in the Save As dialog box.

text block In PageMaker, text that, when selected, is bound by two windowshade handles with loops at the top and bottom. See also *threaded text*.

text tool The tool used in PageMaker to select text for editing and changing type specifications. When the text tool is selected, the pointer looks like an I-beam.

Text Wrap The command on PageMaker's Element menu that enables you to specify the relationship of text to graphics. Text can wrap around a graphic, flow through a graphic, or jump over a graphic. See also *graphic boundary* and *standoff*.

thin space A fixed space half the width of an en space, inserted by pressing Command-Shift-T on a Mac, Ctrl-Shift-T on a PC. Compare *em space, en space,* and *fixed space*.

threaded text Text placed or typed as a single file, connected in PageMaker's memory from one column to the next and from one page to the next. When you cut, add, or move copy in a threaded-text file, PageMaker automatically adjusts subsequent text across as many pages as needed to maintain the link between all the text blocks in the threaded file.

TIP

You can copy a style sheet from one PageMaker document to another. Choose Define Styles from the Type menu, click on Copy, and scroll through your directories to find the file that contains the styles you want to copy. (You can copy only an entire style sheet, not selected styles from it.) To create a customized style sheet as the application default, follow this same procedure when there is no publication open and PageMaker is active. You can use these same procedures with colors.

If you are unable to move a text block, even though you see the four-way directional arrow when you select and drag, you might have extremely long windowshade handles that are being blocked by the edge of the pasteboard. Similarly, when you use the Select All command and are unable to move selected items as far in one direction as you'd like, there's probably something on the pasteboard blocking the movement. In either case, move to a global view (press the Shift key and select Fit in Window) to see the entire pasteboard so that you can shorten the handles or move the obstructing item.

thumbnails Rough sketches of a page design; also miniature pages that you can print by selecting the Thumbnails option in the Print dialog box.

tick marks Marks on rulers showing the increments of measure. The larger the page view in PageMaker, the finer the increments on the ruler.

TIFF Short for Tag Image File Format, a format for electronically storing and transmitting bit-mapped, gray-scale, and color images.

Tile A print option in PageMaker that enables you to print oversize pages in sections, or tiles. Each section is printed on a single sheet of paper; then the various tiles are pasted together to form a complete page.

tint A percentage of black or a color.

tone See *tint.*

Toolbox A small window containing PageMaker's text and graphics tools.

Track In PageMaker, the preset spacing values available through the Track submenu.

trap An overlap of abutting colors that eliminates the possibility of white leaks between the colors if the printing plates are not properly aligned.

trim In PageMaker, the page size defined in the Page Setup dialog box. In commercial printing, the size of the page after it is cut during the binding process.

verso The left-hand page.

vignette A graphic in which the background fades gradually until it blends with the unprinted paper.

weight The density of letters, traditionally described as light, regular, bold, extra bold, and so on.

white space The areas of the page without text or graphics; used as a deliberate element in good graphic design.

widow In PageMaker, defined as the first 1, 2, or 3 lines of a paragraph standing at the end of a column. You can instruct PageMaker to disallow widows through the Paragraph Specs dialog box.

width The horizontal measure of letters, described as condensed, normal, or expanded. You can alter the width of characters through the Set Width option in the Type Specs dialog box.

windowshade handles The horizontal lines with loops in the center and square dots on either end that appear at the top and bottom of a text block selected with the pointer tool.

word spacing The amount of space between words. In PageMaker, you can control the word spacing through the Spacing option in the Paragraph Specs dialog box.

wraparound text Text that wraps around a graphic. Also called runaround text. See also *Text Wrap.*

WYSIWYG An acronym for "What You See Is What You Get." Pronounced "wizzy-wig," it refers to the representation on a computer screen of text and graphic elements as they will look on the printed page.

x-height The height of the main body of a lowercase letter, excluding ascenders or descenders.

zero point The point at which the 0 on the horizontal ruler intersects with the 0 on the vertical ruler.

INDEX

The manuscript for this book was prepared and submitted to Microsoft Press in electronic form. Text files were processed and formatted using Microsoft Word.

Cover design by Darcie Furlan
Cover photograph by Walter Wick
Interior text design by Don Wright and Ronnie Shushan
Principal production art and coordination by Lisa Sandburg
Cover color separations by Wescan Color Corporation, Redmond, WA
Interior color separations by Sprintout, New York, NY

Text composition by Don Wright and Ronnie Shushan in Palatino with display in Helvetica Condensed Black Oblique, using Aldus® Pagemaker® with an Apple® Macintosh®. Final pages were printed by Sprintout at 1270 dpi on a Linotronic 300 with RIP 3 (using Postscript version 51.8). Color pages were printed to film at 2450 dpi.